Psychoneuroimmunology

BEHAVIORAL MEDICINE

Series Editors:

Richard S. Surwit
Redford B. Williams, Jr.
Department of Psychiatry
Duke University Medical Center
Durham, North Carolina

David Shapiro
Department of Psychiatry
University of California, Los Angeles
Los Angeles, California

Robert Ader (Ed.): *Psychoneuroimmunology*

Joel F. Lubar and William M. Deering: *Behavioral Approaches to Neurology*

Richard S. Surwit, Redford B. Williams, Jr., and David Shapiro: *Behavioral Approaches to Cardiovascular Disease*

Psychoneuroimmunology

EDITED BY

ROBERT ADER

Department of Psychiatry
University of Rochester School of Medicine and Dentistry
Rochester, New York

With a Foreword by

Robert A. Good

1981

ACADEMIC PRESS, INC.
Harcourt Brace Jovanovich, Publishers

Orlando   San Diego   New York
Austin   Boston   London   Sydney
Tokyo   Toronto

ACADEMIC PRESS, INC.
Orlando, Florida 32887

United Kingdom Edition published by
ACADEMIC PRESS, INC. (LONDON) LTD.
24/28 Oval Road, London NW1 7DX

Library of Congress Cataloging in Publication Data
Main entry under title:

Psychoneuroimmunology.

   (Behavioral medicine series)
   Includes bibliographies and index.
   1. Immunologic diseases--Psychological aspects.
2. Neuroendocrinology. 3. Neuropsychiatry. 4. Immune
response--Regulation. I. Ader, Robert. II. Series.
[DNLM: 1. Endocrinology. 2. Neurophysiology.
3. Psychophysiology. 4. Allergy and immunology.
QW 504 P974]
RC582.P78   616.07'9   80-2765
ISBN 0-12-043780-5   AACR2

PRINTED IN THE UNITED STATES OF AMERICA

87 88 89   9 8 7 6 5 4

Contents

PART **I**

Psychosocial Factors, Stress, and Disease Processes

Psychosocial Factors in Infectious Disease
S. MICHAEL PLAUT AND STANFORD B. FRIEDMAN

Psychoneuroimmunologic Factors in Neoplasia: Studies in Animals
VERNON RILEY, M. A. FITZMAURICE
AND DARREL H. SPACKMAN

Psychosocial Factors and the Immune System in Human Cancer
BERNARD H. FOX

Emotional and Personality Factors in the Onset and Course of Autoimmune Disease, Particularly Rheumatoid Arthritis
GEORGE FREEMAN SOLOMON

PART II
Psychosocial Factors, Stress, and Immune Processes

Stress and Immunologic Competence: Studies in Animals
ANDREW A. MONJAN

Stress and Immunologic Competence: Studies in Man
JAN PALMBLAD

Immunologic Abnormalities in Mental Illness
GEORGE FREEMAN SOLOMON

PART III
Conditioning Effects

Conditioned Immunopharmacologic Responses
ROBERT ADER AND NICHOLAS COHEN

A Historical Account of Conditioned Immunobiologic Responses
ROBERT ADER

PART IV
Neuroendocrine Influences

Hormonal Influences on Immunologic and Related Phenomena
JOHAN AHLQVIST

Pharmacologic Control of the Hormonally Mediated Immune Response
G. J. M. MAESTRONI AND W. PIERPAOLI

Hypothalamic Influences on Immune Responses
MARVIN STEIN, STEVEN J. SCHLEIFER AND STEVEN E. KELLER

Neurophysiology, Immunophysiology, and Neuroimmunomodulation

NOVERA HERBERT SPECTOR AND ELENA A. KORNEVA

Neuroendocrinology and the Immune Process

DAVID MACLEAN AND SEYMOUR REICHLIN

Neurotransmitters and the Immune System

NICHOLAS R. HALL AND ALLAN L. GOLDSTEIN

Immunologic-Neuroendocrine Circuits: Physiological Approaches
H. O. BESEDOVSKY AND E. SORKIN

Integrated Phylogenetic and Ontogenetic Evolution of Neuroendocrine and Identity-Defense, Immune Functions
WALTER PIERPAOLI

PART V
Epilogue

Mind, Body, and Immune Response
ALASTAIR J. CUNNINGHAM

List of Contributors

Robert Ader (281, 321), Department of Psychiatry, University of Rochester School of Medicine and Dentistry, Rochester, New York 14642

Johan Ahlqvist (355), Department of Pathology, Aurora Hospital, 00250 Helsinki 25, Finland

H. D. Besedovsky (545), Schweizerisches Forschungsinstitut, Medizinische Abteilung, Davos-Platz, Switzerland

Nicholas Cohen (281), Department of Microbiology, University of Rochester School of Medicine and Dentistry, Rochester, New York 14642

Alastair J. Cunningham (609), Ontario Cancer Institute, Toronto, Ontario, Canada M4X 1K9

M. A. Fitzmaurice (31), Department of Microbiology, Pacific Northwest Research Foundation, and Fred Hutchinson Cancer Research Center, Seattle, Washington 98104

Bernard H. Fox (103), Biometry Branch, National Cancer Institute, Bethesda, Maryland 20205

Stanford B. Friedman (3), Division of Child and Adolescent Psychiatry and Division of Behavioral Pediatrics, Departments of Psychiatry and Pediatrics, University of Maryland School of Medicine, Baltimore, Maryland 21201

Allan L. Goldstein (521), Department of Biochemistry, The George Washington University Medical Center, Washington, D. C. 20037

Nicholas R. Hall (521), Department of Biochemistry, The George Washington University Medical Center, Washington, D. C. 20037

Steven E. Keller (429), Department of Psychiatry, Mount Sinai School of Medicine of the City University of New York, New York, New York 10029

Elena A. Korneva (449), Institute of Experimental Medicine, USSR Academy of Medical Sciences, 197022, Leningrad, USSR

David MacLean (475), Division of Endocrinology, Tufts–New England Medical Center, Boston, Massachusetts 02111

G. J. M. Maestroni* (405), Institute of Anatomy, University of Zurich, Zurich, Switzerland

Andrew A. Monjan (185), Department of Epidemiology, The Johns Hopkins University School of Hygiene and Public Health, Baltimore, Maryland 21205

Jan Palmblad (229), Department of Medicine IV, the Karolinska Institute at Södersjukhuset, and the Laboratory for Clinical Stress Research, the Karolinska Institute, Stockholm, Sweden

Walter Pierpaoli† (405, 575), Institute of Anatomy, University of Zurich, Zurich, Switzerland

S. Michael Plaut (3), Division of Child and Adolescent Psychiatry, University of Maryland School of Medicine, Baltimore, Maryland 21201

Seymour Reichlin (475), Division of Endocrinology, New England Medical Center Hospital, Department of Medicine, Tufts University School of Medicine, Boston, Massachusetts 02111

Vernon Riley (31), Department of Microbiology, Pacific Northwest Research Foundation and Fred Hutchinson Cancer Research Center, Seattle, Washington 98104

Steven J. Schleifer (429), Department of Psychiatry, Mount Sinai School of Medicine of the City University of New York, New York, New York 10029

George Freeman Solomon‡ (159, 259), Department of Psychiatry, University of California, San Francisco, Fresno, California 93775

E. Sorkin (545), Schweizerisches Forschungsinstitut, Medizinische Abeilung, Davos-Platz, Switzerland

Darrel H. Spackman (31), Department of Microbiology, Pacific Northwest Research Foundation, and Fred Hutchinson Cancer Research Center, Seattle, Washington 98104

Novera Herbert Spector (449), Neurosciences, UAB Medical Center, University of Alabama Medical Center, Birmingham, Alabama 35294

Marvin Stein (429), Department of Psychiatry, Mount Sinai School of Medicine of the City University of New York, New York, New York 10029

---

*PRESENT ADDRESS: Institute of Pathology, Laboratory of Cellular Pathology, 6604 Locarno, Switzerland.

†PRESENT ADDRESS: Institute for Integrative Biomedical Research Lohwisstrasse 50, 8123 Ebmatingen, Switzerland.

‡PRESENT ADDRESS: Fresno County Department of Health, Medical Education, P.O. Box 11867, Fresno, California 93775.

Introduction to the Series

Behavioral medicine is an emerging field which has undergone nearly explosive growth in the past 5 years. In 1977, the National Institutes of Health sponsored a conference on behavioral medicine at Yale University. The conference adopted the following definition of behavioral medicine: "Behavioral Medicine is an interdisciplinary field concerned with the integration of behavioral and biomedical science knowledge and techniques relevant to health and disease and the application of this knowledge and these techniques to prevention, treatment, and rehabilitation."

The books in this series will provide a medium for the presentation, in depth, of research findings on various topics falling within the domain of behavioral medicine. Each will contain careful reviews of the scientific evidence relevant to each of the specific topic areas. Most volumes will be written by a team of behavioral and biomedical scientists.

This series will constitute a growing and evolving archive documenting the scientific basis of behavioral medicine. As such, its intended audience is broad—ranging from basic research scientists to practicing clinicians.

R.S.S.
R.B.W.
D.S.
Series Editors

Foreword:
Interactions of the Body's Major Networks

Immunologists are often asked whether the state of mind can influence the body's defenses. Can positive attitude, a constructive frame of mind, grief, depression, or anxiety alter ability to resist infections, allergies, autoimmunities, or even cancer? Such questions leave me with a feeling of inadequacy because I know deep down that such influences exist, but I am unable to tell *how* they work, nor can I in any scientific way prescribe how to harness these influences, predict or control them. Thus they cannot usually be addressed in scientific perspective. In the face of this inadequacy, most immunologists are naturally uneasy and usually plead not to be bothered with such things.

Yet we have known for many years—as long as my immunologic memory—that the endocrine glands can influence the development, maintenance, and functions of the lymphocytes—those cells which subserve the immunologic functions. From those earliest days when lymphocytes were being aroused from a sleepy past and linked to immunity, Dougherty and White, for example, were showing that the hormones of the adrenal glands could lyse them. Stress, as it was called for want of a better name, also caused lysis of lymphocytes and thymic involution and great changes in the morphology of the lymphoid tissues.

Certain dwarf mice are short-lived because they fail to develop vigorous immunity functions. Their T and B lymphocytes do not develop normally and these deficiencies can be corrected by replacement hormone therapies.

Everyone knows now, and has for a long time, that mental state and stressful experiences can alter the hormonal milieu of the body, and that this, in turn, can influence the numbers of lymphocytes and even their response to antigens, phytomitogens, or allogeneic cells.

The amazing relationship of brain function to the immunity processes was brought home to me by experiments that my colleagues and I did in 1961. Our observations were never published because, about the time we were completing our experiments, a paper appeared in a British journal reporting similar observations and more. In short, we observed that well-selected hypnotic subjects trained to respond with deep somnolence to hypnotic suggestion could receive signals that influenced greatly their immune responses to simple protein antigens to which they had been made allergic. We used the classical method of the Prausnitz–Küstner Reaction. Serum from a highly allergic donor was injected into the skin of each forearm. Twenty-four hours later, under deep hypnosis at the time of challenge, the suggestion was made that the skin of one arm was not to react to the challenge of the sensitizing antigen while the skin of the opposite arm should respond in the usual way. With each of three well-trained hypnotic subjects, the results were the same. Whereas in the skin of the one arm the reaction showed the usual wheal, erythema, itching, burning, and swelling, the opposite arm showed only a wheal and very minimal erythema. There seemed from these experiments little doubt that manifestations of allergic challenge had been influenced significantly by the mind under the influence of hypnosis. As we began to prepare our scientific report, similar experiments were described by the British investigators; they also claimed to be able to influence a delayed allergic reaction to tuberculin. Although we were crestfallen from having been "scooped" of what we considered an important scientific finding, we were all convinced that the effector limb of allergic immunity could be influenced by the brain. We had our own clear view of poorly understood interactions of brain and immunologic processes.

Through many years as a clinical and laboratory immunologist, I have observed numerous such influences expressing in different ways powerful interactions between brain, mind, endocrinological functions, and immunologic activity. With Franz Halberg and his associates, Fernandes and I have studied the influence of circadian time, reversible simply by changing the hours of light exposure, on the numbers of antibody-producing cells generated by antigenic stimulation. The difference in number of antibody-producing cells generated by antigen injected at one circadian time over another was as much as eightfold. We have also shown profound changes with circadian time of natural killer-cell function, and Halberg and associates have demonstrated the influence of rhythms as disparate as daily, weekly, monthly, and yearly on a wide range of immunologic processes and endocrinologic functions.

Recently, Fernandes and I have carried out experiments that showed that conditioning and regular exercise in mice can influence not only thymus size but quantifiable cellular immune responses to antigens and even the rate of progression of transplanted tumors. We also know that the state of mind produced by crowding our animals can change their immune responses and that acute and chronic involution of the thymus can be effected by stressful experiences, including crowding.

Yes, I am absolutely convinced that the interaction of mind, endocrines, and immunity is real. Of this there can be no doubt.

In the present volume, Ader has collected a remarkable series of contributions from a number of critical scientists which suggest that the science focused on interactions of these three major networks of the body has a serious root structure, and that a burgeoning of research on these issues is about to occur. The scientific results reviewed and presented in the pages of this book leave no doubt that the brain can influence many immunologic processes. The question that remains is *how* these three major networks—the nervous system, the endocrine system, and the immunologic system—interact and, *how,* by understanding these interactions in precise quantitative terms, we can learn to predict and control them. I visualize that the next 10 to 15 years will witness rapid development of the sciences that address such issues.

It will be of greatest importance, at every step in the development of this science and the pharmacology that will no doubt follow from it, that precise quantitative measurements be made and that the experiments conducted—whether with humans or animals—be objectively designed, carefully controlled, and critically interpreted.

ROBERT A. GOOD

Preface

The immune system is a constantly vigilant sentinel dedicated to maintaining the integrity of the individual by discriminating between self and nonself and mediating between host and pathogen. It is an immensely complex system, generally considered to be a primary and autonomous agency of defense determining health and disease. There is a growing awareness, however, of an intimate and relatively unexplored relationship between the immune system and the central nervous system and that an analysis of this relationship might reveal much about the operation of the immune system—and about the brain. It is, after all, our own intellectual limitations that have led to the proliferation of scientific disciplines that have no necessary relationship to a full understanding of adaptive processes, and the study of immune processes as an integrated part of the organism's psychobiological adaptation to its environment represents a constructive dissolution of such arbitrary boundaries. That is what this book is all about. It is a unique volume that gathers together for the first time some of the converging evidence that implicates the central nervous system in the regulation of immune responses.

The data presented in this volume indicate that the assumption of an autonomous immune system is no longer tenable, and that the immune system, like all other physiological systems functioning in the interests of homeostasis, is integrated with other psychophysiological processes; as such, it is subject to regulation or modulation by the central nervous system. These data are composed, first, of the several clinical and experimental reports of the effects of psychosocial factors on the susceptibility or response to disease processes that are thought to involve immune mechanisms. More directly, there is a literature concerning the effects of "stress" on *in vitro* and *in vivo* parameters of immunologic reactivity. A newly discovered (or rediscovered) avenue of research implicating the central nervous system in the modification of immune responses involves the conditioning of immunopharmacologic effects. Finally, there are studies documenting the effects of neurophysiological, neuroendocrine, and neurochemical interventions on immune functions, and vice versa. It is these events, which are demonstrably sensitive to behavioral processes of adaptation and involve the integrative functions of the central nervous system, which constitute the internal milieu within which immune processes take place. These, then, provide a link whereby psychosocial factors can be understood to play a role in influencing immune responses and processes of disease.

Each of these areas is represented in sections of this volume. The individual chapters vary considerably in content, coming, as they do, from totally different biopsychosocial levels of organization. They also vary in form, ranging from the review of empirical data, some of which is reported here for the first time, to speculative analyses of the multiple pathways through which the central nervous system could exert some regulatory effect on immune responses. Of necessity, there is some redundancy. In part, this was unavoidable; in part, the editorial decision to retain some repetition was purposeful. For the behavioral scientists in particular, the complexities of the immune system cannot be assumed to have been mastered, making some repetition desirable. Also, no general description of immune function would suffice to provide the definitions or understanding of those aspects of immune function which are dealt with in different experimental paradigms—and in different chapters. Most importantly this is not a textbook. No pretense is being made that the material included in this volume is yet amenable to the kind of integration that would permit the straightforward, logical sequence of chapters that characterizes the description of an organized body of knowledge. There is, then, no single way to approach the material contained in this book, and no "reader's guide" is possible. At the risk of seeming facetious, I might suggest, however, that some general perspective may be gained by proceeding from the Introduction directly to the Epilogue before delving into the intervening chapters.

Despite their diversity, the chapters in this volume share and communicate the excitement that comes from an appreciation of the opportunities that arise when one brings new combinations of ideas and techniques to bear on the formulation of innovative research for the understanding of natural phenomena.

If, at this point, the data are incomplete and the speculations tentative, they are, nonetheless, sufficiently persuasive to prompt immunologists, endocrinologists, neurophysiologists, neurochemists, pharmacologists, behavioral scientists, and physicians from a variety of clinical disciplines to ask questions that have not been asked before.

Psychoneuroimmunology

PART I

Psychosocial Factors, Stress, and Disease Processes

Psychosocial Factors in Infectious Disease

S. MICHAEL PLAUT
STANFORD B. FRIEDMAN

If you don't get some rest you are going to get sick. [Typical Mother]

It is difficult for many to view infectious disease as a "psychosomatic" process; a "strep throat" conveys, by name alone, the etiologic agent as *beta hemolytic streptococcus*. Yet, the puzzle remains as to why some children develop pharyngitis whereas others, the majority, remain carriers of the organism without manifest disease. Immunologic defenses obviously are relevant, and a classic example of the importance of prior exposure to a specific type of *streptococcus* resulting in immunologic protection is clearly seen in the epidemiology of acute glomerulonephritis. However, to the behavioral scientist, streptococcal disease is but one example of a host–parasite relationship where traditional cause-and-effect—streptococcus causes disease—appears only a partial explanation of disease, and the speculation arises as to whether psychosocial factors conceivably contribute to the development of disease (Meyer and Haggerty, 1962).

GENERAL OVERVIEW

Psychosomatic Medicine

The roots of the notion that psychological factors precipitate or cause disease go back to antiquity. However, recent thinking is heavily influenced by the observations of Alexander (1950). He related psychological factors to

3

seven disease entities (peptic ulcer, ulcerative colitis, hyperthyroidism, regional enteritis, rheumatoid arthritis, essential hypertension, and bronchial asthma). It was thought that a specific psychological conflict was an underlying basis for each of these illnesses. Dunbar (1943) proposed that the conflict was not specific, but rather that a definable personality type was the factor of etiologic importance, and she described disease-related personality profiles. In common to both these investigators was a belief that specific psychological factors caused or predisposed to specific deseases, and thus developed the "theory of specificity." It also led to thinking of psychosomatic diseases as differentiated from those of organic or physical cause. This either–or concept has been repeatedly challenged.

Engel developed, in detail, the notion of multifactorial etiology of disease (Engel, 1954), and later advanced a biopsychosocial model of disease (Engel, 1977). From this perspective, disease has multiple determinants, and in most instances, the search for a single cause of an illness is considered to be overly simplistic.

The extent to which any one etiologic factor—including the psychosocial—contributes to the disease process depends on a number of considerations (Figure 1), each of which will be discussed more fully in "A Multifactorial Approach." First of all, some diseases may be more easily influenced by psychosocial factors than others. There is little or no evidence, for example, that brain tumors in children are affected by such factors. It should be emphasized, however, that the apparent lack of such a relationship may well be due to insufficient study of this possibility. Second, just as the virulence of a pathogen affects the severity of disease, so may the intensity or form of a psychosocial stimulus alter its impact on the disease. Third, individual differences due to genetic or life experiences will modify the impact of any

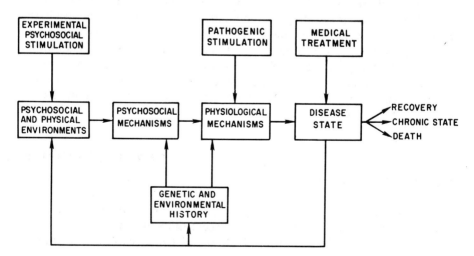

Figure 1. Factors to be considered in a multivariate approach to the study of psychosocial influences on resistance to infectious disease. These are discussed in "A Multifactorial Approach."

etiologic factor on the state of the individual. Fourth, there are temporal or developmental factors that may alter the role of psychosocial stimuli in disease.

Infectious Disease as a Psychosomatic Phenomenon

The possible etiologic role of psychosocial factors in infectious disease is not new, and perhaps Dubos (1955, 1961) more than any other individual, has done more to advance such a hypothesis. He has emphasized that an infectious agent, alone, is usually not sufficient to cause disease, but rather, a multitude of factors must be considered. These include prior exposure to the microorganism and the development of immunity, nutritional status of the host, the presence of other disease, and a wide range of genetic factors. In the fetus and infant, maternal factors, such as the transfer of antibodies across the placenta, have a significant influence on the host's response to infectious agents. Dubos also focused on the importance of other considerations, including the influence of socioeconomic and public health conditions.

Lest the above discussion of the concept of psychosocial factors contributing to disease vulnerability be misunderstood, it must be emphasized that the authors do not deny the relevance of microorganisms to the development of infectious disease! The *dosage* of the pathogen is of particular importance in understanding the relationship of an infectious agent and the biopsychosocial model of disease. For example, in some of our own work, to be more fully described in "Empirical Findings" (Friedman *et al.,* 1965), the effects of environmental stimulation (electric shock preceded by a warning light) upon Coxsackie B infection in adult mice was *only* evident within a relatively narrow dosage range; low doses of virus produced no demonstrable illness under any of the experimental conditions, and high doses produced illness unaffected by experimental manipulation. Such findings, that is, the variable influence of environmental factors, do not negate the potential etiologic role of psychosocial factors and in fact approximate what would be expected in the clinical setting. Psychosocial factors would be predicted to be of most importance when the host–parasite relationship was in delicate balance in terms of whether the host would eliminate the microorganism, a carrier state would develop, or disease would occur.

Possible Mechanisms

Psychosocial factors do not influence disease in some mystic fashion. Rather, the physiological status of the host is altered in some way. Numerous studies over the last two decades clearly demonstrate that psychological stimuli may have a profound influence on a wide range of physiological processes in both the experimental animal and in man (e.g., Friedman and Glasgow, 1966; Mason, 1972). It is *assumed* that these physiological changes, acting simply or in combination, are the underlying mechanisms to which disease vulnerability or susceptibility is related. However, in the opinion of these authors, this relationship has never been definitively established in either the experimental animal or man. In short, it is known that (a) psychological factors influence a wide range of physiological, hormonal, and biochemical responses; and (b) psychological factors influence the natural history of many disease states. However, the mechanism(s) by which psychological factors contribute to the etiology of any given disease is largely speculative. The present volume has grown out of the need to elucidate these mechanisms, and from recent studies demonstrating the extent to which the immune system may be subject to psychosocial influence.

Previous work was stimulated, to a great extent, by the classic animal studies of Selye (1946), and his development of a theory of physiological adaptation. This theoretical framework, the General Adaption Syndrome (GAS), linked environmental stress to a nonspecific adrenocortical response. According to Selye's early formulation, it was this hormonal response which accounted for survival of the animal. The GAS had three stages: (a) alarm reaction; (b) resistance; and (c) exhaustion. Resistance was possible through increased adrenocortical activity. On the other hand, severe and/or prolonged stress could exceed the animal's ability to sustain sufficient adrenocortical secretion, and adrenal cortex "exhaustion" occurred—this led to either disease or death. The characteristics of the disease depended on a multitude of factors, though of major importance was the type of stressor (e.g., exposure to cold, inoculation of endotoxin) used in a given experiment. Central to the discussion is that adrenocortical function was thought to be the primary underlying mechanism linking stress to disease.

The monolithic focus on the adrenal cortex to explain disease caused by stress was oversimplistic, as Selye (1973) himself pointed out. In the area of infectious disease, however, it was tempting to conclude that adrenocortical function was the mediating mechanism between a psychological "stress" and decreased resistance to an infectious agent. It was well known that both adrenal insufficiency and high levels of adrenocortical hormones increased susceptibility to a wide range of infectious diseases. However, such a causative relationship has not been documented in the physiological adrenocortical response to environmental stimulation. Further, Mason (1972) emphasized that the role of other hormones in response to stress has received insufficient attention, due in part to the difficulty in assaying hormonal levels until recently. Further discussion of possible mechanisms may be found under Physiological Mechanisms in "A Multifactorial Approach."

The "State of the Art"

PSYCHOSOMATIC RESEARCH AND BEHAVIORAL MEDICINE

When the literature about psychosocial influences on infection is compared with that regarding such relationships in noninfectious diseases, the relative absence of studies dealing with infectious disease is startling. In fact, some recent reviews of psychosomatic research make no mention of infectious diseases. Many still refer to "psychosomatic disease" as if some illnesses were subject to such influences while others were not. The primary basis for this prevailing attitude is probably most closely related to our traditionally simplistic view of the etiology of disease. "The model of disease causation provided by the germ theory," writes Cassel (1974), "has accustomed us to think in monoetiological, specific terms." As Ader (1974) and Engel (1974) repeatedly emphasized, however, psychosomatic research "deals not with the role of psychosocial factors in *causing* disease, but in *altering individual susceptibility to disease.*" They and others have argued that the etiology of disease is best studied by a multifactorial or interactive approach (e.g., Freyhan, 1976; Friedman and Glasgow, 1966; Levi, 1974; Weiner, 1971). The relevant question is not *whether* a given disease is caused by a pathogenic agent *or* by psychological factors, but rather *to what extent* the disease can be related to each of a number of factors in the history, makeup, and environment of the organism. In statistical terms, we are asking what proportion of total variance is accounted for by each determining factor. Thus, if the "germ" is seen as a "necessary but not sufficient" determinant of disease, and as one of many interacting etiologic factors, "any distinction between psychosomatic and nonpsychosomatic disease is completely arbitrary [Colligan, 1975]." The term "psychosomatic disease" in fact loses its meaning, and justifiably so.

Clinicians working in the field of psychosomatic medicine over the years have often expressed the hope that this multifactorial approach to disease would lead to changes in the attitudes of health care workers toward patients, so they would be seen less as objects and diseases and more as people living in a social context (Engel, 1979; Hinkle, 1956). In fact, the attitude of both public and professional seems to have shifted somewhat in this direction during recent years. Biofeedback clinics have developed and thrived, "wellness" clinics emphasize preventive medicine with their clients, and articles on coping with stress as a way to avoid disease are frequently seen in popular magazines and newspapers. A new field called "behavioral medicine" has developed around this holistic approach to medical care (Schwartz and Weiss, 1977). Recent reviews and theoretical statements in the field reveal considerable variability in their definitions of concepts, literature cited, theoretical orientation, and suggestions and attitudes regarding the application of such knowledge (Levi, 1974; Martin, 1978; Murray, 1977; Nemiah, 1973; Schwab and Schwab, 1975). All of this can only suggest that we still lack the consistent and convincing body of data that would provide the necessary credibility to the field.

THE NEED FOR FURTHER RESEARCH

One of the better known advocates of expanded research on psychosomatic relationships is Norman Cousins, editor of the *Saturday Review,* who fell victim to a severe collagen disease called ankylosing spondylitis. During his recovery process he became convinced of the role of his emotional state in his condition. He concluded that "the will to live is not a theoretical abstraction but a physiologic reality with therapeutic characteristics [Cousins, 1976]," and that "we need to know more not just about the balancing mechanisms inside the human body, but about the phenomenon of repair and the way stress is related to both [Cousins, 1979]."

"That the relation of people to their society and to the people around them can influence the incidence, the prevalence, the course, and the mortality of disease seems clear enough," wrote Hinkle (1973). "The questions at issue are the questions of when they do so, under what circumstances, by what mechanisms, and to what extent. Precise answers to these questions will not be forthcoming without a great deal of scientific effort." Such methodologically sound research efforts will help convince medical educators of the importance of these issues and provide the necessary empirical basis for the humanistic practice of medicine (DiMatteo, 1979; Engel, 1962).

Another rarely discussed value of research in this field is its methodological relevance to other areas of biomedical research which are not directly concerned with psychosocial issues. For example, if it can be shown that the incidence or severity of a given disease is related to the number of animals in a cage or to interpersonal relationships in a human population, these then become variables which should be controlled in other studies in order to minimize variability in the data, reduce the possibility of confounding variables, and facilitate comparisons among the studies of various investigators.

EMPIRICAL FINDINGS

This section will briefly review the human and animal studies which have demonstrated relationships between psychosocial factors and infectious disease. Studies relating such factors to disease in general will also be discussed, because of the methodological importance of recent studies of that type. A growing literature deals with psychosocial aspects of cancer, and this area has been discussed by Riley and Spackman (1981) and by Fox (1981). Autoimmune diseases have been discussed by Solomon (1981).

Human Studies

SPECIFIED DISEASES

Studies relating psychosocial factors to specific infectious diseases began to appear in the literature about 25 years ago, and many of the early studies have been discussed in detail by Friedman and Glasgow (1966). Among the few well-designed clinical studies of that earlier period was one by Greenfield *et al.* (1959), who administered the Minnesota Multiphasic Personality Inventory (MMPI) to 38 college students who had recently recovered from infectious mononucleosis (IM). They found a significant relationship between psychological health (ego strength, as measured by the MMPI) and rate of recovery from IM as determined by an internist using hematologic data. Meyer and Haggerty (1962) followed streptococcal disease in 16 families for over a 12-month period and also administered a rating scale to determine the level of "chronic stress." They reported that high stress scores were related to increases in streptococcus acquisition rate, illness rate, and antistreptolycin O responses. In addition, family episodes judged to be stressful were associated with fourfold increases in the frequency of streptococcal and nonstreptococcal respiratory illness.

There is some evidence that dental disease responds to psychosocial influences. Sutton (1965) found correlations between incidence of acute crown caries and patients' reports of "mental stress." Manhold (1979), using the Bernreuter Personality Inventory, found that "neurotic tendencies" and introversion–extroversion ratios correlated with the incidence of decayed, missing, and fitted teeth and with the severity of periodontal destruction. Jacobs *et al.* (1969) administered a number of pencil and paper tests to students reporting to a college health service, comparing these students with upper respiratory infections with an equal number ($n = 29$) of symptom-free students. Those who became ill and sought medical attention displayed greater evidence of role crisis, personal failure, depression, hostility, and anxiety than the "normals."

Diabetes is an immune-related disorder that has been related to psychosocial factors in a number of studies done over the last 30 years (Kimball, 1971). In one study (Stein and Charles, 1971), a group of diabetic adolescents was found to experience a significantly higher incidence of parental loss and "severe family disturbance" (e.g., severe illnesses, emotional conflict) than their matched controls suffering from other chronic disorders.

In a study done at the West Point Military Academy, Kasl *et al.* (1979) screened 1327 entering cadets for presence of Epstein–Barr Virus (EBV) antibody to infectious mononucleosis (IM). Those cadets with the EBV antibody were eliminated from the study. The remaining (susceptible) cadets were followed for one of three possible outcomes. They might, by evidence of the EBV antibody, indicate that they had become infected (seroconverted). These cadets might or might not contract IM. The third group of susceptible cadets would not indicate evidence of seroconversion. As expected, some of the susceptible cadets became infected (seroconverted) during their stay at the Academy without evidence of illness, whereas others contracted IM. The cadets with IM were characterized as experiencing greater academic pressure than the other susceptible cadets, as defined by their high level of motivation, having fathers who were "overachievers," and by their poor academic performance.

EFFECTS OF LIFE EXPERIENCES ON DISEASE

Most clinical studies in the field of psychosomatic medicine have examined the impact of psychosocial factors on disease in general or on disease behavior (e.g., absenteeism, clinic visits) rather than on specific diseases. While such studies may appear to be of little relevance to the student of a specific infectious disease, they are important for at least two reasons. First, they have led to increasingly improved research design from the point of view of the predictor or behavioral variables. These improvements may be readily applied to future studies which may concentrate more fully on specific infectious diseases or on physiological mechanisms. Second, the data from these studies have repeatedly shown that the behavioral stimulus or experience to which a subject is exposed may not be as important as his ability to cope with the situation. This important consideration will be discussed more fully in "Mediating Variables."

A classic series of early studies relating psychosocial factors to illness was done by Hinkle and his associates, beginning some 30 years ago. Many of these studies were of telephone company employees, and indicated that most illnesses were experienced by a relatively small proportion of workers. Those workers with a high illness–absentee rate reported higher levels of dissatisfaction with life and 12 times the number of minor respiratory illnesses than a control sample of low absence workers (Hinkle and Plummer, 1952).

A recent prospective study followed 185 students over a 40-year period (Vaillant, 1979). Incidence of physical illness was related to such psychological predictors as the number of psychiatric visits, use of mood-altering drugs, occupational progress, job dissatisfaction, and amount of recreation with others. These factors were significantly related to physical health even when such things as use of alcohol and tobacco, obesity, and longevity of ancestors were controlled.

During the past 15 years a substantial proportion of the human research relating psychosocial factors to disease has examined "life change" as a predictor of illness (Petrich and Holmes, 1977; Rahe, 1972). Most of these studies utilize a Schedule of Recent Experience (SRE)—a list of 42 life events, each of which had previously been assigned a value by a normative population on the basis of the amount of adjustment required by the event in question. Examples of items and their assigned values include marriage (50), death of spouse (100), trouble with boss (23), gain of new family member (39), and vacation (13). Subjects are generally given the list and asked to indicate which events have occurred during a given period of time—usually 6–24 months. A score is computed, and then related to incidence or severity of illness. Although there are still a number of conceptual and methodological problems with this technique (Rabkin and Streuning, 1976), some of which will be discussed in "A Multifactorial Approach," this line of research is among the most consistent and systematic in the history of psychosomatic medicine.

As mentioned earlier, most life change studies have considered illness behavior or illness in general, rather than focusing on specific diseases. Wyler *et al.* (1971) developed a Seriousness of Illness Rating Scale (SIRS) which has been used in a number of life change studies (Petrich and Holmes, 1977). A group of illnesses were scaled for seriousness by groups of physicians and non-physicians. SIRS scores for specific patients were found to correlate with life change scores on the SRE. Interestingly, the 17 chronic diseases on the list (of which 3 were infectious) correlated highly with SRE scores over 6 months ($r = 0.54$), 1 year ($r = 0.68$) and 2 years ($r = 0.73$) while 11 acute illnesses (of which 7 were infectious) yielded nonsignificant correlations with SRE scores for those same respective time intervals (Wyler *et al.*, 1971). It may be that acute diseases respond to changes during a shorter time span or are more subject to coping mechanisms not accounted for by the SRE (Rabkin and Streuning, 1976).

Since the SRE is to some extent specific to age as well as a number of socioeconomic variables (Masuda and Holmes, 1978), variations of the scale have been developed for other populations. Heisel *et al.* (1973) devised a scale for children, and found that pediatric patients had higher life change scores than "normal" children over a year previous to the illness. Boyce *et al.* (1977) reported that life change scores were related to the duration of respiratory illness in children ranging in age from 1 to 11 years. Correlations of life change scores with severity of illness were higher in children from families in which the level of family routine was also high, suggesting that such families had more difficulty adjusting to life changes.

Animal Studies

Animal models have provided valuable data concerning the role of psychosocial factors in resistance to disease because of the genetic and experimental homogeneity of the animal populations and the ability to manipulate both psychosocial experience and the nature and extent of pathogenic stimulation (Cassel, 1974; Plaut, 1975; Weiner, 1971).

A series of early studies, begun in 1957, demonstrated effects of psychosocial stimulation—primarily in mice—on resistance to herpes simplex virus, Coxsackie B virus, poliomyelitis virus, vesicular stomatitis virus, *Trichinella spiralis,* and tuberculosis (Friedman and Glasgow, 1966). These and more recent studies (Ader, 1980; Friedman *et al.,* 1969) can be classified into three categories, based on the way in which psychosocial experiences are manipulated. These will be briefly described in the following paragraphs and some specific methodological issues raised by these studies will be discussed in "A Multifactorial Approach."

SOCIAL FACTORS

Some studies have investigated effects of social factors as defined by differential housing, that is, the number of animals in a cage. Plaut *et al.* (1969) infected CD-1 mice with *Plasmodium berghei,* a malarial parasite specific to rodents, and found that the postinoculation life span was inversely related to the number of mice in a cage (Figure 2). Friedman *et al.* (1970) studied the effects of differential housing of mice on resistance to encephalomyocarditis (EMC) virus. A higher proportion of individually housed mice died as compared to mice housed five or more per cage (Figure 3).

Edwards and Dean (1977) housed 960 Swiss-Webster mice in cages of 2, 10, 30, or 60 animals, injecting half the animals with typhoid paratyphoid vaccine. After 7 days, all mice were given an LD:50 dose of *Salmonella typhinium.* The mortality rate was higher among mice housed 30 or 60 per cage than among mice housed 2 or 10 per cage. Correspondingly, mean antibody titers were higher for animals housed 2 or 10 per cage than for those in cages of 30 or 60.

Aside from the differential housing studies, few investigators have related social factors to infectious disease resistance. Two studies demonstrated that

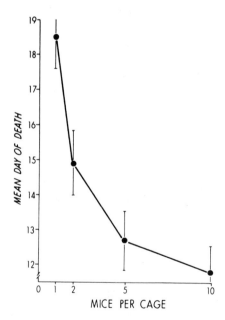

Figure 2. Mean day of death (± *SEM*) in differentially housed CD-1 mice infected with *Plasmodium berghei.* (From "Social Factors and Resistance to Malaria in the Mouse: Effects of Group vs. Individual Housing on Resistance to *Plasmodium berghei* Infection" by S. Michael Plaut, Robert Ader, Stanford B. Friedman, and Albert L. Ritterson, *Psychosomatic Medicine,* 1969, 31, 536–552. Copyright 1969, American Psychosomatic Society, Inc. Reprinted by permission.)

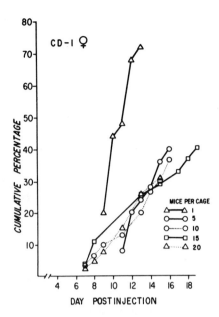

Figure 3. Mortality following inoculation with EMC virus in female CD-1 mice housed 1-20 per cage for 90 days. (From "Differential Susceptibility to a Viral Agent in Mice Housed Alone or in Groups" by Stanford B. Friedman, Lowell A. Glasgow, and Robert Ader, *Psychosomatic Medicine,* 1970, 32, 285-299. Copyright 1970, American Psychosomatic Society, Inc. Reprinted by permission.)

the resistance of mice to the tapeworm *Hymenolepsis nana* was reduced either by intense fighting (Weinman and Rothman, 1967) or by exposure to a cat (Hamilton, 1974).

PROGRAMMED STIMULATION

Regimens of programmed stimulation have been used in many studies in an effort to provide animals with a relatively uniform experience, often with the presumption of an emotional component as a primary factor in the alteration of response to disease. Typically, stimulation involves noxious stimuli, such as relatively mild electric shocks. The shock may or may not be preceded by a warning stimulus (e.g., light or tone), and the animal may or may not be given an opportunity to avoid or escape the noxious stimulus by pressing a lever or performing some other task.

In a pioneering series of experiments, Rasmussen (1969) and his colleagues subjected mice to an avoidance learning task, and observed the effects of this experience on a number of experimentally-induced diseases. In the avoidance learning situation, the animals were placed in a shuttle box apparatus—an elongated cage with a metal grid floor and a barrier separating the two halves of the cage. Every 5 min a light and buzzer were presented to the animal, and the animal was expected to jump the barrier to the other side of the cage. Failure to do so resulted in the presentation of a footshock through the grid floor until the mouse escaped to the other compartment. Rasmussen and his colleagues reported that mice subjected to this procedure displayed increased susceptibility to herpes simplex, poliomyelitis, Coxsackie B, and polyoma virus infections. They also studied accompanying bodily changes (e.g., organ weights) and changes in immune mechanisms such as clearance of foreign particles from the blood, skin graft rejection, and antibody responses to influenza virus vaccine.

Friedman *et al.* (1965) utilized an apparatus similar to that of Rasmussen, but did not permit their animals to escape or avoid the shock. Mice were periodically presented with a 10-sec light followed by an unavoidable, 2-sec shock (paired light–shock). They found that mice inoculated with a Coxsackie B virus and subjected to paired light–shock stimuli lost weight whereas mice who were exposed to shock alone, light alone, or no stimulation did not. Light–shock stimulation in the absence of the virus also had no effect on body weight (Figure 4). Thus, the virus, operating in interaction with the anticipation of a noxious stimulus, decreased resistance to infection. However, when a similar stimulation pattern was presented to mice infected with *P. berghei* malaria, shock *prolonged* life span whether or not preceded by a warning signal (Friedman *et al.*, 1969, 1973). The implications of these different responses to the same stimuli will be discussed in Stress and Coping and Psychosocial Mechanisms under "A Multifactorial Approach."

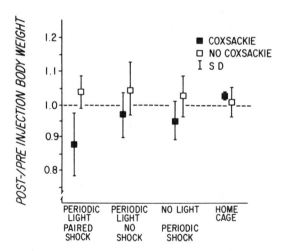

Figure 4. Interactive effects of Coxsackie B virus inoculation and programmed stimulation on weight loss in BALB/cJ mice. (From "Effects of Psychological Stress in Adult Mice Inoculated with Coxsackie B Viruses" by Stanford B. Friedman, Robert Ader, and Lowell A. Glasgow, *Psychosomatic Medicine*, 1965, 27, 361–368. Copyright 1965, American Psychosomatic Society, Inc. Reprinted by permission.)

EFFECTS OF PRIOR EXPERIENCE

The studies of the effects of social factors and programmed stimulation described in the preceding section generally involve experiences imposed concurrently with the animal's exposure to the pathogenic stimulation. Studies with noninfectious disease models indicate that psychosocial stimulation imposed prior to pathogenic challenge can alter subsequent resistance (Ader, 1970). These studies have involved prior stimulation of adult animals as well as prenatal maternal or early postnatal experiences. However, there is little evidence to date of such effects in infectious disease models.

Friedman *et al.* (1969) exposed mice twice daily to 3 min of handling or electric shock stimulation at either 1–21 days or 42–62 days of age, and inoculated them with EMC virus after stimulation was terminated. Mice shocked at age 42–62 days showed a decreased mortality rate compared to animals shocked at the earlier age, handled at either age, or not stimulated. Hotchin *et al.* (1970) reported that mortality of young mice exposed to lymphocytic choreomeningitis virus was altered if maternal behavior was disturbed either by exchanging mothers or providing multiple mothers, and depending on whether the mother was also inoculated with the virus.

A MULTIFACTORIAL APPROACH

The third section of this chapter will be devoted to conceptual and methodological issues important to the design, execution, and interpretation of studies relating psychosocial factors and disease resistance. Figure 1 depicts eight classes of variables important to an understanding of the process by which such relationships occur. A basic study in this field generally takes a "black box" approach, that is, (*a*) the impact of a form of psychosocial stimulation on (*b*) the subjects' state of health or disease is observed under (*c*) a given form of potentially pathogenic stimulation. These three classes of variables may be considered *primary variables* inasmuch as they define the extent of an interrelationship among stimulation, pathogen, and host response. One may then consider the nature of *mediating variables* in that interrelationship, that is, the underlying historical, psychosocial, and physiological mechanisms by which the process takes place, as well as other aspects of the immediate environment to which the host organism is exposed.

Primary Variables

STRESS AND COPING

Just as the "germ theory" has served to inhibit studies relating psychosocial factors to infectious disease, "stress theory" has, to some extent, limited the entire field of psychosomatic research. The assumption, apparently made by many, that "stress" represents only a nonspecific response to stimulation has often led researchers to use the word "stress" to describe virtually any type of stimulation which was applied to their subjects, as if all forms of stimulation were functionally equivalent. Second, the term "stress" typically bears a negative connotation, with the implication that stimuli which, at face value, appear at all noxious are to be avoided. It has been pointed out, however, that each form of stimulation has both nonspecific and specific effects on the organism (Lazarus, 1974; Levi, 1974). Even Selye (1973), the "father" of "stress theory," has emphasized in recent publications that "stress is not something to be avoided"—that is, certain levels of arousing stimuli are both necessary and beneficial to the organism.

It has also been demonstrated that similar forms of noxious or threatening stimulation can increase resistance to some diseases while decreasing resistance to others. As mentioned earlier in Social Factors under "Animal Studies," group housing of mice increases resistance to EMC virus infection while decreasing resistance to malaria. (The bias of investigators in this area can often be determined on the basis of whether the title of their paper refers to effects of "crowding stress" or to "isolation stress.") Similarly, paired light–shock stimulation of mice decreases resistance to Coxsackie B virus (Friedman *et al.*, 1965), but increases resistance to *P. berghei* malaria (Friedman *et al.*, 1973). More recent work from the authors' laboratory has indicated that light–shock stimulation also increases resistance to spontaneous AKR leukemia in mice (Plaut *et al.*, 1980), and blocks increases in blood sugar levels normally resulting from streptozotocin inoculation of mice (Huang *et al.*, in press). These results underscore the value of identifying the mechanisms of these various effects on resistance to disease. They also support the conclusion of some authors that "stress" is of questionable value as a scientifically useful concept (Ader, 1980; Hinkle, 1973; Mason, 1971; Rogers *et al.*, 1979).

It is important to understand, in this context, that the impact of any form of stimulation will depend on how the organism copes with or adapts to the challenge of stimulation (Dubos, 1966). This, in turn, will depend upon the prior experience, background setting, and genetic constitution upon which the stimulation is superimposed (Ader, 1974; Engel, 1974; Martin, 1978). Put in clinical terms, "many times it is more important to know what kind of patient has the disease than what kind of disease the patient has [Rosch, 1979]."

Some of the more recent life change research has demonstrated the importance of the subjects' ability to cope with life changes. The nature and strength of social support systems will affect the impact of life changes (Cassel, 1974; Rabkin and Streuning, 1976). Fairbank and Hough (1979) reported that responses to life changes were dependent on the amount of control their subjects had over these changes.

Weiss (1972) studied the effects of electric shock presented with or without a warning signal on gastric ulceration in rats. The animals were able to avoid or escape the shock by turning a wheel. Weiss found that stimulation schedules characterized by a high response rate and a low level of relevant feedback to the animals led to the highest ulceration rate. For example, rats who could either avoid or escape the shock by turning the wheel displayed a lower level of ulceration than rats who could not avoid or escape shock, but who were electrically "yoked" to the avoidance–escape rats and thus received the *same number of shocks*. In other words, the wheel-turns of the yoked rats resulted in irrelevant feedback. At the same time, however, yoked rats given a warning signal before their shocks had less ulceration than yoked rats who did not get a warning signal. Thus, anticipation and control, that is, the animals' ability or inability to cope with the stimulus situation, was a primary determinant of their resistance to gastric ulceration.

In summary, it is often inappropriate and misleading to make *a priori* value judgments about the consequences of any form of psychosocial stimulation. The subjects' ability to cope with the stimulus in an adaptive way will depend upon its genetic and experiential history, the situation in which the stimuli are presented, and the nature of potentially pathogenic stimulation to which the subject may be exposed. (Further supportive data will be given in the section on Mediating Variables.) In attempting to apply data from this field to clinical situations, efforts to help the patient cope with life events would probably yield more realistic benefits than exhorting him simply to "avoid stress."

DISEASE PARAMETERS

Most discussions of the methodological aspects of psychosomatic research have concentrated on the psychosocial variables rather than on the operational definitions of "disease resistance," as the former have been of primary concern. As the literature in the infectious disease area grows, however, it will be necessary to give more attention to the validity of disease parameters applied to these studies.

In animal studies, one might ask whether psychosocial influences on experimental infection can be generalized to situations involving spontaneous incidence of the same disease. If the endpoint of a study is something other than mortality which can be attributed to the disease in question, the validity of the dependent variable selected must be considered, and it must also be determined that the results can be related to the disease, rather than the psychosocial stimulation alone. For example, Friedman *et al.* (1965) used body weight loss as an index of response to Coxsackie B virus infection. Since it was possible that the light–shock stimulation imposed on the mice might also have resulted in weight loss, some animals were given placebo infections (injections of tissue culture media), thus providing all animals with identical experiences except for the virus itself. It was thus determined that both light–shock stimulation *and* virus infection were necessary for the weight loss to occur (see Figure 4).

Many human studies in this area have observed illness *behavior* (e.g., seeking treatment) as a dependent variable rather than clinical diagnosis (Kasl *et al.*, 1979). Other studies rely on retrospective self-reports of illness. As studies in this area become more refined it may be important to determine the extent to which illness reports, illness behavior, and valid diagnoses are related to each other for any given disease.

Mediating Variables

In order to understand the basis for the effect of any form of psychosocial experience on a given disease, it is important to be aware of the physiological and behavioral mechanisms underlying that effect. The impact of any stimulus will also, as mentioned earlier, depend upon the environmental situation upon which it is superimposed, as well as the genetic and experiential history of the host organism. A classic demonstration of this interrelationship of variables may be found in the writing of Weiner *et al.* (1957), who reported that gastric ulceration rate was dependent on (*a*) the personality profiles of their more than 2000 army inductees, (*b*) their rates of gastric secretion, and (*c*) exposure to social situations which were noxious to given individuals. In parallel studies with rats, Ader (1971) demonstrated that psychological factors, physical stimuli, and genetic predisposition all interacted to determine the rate of gastric ulceration.

SITUATIONAL FACTORS

Two kinds of situational variables are likely to affect the outcome of a study: (*a*) consistent background conditions, and (*b*) experimental procedures. Relevant background conditions may include such things as nutrition, circadian rhythms, temperature, and extraneous stimulation in the immediate environment. For example, Plaut *et al.* (1969) found that the effects of differential housing on malaria infection in mice seen at 21°C, were not seen when room temperature was raised to 27°C. In that same study, it was found that the act of taking a blood sample from the tail of mice on the fifth day after infection with malaria significantly accelerated the rate of mortality. Teodoru and Schwartzman (1956) noted that daily examination of their experimental hamsters decreased their resistance to poliomyelitis infection.

PSYCHOSOCIAL MECHANISMS

Some investigators describe the forms of psychosocial stimulation under study in operational terms (differential housing, light–shock stimulation, handling, life changes), while others describe these variables in more conceptual terms (fighting, crowding, experimental anxiety, novelty). Regardless of which descriptive level is used, it is important to realize that one is really dealing with stimulus complexes. The understanding of any given psychosomatic relationship thus depends ultimately on identification of the elements of the psychosocial stimulation, as operationally defined, which are responsible for the observed effects on resistance to disease.

At times, these stimulus complexes may involve the confounding of psychosocial and "physical" components. Mason (1972) found that hormonal response patterns of monkeys to fasting were altered if animals were provided a nonnutritive food substitute, suggesting that the response to fasting might be partially attributed to such factors as the discomfort of an empty stomach or the fact that the animal caretaker passes the animal by at feeding time.

In other studies it has been shown that subjects' responses to different pathogens are related to different components of the same stimulus complex. The resistance of mice to Coxsackie B virus was affected by paired light–shock stimulation, but not by shock alone (Friedman *et al.,* 1965) (Figure 4). Responses to *P. berghei* malaria, however, were equally affected by light–shock and shock alone (Friedman *et al.,* 1969). Similarly, mortality rate of mice infected with *P. berghei* increased as the number of mice per cage increased from 1 to 10 (Plaut *et al.,* 1969) (Figure 2). However, the percentage of deaths in response to EMC virus was equivalent among mice housed between 5 and 20 per cage (Friedman *et al.,* 1970) (Figure 3). Plaut *et al.* (1969) also demonstrated that population *size,* rather than density, was responsible for the effects of differential housing on malaria infection. They housed different numbers of animals in cages of three sizes and found that mortality rate was related only to the number of animals in a cage and not to the amount of floor area per mouse. In another experiment, mice housed four per cage were separated from each other by a double thickness of wire mesh screening, thus preventing physical contact among the animals. These mice died as slowly as individually housed animals (Figure 5), demonstrating that the increased mortality rate in grouped mice was dependent on the opportunity for physical contact. The knowledge that different aspects of a given form of psychosocial stimulation may affect resistance to different diseases helps explain the fact that the same form of stimulation may increase resistance to one disease and decrease resistance to another.

An increasing number of studies in the "life change" literature are including some more detailed examination of the life change phenomenon in terms of its meaning to the subjects. Mehrabian and Ross (1977) observed illness incidence in undergraduate college students as a function of the extent of life change. In addition, they determined three characteristics of these life changes: (*a*) level of arousal (an out-of-country trip was rated more arousing than a vacation); (*b*) whether the event was pleasurable or unpleasurable (a vacation was rated more pleasurable than the death of a friend); and (*c*) the extent to which the event was submissiveness-inducing (conviction of a crime was more submissiveness-inducing than a promotion at one's job). The authors found that their ability to predict illness was significantly enhanced by

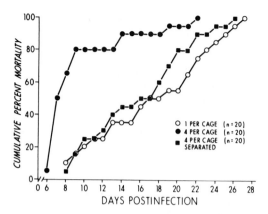

Figure 5. Cumulative mortality in malaria-infected CD-1 mice housed alone, in groups, or in groups without physical contact between animals. (From "Social Factors and Resistance to Malaria in the Mouse: Effects of Group vs. Individual Housing on Resistance to *Plasmodium berghei* Infection" by S. Michael Plaut, Robert Ader, Stanford B. Friedman, and Albert L. Ritterson, *Psychosomatic Medicine,* 1969, 31, 536–552. Copyright 1969, American Psychosomatic Society, Inc. Reprinted by permission.)

taking these factors into account along with the traditionally used "extent of life change" measure. Lin *et al.* (1979) looked at both life changes and social support (e.g., feelings about one's neighborhood, having close friends) as predictors of psychiatric symptoms. Although the extent of life change correlated positively with symptom incidence, the negative correlation of social support with symptom incidence was substantially greater. These studies support the point made earlier, that the impact of any given event will depend on one's ability to cope in an adaptive way.

GENETIC AND ENVIRONMENTAL HISTORY

Levi (1974), in outlining the important factors in a model of psychosocial aspects of disease, refers to the "psychobiological program," that is, one's propensity to react as determined by genetic factors and earlier environmental influences. Friedman and Glasgow (1973) found, for example, that the effects of differential housing on resistance to *P. berghei* malaria observed in CD-1 mice could not be demonstrated in four other mouse strains (Figure 6).

Experiential interactions with psychosocial influences on disease resistance have been shown in other studies. The influence of differential housing on resistance to EMC infection in mice was affected by both preinfection and postinfection housing conditions (Friedman *et al.*, 1970). This was determined by reversing the housing conditions of some mice at or before the time of infection. Using similar methods, however, the effects of differential housing on malaria infection were attributable almost entirely to postinfection housing (Plaut *et al.*, 1969). Similarly, Tobach and Bloch (1956) found that the effects

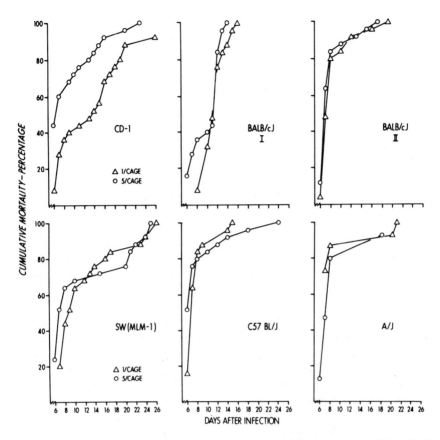

Figure 6. Cumulative mortality of five strains of differentially housed mice infected with *Plasmodium berghei*. (From "Interaction of Mouse Strain and Differential Housing Upon Resistance to *Plasmodium berghei*" by Stanford B. Friedman and Lowell A. Glasgow, *Journal of Parasitology*, 1973, 59, 851-854. Copyright 1973, American Society of Parasitologists. Reprinted by permission.)

of differential housing on resistance to tuberculosis in mice was dependent on postinfection housing conditions. Often, such experiential influences may be "hidden" in the subtle procedural aspects of an experiment. When Friedman *et al.* (1965) first investigated the effects of light-shock stimulation on resistance to Coxsackie B virus infection, no effect of the stimulation on resistance was seen. Since the mice had been in their stimulation cages for only 3 days, the investigators considered the possibility of a "novelty" effect, and, in a second experiment, allowed the mice to adapt to their new cages for 7 days. Under the latter conditions, the stimulation conditions were able to alter the animals' resistance to the virus infection. In a final example, Monjan and Collector (1977) found that sound stimulation could either enhance or depress immunoreactivity, depending on the length of exposure to the stimulation.

A number of life change studies have considered the relationship of life change scores to demographic and personality variables (Uhlenhuth *et al.,* 1974; Garrity *et al.,* 1977; Cleghorn and Streiner, 1979; Hong *et al.,* 1979). Masuda and Holmes (1978), in a review of 19 life change studies, indicated that the impact of life changes on disease could be related to age, marital status, sex, socioeconomic status, ethnicity, education, culture, and prior experience with the event.

PHYSIOLOGICAL MECHANISMS

Perhaps the biggest "missing link" in the field of psychosomatic research is in the paucity of data on physiological mechanisms of the effects of psychosocial factors on resistance to disease. As mentioned earlier the overriding influence of stress theory on this field has led to an excessive concentration on the adrenocortical system as a possible primary mechanism (Friedman and Glasgow, 1966). Mason (1972) has emphasized the value of looking at "overall hormone balance" in determining the state of metabolic activity at any given moment.

Few studies have examined relationships between psychosocial effects on infectious disease resistance and possible physiological mechanisms. Plasma interferon levels and virus titers in blood and selected organs were not able to explain differences in resistance to either rodent malaria (Friedman and Glasgow, 1973) or EMC virus infection (Friedman *et al.,* 1970). Although plasma corticosterone levels were also not related to the psychosocial effects on these diseases, splenectomy was able to eliminate the effect of differential housing on resistance to malaria (Plaut *et al.,* 1971), suggesting some involvement of the reticuloendothelial system (Figure 7).

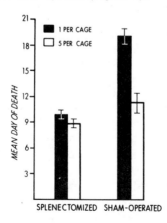

Figure 7. Mortality rates in differentially housed, splenectomized, and sham-operated CD-1 mice infected with *Plasmodium berghei.* (From *"Plasmodium berghei:* Resistance to Infection in Group and Individually House Mice" by S. Michael Plaut, Stanford B. Friedman, and Lee J. Grota, *Experimental Parasitology,* 1971, 29, 47–52. Copyright 1971, Academic Press, Inc. Reprinted by permission.)

In their studies of EMC virus infection in differentially housed mice, Friedman *et al.* (1970) found that females were somewhat more reliably affected by the differential housing, and that a consistently higher mortality rate was seen in male mice at the dosages being used. In subsequent studies, castration of male mice decreased mortality rate to the level of either normal or ovariectomized females, which did not differ from each other (Friedman *et al.*, 1972) (Figure 8). Injections of testosterone into castrated males or females increased mortality rate to the high level of normal males (Figure 9). Mortality rate could also be altered by adrenalectomy or by injection of ovarian hormones, again emphasizing the involvement of many hormone systems and the complexity of mediating factors determining resistance to infection.

The present volume represents an increased emphasis on the immune system as a possible mechanism of such effects. Rogers *et al.* (1979) have recently reviewed the literature relating behavioral factors to the immune system. In pointing out the number of factors (age, sex, race, rhythms) related to measures of immune response, they emphasized the fact that "the immune system is a very complex network, and that there is no simple measure of immunity, but many different measures" must be considered in seeking appropriate mechanisms.

Other studies of possible hormonal mechanisms have demonstrated the importance of variables such as time of day, and time course of response to

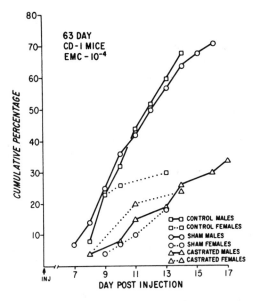

Figure 8. Effects of castration on mortality of CD-1 mice in response to encephalomyocarditis (EMC) virus. (From "Differential Susceptibility of Male and Female Mice to Encephalomyocarditis Virus: Effects of Castration, Adrenalectomy, and the Administration of Sex Hormones" by Stanford B. Friedman, Lee J. Grota, and Lowell A. Glasgow, *Infection and Immunity*, 1972, 5, 637–644. Copyright 1972, American Society for Microbiology. Reprinted by permission.)

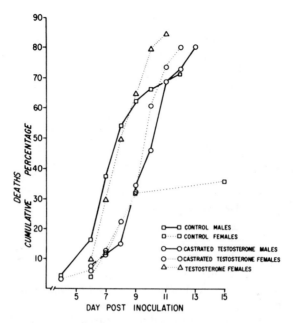

Figure 9. Effect of testosterone on susceptibility to EMC virus in castrated and intact adult CD-1 mice. (From "Differential Susceptibility of Male and Female Mice to Encephalomyocarditis Virus: Effects of Castration, Adrenalectomy, and the Administration of Sex Hormones" by Stanford B. Friedman, Lee J. Grota, and Lowell A. Glasgow, *Infection and Immunity,* 1972, 5, 637–644. Copyright 1972, American Society of Microbiology. Reprinted by permission.)

stimulation in determining hormone levels (Ader *et al.,* 1967; Gruchow, 1979; Plaut and Grota, 1971). Differences between experimental groups may be seen at one time of the 24-hr rhythm but not at another. They may not be seen as baseline responses but may be seen some minutes after a mild stimulus is applied (e.g., handling). Daily susceptibility rhythms to specific infections have been shown as well (Feigin *et al.,* 1969; Shackelford and Feigin, 1973). Attention to such subtle procedural stimuli will not only add to the understanding of such mechanisms, but will also reduce variability in data and facilitate comparison among closely related studies.

RESPONSE TO TREATMENT

The great majority of studies of psychosomatic relationships have dealt with factors determining the onset and course of disease, and virtually no studies have concerned themselves with psychosocial influences on recovery from disease. The disease state will cause changes not only in the physiological state of the patient or animal, but also in social relationships, self-concept, and other psychosocial factors, which may, in turn, alter the disease process by the same mechanisms by which such factors affect disease onset (Imboden, 1972).

In one sense, such studies would seem to have a more practical appeal than the more traditional study in this area, because of the potential of the health professional to influence the psychosocial milieu and, thus, the recovery rate of his patients.

Guidelines for Further Research

As evidenced by the data presented in the previous sections of this paper, research on the psychosocial aspects of infectious disease has been somewhat hampered by our tenacious hold on the germ theory as a means of explaining such diseases, and would benefit greatly by the acceptance of a multivariate approach. Three additional considerations would do much to enhance the rate of progress in this field.

DEFINITION AND COMMUNICATION

It is important that variables be defined in such a way that personal and cultural biases of the investigator are minimized, and that these definitions be clear enough to communicate readily and reliably. "Terms such as 'stress,' 'tension,' 'anxieties,' 'emotional upset,' and the like," writes Engel (1974), "have about as much resolving power today as did 'fevers,' 'catarrh,' or 'dropsy' in bygone eras." A more productive approach would be to describe our forms of stimulation in operational terms initially, and then to attempt to identify the components of stimulation which alter one's resistance to any given pathogenic stimulus.

SYSTEMATIC INVESTIGATION

In order to understand more fully the basis for these psychosomatic relationships, much more attention must be given to the methodological aspects of such studies, and more comprehensive studies must be done involving simultaneous testing of the physiological, psychological, and historical factors involved in these relationships (Hurst *et al.,* 1976; Levi, 1974). With the exception of some of the animal studies and some of the recent research on the effects of life changes on disease, most studies in the infectious disease area have consisted of isolated demonstrations of specific effects with little systematic followup.

INTERDISCIPLINARY COLLABORATION

One of the primary reasons for the absence of systematic research in this area is that the simultaneous investigation of psychosocial and physiological mechanisms generally requires communication and collaboration between workers from various disciplines who can contribute the current methodological expertise required for this research (Ader, 1980; Dworkin, 1969). Hull (1977) recently reviewed over 300 studies published between 1965 and 1974 which related life circumstances to physical illness. These studies came from 8 defined disciplines and were published in 19 different journals. After a factor analytic survey of the antecedents and illnesses studied by the investigators, the disciplines from which they came, and the journals in which they were published, she concluded that this area of work is "inappropriately field bound, and that both investigators and journals are influenced to a surprising degree by historical-traditional considerations in the selection of content."

It would appear that the most effective way to break through such traditional restrictions on thinking and methodology would be to encourage the training of young scientists in this area in settings which expose them to an interdisciplinary milieu (Ader, 1967). This also means that training institutions must be willing to encourage, or at least to allow, their investigators to cross departmental lines freely in setting up such research and training programs. A final area deserving of consideration is that of funding flexibility. There is sometimes a tendency for behaviorally and nonbehaviorally oriented funding agencies to feel that an interdisciplinary training or research application belongs more properly in the "other" camp, resulting in such projects being treated as stepchildren of each agency.

If fruitful, systematic research in this area is to be done, it is vital that appropriate training and research resources be available. Of primary importance, however, is that the role of psychosocial factors in infectious disease be seen as both methodologically valid and clinically relevant. The increasing realization that the immune system is itself subject to psychosocial influences is a major step toward that goal.

REFERENCES

Ader, R. (1967). Training for psychosomatic research: Some views of an experimental psychologist. *Adv. Psychosom. Med.* **5,** 90–99.

Ader, R. (1970). The effects of early life experiences on developmental processes and susceptibility to disease in animals. *In* "Minnesota Symposia on Child Psychology" (J. P. Hill, ed.), Vol. 4, pp. 3–35. Univ. Minn. Press, Minneapolis.

Ader, R. (1971). Experimentally induced gastric lesions: Results and implications of studies in animals. *Adv. Psychosom. Med.* **6,** 1–39.

Ader, R. (1974). The role of developmental factors in susceptibility to disease. *Int. J. Psychiatry Med.* **5,** 367–376.

Ader, R. (1980). Behavioral influences on immune responses. *In* "Perspectives on Behavioral Medicine" (S. Weiss, A. Hurd, and B. Fox, eds.), pp. 1–36. Academic Press, New York.

Ader, R., Friedman, S. B., and Grota, L. J. (1967). 'Emotionality' and adrenal cortical function: Effects of strain, test, and the 24-hour corticosterone rhythm. *Anim. Behav.* **15,** 37–44.

Alexander, F. (1950). "Psychosomatic Medicine." Norton, New York.

Boyce, W. T., Cassel, J. C., Collier, A. M., Jensen, E. W., Ramey, C. T., and Smith, A. H.

(1977). Influence of life events and family routines on childhood respiratory tract illness. *Pediatrics* **60**, 609–615.

Cassel, J. C. (1974). An epidemiological perspective of psychosocial factors in disease etiology. *Am. J. Public Health* **64**, 1040–1043.

Cleghorn, J. M., and Streiner, B. J. (1979). Prediction of symptoms and illness behavior from measures of life change and verbalized depressive themes. *J. Hum. Stress* **5**, 16–23.

Colligan, D. (1975). That helpless feeling: The dangers of stress. *N.Y. Mag.* July 14, pp. 28–32.

Cousins, N. (1976). Anatomy of an illness (as perceived by the patient). *N. Engl. J. Med.* **295**, 1458–1463.

Cousins, N. (1979). Stress. *J. Am. Med. Assoc.* **242**, 459.

DiMatteo, M. R. (1979). A social-psychological analysis of physician–patient rapport: Toward a science of the art of medicine. *J. Soc. Issues* **35**, 12–33.

Dubos, R. (1955). Unsolved problems in the study and control of microbial diseases. *J. Am. Med. Assoc.* **157**, 1477–1479.

Dubos, R. (1961). "Mirage of Health." Doubleday, New York.

Dubos, R. (1966). Man and his environment—biochemical knowledge and social action. *Perspect. Biol. Med.* **9**, 523–536.

Dunbar, H. F. (1943). "Psychosomatic Diagnosis." Harper (Hoeber), New York.

Dworkin, S. F. (1969). Psychosomatic concepts and dentistry: Some perspectives. *J. Peridontol.—Periodontics* **40**, 647–654.

Edwards, E. A., and Dean, L. M. (1977). Effects of crowding of mice on humoral antibody formation and protection to lethal antigenic challenge. *Psychosom. Med.* **39**, 19–24.

Engel, G. L. (1954). Selection of clinical material in psychosomatic medicine. *Psychosom. Med.* **16**, 368–373.

Engel, G. L. (1962). The nature of disease and the care of the patient; the challenge of humanism and science in medicine. *R.I. Med. J.* **45**, 245–251.

Engel, G. L. (1974). Memorial lecture: The psychosomatic approach to individual susceptibility to disease. *Gastroenterology* **67**, 1085–1093.

Engel, G. L. (1977). The need for a new medical model: A challenge for biomedicine. *Science* **196**, 129–136.

Engel, G. L. (1979). The biopsychosocial model and the education of health professionals. *Gen. Hosp. Psychiatry* **1**, 156–165.

Fairbank, D. T., and Hough, R. L. (1979). Life event classifications and the event–illness relationship. *J. Hum. Stress* **5**, 41–47.

Feigin, R. D., San Joaquin, V. A., Haymond, M. W., and Wyatt, R. G. (1969). Daily periodicity of susceptibility of mice to pneumococcal infection. *Nature (London)* **224**, 379–380.

Fox, B. (1981). Psychosocial factors in neoplasia: Studies in man. *In* "Psychoneuroimmunology" (R. Ader, ed.). Academic Press, New York.

Freyhan, F. A. (1976). Is psychosomatic obsolete? A psychiatric reappraisal. *Compr. Psychiatry* **17**, 381–386.

Friedman, S. B., and Glasgow, L. A. (1966). Psychologic factors and resistance to infectious disease. *Pediatr. Clin. North Am.* **13**, 315–335.

Friedman, S. B., and Glasgow, L. A. (1973). Interaction of mouse strain and differential housing upon resistance to *Plasmodium berghei*. *J. Parasitol.* **59**, 851–854.

Friedman, S. B., Ader, R., and Glasgow, L. A. (1965). Effects of psychological stress in adult mice inoculated with Coxsackie B viruses. *Psychosom. Med.* **27**, 361–368.

Friedman, S. B., Glasgow, L. A., and Ader, R. (1969). Psychosocial factors modifying host resistance to experimental infections. *Ann. N.Y. Acad. Sci.* **164**, 381–393.

Friedman, S. B., Ader, R., and Glasgow, L. A. (1970). Differential susceptibility to a viral agent in mice housed alone or in groups. *Psychosom. Med.* **32**, 285–299.

Friedman, S. B., Grota, L. J., and Glasgow, L. A. (1972). Differential susceptibility of male and female mice to encephalomyocarditis virus: Effects of castration, adrenalectomy, and the administration of sex hormones. *Infect. Immun.* **5**, 635–644.

Friedman, S. B., Ader, R., and Grota, L. J. (1973). Protective effect of noxious stimulation in mice infected with rodent malaria. *Psychosom. Med.* **35**, 535-537.

Garrity, T. F., Marx, M. B., and Somes, G. W. (1977). Personality factors in resistance to illness after recent life changes. *J. Psychosom. Res.* **21**, 23-31.

Greenfield, N. S., Roessler, R., and Crosley, A. P. (1959). Ego strength and length of recovery from infectious mononucleosis. *J. Nerv. Ment. Dis.* **128**, 125-128.

Gruchow, H. W. (1979). Catecholamine activity and infectious disease episodes. *J. Hum. Stress* **5**, 11-17.

Hamilton, D. R. (1974). Immunosuppressive effects of predator-induced stress in mice with acquired immunity to *Hymenolepsis nana*. *J. Psychosom. Res.* **18**, 143-153.

Heisel, J. S., Coddington, R. D., Raitz, R., Rappaport, M., and Reams, S. (1973). The significance of life events as contributing factors in the diseases of children. *J. Pediatr.* **83**, 119-123.

Hinkle, L. E. (1956). The influence of the patients behavior and his reaction to his life situation upon the course of diabetes. *Diabetes* **5**, 406-407.

Hinkle, L. E. (1973). The concept of "stress" in the biological and social sciences. *Sci. Med. Man.* **1**, 31-48.

Hinkle, L. E., Jr., and Plummer, N. (1952). Life stress and industrial absenteeism. *Ind. Med. Surg.* **21**, 363-375.

Hong, K. M., Hopwood, M. A., Wirt, R. D., and Yellin, A. M. (1979). Psychological attributes, patterns of life change, and illness susceptibility. *J. Nerv. Ment. Dis.* **167**, 275-281.

Hotchin, J., Benson, L., and Gardner, J. (1970). Mother-infant interaction in Lymphocytic Choriomeningitis virus infection of the newborn mouse: The effect of maternal health on mortality of offspring. *Pediatr. Res.* **4**, 194-200.

Huang, S. W., Plaut, S. M., Taylor, G. A., and Wareheim, L. E. (in press). Effect of stressful stimulation on the incidence of streptozotocin-induced diabetes in mice. *Psychosom. Med.*

Hull, D. (1977). Life circumstances and physical illness: A cross disciplinary survey of research content and method for the decade 1965-1975. *J. Psychosom. Res.* **21**, 115-139.

Hurst, M. W., Jenkins, C. D., and Rose, R. M. (1976). The relation of psychological stress to onset of medical illness. *Annu. Rev. Med.* **27**, 301-312.

Imboden, J. B. (1972). Psychosocial determinants of recovery. *Adv. Psychosom. Med.* **8**, 142-155.

Jacobs, M. A., Norman, M., and Spilken, A. (1969). Relationship of life change, maladaptive aggression, and upper respiratory infection in male college students. *Psychosom. Med.* **31**, 31-44.

Kasl, S. V., Evans, A. S., and Niederman, J. C. (1979). Psychosocial risk factors in the development of infectious mononucleosis. *Psychosom. Med.* **41**, 445-466.

Kimball, C. P. (1971). Emotional and psychosocial aspects of diabetes mellitus. *Med. Clin. North Am.* **55**, 1007-1018.

Lazarus, R. S. (1974). Psychological stress and coping in adaptation and illness. *Int. J. Psychiatry Med.* **5**, 321-333.

Levi, L. (1974). Psychosocial stress and disease: A conceptual model. *In* "Life Stress and Illness" (E. K. Gunderson and R. H. Rahe, eds.), pp. 8-33. Thomas, Springfield, Illinois.

Lin, N., Ensel, W. M., Kuo, W., and Simeone, R. S. (1979). Social support, stressful life events, and illness: A model and empirical test. *J. Health Soc. Behav.* **20**, 108-119.

Manhold, J. H. (1979). Stress, oral disease, and general illness. *Psychosomatics* **20**, 77-83.

Martin, M. J. (1978). Psychosomatic medicine: A brief history. *Psychosomatics* **19**, 697-700.

Mason, J. W. (1971). A re-evaluation of the concept of 'non-specificity' in stress theory. *J. Psychiatr. Res.* **8**, 323-333.

Mason, J. W. (1972). Organization of psychoendocrine mechanisms. A review and reconsideration of research. *In* "Handbook of Psychophysiology" (N. S. Greenfield and R. A. Sternbach, eds.), Holt, Rinehart, and Winston, New York, pp. 3-91.

Masuda, M., and Holmes, T. H. (1978). Life events: Perceptions and frequencies. *Psychosom. Med.* **40**, 236-261.

Mehrabian, A., and Ross, M. (1977). Quality of life change and individual differences in stimulus screening in relation to incidence of illness. *Psychol. Rep.* **41**, 267-278.

Meyer, R. J., and Haggerty, R. (1962). Streptococcal infections in families: Factors altering individual susceptibility. *Pediatrics* **29**, 539-549.

Monjan, A. A., and Collector, M. I. (1977). Stress-induced modulation of the immune response. *Science* **196**, 307-308.

Murray, J. B. (1977). New trends in psychosomatic research. *Genet. Psychol. Monogr.* **96**, 3-74.

Nemiah, J. C. (1973). Psychology and psychosomatic illness: Reflections on theory and research methodology. *Psychother. Psychosom.* **22**, 106-111.

Petrich, J., and Holmes, T. H. (1977). Life change and onset of illness. *Med. Clin. North Am.* **61**, 825-838.

Plaut, S. M. (1975). Animal models in developmental research. *Pediatr. Clin. North Am.* **22**, 619-631.

Plaut, S. M., and Grota, L. J. (1971). Effects of differential housing on adrenocortical reactivity. *Neuroendocrinology* **7**, 348-360.

Plaut, S. M., Ader, R., Friedman, S. B., and Ritterson, A. L. (1969). Social factors and resistance to malaria in the mouse: Effects of group vs. individual housing on resistance to *Plasmodium berghei* infection. *Psychosom. Med.* **31**, 536-552.

Plaut, S. M., Friedman, S. B., and Grota, L. J. (1971). *Plasmodium berghei*: Resistance to infection in group and individually housed mice. *Exp. Parasitol.* **29**, 47-52.

Plaut, S. M., Esterhay, R. J., Sutherland, J. C., Wareheim, L. E., Friedman, S. B., Schnaper, N., and Wiernik, P. H. (1980). Psychological effects on resistance to spontaneous AKR leukemia in mice. *Psychosom. Med.* **42**, 72.

Rabkin, J. G., and Struening, E. L. (1976). Life events, stress, and illness. *Science* **194**, 1013-1020.

Rahe, R. H. (1972). Subjects' recent life changes and their near-future illness susceptibility. *Adv. Psychosom. Med.* **8**, 2-19.

Rasmussen, A. F., Jr. (1969). Emotions and immunity. *Ann. N.Y. Acad. Sci.* **164**, 458-461.

Riley, V., and Spackman, D. (1981). Psychosocial factors in neoplasia: Studies in animals. *In* "Psychoneuroimmunology" (R. Ader, ed.) Academic Press, New York.

Rogers, M. P., Dubey, D., and Reich, P. (1979). The influence of the psyche and the brain on immunity and disease susceptibility: A critical review. *Psychosom. Med.* **41**, 147-164.

Rosch, P. J. (1979). Stress and illness. *J. Am. Med. Assoc.* **242**, 427-428.

Schwab, J. J., and Schwab, R. B. (1975). Social psychiatry and psychosomatics. *Psychosomatics* **16**, 151-154.

Schwartz, G. E., and Weiss, S. M. (1977). What is behavioral medicine? *Psychosom. Med.* **39**, 377-381.

Selye, H. (1946). The general adaptation syndrome and the diseases of adaptation. *J. Clin. Endocrinol.* **6**, 117-230.

Selye, H. (1973). The evolution of the stress concept. *Amer. Scientist* **61**, 692-699.

Shackelford, P. G., and Feigin, R. D. (1973). Periodicity of susceptibility to pneumococcal infection: Influence of light and adrenocortical secretions. *Science* **182**, 285-287.

Solomon, G. F. (1981). Emotional and personality factors in rhemumatoid arthritis and other autoimmune disease. *In* "Psychoneuroimmunology" (R. Ader, ed.). Academic Press, New York.

Stein, S. P., and Charles, E. (1971). Emotional factors in juvenile diabetes mellitus: A study of early life experience of adolescent diabetics. *Am. J. Psychiatry* **128**, 56-60.

Sutton, P. R. N. (1965). The early onset of acute dental caries in adults following mental stress. *N.Y. Dent. J.* **31**, 450-456.

Teodoru, C. V., and Schwartzman, G. (1956). Endocrine factors in pathogenesis of experimental poliomyelitis in hamsters: Role of inoculatory and environmental stress. *Proc. Soc. Exp. Biol. Med.* **91**, 181-187.

Tobach, E., and Bloch, H. (1956). Effect of stress by crowding prior to and following tuberculosis infection. *Am. J. Physiol.* **187**, 399-402.

Uhlenhuth, E. H., Balter, M. B., Lipman, R. S., and Stern, M. (1974). Symptom intensity and life stress in the city. *Arch. Gen. Psychiatry* **31,** 759-764.

Vaillant, G. E. (1979). Natural history of male psychological health: Effects of mental health on physical health. *N. Engl. J. Med.* **301,** 1249-1254.

Weiner, H. (1971). Current status and future prospects for research in psychosomatic medicine. *J. Psychiatr. Res.* **8,** 479-498.

Weiner, H., Thaler, M., Reiser, M. F., and Mirsky, I. A. (1957). Etiology of duodenal ulcer. I. Relation of specific psychological characteristics to rate of gastric secretion (serum pepsinogen). *Psychosom. Med.* **19,** 1-10.

Weinman, C. J., and Rothman, A. H. (1967). Effects of stress upon acquired immunity to the dwarf tapeworm *Hymenolepsis nana. Exp. Parisitol.* **21,** 61-67.

Weiss, J. M. (1972). Psychological factors in stress and disease. *Sci. Am.* **226,** 104-113.

Wyler, A. R., Holmes, T. H., and Masuda, M. (1971). Magnitude of life events and seriousness of illness. *Psychosom. Med.* **33,** 115-122.

Psychoneuroimmunologic Factors in Neoplasia: Studies in Animals

VERNON RILEY
M.A. FITZMAURICE
DARREL H. SPACKMAN

INTRODUCTION

Stress: The Difficulties of Definition

Stress is a widely and somewhat loosely used term for describing a biological response to a novel or difficult situation. There is, thus, an infinite variety of circumstances where this has been used as a convenient term to convey a complex and incompletely understood physiological concept (Mason, 1975a,b; Riley, 1979b; Selye, 1975).

In these studies, we have employed the term "stress" in a more restricted experimental framework. Thus, for purposes of this presentation, we would like to describe our use of this convenient word in terms of specific biochemical and cellular changes that are induced by an emotional activation of the adrenal cortex. Within the restricted biological system that we have examined, the following parameters describe both qualitatively and quantitatively the physiological manifestations of "stress," and their pathological and other consequences in experimental animals.

31

Although stress undoubtedly brings about many biochemical changes, in these studies we have focused our attention on the adrenal cortex and have measured the most conspicuous, and what appears at this time to be the most relevant of the biochemical substances elaborated by this remarkable organ, namely, corticosterone. In the higher primates and man, the equivalent would be cortisol, of course. Immediately following an emotional stimulus, or the perception of a situation that generates anxiety, the adrenal cortex in response to signals from the hypothalamus via the pituitary produces increased quantities of corticosterone. The rapidity of appearance in the plasma and the quantitative extent of this biochemical product can be readily measured by appropriate microassay techniques (Glick *et al.,* 1964; Spackman and Riley, 1978; Spackman *et al.,* 1978).

Secondary manifestations resulting from the elevation of the corticosterone concentrations in the blood plasma are (*a*) lymphocytopenia; (*b*) thymus involution; and (*c*) a corresponding loss of tissue mass of the spleen and peripheral lymph nodes. Details of these cellular and tissue effects will be described in other sections of this chapter; however, it is relevant to note here that the above consequences of stress have significant adverse effects upon important elements of the immunologic defense apparatus. By the appropriate design of experiments, it is possible to demonstrate these effects upon cancer and other disease processes.

Although we favor a conservative attitude in extrapolating biological findings from mice to other species, as biologists we cannot refrain from subscribing to the logical principle that there are many physiological similarities and biochemical relationships among animals belonging to an evolutionary phylum. A reasonable expectation associated with this thesis is that basic biological principles that are further delineated by the study of animal models, may have some application to man.

Many careful investigators have examined the relationships between various forms of stress and neoplastic processes. The formidable difficulties inherent in the establishment of authentic quiescent baseline conditions for experimental animals, however, has complicated the interpretation of many of these earlier studies. In addition, in many cases there was a lack of access to the biochemical and cellular measurements which provide an objective assessment of the basic physiological manifestations of stress.

The resulting failure to obtain consistent results between laboratories tended to undermine confidence in the reliability of research in this difficult but vital field. However, rapid developments in the past few years delineating and characterizing many new facets of immunology, endocrinology, and neurobiology now provide a more effective base for reexamining and determining both the potentialities and the limitations of the effects of stress upon various neoplastic processes.

BACKGROUND

Physiological Effects of Various Stressors upon Immune Competence

Marsh and Rasmussen (1960) observed typical stress syndromes consisting of adrenal hypertropy, thymus involution, leukocytopenia, and a decrease in spleen weight in mice following their daily exposure to shuttle box electric shock, or immobilization. These adverse effects on immunologic elements, and other organs, are consistent with the findings of Riley and Spackman (1976a,b, 1977a). Nieburgs *et al.* (1976, 1979) undertook studies to examine the effects of various types of stress on tumorigenesis at the cellular level. They examined the microscopic changes occurring in the thyroid, thymus, liver, adrenals, stomach, lungs, and testes following a variety of stress stimuli. These included handling, transportation, cold swim, and electric shock. Marked differences were observed in the mitosis of liver cells harvested from stressed rats. Some changes that were observed in animals that had received electric shock for a 2-hr period were absent in animals that had been subjected to the same stress for 24 hr. However, other cellular changes were more prominent in rats at 24 hr following electric shock, and also at various periods following discontinuation of the stress. They reported that stress resulted in a reduction in the numbers of blood lymphocytes, with a decrease in the percentage of small lymphocytes, and a relative increase in the percentage of large lymphocytes. This suggests an alteration in the relative proportion of T and B lymphocytes. The abnormal cellular changes which occurred as a result of cold swim stress, transportation, and handling, persisted longer than those produced by electric shock.

Cancer Immunology, and the CNS

A series of investigations by Khayetsky (1965), Korneva and Khai (1963), Stein *et al.* (1969, 1976), and others have examined the immunological consequences of producing lesions in the anterior hypothalamic area of experimental animals. In general, a lower antibody production was found in such animals as compared to those that had posterior hypothalamic lesions, or with no lesions at all. As a result of these experiments, it was suggested that psychosocial phenomena may modify the immune processes through the central nervous system. The Russian investigators Korneva and Khai (1963) also found that in rabbits with lesions of the hypothalamus, there was a suppression of antibodies and a prolonged retention of antigen in the blood. The implications of this work have been extended by Kavetsky *et al.* (1958, 1966,

1969), through an examination of the relationships between alterations in the central nervous system and subsequent malignancies. They also reported that it is possible to alter the course of hormone-dependent tumors by procedures that act upon the hypothalamus. Not all authors have observed a direct relationship between the host immunological status and cancer. It has been reported, for example, that the immunological state of the host did not seem to affect the development of either the primary tumor or of metastases in mice inoculated with the Lewis lung carcinoma.

The Effects of Various Stressors on
Virus-Induced and Transplantable Tumors

Reznikoff and Martin (1957) studied the influence of electric shock on the incidence of spontaneous mammary tumors in C3H mice that carried the mammary tumor virus (MTV), in comparison with similar C3H mice in which the virus was absent. Half of the animals in each of the two groups were stressed by daily intermittent electric shock for periods ranging from about 6 months to over a year. The authors reported that mice without a predisposition to mammary cancer as a result of the absence of MTV, did not in any instance develop tumors, even when exposed to shocks; whereas more than 75% of the "stressed" animals with MTV, and a comparable percentage of the MTV-infected controls, developed mammary tumors. The tumors appeared earlier, however, in the "stressed" group of MTV-infected mice. These findings were discussed by the authors with the caution that they were preliminary and required confirmation. The results are, however, consistent with reports from our laboratory (Riley, 1975; Riley et al., 1975; Riley and Spackman, 1977a), indicating that protective, low stress animal housing significantly reduced mammary tumor incidence, when compared with that observed in similar mice housed in conventional facilities known to induce chronic or intermittent stress.

Solomon and Amkraut (1979) and Solomon et al. (1980) have demonstrated varied effects of stress on the development of Moloney sarcoma virus (MSV)-induced tumors. Their observations include both enhancement and suppression of tumor growth by different stress systems. For example, the stress of 4 hr per day of random brief electric shocks administered successively for 3 days prior to inoculation with MSV reduced the incidence and size of tumors. However, when shocks were continued during the course of tumor growth, spontaneous regression was somewhat delayed, but both incidence and tumor size eventually equaled those of the controls. On the other hand, when mice were subjected to 3 days of electric shock stress following MSV inoculation, a significant increase in tumor size was observed.

The role of immunologic competence in host resistance to virus-induced tumor development is supported by the observation of Fefer *et al.* (1968) that immunologically immature mice less than 2 weeks of age inoculated with Moloney sarcoma virus all succumb; whereas immunocompetent mice 4 weeks of age or older, when injected with MSV, develop sarcomas which grow progressively for 1 or 2 weeks and then are rejected, with survival of the hosts. This has been confirmed and extended by Riley *et al.* (1978a; see also Hirsch, 1974).

Marsh *et al.* (1959) studied the effect of repeated brief exposures to stress on the growth of the transplantable Ehrlich carcinoma. A series of experiments were performed in which mice that had been injected subcutaneously with Ehrlich tumor cells were subjected to stress either by an electric shock shuttle box technique, or by immobilization. In 5 out of the 8 experiments, significantly smaller tumors were observed in the stressed animals than in the controls. Two of the remaining three experiments yielded statistically nonsignificant results, but in the same direction, and one experiment showed a significant increase in the size of the tumors in the stressed mice. Uncontrolled experimental variables which may account for these puzzling discrepancies are discussed in a separate section of this chapter.

Effects of Various Stressors
on Chemically-Induced Tumors

Sakakibara (1966) studied the effects of bright light, compared with total darkness, or normal laboratory light, on chemical carcinogenesis. A 20-week course of dimethylbenzanthracene (DMBA), administered through the diet, was given to mice that were 11 weeks old at the start of the experiment. The animals were divided into four groups: One group was exposed to flashing lights, at 1000 lux, with the light being switched on and off 30 times per min for 8 hr a day. In these mice, liver tumors developed with an average latent period of 15 weeks, and a tumor incidence of 79%. In mice exposed to steady fluorescent light of the same intensity and for the same time period, the tumors developed in 16 weeks, and the incidence was 64%. Similar mice kept in darkness developed tumors in an average of 18 weeks with an incidence of 24%. Mice which were termed "controls" were kept under natural room light, and in this case tumors developed in 18 weeks with an incidence of 36%. The authors attributed the shortened latent periods and increased tumor incidence in the mice exposed to flashing or continuous light as the consequences of a stress response. The observation of Khayetsky (1965) that continuous light resulted in hypothalamic and pituitary disturbances may be relevant.

Cooley *et al.* (1976) compared the effects of electric shock, immobilization, and group-housing on the growth of DMBA-induced tumors. They found that electric shock and immobilization inhibited the growth of these tumors through activation of a sympathetic adrenal medullary response, whereas the group-housed rats exhibited high steroid levels, which were responsible for enhanced tumor growth. Their observations on the inhibition of DMBA-induced tumors following immobilization are in agreement with the results of Marsh *et al.* (1959), who observed an inhibition of Ehrlich ascites tumors in mice, and Guillon *et al.* (1970), who observed a delayed appearance of DMBA-induced mammary tumors following immobilization. However, Newberry *et al.* (1972) observed that forced restraint failed to influence the average size of the DMBA-induced tumors that appeared in their rats.

The effects of electric shock applied intermittently over various prolonged periods were studied by Newberry (1976), Newberry and Sengbusch (1979), and Nieburgs *et al.* (1976, 1979). Both research groups employed DMBA-induced mammary tumors in rats. In Newberry's experiments, shocks applied for 25 consecutive days had no effect upon tumor incidence. However, reduced tumor incidence was observed when the shocks were applied for 40 or 85 days.

Nieburgs' group found that tumor incidence was decreased following 90 days of shock treatment, and increased when the shocks were applied for 150 days. Similar effects on tumor incidence were found in rats exposed to handling stress for 90 and 150 days. However, handling for 90 days resulted in a decrease in average tumor size, whereas electric shock treatment given over the same time period was associated with an increased tumor size. Some of these timing effects may be related to a cycling of immune suppression followed by immune enhancement, similar to the observations of Monjan and Collector (1977), which are discussed in a separate section of this chapter.

Effects of Isolation and Cage Crowding

Andervont (1944), Muhlbock (1950, 1951), and Henry *et al.* (1975) investigated the influence of population density on spontaneous mammary tumor latent periods. Mice reared in isolation were compared to those raised in groups. The isolation-reared mice developed mammary tumors earlier than did analogous mice raised in social groups. In view of other studies, these results might be interpreted as demonstrations that prolonged isolation-rearing modifies the immunologic capacity of the animals to cope with either the mammary tumor virus (MTV), or the malignant cells transformed by the virus.

In a related inquiry, Glenn and Becker (1969) studied the influence of varying the housing congestion on immunocompetence in Swiss Webster female mice. They found that animals housed singly showed a significantly less vigorous humoral immune response to challenge by 0.1% BSA than did similar mice that were housed in larger groups. This suggests that the immune capabilities of the mice housed singly were impaired in comparison with those mice living in a more "normal" crowded social situation. These observations may be interpreted as being consistent with the results of Henry and Santisteban (1971) and Henry *et al.* (1972, 1975), who found that isolation-rearing handicapped mice in coping with stressful situations imposed later in life. Such observations would also seem to be consistent with those of Andervont (1944) and Muhlbock (1950, 1951).

Dechambre and Gosse (1968, 1971) studied the influence of population density on the survival time of mice bearing two varieties of transplanted tumors. Virgin female C57BL/6 mice, bearing subcutaneous implantations of B-16 melanoma, were employed in one experimental series. Dechambre and Gosse made the observation that survival time was longer when the mice were caged individually, in contrast to mice caged in groups of 10. Similar effects upon mice bearing Krebs-2 ascites carcinoma were also described. However, in a later report (1973), the same authors concluded that an abrupt change in social environment, either from isolation (single mouse per cage) to a group of 10 mice per cage, or vice versa, resulted in adrenal hypertrophy and increased growth of implanted Krebs-2 ascites tumors. Since the physiological response was the same whether the environmental change involved a decrease or an increase in population density, it was concluded by the authors that mice perceive such environmental changes as stressful.

Consequences of Early Experiences of Rodents

Newton (1974, 1975) and Newton *et al.* (1962) reported that tactile and visual experience, such as handling in the first few days of life, exposure to light, and closeness to the mother, lead to significant alterations in the animals' response to stress. The parameters examined were emotional reactivity, weight gain, and learning behavior. It was suggested that influences on the developmental process are more subtle than has heretofore been realized.

Santisteban and Henry (1971) and Henry *et al.* (1972, 1975) also found that early experience has a profound effect upon the subsequent ability of mice or rats to cope with psychosocial stress. As an example, mice that were reared in isolation between 4 and 12 weeks of age, and then placed in a competitive "population cage" where they were subjected to the stress of frequent confrontation and social integration, developed hypertension, cardiovascular diseases, heart enlargement, and other pathologies, more rapidly than mice that were raised in a competitive environment in cages containing 8–10 mice. Exposure of isolation-reared female mice to subsequent psychosocial stress enhanced mammary tumor incidence, as compared to mice reared under more normal circumstances.

Solomon and Amkraut (1979) found that rats handled from birth responded more vigorously to primary challenge with the potent antigen flagellin at 9 weeks of age, and also to a booster immunization 4 weeks later, when compared with nonhandled controls. This was in contrast to their finding that stress administered to adult animals was immunosuppressive, when measured by their response to flagellin administered both immediately prior to and subsequent to stress.

A series of related papers by Levine (Levine and Cohen, 1959; Levine, 1967), Ader and Friedman (1964, 1965a,b), Ader and Grota (1969), Friedman and Ader (1965), Friedman *et al.* (1965, 1969), La Barba (1970), La Barba *et al.* (1967, 1970a,b), have also examined the influence of early experience on the subsequent ability of animals to cope with stress. For example, Ader and Friedman (1964, 1965a,b) found that the handling of infant rats during their first week of life delayed the appearance of transplanted Walker 256 tumors, but increased the mortality, following inoculation of 60-day-old rats with Walker 256 tumor cells. Handling or manipulation was frequently used as a stressor for young rats by these investigators. However, the effects of early weaning, electric shock, and other methods such as restraint were also examined. A great deal of inconsistency and apparent experimental contradiction appeared in these copious data; it is presumed that the many experimental variables among the various laboratories may be responsible for the seeming lack of agreement in the data.

Otis and Scholler (1967) exposed young mice and rats for short periods daily to electric shock either to the body surface or by convulsive shock to the brain. The shock exposures were administered over a short period between birth and 24 days of age. This was followed either by implantation of transplantable tumors, or tumor induction by chemical or viral agents. The experimental results failed to support the findings of other investigators, namely, that repeated electric shocks given to infant rodents resulted in a subsequent lowered resistance to cancer-producing agents, and a decrease in the latent period of spontaneous tumors. There are a number of possible explanations for such discrepant results, which are discussed in another section of this chapter.

Effects of Temperature on Spontaneous or Viral-Induced Tumors

Fuller *et al.* (1941) studied the effect of several environmental temperatures on spontaneous tumors in mice. Various groups of virgin female DBA mice were kept under conditions of moist warmth at 90–91° F (32–33° C), or in a cooler environment of 65° F. They reported that the tumors which appeared under the moist warm environmental conditions grew more slowly and took over twice as long to kill their hosts as did tumors in animals maintained at the cooler temperature. The average of the time required between the appearance of the tumors and the deaths of the animals were 28 days at 65° F, 47 days at 70–75° F, and 60 days at 90–91° F.

Wallace *et al.* (1944) also examined the influence of environmental temperature on the incidence and course of spontaneous mammary tumors, employing C3H mice carrying the Bittner virus (MTV). The virgin mice employed in these experiments exhibited an increase in tumor incidence in "cool" environments of 68° F (20° C), as compared with "hot" environments of 91° F (33° C). However, once the tumors appeared, they killed the hosts residing in the higher temperatures more quickly. Multiple tumors in the C3H mice were four times more frequent among the "cool room" mice than among those kept at 91° F, possibly as a result of their longer survival periods.

If stress is evoked to explain the effects of temperature on the spontaneous tumors, then low and normal temperatures would appear to be more stressful than high temperatures. However, the authors felt that the lower tumor incidence observed in warm environments represented a tumor suppression rather than merely a delay in tumor appearance. They compared their findings with the reported epidemiological rate of human cancer deaths by age groups in northern states compared with southern states, and pointed out that cancer rates in the north rise much more rapidly with advancing age than cancer rates in the south.

Of possible relevance, Newell and Waggoner (1970) carried out epidemiological investigations on cancer mortality and environmental temperature in the United States. They suggested that geographical differences in cancer mortality could be associated with both artifacts and indirect causative factors, rather than reflecting a direct environmental effect of temperature on cancer risk, and concluded that the statistical differences require careful interpretation.

Temperature Influences upon Chemically Induced Tumors

Young (1958) studied the effect of temperature on the production of DMBA-induced mammary tumors, employing noninbred, specific pathogen-free rats. One group was maintained at a "warm" temperature of 32° C (90° F), while the other group was maintained at a "low" temperature of 5° C (40° F). All animals were on a standard diet, and exposed to equal periods of light and darkness. A single dose of DMBA (30 mg, orally in corn oil) was administered to the mice at 50 days of age. The earliest mammary tumors occurred in the "warm" temperature group, and appeared 5.5 weeks after DMBA administration. Those rats maintained at the "low" temperature developed tumors 2 weeks later. The total mammary tumor incidence at 120 days following DMBA administration was 26 out of 39 animals (67%) in the "warm" temperature group, as compared to only 16 out of 39 rats (41%) in the "low" temperature group.

Wallace *et al.* (1942) performed analogous experiments employing subcutaneous injections of methylcholanthrene (MCA) to induce sarcomas in C3H mice under two environmental conditions: specifically, "warm–humid" compared with normal laboratory temperatures. Tumors arose earlier in the mice held in the warm environment of 92° F (33° C), as compared with their litter mates maintained at 65° F (18° C). The average sarcoma latent period was 10 weeks in the "warm" room, as compared to 12 weeks in the "cool" room.

In a separate experiment by Wallace *et al.* (1942), one of the MCA-induced tumors was transplanted into C3H mice and maintained in the two thermal environments. When the tumor was implanted subcutaneously, the sarcomas grew rapidly in the "warm" room, but grew slowly or regressed in the "cool" room. When injected intramuscularly, the sarcomas grew with equal rapidity in both environments.

The higher tumor incidences and shortened latent periods observed for chemically-induced tumors following the administration of MCA or DMBA to mice maintained at high temperatures might be ascribed to stress induced by these temperatures. However, since exposure to cold has also been considered to be stressful, other physiological mechanisms may account for the more rapid development of chemically induced tumors in hosts exposed to warm temperatures.

EXPERIMENTAL OBSERVATIONS
MADE IN OUR LABORATORY

Alteration of Mammary Tumor Incidence
as a Function of Environmental Stress

For many years C3H female mice harboring the mammary tumor virus (MTV) from birth have been employed for various experimental purposes (Andervont, 1944; Muhlbock, 1950, 1951; Riley, 1975; Riley *et al.*, 1975; Riley and Spackman, 1977a; Wallace *et al.*, 1944).

In Figure 1, experimental groups A and B are depicted by the two upper curves that illustrate the statistically significant differences found in mammary tumor latent periods and final mammary tumor incidence in parous and nonparous C3H mice held under standard housing conditions. Both groups were housed in stainless steel "shoe box" containers on open racks in a communal animal room that was subject to the daily activities of cage cleaning, bleeding procedures, rack movement, and other stress-inducing experimental manipulations of animals in the same room. Both groups were thus exposed to the usual dust, noise, drafts, odors, and recirculating pheromones.

The experimental results obtained under these conventional environmental conditions are in contrast to the extended mammary tumor latent periods observed in mouse group C, represented by the lower curve. These animals were analogous to the nonparous mice of group B, but important modifications were made in their housing, and thus in their exposure to chronic stress.

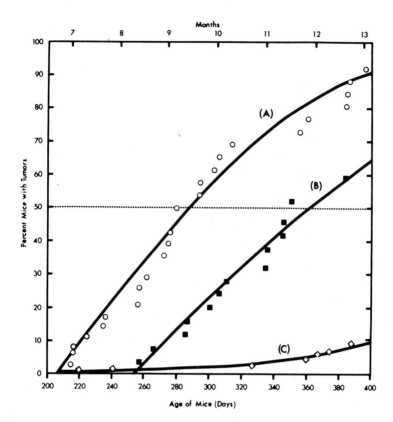

Figure 1. Mammary tumor incidence and latent periods of C3H/He female mice maintained under various environmental conditions. (A) Parous mice housed under conditions of daily stress. (B) Nonparous mice housed under the same conditions of daily stress. (C) Nonparous mice housed under environmental conditions of low stress.

Unlike groups A and B, group C mice were housed in plastic cages with bedding and were maintained within specially designed protective enclosed ventilated shelves. They also experienced less thermal fluctuation and greater precision in the control of equal light–dark cycles.

These low stress residential changes are presumed to have had a beneficial influence on the immunologic surveillance capabilities of the mice in group C by a retention of the integrity of their thymus, and a normal maintenance of their T cell population. Other unknown factors contributing to cancer cell surveillance and immunologic competence may also have benefited from the low-stress environment.

Thus, as a practical demonstration of the pathological effects of chronic environmental stress, the data of Figure 1 illustrate the significant differences obtained in mammary tumor incidence and latent periods in genetically susceptible mice carrying the Bittner mammary tumor virus, when maintained under various environmental and experimental conditions. For example, the median latent period for the parous mice in group A housed in conventional facilities was 276 days as compared to 358 days for the companion group B consisting of nonparous mice. In contrast, the nonparous group C mice housed in low stress protective facilities had a median latent period of 566 days, a significant extension over both groups A and B ($p < .001$).

Protective Animal Housing
as an Essential Research Component

It is clear from the data shown in Figure 1 that critical experimental work cannot be done in the field of psychoneurobiology using conventional animal housing facilities, since they are not suitable for the maintenance of normal quiescent baseline values of stress-associated hormonal and cellular elements that influence or control physiological and pathological processes. We have therefore designed animal facilities which not only serve the experimental needs of our physiological stress research but, in addition, provide safer facilities for working with either infectious or allergenic agents (Riley, 1972, 1978; Riley and Spackman, 1977a). The essential principles of low stress animal facilities are illustrated by the prototypes shown in Figure 2.

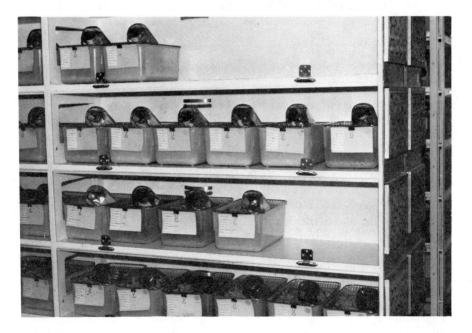

Figure 2. Protective mouse facilities. Each shelf is independently ventilated, and enclosed with noise-suppressing, hinged plexiglass doors. No odors, pheromones, or infectious aerosols are recirculated within the room, or through the laminar-flow shelving.

From the standpoint of the low-stress environment that is essential for careful biological research involving animals, these individually ventilated shelf units offer several beneficial features. For example, the enclosed shelves provide a substantial degree of soundproofing, which is of significance since it has been established that animals are stressed by a wide variety of noises which stimulate immunologically adverse neuroendocrine reactions (Henry, 1967; Jensen and Rasmussen, 1963; Monjan and Collector, 1977; Sze, 1970). Stressful noises and periodic cage motion are prevalent in most conventional animal rooms, particularly where there are rolling metal racks employed for supporting either plastic or metal cages, loud radios, shouting, routine cage cleaning with rough handling, and other noisy and stressful operations.

Corticosterone Levels in Mice Housed
in Conventional and Low-Stress Animal Facilities

As a consequence of several interrelated developments, it has been demonstrated that experiments using mouse models for the study of immunologic and neoplastic relationships are frequently compromised by the inadvertent and unappreciated stress that is present when mice are maintained in conventional housing facilities and handled in the usual manner. This is illustrated by the mammary tumor data shown in Figure 1.

The protective animal facilities shown in Figure 2 constitute one of the important conditions that permitted our work upon environmental and anxiety stress to be placed on a quantitative basis. It is such quiescent conditions that permit the low baseline values of 0–35 ng/ml for plasma corticosterone to be obtained. In contrast, plasma corticosterone values observed in mice maintained in conventional communal animal rooms where the animals are routinely exposed to rack motion, cage cleaning, noise, drafts, dust, odors, pheromones, and experimental manipulation have usually been in the range of 150–500 ng/ml. This constitutes an elevation of ten to twenty times the quiescent plasma corticosterone level. Such physiological corticosterone elevations cause thymus involution, lymphocytopenia, alterations in amino acid metabolism, and may produce various effects upon tumor growth, latent periods, and incidence (Monjan and Collector, 1977; Spackman and Riley, 1974, 1976; Spackman et al., 1975). These effects imply that animals housed under conventional, nonprotective conditions may have a relatively impaired immunocompetence.

A subenvironmental factor to be considered in maintaining mice under optimal conditions is the type of holding cage to be employed within the animal facilities. For example, we have compared plasma corticosterone levels of mice housed in hanging wire-bottom cages and analogous mice housed in plastic cages with corn-cob bedding. Both types of holding cages were maintained within the same low-stress protective facilities. A statistically significant plasma corticosterone elevation ($p < .005$) was observed in the mice housed in the wire-bottom cages. In addition to the hormone increase, a differential adrenomegaly ($p < .01$) and a shortening of life span was observed ($p < .0001$). These data strongly suggest that wire-bottom cages are stressful for mice, even when employed within protective facilities. Other environmental factors which may affect experimental results have been discussed by Vessell *et al.* (1976).

Stresslike Effects Generated
by Near Proximity of Male and Female Mice

Figure 3 demonstrates that mice housed in separate cages, but in proximity to cages of mice of the opposite sex, exhibited a four- to sevenfold increase in plasma corticosterone level. Male mice were less affected when observed over a long period. These data indicate that the mixing of the sexes within the same facility, even if housed in separate cages, may have physiological consequences that can distort biochemical and immunlogic parameters. It should be recognized, of course, that these effects might not be observed under the nor-

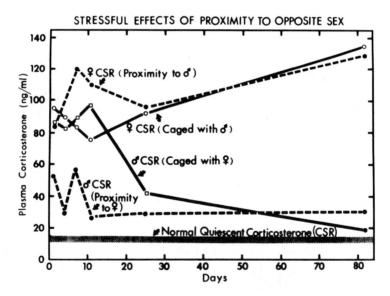

Figure 3. Corticosterone (CSR) alterations in mice exposed to the opposite sex. Plasma corticosterone levels of adult mice caged with mice of the opposite sex are compared with the hormone levels of analogous mice caged in the vicinity of such cages, but containing only one sex in each cage. Female corticosterone values were obtained from nonpregnant individuals only. All mice were housed 5 per cage in standard plastic cages with corn-cob bedding, and maintained in enclosed, individually ventilated shelves with laminar airflow. The "normal quiescent" corticosterone levels were established for normal quiescent mice housed in the complete absence of the opposite sex.

mally stressful conditions of a conventional animal room, where the mice may have corticosterone elevations five- to twentyfold above normal.

Rapidity of Corticosterone Elevation
Following Environmental Stress

Figure 4 illustrates the profound hormonal consequences that an extremely mild handling is capable of inducing in normal quiescent mice. The cluster of unconnected points at the bottom left hand corner of the figure are the quies-

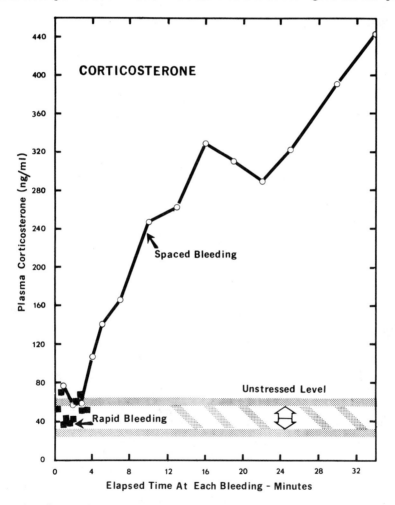

Figure 4. Influence of animal capture and handling upon the concentration of stress-induced corticosterone elevations in the plasma of normal mice as a function of time. The ascending linear curve demonstrates the rapidity of the physiological response to stress as measured by the corticosterone parameter. Both groups of mice were bled by the orbital bleeding technique.

cent plasma corticosterone values of individual mice that are obtained when a group of 10 animals is removed from protective storage and the mice bled by the rapid orbital bleeding technique (Riley, 1960) within 3½ min. This short time period is insufficient for the overt expression of fear or anxiety to be manifested biochemically by an elevation of plasma corticosterone. However, when similar cages of mice were removed from protective storage, and one animal was randomly captured and bled every 2 or 3 min, the ascending curve shows the rate at which corticosterone becomes elevated in the blood plasma of such stressed animals. This corticosterone elevation is induced, not merely by the bleeding procedure itself, but by the anxiety induced in the entire cage population during the sequential capture of each mouse.

Similar effects have been observed in each of four different mouse strains tested (BDF, BAF, C3H, and CBA), as well as in mice of different ages, specifically young mice 7 weeks of age and mice 24 months old. These data have led to the recognition that quiescent corticosterone levels can be obtained only when the blood samples are obtained within 3½ min following removal of the animals from protective storage.

Intercage Communication of Anxiety?

Six standard plastic cages containing 5 mice each were removed from their low stress, enclosed housing shelves and were placed together on an open shelf adjacent to the work bench where the mice were bled. Blood samples obtained from the 5 mice in each cage by the orbital bleeding route were pooled and the plasma corticosterone concentrations were determined.

As shown in Figure 5, this procedure was repeated with four separate series of six cages, plus an additional single cage. The data shown in Figure 5 demonstrate that the pooled plasma corticosterone level of the mice in the first cage (dashed bar) of each group was significantly lower ($p < .0005$) than those of the subsequently bled five cages (solid bars).

Of further interest, when the pooled corticosterone values of the various groups were averaged and plotted as a function of their order of bleeding (first-bled cages, second-bled cages, and so forth), as shown in Figure 6, a statistically significant ($p < .01$) trend was observed.

The data presented in Figure 4 illustrate the rapid expression of anxiety that occurs within a group of animals in a single cage, following the capture of one or more of the inmates. An extension of this intracage phenomenon to possible intercage communication is illustrated by the data shown in Figures 5 and 6, with several interesting but uncertain implications.

Interpretation of these observations requires consideration of at least two separate mechanisms. The simple act of removing the cages of mice from their protective shelves and carrying them to the workbench is probably a sufficient

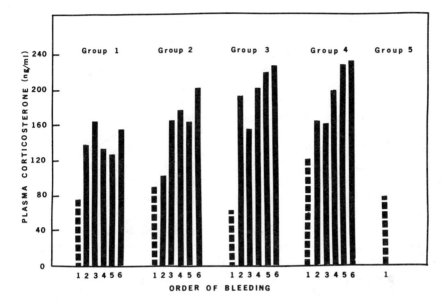

Figure 5. Effects of cage transport and/or intercage communication. See text for procedure. The corticosterone concentration in the pooled plasma from the mice in the first cage (dashed bar) of each group was significantly lower than those of the subsequently bled five cages (solid bars). ($p < .0005$; Student's t test).

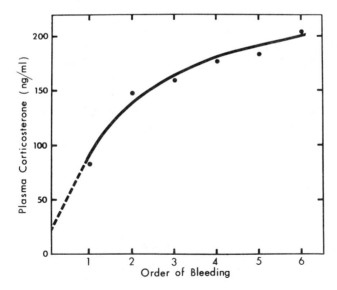

Figure 6. Corticosterone concentration in the plasma of mice held for various periods in their cages on an open shelf in the vicinity of sequential bleeding operations. Each point on the curve represents the average corticosterone concentration of four cages of mice at their sequential bleeding time. The systematic differences in corticosterone levels as a function of bleeding order are statistically significant ($p < .01$; determined by analysis of variance).

disturbance to initiate an anxiety state that could elevate the plasma corticosterone by 100%. This is the simplest explanation.

However, the data of Figure 6 carries an added implication of potential interest. It has been demonstrated that rodents and certain other animals are capable of communicating through the use of supersonic signals (Anisko *et al.*, 1978; Noirot, 1966, 1968; Sales, 1972a,b; Sales and Pye, 1974; Voss, 1980). Some of our studies reported elsewhere (Riley *et al.*, 1981), diminish the plausibility of the role of pheromones (Gleason *et al.*, 1969) in stress signal communication. Therefore, if the systematic increase in corticosterone shown in Figure 6 results from either handling of the cages or the reception of supersonic signals from the first-handled mice, then these effects must be considered as an additional factor or complication in the design of sophisticated biological experiments.

Such phenomena further demonstrate the dual need for quiescent protective animal facilities and the employment of appropriate animal handling techniques in most biologic studies, especially if optimal immunocompetence and normal physiology is of relevance to the experiment (see Fortier, 1958; Riley, 1972, 1978, 1979a,b; Riley and Spackman, 1976a,b, 1977a,b, 1978a; Riley *et al.*, 1975, 1979a, 1981.)

The Necessity for Mouse Equilibration
Following Shipping

As shown in Figure 7, plasma corticosterone levels are elevated tenfold in mice during and after air shipment, and thymus involution is initiated as expected in response to the increased corticoid concentrations. The physiological effects induced by shipping stress take approximately 2 weeks to return to quiescent levels after the mice are placed in protective facilities. The timecourse of recovery is shown in Figure 7. It is therefore our practice to allow animals to equilibrate for at least 2 weeks prior to their being placed in experiments. A persuasive example is shown in Figure 8. This figure illustrates the differences in host mortality rates ($p < .005$) if tumors are implanted into newly received mice as compared to analogous equilibrated mice.

Benign Stress-Inducing Machine

The contradictory results of previous studies on stress have demonstrated the need for a simple, reproducible, and nontraumatic means for inducing controlled stress in experimental animals. Such stress should be produced without significantly activating hormonal systems other than those of the adrenal cortex (or medulla in some cases), depriving the animals of free access to food and water or subjecting them to unnecessarily harsh treatment.

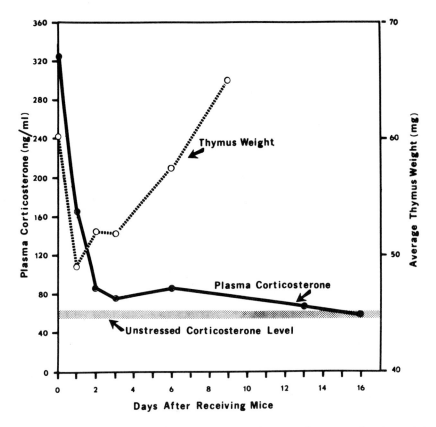

Figure 7. Manifestations of shipping stress in mice. Plasma corticosterone elevation and thymus involution were observed in mice received in our laboratory approximately 48 hr following initiation of air shipment. These data demonstrate the need for rodents to equilibrate for a minimum of 2 weeks in protective, low stress housing prior to use in critical experimentation. The shaded area at the bottom of the Figure represents the range of normal quiescent plasma corticosterone levels.

Figure 9 shows a simple stress-inducing device that provides a controlled, readily reproducible form of quantifiable stress, and permits automatic programming for a wide variety of intermittent stress/rest intervals. This machine is a modified phonograph turntable having the four standard speeds of 16, 33.3, 45, and 78 rpm. The instrument has been designed so that an entire cage of animals can be rotated without changing the familiar arrangement of their living quarters. Thus, with this benign stressing device it is not necessary to submit the animals to a novel environment, or to alter the availability of their food and water, inasmuch as the slow rotational speeds permit the animals to move about their cage and to continue eating and drinking. In this respect it may be noted that the maximum lateral gravitational force experienced by the mice is less than one *g*. This stress-inducing instrument is thus not a centri-

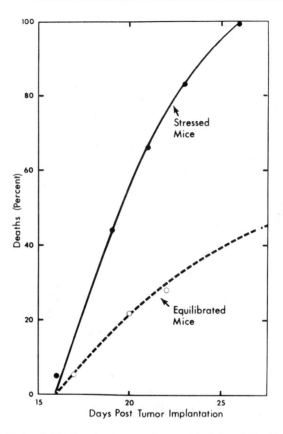

Figure 8. The effects of shipping stress upon mouse survival time following implantation of C3H/Bi female mice with the 6C3HED lymphosarcoma. The stressed mice were implanted with the tumor immediately following air shipment, when their corticosterone levels were high, as shown in Figure 7. The equilibrated mice received the same tumor preparation, but they had been held in our low stress protective facilities for 35 days prior to tumor implantation. The minor difference in age between the two groups has no significant influence on tumor-bearing host survival. The observed differences in mortalities were highly significant statistically ($p < .005$, determined by chi-square analysis).

fugal device in the usual sense, but is essentially a mechanical means for inducing mild spatial disorientation, and possibly vertigo or dizziness, with an associated anxiety that activates the adrenal cortex, resulting in a prompt elevation of plasma corticosterone.

The ability of this instrument to induce both controlled and variable intensities of stress is shown in Figure 10, where plasma corticosterone values are plotted against the various rotational speeds. It may be seen that following the rotation of separate groups of mice at each of the four speeds, a graded and systematic increase in plasma corticosterone was observed (Riley *et al.*, 1979a). For most stress-inducing purposes in the experiments reported here,

Figure 9. A programmable stress-inducing machine. Entire cages of mice are slowly rotated at predetermined speeds and for various periods of intermittent rotation and rest. Automatic timers control the rotation/rest time ratios, which permits the mice to be quantitatively stressed in their home cages without depriving them of access to food and water, or employing any physical restraint. The machine can be programmed for any length of time and rotational periodicity required by the experimental design.

the intermediate speed of 45 rpm was employed. For prolonged stress exposures, the animals were usually rotated for 10 min followed by a 50-min rest. This, or other on/off cycles, can be repeated for any desired periodicity, or for any time sequence by employing preprogrammed automation.

An ability to control the magnitude of the stress stimulus, and to actually quantify stress-induction in terms of the biochemical and cellular response of the stressed subject has been an important development in placing our stress studies on a quantitative and easily repeatable basis. For example, the acquired data on stress-associated lymphocytopenia, thymus involution, and other physiological and neoplastic responses have been accomplished with the aid of this simple but highly effective instrumentation.

It is assumed that the adrenal medulla is not significantly activated by this mild stress, or in any case, does not interfere with the specific stress effects associated with adrenal cortical activation. However, participation of the adrenal medulla, with a release of potent CNS-active catecholamines, occurs in rodents under more intense stressful conditions, especially if fear or rage is the inciter (Cannon, 1929; Harlow and Selye, 1937; Henry, 1977; Henry and Stephens, 1977).

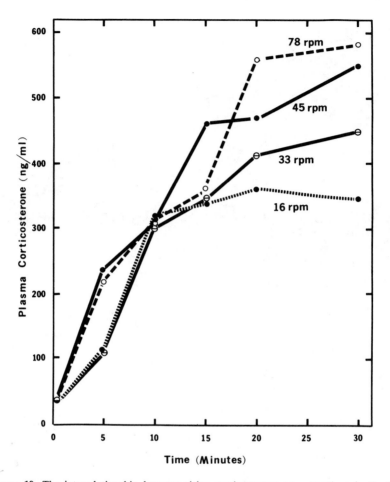

Figure 10. The interrelationship between rising corticosterone concentrations in the blood plasma and the speed and duration of cage rotation employing the stress-machine shown in Figure 9. If the equilibrium values of corticosterone that are obtained between 20 and 30 min of rotation are plotted as a function of rotational speed (rpm), a straight-line relationship is obtained.

Stress-Induced Lysis of Cells and Tissues

Figure 11 shows the effect of programmed stress-inducing rotation (10 min out of the hour at 45 rpm) on the leukocyte count. It is relevant to note that this stress-induced leukocytopenia immediately follows, and is a consequence of the elevated plasma corticosterone levels induced by the anxiety stress.

This alteration in an important cellular component is a key factor in bringing about an impairment of the host immunologic apparatus. It is particularly relevant to note that the majority of the circulating mouse leukocytes are T

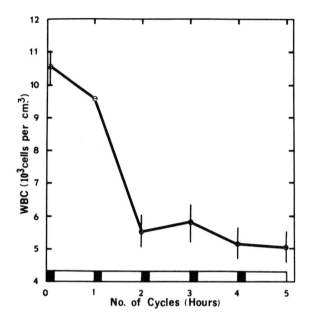

Figure 11. Leukocytopenia induced by mild, nontraumatic rotational stress at 45 rpm during five 60-min cycles consisting of 10 min of rotation followed by 50 min of rest. An approximate 50% leukocytopenia was produced by the end of the second cycle, and was maintained throughout the 5 hr of intermittent stress. Vertical lines through each point represent standard errors.

cells, and this induced lymphocytopenia is thus indicative of a reduction of a critical component of the host defense system. This rapid loss of T cells acquires special significance in view of the substantial damage also done to the thymus, which prevents or delays processing of replacement T cells. Thus, in terms of the sequence of events, increased concentrations of corticosterone appear in the blood within a few minutes following anxiety stress stimuli; this, in turn, brings about circulating lymphocyte damage within 1 or 2 hr. Thymus involution follows; however, the disintegration of the solid organ requires more time, but a measurable weight loss occurs within less than 24 hr. The time course of this hormonal action upon the thymus is shown in Figure 12.

Effects of Stress-Induced Corticosteroid Elevations
upon Amino Acid Metabolism and Protein Synthesis

One of the important physiological effects of corticosteroids is their influence on amino acid metabolism and on protein synthesis. Elevated blood levels of these hormones, resulting either from various stress-inducing conditions, or from the injection of specific corticosteroids, significantly alter the levels of amino acids in physiological fluids and tissues, as shown in Tables 1

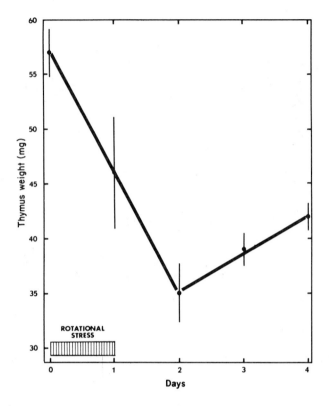

Figure 12. Thymus involution resulting from anxiety-stress induced by rotation. Evidence indicates that the thymocytes are lysed by the increased concentrations of plasma corticosterone which accompany stress. The anxiety stress was induced by spatial disorientation by rotating the entire mouse cage slowly at 45 rpm for 10 min out of each hour for a 24-hr period.

and 2 and Figure 13. Tables 1 and 2 list plasma amino acid changes in mice following a 24-hr rotation period, while Figure 13 is a collocated profile showing changes in specific amino acids excreted in the urine during and following a similar 24-hr rotation. Of relevance, the plasma corticosterone levels at the end of the rotation periods were 350 ng/ml, which represents a tenfold increase over normal quiescent levels. Conspicuous amino acid changes occurring in the urine include the decreased concentration of lysine, and in contrast, the elevations of glutamic acid, alanine, valine, leucine, tryptophan, phenylalanine, tyrosine, and isoleucine. Preliminary studies indicate that stress also induces significant changes in amino acid concentrations in brain tissue (D. H. Spackman and V. Riley, unpublished data), presumably mediated through elevated corticosteroids. For a description of the methods employed for amino acid analysis, see Spackman (1969) and Spackman *et al.* (1958).

Although others have observed that elevated levels of corticosteroids result

TABLE 1
Amino Acids Exhibiting an Increased Concentration in the
Plasma Following Rotation-induced Stress

Amino acid	Percentage of increase
Alanine	30
Lysine	28
Hydroxyproline	28
Histidine	24
l-methylhistidine	26
Aspartic acid	21
Glutamine	19
Tyrosine	17
Methyllysine	17
Methionine	15
Asparagine	14
Cystine	12

The intermittent rotation consisted of 10 min of rotation at 45 rpm each hour. The plasma corticosterone levels at the end of the rotation period were 350 ng/ml. BDF female mice were employed.

in an increased excretion of urinary nitrogen and a negative nitrogen balance (White *et al.,* 1968), the mechanisms have not been clearly defined. Probably both an inhibition of protein synthesis and increased protein catabolism occur, resulting in the observed elevated concentrations of plasma amino acids, as well as an increased gluconeogenesis utilizing the released amino acids (Turner and Hagnara, 1971). Such alterations in amino acid metabolism may have potential influences upon disease processes, through their adverse effects on the synthesis of enzymes and cellular proteins necessary for optimum immune surveillance. Jose and Good (1973), for example, have reported that the restriction of certain essential amino acids in the diet severely depresses specific humoral antibody responses.

TABLE 2
Amino Acids Showing a Decreased Concentration in the
Plasma Following Rotation-Induced Stress

Amino acid	Percentage of decrease
α-Aminobutyric acid	56
Citrulline	15
Proline	12

The intermittent rotation consisted of 10 min of rotation at 45 rpm each hour. The plasma corticosterone levels at the end of the rotation period were 350 ng/ml. BDF female mice were employed.

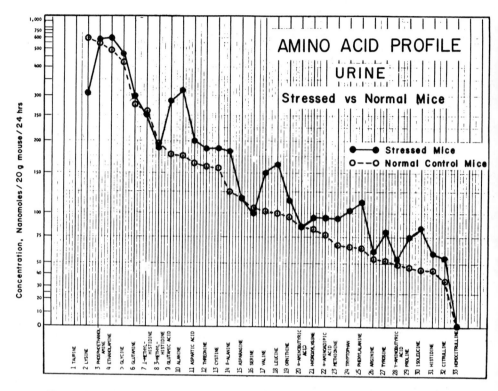

Figure 13. Amino acid concentration profiles of the urine of mildly stressed mice as compared with urine from normal quiescent control animals. The anxiety stress was induced under highly controlled experimental conditions using a slow-speed rotational device at 45 rpm intermittently for 24 hr. The rotational intermittence was controlled automatically and was programmed for 10 min rotation and 50 min rest each hour. Food and water were available at all times during the 24-hr period.

Thymus Involution: Comparison of the Effects of an Exogenous Corticosteroid, Rotational Stress, and LDH Virus Infection

Figure 14 illustrates and compares the influence of three distinct stress inducers on the involution of the thymus. Panel A shows the effect of the benign lactate dehydrogenase elevating virus (LDH virus) on thymus involution as a function of time during the first 96 hr following infection, while Panel B shows that a similar effect can be obtained following the injection of a single dose of the synthetic corticoid, dexamethasone (DMS). Similar effects on the thymus were obtained following the induction of anxiety stress by the slow rotation of mice, as indicated by Panel C.

The LDH virus is a useful biological tool for inducing moderate immunologic alterations in either normal or tumor-bearing mice (Riley, 1973,

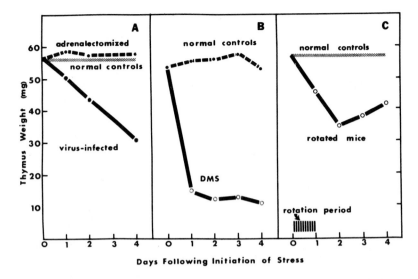

Figure 14. Thymus involution variously induced by (A) an infectious agent, specifically, the LDH virus; (B) a synthetic corticoid, dexamethasone (DMS); and (C) anxiety stress associated with the disorienting effects of the slow rotation of an entire cage of mice. (A) The LDH virus was inoculated on day 0 into both intact and adrenalectomized female BAF mice. The regression line of the thymus weights of the virus-infected intact mice was fitted by the method of least squares; its difference from the response of the virus-infected adrenalectomized mice, and normal thymus weights, was statistically significant ($p < .001$). (B) Thymus involution was produced in this experiment by a single injection of a relatively insoluble pellet of DMS, providing a total dose of 50 mg/kg, which was absorbed over an extended period, maintaining elevated but physiological levels. (C) Thymus destruction resulting from stress associated with cage rotation at 45 rpm for 10 min out of each hour for a 24-hr period. During this mild stress period the plasma corticosterone was elevated approximately fivefold over normal quiescent levels.

1974a,b; Riley and Spackman, 1976a,b; Fitzmaurice *et al.*, 1972; Santisteban and Riley, 1973). This ubiquitously distributed virus appears to function indirectly as an immunosuppressant through its adverse effects upon T and B cells (Howard *et al.*, 1969). The destruction of thymus tissue and T cells in LDH virus-infected mice is undoubtedly brought about through an elevation in plasma corticosterone levels during the acute phase of viral infection (Spackman and Riley, 1974).

The data of Figure 14 indicate that when natural or synthetic glucocorticoids are present in the blood at concentrations above normal, irrespective of the inducing agent, they have a similar lytic effect upon lymphatic tissues such as the thymus, nodes, and spleen, as well as upon the peripheral lymphocytes. Since these cellular elements are important components in immunologic defense, the potential consequences of their impairment or depletion on latent pathological processes seem obvious.

These data support and are consistent with the hypothesis that a logical sequence of biochemical and cellular events lead from stressful stimuli to the impairment of immunologic competence, followed by the enhancement of various pathological conditions, including certain neoplastic processes.

Circadian Influences on Plasma Corticosterone Levels in LDH Virus-Infected and Normal Mice

Figure 15 shows the results of an experiment in which blood samples were obtained at 2-hr intervals for a 24-hr period. Each point represents the corticosterone level of plasma pooled from 5 mice. All mice received either an LDH virus inoculation, or a matching saline injection at 9 A.M. Separate groups of mice were bled at the various times indicated in order to eliminate the stress-inducing effects of repeated bleedings. The increased plasma corticosterone induced by the LDH virus during the initial 24 hr of acute viral infection, as well as the circadian corticosterone rhythm exhibited by the normal mice, are illustrated in this Figure.

In contrast to the modest twofold elevation of plasma corticosterone observed following the early morning inoculation of the LDH virus, injection of the virus just prior to the nocturnal portion of the corticosterone cycle produced the unexpected results shown in Figure 16. While plasma corticosterone levels in the untreated and saline-injected control groups exhibited the expected circadian pattern, the LDH virus-infected group exhibited extremely

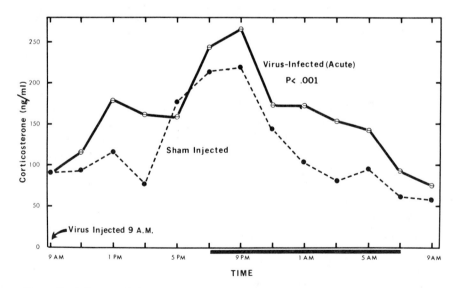

Figure 15. Influence of the LDH virus upon the plasma corticosterone levels during a 24-hr period, following inoculation of the virus at 9 A.M. The difference between the two curves is statistically significant ($p < .001$). These data demonstrate the circadian variations of plasma corticosterone in normal (sham-injected) as well as virus-infected mice.

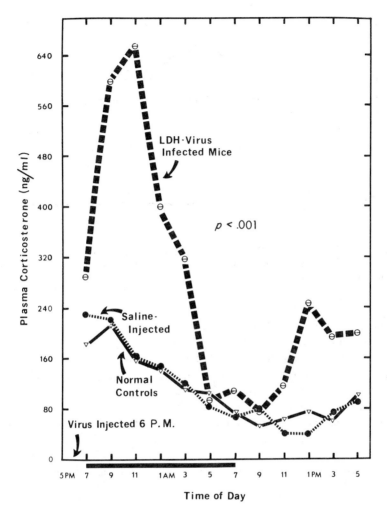

Figure 16. Influence of the LDH virus on circadian plasma corticosterone levels following inoculation of the virus just prior to the natural nocturnal increase at 6 P.M. These differences are statistically significant. The corticosterone levels of the sham-injected and normal controls correspond to those levels expected as a result of the normal circadian rhythm.

high levels of plasma corticosterone 5–6 hr following inoculation. In addition, a second recurrent corticosterone peak was observed from 19 to 24 hr following the virus inoculation. The occurrence of these corticoid peaks is consistent with the subsequently observed lymphocytopenia and thymus involution associated with the acute phase of the LDH virus infection.

The acute LDH virus-induced elevations of plasma corticosterone persist for 1–3 days. In contrast, Figure 17 shows that the plasma corticosterone values found in chronically infected mice during a 24-hr period, beginning 4 days following virus infection, are not significantly different from those of the

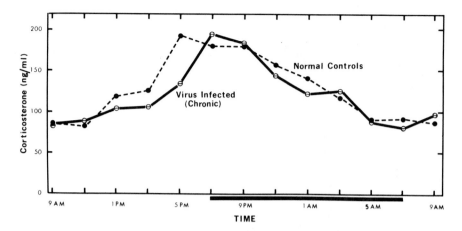

Figure 17. Absence of the LDH virus effect upon plasma corticosterone levels during the chronic phase of viremia, 4 days after virus inoculation. Under these experimental conditions no significant difference was found between the corticosterone levels in normal and virus-infected mice.

controls. It is thus concluded that the high corticosterone levels associated with the virus are found only during the acute, early phase of LDH virus infection, and that the destruction of thymus tissue continues after plasma corticosterone concentrations return to normal. A similar corticosterone-associated thymus involution has also been observed following shipping stress or slow rotation. See Figures 7, 12, and 14.

Figure 17 also shows the circadian rhythm of plasma corticosterone levels in normal unstressed mice. The chronobiology of the LDH virus is relevant to stress and neoplasia inasmuch as this virus produces several features of a typical stress syndrome and can influence specific malignant processes.

Effects of Chemically Simulated Stress
upon LDH Virus Titers

Figure 18 shows the physiological consequences of a single injection of the synthetic corticoid dexamethasone (DMS) upon the thymus weights, as well as a DMS-induced enhancement in the equilibrated LDH virus titer levels in mice chronically infected with this persistent virus.

The original elevated corticosterone levels induced in the plasma during the acute phase of the LDH virus infection return to normal in 1 or 2 days, which is followed by a drop in virus titer from approximately 10^{10} to 10^6 ID_{50}/ml. The DMS-induced increase in virus titer to the high level usually seen only during the acute phase of the infection, suggests that various stress-induced corticosterone elevations may potentiate other viruses, or certain virus-induced tumors, by activating latent carcinogenic viruses, or by increasing the titers

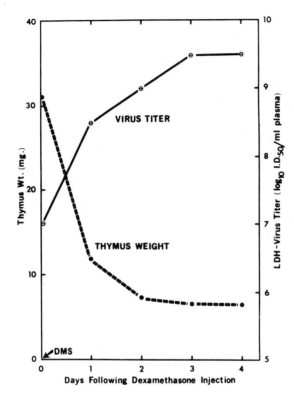

Figure 18. Effects of the synthetic corticoid, dexamethasone, upon thymus weight and LDH virus titers. BDF female mice chronically infected with the LDH virus were injected with a slowly releasing pellet of dexamethasone (1 mg/20 gm mouse) 7 days following infection with the virus. The low, chronic virus titers are increased to a level normally observed only during the acute phase of the infection when corticosterone levels are high.

of such viruses that are present in a low-titer chronic state. The Bittner mammary tumor virus (MTV) in C3H mice is an example. The enhancement of oncogenic viruses and their neoplastic processes by the LDH virus has been previously reported (Riley and Spackman, 1976b). Of relevance to these phenomena are reports by Chang and Rasmussen (1965) and Jensen (1968b), indicating that stress may suppress interferon production in virus-infected mice. Yamada *et al.* (1964) also reported on the effects of stress on the relative susceptibility to viral infections.

Enhancement of Tumor Growth by Virus-Induced or Biochemically Simulated Stress

Melanomas have a reputation for unpredictable clinical behavior. Cumulative data suggest that certain melanomas may generate an immunologic response in the host that occasionally results in either a temporary or permanent regression of the malignant lesions (Cochran *et al.*, 1972; Nicholls, 1973). Thus it appears that such tumors are either capable of eliciting a specially vigorous host immunologic response, or may at times exist in a more fragile histocompatible equilibrium with the host, and are therefore more susceptible to an ordinary immune response.

Figure 19 illustrates the differential influence of LDH virus infection upon the behavior of a slowly growing nonpigmented variant of the B-16 melanoma, as compared to the more rapidly growing, uncontrolled pigmented B-16 melanoma. Apparently, transformation from the pigmented to a nonpigmented state results, in this case at least, in a tumor with less histocompatibility than the original pigmented tumor. The growth rate of this tumor is significantly less than its pigmented counterpart, and its tendency to undergo spontaneous regression also distinguishes it from the more histocompatible pigmented version. The suppressible nonpigmented melanoma thus is a suitable experimental model for detecting the influence of subtle immunologic modifiers. This is demonstrated by the increased growth rate of this tumor in mice acutely infected with the LDH virus, which has modulating effects upon host immunocompetence. In contrast, the rapidly growing pigmented mela-

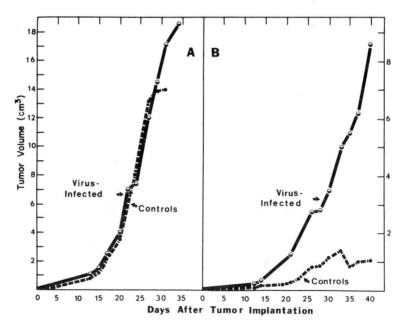

Figure 19. Comparison of the lack of influence upon tumor growth by an acute LDH virus infection upon a rapidly growing pigmented B-16 melanoma, as shown in (A), in contrast to the virus-induced enhancement of the growth of a partially host-suppressed nonpigmented variant of B-16 origin, illustrated in (B). Similar tumor suspensions were implanted in all groups using BDF female mice between 10 and 14 weeks of age. Tumor growth was determined by three-dimensional caliper measurements.

noma exhibited essentially the same rate of growth in both virus-infected and control mice.

Figure 20B indicates that the LDH virus has an enhancing effect upon the growth of the 6C3HED lymphosarcoma, whose degree of syngeneity with the C3H/He mice employed is imperfect (see Table 3). Again, in this instance, acute infection with the LDH virus enhanced tumor growth rate and increased the percentage of progressively growing tumors following transplantation. At 30 days after tumor implantation, 5 of 10 tumors in the noninfected mice had completely regressed, while in the virus-infected group, only 1 out of 10 had regressed. In respect to survival, 9 out of the 10 uninfected mice were alive, but only 3 out of 10 of the virus-infected animals.

Figure 20A shows the hormonal-mediated enhancement of tumor growth produced by the direct administration of dexamethazone (DMS). This synthetic corticoid functions in a manner similar to the natural elevated corticosterone that results from acute infection with the LDH virus. Thus a significant enhancement of tumor growth resulted either from infection with a benign virus, or the administration of a synthetic hormone closely related to a natural

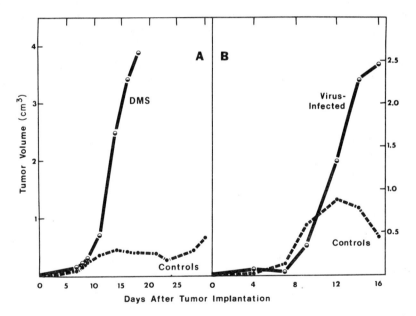

Figure 20. Demonstration of the tumor-enhancing effects of two varieties of "stress" on the 6C3HED lymphosarcoma. (A) shows the consequences of synthetic corticoid administration by the implantation of a single dose of a long-acting preparation of dexamethasone (DMS). This chart shows the tumor enhancement which occurs as a result of corticoid-induced impairment of the host's immunological apparatus. A similar tumor enhancement may be observed in (B), following inoculation of the "stress-inducing" LDH virus. The DMS and the LDH-virus injections were both administered on the same day as the implantation of the 6C3HED lymhosarcoma into the C3H/He mice.

hormone associated with stress. These results are consistent with the working hypothesis that all of these entities have similar damaging effects upon the immunologic competence of the tumor-bearing host.

Since the LDH virus will enhance the growth of certain "stress-sensitive" tumors regardless of whether it is intentionally inoculated or transmitted as an inadvertent contaminant, it should be emphasized that efforts to study the effects of stress upon such an unsuspectedly contaminated tumor would probably be confusing and difficult to evaluate (Riley, 1974a; Riley *et al.*, 1978b).

Effect of Tumor Syngeneity and Mouse Substrain Effects on the Growth of Certain Tumors

Table 3 compares various parameters of tumor growth following the implantation of the 6C3HED lymphosarcoma into C3H/He and C3H/Bi mice. This tumor is obviously more histocompatible with the C3H/Bi substrain, than with the C3H/He mice, which is demonstrated by differences in the percentage of tumor regressions. The C3H/He substrain is thus more useful for detecting and measuring subtle, stress-induced impairment of immunocompetence, which is reflected by an enhanced growth of the 6C3HED tumor in this substrain. The C3H/Bi substrain is less useful in this respect, since there is less natural host capability for containment of the growth of the tumor, which thus proceeds with equal rapidity in both stressed and non-stressed mice of this substrain.

TABLE 3

Effect of Mouse Substrain on the Growth Behavior of the 6C3HED Gardner Lymphosarcoma in C3H Mice

Parameters measured	C3H/He mice	C3H/Bi mice
Tumor regressions[a]	100%	0%
Tumor-associated deaths[b]	0%	100%
Maximum tumor volume attained (cm³)[c]	0.8 ± 0.3	2.3 ± 0.8
Mean tumor latent period[d] (days ± s.d.)	6.0 ± 0.1	6.1 ± 0.3

[a] The median regression time of the tumors in the C3H/He mice was 21 days after implantation, and all tumors in this substrain had regressed by 35 days after implantation.

[b] The median survival time of the C3H/Bi mice was 33 days, following tumor implantation, and all C3H/Bi mice were dead by 37 days after implantation.

[c] In the C3H/He mice, maximum tumor volumes were attained between 16 and 19 days following implantation, after which the tumors in this substrain regressed. In the C3H/Bi mice, maximum tumor volumes were observed just prior to the deaths of the mice, which occurred between 23 and 35 days after implantation.

[d] All mice were females, 9 weeks of age, housed 10 per cage in standard plastic cages with corncob bedding. The cages were maintained within low stress, protective facilities.

Effects of Various Stress Stimuli
on the Behavior of Virus-Induced Moloney Tumors

Figure 21 compares the effects of (*a*) rotational stress; (*b*) infection with the LDH virus; and (*c*) implantation of a single, slow-release depot of corticosterone upon the growth behavior of tumors induced by the Moloney sarcoma virus (MSV). The enhanced growth is expressed by significantly larger maximum tumor volumes attained in all three experimental groups as compared with the untreated MSV-inoculated controls (*p* < .001) for all three experimental modalities).

The enhancing effects of these forms of stress are highly dependent upon

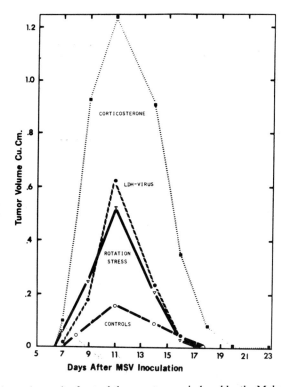

Figure 21. Enhanced growth of autochthonous tumors induced by the Moloney sarcoma virus (MSV) following (*a*) rotation-induced stress; (*b*) infection with the LDH virus; and (*c*) implantation of a single slow-release pellet of exogenous corticosterone. The rotated group of mice was subjected to intermittent rotation (45 rpm, 10 min rotation, 50 min rest per hour) for a total period of 72 hr, starting on the day of MSV inoculation. The LDH virus-infected group was inoculated with the LDH virus on the same day that the MSV inoculation was performed. The mice given exogenous corticosterone were implanted subcutaneously in the left hip with a slow-release corticosterone-spermaceti pellet, also on the day of MSV inoculation. The BALB/c female recipient mice were inoculated intramuscularly in the right hip with 0.05 ml of Moloney sarcoma virus inoculum. All mice were housed in plastic cages, 10 per cage, within low stress protective facilities.

the timing of the stressors relative to MSV inoculation. For example, rotation stress when applied from the fourth through sixth days following MSV inoculation, resulted in a significant enhancement of tumor growth. However, this was of lesser magnitude than that observed following rotation for the same length of time but initiated on the day of MSV inoculation. In contrast, rotation stress applied 3 days prior to MSV inoculation resulted in an inhibition of the MSV-induced tumors. Similar timing effects may be responsible for the stress-induced inhibition of SJL/JDg neoplasia reported by Crispens (1976; also see Jensen, 1968a; Amkraut and Solomon, 1972).

Our interpretation of these phenomena is consistent with other related data, namely, that all of the above stress stimuli cause an indirect impairment of immunocompetence. Such impairment may be followed by recovery of the immunologic elements, followed by an overshoot resulting in a temporary immunologic enhancement.

Enhancement of Tumor Growth
Following Rotation-Induced Stress

Figure 22 shows the influence of intermittent rotation-induced stress on the subsequent growth rate of the 6C3HED lymphosarcoma in C3H/He mice. In this experiment the tumor-bearing mice were exposed to a mild disorienting rotation at 45 rpm for 10 min out of each hour during the first 6 days following subcutaneous implantation of the transplantable lymphosarcoma. A logical interpretation of these observations suggests that those animals receiving such rotational stress had some elements of their immunologic competence compromised which permitted this stress-sensitive tumor to grow at a more rapid rate than occurred in the control animals. The latter presumedly possessed an immunologic capability to restrain the optimal growth of this tumor. Such a stress-induced decrease in immunologic competence is a logical and consistent theoretical consequence of the T-cell damage that is associated with the plasma corticosterone elevation induced by anxiety stress.

Effects of the Timing of Simulated Stress
Relative to Tumor Behavior

Figure 23 provides evidence concerning the effects of the timing of stress with respect to its influence upon neoplastic behavior. In this experiment the neuroendocrine pathways were intentionally bypassed and some of the biochemical and cellular features of physiological stress were simulated by the administration of a potent synthetic corticoid. In this experiment, a single injection of fluocinolone acetonide (FCA), which is closely related chemically to dexamethasone, was administered to different groups at systematic inter-

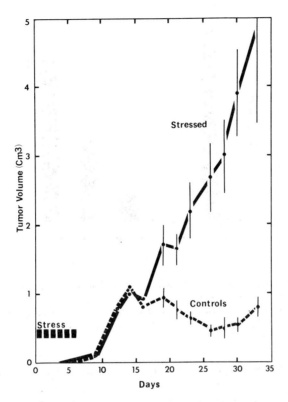

Figure 22. Stress-associated influences on tumor growth in mice exposed to an intermittent course of mild anxiety stress. The stress was induced by slow rotation at 45 rpm for 10 min out of each hour during the first 6 days following tumor implantation. The tumor was the 6C3HED lymphosarcoma in C3H/He female mice. Food and water were available ad libitum during the course of the experiment.

vals following transplantation of the 6C3HED lymphosarcoma into C3H/He mice.

When a single dose of the corticoid was administered 7 days following tumor implantation, no tumor regressions occurred, which was indicative of an induced impairment in the host immunocompetence. This was in contrast to 70% regressions observed in the untreated control mice, illustrating partial immunological control of the tumor by the unstressed host. However, this corticoid effect was systematically diminished when the FCA was administered at later times in the course of the tumor process. These data may be interpreted as a demonstration of the impairment inflicted upon the host immunologic apparatus by elevated adrenal corticoids, whether endogenous or administered. The quantitative expression of this impairment by a decrease in percentage of tumor regressions, however, is dependent upon the number of viable tumor cells remaining at the time of corticoid administration.

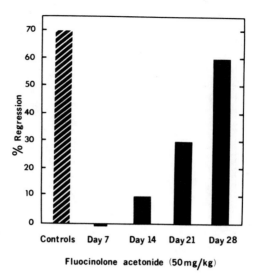

Figure 23. The influence of a synthetic adrenocorticoid in preventing or inhibiting the normal regression of established 6C3HED lymphosarcomas transplanted in C3H/He female mice. The synthetic glucocorticoid was fluocinolone acetonide (FCA) implanted intraperitoneally as a slow-release suspension of slight solubility, at the times indicated following tumor implantation. Ten mice were employed in each group.

This is further demonstrated by Figure 24, which shows the differences in tumor growth rates resulting from FCA injections at various times following tumor implantation. Maximum tumor growth enhancement occurred following a single FCA dose at 7 days following tumor implantation. Similar effects were observed when the compound was injected 14 or 21 days postimplantation, while no effect on tumor growth was observed if treatment was delayed until 28 days after implantation. This experiment illustrates that the timing of stressful stimuli may be critical with respect to their optimal or even tangible effects upon stress-responsive tumors.

Chronic Psychosocial Confrontations: Effects upon Survival of Tumor-Bearing Mice

In an effort to determine the physiological effects of the psychosocial stress induced by enforced mouse to mouse confrontation, three standard plastic cages were interconnected with cylindrical passageways. The three-cage complex contained only one food hopper which was located in the central cage; a water bottle was located in each of the other two cages. In essence, this is a linear version of the Henry–Santisteban circular "population cage" (Henry and Santisteban, 1971).

There was only a slight increase in the growth rate of the 6C3HED lympho-

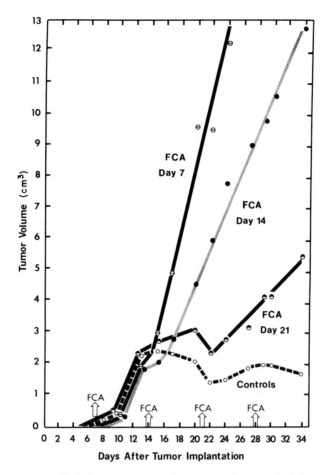

Figure 24. Systematically different tumor growth rates resulting from the injection of a single, slow-release dose of synthetic corticosteroid at various times with respect to tumor implantation. The groups of mice are the same as those shown in Figure 23. Those mice receiving FCA on the twenty-eighth day postimplantation exhibited a tumor growth behavior that was indistinguishable from that of the untreated tumor-bearing controls.

sarcoma in C3H/He female mice in these cages, as compared to analogous tumor-bearing mice in a single standard plastic cage containing its own food hopper and water bottle. However, as indicated in Table 4, 36% of the mice in the population complex were dead by day 47 following tumor implantation, compared to no deaths in the tumor-bearing mice that were housed in the single cage ($p < .001$). These results are consistent with observations on the physiological effects of psychosocial stress, made by Santisteban (1978), Santisteban and Henry (1971), and Santisteban et al. (1979). The overall population density of both groups was the same, or at least the amount of space available was identical. However, mice tend to cluster together, which con-

TABLE 4

Effect of Psychosocial Stress upon Deaths in Tumor-Bearing Mice

Cage type	Number of mice	Percentage of deaths at 47 days[c]	p value[d]
Standard single plastic cage[a]	10	0	
Three-cage complex	30	36	$p < .001$

[a] Mice in the single standard plastic cage were housed 10 per cage.

[b] The three-cage, intercommunicating complex had two water bottles and a single food hopper separately located to enforce social confrontation. It should be noted that the available space in terms of population density was the same in the single cage and the three-cage population complex. Both groups were housed in the same type of plastic cages, and held within the protective, low stress enclosed shelves.

[c] The percentage of deaths was determined 47 days following implantation of the Gardner 6C3HED lymphosarcoma into C3H/He female mice.

[d] The probability value was determined by the chi-square method.

serves body heat, and thus there is a voluntary alteration in actual population density during the huddling periods. Both types of caging were mounted within the enclosed, low stress shelves having laminar airflow.

Population Density Experiments

It is important for the investigator to know what physiological effects, if any, various numbers of animals housed in a standard cage will have upon the results of an experiment. In order to minimize fighting, or for other reasons, some investigators house their mice or rats 1 per cage, while others engaged in similar studies may have various numbers ranging from 2 to 10 per cage.

Several investigators have described the seemingly stressful effects of "cage crowding," and the alleged consequential influences on the growth or incidence of various tumors, or upon other disease processes, presumedly due to alterations in the immunological competence of the hosts (Green et al., 1967; Levine, 1967; Dechambre and Gosse, 1968, 1971, 1973; Muhlbock, 1950, 1951; Vessey, 1964).

We have undertaken experiments to re-examine this question utilizing protective, low stress facilities, and minimal stress-inducing handling techniques. These facilities and this experimental approach provides an opportunity to control a number of the known forms of environmental stress in carrying out such population density studies.

The experiments were designed to determine the different levels of anxiety stress that might occur among mice caged in groups of either 1, 2, 3, 5, 10, 15, or 20, and held for relatively long periods in standard plastic cages. There were no mice of the opposite sex either in the cages or in the immediate vicinity, and thus there was no obvious source of sex-related pheromones or other signals which could provide uncontrolled stress-inducing circumstances within the laminar airflow shelves. See Figure 3 for effects of proximity to opposite sex.

Absence of Effects of Population Density upon Plasma Corticosterone Levels

It has been shown in these studies that various population densities of caged mice do not constitute in themselves a basis for "cage-crowding stress." This was first demonstrated by a failure to detect differential levels of plasma corticosterone (CSR) in female mice caged either 1, 2, 3, 5, 10, 15, or 20 per standard plastic cage for various time intervals. It was expected, however, that quite different effects would be observed when employing more competitive and quarrelsome male mice under analogous experimental circumstances. It was thus surprising to observe that increasing cage population densities of males also failed to exhibit elevated plasma corticosterone levels. Figure 25 illustrates the similarity of plasma corticosterone levels in both male and female C3H/He mice when housed in various population densities.

Effects of Population Density upon Relative Food Consumption

In addition to the corticosterone data, Figure 25 also shows that the differences in food consumption observed with females maintained under conditions of various population densities also applies to male mice. These data show an unexpected systematic difference in individual daily food consumption, which is expressed as a concave curvilinear function of population density. Mouse weight was taken into consideration in the plotting of these data.

Our interpretation of these observations is that the low stress, protective animal facilities, in conjunction with our experimental design, have permitted a sensitive quantitative detection of the homeostatic thermal regulatory mechanism that controls caloric intake as a function of body temperature. It is obvious that body heat loss occurs more rapidly in mice residing alone, or in small numbers, as compared with the preservation of body heat in high density populations where huddling and multiple body contacts occur. The radiant surface area of a typical mouse cluster is, of course, smaller on a per mouse basis.

Other possible explanations for these observations have been considered and experimentally examined; however, the constant body weight data shown in Figure 26 and the absence of hierarchical-imposed mouse weight differences due to food competition are all consistent with the homeostatic caloric requirement hypothesis. Irrespective of the mechanism, these observa-

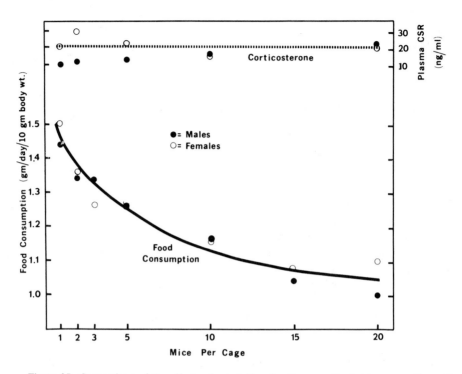

Figure 25. Comparison of the effects of population density upon the food consumption and daytime plasma corticosterone levels of male and female mice. Food consumption is plotted per 10 gm of body weight, to correct for body weight differences between male and female mice. Food consumption was determined by weighing the food hoppers three times per week; each food consumption point represents the mean over a 4-week period. Duplicate corticosterone assays of plasma pooled from five mice were determined on days 11, 18, 25, 32, 39, 47, and 53 after the initial experimental caging. Each corticosterone point represents the mean of these determinations. C3H/He male and female mice were housed in separate but similar low stress protective facilities.

tions are relevant to the experimental design of nutritional, neoplastic, and related experiments where caloric intake is of importance. In this respect, it is appropriate to recall the multiple influences upon carcinogenic and related processes that have been reported, by varying food intakes (Herbst *et al.,* 1960; Sprunt and Flanigan, 1956; Tannenbaum, 1940; Tannenbaum and Silverstone, 1953; Visscher *et al.,* 1942) and temperature conditions (Fuller *et al.,* 1941; La Barba *et al.,* 1970; McVay, 1968; Wallace *et al.,* 1942, 1944; Young, 1958).

In contrast to the absence of any detectable influence of cage population density upon plasma corticosterone, there is a statistically significant increasing trend in adrenal weight as a function of the number of female mice per cage ($p < .01$), which is shown in Figure 26. Several hypotheses may be considered to rationalize these findings. One possibility is that changes in adrenal

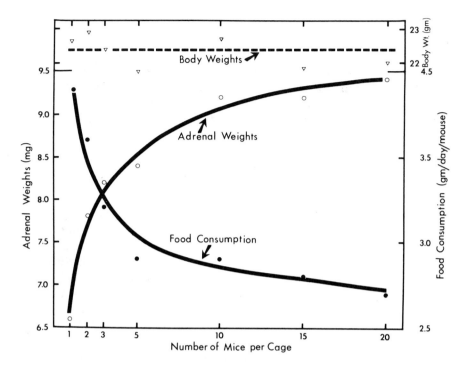

Figure 26. Effects of population density upon food consumption, body weights, and adrenal weights of C3H/He female mice. Adrenal weights were determined 5 weeks following initiation of the population density experiments. Each adrenal weight point represents the median value of adrenals from five randomly selected mice. A test for trend yielded $p < .01$, indicating that significantly higher adrenal weights were observed in those mice residing in the cages containing larger numbers of animals. Body weights were determined on days 11, 18, 25, and 33 after caging, and averaged; each body weight point represents the average of 10–20 mice.

weight under these circumstances may be a more sensitive parameter of stress over a prolonged period than daytime plasma corticosterone levels, which may not express the full nocturnal range of corticosterone response. Another possibility that should be considered is that the increase in adrenal weight is an expression of adrenal medulla hyperplasia rather than adrenal cortex activation. The adrenal cortex is, of course, the tissue involved in the production of corticosterone, whereas the adrenal medulla is concerned with the production of catecholamines, the most conspicuous being epinephrine and norepinephrine.

Henry *et al.* (1975) have evidence that the physiological effects of stress can be divided into two separate categories, with mild anxiety-stress being primarily associated with activation of the adrenal cortex, whereas stress involving fright or fury as in fighting animals, or in the establishment of social hierarchy, involves the adrenal medulla and the production of catecholamines, rather than, or in addition to, the adrenal cortex and glucocorticoid elevation. Histological examination of the adrenals, carried out under similar experimental conditions, is obviously required to determine which elements are responsible for the tissue hyperplasia. Another reasonable explanation is that the plasma samples which were obtained at 9 A.M. to 11 A.M. for corticosterone assay do not accurately reflect the integrated 24-hr corticosterone levels, especially those levels occurring during the nightly competitive feeding period.

Effects of Population Density upon Tumor Growth

A part of the testing procedure for detecting possible effects of cage crowding included challenging the mice with tumor transplants, and monitoring the animals for percentage of tumor incidence, tumor latent periods, tumor growth rates, and mouse survival times. One of the tumor types that had been reported to be responsive to cage crowding was the transplantable B-16 mouse melanoma (Dechambre and Gosse, 1971). A similar experiment was undertaken using the same tumor type, as follows: On experimental day 29 following initiation of a population density experiment involving 1, 2, 3, 5, 10, 15, or 20 BDF female mice per cage, all of the animals were implanted with the B-16 pigmented melanoma. Tumor measurements were made twice a week in order to determine relative tumor growth rates. Tumor latent periods were also determined, as well as the survival times of the hosts. In contrast to the report of Dechambre and Gosse, under the circumstances of our experiment there was no significant influence of population density on the tumor growth rates, or the survival times of the tumor-bearing hosts (Riley and Spackman, 1977b). Thus, in our experiment, the growth behavior of this particular tumor was essentially the same in mice housed individually as in those mice that were housed 20 to a cage, as well as in the other intermediate population densities. This is consistent with our observation of a lack of effect of LDH virus-induced stress upon the pigmented B-16 melanoma, as shown in Figure 19A.

In contrast to the apparent lack of effect of population density upon the pigmented B-16 melanoma, Figure 27 shows the effects of population density upon the growth of the 6C3HED lymphosarcoma in C3H/He female mice. These effects are demonstrated by differences in the maximum tumor volumes that were attained in the various population density groups. This illustration again shows the effects of population density upon food consumption prior to tumor implantation. It is unclear whether the effects of population density upon the growth of this tumor may be related to the earlier differences in food consumption and caloric intake, or to the observed differences in adrenal size shown in Figure 26, or to other inapparent factors. However, this tumor–host model has been shown to be sensitive to several forms of stress, as indicated by Figures 8, 20, 22, 23, 24, and 27, as well as by Tables 3–6.

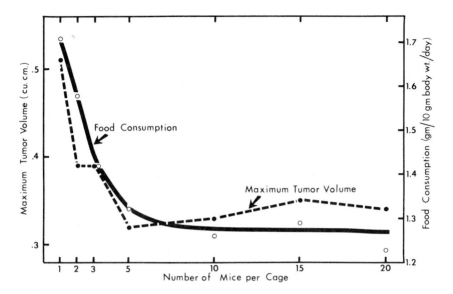

Figure 27. Effects of population density upon food consumption and subsequent maximum tumor volumes in female C3H/He mice. The largest lymphosarcomas were observed in the isolated female mice, while the smallest tumors were found in the female mice housed 5 per cage ($p < .005$). Each food consumption point represents the mean of determinations made at 3 or 4 day intervals during the period from 3 to 36 days following the initiation of the various population densities. Subsequently, on day 56 of the experiment, all mice were implanted with the 6C3HED lymphosarcoma.

Effects of Population Density upon Tumor Regressions

Since tumor regression in a properly balanced tumor–host model is a good index of immune competence, we examined that parameter as one means for determining the optimal population of mice per standard plastic cage. The results of these experiments were unexpected. The tumor regression rate of the 6C3HED lymphosarcoma in C3H/He female mice in cages having only one animal per cage was 60%. This was in contrast to other population densities of 2, 3, 5, 10, 15, or 20 mice per cage, which had a range of 80–100% regressions, with an average of 93% ($p < .001$). Thus, based upon the ability of female mice to reject a tumor challenge, all tested densities of group housing were preferable to that of single animal isolation (See Table 5).

As shown in Table 6, male C3H/He mice housed 1 or 2 per cage had a lesser ability to reject the 6C3HED lymphosarcoma than did those housed 3, 5, 10, 15, or 20 per cage. Unlike female mice, male mice housed 2 per cage exhibited no advantage over isolated mice, with respect to tumor growth. It therefore appears that for optimum immunocompetence, male mice should not be housed either 1 or 2 per cage. However, any number over 2 per cage, up to 20

TABLE 5
Effects of Isolation upon Percentage of Tumor Regressions in Female C3H/He Mice

Number of mice per cage	Tumor regressions[a] (%)	Probability[b]
1	60	
2, 3, 5, 10, 15, or 20	93	$p < .001$

[a] The Gardner 6C3HED lymphosarcoma was implanted into C3H/He female mice 56 days after initiation of the various population densities. Percentages of tumor regressions were determined on day 25 after tumor implantation.

[b] The probability value was determined by the chi-square method, comparing the data from one mouse per cage with the combined data from 2, 3, 5, 10, 15, or 20 mice per cage.

TABLE 6
Effects of Population Density upon Percentage of Tumor Regressions in Male C3H/He Mice

Number of mice per cage	Tumor regressions[a] (%)	Probability[b]
1	70	
2	65	
1 or 2 (combined data)	67.5	
3, 5, 10, 15, or 19 (combined data)	84.6	$p < .01$

[a] The Gardner 6C3HED lymphosarcoma was implanted into C3H/He male mice 56 days after initiation of the various population densities. Tumor regressions were determined on day 25 after tumor implantation.

[b] The probability value was determined by the chi-square method, comparing the data from 1 or 2 mice per cage (combined data) with the combined data from 3, 5, 10, 15, or 19 mice per cage.

per cage, yielded similar results, with no optimum number per cage within this range detected.

Despite the significant difference in tumor regressions, housing male mice 1 or 2 per cage had no observable influence upon daytime plasma corticosterone levels. It was noted, however, that male mice housed 2 per cage exhibited a lower food consumption and somewhat lighter body weights than did those housed 1 or 3 per cage.

Observation of Stresslike Effects Following Exposure of Mice to Microwaves

Studies were undertaken to obtain objective information on possible interactions between radio frequency (RF) radiation and biological materials, specifically, changes in cells, tissues, organs, and implanted tumors, as measured in a suitable experimental animal model (Riley et al., 1978c, 1979b; Guy and Chou, 1975).

In order to introduce and to maintain maximum control of the more critical experimental conditions in these studies, a mouse tumor–host model was employed (Riley *et al.*, 1978c, 1979b). The logic that was followed in selecting this particular model stemmed from a concern that some of the earlier reports which ascribed certain physiological and pathological changes in both humans and experimental animals to RF exposures, may not have been adequately controlled with respect to physiologically perturbing stress factors. These questions have arisen partly because some of the RF-associated biological changes reported have been similar to recognized stress effects (Riley and Spackman, 1978a,b).

Also of relevance, a number of reports concerning the physiological effects of microwaves and other RF frequencies, have implicated the immunologic apparatus of experimental animals *in vivo,* or certain elements of the immune system *in vitro* (Czerski, 1975; Szmigielski, 1975). As a consequence of the accumulating evidence that immunologic competence might be modified during or following exposure to RF fields or to microwave radiation, a series of experiments was designed to detect the possibility of observing subtle RF influences on the immunocompetence of a specially selected mouse model.

Other studies described in this chapter have demonstrated the sensitivity of certain tumor–host relationships for expressing either impairment or enhancement of the immunologic system of the mouse. Thus, by appropriate selection of a tumor–host model where the immunologic capacity of the host is in equipoise with the tumor, small alterations in the immune competence of the host are reflected by quantifiable changes in the behavior of the tumor. Such alterations may be determined by a comparison of various parameters of the RF-exposed host and its tumor with suitable sham-exposed controls. Those tumor–host parameters that have been most useful are (*a*) the tumor latent periods; (*b*) tumor growth rates; (*c*) maximum tumor volumes; (*d*) the number and rate of tumor regressions; and (*e*) the survival time of the tumor-bearing hosts.

The summary data reported here are derived only from tumor regression observations. Negative findings would presumedly indicate that exposure of the mice to RF radiation has not influenced the animals' immunocompetence as detectable by this sensitive system. The detection and measurement of either impairment or enhancement of the immune system in mice exposed to RF radiation, in comparison with the sham-exposed controls, suggest that either the RF energy, or some characteristic of the exposure techniques have brought about an alteration in the host immune system (Riley and Spackman, 1978a,b).

The following experiment illustrates some of the results obtained with this model. Figure 28 illustrates the differential tumor regression behavior of the various experimental groups of C3H/He mice. This particular parameter seems to be the most sensitive and responsive in respect to the behavior of the

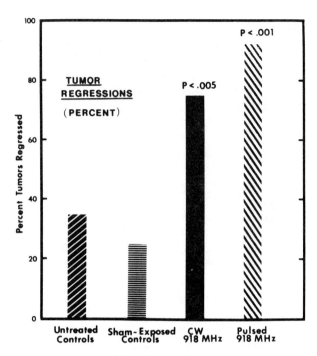

Figure 28. Tumor regressions associated with chronic exposure of C3H/He mice to microwaves (918 MHz RF radiation). The irradiated mice were exposed to 10 mW/cm^2 for 2 hr per day, 5 days per week, for an 8-week period. 6C3HED tumors were implanted 8 days following discontinuance of the RF exposures. The regression percentages were observed on day 21 following tumor implantation; Probability values were determined by the chi-square procedure.

tumors in the RF-radiation-exposed group as compared with the sham-exposed controls. It may be noted that tumor regressions occurred in a significantly higher percentage of those animals that were previously exposed to continuous wave (CW) and pulsed RF radiation than in either the untreated controls or sham-exposed but nonirradiated control animals.

Although there appears to be a higher percentage of tumor regressions in those animals exposed to the pulsed mode as compared with the CW mode, the differences between these two groups are not statistically significant.

Analyzing the data from a somewhat different perspective, Table 7 shows a comparison of the tumor regressions occurring in the various groups from the standpoint of the average time that was required for 50% of the mice to regress their tumors. Again, it may be noted that those animals exposed to either pulsed or CW modes employed a significantly shorter time period for the regression of their tumors than that required for either the untreated or sham-exposed controls. The probability value for these differences was $p < .001$. These two sets of data are thus consistent.

TABLE 7
Comparison of Tumor Regressions between Control and Irradiated C3H/He Mice[a]

Treatment	Number of mice	Time required for 50% of the mice to regress their tumors (Days)[b]	Probability[c]
Untreated controls	20	24	NS
Sham-exposed controls	12	25	Reference
Chronic 918 MHz (Pulsed)	12	21	$p < .001$
Chronic 918 MHz (CW)	12	21	$p < .001$

[a] Irradiated mice received $10 \, mW/cm^2$ for 2 hr per day (5 days/week) for an 8-week period, at a frequency of 918 MHz.
[b] Tumors were implanted 8 days following discontinuance of microwave exposure.
[c] Probability values were obtained using the chi-square test for the distributions of the regression times.

CONSIDERATIONS RELEVANT TO EXPERIMENTAL DESIGN OF STUDIES ON STRESS

Probable Causes of Experimental Contradictions

It is apparent from an examination of the inconsistent results obtained in earlier studies by various investigators, that the experimental nuances and complexities of the effects of various forms of stress on cancer have heretofore exceeded our ability to evaluate the relative potencies of the experimental variables involved and to provide all of the necessary experimental conditions and controls. It appears that these difficulties have arisen from a variety of unappreciated experimental factors.

The Rapid Physiological Response to Handling-Induced Stress

One troublesome aspect has been a failure to appreciate the extreme sensitivity and rapidity of response of experimental animals exposed to experimental, manipulative, or environmentally-induced stress. Critical phases of the stress syndrome are initiated within a few minutes following the slightest disturbance of mice. The physiological consequences of this stress may continue for hours or even days, depending upon the nature, severity, and duration of the stressful stimulus.

The rapid physiological response to handling-induced anxiety stress is indicated by the measurable elevation in plasma corticosterone levels observed only minutes after the animals have been agitated by simple capturing procedures. This is illustrated by the rapidly ascending corticosterone curve in Figure 4, which demonstrates that the response to handling is so rapid that its biochemical manifestation in the form of plasma corticosterone elevation is initiated within $3\frac{1}{2}$ minutes. This imposes a rigorous time limitation upon the investigator to obtain blood samples for establishing the baseline levels of plasma corticosterone in his control animals as well as for measuring the physiological effects of experimentally induced stress. Rapid rises in plasma corticosterone can be generated by the routine process of capturing animals for injections, cage transfer, bleeding, or other experimental procedures, or even by simply transporting the animals from their protective holding facilities to the laboratory bench. Unless these operations are carried out in less than a 4-min period, anxiety stress will be manifested by initiation of the typical physiological stress syndrome, resulting in elevated plasma corticosterone levels. If sufficient time elapses, leukopenia and eventually thymus involution will occur.

Anxiety Stress and Impairment of the Immune System

The most persuasive explanation, based upon the results of our studies (Riley and Spackman, 1976a, 1977a, 1978a; Riley et al., 1979a; Spackman and Riley, 1974, 1975, 1976, 1977, 1978; Spackman et al., 1974, 1978; Santisteban et al., 1977, 1978), as well as those of others (Ader and Grota, 1969; Henry, et al., 1975; Jonas, 1966; Khalestkaia, 1954; Mason, 1968, 1974, 1975a,b; Monjan and Collector, 1977; Raushenbakh, 1952; Ray and Pradhan, 1974; Schwartz, 1969; Weiss, 1973; Weston, 1973) for the tangible effects of psychosocial or anxiety stress upon tumor processes appears to be related to the immunological impairment resulting from elevated levels of plasma adrenal corticoids. There is abundant evidence that the basic cellular elements constituting the immunological apparatus, including macrophages, T cells, and B cells, are all subject to modification, impairment, and/or destruction by specific adrenal cortical hormones (Gisler and Schenkel-Hullinger, 1971; Monjan and Collector, 1977; Santisteban, 1958, 1959, 1970; Santisteban and Dougherty, 1954; Santisteban et al., 1969, 1972; Santisteban and Riley, 1973). A particularly conspicuous cellular effect of these stress-elevated hormones is thymus involution. The lymphocytopenia resulting from stress-induced plasma corticosterone undoubtedly indicates destruction of T cells and probably also B cells (Gisler et al., 1971; Jensen, 1969; Monjan and Collector,

1977; Solomon and Amkraut, 1972, 1979; Solomon, *et al.*, 1980), although organ sequestration has also been cited to account for some of the white cell disappearance.

Adrenal corticoid-induced immunological impairment thus logically accounts for the enhancement of tumor growth in mice stressed by rotation (Figures 21 and 22), as well as the shorter survival interval in tumor-bearing mice stressed as a result of cross-country air shipment (Figure 8), or psychosocial confrontation and competition (Table 4). Since the administration of synthetic corticoids has demonstrable effects upon tumor growth, regression, and host survival, similar to that produced by stress, as shown in Figures 19, 20, 23, and 24, this mechanism is a plausible explanation for the physiological effects of certain forms of stress resulting in the enhancement of some tumor processes.

Increases in Cancer Incidence as a Consequence of T-Cell Deficiency

Thymectomy or treatment with antilymphocytic serum results in increased tumor incidence in animals inoculated with viruses such as polyoma or SV40. In contrast, if the ablated T-cell system is replaced by thymus grafting, or by inoculations of syngeneic lymphocyte suspensions containing mature T cells, most of the tumors are suppressed, and the observed incidence is much lower (Klein, 1975). These results support the hypothesis that the increased tumor incidence of the immunologically impaired animals was related specifically to a T-cell deficiency (Archer and Pierce, 1961; Comsa and Hook, 1973; Habel, 1963; Hellström *et al.*, 1971; Prehn, 1969). Further supporting evidence, derived from the adverse effects of genetically determined immunodeficiency, is the increased tumor incidence in patients with the Wiskott–Aldrich syndrome, or with ataxia–telangiectasia. Both of these genetic diseases affect the T-cell system adversely. Also, patients receiving long-term immunosuppression in order to maintain kidney transplants have an increased tumor incidence compared with the normal population. The accumulated data thus indicate that any compromise of T cell status permits an increased risk of incipient neoplastic processes escaping immunological containment. This applies to immunosuppression induced by stress as well as by other means.

Effects of Chronic Stress: Immunosuppression Followed by Immunoenhancement

Figure 29 shows the results of an experiment by Monjan and Collector (1977), in which immunosuppression was followed by subsequent immunoenhancement during chronic nocturnal exposure of mice to an intermittent auditory stress. When the responsiveness of splenic B cells and T cells from

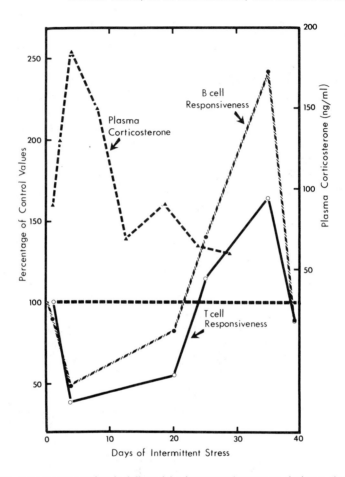

Figure 29. Immunosuppression is followed by immunoenhancement during a chronic stress experiment. Plasma corticosterone levels were elevated during the period of immunosuppression, but dropped as the animals apparently became adapted to the chronic stress. This Figure is a re-plot of the Monjan and Collector (1977) data, and is used here with permission.

such mice to mitogens was assayed *in vitro,* both types of cells displayed similar patterns of immunosuppression followed by immunoenhancement. Plasma corticosterone levels were assayed in a separate similar experiment. The observed cellular immunosuppression was probably a consequence of elevated corticosterone levels (Santisteban and Dougherty, 1954; Spackman *et al.,* 1975). However, the mechanisms underlying the subsequent immunoenhancement are less clear. Many humoral factors, including somatotropin and thyroxin, exhibit increased plasma concentrations during long-term exposure to environmental stressors (Solomon and Amkraut, 1979; Pierpaoli *et al.,* 1969; Mason, 1974, 1975c). It was postulated by Monjan and Collector that the delayed immunoenhancement during exposure to chronic stress might be due to the elevation of one or more such circulating factors which stimulate lymphocyte reactivity through activation of the cyclic nucleotide guanosine 3′, 5′-monophosphate.

The phenomenon of alternating immunosuppression and immunoenhancement during exposure to chronic experimental or environmental stress may account for some of the conflicting reports regarding enhancement versus inhibition of carcinogenesis, tumor development, incidence, or regressions in experimental animals exposed to other varieties of chronic stresses. For example, Newberry and Sengbusch (1979) have reported that when rats were exposed to severe electric shock stress for either 40 or 85 consecutive days the incidence of tumors resulting from DMBA injections was reduced; however, 25 days of the same stress did not significantly influence the number of tumors as compared with the untreated controls.

The data in Figure 30 illustrate another example of either stress-induced im-

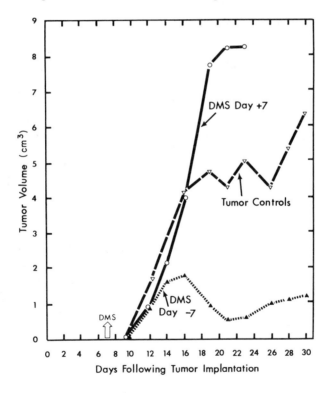

Figure 30. Comparative tumor response following administration of a synthetic corticosteroid at various times in respect to tumor implantation. The synthetic adrenocorticoid was dexamethasone (DMS), which was injected intraperitoneally at a dose of 50 mg/kg suspended in 0.9% NaCl. The 6C3HED lymphosarcoma was implanted as a cell suspension in the hip. Ten C3H/He females were used in each group. DMS injected 1 week prior to tumor implantation appears to have enhanced the immunological competence of the host, as indicated by the suppression of tumor growth as compared with the untreated tumor-bearing controls. In contrast, when DMS was injected 7 days following tumor implantation, there is evidence of immunosuppression, based upon the enhanced growth rate of the tumors.

pairment or enhancement of immunologic competence, depending upon the timing of the application of stress, or its simulation by the injection of a synthetic corticoid such as dexamethasone. In this experiment, both tumor suppression and tumor enhancement were observed, depending upon the time of injection of the DMS. If dexamethasone was administered 7 days prior to tumor implantation, the immunocompetence of the host appeared to be enhanced since the tumor was suppressed in comparison with the growth of the untreated control tumors. When the DMS was administered 7 days after implantation of the tumor there appeared to be immunologic impairment since the tumor escaped, grew rapidly, killing the biochemically stressed hosts. This is a further demonstration of experimental factors that change the end result merely as a function of the timing of the various events.

Circadian Rhythms Affecting Plasma Levels of Adrenal Corticoids

All living organisms exhibit circadian rhythms in certain of their biological and biochemical control systems. Circadian fluctuations in plasma corticosterone concentrations in mice who, of course, are nocturnal creatures, amount to a three to fivefold increase between the early morning low plasma concentration and the evening high concentrations, as shown in Figure 15 (Riley and Spackman, 1976b). Man, by comparison, exhibits high plasma cortisol levels between 6 A.M. and noon, and the lowest concentrations late in the evening. Thus, the time of day at which stress-affected plasma hormone levels are determined is relevant in experimental design and reporting.

The phenomenon of circadian hormone fluctuation indicates a need for a 24-hr measurement of adrenal cortical activity. This measurement may be made simpler and more accurate by a noninvasive technique of urine collection over a 24-hr or other appropriate interval, followed by chromatographic separation and fluorescent analysis for stress-associated adrenal cortical metabolites (D. H. Spackman, unpublished data; Riley et al., 1980). Since it is possible that daytime corticosterone levels may not reflect accurately the degree of stress imposed upon nocturnal rodents, such an integrative 24-hr measurement represents a possible means for detecting even the subtle nighttime stress.

The phase of the circadian cycle during which experimental stresses are initiated may greatly affect the subsequent influences of such stress on the physiological, biochemical, cellular, and immunologic events under consideration. For example, the data of Figure 15, when compared to those of Figure 16, provide an indication of the dramatic corticosterone differences resulting from experimental timing. The LDH virus, when inoculated at 5 P.M., just prior to the nocturnal increase in corticosterone, produces peak corticosterone levels much higher than those resulting from a similar virus inoculation made at 9 A.M. (Riley and Spackman, 1976b). Thus the timing of experimental stress may be of critical importance. Such subtle procedural differences may also account for many of the apparent contradictions in the literature. Therefore, the time of day at which experimental stresses are initiated should be both regulated and recorded. It is now known that the time of day that therapeutic drugs are administered also relates to their efficacy. Additional studies of such rhythmic physiological phenomena may result in further insights into demonstrating relationships between stress and neoplastic diseases.

Experimental Stress Superimposed upon Environmental Stress

The foregoing data illustrate the potential pitfalls associated with superimposing experimental stress upon animals that are already stressed due to environmental factors or handling techniques. It can now be readily demonstrated that uncontrolled environmentally-induced stresses may produce physiological conditions that either negate or complicate the interpretation of the experimental results. For example, wire-bottom cages in themselves are stressful, as is the environment of conventional communal animal facilities. Thus, interpretation of experimental data obtained from rodents housed under one or both of these conditions would obviously be risky and difficult. Supplemental anxiety induced by mild experimental stresses such as brief handling or slow rotation, which produce dramatic effects in quiescent animals, may have no apparent differential effect upon mice already undergoing chronic environmental stress in an animal facility where they are exposed to daily experimental and house-keeping procedures. It is thus essential to employ housing and caging conditions, as well as special handling procedures which provide pre-experimental quiescent animals, as well as permanently nonstressed controls.

The noninvasive procedures that we are developing for the measurement of biochemical parameters in stressed and control animals include the design of a special plastic cage for the collection of noncontaminated 24-hr urine specimens or other appropriate sampling periodicities. The urine thus collected can be analyzed for amino acids, as shown in Figure 13, or for urinary corticoid metabolites, which increase as a result of stress-induced elevations of plasma adrenal cortical hormones (Riley et al., 1981).

Multiple Physiological Responses to Severe Experimental "Stress"

It must, of course, be assumed that physiological phenomena are not as simple as implied by most experimental protocols, and it is thus prudent to be aware that several varieties of physiological responses may occur during the most carefully controlled experiments. A special problem would be an experiment that employs rigorous "stress."

Activation of the adrenal medulla, or of other hormonal and metabolic systems, depends upon the nature of the "stressor" and/or the intensity of the procedures employed (Henry and Santisteban, 1971; Henry et al., 1972, 1975; Mason, 1968, 1974, 1975a,b,c; Mason et al., 1957). It has been established that mild anxiety is capable of rapidly activating the adrenal cortex, resulting in the production of substantial elevations in circulating corticoids (Mason, 1974, 1975c; Spackman and Riley, 1976; Spackman et al., 1975). However, the question arises as to what additional physiological events may occur if the experimental procedures also generate fear or anger, which activate the adrenal medulla (Henry et al., 1971, 1972, 1975), or interfere with the nutritional state or the metabolism of the experimental subject (Mason, 1974, 1975c).

A significant elevation in plasma corticosterone levels, as well as changes in other elements of the stress syndrome such as leukocytopenia, reductions in thymus, spleen, and lymph node weights, occurred in mice following either food or water deprivation for 48 hr (V. Riley and D.H. Spackman, unpublished observations, 1975). Interestingly, however, Mason (1974) has shown that corticosteroid elevations occur in monkeys completely deprived of food for 3 days but not in those given a non-nutritive but pleasantly flavored placebo, indicating that emotional factors may have been responsible for the stress syndrome induced by fasting. The monkeys receiving the non-nutritive placebo for 3 days, however, exhibited several other severe metabolic alterations, including elevations in urinary epinephrine and thyroid hormone levels, a decrease in gonadal hormone production, and a decrease in plasma insulin and glucose levels (Mason, 1974).

Deprivation of certain amino acids in the diet has been reported to cause an impaired synthesis of antibodies, and thus interference with immunologic competence (Jose and Good, 1973). It has also been shown that caloric restriction can alter tumor incidence and growth rates, and has other influences upon disease processes (Tannenbaum, 1940; Tannenbaum and Silverstone, 1953; Rusch, 1944; Visscher et al., 1942). An experimental design which results in the inadvertent alteration of food intake may thus introduce many complicating factors, making it difficult to sort out the unintended influences of nutritional modification from the physiological effects of the experimental treatment.

While the simple procedure of restraining an animal undoubtedly causes anxiety stress, physically imposed immobilization also alters a number of other physiological functions. Mason (1974, 1975c) has shown that sustained chair restraint of monkeys results in elevations in corticosteroids, ephinephrine, norephinephrine, and thyroid hormone, with concomitant decreases in insulin and gonadal hormones. If the immobilization is prolonged, the nutritional and metabolic status of the animal will be compromised, and alterations in breathing and blood flow may also occur. Such forced immobilization is thus an experimental stressor that should be employed with the knowledge that undesired elements may intrude into experiments that are designed to measure the effects of emotional stress.

Some of the earlier experiments on stress and cancer employed harsh experimental stimuli, such as repeated surgical trauma, ether anesthesia, chilling, swimming in cold water to exhaustion, heating, and other physical insults. Again, such harsh means for inducing anxiety stress are not necessary, and may have the additional disadvantage of defeating the aims of the experiment. When such processes exceed the physiological thresholds, causing metabolic exhaustion, shock, or actual injury, many biochemical processes other than those activated by mild psychosocial or anxiety stress may be either stimulated or suppressed. For example, exposure of monkeys to gradually decreasing temperatures over a 1-week period resulted in elevations in corticosteroids, ephinephrine, norephinephrine, thyroid, and growth hormones (Mason, 1974). On the other hand, exposure to heat (30° C over a 2-week period) caused decreased levels of the same hormones (Mason, 1974). The biological consequences of these treatments thus have uncertain relationships to the specific physiological sequence of events induced by mild anxiety stress (Riley *et al.*, 1979a; Mason, 1974).

It is thus appropriate to assess the potential physiological effects of severe "stress," which substantially exceeds the mild anxiety that is adequate to activate the adrenal cortex producing a typical stress syndrome. To avoid experimental complications, it seems desirable to induce controlled stress by the mildest possible procedures that will produce elevated levels of circulating adrenal corticoids, and thus bring about a significant impairment of immunologic competence, as indicated by thymus involution, lymphocytopenia, and other effects upon the host immunologic apparatus.

Metabolic Effects of Population Density

Another experimental factor to be considered is the number of animals employed per cage. As shown in Figures 25, 26 and 27, a sensitive homeostatic thermal mechanism appears to be operating, based upon a regulatory feedback that controls caloric intake as a function of body weight maintenance requirements. This mechanism is influenced by the caloric requirements of mice that retain or lose body heat depending upon the population density in their cage. The multiple influences upon tumor growth and carcinogenic processes that have been reported for various caloric intakes (Riley, 1979b, Riley *et al.*, 1979a, 1981; Sprunt and Flanigan, 1956; Tannenbaum, 1940; Tannenbaum and Silverstone, 1953) and temperature conditions (Fuller *et al.*, 1941; Wallace *et al.*, 1942, 1944; Young, 1958), are relevant to the selection of appropriate experimental population densities.

The most rewarding studies of stress should be directed toward an increased understanding of the underlying physiological phenomena. For example, the maximum tumor volume data of Figure 27 suggest that there may be subtle effects of population density upon host physiology. However, these effects may not be explained in terms of the known physiological effects of elevated corticosterone, since the daytime corticosterone levels remained the same for all of the population densities tested in this experiment.

It remains unclear as to whether the differential food consumption due to varying homeostatic thermal requirements has given rise to the differential tumor response, or whether some physiological mechanism indicated by the significant adrenal weight trend shown in Figure 26 may be responsible. The complexities of these interrelationships are further emphasized by this relatively simple experiment.

In addition, unlike the maximum tumor volumes, the tumor regression data shown in Tables 5 and 6 indicate that yet another physiological mechanism may be operating in mice that are housed singly, since the tumor regression data exhibited a different pattern, with respect to population density, from that of the maximum tumor volume data. The physiological mechanism underlying the adverse effects of isolation upon tumor behavior, unlike the consistent effects of rotation, shipping, and psychosocial confrontation, does not appear to depend upon increased levels of adrenal cortical hormones. Thus, this experiment indicates the presence of several metabolic mechanisms, none of which would have been apparent under adverse housing or stressful environmental conditions, or if a less sensitive tumor–host model had been employed.

The Age and Sex of the Experimental Animals

Differences in response to transplantation of nonsyngeneic tumors as a function of age have been reported by Teller et al. (1964). They have observed that old mice are more receptive to heterotransplantation, which indicates a reduced immunologic competence in older animals. Also, there is an increased incidence of mammary tumors in older C3H mice infected with the Bittner virus. Generally speaking, the thymus is larger in young animals and tends to atrophy with age. Thus, experiments involving thymus involution and impaired T cell functions may be performed most effectively in young adult mice. However, insofar as tumor behavior is concerned, age differences in mice between 6 and 30 weeks of age appear to be insignificant.

Sex effects are apparent in some stress studies. For example, the data of Figure 3 indicate that female mice are more responsive to the presence of the opposite sex, in terms of corticosterone production, than are males. Such influences are seen even when the two sexes are not in the same cage, but merely in proximity to each other in the same room. The significance of this phenomenon in terms of tumor behavior has not been tested in our laboratories. However, it is quite possible that females when housed separately will respond to a tumor challenge quite differently than when housed alongside cages of male mice.

The Handling and "Gentling" of Young Rodents:
Stress Adaptation

Our studies have shown that conventional experimental handling of adult mice is highly stressful as expressed by the detrimental physiological and immunologic consequences. However, it has also been reported that the daily handling of rats, starting at an early age, conditions them to stress-adaptation as shown by their more normal immunologic responses later in life. It is therefore important to distinguish between the effects of occasional, stressful handling, and the long-term consequences of an early and systematic intentional "gentling" procedure, which begins at an early age, takes place over a substantial period of time, and has future conditioning potential.

Tumor-Host Syngeneity and the Selection
of Effective Tumor-Host Models

Although there has been understandable controversy over the role of immunologic surveillance in controlling cancer and other diseases, accumulated data have now resulted in a preponderance of opinion that such protective monitoring is an immunologic reality (Burnet, 1970, Keast, 1970; Prehn, 1963, 1969). George Klein (1975) has suggested that immune surveillance may be most effective against tumor-associated antigen systems that have been regularly encountered by the species during evolutionary processes. Of possible relevance, tumors induced by chemical carcinogens introduced by the recent events of industrialization, are relatively unaffected by immunologic mechanisms. Accumulated data suggest that such chemically-induced tumors respond differently to experimental stress than do the more immunoresponsive tumors resulting from oncogenic viruses, such as murine mammary carcinoma or Moloney virus-induced sarcoma.

In experiments utilizing measurement of the incidence and/or growth rate of a transplantable tumor for studying the effects of stress on immunocompetence, selection of the proper tumor type is critical. Rapidly growing tumors that are syngeneic with the host, such as the rapidly growing B-16 pigmented melanoma shown in Figure 19A, do not respond to stress or to other mild impairments of the immune system. However, the slowly growing nonpigmented variant is responsive to the host's control, and is thus capable of responding to the biochemical events induced either by anxiety stress or by inoculation with a "stress"-inducing virus. Figure 20 shows another nonsyngeneic tumor, the 6C3HED lymphosarcoma growing in C3H/He mice, responding similarly to both dexamethasone (DMS) and LDH virus infection. This tumor–host model is also responsive to rotational-induced anxiety stress, as shown in Figure 22. However, when the same tumor is implanted into C3H/Bi mice, a more compatible substrain, it grows rapidly even in unstressed animals and does not respond to corticosterone or DMS-induced immunoimpairment (see Table 3). Thus, rapidly growing tumors, such as the pigmented melanoma in Figure 19A, or the Gardner lymphosarcoma growing in C3H/Bi mice, will not respond to the presence of stress. Such differences in host–tumor compatibility and sensitivities may also explain many of the apparent discrepancies reported in the literature.

"Stress"-Associated Inhibition of Neoplastic Processes

In contrast to the usual observation of neoplasm enhancement, the most conspicuous inhibitory effects of "stress" upon tumor processes have been reported in experiments involving tumors that have been induced by chemical carcinogens such as DMBA or MCA. The stress has usually been produced by electric shock or long-term daily restraint. These results pose the interesting question as to whether there is something unique about the response of chemically-induced tumors to immune processes, as suggested by George Klein (1975), or whether the unexpected results are due to the nature of the stressor systems, or complications due to extrinsic factors such as reduced caloric intake, or the chronic stress of the animals if they were maintained in conventional facilities.

Another possible explanation for stress-induced inhibition of cancer processes is inherent in the work of Monjan and Collector (1977), who have shown that chronic stress is capable of inducing an immunoenhancement following the initial corticosteroid-induced immunoimpairment (Figure 29).

Biologic Interactions

Figures 19A and 20B illustrate the synergisms between the LDH virus and two nonsyngeneic tumors. As a consequence of LDH virus infection, these tumors behave as though they were compatible with the host (Spackman and Riley, 1974, 1975; Riley and Spackman, 1976a).

Specific influences imposed by the ubiquitous LDH virus that may alter or compromise experiments involving neoplasia or immunologic responses include the following: (a) elevations of plasma corticosterone during the acute phase of infection (Spackman and Riley, 1974; Riley and Spackman, 1976b); (b) subsequent partial temporary thymus involution (Santisteban, 1970; Santisteban et al., 1972); (c) lysis of circulating lymphocytes, presumably T cells (Fitzmaurice et al., 1972; Howard et al., 1969; Riley, 1973); (d) dual effects upon the spleen, namely, a destruction of small lymphocytes in thymus-dependent regions concomitant with a continuous immunoblast proliferation in the thymus-independent regions, resulting in a moderate hyperplasia (Fitz-maurice *et al.*, 1972; Santisteban *et al.*, 1972); (*e*) enhancement of spleen antibody-forming cells during acute infection, followed by inhibition during the subsequent life-long chronic phase of the infection (Riley *et al.*, 1976b); (*f*) alterations in the incidence of tumors induced by certain oncogenic viruses (Riley and Spackman, 1976b; Riley *et al.*, 1966, 1978a); (*g*) reduction in regression rates of certain virus-induced tumors (Riley and Spackman, 1976b); (*h*) enhancement of growth rates of certain nonsyngeneic transplantable tumors (Riley and Spackman, 1976a); (*i*) a three to twentyfold enhancement in the production of spleen tumor foci following intravenous inoculation of Friend virus (Riley and Spackman, 1976b; Turner *et al.*, 1971); and (*j*) an impairment of the clearance of certain enzymes from the plasma, with a concomitant increased influx of enzymes into the plasma, which persists for the lifespan of the infected mouse. In the presence of a growing tumor, these physiological alterations result in a synergistic increase in the levels of certain endogenous enzymes, notably lactate dehydrogenase (LDH), that may amount to more than one hundredfold over normal values (Riley, 1974a,b; Riley and Spackman, 1976b; Riley *et al.*, 1978b). Some of these and other effects of LDH virus infection are itemized in Tables 8 and 9. It would be pre-

TABLE 8
Various Physiological and Biochemical Differences Capable of Affecting Immunologic Competence in Normal Mice and Those Infected with LDH Virus

Parameters measured	Normal mice (No LDH virus)	Virus-infected mice
Plasma corticosterone levels	Normal	2 to 20-fold[a] increase
Thymus weight	Normal	50% weight loss[b]
Peripheral lymphocytes	Normal	70% depletion[c]
Spleen weight	Normal	30% weight increase
Peripheral nodes (weight)	Normal	50% weight increase
Carbon clearance (K rate)	.016	.006
Macrophage integrity	Normal	Impaired
Spleen antibody-forming cells (plaques per spleen), relative numbers		
Acute infection	1	10
Chronic infection	15	1
Plasma LDH level[d]	200–400	2,000–4,000
In tumor-bearing mice	200–2,000	10,000–100,000
Clearance of exogenous enzymes (T½)		
Lactate Dehydrogenase (LDH)	12 hr	24 hr
Asparaginase	2–4 hr	20–25 hr

[a] First 48 hr following infection.
[b] Four days following infection.
[c] Four days following infection.
[d] Wroblewski units.

TABLE 9
Differences in Tumor Responses in the Presence or Absence of the LDH Virus

Parameters measured	Noninfected mice (No LDH virus)	LDH virus infected mice
Tumor incidence		
Harvey sarcoma virus	25%	100%
Moloney sarcoma virus	34%	83%
Tumor regression rates		
Harvey sarcoma	100%	0%
Moloney sarcoma	66%	17%
6C3HED lymphosarcoma in C3H/He mice	100%	0%
Tumor Growth Rate		
Amelanotic variant of B-16 melanoma	Slow	Rapid
Friend virus spleen foci (Number per spleen)	8	24
Host survival following treatment with 250 IU/kg of EC-2 asparaginase (6C3HED Lymphosarcoma in C3H/Bi Mice)	0%	100%

sumptuous to assume that this is the only inconspicuous infectious entity capable of such physiological influences (Gotlieb-Stematsky *et al.*, 1966; Tisdale, 1963; Turner *et al.*, 1968; Wheelock, 1966, 1967; Youn and Barski, 1966).

Therapy for Stress Effects?

Since the adverse effects of the stress syndrome are a scientific reality despite the many contradictions in the published experimental data, it is relevant to consider what therapeutic possibilities may exist for blocking the undesirable physiological effects of either acute or chronic stress. If we accept the hypothesis that the host response to stressful stimuli results in adrenal cortical hypersecretion, which produces lympholytic activity resulting in a depression of cell-mediated and possibly humoral immune reactions, and that such immune depression is responsible for an escape or encouragement of tumor activity in stressed animals, then it is obvious that it would be both desirable and possible to block the adverse biochemical effects of stress.

Seifter *et al.* (1973b, 1976) Lazarus *et al.* (1963), and Reitura *et al.* (1973) have tested this hypothesis directly and have demonstrated that metyrapone, a chemical that inhibits corticosterone production, prevented the typical stress syndrome, and increased the resistance of stressed mice to a murine sarcoma virus. Since this compound directly inhibits glucocorticoid synthesis, its administration may have some undesirable hormone depletion effects. However, there may be other more suitable substances which can accomplish the desired therapy by competing for the receptor sites of target tissues, and thus block the destructive effects of elevated levels of corticoids without depleting important hormones below normal physiological levels. Steroids such as deoxycorticosterone, for example, have such competitive capacities for tissue receptor sites and may thus be beneficial. It has also been suggested that vitamin A may have such a capacity (Reitura et al., 1973). Other natural substances, such as progesterone, may have a competitive capacity to prevent the adverse effects of cortisol or corticosterone. An expansion of these and related studies would seem to be justified, and might reduce the hazards of stress without at the same time altering the beneficial functions of the adrenal corticoids and other hormones associated with the stress syndrome. Irrespective of the ultimate consequences of these specific leads, the relationships between stress-associated modulations of pathological processes and the effects of stress on the thymus and on the circulating T and B cells, deserve serious concern by investigators.

SUMMARY

Some of the biological consequences of emotional or anxiety stress result in adverse influences upon identifiable elements of the mouse immune system. This report describes some of our studies concerning the mechanisms associated with these phenomena. Experimental animal models have been devised to examine the nature of these detrimental effects of mild anxiety stress upon immunocompetence with resulting enhancement of various pathological processes.

By utilizing an appropriate tumor–host model having an immunologic equipoise that permits the detection of modest changes in the immunocompetence of the host, we have demonstrated the tangible increased risk of the stressed subject with respect to either incipient or overt malignancies.

The most conspicuous biochemical substance participating in these events as a common denominator in stress phenomena, is elevated plasma corticosterone. This "stress" hormone is also elevated during or following certain inconspicuous viral infections. Analogous to the consequences of mild psychoneural stress, benign infectious agents, such as the LDH virus, can induce a similar increased risk for the host with respect to an increased susceptibility to certain neoplastic processes. This virus thus simulates both the biochemical and pathological effects of anxiety stress.

We have shown further in these studies that certain controlled pathological processes respond similarly to increases in corticosterone whether the source is (a) stress-induced psychoneurological activation of the adrenal cortex; (b) elevation during a viral infection; or (c) the direct administration of exogenous natural or synthetic corticoids.

This report demonstrates that following all of these diversely stimulated increases in plasma corticosterone, a resulting lymphocytopenia, thymus involution, and adverse effects upon the spleen, lymph nodes, and other elements of the immunologic apparatus can be observed. The primary effects of stress upon the cancer process thus appear to be associated with stress-induced changes in host immunologic surveillance and competence.

Technical prerequisites for these studies have included the development of new protective animal facilities. Such low stress housing has provided experimental animals having a quiescent, low stressed physiological state not found in animals maintained in most conventional animal housing facilities. Utilization of special handling techniques and the recognition of vital physiological time factors were essential to minimize confusing experimental pitfalls.

The construction of a simple rotational stress-machine for inducing mild nontraumatic stress stimuli that are quantifiable, has provided a useful means for exposing animals to a controlled and measured amount of stress. This instrumentation has thus permitted the introduction of programmable stress stimuli which can, in turn, be equated or correlated with resulting changes in physiological, biochemical, and cellular targets.

Microassays have been developed which permit precise measurements of corticosterone and related compounds. These, together with the use of appropriate quantitation to monitor the changes which occur in the various internal organs as a physical consequence of anxiety stress, combine to provide experimental means for the quantitation of stress and its effects.

The availability of these new technologies has permitted the acquisition of reproducible data, a firm basis for reasonable interpretations of stress-associated observations, and new insight into the importance of stress in awakening pathological processes. These studies also provide information concerning the limitations of stress in promoting or enhancing cancer processes and other pathologies.

REFERENCES

Ader, R., and Friedman, S. B. (1964). Social factors affecting emotionality and resistance to disease in animals. IV. Differential housing, emotionality, and Walker 256 carcinosarcoma in the rat. *Psychol. Rev.* **15,** 535–541.

Ader, R., and Friedman, S. B. (1965a). Social factors affecting emotionality and resistance to disease in animals. V. Early separation from the mother and response to a transplanted tumor in the rat. *Psychosom. Med.* **27,** 119–122.

Ader, R., and Friedman, S. B. (1965b). Differential early experiences and susceptibilities to transplanted tumors in the rat. *J. Comp. Physiol. Psychol.* **59,** 361–364.

Ader, R., and Grota, L. J. (1969). Effects of early experience on adrenocortical reactivity. *Physiol. Behav.* **4,** 303–305.

Amkraut, A., and Solomon, G. F. (1972). Stress and murine sarcoma virus (Moloney)-induced tumors. *Cancer Res.* **32**, 1428–1433.

Andervont, H. B. (1944). The influence of environment on mammary cancer in mice. *J. Natl. Cancer Inst.* **4**, 579–581.

Anisko, J. J., Suer, S. F., McClintock, M. K., and Adler, N. T. (1978). Relation between 22-kHz ultrasonic signals and sociosexual behavior in rats. *J. Comp. Physiol. Psychol.* **92**, 821–829.

Archer, O., and Pierce, J. C. (1961). Role of thymus in development of the immune response. *Fed. Proc., Fed. Am. Soc. Exp. Biol.* **20**, 26.

Burnet, M. (1970). Cellular Immunology Books One and Two. Melbourne University Press, Cambridge University Press.

Cannon, W.B. (1929). "Bodily Changes in Pain, Hunger, Fear and Rage," 2nd ed. Appleton, New York.

Chang, S.S., and Rasmussen, A.F., Jr. (1965). Stress-induced suppression of interferon production in virus-infected mice. *Nature (London)* **205**, 623.

Cochran, A.J., John, U.W., and Gothoskar, B.P. (1972). Cell mediated immunity in malignant melanoma. *Lancet* **1**, 1340–1341.

Comsa, J., and Hook, R.R., Jr. (1973). Thymectomy. *In* "Thymic Hormones" (T.D. Luckey, ed.), pp. 1–18. University Park Press, Baltimore, Maryland.

Cooley, B., Henry, J.P., and Stephens, P.M. (1976). Enhancing effects of psychosocial stimulation on experimental mammary tumors. *Abstr., Int. Symp. Detect. Prev. Cancer, 3rd, 1976,* 36.

Crispens, C.C., Jr. (1976). Apparent inhibitory influence of stress on SJL/(JDg neoplasia. *Psychol. & Psychiatry* **4**, 169.

Czerski, P. (1975). Microwave effects on the blood-forming system with particular reference to the lymphocyte. *Ann. N.Y. Acad. Sci.* **247**, 232–242.

Dechambre, R.P., and Gosse, C. (1968). Influence of population density on mortality in mice bearing transplanted tumors. *C. R. Hebd. Seances Acad. Sci.* **267**, 2200–2202.

Dechambre, R.P., and Gosse, C. (1971). Influence of an isolation stress on the development of transplanted ascites tumors in mice. Role of the adrenals. *C. R. Hebd. Seances Acad. Sci.* **272**, 2720–2722.

Dechambre, R.P., and Gosse, C. (1973). Individual versus group caging of mice with grafted tumors. *Cancer Res.* **33**, 140–144.

Fefer, A., McCoy, J.L., Perk, K., and Glynn, J.P. (1968). Immunologic, virologic, and pathologic studies of regression of autochtonous Moloney sarcoma virus-induced tumors in mice. *Cancer Res.* **28**, 1157.

Fitzmaurice, M.A., Riley, V., and Santisteban, G.A. (1972). Biological synergism between the LDH-virus and *Eperythrozoon coccoides:* Studies on the mechanism. *Pathol.-Biol.* **20**, 743–750.

Fortier, C. (1958). Sensitivity of the plasma free corticosteroid response to environmental change in the rat. *Arch. Int. Physiol.* **66**, 672.

Friedman, S.B., and Ader, R. (1965). Parameters relevant to the experimental production of "stress" in the mouse. *Psychosom. Med.* **27**, 27–30.

Friedman, S.B., Glasgow, L.A., and Ader, R. (1965). Psychosocial factors modifying host resistance to experimental infections. Annals N.Y. Acad. Sci. **164**, 381–393.

Friedman, S.B., Glasgow, L.A., and Ader, R. (1969). Psychosocial factors modifying host resistance to experimental infections. Annals N.Y. Acad. Sci. **164(2)**: 381–393.

Fuller, R.H., Brown, E., and Mills, C.A. (1941). Environmental temperatures and spontaneous tumors in mice. *Cancer Res.* **1**, 130–133.

Gisler, R.H., and Schenkel-Hullinger, L. (1971). Hormonal regulation of the immune response. II. Influence of pituitary and adrenal activity on immune responsiveness *in vitro. Cell. Immunol.* **2**, 646.

Gisler, R.H., Bussar, A.E., Mazie, J.C., and Hess, R. (1971). Hormonal regulation of the immune response. I. Induction of an immune response *in vitro* with lymphoid cells from mice exposed to acute systematic stress. *Cell. Immunol.* **2**, 634.

Gleason, K. K., and Reynierse, J. (1969). The behavioral significance of pheromones in vertebrates. *Psychol. Bull.* **71**, 58–73.

Glenn, W.G., and Becker, R.E. (1969). Individual versus group housing in mice: Immunological response to time and phase injections. *Physiol. Zool.* **42**, 411–416.

Glick, D., von Redlick, D., and Levine, S. (1964). Fluorometric determination of corticosterone and cortisol in 0.02–0.05 milliliters of plasma or submilligram samples of adrenal tissue. *Endocrinology* **74**, 635–655.

Gotlieb-Stematsky, T., Karbi, S., and Allison, A. C. (1966). Increased tumor formation by polyoma virus in the presence of nononcogenic viruses. *Nature (London)* **212**, 421–422.

Green, S., Diefenbach, K., and Santisteban, G. A. (1967). Comparison of the adrenocortical responses to the stressing effects of crowding and life in a complex environment in CBA mice. *Anat. Rec.* **157**, 2.

Guillon, J. C., Gentil, A., Lasne, C., and Chouroulinkov, I. (1970). Influence de la cohabitation sur la cancerologie mammaire par le 7,12-dimethl-benz[a]anthracene. *C. R. Hebd. Seances Acad. Sci.* **240**, (7), 1066–1068.

Guy, A. W., and Chou, C. K. (1975). System for quantitative chronic exposure of a population of rodents to UHF fields. (C.C. Johnson and M.L. Shore, eds.), HEW Publ. (FDA) 77–8011, pp. 389–422. US Govt. Printing Office, Washington, D.C.

Habel, K. (1963). Immunologic aspects of oncogenesis by polyoma virus. *In* "Conceptual Advances in Immunology and Oncology" pp. 486–502. Harper and Row, New York.

Harlow, C. M., and Selye, H. (1937). The blood picture in the alarm reaction. *Proc. Soc. Exp. Biol. Med.* **36**, 141–144.

Hellström, I., Sjögren, H. O., Warner, G., and Hellström, K. E. (1971). Blocking of cell-mediated tumor immunity by sera from patients with growing neoplasms. *Int. J. Cancer* **7**, 226–237.

Henry, J. P. (1977) Personal communication.

Henry, J. P., and Santisteban, G.A. (1971). The induction of arteriosclerosis by psychosocial factors in CBA mice: Observations on the heart, aorta, and kidneys. *Arteriosclerosis* **14**, 203–218.

Henry, J. P., and Stephens, P. M. (1977). "Stress, Health, and the Social Environment." Springer-Verlag, New York.

Henry, J. P., Ely, D. L., and Stephens, P. M. (1972). Mental factors and cardiovascular disease. *Psychiatr. Ann.* **2** (7), 25–71.

Henry, J. P., Stephens, P. M., and Watson, F. M. C. (1975). Force breeding, social disorder and mammary tumor formation in CBA/USC mouse colonies. A pilot study. *Psychosom. Med.* **37**, 277–283.

Henry, J. P., Kross, M. E., Stephens, P. M., and Watson, F. M. C. (1975). Evidence that differing psychosocial stimuli lead to adrenocortical or adrenal medullary stimulation. International Symposium on Catecholamines and Stress, Bratislava, Czechoslovakia, July 1975.

Henry, J. P., Watson, F. M. C., Kross, M. E., and Stephens, P. M. (1974). Influence of the adrenal nervous supply upon levels of plasma corticosterone during prolonged psychosocial stimulation. *Fed. Proc.* **33**, 370.

Henry, K. R. (1967). Audiogenic seizure susceptibility induced in C57 BL/6J mice by prior auditory exposure. *Science* **158**, 938–940.

Herbst, A. L., Yates, F. E., Glenister, D. W., and Urquhart, J. (1960). Variations in hepatic inactivation of corticosterone with changes in food intake: An explanation of impaired corticosterone metabolism following noxious stimuli. *Endocrinology* **67**, 222.

Hirsch, M. S. (1974). Immunological activation of oncogenic viruses: Interrelationship of immunostimulation and immunosuppression. *Johns Hopkins Med. J., Suppl.* **3**, 177–185.

Howard, R. J., Notkins, A. L., and Mergenhagen, S. E. (1969). Inhibition of cellular immune reactions in mice infected with lactate dehydrogenase virus. *Nature (London)* **221**, 873–874.

Jensen, M. M. (1968a). The influence of stress on murine leukemia virus infection. *Proc. Exp. Biol. Med.* **127**, 610.

Jensen, M. M. (1968b). Transitory impairment of interferon production in stressed mice. *Proc. Soc. Exp. Biol. Med.* **128**, 174.

Jensen, M. M., and Rasmussen, A. F., Jr. (1963). Stress and susceptibility to viral infection. II. Sound stress and susceptibility to vesicular stomatitis virus. *J. Immunol.* **90**, 21.

Jonas, A. D. (1966). Theoretical considerations concerning the influences of the central nervous system on cancerous growth, *Ann. N.Y. Acad. Sci.* **125** (3), 856-864.

Jose, D. G., and Good, R. A. (1973). Quantitative effects of nutritionally essential amino acid deficiencies upon immune responses to tumors in mice. *J. Exp. Med.* **137**, 1-9.

Kavetsky, R. E. (1958). "Tumors and the Nervous System." Gos. Meditsinskoe Izd., Kiev, USSR (in Russian).

Kavetsky, R. E., Turkevich, N. M., Balisky, K. P. (1966). On the psychophysiological mechanisms of the organism's resistance to tumor growth. *Ann. N.Y. Acad. Sci.* **125** (3), 933-945.

Kavetsky, R. E., Turkevich, N. M., Avimeva, R. M., and Khayetsky, I. K. (1969). Induced cancerogenesis under various influences on the hypothalamus. *Ann. N.Y. Acad. Sci.* **164** (3), 517-519.

Keast, D. (1970). Immunosurveillance and cancer. *Lancet* **2**, 710-712.

Khalestkaia, F. M. (1954). The influence of excessiveness of activity of the nervous system on the development of individual tumors in mice. *Zh. Vyssh. Nervn. Deat. im I.P. Pavlova* **4**, 869-876.

Khayetsky, I. K. (1965). The influence of hypothalamo-pituitary disturbances produced by continuous light on development of induced mammary tumors in rats. *Vopr. Eksp. Onkol.* **1**, 87-94.

Klein, G. (1975). Immunological surveillance against neoplasia. *Harvey Lect.* **69**, 71-102.

Korneva, E. A., and Khai, L. M. (1963). Effect of destruction of hypothalamic areas on immunogenesis. *Fiziol. Zh. SSSR im I.M. Sechenova* **49**, 42.

La Barba, R. C. (1970). Experimental and environmental factors in cancer. A review of research with animals. *Psychosom. Med.* **32**, 259-275.

La Barba, R. C., Martini, J., and White, J. (1967). The effect of maternal separation on the growth of Erhlich carcinoma in the BALB/c mice. *Psychosom. Med.* **31**, 129-133.

La Barba, R. C., Klein, M., White, J. L., and Lazar, L. (1970a). The effects of early cold stress and handling on the growth of Ehrlich carcinoma in the BALB/c mice. *Dev. Psychol.* **2**, 312.

La Barba, R. C., White, J. L., Lazar, L., and Klein, M. (1970b). Early maternal separation and the response to Ehrlich carcinoma in BALB/c mice. *Dev. Psychol.* **3**, 78-80.

Lazarus, L., Georgy, E. P., and Stuart, M. (1963). Effect of varying doses of methopyrapone (Metopirone) on the secretion rate of cortisol. *J. Clin. Endocrinol. Metab.* **23**, 773-775.

Levine, S. (1967). Maternal and environmental influences on the adrenocortical response to stress in weaning rats. *Science* **156**, 258-260.

Levine, S., and Cohen, C. (1959). Differential survival to leukemia as a function of infantile stimulation in DBA/2 mice. *Proc. Soc. Exp. Biol. Med.* **102**, 53-54.

Marsh, J. T., and Rasmussen, A. F., Jr. (1960). Response of adrenals, thymus, spleen, and leukocytes to shuttle box and confinement stress *Proc. Soc. Exp. Biol. Med.* **104**, 180-183.

Marsh, J. T., Miller, B. E., and Lamson, B. G. (1959). Effect of repeated brief stress on the growth of Ehrlich carcinoma in the mouse. *J. Natl. Cancer Inst.* **22**, 961.

Mason, J. W. (1968). A review of psycho-endocrine research on the pituitary–adrenal cortical system. *Psychosom. Med.* **30**, 576.

Mason, J. W. (1974). Specificity in the organization of neuroendocrine response profiles. *In* "Frontiers in Neurology and Neuroscience Research" (P. Seeman and G. M. Brown, eds.), pp. 68-80.

Mason, J. W. (1975a). A historical view of the stress field. Part I. *J. Hum. Stress.* **1**, 6-11.

Mason, J. W. (1975b). A historical view of the stress field. Part II. *J. Hum. Stress.* **1**, 22-36.

Mason, J. W. (1975c). Emotion as reflected in patterns of endocrine regulation. *In* "Emotions—Their Parameters and Measurement" (L. Levi, ed.), pp. 143-181. Raven, New York.

Mason, J. W., Harwood, T., and Rosenthal, N. R. (1957). Influence of some environmental factors on plasma and urinary 17-hyroxycorticosteroid levels in the Rhesus monkey. *Am. J. Physiol.* **190**, 429.

McVay, J. R. (1968). Environmental temperature and death-rate from intestinal neoplasms. *Lancet* **2**, 1393.

Monjan, A. A., and Collector, M. I. (1977). Stress-induced modulation of the immune response. *Science* **196**, 307–308.

Mühlbock, O. (1950). Effect of environment on development of cancer: Studies on mammary cancer in mice. *Ned. Tijdschr. Geneeskd.* **94**, 3747–3752.

Mühlbock, O. (1951). Influence of environment on the incidence of mammary tumors in mice. *Acta. Unio Int. Cancrum* **7**, 351.

Newberry, B. H. (1976). Inhibitory effects of stress on experimental mammary tumors. *Abstr. Int. Symp. Detect. Prev. Cancer, 3rd,* 1976, 35.

Newberry, B. H., and Sengbusch, L. (1979). Inhibitory effects of stress on experimental mammary tumors. *Cancer Detect. Prev.* **2** (2), 225–233.

Newberry, B. H., Frankie, G., Beatty, P. A., Maloney, B., and Gilchrist, J. (1972). Shock stress and DMBA-induced mammary tumors in mice. *Psychosom. Med.* **34**, 295–303.

Newell, G. R., and Waggoner, D. E. (1970). Cancer mortality and environmental temperature in the United States. *Lancet* **1**, 766–768.

Newton, G. (1964). Early experiences and resistance to tumor growth. *In* "Psychosomatic Aspects of Neoplastic Disease" (D. M. Kissen and L. L. LeShan, eds.), p. 71. Lippincott, Philadelphia, Pennsylvania.

Newton, G., Bly, C. G., and McCrary, C. (1962). Effects of early experience on the response to transplanted tumors. *J. Nerv. Ment. Dis.* **134**, 522–527.

Nicholls, E. M. (1973). Development and elimination of pigmented moles, and the anatomical distribution of primary malignant melanoma. *Cancer* **32**, 191–195.

Nieburgs, H. E., Weiss, J., Navarrete, M., Grillione, G., and Siedlecki, B. (1976). Inhibitory and enhancing effects of various stresses on experimental mammary tumorigenesis. *Abstr., Int. Symp. Detect. Prev. Cancer, 3rd,*. 1976, 50.

Nieburgs, H. E., Weiss, J., Navarrete, M., Strax, P., Teirstein, A., Grillione, G., and Siedlecki, B. (1979). The role of stress in human and experimental oncogenesis. *Cancer Detect. Prev.* **2** (2), 307–336.

Noirot, E. (1966). Ultrasounds in young rodents. I. Changes with age in albino mice. *Anim. Behav.* **14**, 459–462.

Noirot, E. (1968). Ultrasounds in young rodents. II. Changes with age in albino rats. *Anim. Behav.* **16**, 129–134.

Otis, L. S., and Scholler, J. (1967). Effects of stress during infancy on tumor development and tumor growth. *Psychol Rep.* **20**, 167–173.

Pierpaoli, W., Baroni, C., Fabris, N., and Sorkin, E. (1969). Hormones and immunologic capacity. II. Reconstitution of antibody production in hormonally deficient mice by somatotrophic hormone, thyrotropic hormone, and thyroxin. *Immunology* **16**, 217–230.

Prehn, R. T. (1963). Role of immune mechanisms in biology of chemically and physically induced tumors. *In* "Conceptual Advances in Immunology and Oncology," pp. 475–485. Harper and Row, New York.

Prehn, R. T. (1969). The relationship of immunology to carcinogenesis. *Ann. N.Y. Acad. Sci.* **164** (3), 449–457.

Rasmussen, A. F., Jr., Spencer, E. S., and Marsh, J. T. (1957). Increased susceptibility to Herpes simplex in mice subjected to avoidance-learning stress or restraint. *Proc. Soc. Exp. Biol. Med.* **96**, 183.

Rasmussen, A. F., Jr., Hildemann, W. H., and Sellers, M. (1963). Malignancy of polyoma virus infection in mice in relation to stress. *J. Natl. Cancer Inst.* **30**, 101.

Raushenbakh, M. O., Zhorova, E. M., and Khokhlova, M. P. (1952). The influence of overstraining of the central nervous system in mice on the development of experimental leukocytosis. *Arkh. Patol.* **14**, 23–31.

Ray, P., and Pradhan, S. N. (1974). Growth of transplanted and induced tumors in rats under a schedule of punished behavior. *J. Natl. Cancer Inst.* **52**, 575–577.

Reitura, G., Seifter, J., Zisblatt, M., Levenson, S. M., Levine, N., and Seifter, E. (1973). Metapyrone-inhibited oncogenesis in mice inoculated with a murine sarcoma virus. *J. Natl. Cancer Inst.* **51**, 1983–1985.

Reznikoff, M., and Martin, D. E. (1957). The influence of stress on mammary cancer in mice. *J. Psychosom. Res.* **2**, 56.

Riley, V. (1960). Adaptation of orbital bleeding technique to rapid serial blood studies. *Proc. Soc. Exp. Biol. Med.* **104**, 751–754.

Riley, V. (1966). Spontaneous mammary tumors: Decrease of incidence in mice infected with an emzyme-elevating virus. *Science* **153**, 1657–1658.

Riley, V. (1972). Protective ventilated shelves for experimental animal storage. *Proc. 23rd Annu. Sess. Am. Assoc. Lab. Anim. Sci.* No. 22A.

Riley, V. (1973). Persistence and other characteristics of the lactate dehydrogenase-elevating virus (LDH-virus). *Prog. Med. Virol.* **18**, 198–213.

Riley, V. (1974a). Biological contaminants and scientific misinterpretations. *Cancer Res.* **34**, 1752–1754.

Riley, V. (1974b). Erroneous interpretation of valid experimental observations through interference by the LDH-virus. *J. Natl. Cancer Inst.* **52**, 1673–1677.

Riley, V. (1975). Mouse mammary tumors: Alteration of incidence as an apparent function of stress. *Science* **189**, 465–467.

Riley, V. (1978). Stress and cancer: Fresh perspectives. *Proc. Int. Symp. Detect. Prev. Cancer, 3rd,* 1976, 1769–1776. Marcel Dekker Inc., New York.

Riley, V. (1979a). Introduction: Stress–cancer contradictions: A continuing puzzlement. *Cancer Detect. Prev.* **2**, No. 2, 159–162.

Riley, V. (1979b). Cancer and stress: Overview and critique. *Cancer Detect. Prev.* **2**, No. 2, 163–195.

Riley, V. Fitzmaurice, M. A., and Spackman, D. H. (1981). Biobehavioral factors in animal work on tumorigenesis. *Proc. Acad. Behav. Med. Res.* (S. Weiss, ed). pp. 183–214. Academic Press, New York.

Riley, V., Fitzmaurice, M. A., and Spackman, D. H. (1981). Animal models in biobehavioral research. Effects of anxiety stress on immunocompetence and neoplasia. *In* Perspectives in Behavioral Medicine (S. Weiss, et al, ed.) Academic Press, New York. (In Press).

Riley, V., and Spackman, D. H. (1976a). Melanoma enhancement by viral-induced stress. *In* "The Pigment Cell; Melanomas: Basic Properties and Clinical Behavior" (V. Riley, ed.), Vol. 2, pp. 163–173. Karger, Basel.

Riley, V., and Spackman, D. H. (1976b). Modifying effects of a benign virus on the malignant process and the role of physiological stress on tumor incidence. *Fogarty Int. Cent. Proc.* **28**, 319–336.

Riley, V., and Spackman, D. H. (1977a). Housing stress. *Lab Anim.* **6**, 16–21.

Riley, V., and Spackman, D. H. (1977b). Cage crowding stress: Absence of effect on melanoma within protective facilities. *Proc. Am. Assoc. Cancer Res.* **18**, 173.

Riley, V., and Spackman, D. H. (1978a). Enhancing effects of anxiety-stress on the neoplastic process in mice. Abstracts *Int. Cancer Congr., 12th, 1978, 2,* 134.

Riley, V., and Spackman, D. H. (1978b). Simulation of RF and microwave biological effects by handling and housing-induced stress of experimental animals. *Int. Union Radio Sci.* Abstracts OS:2, p. 63.

Riley, V., Fitzmaurice, M. A., and Loveless, J. D. (1966). Decrease in "spontaneous" mammary tumor incidence. *Proc. Am. Assoc. Cancer Res.* **7**, 59.

Riley, V., Spackman, D. H., and Santisteban, G. A. (1975) The role of physiological stress on breast tumor incidence in mice. *Proc. Am. Assoc. Cancer Res.* **16**, 152.

Riley, V., Braun, W., Ishizuka, M., and Spackman, D. H. (1976a). Antibody-producing cells: Virus-induced alteration of response to antigen. *Proc. Natl. Acad. Sci. U.S.A.* **73**, 1707-1711.

Riley, V., Spackman, D. H., Fitzmaurice, M. A., Santisteban, G. A., McClanahan, H., Louthan, S., Dennis, M., and Bloom, J. (1976b). Enhancement and inhibition of lymphosarcoma by fluocinolone acetonide. *Proc. Am. Assoc. Cancer Res.* **17**, 161.

Riley, V., Spackman, D. H., Hellström, K. E., and Hellström, I. (1978a). Growth enhancement of murine sarcoma by LDH-virus, adrenocorticoids, and anxiety stress. *Proc. Am. Assoc. Cancer Res.* **19**, 57.

Riley, V., Spackman, D. H., Santisteban, G. A., Dalldorf, G., Hellström, I., Hellström, K. E., Lance, E. M., Rowson, K. E. K., Mahy, B. W. J., Alexander, P, Stock, C. C., Sjögren, H. O., Hollander, V. P., and Horzinck, M. C. (1978b). The LDH-virus: An interfering biological contaminant. *Science* **200**, 124-125.

Riley, V., Guy, A. W., Spackman, D. H., and Chou, C. K. (1978c). Neoplastic cells as sensitive targets for examining the biological and pathological effects of RF and microwave irradiation. *Int. Union Radio Sci. Abstr. OS* **2**, 93.

Riley, V., Spackman, D. H., McClanahan, H., and Santisteban, G. A. (1979a). The role of stress in malignancy. *Cancer Detect. Prev.* **2**, No. 2, 235-255.

Riley, V., Spackman, D. H., Fitzmaurice, M. A., Guy, A. W., and Chou, C. K. (1979b). An experimental model for detecting and amplifying subtle RF field-induced cell injuries. *Int. Union Radio Sci. Abstr. BEMS* p. 433.

Rusch, H. P. (1944). Extrinsic factors that influence carcinogenesis. *Physiol. Rev.* **24**, 177-204.

Sakakibara, T. (1966). Effects of brightness or darkness on carcinogenesis. *Nagoya Shiritsj Daigaku Igakkai Sasshi* **19**, 525-557.

Sales, G. D. (1972a). Ultrasound and mating behavior in rodents with some observations on other behavioural situations. *J. Zool.* **168**, 149-164.

Sales, G. D. (1972b). Ultrasound and aggressive behavior in rats and other small mammals. *Anim. Behav.* **20**, 88-100.

Sales, G. D., and Pye, D. (1974). Ultrasound in rodents. *In* "Ultrasonic Communication by Animals," pp. 149-201. Chapman & Hall, London.

Santisteban, G. A. (1958). Studies on the relationships of the acute involution of lymphatic organs to the severity of stress stimuli. *Anat. Rec.* **130**, 2.

Santisteban, G. A. (1959). Comparison of the influences of various forms of stress stimuli upon the adrenocortico-thymico-lymphatic system in CBA mice. *Anat. Rec.* **133**, 331.

Santisteban, G. A. (1968). Studies of the functional development of the adrenal cortex. *Anat. Rec.* **160**, 2.

Santisteban, G. A. (1978). Adrenal cortical and cardiovascular responses to psychosocial stress in CBA mice and albino rats. *Anat. Rec.* **190**, 530.

Santisteban, G. A., and Dougherty, T. F. (1954). Comparison of the influences of adrenocortical hormones on the growth and involution of lymphatic organs. *Endocrinology* **54**, 130-146.

Santisteban, G. A., and Henry, J. P. (1971). The induction of arteriosclerosis by psychosocial factors in CBA mice: Observations on the heart, aorta, and kidneys. *Anat. Rec.* **169**, 2.

Santisteban, G. A., and Riley, V. (1973). Thymo-lymphatic organ response to the LDH-virus. *Proc. Am. Assoc. Cancer Res.* **14**, 112.

Santisteban, G. A., Guslander, C., and Willhight, K. (1969). Studies on the maturation of the adrenal cortical-lymphatic tissue interrelationships. *Anat. Rec.* **163**, 2.

Santisteban, G. A., Riley, V., and Fitzmaurice, M. A. (1972). Thymolytic and adrenal cortical responses to the LDH-elevating virus. *Proc. Soc. Exp. Biol. Med.* **139**, 202-206.

Santisteban, G. A., Riley, V., and Spackman, D. H. (1977). Stress related factors in the neoplastic process. *Proc. Am. Assoc. Cancer Res.* **18**, 172.

Santisteban, G. A., Riley, V., Spackman, D. H., Dennis, M., Grytting, A., and Fitzmaurice, M. A. (1978). Influence of common environmental factors upon the neoplastic process. *Proc. Am. Assoc. Cancer Res.* **19**, 57.

Santisteban, G. A., Adams, D. R., and Katora, K. (1979). Psychosocial stress, adrenal corticoids, and hypertension in rats. *Anat. Rec.* **193**, 674.

Schwartz, R. S. (1974). Defective immune responses and malignancy. *Johns Hopkins Med. J.,* *Suppl.* **3**, 173–176.

Seifter, E., Rettura, G., Zisblatt, M., Levenson, S. M., Levine, N., Davidson, A., and Seifter, J. (1973a). Enhancement of tumor development in physically-stressed mice inoculated with an oncogenic virus. *Experientia* **29**, 1379–1382.

Seifter, E., Zisblatt, M., Levine, N., and Rettura, G. (1973b). Inhibitory action of vitamin A on a murine sarcoma. *Life Sci.* **13**, 945–952.

Seifter, E., Cohen, M. H., and Riley, V. (1976). Of stress, vitamin A, and tumors. *Science* **193**, 74–75.

Selye, H. (1975) Confusion and controversy in the stress field. *J. Hum. Stress (June),* pp. 37–44.

Solomon, G. F., and Amkraut, A. A. (1972). Emotions, stress, and immunity. *Front. Radiat. Ther. Oncol.* **7**, 84–96.

Solomon, G. F., and Amkraut, A. A. (1979). Neuroendocrine aspects of the immune response and their implications for stress effects on tumor immunity. *Cancer Detect. Prev.* **2**, (2), 197–224.

Solomon, G. F., Amkraut, A. A., and Rubin, R. T. (1980). Stress and psycho-immunological response. *Proc. Acad. Behav. Med. Res.* (S. Weiss, ed). Academic Press, New York.

Spackman, D. H. (1969). Improved resolution in amino acid analysis in cancer therapy studies. *Fed. Proc., Fed. Am. Soc. Exp. Biol.* **28**, 898.

Spackman, D. H., and Riley, V. (1974) Increased corticosterone, a factor in LDH-virus induced alterations of immunological responses in mice. *Proc. Am. Assoc. Cancer Res.* **15**, 143.

Spackman, D. H., and Riley, V. (1975). Stress effects of the LDH-virus in altering the Gardner tumor in mice. *Proc. Am. Assoc. Cancer Res.* **16**, 170.

Spackman, D. H., and Riley, V. (1976). The modification of cancer by stress: Effects of plasma corticosterone elevations on immunological system components in mice. *Fed. Proc., Fed. Am. Soc. Exp. Biol.* **35**, 1693.

Spackman, D. H., and Riley, V. (1978). True adrenal glucocorticoid values in experimental animals: Implications for cancer research. *Proc. Int. Cancer Congr. 12th, 1978* Abstracts, Vol. 2, p. 26.

Spackman, D. H., Stein, W. H., and Moore, S. (1958). Automatic recording apparatus for use in the chromatography of amino acids. *Anal. Chem.* **30**, 1190–1206.

Spackman, D. H., Riley, V., Santisteban, G. A., Kirk, W., and Bredburg, L. (1975). The role of stress in producing elevated corticosterone levels and thymus involution in mice. *Abstr. Int. Cancer Congr., 11th, 1974* Vol. 3, pp. 382–283.

Spackman, D. H., Riley, V., and Bloom, J. (1978). True plasma corticosterone levels of mice in cancer/stress studies. *Proc. Am. Assoc. Cancer Res.* **19**, 57.

Sprunt, D. H., and Flanigan, C. C. (1956). The effect of malnutrition on the susceptibility of the host to viral infection. *J. Exp. Med.* **104**, 687–706.

Stein, M., Schiari, R. C., and Luparello, T. J. (1969). The hypothalamus and immune processes. *Ann. N.Y. Acad. Sci.* **164** (2), 463–472.

Stein, M., Schiari, R. C., and Camerino, M. (1976). Influence of brain and behavior on the immune system. *Science* **191**, 435–440.

Stern, E., Mickey, M., and Gorski, R. (1969). Neuroendocrine factors in experimental carcinogenesis, *Ann. N.Y. Acad. Sci.* **164**, (2), 494–508.

Sze, P. (1970). Neurochemical factors in auditory stimulation and development of susceptibility to audiogenic seizures. *In* "Physiological Effects of Audible Sound" (B. Welch and A. Welch, ed.) Plenum, New York.

Szmigielski, S. (1975). Effect of 10-cm (3GHz) electromagnetic radiation (microwaves) on granulocytes in vitro. *Ann. N.Y. Acad. Sci.* **247**, 275–281.

Tannenbaum, A. (1940). The initiation and growth of tumors, I. The effects of underfeeding. *Am. J. Cancer* **38**, 335–350.

Tannenbaum, A., and Silverstone, H. (1953). Nutrition in relation to cancer. *Adv. Cancer Res.* **1**, 451–501.

Teller, M. N., Stohr, G., Curlett, W., Kubisek, M. L., and Curtis, D. (1964). Ageing and cancerigenesis. I. Immunity to tumor and skin graft. *J. Natl. Cancer Inst.* **33**, 649–656.

Tisdale, W. A. (1963). Potentiating effect of K-virus on mouse hepatitis (MHV-S) in weanling mice. *Proc. Soc. Exp. Biol. Med.* **114**, 774–777.

Turner, C. D., and Hagnara, J. T. (1971). "General Endocrinology," 5th ed., pp. 382–383. Saunders, Philadelphia, Pennsylvania.

Turner, W., Chirigos, M. A., and Scott, D. (1968). Enhancement of Friend and Rauscher leukemia virus replication in mice by Guaroa virus. *Cancer Res.* **28**, 1064–1073.

Turner, W., Ebert, P. S., Bassin, R., Spahn, G., and Chirigos, M. A. (1971). Potentiation of murine sarcoma virus (Harvey) (Moloney) oncogenicity in lactic dehydogenase-elevating virus-infected mice. *Proc. Soc. Exp. Biol. Med.* **136**, 1314–1318.

Vessell, E. S., Lang, C. M., White, W. J., Passananti, G. T., Hill, R. N., Clemens, T. L., Liu, D. K., and Johnson, W. D. (1976). Environmental and genetic factors affecting the response of laboratory animals to drugs. *Fed. Proc., Fed. Am. Soc. Exp. Biol.* **35**, 1125–1132.

Vessey, S. H. (1964). Effects of grouping on levels of circulating antibodies in mice. *Proc. Soc. Exp. Biol. Med.* **115**, 252.

Visscher, B., Ball, Z., Barnes, R. H., and Silvertsen, I. (1942). The influence of caloric restriction upon the incidence of spontaneous mammary carcinoma in mice. *Surgery* **11**, 48–55.

Voss, W. A. G. (1980). Personal communication (Ultrasonic communication in mice).

Wallace, E. W., Wallace, H. M., and Mills, C. A. (1942). Effect of climatic environment upon the genesis of subcutaneous tumors induced by methylcholanthrene and upon the growth of a transplantable sarcoma in C3H mice. *J. Natl. Cancer Inst.* **3**, 99–110.

Wallace, E. W., Wallace, H. M., and Mills, C. A. (1944). Influence of environmental temperature upon the incidence and course of spontaneous tumors in C3H mice. *Cancer Res.* **4**, 279–281.

Weiss, D. W. (1969). Immunological parameters of the host–parasite relationship in neoplasia. *Ann. N.Y. Acad. Sci.* **164**, (2), 431–448.

Weston, B. J. (1973). The thymus and immune surveillance. *Contemp. Top. Immunobiol.* **2**, 237–263.

Wheelock, E. F. (1966). The effects of non-tumor viruses on virus-induced leukemia in mice: Reciprocal interference between Sendai virus and Friend leukemia virus in DBA/2 mice. *Proc. Natl. Acad. Sci. U.S.A.* **55**, 774–780.

Wheelock, E. F. (1967). Inhibitory effects of Sendai virus on Friend virus leukemia in mice. *J. Natl. Cancer Inst.* **38**, 771–778.

White, A., Handler, P., and Smith, E. L. (1968). "Principles of Biochemistry," 4th ed., pp. 936, 964. McGraw-Hill, New York.

Yamada, A., Jensen, M. M., and Rasmussen, A. F., Jr. (1964) Stress and susceptibility to viral infections. III. Antibody response and viral retention during avoidance–learning stress. *Proc. Soc. Exp. Biol. Med.* **116**, 677.

Youn, J. K., and Barski, G. (1966). Interference between lymphocytic choriomeningitis and Rauscher leukemia in mice *J. Natl. Cancer Inst.* **37**, 381–388.

Young, S. (1958). Effect of temperature on the production of induced rat mammary tumors. *Nature (London)* **219**, 1254–1255.

Psychosocial Factors and the Immune System in Human Cancer

BERNARD H. FOX

INTRODUCTION

This discussion bears on the broader topic of psychosocial factors (PF) and incidence of cancer, but focuses on an intermediate element, immunity, that is often but not always relevant to the topic. The present subject must be broken into its components before one can find an integrated relationship among those components. During that breaking down and during that looking we may be led to some tentative inferences regarding cancer and PF, but not to any firm conclusions. The discussion will deal mostly with endogenous psychosocial etiology of cancer ("endogenous" is used here to mean arising from internal states stemming directly from influence on or by the psyche). Even though we may have some doubts, we are being drawn closer and closer, in view of recent studies, to the firm position that PF in the human may indeed affect cancer incidence. But we are not yet securely at that position.

For purposes of clarification, as in a previous paper (Fox, 1978, p. 47), PF that lead to behavior changes where behavior induces carcinogenesis from an external source (exogenous psychosocial etiology of cancer) will be considered as any other carcinogen—an interfering or irrelevant source of cancer. For example, the personality that leads to greater risk of smoking is irrelevant if the ultimate cause of the greater risk is the smoking, not internal events associated

103

PSYCHONEUROIMMUNOLOGY   ISBN 0-12-043780-5 with the personality. If, however, some psychic state changes the person so that he is more susceptible to carcinogens in general or to particular ones (e.g., smoking), that state would be considered an endogenous psychosocial etiologic agent.

The topic of this discussion is important. During the last 20 years many papers have appeared and conferences have been held where the immune system (IS) has been called on as the mediating element in claimed psychosocial etiology of cancer. Etiology implies cause. If only an association were posited, there would be no need to call on a mediator. But conversely, if a mediator is named, one infers an intent to go beyond mere association to cause and effect. It is, therefore, important to examine some of the claimed sources of relationship of the human psyche to increased risk of cancer. Before about 1978, many of these papers cited speculative, usually rather general, immunologic relationships to human cancer in justification of the etiologic role of PF; not one cited a clear, proven relationship. For example, see both conferences on psychophysiological aspects of cancer (Bahnson, 1969; Bahnson and Kissen, 1966). It is, therefore, important to examine the state of affairs in the relationship: PF–immune function–cancer and see if it can be labeled as more than speculative.

An attempt will be made to lay out the psychosocial states and changes that could affect carcinogenesis in the human, and to note data that do or do not lend support to such influence. Effects of the psyche on the progress of cancer probably involve different biologic issues from those contributing to cancer causation, and will not be addressed.

CARCINOGENESIS

The conventional wisdom has been that carcinogenesis results from a critical mutation, effectively a permanent change in the identity of the substructures in DNA or RNA. The attention paid to bacterial mutagenicity tests for carcinogens (Ames *et al.*, 1973) reflects this view. It has recently been subject to considerable question, however, with the suggestion that less fundamental transformations are able to lead to cancer (Holliday, 1979; Rubin, 1980). Be that as it may, those changes can be brought about by ionizing radiation such as X-rays or ultraviolet (UV) rays (recent epidemiologic studies even implicate nonionizing radiation or fields, Leeper, 1980; Wertheimer and Leeper, 1979); chemical reactions; viral invasion; direct hormonal action, at least in the mouse (Huseby, 1980); indirect hormonal action; genetic attributes; physical status, for example, by chemically inert asbestos fibers (Selikoff and Hammond, 1979) or implanted inert film (Brand, 1975, 1976); injury to tissue of specific kinds (e.g., Davies, 1975, pp. 374–378); immunogenic competence (Kersey and Spector, 1975); and possibly aging alone, although if the last is true, the mechanisms are not understood.

In order to increase or decrease the effect of these phenomena, PF must alter the physical or chemical stimulus; yield a state of the organism that makes the cell change (mutation or transformation) more or less likely to occur; or affect the change by direct means (faulty or good repair of DNA) or indirectly (e.g, enhance by blocking immune effectors or remove the transformation by cell lysis). The transformation is often one in a series of such alterations, an early one of which can be transformation to a not yet malignant altered tissue cell (e.g., actinic keratosis or colonic polyp). Sometimes a tissue variation appears at birth, such as a skin nevus. The theory of multistage cancer induction has been examined with some care (e.g., Armitage and Doll, 1957; Day and Brown, 1980; Whittemore and Keller, 1978), but convergence toward consensus is only just approaching (e.g., Moolgavkar and Venzon, 1979; Moolgavkar et al., 1980).

Radiation

Some carcinogenesis takes place by energy application that directly affects the cell (e.g., ionizing radiation). Indications are that RNA or DNA is transformed. Within a certain time, up to 48 hr after irradiation *in vitro*, if division and growth were inhibited, almost all cells survived, and remained nonmalignant when finally stimulated to grow (Little, 1977). When stimulated to grow earlier than this, however, surviving cells suffered no *apparent* morphological change, but some later transformed to morphologically different cells that were malignant, radiation damage apparently being genetically fixed. The maximum transformation effect was seen if growth was stimulated 3 hr after irradiation. Little theorizes that DNA is damaged by the radiation and immediately starts a repair process. A rapid repair takes place, he thinks, but the process is error-prone and results only in a quick, but faulty repair. Then another, but slower, repair mechanism acts on faulty repairs and corrects them fully or almost fully. If the latter cannot be completed, faults remain and are transmitted to succeeding generations. In his study the number of transformations per cell rose exponentially up to about 400 rads, but stayed constant beyond that. Of course, the number of cells surviving fell rapidly with dosage increase and that fall became exponential below about 50% survival, which took place at about 200 rads. These numbers may not apply to all cells, to all species, and under all conditions, but the theory is very likely to apply *in vivo*. In order to fix the damage as heritable, no more than one, or at most two, divisions were sufficient in the case of damage due to radiation (Borek and Sachs, 1968), chemicals (Kakunaga, 1975), and SV-40 virus (Todaro and Green, 1966). The malignant expression, however, did not come until 10–12 divisions after irradiation (Little, 1977), or until about 3 divisions after methylcholanthrene treatment (Kakunaga, 1975).

Several noncarcinogenic agents potentiated radiation effects. One is the well-known promoter (an agent that alone does not cause malignant transformation but does after another agent, an initiator, has changed the cell's susceptibility), the phorbol ester 12-O-tetradecanoyl-phorbol-13-acetate (TPA). After UV treatment *in vitro* with dose levels leading to no transformed foci, TPA exposure led to transformation (Mondal and Heidelberger, 1976). Similar results emerged with X-radiation followed by TPA. Among the important noncarcinogenic promoters relevant to this discussion, syngeneic interferon *in vitro* potentiated X-ray transformation when present during the period of expression (Brouty-Boye and Little, 1977). Human interferon did not affect it.

Radiation and benzo(a)pyrene, a major carcinogen in tobacco smoke, are synergistic, that is, their combination yields a greater proportion of transformed cells than the sum of the singly applied stimuli. This is true whether one was applied first, followed by the other, or vice-versa (Terzaghi and Little, 1974). Lastly, oncogenic virus effects are enhanced by X-irradiation (Pollock and Todaro, 1968; Stoker, 1963).

One can conclude, to use Little's own words (1977, p. 937): "(1) Appropriate stimuli to and capacity for cell proliferation in irradiated cell populations are major determinants in the fixation and expression of transformational damage. (2) The ultimate carcinogenic effect of radiation may depend largely on factors secondary to the initial DNA damage."

In terms of our objective, we can only speculate, in respect to radiation, about the role of immune process on the one hand and behavior on the other. To the extent that viruses may (remembering that only few viruses have been studied for interaction with radiation) so interact, psychic factors may lead to their increased activity (Henry and Stephens, 1977, p. 162). If they are oncogenic (see the discussion of viruses); if their proliferation is enhanced by stress of one kind or another; if that particular stress occurs at an appropriate time before or after the radiation (cf. Little, 1977, above); and if the radiation is of an appropriate strength, then there *might* be an enhancement of cancer induction. What are the odds of all these things happening together?

Second, if the cited interferon findings (Brouty-Boye and Little, 1977) are valid for man; if an infection stimulates the body to produce interferon; if the radiation is at proper strength; if the interferon appears at an appropriate time, possibly before, much more probably after, the irradiation; and if the interferon remains active for an appropriate length of time, then there *might* be an enhancement of cancer induction. Again, what are the odds of all these things happening together?

Let us go through the same conceptual paradigm for promoters that we might ingest or be exposed to. In this case the promoter needs one additional condition. It must make contact with the irradiated cells. If the foot is X-rayed, will benzo(a)pyrene contact the bone marrow? No. Will it contact blood cells that are formed there and circulate? Possibly. In the end we ask the same question. What are the odds that all these (as above) things will happen together?

It would be foolhardy to try to answer realistically with a number. We do not know enough. But it would be equally foolhardy to say that the odds are nil. Merely to say the odds are not nil needs a positive answer to *all* of the conditions in any of the case mentioned above. We do not know if human cancer-producing viruses interact with radiation as described. We do not know if the *in vitro* phenomena observed are also valid *in vivo humano*. We do not know if the attendant circumstances or time periods or concentrations are the same *in vivo humano* as *in vitro*. The most we can say is that among people who have been exposed to X-rays, and have gotten cancer, a few cases might have come about by virtue of the unlikely simultaneity and concatenation of events described above.

And even if it is so, imagine the scope and complexity of research in the human necessary to change that possibility, as theory, to likelihood, as epidemiologic inference. To add to the problem, other kinds of radiation have been implicated as stimulants to cancer other than skin—electric fields around high voltage sources (Wertheimer and Leeper, 1979).

Chemical Carcinogenesis

Most chemical carcinogenesis is thought to result from the action of strongly electrophilic—that is electron-deficient—substances on information-carrying molecules of the cell—DNA or RNA (Miller and Miller, 1977). A few of these substances can affect DNA or RNA directly (e.g., alkylating agents), but most do so by being created from some proximate carcinogen, not itself altering DNA or RNA, and yielding an ultimate electrophilic metabolite, which does act on either of these macromolecules (Miller, 1970).

This conclusion derives from experiments on mutagenesis under various conditions. It is known from carcinogenesis experiments that almost all carcinogens are mutagens, but not all mutagens are carcinogens. The cellular target for carcinogens is not yet clearly defined—DNA? RNA? protein?—and may be variable, depending on the carcinogen, the state or identity of protein, DNA, or RNA target, or other phenomena. Moreover, because cancer induction can proceed through an initiator–promoter sequence (Boutwell, 1974), and because it can proceed through a more general nonconditional stepwise sequence, it is hard to identify the precise intracellular target(s) of various carcinogens.

For present purposes the exact identity of the target is not relevant. More important is the fact that the mechanism of transformation of procarcinogens to intermediate to ultimate carcinogens is controlled by enzymes. Such enzymes appear at various levels of activity in different people and in different tissues. Thus, part of the reason for person A getting lung cancer from smoking and not person B could be such a difference in activating enzyme(s). For example, an important transformation is that from the procarcinogen benzo(a)pyrene. A number of different human tissues have been studied that express the activity of the transforming enzyme mixture called aryl hydrocarbon hydroxylase (AHH): liver (Kuntzman *et al.,* 1966), lung (Grover *et al.,* 1973), macrophages (Cantrell *et al.,* 1973), cultured monocytes (Bast *et al.,* 1974) and mitogen-stimulated leukocytes (Busbee *et al.,* 1972). In each of these tissues high variability has been found among individual levels of enzyme activity. Because AHH was not known to be a mixture when most of these studies were done, and for other possible reasons, various attempts to verify the view that the hereditary expression of this enzyme group determines lung cancer susceptibility have been less than uniformly successful (Mulvihill, 1979, p. 120). It is broadly believed by geneticists oriented toward cancer etiology and epidemiology (Mulvihill, 1980) that individual enzyme activity levels are importantly, although not exclusively (Kouri and Nebert, 1977), determined by genes.

If they exist, genetic variations in enzyme activity would allow a neat explanation of part of the reason that one person succumbs to the carcinogenic effects of substance a, another to those of substance b, and a third to neither. Now we come to speculation again. If the genes associated with strong (or weak) proliferation of the relevant carcinogen-producing enzyme are also associated with particular personality traits, then those traits might be associated with increased (or decreased) cancer risks for the particular cancers produced by that carcinogen. But see the problem. To begin with, only a few such enzymes have been connected with genes. Moreover, no gene has been connected with any personality trait (except those associated with severe genetic disturbances such as Lesch-Nyhan syndrome or Down's syndrome). So the whole concept is speculative at this point. We can come to no conclusion regarding influence of PF on induction of cancer through exogenous carcinogens. We do, however, have a highly speculative, extremely uncertain mechanism by which it could happen.

Viruses

It is clear that viruses, both animal and human, can cause cancer in *animals.* A series of virus types are known and the necessary steps have been taken to show that they can indeed do this. Among them are various DNA viruses called oncodna viruses—papovaviruses (papilloma, polyoma, and SV-40 viruses), adenoviruses, and herpesviruses; and various RNA viruses called oncornaviruses—type C, type B, feline and bovine leukemia, mouse mammary tumor. No absolute proof exists, however, that any virus can cause *human* cancers; nevertheless there is much suggestive evidence. In particular, the epidemiologic evidence is strong for certain DNA viruses. The cancers are Burkitt's lymphoma (Epstein–Barr, or EB virus), nasopharyngeal carcinoma (EB virus), cervical cancer (herpesvirus 2), and liver cancer in certain African peoples (hepatitis B virus). Evidence for RNA viruses is relatively weak. Our present knowledge suggests that even if viruses can cause certain cancers, they do not constitute a major portion of the total human cancer burden. In those cases where virus-caused cancer exists, a connection with stress and the immune process, if present at all, is likely to be stronger than that with other carcinogens. The reason is that most or all virus-induced cancers, at least in animals, express antigens on the cell surface and are therefore susceptible to IS reaction, whereas cancers induced through other means express detectable antigens less often than those induced by viruses and may not be so susceptible to IS attack as virus-induced cancers.

Viruses cause cancer in general by adding a few viral genes to the cellular genome, that is, the full set of the chromosomes of a cell. Two stable characteristics of all cells transformed by adenoviruses are the continued expression of a virus-induced tumor antigen and the retention of at least part of the virus genome, integrated into host DNA. But these, like other viruses, are variably oncogenic, both as to degree and as to animal strain. Transformation results from random integration of fragments of viral DNA, but tumorigenic properties in such transformed cells only arise after a further genetic change in the host—mutation or possibly an epigenetic change. This minimum two-step process is consistent with epidemiologic multi-stage theories. (Whittemore and Keller, 1978).

After invasion of a cell the virus may and may not duplicate and shed viruses for invasion of other cells. If the virus incorporates some genes into the genome it will produce an antigen on the surface of the cell, in the cytoplasm, or in the nucleus. If a tumor results, there will always be a cell-surface antigen in the case of oncodnaviruses as well as some nuclear or cytoplasmic antigens. A given tumor antigen is virus-specific, appearing in different species infected with the same virus. Oncornaviruses also always have antigens, but whether they come from the host cell or the virus itself is unclear. It is very difficult to separate these because of a major difference in DNA and RNA viruses. In the former, either the virus duplicates itself in the cell and kills it by lysis, or it does not duplicate itself, staying in the cell's chromosome(s) and rendering the cell malignant. Thus, cell–derived surface antigens are distinguishable from virus antigens. In RNA viruses there is duplication of the virion in the cell, and either its daughters emerge directly or there may be a cell membrane bud containing the virus that pinches off and then releases the virus. Cell–derived surface antigens are therefore not easy to distinguish from virus antigens (Ristow and McKhann, 1977, pp. 125–132).

At this point the differences among initiation, promotion, and growth become fuzzy. If a virus invades, its mere presence is probably not the stimulus to produce interferon and consequent increased natural killer (NK) cells activity, but rather, the ability of the virus to replicate is, since inactive and killed virus does not induce NK activity rise (Herberman and Holden, 1978, p. 320). If that is the case, cell invasion is necessary, and the reaction to cell surface antigen, which appears as a result of the viral invasion, causes attack by various immune processes. If the cell replicates a few times and is then killed by virtue of stimulated cytotoxic processes, is that prevention of carcinogenesis? On the other hand, if a cytotoxic reaction is reduced or prevented, is that stimulation of carcinogenesis or is it stimulation of tumor that has already formed? If initiation takes place, but promotion is a function of events occurring days or years later, are the effects of these events, whether positive or negative, part of the carcinogenic process or the tumor development process? The problem is clear. Carcinogenesis is probably a stepwise process, but because the elements in it may be graded, and are often stochastic in nature, for some purposes it can be regarded as a continuous process from the first relevant event to full-blown metastasis.

The issue in this section has to do with whether viral invasion can yield cancer in humans and whether, given that it can, PF can influence that probability through the immune system. We already know that in animals stress can activate a resident virus and yield disease (Meyer, 1942; Riley, *et al.*, 1979), or may not increase reactivity to an oncogenic virus (Rasmussen *et al.*, 1963). In man, since viruses are believed to cause only a few cancers, even if the same phenomenon were to obtain—that is, stress-provoked activation of an oncogenic virus—it would contribute very little to the total incidence of cancer. The reasoning is as follows.

If viral effect comes from stress, whether due to removal of protective lymphocytes, or reduction of antibody, or stimulation of suppressor cells, then any effect would better be observed in those specific diseases that are suspected of being viral. To investigate research questions on possible viral cancers, there is an adequate number per year of cervix cases for a prospective study (12.6/100,000 women), but probably not enough hepatoma cases (2.1/100,000 persons), Burkitt's lymphoma cases (all lymphomas together have a rate of 1.7/100,000 persons) or nasopharyngeal cancer cases (0.5/100,000 persons) (Young *et al.*, 1978). Most human stress studies have used all cancer types, although several workers in the psychosocial area have restricted themselves to single diseases (e.g., cervix, Schmale and Iker, 1966; breast, Greer *et al.*, 1979; lung, Kissen, 1967). One rather important study has investigated cervix cases in relation to life stress, Graham *et al.* (1971). Using a control group of whom two-thirds were cancer cases, they excluded other reproductive organ cancer cases from the controls. Stressful life history events did not distinguish cervix cases from controls. Although biased in respect to testing certain other hypotheses (Fox, 1978, p. 85), the study was not biased for this question. No prospective study on stress in presumably viral cancer is known.

We are in the dark. The little indication there is (Graham *et al.,* 1971) shows no apparent effects. Theory, in terms of overall prevalence data, suggests that even if an effect is present, it makes up so small a proportion of all cancer as to be negligible—6.7 + 2.1 + .5 per 100,000 persons (rates given are for both sexes combined) per year, or 9.3/100,000. When compared with all cancers, whose annual rate is 324.4/100,000, this gives only 2.9% of all cancers that are even *able* to be influenced by stress effect on viral expression, so far as our present knowledge goes. To that fact is added the probability that a large number of people who get those cancers will do so whether stressed or not (Fraumeni, 1975). The net conclusion is that the effect of stress, as the active element of PF for these cancers, could probably not be detected in any study conceived to be feasible today, due to its tiny contribution, even if that contribution were real—which we do not know. To make the point even more convincing, any stress effects that *improve* immune resistance to virus invasion will cloud the results even more, since such events will increase the number of persons with high stress in the controls.

Hormones

While it is clear that sex-related hormones such as estradiol (e.g., Huseby, 1980), or diethylstilbestrol (e.g., Kurland *et al.,* 1975), can induce animal malignancy directly, experimental doses in these demonstrations are usually very large. In the normal course of events the local concentration of hormones would never approach such levels. Prolactin is known to bear on growth of cancer, but has been clearly implicated in carcinogenesis only in animals. It has been shown that immune response to allogeneic (genetically foreign) lymph node injection quickly raised the level of two gonadotropins, luteotropic hormone and follicle-stimulating hormone, which in turn caused a hormone-dependent transformation of cells to antibody-forming cells. If a combination of drugs blocked the appearance of the gonadotropins, the subsequent creation of antibodies was prevented (Pierpaoli and Maestroni, 1977).

Male hormones have been looked at sketchily. For example, testosterone in the mouse can facilitate the development of an ultimate carcinogen from a procarcinogen (Bakshi *et al.,* 1977). Can we say anything about that in man? Can we relate that fact to the appearance of twice as many kidney tumors in men as women after age 30? Perhaps not. Nevertheless it would be foolhardy to ignore that finding or the one by Mehta *et al.* (1980) that in the mouse, androgen receptors in the colon are strongly implicated in susceptibility to colon cancer.

In man, Rampen and Mulder (1980) suggested androgen dependency of survival in human metastatic melanoma. The role of estrogens in survival of postmenopausal breast cancer patients is well known. Wakisaka *et al.* (1972) showed an interesting relationship of sex hormones, supported by patient and population distributions, of alopecia of maturity and that of age, to stomach cancer in Japanese.

In humans, considerable theoretical evidence points to a long-term effect of estrogens as one of the potentiators or even one of the contributing causes of cancers of the human breast (MacMahon *et al.*, 1973), ovaries, and endometrium, and of certain renal cancers. In animals, besides these, effects have also been found in cervix, pituitary, testicle, and bone marrow. In describing the background of this question, Hertz (1977) makes the following statement: "This author knows of no other pharmacological effect so readily reproducible in such a wide variety of species which has been generally regarded as potentially inapplicable to man." First, doses used in animal work are usually far greater than those in the human. They are frequently so high, in fact, that a dose–response curve is often not possible to obtain. Since it requires a substantial part of the lifetime of a rodent to yield tumors, age at onset is confounded with duration of exposure. The genetic strain of the animal is critical, and if it is possible to draw inferences from strains of high and low susceptibility, a parallel genetic situation in the human cannot be found; our breeding is too mixed. Moreover, viral transformation, which appears in rodent breast cancers but is questionable in human, interacts with genetic susceptibility.

Inferences about humans come from looking at the lower risk in hysterectomized populations (Burch *et al.*, 1974); diethylstilbestrol (DES) exposure of pregnant women yielding elevated risk of vaginal adenocarcinoma in daughters (e.g., Greenwald *et al.*, 1971); reduced incidence of breast cancer after ovariectomy in young women; the effectiveness of progesterone, an estrogen antagonist, in inducing regression of endometrial hyperplasia as well as carcinoma; the greater risk of breast cancer among postmenopausal women treated with estrogen than among those not so treated (Zeil and Finkle, 1975), and the extensive epidemiologic data on breast cancer incidence and mortality (Kelsey, 1979; MacMahon *et al.*, 1973). A mechanism underlying the proposed influence of estrogens on breast cancer has recently been hypothesized in humans (Korenman, 1980), but there is conflicting evidence even in the basic theory (Kelsey, 1979; Trichopoulos *et al.*, 1980).

In breast cancer, relationship to immune function is very unclear in the human, in view of the lack of prospective data. Merely showing that cell-mediated immune function is depressed in advanced breast cancer (Tee and Pettingale, 1974) and that humoral antibody response is usually unaffected is not very helpful, especially since we are not sure whether the former response is depressed early in the disease. In particular, Pettingale *et al.*, (1977b) remark that in a study of women with breast cancer compared with those having benign conditions, the serum immunoglobulins G, A, M, and E were found not to show differences between the two groups before operation, or postoperatively at 3 months, 1 year, and 2 years. They conclude that there is a secondary defense reaction against increasing tumor load, and that the data do not support the theory that an early depression in immunoglobulin metabolism plays a part in the pathogenesis of breast cancer. A similar failure to predict for recurrence or prognosis was found by Teasdale *et al.,* (1979) when they tested for white blood count, absolute and percentage lymphocyte counts, IgG, IgA, IgM, lymphocyte transformation with phytohemagglutinin, and delayed cutaneous hypersensitivity to tuberculin protein and to dinitrochlorobenzene.

Susceptibility to many types and sites of tumor can be increased in animals by stress through hormonal action, mostly corticosteroids. Likewise, stress can inhibit tumors, depending on several factors like time of stimulation (Newberry, 1978), duration of stimulation (Kališnik *et al.,* 1979), and type of stimulation. It is also probable that stress effects in certain cases arise through action on cellular metabolites that process the transformation of procarcinogens or proximate carcinogens to ultimate carcinogens (Boyd *et al.,* 1979) rather than through the immune system. Riley's (1979) review of stress and cancer in animals is instructive, but irrelevant to man so far as the immune system is concerned.

Studies indicating relevance of catecholamines in respect to immune function in the human are fewer than those relating adrenocortical hormones to immune surveillance. Nevertheless, under many conditions catecholamines may have effects. For example, it is known that for about 10 days following surgery several immune functions are depressed: leukocyte migration inhibition; mitogen responsiveness; cytotoxicity; and antibody-dependent cellular cytotoxicity (Cochran, 1978, p. 247). Cochran (1978) says that the mechanism of these effects is not known. He points out that steroid levels are known to rise during operation, but their time kinetics do not follow the usual postsurgery immune depression. However, Munster (1976) hypothesizes that suppressor cells are strongly stimulated to protect against probable autoimmune responses following cell fragment exposure attending trauma.

Again we find some possible inferences, but the elements leading to meaningful conclusions are connected by long, logically fragile threads. During surgery immune function, for a time, is depressed. If a carcinogenic stimulus is present during that time, maybe an unprotected transformation can take place. During surgery, steroid levels rise. Possibly the depressed immune function is associated with such a rise. During stressful events and during occasions of poor coping, steroid levels rise. Therefore, following stressful events the chance of cancer inception is greater. First, the syllogism is faulty: *post hoc, ergo propter hoc.* More important, though, the possibilities and variations of potential explanation are so many that there is no point in even discussing them in the above conceptual structure.

Nor can we make much of the finding that the catecholamines, epinephrine and norepinephrine, are almost absent from malignant human tissue. When they examined tumors from liver, kidney, pylorus, colon, bronchi, breast, ovary, and testis, Børresen *et al.,* (1980) observed no more than 3.6% of the amount of norepinephrine found in normal tissue. Epinephrine concentrations correlated highly with norepinephrine ($r = 0.96$). Børresen *et al.* attribute the absence to the lack of, or low density of, or failure to respond to, sympathetic innervation. In fact, it is just this failure to respond that may form part of the basis of cancer screening by use of a stress-provoked blanching of breast tissues surrounding a tumor and the failure to blanch in tumorous tissue. A thermographic device detects and locates such a reaction (Snyder *et al.*, 1979). It should be noted, however, that if there is lack of innervation, which is not universally held to be proved, it does not prevent the existence of catecholaminic effects on vascular constriction in tumors by direct action from the circulating blood (Mattson *et al.*, 1980). It is obvious that vascular effects may influence spread of growth of tumors, but probably not carcinogenesis. Catecholamines affect rate of cell division, hence might affect mutation rate, and certainly do affect repair rate of DNA breakage.

Lastly, colon crypt cells and colon tumors in rats have been shown to be influenced by adrenergic hormones, both stimulatory and inhibitory effects being observed (Tutton and Barkla, 1980). Tumors, however, were not influenced by autonomic neural stimulation, whereas crypt cells responded both to endocrine and neural stimulation.

In respect to glucocorticoids, a few studies on animals and man yielded mixed results on natural killer cell activity after stimulation with corticosteroids (Herberman and Holden, 1978). Steroids given experimentally are known to affect DNA function after binding to cell membranes: they lyse certain lymphocytes, and inhibit lymphocyte development. But no connection has been made to human response.

It is quite clear that hormonal changes in animals can and do bring about increased and decreased susceptibility to cancer. Whether this is associated with stress hormones (LaBarba, 1970; Riley, 1975, 1980) or sex hormones is not important for demonstration of the point. But by and large, however many hormonally based changes might be found in animals, they can only tentatively, if at all, be extrapolated to the human. Moreover, so many changes that increase as well as decrease immune reactivity have been found in animals that it would be conceptually very hazardous to say that this or that stressful event will be duplicable (except where experimental conditions have been very carefully controlled); or, having observed an important result in the animal, that it will be duplicable in man.

Kripke and Boros (1974) described a series of studies in which various adrenocorticoid hormones (mostly cortisone) were examined for effect on incidence of cancer. Prednisolone, dexamethasone, triamcinolone, and methylprednisolone decreased incidence of sarcomas in the Swiss mouse (Nakai, 1961; Qureshi and Zaman, 1966). In fourteen studies where cortisone, hydrocortisone, or cortisone acetate were used (Kripke and Boros, 1974, pp. 899–900), the incidence of cancer decreased in four studies, increased in nine studies, and was unchanged in one study. In seven studies the carcinogen was applied topically to the skin, in one subcutaneously, in one as whole body radiation, in one through diet, in two in the cheek pouch, in one implanted in the submaxillary gland, and in one study the authors failed to describe the route of application. The variability in results, depending on various circumstantial factors, was enormous. A good example is the circadian change. Sabes *et al.*, (1963) reported giving single doses of dimethylbenzanthracene and cortisone, injected into the submandibular salivary gland of hamsters. When given in the afternoon, cortisone had no perceptible effects of the usual appearance of sarcomas, but when the injections were given in the morning, cortisone prevented the development of salivary gland sarcomas.

Hormones can influence the expression of viral particles. In mice, during early pregnancy, viral particles are produced under the combined action of hypophyseal and ovarian hormones, and during lactation mammotropin and cortisol cause viral expression, but not the former two hormones (Lasfargues and Feldman, 1963). Glucocorticoids can cause an increase in mammary tumor virus (Shyamala and Dickson, 1976) and this effect can be inhibited by progesterone (McGrath, 1971). None of this, of course, can be used by the theorist relating psychosocial conditions to cancer in humans since, in a broad-ranging review Pimentel (1979) says "The present state of knowledge, or ignorance, in the field of human oncovirology would make any definite conclusion appear as hazardous."

Genetic Attributes

The variable susceptibility to cancer among different species has been well documented. For example, Hayes examined the comparative epidemiology among dogs, cats, and humans for cancer incidence at various sites (Hayes, 1978). He also remarked on differences in susceptibility among breeds, where these showed interesting features. As one would expect, there are similarities and differences. For example, ovarian cancer, except for tissue differences, shows epidemiologic similarity in dogs and humans as to frequency, but the age-related incidence is different in the two species. Dogs show an increasing incidence for epithelial tumors, as do humans, but in dogs granulosa-theca cell tumors have a generally constant risk from 4 to 15 years, followed by a rise. Mammary gland tumors are the most common type in female dogs and humans, but are relatively rare in cats. Testicular cancers are relatively infrequent in men, except for those in their late twenties, when it is the most frequent of all tumors. In animal hospitals testicular cancers are the second most frequent tumor for all ages combined. Several breeds have excessive risk, but they differ in the tumor cell types for which they are at risk: the Boxer is at excess risk for three cell types, the Weimaraner for two, and the Shetland Sheepdog and German Shepherd for one. When rats and mice are compared in respect to identical chemicals, out of 250 substances tested, 38% were noncarcinogenic in both species, 44% carcinogenic in both, 7% carcinogenic in rats only, and 8% in mice only. An additional 2% showed differences from other species, but the study (Purchase, 1980) did not describe the number of substances in which more than two species were tested and did not differ. Among substances carcinogenic in both species, 64% showed tumors with at least one common site. These data came from a large number of published articles, using different strains, dosages, and routes of administration.

As for strain differences, we find variations. When C. C. Little, who founded the Jackson Laboratory, developed the first strain of inbred mice (DBA) in 1929, he set in motion a massive scientific movement that is still going strong. These mice were susceptible to noise-induced epileptic seizures and breast cancers. Since then many other strains, with different site susceptibilities, both high and low, have been developed. Most are highly susceptible rather than resistant to various tumors. Of particular interest among the latter are the low cancer strains CBA/Ht and WHT/Ht used by Hewitt et al., (1976), about whom more below. A few examples of strain variation will suffice. Boraschi and Meltzer (1979) showed that among 22 mouse strains, 8 failed to develop tumoridical capacity in macrophages by 7 days after intraperitoneal BCG infection. Stutman (1972) showed that after giving antimouse lymphocyte serum (ALG) to C3Hf and to I mice and to their F_1 and F_2 generations and backcrosses, ALG gave different results in terms of resisting tumorigenicity of 3-methylcholanthrene. Antigenicity was about the same, but there were "absolutely resistant" strains and "relatively sensitive" strains. These effects correlated with host genotype at certain geneic loci. Kärre et al. (1980) showed that a substrain of the C57BL mouse, a mutation with a recessive "beige" (bg^J) gene, has very low NK (natural killer) cell activity. Normal $+/bg$ littermates were relatively resistant to small threshold doses of one virally and one chemically induced leukemia, whereas the recessive bg/bg mice, deficient in the rapidly acting NK cell defense response, developed well-growing tumors faster and more easily than the normals. MacKenzie and Garner (1973) described 749 tumors from six strains of rats raised at seven laboratories. The tumors came from 24 sites with an average of 3.25 tissue types for each site, ranging from 1 to 11. Major differences in incidence rates were observed among the strains. For example, the range of percentages of animals in the different strains having various tumors was as follows: pituitary, from 17.9 to 3.3; mammary in female rats, from 39.8 to 6.7; thyroid, from 6.7 to 0.5; adrenomedullary, from 9.7 to 0; and adrenocortical, from 7.1 to 0. For most of these there was clearly no statistical question of chance events, although multiple comparison tests were not indicated. The extremity of the differences in the percentages can be gauged from the number of rats forming the source pool for each tumor type: they ranged from an average of 190 per source for breast tumors to 313 per source for adrenocortical tumors. The authors say, "The incidence of tumors in 'Sprague–Dawley' rats from different commercial sources varied as much from each other as from the other 'strains'." It is likely, of course, that factors other than genetic were involved to some extent in this picture—diet, husbandry, and incidental disease. However, the picture is consistent with substantial strain differences, since contract requirements set up by the Army related to diet, housing, and age, thus tending to standardize effects of those variables somewhat.

Caution, of course, is advised in drawing inferences from different experiments on the same strain. For example, Sabine et al. (1973) report that in two strains of mice there was an almost 100% incidence of liver and mammary tumors in the United States, but when such mice were bred and reared in Australia, they had an almost 0 incidence, particularly after the first generation. When one of the first strains was reared in Australia, but with United States feed, their tumor incidence rose somewhat; with United States feed and bedding, they showed an almost 100% incidence. The bedding in the United States, cedar shavings, was considered to be the carcinogenic culprit (Sabine et al., 1973; Schoental, 1974), but this interpretation was not accepted (Heston, 1975), the influence of mites being suggested instead. One might consider the implications of these findings for various laboratories doing work on carcinogens. For a carcinogen having relatively small excess relative risk, as is likely to be true in the case of stress, such physical considerations can be troublesome confounders, and may even, in some cases, explain some of the apparent carcinogenic effects of stress.

The last level of variability is between individuals within strains. The mere observation of the fact that some animals get cancer earlier than others, or the concept of a survival curve, says there are differences in apparently genetically identical individuals. The question that concerns us now is "Why?" Up to now we have only been able to speculate, and people's ideas have seemed to reside in variation in immune resistance, mostly. They shouldn't, since at least two other phenomena are extremely important in the decision by fate that a certain animal will get a thriving tumor at a particular time: the efficacy of DNA repair mechanisms in the face of a break, deletion, dimerization or translocation; and the abundance of various genetically determined blood and tissue substances involved in the metabolism of proximate to ultimate carcinogens—particularly enzymes. Nevertheless, Prehn (1979) attempted to examine the immunologic contribution to differences in susceptibility to carcinogenesis among mice from a single genotype. He reduced the immune response in experimental mice, either by X-radiation and thymectomy or by reducing the immunogenicity with use of low dosage carcinogen (0.5% methylcholanthrene), instead of the standard dosage of 5%. After implanting four subcutaneous methylcholanthrene wafers, when the first tumor appeared at a wafer, he excised it, and the corresponding wafer of a matching animal without tumor was also excised. The question was whether the next appearing tumor arose more often in the animal whose tumor was removed than in the previously nonreacting animal. When the dose was high, that did happen. But when the dose was low, or when the animals were X-radiated and thymectomized, thereby presumably reducing immune responsiveness, the next tumor arose randomly, favoring neither the animal with an earlier tumor nor the animal that had not borne such a tumor. Prehn concludes that this phenomenon suggests that the prior immune state of the animal, as indicated by its initial susceptibility to tumor, governed its preferential susceptibility to a second tumor. When the immune status was equalized, he maintained, by reducing immune competence in both matched animals, there was no longer a preferential occurrence of tumor in the putatively less competent animal. Prehn points out that these results are not consistent with results obtained in his own laboratory, where X-radiation plus thymectomy did not affect significantly the incidence of methylcholanthrene-induced tumors regardless of the concentration (Lawler and Prehn, 1980). However, if a tiny amount of spleen cells mass were restored to the animal, oncogenesis was accelerated. He suggests that this phenomenon might form the immunologic basis for the phenotypic differences shown in his first described paper. Later work would suggest that suppressor cells were active when spleen was restored.

In mouse models it is clear that genetic susceptibility varies considerably from strain to strain (cf., Hewitt's use of highly cancer-resistant strains, Hewitt et al., 1976). One would suspect that the same situation holds in other animals, but so far as the human is concerned, to establish that fact in the same way that one does for animals is patently impossible. One can use analogous devices, however. Nevertheless, because these involve many uncontrolled sources of variation, the conclusions to be drawn in the human case are not so secure as those deducible from the animal model, in some cases.

Mulvihill (1977) has laid out a general mutant genetic repertory of neoplasia in humans. Nearly all histologic types of tumor are represented, and a substantial number of all known single gene traits in humans can be manifested as neoplasia. In many, neoplasia is only an occasional feature, but in some it is invariable. Since it is not possible to distinguish tumor characteristics as defining those deriving from genetic sources, the determination that they are indeed of genetic origin must be made on other grounds—usually by recognizing other features of the trait or syndrome in the patient or family. A broader view of the whole topic of the genetic contribution to susceptibility to cancer can be gained from Mulvihill et al. (1977) and the section on host factors in Fraumeni (1975). Other data demonstrate familial predisposition to particular cancers without an identifying gene character (e.g., Lynch and Krush, 1973). The most convincing demonstration of this comes from pedigree analyses, although twin studies and retrospective studies, subject to methodological problems though they are, contribute some insights to the issue (Anderson, 1975).

Recently a number of studies have addressed the investigation of genetic clues to cancer in the area of immunologic processes. For example, Hersey et al. (1979) showed that Rh-negative normal subjects and melanoma patients had higher natural killer cell cytotoxicity than Rh-positive patients. Dean et *al.* (1979) showed that in four families with a genetic dysplastic mole that predisposes to melanoma, *in vitro* response to pooled alloantigens in the one-way mixed leukocyte culture was diminished, and there was a tendency to reduced B-lymphocyte and T-lymphocyte levels. These were found not only in family members but also in unaffected blood relatives and spouses, when compared with controls. The implications for genetic association are clear, although they do not lead to certainty. Dworsky *et al.,* (1978) showed that healthy blood-related members of families with multiple lymphoreticular neoplasms showed elevated IgM levels and reduced responses to the T-cell mitogen concanavalin A. Bouillenne and Deneufbourg (1979) showed a positive correlation between breast cancer in menopausal nulliparous women and elevated frequency of HLA-A28. There is a suspicion that susceptibility to nasopharyngeal cancer is associated in the Chinese with genetic factors. For example, Henderson *et al.* (1976) found that the risk for this cancer increased among those of this group with HLA-A2 and less than two antigens at the B locus, suggesting a genetic variation in susceptibility. A similar finding emerged from the work of Simons *et al.,* (1974). But in the cross-validation (Terasaki *et al.,* 1977) of an earlier study (Takasugi *et al.,* 1973), Terasaki reports "The general conclusion . . . that HLA is not strongly associated with cancer is confirmed."

One classic work on immunodeficiency was done by Kersey *et al.,* who counted the cancer occurrences associated with various kinds of childhood primary immunodeficiency diseases (1973).

An interesting finding of possible genetic importance is that of Hopkin and Evans (1980), who found differences in genetic damage to lymphocytes caused by smoke in different groups with and without lung cancer, and with differing smoking durations. A possible explanation lies in the different genetic susceptibilities of the various groups to such damage, although the authors concede the possibility of gross differences in actual smoking history to explain the findings rather than genetic ones. On the basis of negative findings relating normals, cancer patients, and the latter's progeny, Paigen *et al.* (1977) reject the genetic transmissibility of AHH (aryl hydrocarbon hydroxlase) as one basis for increased susceptibility to lung cancer, although Kellermann *et al.* reported evidence for it (1973). The role of AHH and other enzymes associated with an *Ah* locus gene in affecting cancer susceptibility in the mouse, however, is virtually certain (Kouri and Nebert, 1977; Poland and Kende, 1977; Thorgeirsson *et al.,* 1977).

Diseases associated with immune depression include those involving B and T lymphocytes. Bruton's agammaglobulinemia involves only B-lymphocyte defects. Most primary immunodeficiency diseases associated with increased cancer risk involve both B and T cell deficiencies. Among these are severe combined immune deficiency of infancy; Wiskott-Aldrich syndrome, an X-linked disorder (females are clinically normal carriers, but the manifest disease appears in males); ataxia-telangiectasia; and variable, or late-onset, immunodeficiency, which appears at unpredictable ages, often not until late adulthood. Few individuals with these diseases, except the last, survive until adulthood, succumbing, for the most part, to infections or malignancy. In a table of these diseases against type of cancer, Kersey and Spector (1975) describe percentage of deaths due to cancer among all deaths among immune disease-suffering children versus unselected children. In the following, from their data, the percentage of unselected children in the United States from 1960 to 1966 who died of the named cancer is given first, then a similar percentage for children with primary immunodeficiency disease (PID): leukemia, all types—48, 16; central nervous system—16, 2; lymphoreticular—8, 67; bone—4, 2; other—24, 2. The disparity is quite clear. Ninety-two percent of the cancers afflicting the PID sufferers were lymphoreticular or leukemic; 56% of the cancers afflicting unselected children were these two diseases. When all ages in the general population are examined, these two account for only 7.8% of all cancers identified, excluding nonmelanotic skin and cervical cancer *in situ*.

These immune deficiency diseases, it must be emphasized, are not common. Their occurrence rates range from 1 case in several hundred births to 1 in 100,000 or more births, and in most such diseases only a fraction of those having the disease get cancer (in a few, most or all get cancer). The explanations of how genetic characteristics predispose to cancer are not well advanced. In a few cases specific mechanisms have been adduced. For example, in xeroderma pigmentosum, a disease involving skin lesions and ultraviolet sensitivity, it is known that the mechanism for DNA repair is faulty, and many basal cell tumors arise. A mutation is involved and the failure of cellular differentiation—not the presence of dedifferentiation (Pierce, 1977)—associated with cancer often follows mutations. The repair process takes place by a series of enzymatic actions (Lehmann, 1979). A dimer is created in the DNA strand by ultraviolet rays striking the skin. It distorts the DNA. An endonuclease (which turns out to involve several enzymes) nicks the DNA very close to the dimer, an exonuclease removes the nicked portion, DNA polymerase fills the gap, and DNA ligase stitches it together. (See section on "Carcinogenesis and Related Processes.")

Except for the small numbers of cancer cases that reflect single gene dominant and recessive traits—although the types of those may number more than 200 (Mulvihill, 1977)—most cancer is polygenic. Moreover, since that is so, most cancers that appear as a result of genetic manifestation do so with apparently graded probability. It is true that the number of cases of familial cancer, in which the occurrence of cancer in a family far exceeds its expectation, is small. Yet the absence of a large number of such families does not negate the notion that individual families, having a mix of susceptibilities, may produce individuals with a chance emergence of greater susceptibility to a particular cancer. These sporadic cases are clearly suspected, but are extremely difficult to isolate as genetic because of the environmental likenesses within families. Twin studies show a clear excess of concordance of leukemia in children among monozygotic (MZ) twins versus dizygotic (DZ)—16.7% versus 0 in one study and 25.0% versus 0 in another (Nance, 1977). MZ twins did not show a strong excess, except in ovarian cancer, for other individual sites. Nor, as would be expected, is there an excess for cancer in general. However, the prevalence of ovarian cancer in women who have a male twin is three times that of women who have a female twin: 0.67% as against 0.23%. These studies are not necessarily conclusive, if the Knudson two-hit model [(1975), requiring at least two transformations for a cell to become malignant] is valid in certain of the cases but not in others. In those where it is valid, genetic conditions provide the first hit, or transformation, and a random transformation provides the second. The interval between occurrence of a cancer in one twin and that in another twin was measured. In Keith and Brown's data (1971) the results indicated the possibility of two kinds of leukemia—full genetic and one with first step genetic but second environmental. There is little here to show strongly that genetic defects are a major force in predicting adult cancers, but in childhood ones they are almost certain to be.

Many cancers arise because the genetics of the *individual* predispose to cancer in the presence of adequate carcinogenic stimulus. For the same stimulus, only certain people will get cancer, assuming they do not die of something else first. Witness the rate of lung and other smoking-related cancers—larynx, mouth, bladder, pancreas. The presumption is that those who do get cancer, for similar exposure to carcinogens, have a certain aggregation of genes that involve greater susceptibility than others. Such susceptibility may reside in the enzymes processing carcinogenic chemicals; the efficiency of DNA repair enzymes; the tendency to produce certain hormones in the presence of various stimuli; the ratio of various hormones to each other; the basic level of various components of the immune system such as NK cells, immunoglobulins, suppressor cells, and macrophages; or other abnormalities. In addition, there is a wide range of exposure to a variety of carcinogens, leading to even more variability of susceptibility. Thus, there is a distribution of probabilities of cancer occurrence based on internal susceptibility and cancer stimulation by various carcinogens.

Psychosocial factors are essentially two elements: psychological attributes, whether inborn or learned, that are relatively stable aspects of the person and stay more or less the same whatever the local circumstance—called traits for convenience; and psychological attributes that are transitory, called states. Discussion of states will be deferred to the section on Inferences in the Human. A trait can be genetic or acquired. Any genetic quality that increases cancer susceptibility must be associated with a PF trait if one is to ascribe a relationship between trait and cancer. Many such traits are exogenous PF, which themselves must be eliminated, or whose effect must be eliminated, before asking whether they are also endogenous. Where they are also endogenous, some connection with cancer must be shown.

Most psychological studies purporting to show such connection have not been well controlled for external carcinogenic exposure. But far more important, most such studies have shown no connection between the trait and a known cancer suppressive or enhancing state.

From the facts relating to genetic, or at least, trait phenomena, one would expect that if there is a connection with cancer-affecting physiological states and these phenomena, they are very likely to be site-specific. That is, only sites affected by the particular genetic event will be discriminable. For example, one mix of enzyme effects leads to susceptibility to lung cancer if a certain carcinogen is there strongly (e.g., smoking). But it does not lead there for X-rays. Other sites are relatively protected against. For a certain genetic mix, a certain hormone combination tends to breast cancer, and also ovarian and uterine body cancer, since epidemiologically these susceptibilities are correlated. It would be very difficult, if trait phenomena are indeed site–specific, to pick out any single psychological set of features and relate it to cancer in general—or even to any single cancer with which it is putatively connected, unless that cancer is the specific dependent variable.

There is one exception. It is a connection with a bodily reaction that is broad-gauge in its cancer-enhancing or protective function. For example, if NK cells are connected to a genetically controlled PF, and they, in turn, affect sensitivity to several kinds of cancer, such a relationship might be discovered.

An alternative hypothesis—or rather, one that complements the above—is that PF may not trigger a cancer in which mild predisposition exists, but merely cause an advance in time for an event whose probability is high to begin with.

CARCINOGENESIS AND RELATED PROCESSES

As mentioned in the preceding section, cancer is usually induced in a cell by a mutagenic process,[1] whether the agent involved is radiation, a virus,

---

[1] This term is used in its broadest sense. The addition to a DNA strand of a methyl group may not be considered to be a mutation (e.g., Holliday, 1979), but these, or DNA breaks, or other minor phenomena will be encompassed in the term as used here. It is recognized that transformed cells can revert back to normal ones, but if they replicate as different cells, as in the case of the cancer cell, there is the presumption of a basic genetic change. Epigenetic changes, for example, in membrane transmissibility or in cytoplasm, are important in this picture, (Rubin, 1980), so the issue is in part definitional. To avoid complication, the view that cancer, for the most part, results from mutation will be assumed here as an operating principle in spite of important evidence to show that other conditions may contribute or even be sufficient by themselves for carcinogenesis (Rubin, 1980).

transformation from an already different genetic state, action by a chemical—hormone, pesticide, whatever—or aging, although some of the processes affecting the aging cell are very similar to those inducing cancer. When such an agent impinges on the cell it does not necessarily result in cancer, even a temporary one that is soon eliminated by defenses. In fact, it is usually the case that the transformation is not cancerous, and we get tissue changes associated with various diseases. For example, when most viruses invade they result in noncancerous viral diseases (e.g., mononucleosis, hepatitis, colds, viral pneumonia). Or the tissue looks different, as in age spots or warts. Only certain ones, called oncogenic viruses, affect tissue in such a way as to result in a precursor to cancer or in a frank malignancy directly. The same is true of most chemicals. The bulk of them are not carcinogenic. So with radiation. High dosage is needed to get a large enough number of cases to show a detectable excess relative risk, let alone a substantial excess. Why, then, does the occasional cancer appear in association with these carcinogens?

Chance plays an extremely large part in this picture, although the probability of a malignancy resulting from a stimulus by a carcinogen is raised or lowered by various states of the organism (Miller, 1980). Within the broad status of susceptibility in the organism, chance rides, in part, on top of that susceptibility and determines when and in what organ a malignancy will appear. Thus, two determinable states, in theory, form the baseline for susceptibility: first, the state of the organism; and second, the strength of the carcinogenic stimulus, since the probability of cancer is always (or almost always) a direct function of the dose received, that is, there is a dose–response relationship.

Many factors affect the state of the organism in respect to the probability that a carcinogen will enter the cell and cause a transformation that is itself malignant or precedes one. The latter transformation may or may not eventuate in a malignant further transformation. For example, if an organism has excess fat, it may provide a larger load of fat-soluble carcinogen that might be stored over long periods and provide low-level but extended contact with cells. During certain times of life, (e.g. during pubertal and prepubertal years in girls), exposure to certain carcinogens such as strong radiation imposes greater risk than at other times of life (Korenman, 1980). If a woman has a large number of estrogen receptors in the breast and it contains an early–stage malignant tumor, the prognosis is better than it would be if the estrogen receptor count is low (Cooke et al., 1979). If a hamster has been fed certain retinoids, especially vitamin A, then tumor of the cervix and of the respiratory tract are inhibited (Chu and Malmgren, 1965). If a woman starts sexual activity very early and has many partners, the risk of her getting cervical cancer rises (Kessler, 1974). If a person smokes, his or her chance of getting lung cancer rises. Examples of increased and decreased susceptibility to cancer are legion.

One can regard such susceptibility changes as the first factor in a series that determines whether cancer will appear. The factors include genetics, exposure to carcinogens, and certain biologic phenomena linked to metabolism, to some extent affected by diet. In particular, eating little tends to avoid excess risk of cancer, possibly, some have theorized, because free radicals are not increased in the environment of dividing cells by heightened metabolism, but also because the actual number of cell divisions is smaller, thereby also reducing the number of occasions when the cell, through that division, can immortalize an oncogenic mutation and prevent repair. Antioxidants such as BHA, butylated hydroxyanisole, inhibit the formation of mouse tumors induced by chemical carcinogens (Wattenberg, 1972).

The classes of carcinogens have already been mentioned. The ultimate stage, a transformed cell that is stably regenerative and can lead to metastasis, can be reached by several routes: radiation breaks a DNA component, or splits a molecule, or polymerizes two pyrimidines; a chemical carcinogen acts on cell elements—DNA or RNA or cell protein—and replication perpetuates the cancerous type; a virus invades and part of its genome attaches to a DNA strand or substitutes for a portion; speculatively, a substance may affect cell reactivity so that cell membrane character changes, and virus or carcinogen can activate more easily.

In these processes certain mechanisms, both protective of and dangerous to the organism, are active.

DNA Repair

In the case of ultraviolet radiation, for example, adjacent pyrimidines in one DNA strand are joined, causing covalent dimerization, a state that can be carcinogenic (Hart *et al.*, 1977). In the healthy human this state provokes a repair process called excision repair (Cleaver, 1977). At least seven enzymes are involved in this type of repair, and poor or no supply of any one or combination could, in theory, cause failure of repair. Therefore, genetic characteristics, presumably governing the presence or activity of these enzymes, could produce increased susceptibility to repair failure and hence to cancer. Several clear-cut diseases of this nature are known (Friedberg *et al.*, 1979). For example, in persons afflicted with xeroderma pigmentosum (XP), the repair process is genetically faulty, and UV causes many skin cancers. In X-ray exposure, nucleic acid bases are damaged and DNA strands are actually broken. We do not know whether the same enzymes make repairs as in skin damage, but we do know that X-ray damage is much more disturbing to cellular function than dimerization, since ataxia telangiectasia patients are extremely sensitive to such damage, quickly dying of cancer after exposure to gamma-ray or X-ray therapy given for other diseases. When a break, damage, disturbance, or chemical alteration appears from other sources (e.g., an ultimate carcinogen), are other enzymes involved which can become dysfunctional on genetic or metabolic grounds, thus increasing risk of cancer? Contrarily, are there mutations or genetic types that produce super-repair capabilities, thus reducing cancer susceptibility to cellular alterations leading to cancer (e.g., Cleaver, 1977, p. 360)?

When DNA damage occurs, but the cell cycle is in a phase such that excision repair is interrupted by cell division, a daughter cell is formed with a persistent DNA fault. DNA synthesized on such a damaged template is smaller than normal size. The small pieces are joined to give full-sized strands by postreplication repair. When there are such gaps in daughters that form opposite dimers of parental strands, they can be filled by recombinational events, copying from parental undamaged strands. The process is much slower than prereplication repair. When recombination is faulty, so is postreplication repair, and it is error-prone. Preillumination by UV enhances postreplication repair, and reduces mutagenesis (Hart *et al.*, 1977). DNA retaining errors due to faulty postreplication repair can be procarcinogenic or carcinogenic. Particularly noteworthy, at low doses of UV, where repair capabilities are not yet fully utilized, all or most dimers formed by the UV are repaired. With increasing dose the repair capability becomes saturated, and only a certain maximum number of damaged strands are repaired. The remainder stay as dimers, and may or may not be repaired in later postreplication repair. This kind of data might explain why no differences in cancer incidence are found among locales with different ground and cosmic ray exposure involving radiation damage, sometimes with severalfold exposure differences. The exposure levels would all be well below the saturation point, so that all breaks are equally well taken care of by repair processes. Extrapolation to other radiation situations must be made cautiously. For example, radon on a dust particle continues to bombard many cells in one place again and again, usually in the lung, and involves high probability that some of the damage occurs just before a division. When this happens, there is heightened chance that an original area of damage will be hit again with a radiation particle, further damaging the DNA—perhaps bringing about the second of the two-stage transformation necessary in carcinogenesis. Uranium miners are particularly subject to this process, since radon gas, a product of uranium, adheres to dust particles; these workers are therefore subject to considerably elevated cancer risk.

The Immune System

The immune system (IS) operates to protect against invasion by foreign substances or organisms by various means. Major histocompatibility complex, a chromosome region (called HLA in man), controls in part immune responsiveness and development, and susceptibility to disease; various elements of immune behavior are under genetic control and display differences that could result in different sensitivities to viral or other transformation. Cells active against tumors are known as effector cells. We know of at least four classes: B lymphocytes, derived from bone marrow, that carry certain antibodies—immunoglobulins—on their surface; T lymphocytes, derived from the thymus; macrophages; and polymorphonuclear leukocytes. They interact in complex ways with antibodies. In addition, other cells and subclasses of these that perform many functions are known (e.g., helper cells and suppressor cells). Killer cells are a class of lymphocytes, a subclass being natural killer (NK) cells and another being primed macrophages. Originally called null cells, having neither T- nor B-cell characteristics, NK cells are now believed to derive from T-cell lineage (Herberman and Holden, 1979). Other antitumor elements are various substances such as macrophage migration inhibition factor, which keep cell-killing macrophages from wandering away from their target; antibodies reacting against antigens; interferons, which activate NK cells and are also viral antagonists in their own right (Bloom, 1980); and complement, a term for a variety of chemicals produced in the body which, when jointly activated with an appropriate antibody, can cause lysis in a cell with a given antigen. For example, only one molecule of the immunoglobulin (IgG) can trigger the production of complement sufficient to cause lysis in one cell, but many more of IgG are needed (Henney, 1977, p. 60). The whole system is incredibly complex, with positive and negative feedback abounding. Cells with other functions exist, such as helper cells and memory cells.

Functions of elements of the IS in cancer have been well described in several sources (Castro, 1978; Gilbert, 1972; Green et al., 1977; Hiatt et al., 1977; Walters, 1978). In addition, some good discussions of the IS as it relates to cancer and stress have appeared (Morrison, 1980b; Solomon and Amkraut, 1979; Wayner et al., 1979). It will therefore not be fruitful to describe the IS in detail here. Certain points can be made, however.

The immune surveillance theory of Burnet (1970), amended in 1970 from his earlier view of 1957 (Burnet, 1957), while discredited in both of these forms (Stutman, 1972; Prehn, 1974; Morrison, 1980b; Solomon and Amkraut, 1979; Wayner et al., 1979), is not wholly discredited, and maintains partial validity, although with important exceptions and alterations (Herberman and Holden, 1978; Wayner et al., 1979). The immune system may sometimes stimulate cancer growth (Prehn, 1974); it is thus possible for stress to reduce cancer risk by virtue of suppressing the cancer-stimulating elements of the IS. Moreover, the immune system may function as a holding device. That is, a minimal cancer can develop, but not go on to major growth, being contained in a quiescent state by the IS, only to become active under certain conditions (Noble and Hoover, 1975; Wheelock et al., 1969).

The stimulatory action comes about through the action of suppressor cells which are proliferated in the thymus in mice. A good general review has been given by Broder and Waldmann (1978). These cells apparently have three major original functions: to avoid destructive hyperimmune response to antigens in general, (e.g., following injury); and to avoid destructive autoimmune responses. They, and the substances forming their active principles, are genetically controlled, and in mice it is believed that the I–J area of the H-2 histocompatibility complex is the locus of that control. Anaclerio *et al.* (1980) have shown that some cytotoxic chemotherapeutic agents, (e.g., cyclophosphamide), depress suppressor cell activity, thus increasing their own tumor-killing effect by permitting the IS to exercise its effect more strongly. Suppressor T cells involved in enhancement of tumor growth were tested for specificity in one system and found to be tumor-specific. They did not suppress IS activity toward tumors at different sites (Broder and Waldmann, 1978). Other suppressor cells are known—macrophages and monocytes (Kirchner, 1978). Reduced cellular immunity was observed in hereditary as well as sporadic colon cancer patients and some of their healthy relatives, probably associated with macrophage suppressors, since elimination of these increased lymphocyte immune response in the cases. Similar phenomena did not appear in patients with hereditary polyposis or their relatives. This is an important observation, supporting the main thesis of this paper (see section on Integration). Hydrocortisone increased suppressor cell activity for Lewis lung carcinoma in mice. X rays have been found to reduce suppressor cell activity. This may be one reason for the efficacy of X rays as therapy. The carcinogenic potential of X rays is independent of this phenomenon, and may even be exercised simultaneously with its enhancement of immune function. In particular, X rays of the spleen enhance immune function, since it stores suppressor cells.

The last important element of the IS to be discussed is natural killer (NK) cells (Herberman and McIntire, 1979). These recently discovered and investigated cells have a T-cell origin. They can be activated by interferon, and can be made inactive by suppressor cells (Herberman and Holden, 1978, p. 454). NK cells have been shown to be sensitive to antigens that other IS cells do not recognize, and indeed, while not completely nonspecific, are reactive to a fairly wide range of antigens (Huddlestone *et al.,* 1979). NK cells are known to kill tumor cells. Their importance lies in the fact that they are an IS resource acting somewhat independently from the usual T cell. In the nude mouse strain, immune reactivity by T cells is quite low, yet these animals are not particularly prone to cancer. It has been shown that their NK cell activity is one important source of cancer defense. NK cells are known in the human, and perform quite similarly to those in rodents (Herberman and Holden, 1978). There are enough differences, however, to prevent quick extrapolations from animal experiments.

INFERENCES IN THE HUMAN

On the basis of the parallelism of a number of functions and processes in the human and in various animals, one is tempted to infer a high probability that PF do the same thing in humans that they do in animals. Two things have to be done before that inference is judged. First, we must break down the element PF in the sequence PF—immune function—cancer (see Introduction), and second, we must describe the usual sequences of events in the human that are thought to take place in carcinogenesis. The latter has already been done. As part of the judgment itself we shall look at the various immune elements and processes.

In animals, PF may, as in humans, consist of two parts: effect of environmental disturbance to the nervous system, usually involving a stressor—physical or psychological—that provokes a departure from normal homeostasis (shall we call it heterostasis?); and a difference in "personality" of the animal from that of another, presumably connected with some bodily attribute that yields differential susceptibility to carcinogenesis. There are very many stressors in the literature, and a goodly number have been examined in respect to their association with initiation of cancer in animals (Riley, 1979). Extremely few workers have gone the route of looking at all three elements in their experiments: PF, immune function, and carcinogenesis. Nevertheless, one might presume that some events intervening between stress and cancer have to do with the immune system (IS). The problem is that in order to draw inferences about the relationship, events in the IS must have been measured. So far as "personality" in the animal is concerned, the usual hypothesis is that most of the behavioral characteristics of animals except those deliberately imposed by the experimenter, such as conditioned responses, are hereditary. Whether this is true is of some, but not overriding, importance. Even if many such characteristics are learned, or acquired by virtue of the circumstances attending the life history of the organism (type of food available, presence of slow poisons in bedding, ambient temperature, crowding status of the rodent colony, and the like), and even if these influences depart so little from the norm as not to be particularly stressful, the route to cancer susceptibility must be examined in terms of the same variables. They include the nature and strength of carcinogenic stimuli, cell transformation sequences, time relations, the hormonal picture, all the protective mechanisms of any organism—DNA repair, metabolism of carcinogenic substances, immune detection and reaction,—and the routes through which these behavioral characteristics can operate to affect cancer susceptibility. A number of such behaviors have been documented (Fox, 1978, p. 57, for some references; Hirsch, 1967): maze-running ability, gregariousness, avoidance conditioning tendencies, emotionality, aggressiveness. However, I know of no studies that have related such characteristics to cancer susceptibility, except a series of Russian ones that are unfortunately lacking in detail (see Corson, 1966; Kavetskii, 1958). The major "personality" characteristic mentioned in Kavetskii's work (Chapter 3) is "strength" or "weakness" of the higher nervous system, by which is meant ease or difficulty of being conditioned. The mouse or rabbit was the animal used most often, usually the mouse, with animal samples on the order of three or four. It would be hazardous to draw inferences about cancer and conditionability from such studies. In general, there seems to be as great a dearth of material relating behavioral characteristics in the animal to either immune processes or to cancer initiation as in the human. The other facet of PF, stress, has been examined extensively in animals, as has already been mentioned, and to repeat quickly, the majority of stressors lead to earlier cancers in carcinogen-stimulated cases, but a substantial number of studies show that stress can delay cancer appearance beyond the time when it appeared in controls. Relatively little work has been done on the appearance of spontaneous tumors in association with stress, but that which has (e.g., Riley, 1975) usually shows earlier spontaneous tumors among the stressed than the nonstressed.

Inferences from Animal Studies

Usually rodents are chosen for cancer studies, partly because they have short life-spans, allowing tumors to appear within months rather than years; partly because it is much less expensive to maintain them than large animals; partly because pure strains have been developed; and partly because their physiology is not extremely different from that of humans, and in many ways is identical. Nevertheless differences in cancer susceptibility exist, as has already been mentioned in the section on genetics. Here it is appropriate to extend the story of those differences and to point out that it is even hazardous to assume homogeneity *within* strains but *across* carcinogens and organ sites. Pavelić and Hršak (1978) examined the effects of four immunosuppressants—cyclophosphamide, cortisone acetate, irradiation, and Ehrlich ascites fluid (EAF) on the growth of six transplanted tumors—Ehrlich tumor, thymoma, methylcholanthrene–induced fibrosarcoma, B-16 melanoma, lymphatic leukemia, and myeloid leukemia. Thymoma and Ehrlich tumor growth were regularly enhanced. Fibrosarcoma and melanoma growth were retarded in mice pretreated with X-rays or EAF, but remained unchanged when pretreated with either drug. EAF enhanced growth of lymphoid leukemia, but neither type of leukemia was affected by any other treatment. They conclude that there is no rule as to how immunosuppression in the host will influence tumor growth. They feel that tumor type governs more strongly the effect of treatment on growth than type of treatment.

In the face of such variation we might ask, how can one extrapolate to the human, or compare results with other animals? When considering other species it is usually the case that one or a few characteristics display similar features in that species and in man, and for those characteristics the animal is chosen as a model for extrapolation to man. The Armed Forces Institute of Pathology maintains a registry of comparative pathology, and animal models in human disease have been compiled in a handbook with as many as 180 models, which have to include strains to account for that many models (Jones *et al.,* 1979). Overall IS function is consistent among all mammalian species, of course. However, the IS characteristics and responses in man and animal differ considerably in certain respects, and prevent facile inference about humans from animal stress experiments, especially rodent studies. Some pertinent differences are

1. Rodent strains have been bred because of special characteristics (e.g., the nude mouse lacks an immune responsiveness to heterografts, and will not reject them). How far can one extrapolate to the average human from such single strains? The human population is highly outbred, so that almost certainly, if there were a human strain comparable to the mouse strain being experimented on, it would appear in very low numbers. (Humans have probably never achieved the degree of inbreeding of specific mouse strains, involving on the order of 30 generations of brother–sister matings.) Whatever conclusions might be drawn from the mouse strain could be quite consistent with most human biologic responses or it could be consistent only with that tiny proportion that is comparable. Essentially the experimenter is gambling, when he does an experiment, that there will be substantial carry-over to the human, since most animal work is directed to discovering phenomena that can be generalized to the human.

2. Most stress experiments on rodents involve transplants of tumors or large dosages of carcinogens or strong treatment with X-rays. These, for the most part, result in emergence of tumors with strong antigens. On the other hand, most human tumors are spontaneous, with considerably weaker (presently detectable) antigenic stimulus.

3. Hormonal levels differ among strains (Russfield, 1966) and in different cage environments, often yielding different results in tumor incidence and latency. Different stress baselines no doubt exist [e.g., Riley (1975), but the results of Chino *et al.* (1971), pose mild questions about Riley's findings].

4. A large number of spontaneous cancers in the rodent are viral, while very few are even strongly suspected of being viral in the human—see the section on viruses under Carcinogenesis—let alone fully confirmed. Since viral cancer in the mouse tends to express antigens clearly, the immune process represented by the usual mechanism of the antigen being recognized by lymphocytes and stimulating antibody, T-cell and macrophage response in the classical way would be active in the mouse. But the human, in whom surface antigens are far fewer (with present detection techniques), might have mechanisms that differ at least in quantity (different responsiveness, different thresholds, different feedback controls, etc.) from those of the rodent, and possibly in quality [structural recognition (H.T. Holden, personal communication, 1980), electric potential, etc.] Again, at the very least, caution is dictated by virtue of these facts.

5. Viral activation under the stimulus of stress remains a distinct possibility

in humans, and is not being ignored here, but it has not received much attention, as such things go, in the experimental or epidemiologic cancer literature. Riley *et al.* (1980) have shown that unsuspected viruses can confound seriously the results of mouse stress experiments. We do not know whether similar phenomena exist in man, although Fraumeni (1979) plays down the roles of viruses in human cancers, pointing out the fact that immunodeficiency in animals enhances viral cancers, and this seems not to be so in man, in view of item 7, below.

6. The life history of immune function in some rodent strains differs from that of others. For example, C3H mice do not lose much reactivity to hemagglutinin challenge with age, as opposed to C57BL mice and the F_1 generation of the AKR × C57BL cross (Metcalf, 1966, p. 75). He says, further, "It is well known that thymectomy performed on mice in adult life does not lead to any shortening of their mean life-span and in some cases (e.g., in high leukemia strain AKR mice) thymectomy may even prolong the mean life-span." In the human the maximum average weight of the thymus (about 35 gm) is reached between 11 and 15 years of age, after which the thymus begins not only to lose weight markedly, but also suffers a far more extreme decline in the relative proportion of active tissue devoted to its apparent function. From a maximum at age 15, by age 22 the thymus loses half its weight, after which the loss is more gradual. By age 70 it is down to one-fourth of the maximum weight reached at puberty. The parenchyma (essential, active portion of tissue) drops from a weight of about 30 gm to less than 2 gm at age 70 (Goldstein and Mackay, 1969, pp. 128–129). It is not unreasonable to think that functional loss, although not proportional to parenchymal weight, at least bears a direct relationship to weight. If cancer incidence were the criterion this hypothesis might seem reasonable, but in respect to other diseases it is not at all clear that the hypothesis is valid.

The probability that thymus in the adult human who is not yet old has little to do with cancer susceptibility can be demonstrated by data from Vessey *et al.* (1979). Basing their study on the fact that recent theory suggests myasthenia gravis to be an autoimmune disease, and that treatment often includes thymectomy, they examined cancer frequency among patients so treated. Aggregrating years since thymectomy from 0 to 20 among 381 patients, they observed 11 extrathymic tumors and expected 8.78 ($p \cong 0.5$), showing no appreciable difference.

Both Seifter (1976) and Riley *et al.* (1979) point to thymic involution as an interesting phenomenon attending stress and adrenohyperplasia in mice, but make no remark about its role in tumor growth. Thymus regression has been noted as an accompaniment to corticoid substances (Dougherty, 1952; Gordon, 1955) and to stress, whether viral or bacterial infection, or injury (Seifter, 1980), and Riley *et al.* (1979) confirm that regression. Even in mice, however, it is only when thymectomy takes place in very young pups that cancer is immediately affected. Leukemia is remarkably reduced and other tumors are increased as the animal grows (Goldstein and Mackay, 1969). However, when thymectomy takes place in the adult, as in humans, little or no increase in cancer susceptibility seems to take place. Similarly, in the dog, immune capacity is little affected by thymectomy even at birth (mostly because peripheralization occurs before birth.) In the mouse it happens in the first month or so of life, and in the rat just about at birth, leading to irregular effects of thymectomy shortly after birth in that animal (Good and Gabrielsen, 1964, p. 434).

In spite of the strong parallelism in life history and apparent function in rodent and human thymus (although Metcalf's observations [1966] of strain differences in immune reactivity suggest great caution before extrapolating to humans), there is a major difference in immune reactivity between the human and the rodents most studied. In a very provocative review Claman (1972) describes species differences in susceptibility to glucocorticoids, a division being made between corticoid-sensitive and corticoid-insensitive species. He says that the first group includes the mouse, rat, hamster and rabbit, the second the guinea pig, monkey, and man. The differentiation is usually based on the relative ease of producing lymphoid depletion after a given regimen of systemic glucocorticoids. He stresses, "The differentiation is of great importance. As it happens, most of the information on the effects of steroids on lymphoid cells and immunologic processes have been gathered from experiments on steroid-sensitive species. Therefore, extrapolation of the results of these experiments to man (a steroid-resistant species) should be done with caution." Describing a series of experiments by various investigators in regard to thymic and lymphocytic sensitivity in the various species, Claman (1972) concludes that relatively small doses in sensitive species are enough to produce substantial reduction in thymic size and in number of surviving lymphocytes, while in the steroid-resistant species, although glucocorticoids can suppress manifestations of cell-mediated immunity, large doses or prolonged treatment are required to do so.

In view of the considerable interest in corticosteroids as possible depressants of lymphocyte function in relation to cancer incidence and progress, it is noteworthy that even in steroid-sensitive species, the bulk of the cells killed are incapable of immune response; they reside in the thymic cortex, and are only immature, potential immune responders. None or practically none of the mature, immune competent lymphocytes are killed (Claman, 1972). This fact may explain some of the time relationships observed in rodent studies. Further to complicate these time relations, steroids are known to inhibit tumor growth by eliminating precursors of suppressor cells (Schechter and Feldman, 1977). They have many other effects, variably influencing the potential appearance or progress of cancer (Claman, 1972, p. 394).

7. When rodents are immunosuppressed they acquire malignancies without important restriction of site except for the specificity imposed by their strain susceptibility and the viral type (e.g., Bittner virus produces mammary

tumor). On the other hand, when humans are immunosuppressed, the majority of the tumors resulting are lymphoreticular. The focus of the immunosuppressive stimulus—radiation, chemotherapeutic adjuvant, transplant rejection suppressor—is the IS itself: reticuloendothelial cells and lymphocytes. They are the organs that are affected by the immunosuppressant and they are the organs that suffer the malignancy. It is true that there is an excess of risk of other tumors, but it is relatively small. Hoover (1977) examined data from 16,290 patients who survived more than a month after transplantation, in which immunosuppression is used to prevent rejection of the grafted organ. He found, counting *de novo* cancers only (he excluded 11 cases where a cancer had unknowingly been transplanted), that lymphoma occurred 19 times as often as it did in the general population, and that the major contributor in this elevated risk was reticulum cell sarcoma, an IS cell malignancy, whose relative risk was about 150. This figure is from a determination made 5 years after that of Hoover and Fraumeni's (1973) preliminary data on the same cohort when the figure was 350. The risk of other cancer was about twice that expected, although the longer a patient survived the greater his or her risk of incurring a nonlymphatic cancer. One can marshal arguments to reduce the magnitude of these figures somewhat (Hoover, 1977), but the major point remains: the apparent discrepancy between the behavior of cancer incidence in rodents and in man after similar kinds of immunosuppression. That discrepancy could signal a major difference in the inference patterns that could be applied to humans when theoretical inductions are attempted on the basis of stress as an immunosuppressant. At the very least it suggests great caution in claims that, based on animal findings, stress in humans might be expected to lead to increased risk of cancer.

8. The epidemiology of tumors differs markedly among animals, as has already been shown in regard to tumor transplantation and immune response. Also, we know that long-lived mouse strains live more than twice as long as short-lived (Storer, 1966). Human offspring of long-lived parents tend to outlive offspring of short-lived parents (Upton, 1977). Pontén (1977), citing Crowley and Curtis (1963), showed the inverse relationship of survival and number of chromosome breaks, the latter of which in turn are positively related to cancer susceptibility. Dawe (1973) presented the variable incidence of many different tumor types characteristic of many different mouse strains. The inference of the above is that if stress rides on top of a tendency to get or not get tumors, it will probably exert considerably less influence than the basic tendency.

On the other hand, we have a most important further inference. If any personality characteristic is indeed related to one of the genetic attributes that affect cancer susceptibility, one can at least predict altered susceptibility from an endogenous PF source. The relationship, however, remains to be demonstrated even for one attribute.

9. In drawing inferences about humans from animals, care must be used,

since human tumors heterografted to nude mice grow more rapidly than in the human host (Mattern *et al.,* 1980). This finding by itself may be explainable on grounds of T–cell deficiency (Borysenko, 1981) or of cell cycling in tumors of different sizes (Mattern *et al.,* 1980). Nevertheless it suggests examining a deduction made by Peto (1977, pp. 1413–1414). He pointed out that there is a theoretical negative relationship between the rate of carcinogenesis and weight of species as well as between rate and evolutionary stage. If duration of exposure to carcinogens (*a*) and opportunity for cell transformation as measured by number of body cells (*b*) are used to estimate relative susceptibility, he points out that (*a*) is 30 times as great in man as in mouse and that (*b*) is about 1000 times as great in man (although we don't know the number of stem cells, which is where cancer begins; they are the precursors to all differentiated cells in mammals.) Since the rate of cancer incidence is as the fourth to sixth power of age (except for cancer of the prostate, whose incidence is as the eleventh power), 30 times the duration of exposure gives, at a minimum, $30^{4.1} = 1$ million, and 1000 times that for cell frequency is about 1 billion. Thus, humans should have an incidence rate about 1 billion times that of the mouse. Yet the incidence rates are separated by no more than a third of an order of magnitude, for equivalent age fractions. This phenomenon suggests extreme caution in describing mechanisms and comparing susceptibilities, rates of growth, and effects of carcinogens. We should be very reluctant to make claims as to the action of PF as carcinogens or at least, if they are indeed carcinogenic, as to their mechanisms.

10. When tumor transplants are involved, as in many stress studies on animals, the behavior of the immune system is focused on a different bodily insult from that which occurs with gradual exposure to a carcinogen such as repeated X-rays or cigarette smoke. In contrast to the human case a relatively large tumor mass is usually involved; it is almost certain to have antigenic expression; and the phenomena of enzymatic cell repair and enzyme metabolism to an ultimate carcinogen are not involved. But most important of all, a surgical trauma is involved that does not appear in the carcinogenesis of most human tumors. Surgical trauma itself leads to increased metastasis (Simon *et al.,* 1980), and causes severe immunosuppression, possibly by activation of suppressor cells (Munster, 1976). It must be pointed out, however, that if such traumata affect susceptibility by virtue of corticoid hormones, and psychic stress also produces such hormones, the just-mentioned contrast would be less valid as contrast.

While the ten points of contrast just described tell us to be cautious about drawing too close a parallel between the interactions among stress, immune system, and cancer in man and in animals, there are still fundamental likenesses among most mammalian carcinogenic processes and IS's that overbear the differences in respect to certain conclusions about PF and cancer. These likenesses overall are more important than the differences overall. One can compare them to the stems or roots in a language, and the differences to the inflectional changes. The most important ones are

1. Cancers are induced by the same mechanisms, in general, in man and other animals Falk (1980), as outlined earlier (see the section on Carcinogenesis). They involve mutagenic, quasi-mutagenic, and epigenetic changes in the cell (Dedrick and Bischoff, 1980).

2. Except for a few special situations malignant tumors are believed to arise from a single cell in all organisms. All that we know points to the fact that, within a matrix of a range of environmental and genetic predispositions, transformation of that cell to malignancy is a matter of chance (Miller, 1980).

3. The more inbred an animal line is, up to a functionally asymptotic state, the more clearly is the level of cancer susceptibility manifested. In experimental animals this has been clearly demonstrated. In man, data on distant and close relatives in susceptible families bear this out, as do twin studies (Nance, 1977).

4. The genetic predisposition to low or high cancer susceptibility appears within an inbred line following the chance manifestations of the first, second, third, . . . , nth generations. The asymptotically common generations have a certain mix of geneic features bearing on cancer susceptibility. These features relate to carcinogen-processing enzymes; DNA repair mechanisms; basic activity level and abundance of various immune processes and structures such as immunoglobulins, killer cells, natural killer cells, macrophages, suppressor cells, memory cells, helper cells, and the like; various IS lymphokines and factors such as migration-inhibition factor, chemotactic factor, macrophage-activating factor, and interferon; tendency to proliferate various hormones under stress or other circumstances. These factors are found in man and in all mammals so far investigated for them.

5. Of those chemicals known to be carcinogenic to man, some 90% are also carcinogenic to some other mammals.

6. Carcinogens do the same things in man that they do in animals: attach to DNA strands, break them, prevent repair or reduce its rate, polymerize DNA bases, etc.

7. Stress in man, for the hormones that have been tested, provoke the same hormonal responses that have been observed in animals, with quantitative differences.

8. Within limits, and subject to certain major questions, hormones do the same things to the human IS that they do to the animal IS. Many of the mechanisms are the same, for example, occupation by hormones of lymphocytic hormonal receptor sites. These include both extraneural ones and those with major representation in the brain.

9. The overall epidemiology of animals' cancer, as well as their cancer etiology, are broadly comparable in rates, and conceptually quite comparable as to mechanism.

Inferences from Human Studies

Partly because the human cannot be manipulated experimentally, but
mostly because the relationship of PF to cancer with consideration of the IS,
or of PF to the IS with consideration of cancer, has only recently become a
matter of increasing interest, very few studies on those topics have been done.
This is not the place to deal with studies on PF and human cancer without
consideration of the IS. Much has been written on such studies (cf. Bahnson,
1969; Bahnson and Kissen, 1966; Fox, 1978; Morrison, 1980a, b). A couple of
hundred titles on the topic could be compiled.

The better known among the relevant studies in the human are those of Bartrop *et al.* (1977), Palmblad *et al.* (1979), and Pettingale *et al.* (1977a). Bartrop *et al.* (1977) examined immune responsiveness of 26 recently widowed
women at 2 weeks and 6 weeks after the spouse's death. Responses to
phytohemagglutinin (PHA) and to concanavalin A (con A) were measured, as
well as T and B cell numbers, four immunoglobulins, presence of autoantibodies, delayed hypersensitivity, and assays for thyroxine, triiodothyronine, cortisol, prolactin, and growth hormone. Except for the first
two, none of the measures showed a difference. Controls and bereaved differed in response to 10–20 μg/ml of PHA at both 2 and 6 weeks: the response
in the bereaved was lower at 6 than at 2 weeks for 100 μg/ml of PHA; and at 6
weeks the controls and the bereaved group differed in response to con A for 5
and for 50 μg/ml. Although Bartrop *et al.* did not find significance at 1
μg/ml, there was a difference between groups in the same direction as was
found for 5 and 50 μg/ml. One is inclined to trust the validity of such differences in spite of the fact that at least 20 separate tests were made, and that
one would expect some significant results by chance. The reason is the consistency of the differences in the curves overall in the PHA and con A determinations. What this finding means for incidence of cancer is anyone's guess,
since the direct prediction of prognosis has been looked at, to my knowledge,
only for those already suffering from cancer (e.g., Cummings *et al.,* 1978). I
know of no direct data on animals or humans that have predicted altered incidence of cancer with lowered mitogenic responsiveness to these two
chemicals. Indirect evidence with *increased* mitogenic responsiveness points to
greater susceptibility to at least one cancer, Hodgkin's disease (HD). *Increased* response to the mitogen PHA was found in a population that had
been discovered to have a clustering of HD with a relative risk of incidence of
9.4 and of mortality of 6.4 (Schwartz *et al.,* 1978). Many of the townspeople
had been exposed to an excess of PHA in dust from a local grain elevator
holding navy beans, where the PHA could have acted like an antigen. There is
a question about the stability of the results of Bartrop *et al.* (1977), since
R.W. Bartrop (personal communication, 1979) told me of his desire for cross-
validating data, given the difficulties in the technique. Others have corroborated his worries, pointing out that in looking at T-cell levels the problem

lies with incubation duration (Whitehead *et al.*, 1978). Incubation time was the very issue about which Bartrop raised questions in regard to the reliability of his own findings on PHA and con A responsiveness. But in his favor, there is recent evidence consistent with his, to be discussed below (see Schleifer *et al.*, 1980).

Palmblad and coworkers did a series of studies on fasting and sleep deprivation. Only the latter topic concerns us here, since food deprivation may yield results that interact with stress results. In one experiment Palmblad *et al.* (1979) examined immune response to 48 hr of sleep deprivation in 12 healthy young men. As did Bartrop *et al.* (1977), they looked at reaction to PHA stimulation, but also at granulocyte function and adherence. All three functions were depressed compared with the predeprivation values. Five days after vigil none differed significantly from predeprivation levels. In another study Palmblad *et al.* (1976) measured phagocytosis and interferon-producing capacity of leukocytes in 8 healthy women, mean age 33, following 77 hr of sleep deprivation with performance tests on a simulated shooting range and authentic battle noise at 95 decibels. After $2\frac{3}{4}$ hr of this, a question period followed, with time for eating, voiding, etc. Then the stress was begun again. Adrenalin rose during the experiment and stayed high. Noradrenalin was irregularly higher during the experiment than postvigil (5 days after). Cortisol first rose somewhat, then fell considerably 5 days after the vigil. Interferon-producing capability of leukocytes rose during the exercise, both in respect to blood volume and per million leukocytes. Phagocytosis dropped early in the vigil, rose again, and 5 days after vigil it exceeded the previgil value.

In a group of breast-diseased patients interviewed before biopsy, Pettingale *et al.* (1977b), measuring four immunoglobulins, IgA, IgE, IgG, and IgM, found significantly higher levels of IgA among women who suppressed anger than among others. These higher levels tended to persist through the 2 years the cohort Ig levels were measured, although significance levels less than .05 were found clearly only in preoperative and 3-month determinations among cancer patients and in preoperative determinations in benign patients. When degree of metastatis was measured (Pettingale *et al.*, 1977a) there was a significant correlation between immunoglobulin levels and extent of metastatic disease ($r = .29$ for IgA at 1 year and $r = .26$ for IgM at 3 months postoperatively, $p < .05$ for both). They concluded that Ig levels were probably not predictive of cancer incidence, but that IgA could identify disease progress to some degree. Since IgA levels among anger-suppressors were elevated both in the benign group and the malignant group (Pettingale et al, 1977a), we cannot say that this attribute discriminated the groups. And since none of the immunoglobulins discriminated the benign and cancer groups, no connections can be made between the psychological measure and cancer incidence.

Since those three studies a series of more recent ones have been done on humans.

Rogentine *et al.* (1979), looking at melanoma patients, included Ig data in their determinations. However, since these were associated with clinical trials, they have not been analyzed: the last patients are just now being completed. The data will be available, and will be related to various measures, MMPI personality scores, Locus of Control scores, and Holmes–Rahe data, as already measured (Fox *et al.,* 1978).

Bahnson (1979) did some exploratory measurements on immune function and psychological measures, but since only a few subjects were tested, he is, quite properly, unwilling to publish results that cannot be deemed representative of any population.

Greene *et al.* (1978) examined 33 subjects who were given a nasal exposure to influenza virus, with measures of symptoms and signs, the College Schedule of Recent Events, the associated Life Change Units (LCU), and the Profile of Mood Status (POMS). Immune measures taken were nasal virus shed, nasal wash interferon (INF), and hemagglutination inhibition antibody titer (HAI). Also, on 25 subjects, lymphocyte transformation (LTN) and lymphocyte cytotoxicity (LCT) response rates were measured. The principal purpose of the study was to test the effect of a drug, isoprinosine, on progress of influenza. Age, sex, and drug were not significantly correlated with clinical or immune measures. Some relationships among the POMS scores were observed. Other substantive correlations were as follows: LCU versus LCT, $r = -0.42, p. < .035$; LCU versus LTN, $r = -0.28, p < .18$; Tension versus INF, $r = 0.31, p < .08$; Vigor versus LCT, $r = -0.32, p < .12$. They hypothesized that negative moods would go along with lowered immune response. Instead, combined LCU and Vigor correlated with LCT, $r = -0.54, p < .006$, and with HAI, $r = 0.35, p < .045$. They concluded that not only negative, but also positive moods should be included in psychosocial measures, and that not only humoral but also cellular immune status should be measured.

Locke and Heisel (1977) examined one type of humoral immune response (hemagglutination inhibition antibody titer) in relation to the Holmes and Rahe Schedule of Recent Events and the Profile of Mood Status (POMS) in 124 subjects who received swine flu vaccine. Postimmunization antibody levels and the following variables were compared, no relationship being observed: life stress for the preceding month or year; POMS depression or anxiety; repressed hostility, social withdrawal or feelings of helplessness or hopelessness on POMS-derived scales.

In pursuit of their supposition about cellular immunity, Locke *et al.* (1979) carried out what I consider to be an extremely important study. They argued that stress may be associated in the human with cell-mediated immune function, and measured natural killer cell activity (NKCA) in association with life-change stress (LCS) and psychiatric symptoms. 108 healthy male student volunteers were chosen from 457 to yield equal numbers of subjects experiencing high, medium, and low LCS. Measures taken were individual LCU's or life change units (ILCU), that is, judgments of degree of readjustment required for each LCS event; the Hopkins Symptom Checklist, describing somatic, cognitive, affective, and other behavioral symptoms (Sx) in the past week; and NKCA. Each subject's experiences on a list of 43 events were self-checked for the last 2 weeks before blood sampling, the past month, and the past year (excluding the past month). ILCU's were summed to get a continuous score on overall subjective LCS impact. NKCA was not related to high or low LCS levels. A significant interaction appeared between LCS and Sx level for the year-long interval but not for the shorter intervals. Apparently "chronic" stress was associated with Sx. When level of LCS and Sx level were examined jointly, NKCA, going from high to low, was in this order: low Sx, high LCS; low Sx, low LCS; high Sx, low LCS; and high Sx, high LCS. The last differed from the first at $p = .14$ and from the third at $p = .021$, using a multiple comparison test. In further analysis they effectively removed the possibility that the low NKCA was associated with perceived or recollected somatic symptoms. Moreover, in the NKCA group 1 year LCS and current Sx were distinctly correlated ($r = 0.59$, $N = 27$, $p < .001$), but questionably or not at all in the high NKCA group ($r = 0.29$, $p < .15$). The observed relationships, while clear, were not overwhelming, as was also true of the observed differences.

In a further analysis, MMPI scores in these subjects were related to NKCA. In the clinical scales, comparison of the groups in the highest and lowest quartiles of NKCA showed that in all ten clinical scales the lowest group displayed more psychopathology than the highest. Among these and three validity scales, however, only PD (psychopathic deviate), PA (paranoia) and PT (psychasthenia) were significant at $p < .05$. Out of 12 research scales, 4 were significant at $p < .05$ (two anxiety scales, A and AT; dependency, DY, and maladjustment, MT), and another 2 at $.05 < p < .10$. Further, in 11 of these scales (exception: RE = repression, $p < .06$), subjects in the lowest quartile of NKCA obtained higher average scale scores than those in the highest quartile. While the meaning of the following relation is not clear, it is impressive to note that of the 22 clinical and research scales, in only one (RE) did the high NKCA quartile display a higher score than the low NKCA quartile. The findings are consistent with the hypothesis of Locke et al. (1979) that the low NKCA group was less psychologically healthy than the high NKCA group.

Pursuing Locke's work, McClelland et al. (1980), cited by McClelland and Jemmott (1980) found that in Locke's cohort, subjects high in need for power scored higher on an affective symptoms measure and lower on NK cell level if they reported more rather than fewer life events challenging to their power status.

Roessler et al. (1979) examined level of antibody titer in 71 subjects given A-Texas, B-Hong Kong, and A-Russian influenza vaccines. He related ego strength and stressful life events of these subjects to their antibody titers. Those with high ego strength displayed higher titers. No relationship of titer to events was found, nor was there any significant interaction. In an attempt to cross-validate this result, Roessler (1980) redid the experiment, but the result did not verify the initial findings. He speculated that since the first group had been selected in part for a wide range of ego strength, such extremes might have permitted lesser contrasts to show up. The second group had a narrow range of ego strength and might, he thought, have had too narrow a range for the effect of ego strength to be evident. Such restriction of range is well known to reduce relational statistics to low values and to reduce or eliminate evidence of mild contrasts.

Schleifer *et al.* (1980) reported pre- and 5–7 week postbereavement function in six men whose wives were terminally ill with breast cancer. They measured total lymphocytes in blood, percentage and number of B and T lymphocytes, and response of blood lymphocytes *in vitro* to the mitogens PHA, con A, and that from pokeweed (PWM). Stein (1980) reported no difference in the prebereavement measures and those taken 1 month before, an important base control, showing stability of the prebereavement measures. When pre- and postbereavement measures were compared, no differences were found for numbers and proportions of either of the lymphocytes or their total, but dose–response curves for PHA and PWM were significantly different (repeated measurements analysis of variance), both at $p < .01$, and con A differed at $p < .13$ Measures taken at 2–3 weeks postbereavement on four men showed results similar to those at 5–7 weeks, both lower than prebereavement. A control group of nine men without bereavement measured on the same test days as the bereaved group showed no significant differences in mitogen response pre- and postbereavement.

Results of some experiments involving stress, interferon, and viral stimulation may be explainable by the following combination of facts: NK cells are strongly active against viruses, sometimes against antigenic cells from new tumors, and sometimes, because the reaction is too fast for the latter, against cells apparently without surface antigens; interferon production activates NK cells; stress tends to activate passive or resident viruses; viruses are a potent stimulus to interferon production [in fact, Palmblad *et al.* (1976) used that fact in assaying interferon production capability of leukocytes by challenging with a standard Sendai virus dose]; and last, adrenocortical hormones reduce both interferon (Rytel and Kilbourne, 1966) and NK cell activity (Herberman and Holden, 1978, p. 344). When coupled with the time relations among these and the fact that in the presence of depressed thymic function NK activity rises, at least in mice, it may be possible to make sense of some of the results by animal experimenters who found that, associated with imposed stress, the take of tumor transplants or the growth of tumors from carcinogens are sometimes increased and sometimes decreased, and in humans (e.g., Palmblad *et al.*, 1976) the same might be said of immune response. For example, in the experiment by Solomon *et al.* (1967), the release of resident viruses by stress given before virus infection could easily have raised the interferon level such that, when virus was added after 5 hr, the blood might have been primed, interferon might already have been high due to early virus release, and a normal interferon rise associated with virus injection might have ridden on top of an existing one, giving, as was observed, a significantly higher total titer than was found with virus injection alone or stress giver *after* virus injection (Solomon *et al.*, 1967, Table I). The time relations are consistent with such events.

This kind of speculation, which has not been thoroughly thought out, plus many more data are needed to make sense of the human and animal results on immune response to stress. The speculative train of events is not inconsistent with the findings of Jensen (1968), or Chang and Rasmussen (1965), who showed a fall of interferon during stress, but reasons for such a transitory fall when blood taken during stress is stimulated with virus, as opposed to the rise shown by Solomon *et al.* (1967), should be explored. The data of Bartrop *et al.* (1977) and of Schleifer *et al.* (1980) are provocative, and show immune system changes that could, under some conditions, affect cancer induction. But other data related to bereavement consistently show excess appearance of disease within the first 6 months or year after bereavement, and little excess thereafter (Jacobs and Ostfeld, 1977). Since the time course of development of cancer to detectable size is on the order of years, bereavement could not have triggered the induction of either a precursor to cancer or cancer itself. Several explanations have been offered based on tendency to report illness after and not before bereavement, or excess risk of the bereaved because of common environment, and the like. I have not read, though, of the possibility that a tumor large enough to be seen and detected had been dormant, and became reactivated under the emotional trauma of bereavement. All three explanations are consistent with the observations of Bartrop *et al.* and of Schleifer *et al.* I favor the first two, because of the great reluctance of oncologists to believe in a general dormancy theory. Perhaps occasional cancers might display such a phenomenon, but not a percentage substantial enough to show up in these studies. For that to happen, the relative risk must be 2 or greater, in view of the small number of cases in most bereavement studies. This means that half of the observed follow-up cancers would have had to be of the dormant type and reactivated, far too great a proportion.

The verification by Schleifer *et al.* (1980) of the findings by Bartrop *et al.* (1977), although in men rather than women, lends weight to the probable basis of increased disease among the bereaved being the IS. Although neither group of authors mentioned cancer, their demonstration gives a limited rationale for any cancer excess if later investigation should show that particular kinds of tumors are more likely to appear following bereavement.

Palmblad *et al.* (1976, 1979) found IS changes with stress. Depression of function with PHA stimulation is not of particular relevance to cancer, although it may well be. Principally the demonstration of IS reaction on a short-term basis among healthy people is shown, a finding to be added to the store of other human results and entered into a general theory. Perhaps the most unexpected finding was that interferon-producing capability rose during the simulation exercise, although its significance is not clear at this point.

The data of Pettingale *et al.* (1977b), stemming from cancer patients, are more useful in drawing conclusions about prognosis than about carcinogenesis, as the authors remarked. It is, however, one of the few human studies relating PF to IS events, and will enter the store of human studies as with Palmblad *et al.* (1976, 1979).

The study by Rogentine *et al.* (1979) and the associated one by Fox *et al.* (1978) merit the same remarks as those for Pettingale *et al.* (1977a,b).

Greene *et al.* (1978) found interesting data that must be followed up. If lymphocyte toxicity or lymphocyte transformation capabilities are related to mood, one finds many questions regarding other PF, other IS functions, state or trait status, and the like.

Of all the studies, those by Locke and Heisel (1977) and Locke *et al.* (1979) are most provocative. We have clear evidence of NK cell involvement in cancer protection (Herberman and Holden, 1978), and a relationship such as Locke *et al.* found could signal fundamentally important data for psychosomatic research in cancer. The most important ultimate question yet to be answered, assuming reliability and to some extent, validity of the PF measures, is whether low NK activity is an indicator of later good or poor reactivity to cancer induction and of what tumors it is such an indicator. Human epidemiology will have to wait for large, relatively long-term studies. In animals low NK reactivity strains are known to exist, but since the detection of such activity depends on a particular target cell used in the reactivity test, that alone does not guarantee broad-scale low reactivity. In fact, no consistency has been found. Using various other tumor target cells, Herberman and Holden (1978, p. 313) found considerable variation, and could not characterize any single mouse strain as generally nonreactive. The same issue must surely apply in the human case. We would probably be correct in saying that low NK reactivity is valid for a limited and probably specific group of tumor lines, but not for others, *within each person*. The distribution of reactivities is an important future project, to be followed by long-term studies such as those mentioned previously, with their associated PF measures.

Roessler *et al.* (1979) measured antibody titers to flu vaccines. In view of his inconsistent results on cross-validation (for which he is to be strongly commended, since that kind of experimental care is rare), one must wait for further clarification of results. If he verifies his earlier data in an appropriate sample, this result will be consistent with those of Locke and colleagues, and add strength to the same broad implications of their respective findings.

As has been recorded many times, a large number of studies exist showing an excess of illness among people who have been subjected to stresses of various kinds. A number of these in compiled form such as books are mentioned in Fox (1978, p. 87). With a few exceptions (e.g., Canter *et al.*, 1972), most of the studies on humans done up to fairly recent years have not dealt with immune function, but rather its manifestations in illnesses of various kinds. Even if a connection could have been made on rational grounds in these studies, on the basis that illness involving infection also involves the immune system, the connection to cancer could not at all be made. At this stage those studies are not of much use for the present analysis; they may be as we progress in the field.

INTEGRATION

The basic message emerging from the above data is that both components of PF—stable characteristics of people and stresses—are associated with both increased and decreased susceptibility to cancer. The animal data clearly show both stimulation of tumor growth and earlier appearance, as well as inhibition and delay. Perhaps there is more of the former pair than the latter. Likewise, animal studies show both stimulation and inhibition of IS function. To whatever degree IS controls carcinogenesis, these mixed results are consistent with the mixed cancer induction results just mentioned. The mechanisms are many. One is the activity of NK cells, that seem to act in partial independence of the usual T-cell population and its adjunctive cells. Such independence means that in many cases, where stress would be thought to depress the T-cell group of immune elements, it might have no effect or a stimulating effect on NK cells. Another is suppressor cells, whose activity seems to be the basis for many phenomena that seemingly contradict the immunosurveillance proposed by Burnet (1970).

Several arguments can be advanced to show that stress is likely to have a relatively small effect on carcinogenesis when placed beside the other factors that tend to induce cancer.

The first point is evidence that, if PF had strong effects, there is at least an important limitation on that strength. First, a lemma. We must assume that PF and/or the ability to cope with exogenous PF, hence level of endogenous PF, have varied little over the last 6 or so decades. If there has been a substantial trend of PF or their endogenous stressful results, say upward, three things would all have been true. For the last 5 decades (allowing 10 yr as latent period), those cancer sites whose mortality among United States whites has been rising (e.g., pancreas and lung [Devesa and Silverman, 1978]) would have suffered a smaller than apparent rise due to environmental variables. Those whose mortality has been falling (e.g., cervix and stomach) would have suffered a larger than apparent drop. But those whose level has been steady (e.g., breast and colon) would have had to drop due to other causes precisely enough to compensate for the rising trend in PF in order to stay stable. These sites are not the only ones to stay stable. For all others, an exactly similar compensatory drop would have had to take place, if PF were not particularly selective. If they are selective, we have no way of knowing which sites are affected by PF except to exclude most of the stable ones—colon and breast are, by the way, among those sites with the highest mortality rates among all cancer rates. The lemma of little or no variation is proved. If there is little variation, then we can show that the effect of PF is limited to the most infrequent cancers, all the rest having environmental sources to raise them to any substantial amount. This will be true unless PF are selective. The biology of cancer tends to support that position if indeed PF do help in causing cancer, since different organs are differently endowed with those features that PF can affect: hormone receptor sites, enzyme concentration, type of innervation, etc.

A second point is of some interest. Most epidemiologic variables are unidirectional; that is, they are either carcinogenic or protective. In this case we have seen that in animals stress can help, harm, or have no effect. Speculatively, the same holds true for humans. If the effects were equally divided toward helping or hurting, the net result, without a discriminating stratifier, would be neutral in the overall population, probably with a symmetric distribution around zero effect. If there were an excess of one over the other, the net result would be the algebraic sum of the two. In either case the yield would be an underestimate of the magnitude of that sum. Of course, in any individual case the net result is deterministic, with only one result, good or bad. But in our ignorance about the state of the determiners of that result we can only deal with an aggregate result on many organisms. It is obvious that what is needed is not only well-controlled prospective studies, but also information, both in animal and human, that will help identify the conditions under which stress or other PF will tend toward helping or harming.

I tend to think, although this conjecture is subject to some question, that there may be a greater underestimation of helpful effects than harmful because the degree of helping is hidden by the fact that in a helpful direction there is no threshold of crossover, that is, no indicator of difference between weak and strong help, both tending to no cancer; whereas in a harmful direction there is a threshold of crossover, namely going from no cancer to cancer, which makes easier the identification of harmful effects.

The third point is not quite central to the argument, but is still important. In view of the estimates by Peto (see item 7, Inferences from Animal Studies), one is inevitably led to the speculation that with ascent of the phylogenetic ladder, man, the elephant, the bovine, and other large animals must have developed more efficient means for coping with the increased number of cancers to be expected by virtue of their greater longevity and larger size. These means probably include more and perhaps different enzymes for metabolizing carcinogens [see Ramsey and Gehring (1980) for current ideas on the physical chemistry of such metabolic processes]; specialized and perhaps new DNA repair sytems, for example, the excision repair system missing in the usual xeroderma pigmentosum (XP) patient is also missing in mice, but they do not get extreme carcinogenic sensitivity to UV radiation as do XP humans); devices for reducing carcinogenic initiation and promotion, such as free radical reducers; body temperature, which certainly reduces the metabolic rate and, as has been shown (Lindahl and Nyberg, cited in Hart and Setlow, 1974), reduces the rate of DNA damage associated with normal body heat: the higher the body temperature the more the DNA damage (but repair is faster); and the like. Beyond the actual and possible changes noted above, increased enzyme control and better repair very likely involve a larger number of genes to exercise those controls, and more genes allow the existence of breaks, with greater cancer susceptibility. Assuming no difference in cancer incidence in mouse and man for equivalent longevity fractions, the latter had to accommodate his defense system even more to deal with such breaks.

Peto (1977, p. 1413) doubted that the biology of mouse and man differed so much as to accommodate to a billionfold difference in risk. Perhaps he is right. But he did not consider certain things that could affect that difference. I will mention only the two most important, in my opinion: First, many, perhaps even most, spontaneous mouse tumors are viral; most human are not. Every viral tumor appearing in mouse but not in man is subject to the billionfold difference. For comparability, they must be subtracted from mouse incidence rates. Second, if a protective device such as a DNA repair system is improved, its activity, being continuous, must display close to the identical power functions with age or exposure to carcinogens that Peto described for cancer risk, since its activity, except for periods of mitosis, when repair may not take place, exactly parallels every DNA break, up to the ages where its efficiency may decline. This phenomenon alone could account for a substantial part of the compensatory protective capability of the human. In support of the view that the DNA repair system for UV radiation damaged tissue has improved, Hart and Setlow (1974) have done the precise experiment to examine the question of whether excision repair rate is a positive function of species longevity. They determined that log of longevity, using seven species, varies linearly with the rate of DNA repair for each of the three UV doses used to induce DNA breakage. The lower the dosage, the steeper the relationship. Although Hart and Setlow (1974, p. 2172) are careful to say that this mechanism alone does not account for the life-span differences among species, it could contribute a great deal to the explanation of differences in rate of cancer incidence among species when considered in absolute time terms.

Parenthetically, if tissue dysfunction due to numbers of DNA breaks and levels of repair among the species, including cancer of course, forms a substantial part of the reasons for death, it is clear that we cannot talk about whether species A has kept up with species B, since the argument would become circular. *A posteriori*, man would have *had* to keep up with the mouse in the end product of numbers plus levels, since those numbers and levels would have forced the lifespans of both species.

Looking at the process of chemical carcinogenesis, we see that the IS stands only as a *third* line of defense. The first line is metabolic protection. Do we have a good enough level of enzymes that break down carcinogenic substances before they can induce a transformation? Conversely, do we have a sufficiently low level of those that process precarcinogens to carcinogens? Are we at greater risk because we have been "blessed" with an overabundance of the latter enzymes? The second line of defense is the DNA repair system. Because of the constant barrage of DNA-breaking or deforming stimuli—heat, radiation, chemical carcinogens, viruses—we would be subject to cancer at many times the rates observed, if these systems did not exist. Only then do we come to the IS as a line of defense. For radiation the IS is a second line of defense, and for viral attack, it is both first and second, since viruses can be attacked before they invade cells as well as the antigenic cell. But the main function of the IS occurs after there is incorporation of the carcinogen's result into the cell.

We are thus led to an inference that seems to have some importance in addressing the problem of this discussion.

We have been uncertain as to how much to extrapolate from the animal to the human. The species differences described above say to be cautious; the similarities say that broad-gauge equivalence can be expected. But we have had no directionality: that is, will humans have more or fewer cancers than animals if stressed equally? Will stress be more or less important in animal and man? We will ignore for the moment our inability to equate stresses. The principle is at stake. This discussion on rate of repair in the various species allows us to draw at least one inference, even though the final answer to the directionality question cannot be educed.

Theory regarding effect of stress has thus far focused on hormonal effect on the immune system (Bahnson, 1969), with perhaps some direct influence from the brain on neuronal terminals or glands such as the thymus.

Hart and Setlow demonstrated an exponential effect of repair capabilities on longevity in man and other animals for equal repair times. Cancer is an important part of the limits on such longevity. It is also known (Shakney, 1980) that the reproductive cycling time of human cells is much longer—geometric mean (GM) about 24–96 hr and range about 12–1000 hr—than that of mouse cells—GM about 10–16 hr and range about 8–100 hr. Thus, on two grounds repair in man is more efficient than in mouse in preventing cancer. It follows that in the absence of any other knowledge, if we assume that the immune responses in the two species have equal capabilities as well as the enzyme responses, the former contribute a smaller proportion of cancer-preventing effect in man than in mouse. The concept is formalized in the following. Let us designate man's carcinogen-processing enzyme effects as x, his repair effects as y and his IS effects as z; and mouse's corresponding effects as x', y', and z'. In a pure additive model the total cancer-preventing effects—call them E in man and E' in mouse—are $E = x + y + z$, and $E' = x' + y' + z'$.

We assume that

$$x = x', z = z'. \text{ It follows that if } y > y',$$

then

$$E > E', \text{ and } z/E < z'/E'.$$

In a purely multiplicative model $E = xyz$ and $E' = x'y'z'$. Now the contribution of z to E is

$$z/E = z/(xyz) = 1/(xy),$$

and of z' to E' is

$$z'/E' = z'/(x'y'z') = 1/(x'y').$$

Now if $x = x', z = z'$, and $y > y'$,

then

$$z/E < z'/E', \text{ since } 1/(xy) < 1/(x'y').$$

It can be shown that for any model combining additivity and multiplicativity, $z/E < z'/E'$, under the above assumptions.

Again, in the absence of any other information, if we assume equal effects of stress in the species, then the influence of stress in animals, whether it increases or decreases cancer susceptibility, is proportionately greater than in man because it acts principally on the immune system, which, under our assumptions, we have just shown to contribute a greater relative proportion of influence in mouse than it does in man. Thus, all other things equal, we could conclude that the effects of stress will be more perceptible in mouse in the overall picture of spontaneous cancer incidence than it is in man. Perhaps that is why, thus far, we have been able to find effects of stress in animals much more convincingly than in man.

Lest the reader gloss over the precise wording of the above, I did *not* say that stress has a more powerful effect in mouse than in man. Note the words, ". . . if we assume equal effects of stress in the two species. . . ." The above conclusions were derived subject to that assumption. If stress is, however, truly more powerful in man than in mouse, either positively or negatively, the net outcome would depend on the relative balance of influence. The paradigm would hold only until a crossover point were reached, and the conclusion would be reversed if we found out that stress is so much more powerful in its influence in man than in mouse as to overbear the excess relative importance of repair efficiency in man. This question remains to be determined (Ader, 1980).

In sum, first there is good reason to think that PF, both trait and state, affect the probability of a person getting cancer, but that they do so both damagingly and protectively. In any given case we cannot be sure which it will be, if they do, because the data on humans are not available, and because we cannot yet, even tentatively, make more than extremely ad hoc predictions in animals, let alone extrapolate to humans.

Second, the contribution of PF to cancer incidence is probably relatively small.

Third, the effect of PF, if it exists, is almost certainly specific to certain organ sites, and depends on several things. We do not know for what strain of animal or person, what attending circumstances, or what other determiners any given site will be more likely to be affected, if PF have an effect.

Fourth, compared to other protective or damaging biologic events, PF contribute a smaller proportion in humans than in animals, assuming there is a contribution.

The above summary is tentative, but I myself lean toward the view that these phenomena are indeed true, although I am not yet fully convinced.

ACKNOWLEDGMENTS

I would like to acknowledge with thanks discussions with several people who have given me the benefit of their knowledge and insight: Drs. J. Borysenko, M. Borysenko, P. Gullino, R. B. Herberman, H. T. Holden, and J. J. Mulvihill; and the help of C. Gonzales and S. Riddle, who contributed substantially to the production of this work.

REFERENCES

Ader, R. (1980). University of Rochester School of Medicine, Rochester, New York (personal communication).

Ames, B. N., Durston, W. E., Yamasaki, E., and Lee, F. D. (1973). Carcinogens are mutagens: A simple test system combining liver homogenates for activation and bacteria for detection. *Proc. Natl. Acad. Sci. U.S.A.* **70**, 2281–2285.

Anaclerio, A., Conti, G., Goggi, G., Honorati, M. C., Ruggeri, A., Moras, M. L., and Spreafico, F. (1980). Effect of cytotoxic agents on suppressor cells in mice. *Eur. J. Cancer* **16**, 53–58.

Anderson, D.E. (1975). Familial susceptibility. *In* "Persons at High Risk of Cancer" (J. F. Fraumeni, Jr., ed.), pp. 39–54. Academic Press, New York.

Armitage, P., and Doll, R. (1957). A two-stage theory of carcinogenesis in relation to the age distribution of human cancer. *Br. J. Cancer* **11**, 161–169.

Bahnson, C.B., ed. (1969). Second Conference on Psychophysiological Aspects of Cancer. *Ann. N.Y. Acad. Sci.* **164**, 307–634.

Bahnson, C. B., (1979). Jefferson Medical College, Philadelphia, Pennsylvania (personal communication).

Bahnson, C. B., and Kissen, D. M., eds. (1966). Psychophysiological aspects of cancer. *Ann. N.Y. Acad. Sci.* **125**, 773–1055.

Bakshi, K., Brusick, D., Bullock, L., and Bardin, C. W. (1977). Hormonal regulation of carcinogen metabolism in mouse kidney. *In* "Origins of Human Cancer" (H. H. Hiatt, J. D. Watson, and J. A. Winsten, eds.), Book B, pp. 683–695. Cold Spring Harbor Lab., Cold Spring Harbor, New York.

Bartrop, R. W. (1979), personal communication.

Bartrop, R. W., Luckhurst, E., Lazarus, L., Kiloh, L.G., and Penny, R. (1977). Depressed lymphocyte function after bereavement. *Lancet* **1**, 834–836.

Bast, R. C., Whitlock, J. P., Miller, A., Rapp, H. J. and Gelboin, H. V. (1974). Aryl hydrocarbon (benzo[a]pyrene) hydroxylase in human peripheral blood monocytes. *Nature* **250**, 664–665.

Bloom, B. (1980). Interferon and the immune system. *Nature (London)* **284**, 593–595.

Boraschi, D., and Meltzer, M. S. (1979). Macrophage activation for tumor cytotoxicity: Genetic variation in macrophage tumoricidal capacity among mouse strains. *Cell. Immunol.* **45**, 188–194.

Borek, C., and Sachs, L. (1968). The number of cell generations required to fix the transformed state in X-ray-induced transformation. *Proc. Natl. Acad. Sci. U.S.A.* **59**, 83–85.

Børresen, T., Palmgren, N., and Christensen, N. J. (1980). Absence of catecholamines in malignant tumors. *Eur. J. Cancer* **16**, 123–125.

Borysenko, M. (1981). Personal communication. Tufts U. School of Med., Boston, MA.

Bouillenne, C., and Deneufbourg, J.M. (1979). Positive correlation between breast cancer incidence and HLA antigens. *Oncology* **36**, 156–159.

Boutwell, R. K. (1974). The function and mechanism of promoters in carcinogenesis. *Crit. Rev. Toxicol.* **2**, 419–433.

Boyd, S. C., Sasame, H. A., and Boyd, M. R. (1979). High concentrations of glutathione in glandular stomach: Possible implications for carcinogenesis. *Science* **205**, 1010–1012.

Brand, K. G. (1975). Foreign body-induced sarcomas. *In* "Cancer: A Comprehensive Treatise" (F. F. Becker, ed.), Vol. 1, pp. 485–511. Plenum, New York.

Brand, K. G. (1976). Diversity and complexity of carcinogenic processes: Conceptual inferences from foreign-body tumorigenesis. *J. Natl. Cancer Inst.* **57**, 973–976.

Broder, S., and Waldmann, T. A. (1978). The suppressor-cell network in cancer. *N. Engl. J. Med.* **229**, 1281–1284, 1335–1341.

Brouty-Boye, D., and Little, J. B. (1977). Interferon enhances X-ray-induced transformation *in vitro*. *Cancer Res.* **37**, 2714–2716.

Burch, J. C., Byrd, B. F., and Vaughn, W. K. (1974). The effect of long-term estrogen on hysterectomized women. *Am. J. Obstet. Gynecol.* **118**, 778–782.

Burnet, F. M. (1957). Cancer—a biological approach. *Br. Med. J.* **1**, 779–786, 841–847.

Burnet, F. M. (1970). "Immunological Surveillance." Pergamon, Oxford.

Busbee, D. L., Shaw, C. R., and Cantrell, E. T. (1972). Aryl hydrocarbon hydroxylase induction in human leukocytes. *Science* **178**, 315–316.

Canter, A., Cluff, L. E., and Imboden, J. B. (1972). Hypersensitive reactions to immunization inoculations and antecedent psychological vulnerability. *J. Psychosom. Res.* **16**, 99–101.

Cantrell, E. T., Warr, G. A., Busbee, D. L., and Martin, R. R. (1973). Induction of aryl hydrocarbon hyroxylase in human pulmonary alveolar macrophages by cigarette smoking. *J. Clin. Invest.* **52**, 1881–1884.

Castro, J. E. (1978). "Immunological Aspects of Cancer." University Park Press, Baltimore, Maryland.

Chang, S. S., and Rasmussen, A. F. (1965). Stress-induced suppression of interferon production in virus-infested mice. *Nature (London)* **205**, 623–624.

Chino, F., Makinodan, T., Lever, W. E., and Peterson, W. J. (1971). The immune systems of mice reared in clean and in dirty conventional laboratory farms. I. Life expectancy and pathology of mice with long life-spans. *J. Gerontol.* **26**, 497–507.

Chu, E. W., and Malmgren, R. A. (1965). An inhibitory effect of vitamin A on the induction of tumors of forestomach and cervix in the Syrian hamster by carcinogenic polycyclic hydrocarbons. *Cancer Res.* **25**, 884–895.

Cleaver, J. E. (1977). Human diseases with *in vitro* manifestations of altered repair and replication of DNA. *In* "Genetics of Human Cancer" (J. J. Mulvihill, R. W. Miller, and J. F. Fraumeni, Jr., eds.), pp. 355–363. Raven, New York.

Cochran, A. J. (1978). *In vitro* testing of the immune response. *In* "Immunological Aspects of Cancer" (J. E. Castro, ed.), pp. 219–266. University Park Press, Baltimore, Maryland.

Cooke, T., George, D., Shields, R., Maynard, P., and Griffiths, K. (1979). Oestrogen receptors and prognosis in early breast cancer. *Lancet* 1, 995–997.

Corson, S. A. (1966). Neuroendocrine and behavioral response patterns to psychologic stress and the problem of the target tissue in cerebrovisceral pathology. *Ann. N.Y. Acad. Sci.* 125, 890–918.

Crowley, C., and Curtis, H. (1963). The development of somatic mutations in mice with age. *Proc. Natl. Acad. Sci. U.S.A.* 49, 626–628.

Cummings, K. B., Kodera, T., and Bean, M. A. (1978). *In vitro* immune parameters in relation to clinical course in transitional cell carcinoma. *Natl. Cancer Inst., Monogr.* 49, 78–1460.

Davies, J. N. P. (1975). Overview: Geographic opportunities and demographic leads. *In* "Persons at High Risk of Cancer" (J. R. Fraumeni, Jr., ed.), pp. 373–381. Academic Press, New York.

Dawe, C. J. (1973). Comparative neoplasia. *In* "Cancer Medicine" (J. F. Holland and E. Frei, eds.), pp. 193–240. Lea & Febiger, Philadelphia, Pennsylvania.

Day, N. E., and Brown, C. C. (1980). Multistage models and primary prevention of cancer. *J. Natl. Cancer Inst.* 64, 977–989.

Dean, J. H., Greene, M. H., Relmer, R. R., LeSane, F. V., McKeen, E. A., Mulvihill, J. J., Blattner, W. A., Herberman, R. B., and Fraumeni, J. F., Jr. (1979). Immunologic abnormalities in melanoma-prone families. *J. Natl. Cancer Inst.* 63, 1139–1145.

Dedrick, R. L., and Bischoff, K. B. (1980). Species similarities in pharmacokinetics. *Fed. Proc., Fed. Am. Soc. Exp. Biol.* 39, 54–59.

Devesa, S. S., and Silverman, D. T. (1978). Cancer incidence and mortality trends in the United States: 1935–74. *J. Natl. Cancer Inst.* 60, 545–571.

Dougherty, T. F. (1952). Effect of hormones on lymphatic tissue. *Physiol. Rev.* 32, 379–401.

Dworsky, R., Baptista, J., Parker, J., Chandor, S., Noble, G., Herrmann, K., Henle, W., and Henderson, B. (1978). Immune function in healthy relatives of patients with malignant disease. *J. Natl. Cancer Inst.* 60, 27–30.

Falk, H. L. (1980). Extrapolating carcinogenesis data from animals to humans. *Fed. Proc., Fed. Am. Soc. Exp. Biol.* 39, 76–80.

Fox, B. H. (1978). Premorbid psychological factors as related to cancer incidence. *J. Behav. Med.* 1, 45–133.

Fox, B. H., Boyd, S., van Kammen, D., and Rogentine, G. N. (1978). Further analysis of psychological variables in predicting relapse after stage II melanoma surgery. Presented at the Third International Symposium on Psychobiologic, Psychophysiologic, Psychosomatic and Sociosomatic Aspects of Neoplastic disease, Bohinj, Yugoslavia.

Fraumeni, J.F. (1975). "Persons at High Risk of Cancer." Academic Press, New York.

Fraumeni, J. F. (1979). Epidemiological studies in cancer. *In* "Carcinogens, Identification and Mechanisms of Action" (A. C. Griffin and C. R. Shaw, eds.), pp. 51–63. Raven, New York.

Friedberg, E. C., Ehmann, U. K., and Williams, J. I. (1979). Human diseases associated with defective DNA repair. *Adv. Radiat. Biol.* 8, 85–174.

Gilbert, J. R., ed. (1972). Conference on immunology of carcinogenesis. *Natl. Cancer Inst. Monogr.* 35.

Goldstein, G., and Mackay, I. R. (1969). "The Human Thymus." Warren H. Green, Inc., St. Louis, Missouri.

Good, R. A., and Gabrielsen, A. B., eds. (1964). "The Thymus in Immunobiology." Harper (Hoeber), New York.

Gordon, A. S. (1955). Some aspects of hormonal influences upon the leukocytes. *Ann. N.Y. Acad. Sci.* 59, 907–927.

Graham, S., Snell, L., Graham, J., and Ford, L. (1971). Social trauma in the epidemiology of cancer of the cervix. *J. Chronic Dis.* 24, 711–725.

Green, I., Cohen, S., and McCluskey, R. T., eds. (1977). "Mechanisms of Tumor Immunity." Wiley, New York.

Greene, W. A., Betts, R. F., Ochitill, H. N., Iker, H. P., and Douglas, R. G. (1978). Psychosocial factors and immunity; a preliminary report. *Psychosom. Med.* **40**, 87 (abstr.).

Greenwald, P., Barlow, J. J., and Nasca, P. C. (1971). Vaginal cancer after maternal treatment with synthetic estrogens. *N. Engl. J. Med.* **285**, 390-393.

Greer, S., Morris, T., and Pettingale, K. W. (1979). Psychological response to breast cancer: effect on outcome. *Lancet* **2**, 785-787.

Grover, P. L., Hewer, A., and Sims, P. (1973). K-region epoxides of polycyclic hydrocarbons: Formation and further metabolism of benz(a)anthracene 5, 6-oxide by human lung preparations. *FEBS Lett.* **34**, 63-68.

Hart, R. W., and Setlow, R. B. (1974). Correlation between deoxyriboneucleic acid excision-repair and life-span in a number of mammalian species. *Proc. Natl. Acad. Sci. U.S.A.* **71**, 2169-2173.

Hart, R. W., Setlow, R. B., and Woodhead, A. D. (1977). Evidence that pyrimidine dimers in DNA can give rise to tumors. *Proc. Natl. Acad. Sci. U.S.A.* **74**, 5574-5578.

Hayes, H. M., Jr. (1978). The comparative epidemiology of selected neoplasms between dogs, cats, and humans. A review. *Eur. J. Cancer* **14**, 1299-1308.

Henderson, B. E., Louie, E., Jing, J. S. H., Buell, P., and Gardner, M. B. (1976). Risk factors associated with nasopharyngeal carcinoma. *N. Engl. J. Med.* **295**, 1101-1106.

Henney, C. S. (1977). Mechanisms of tumor cell destruction. *In* "Mechanisms of Tumor Immunity" (I. Green, S. Cohen, and R. T. McCluskey, eds.), pp. 55-86. Wiley, New York.

Henry, J. P., and Stephens, P. M. (1977). "Stress, Health, and the Social Environment." Springer-Verlag, Berlin and New York.

Herberman, R. B., and Holden, H. T. (1978). Natural cell-mediated immunity. *Adv. Cancer Res.* **27**, 305-377.

Herberman, R. B., and Holden, H. T. (1979). Natural killer cells as antitumor effector cells. *J. Natl. Cancer Inst.* **62**, 441-445.

Herberman, R. B., and McIntire, K. R., eds. (1979). "Immunodiagnosis of Cancer," Vols. 1 and 2. Dekker, New York.

Hersey, P., Edwards, A., Trilivas, C., Shaw, H., and Milton, G. W. (1979). Relationship of natural killer-cell activity to rhesus antigens in man. *Br. J. Cancer* **39**, 234-240.

Hertz, R. (1977). The estrogen-cancer hypothesis with special emphasis on DES. *In* "Origins of Human Cancer" (H. H. Hiatt, J. D. Watson, and J. A. Winsten, eds.) Book C, pp. 1665-1673. Cold Spring Harbor Lab., Cold Spring Harbor, New York.

Heston, W. E. (1975). Testing for possible effects of cedar wood shavings and diet on occurrence of mammary gland tumors and hepatomas in C3H-A^{vy} and C3H-A^{vy}fB mice. *J. Natl. Cancer Inst.* **54**, 1011-1014.

Hewitt, H. B., Blake, E. R., and Walder, A. S. (1976). A critique of the evidence for active host defence against cancer, based on personal studies of twenty-seven murine tumours of spontaneous origin. *Br. J. Cancer* **33**, 241-258.

Hiatt, H. H., Watson, J. D., and Winsten, J. A., eds. (1977). "Origins of Human Cancer" Books A, B, and C. Cold Spring Harbor Lab., Cold Spring Harbor, New York.

Hirsch, J. (1967). "Behavior-Genetic Analysis." McGraw-Hill, New York.

Holden, H. T., personal communication, 1980.

Holliday, R. (1979). A new theory of carcinogenesis. *Br. J. Cancer* **40**, 513-522.

Hoover, R. (1977). Effects of drugs—immunosuppression. *In* "Origins of Human Cancer" (H. H. Hiatt, J. D. Watson, and J. A. Winsten, eds.), Book A, Vol. 4, pp. 369-379. Cold Spring Harbor Lab., Cold Spring Harbor, New York.

Hoover, R., and Fraumeni, J. F., Jr. (1973). Risk of cancer in renal-transplant recipients. *Lancet* **2**, 55-57.

Hopkin, J. M., and Evans, H. J. (1980). Cigarette smoked-induced DNA damage and lung cancer risks. *Nature (London)* **283**, 388–390.

Huddlestone, J.R., Merigan, T. C., Jr., and Oldstone, M. B. A. (1979). Induction and kinetics of natural killer-cells in humans following interferon therapy. *Nature (London)* **282**, 417–419.

Huseby, R. A. (1980). Demonstration of a direct carcinogenic effect of estradiol on Leydig cells of the mouse. *Cancer Res.* **40**, 1006–1013.

Jacobs, S., and Ostfeld, A. (1977). An epidemiological review of bereavement. *Psychosom. Med.* **39**, 344–357.

Jensen, M. M. (1968). Transitory impairment of interferon produced in stressed mice. *J. Infect. Dis.* **118**, 230–234.

Jones, T. C., Hackel, D. B., and Migaki, G., eds. (1979). "Handbook: Animal Model of Human Disease." Registry of Comparative Pathology, Armed Forces Institute of Pathology, Washington, D.C.

Kakunaga, T. (1975). The role of cell division in the malignant transformation of mouse cells treated with 3-methylcholanthrene. *Cancer Res.* **35**, 1637–1642.

Kališnik, M., Vraspir-Porenta, O., Logonder-Mlinšek, Zorc, M., and Pajntar, M. (1979). Stress and Ehrlich ascites tumor in mouse. *Neoplasma* **26**, 483–491.

Kärre, K., Klein, G. O., Kiessling, R., Klein, G., and Roder, J. C. (1980). Low natural *in vivo* resistance to syngeneic leukemias in natural killer-deficient mice. *Nature (London)* **284**, 624–626.

Kavetskii, R. E., ed. (1958). "The Neoplastic Process and the Nervous System." State Medical Publishing House, Kiev (translated from the Russian and available from the National Technical Information Service, Springfield, VA 22151, No. 60–21860).

Keith, L., and Brown, E. (1971). Epidemiologic study of leukemia in twins (1929–1969). *Acta Genet. Med. Gemellol.* **20**, 9–20.

Kellermann, G., Shaw, C. R., and Luyten-Kellermann, M. (1973). Aryl hydrocarbon hydroxylase inducibility and bronchogenic carcinoma. *N. Engl. J. Med.* **289**, 934–937.

Kelsey, J. L. (1979). A review of the epidemiology of human breast cancer. *Epidemiol. Rev.* **1**, 74–109.

Kersey, J. H., and Spector, B. D. (1975). Immune deficiency diseases. *In* "Persons at High Risk of Cancer" (J. J. Fraumeni, Jr., ed.), pp. 55–66. Academic Press, New York.

Kersey, J. H., Spector, B. D., and Good, R. A. (1973). Primary immunodeficiency diseases and cancer: The immunodeficiency-cancer registry. *Int. J. Cancer* **12**, 333–347.

Kessler, I. I. (1974). Perspectives on the epidemiology of cervical cancer with special reference to the herpesvirus hypothesis. *Cancer Res.* **34**, 1091–1110.

Kirchner, H. (1978). Suppressor cells of immune reactivity in malignancy. *Eur. J. Cancer* **14**, 453–459.

Kissen, D. M. (1967). Psychosocial factors, personality and lung cancer in men aged 55–64. *Br. J. Med. Psychol.* **40**, 29–43.

Knudson, A. G. (1975). Genetics of human cancer. *Genetics* **79**, Suppl., 305–316.

Korenman, S. (1980). Oestrogen window hypothesis of the aetiology of breast cancer. *Lancet* **1**, 700–701.

Kouri, R. E., and Nebert, D. W. (1977). Genetic regulation of susceptibility to polycyclic-hydrocarbon-induced tumors in the mouse. *In* "Origins of Human Cancer" (H. H. Hiatt, J. D. Watson, and J. A. Winsten, eds.), Book B, pp. 811–835. Cold Spring Harbor Lab., Cold Spring Harbor, New York.

Kripke, M. L., and Boros, T. (1974). Immunosuppression and carcinogenesis. *Isr. J. Med. Sci.* **10**, 888–903.

Kuntzman, R., Mark, L. C., Brand, L., Jacobson, M., Levin, W., and Conney, A. H. (1966). Metabolism of drugs and carcinogens by human liver enzymes. *J. Pharmacol. Exp. Ther.* **152**, 151–156.

Kurland, G., Christensen, A. K., and Huseby, R. A. (1975). Changes in fine structure accompanying estrogen tumorigenesis of Leydig cells in the mouse testis. *Cancer Res.* **35,** 1671-1686.

LaBarba, R. C. (1970). Experiential and environmental factors in cancer: A review of research with animals. *Psychosom. Med.* **32,** 259-276.

Lasfargues, E. Y., and Feldman, D. G. (1963). Hormonal and physiological background in the production of B particles by the mouse mammary epithelium in organ cultures. *Cancer Res.* **23,** 191-196.

Lawler, E. M., and Prehn, R. T. (1980). Influence of immune status of host on immunogenicity of tumors induced with two doses of methylcholanthrene. In preparation. Jackson Laboratory, Bar Harbor, Maine.

Leeper, E. (1980). Re: "Electrical wiring configurations and childhood leukemia in Rhode Island." *Am. J. Epidemiol.* **111,** 461-462.

Lehmann, A. (1979). Genetic clues to cancer. *New Sci.* **84,** 686-688.

Little, J. B. (1977). Radiation transformation *in vitro*: Implications for mechanisms. *In* "Origins of Human Cancer" (H. H. Hiatt, J. D. Watson, and J. A. Winsten, eds.), Book B, pp. 923-939. Cold Spring Harbor Lab., Cold Spring Harbor, New York.

Locke, S. E., and Heisel, J. S. (1977). The influence of stress and emotions on the human immune response. *Biofeedback Self-Regul.* **2,** 320 (abstr.).

Locke, S. E., Hurst, M. W., Heisel, J. S., Kraus, L., and Williams, R. M. (1979). The influence of stress and other psychosocial factors on human immunity. Presented at *Am. Psychosom. Soc. Meet.* (Unpublished) Dept. Biol. Sci. & Psychosom. Med., Boston U. School of Medicine, Boston, MA.

Lynch, H. T., and Krush, A. J. (1973). Genetic factors in families with combined gastrointestinal and breast cancer. *Am. J. Gastroenterol.* **59,** 31-40.

McClelland, D. C., and Jemmott, J. B., III. (1980). Power motivation, stress and physical illness. *J. Human Stress* **6,** 6-15.

McClelland, D. C., Locke, S. E., Williams, R. E., and Hurst, M. W. (1980). "Power motivation, distress and immune function." Unpublished report, Dept. of Biological Sci. and Psychosom. Med., Boston U. School of Med., Boston, MA.

McGrath, C. M. (1971). Replication of mammary tumor virus in tumor cell cultures: Dependence on hormone-induced cellular organization. *J. Natl. Cancer Inst.* **47,** 445-467.

MacKenzie, W. F., and Gardner, F. M. (1973). Comparison of neoplasms in six sources of rats. *J. Natl. Cancer Inst.* **50,** 1243-1257.

MacMahon, B., Cole, P., and Brown, J. (1973). Etiology of breast cancer: A review. *J. Natl. Cancer Inst.* **50,** 21-43.

Mattern, J., Wayss, K., Haag, D., Toomes, H., and Volm, M. (1980). Different growth rates of lung tumours in man and their xenographs in nude mice. *Eur. J. Cancer* **16,** 289-291.

Mattson, J., Alpsten, M., Appelgren, L., and Peterson, H. I. (1980). Influence of noradrenaline on local tumour blood flow. *Eur. J. Cancer* **16,** 99-102.

Mehta, R. G., Fricks, C. M., and Moon, R. C. (1980). Androgen receptors in chemically-induced colon carcinogenesis. *Cancer* **45,** 1085-1089.

Metcalf, D. (1966). "The Thymus. Recent Results in Cancer Research." Springer-Verlag, Berlin and New York.

Meyer, K. F. (1942). The ecology of psittacosis and ornithosis. *Medicine (Baltimore)* **21,** 175-206.

Miller, D. G. (1980). On the nature of susceptibility to cancer. *Cancer* **46,** 1307-1318.

Miller, J. A. (1970). Carcinogenesis by chemicals: An overview. *Cancer Res.* **30,** 559-576.

Miller, J. A., and Miller, E. C. (1977). Ultimate chemical carcinogens as reactive mutagenic electrophiles. *In* "Origins of Human Cancer" (H. H. Hiatt, J. D. Watson, and J. A. Winsten, eds.), Book B, pp. 605-627. Cold Spring Harbor Lab., Cold Spring Harbor, New York.

Mondal, S., and Heidelberger, C. (1976). Transformation of $C3H/10T\frac{1}{2}$ C18 mouse embryo fibroblasts by ultraviolet irradiation and a phorbol ester. *Nature* **260,** 710-711.

Moolgavkar, S. H., and Venzon, D. J. (1979). Two event models for carcinogenesis: Incidence curves for childhood and adult tumors. *Math. Biosci.* **47**, 55–77.

Moolgavkar, S. H., Day, N. E., and Stevens, R. G. (1980). Two stage model for carcinogenesis: Epidemiology of breast cancer in females. *J. Natl. Cancer Inst.* **65**, 559–570.

Morrison, F. R. (1980a). Psychosocial factors in the etiology of cancer. Ph.D. Dissertation, University of California at Berkeley.

Morrison, F. R., and Pattenbarger, R. S., Jr. (1980b). Epidemiologic aspects of biobehavior in the etiology of cancer: A critical review *In* "Perspectives on Behavioral Medicine" (S. M. Weiss, J. A. Herd, and B. H. Fox, eds.), pp. 135–161. Academic Press, New York (in press).

Mulvihill, J. J. (1977). Genetic repertory of human neoplasia. *In* "Genetics of Human Cancer" (J. J. Mulvihill, R. W. Miller, and J. F. Fraumeni, Jr., eds.), pp. 137–143. Raven, New York.

Mulvihill, J. J. (1979). Host factors in human lung tumors: An example of ecogenetics in oncology. *J. Natl. Cancer Inst., Monogr.* **52**, 115–121.

Mulvihill, J. J. (1980). National Cancer Institute, Bethesda, Maryland (personal communication).

Mulvihill, J. J., Miller, R. W., and Fraumeni, J. F., Jr., eds. (1977). "Genetics of Human Cancer." Raven, New York.

Munster, A. M. (1976). Post-traumatic immunosuppression is due to activation of suppressor T cells. *Lancet* **1**, 1329–1330.

Nakai, T. (1961). Influence of small doses of various corticosteroids on the incidence of chemically induced subcutaneous sarcomas in mice. *Cancer Res.* **21**, 221–222.

Nance, W. E. (1977). Relevance of twin studies in cancer research. *In* "Genetics of Human Cancer" (J. J. Mulvihill, R. W. Miller, and J. F. Fraumeni, Jr., eds.), pp. 27–38. Raven, New York.

Newberry, B. H. (1978). Restraint-induced inhibition of 7, 12-dimethylbenz-(a)anthracene-induced mammary tumors: Relation to stages of tumor development. *J. Natl. Cancer Inst.* **61**, 725–729.

Noble, R. L., and Hoover, L. (1975). A classification of transplant tumors in Nb rats controlled by estrogen from dormancy to autonomy. *Cancer Res.* **35**, 2935–2941.

Paigen, B., Gurtoo, H. L., Minowada, J., Houten, L., Vincent, R., Paigen, K., Parker, N. B., Ward, E., and Hayner, N. T. (1977). Questionable relation of aryl hydrocarbon hydroxylase to lung cancer risk. *N. Engl. J. Med.* **297**, 346–350.

Palmblad, J., Cantell, K., Strander, H., Froberg, J., Karlsson, C., Levi, L., Granstrom, M., and Unger, P. (1976). Stressor exposure and immunological response in man: Interferon producing capacity and phagocytosis. *J. Psychosom. Res.* **20**, 193–199.

Palmblad, J., Petrini, B., Wasserman, J., and Akerstedt, T. (1979). Lymphocyte and granulocyte reactions during sleep deprivation. *Psychosom. Med.* **41**, 273–278.

Pavelič, K., and Hršak, I. (1978). Effects of immunosuppression on the growth of six murine tumors. *Z. Krebsforsch.* **92**, 147–156.

Peto, R. (1977). Epidemiology, multistage models, and short-term mutagenicity tests. *In* "Origins of Human Cancer" (H. H. Hiatt, H. D. Watson, and J. A. Winsten, eds.), Book C, pp. 1403–1428. Cold Spring Harbor Lab., Cold Spring Harbor, New York.

Pettingale, K. W., Greer, S., and Tee, D. E. H. (1977a). Serum IGA and emotional expression in breast cancer patients. *J. Psychosom. Res.* **21**, 395–399.

Pettingale, K. W., Merrett, T. G., and Tee, D. E. H. (1977b). Prognostic value of serum levels of immunoglobulins (IgG, IgA, IgM, and IgE) in breast cancer: A preliminary study. *Br. J. Cancer* **36**, 550–557.

Pierce, G. B. (1977). Relationship between differentiation and carcinogenesis. *J. Toxicol. Environ. Health* **2**, 1335–1342.

Pierpaoli, W., and Maestroni, G. J. M. (1977). Pharmacological control of the immune response by blockade of the early hormonal changes following antigen injection. *Cell. Immunol.* **31**, 355–363.

Pimentel, E. (1979). Human oncovirology. *Biochim. Biophys. Acta* **560**, 169–216.

Pollock, E. J., and Todaro, G. J. (1968). Radiation enhancement of SV40 transformation in 3T3 and human cells. *Nature (London)* **219**, 520–521.

Poland, A., and Kende, A. The genetic expression of aryl hydrocarbon hydroxylase activity: Evidence for a receptor mutation in nonresponsive mice. *In* "Origins of Human Cancer" (H. H. Hiatt, J. D. Watson, and J. A. Winsten, eds.). Book B. pp. 847–867. Cold Spring Harbor Lab., Cold Spring Harbor, New York.

Pontén, J. (1977). Abnormal cell growth (neoplasia) and aging. *In* "Handbook of the Biology of Aging" (C. E. Finch and L. Hayflick, eds.), pp. 536–560. Van Nostrand-Reinhold, Princeton, New Jersey.

Prehn, R. T. (1974). Immunological surveillance: Pro and con. *Clin. Immunobiol.* **2**, 191–203.

Prehn, R. T. (1979). Immunological basis for differences in susceptibility to hydrocarbon oncogenesis among mice of a single genotype. *Int. J. Cancer* **24**, 789–791.

Purchase, I. F. H. (1980). Inter-species comparisons of carcinogenicity. *Br. J. Cancer* **41**, 454–468.

Qureshi, S. A., and Zaman, H. (1966). The effect of small doses of prednisolone on the incidence of subcutaneous sarcomas induced by 3-methylcholanthrene in virgin female Swiss mice. *Cancer Res.* **26**, 1516–15.

Rampen, F. H. J., and Mulder, J. H. (1980). Malignant melanoma: An androgen-dependent tumour? *Lancet* **1**, 562–565.

Ramsey, J. C., and Gehring, P. J. (1980). Application of pharmacokinetic principles in practice. *Fed. Proc., Fed. Am. Soc. Exp. Biol.* **39**, 60–65.

Rasmussen, A. F., Hildemann, W. H., and Sellers, M. (1963). Malignancy of polynoma virus infection in mice in relation to stress. *J. Natl. Cancer Inst.* **30**, 101–112.

Riley, V. (1975). Mouse mammary tumors: Alteration of incidence as apparent function of stress. *Science* **189**, 465–467.

Riley, V. (1979). Cancer and stress: overview and critique. *Cancer Detect. Prev.* **2**, 163–195.

Riley V. (1980). Biobehavioral factors in animal work on tumorigenesis. *In* "Perspectives on Behavioral Medicine" (S. M. Weiss, J. A. Herd, and B. H. Fox, eds.), pp. 183–214. Academic Press, New York (in press).

Riley, V., Spackman, D., McClanahan, H., and Santisteban, G. A. (1979). The role of stress in malignancy. *Cancer Detect. Prev.* **2**, 235–255.

Riley, V., Fitzmaurice, M. A., and Spackman, D. H. (1980). Animal models in biobehavioral research: effects of anxiety stress on immunocompetence and neoplasia. *In* "Perspectives in Behavioral Medicine" (S. M. Weiss, J. A. Herd, and B. H. Fox, eds.), pp. 371–400. Academic Press, New York (in press).

Ristow, S., and McKhann, C. R. (1977). Tumor-associated antigens. *In* "Mechanisms of Tumor Immunity" (I. Green, S. Cohen, and R. T. McCluskey, eds.), pp. 109–145. Wiley, New York.

Roessler, R. (1980). Baylor College of Medicine, Houston, Texas (personal communication).

Roessler, R., Cato, T. R., Lester, J. W., and Couch, R. B. (1979). Ego strength, life events and antibody titer. *Am. Psychosom. Soc. Meet.* (Unpublished). Baylor College of Medicine, Houston, Texas.

Rogentine, G. N., Jr., van Kammen, D. P., Fox, B. H., Docherty, J. P., Rosenblatt, J. E., Boyd, S. C., and Bunney, W. E. (1979). Psychological factors in the prognosis of malignant melanoma: A prospective study. *Psychosom. Med.* **41**, 647–655.

Rubin, H. (1980). Is somatic mutation the major mechanism of malignant transformation? *J. Natl. Cancer Inst.* **64**, 995–1000.

Russfield, A. B. (1966). "Tumors of Endocrine and Secondary Sex Organs." U.S. Dept. of Health, Education, and Welfare, Washington, D.C.

Rytel, M. W., and Kilbourne, E. F. (1966). The influence of cortisone on experimental viral infection. *J. Exp. Med.* **123**, 767–775.

Sabes, W. R., Chaudhry, A. P., and Gorlin, R. J. (1963). Effects of cortisone on chemical carcinogenesis in hamster pouch and submandibular salivary gland. *J. Dent. Res.* **42**, 1118–1130.

Sabine, J. R., Horton, B. J., and Wicks, M. B. (1973). Spontaneous tumors in C3H-A and C3H-A fB mice: High incidence in the United States and low incidence in Australia. *J. Natl. Cancer Inst.* **50**, 1237–1242.

Schleifer, S. J., Keller, S. E., McKegney, F. P., and Stein, M. (1980). Bereavement and lymphocyte function. Paper given at *Am. Psychiatr. Assoc. Meet.* (Unpublished). Dept. of Psychiatry, Mt. Sinai School of Med., New York, N.Y. 10029.

Schmale, A. H., and Iker, H. P. (1966). The effect of hopelessness and the development of cancer. I. Identification of uterine cervical cancer in women with a typical cytology. *Psychosom. Med.* **28**, 714–721.

Schoental, R. (1974). Role of podophyllotoxin in the bedding and dietary zearalenone on incidence of spontaneous tumors in laboratory animals. *Cancer Res.* **34**, 2149–2420.

Seifter, E. (1976). Of stress, vitamin A, and tumors. *Science* **193**, 74–75.

Seifter, E. (1980). Albert Einstein College of Medicine, New York (personal communication).

Selikoff, I. J., and Hammond, E. C., eds. (1979). Health hazards of asbestos exposure. *Ann. N.Y. Acad. Sci.* **330**, 1–814.

Shackney, S. E. (1980). National Institutes of Health, Bethesda, Maryland (personal communication).

Shyamala, G., and Dickson, C. (1976). Relationship between receptor and mammary tumor virus production after stimulation of glucocorticoid. *Nature (London)* **262**, 107–112.

Simon, R. H., Lovett, E. J., III, Tomaszek, D., and Lundy, J. (1980). Electrical stimulation of the midbrain mediates metastic tumor growth. *Science* **209**, 1132–1133.

Simons, M. J., Wee, G. B., Day, N. E., Morris, P. J., Shanmugaratnam, K., and De-Thé, G. B. (1974). Immunogenetic aspects of nasopharyngeal carcinoma. 1. Differences in HL-A antigen profiles between patients and control groups. *Int. J. Cancer* **13**, 122–134.

Snyder, R. E., Watson, R. C., and Cruz, N. (1979). Graphic stress telethermometry (GST^{TM}). *Am. J. Diagn. Gynecol. Obstet.* **1**, 197–201.

Solomon, G. F., and Amkraut, A. A. (1979). Neoendocrine aspects of the immune response and their implications for stress effects on tumor immunity. *Cancer Detect. Prev.* **2**, 179–224.

Solomon, G. F., Merigan, T. C., and Levine, S. (1967). Variation in adrenal cortical hormones within physiologic ranges, stress, and interferon production in mice. *Proc. Soc. Exp. Biol. Med.* **126**, 74–79.

Stein, M. (1980). Mount Sinai School of Medicine, New York (personal communication).

Stoker, M. (1963). Effect of X-irradiation on susceptibility of cells to transformation by polyoma virus. *Nature (London)* **200**, 756–758.

Storer, J. B. (1966). Longevity and gross pathology at death in twenty-two inbred mouse strains. *J. Gerontol.* **21**, 404–409.

Stutman, O. (1972). Immunologic studies on resistance to oncogenic agents in mice. *Natl. Cancer Inst., Monogr.* **35**, 107–115.

Takasugi, M., Terasaki, P. I., Henderson, G., Mickey, M. R., Menk, H., and Thompson, R. W. (1973). HL-A antigens in solid tumors. *Cancer Res.* **33**, 648–650.

Teasdale, C., Hillyard, J. W., Webster, D. J. T., Bolton, P. M., and Hughes, L. E. (1979). Pretreatment general immune competence and prognosis in breast cancer. A prospective 2-year follow-up. *Eur. J. Cancer* **15**, 975–982.

Tee, D. E. H. and Pettingale, K. W. (1974). Breast cancer and the immune response. *Br. J. Surg.* **61**, 775–777.

Terasaki, P. I., Perdue, S. T., and Mickey, M. R. (1977). HLA frequencies in cancer: a second study. *In* "Genetics of Human Cancer" (J. J. Mulvihill, R. W. Miller, and J. F. Fraumeni, Jr., eds.), pp. 137–143. Raven, New York.

Terzaghi, M., and Little, J. B. (1974). Interactions between radiation and benzo(a)pyrene in an *in vitro* model for malignant transformation. *In* "Experimental Lung Cancer: Carcinogenesis and Bioassays" (E. Karbe and J. F. Parks, eds.), pp. 497–506. Springer-Verlag, Berlin and New York.

Thorgeirsson, S. S., Wirth, P. J., Nelson, W. L., and Lambert, G. H. (1977). Genetic regulation of metabolism and mutagenicity of 2-acetylaminofluorene and related compounds in mice. *In* "Origins of Human Cancer" (H. H. Hiatt, J. D. Watson, and J. A. Winsten, eds.), Book B, pp. 869–886. Cold Spring Harbor Lab., Cold Spring Harbor, New York.

Todaro, G. T., and Green, H. (1966). Cell growth and the initiation of transformation. *Proc. Natl. Acad. Sci. U.S.A.* **55**, 302–308.

Trichopoulos, D., MacMahon, B., and Brown, J. (1980). Socioneconomic status, urine estrogens, and breast cancer risk. *J. Natl. Cancer Inst.* **64**, 753–755.

Tutton, P. J. M., and Barkla, D. H. (1980). Neural control of colonic cell proliferation. *Cancer* **45**, 1172–1177.

Upton, A. C. (1977). Pathobiology. *In* "Handbook of the Biology of Aging" (C. E. Finch and L. Hayflick, eds.), pp. 513–535. Van Nostrand-Reinhold, Princeton, New Jersey.

Vessey, M. P., Doll, R., Norman-Smith, B., and Hill, I. D. (1979). Thymectomy and cancer: A further report. *Br. J. Cancer* **39**, 193–195.

Wakisaka, J., Inokuchi, T., and Kakizoe, K. (1972). Correlation between cancer of the stomach and alopecia. *Kurume Med. J.* **19**, 245–251.

Walters, H. (1978). "Handbook of Cancer Immunology," Vol. 1. Garland STPM Press, New York.

Wattenberg, L. W. (1972). Inhibition of carcinogenic and toxic effects of polycyclic hydrocarbons by phenolic anti-oxidants and ethoxyquin. *J. Natl. Cancer Inst.* **48**, 1425–1430.

Wayner, L., Cox, T., and Mackay, C. (1979). Stress, immunity and cancer. *In* "Research in Psychology and Medicine" (D. J. Osbourne, M. M. Gruenberg and J. R. Eiser, eds.), Vol. 1, pp. 108–116. Academic Press, New York.

Wertheimer, N., and Leeper, E. (1979). Electrical wiring configurations and childhood cancer. *Am. J. Epidemiol.* **109**, 273–284.

Wheelock, E. F., Caroline, N. L., and Moore, R. D. (1969). Suppression of established Friend virus leukemia by statolon. *J. Virol.* **4**, 1–6.

Whitehead, R. H., Roberts, G. P., Hughes, L. E., and Thatcher, H. (1978). Importance of methodology in demonstrating depression of T-lymphocyte levels. *Br. J. Cancer* **37**, 28–32.

Whittemore, A. S., and Keller, J. B. (1978). Quantitative theories of carcinogenesis. *SIAM Rev.* **20**, 1–30.

Young, J. L., Jr., Asire, A. J., and Pollock, E. S. (1978). "Cancer Incidence and Mortality in the United States, 1973–1976." U.S. Dept. of Health, Education and Welfare, National Cancer Institute, Bethesda, Maryland.

Zeil, H. K., and Finkle, W. D. (1975). Increased risk of endometrial cancer among users of conjugated estrogens. *N. Engl. J. Med.* **293**, 1167–1170.

Emotional and Personality Factors in the Onset and Course of Autoimmune Disease, Particularly Rheumatoid Arthritis

INTRODUCTION

Correlations among personality variables, life events, psychological defenses, affects, and various disease states are many in psychosomatic literature. Controversy persists about the specificity of emotional factors for particular diseases and about the role of disease itself in inducing observed personality traits. Resolution of such disputes hopefully will emerge from predictive studies and from a greater understanding of physiological mechanisms, particularly neuroendocrine, by which environmental factors and mental events may play a role in the pathogenesis of disease. Even disease with known "etiologic agents" are multifactoral in cause, involving genetic, behavioral, nervous, endocrine, and immune interrelationships (Salk, 1962).

Host resistance and immunity and their relationship to stress and integrity of psychological defenses may provide an underlying and unifying principle relating emotional factors in onset and course of infectious diseases, in which humoral immunity plays an important defensive role, and of cancer, the resistance to which increasing evidence finds to be related to cellular immunity that may function as a surveillance mechanism against the neoplastic cell whether induced by radiation, carcinogen, or chance somatic mutation. The following quotes are relevant. "To develop chronic active pulmonary tuber-

159

Copyright © 1981 by Academic Press, Inc.
All rights of reproduction in any form reserved.
ISBN 0-12-043780-5

culosis a person needs some bacilli, some moderately inflammable lungs (not celluloid like the guinea pig's nor asbestos like the elephant's) and some internal or external factor which lowers the resistance to the disease" (Day, 1951). "Perhaps some event reducing immunologic competence at a critical time may allow a mutant cell to thrive and grow" (Habel, 1963).

Autoimmune diseases comprise a variety of conditions in which "horror autotoxicus" fails, and humoral or cellular immunity to some component(s) of self occurs. Autoimmune diseases are generally agreed to include rheumatoid arthritis, thyroiditis, acquired hemolytic anemia, systemic lupus erythematosus, myasthenia gravis, polyarteritis nodosa, and polymyositis. Autoimmunity has been implicated in demyelinating diseases, including multiple sclerosis, Graves' disease, idiopathic thrombocytopenic purpura, ulcerative colitis, and may play a role in some cases of pernicious anemia, diabetes, and Addison's disease (Sampter and Alexander, 1965). The role of autoantibodies themselves in producing the lesions in autoimmune diseases remain uncertain, and they may even have a protective effect (Paterson et al., 1965). Clinically and serologically, there are many overlapping features and unclear boundaries among the diseases. Autoimmune diseases seem to be associated with states of relative immunologic deficiency (Fudenberg, 1968). These diseases occur with relative frequency in patients and in experimental animals with immunologic deficiency states and with neoplastic diseases of immunologically competent cells. Recent work suggests that the critical immunologic deficiency in autoimmune disease is a lack of suppressor T-cell function, which serves an immunoregulatory function (Reinherz et al., 1979; Allison et al., 1971). Genetic susceptibility, viruses, and a defective immune system all appear to be involved in the complex etiology of autoimmune diseases. Autoimmune damage may result from specific autoantibodies, self-directed immunologically competent cells, or deposition of antigen–antibody complexes (MacKay, 1964).

This volume amply documents evidence for a role of the central nervous system in regulation of immunity, including discussions of the hypothalamus and the immune system, conditioning of immune responses, and evidence for immunologic abnormalities in conjunction with mental illness. Other chapters outline the effects of stress on immunologic competence in men and animals. It is my hypothesis that stress, more correctly, its subjective equivalent "strain" or emotional distress, may influence the function of the immunologic system via central nervous system and neuroendocrine mediation. Such experientially altered immunologic competence may play a role in the specific immunologic deficiency state related to autoimmunity. This chapter serves the function of documenting evidence that personality traits may predispose toward autoimmune disease, particularly rheumatoid arthritis, and that emotional stress and decompensation of psychological defenses may play a role in its onset and course. It is gratifying to realize that considerable research evidence for links among emotions immunity and disease is developing, a speculative hypothesis originally introduced by Solomon and Moos in 1964.

Great recent strides in understanding the enormously complex immune system have made far more feasible an unraveling of the influences of various neuroendocrines and neurotransmittors on specific components of the immune response, recently reviewed by Solomon et al. (1979), by Rogers et al. (1979); and by Solomon and Amkraut (1981).

REVIEW OF THE LITERATURE ON PSYCHOSOMATIC ASPECTS OF RHEUMATOID ARTHRITIS

Moos (1963) reviewed published reports on personality involving data over 5000 patients with rheumatoid arthritis appearing in the literature. Many early investigators who did not utilize control groups agreed that emotional factors played a role in rheumatoid arthritis but differed in which factors were cited. Worry, pressure of work, marital disharmony, and real or threatened loss of relatives could be documented immediately prior to onset of disease in nearly half the cases of one series (Ellman and Mitchell, 1936). Twenty rheumatoid arthritics were described as decent looking, quiet, cheerful, reliable, conscientious, tending to hold the same job, self-limited, and restricted in their expression of feelings and frigid (Halliday, 1942). Halliday's patients described their parents as strict and described themselves as shy and retiring in school, self-sacrificing, as having few friends but being loyal to them, and as being orderly, punctual, tidy, and clean. An interview study of 43 arthritics concluded that they were immature, dependent, perfectionistic people who tried to please and that the onset of their disease was often preceded by separation or loss of support (Robinson, 1957).

A psychoanalytic study of eight cases found a constant personality present before the onset of disease (Ludwig, 1955). Rheumatoid arthritics were extremely dependent, felt inadequate, had difficulty coping with their environment and with other people, and were severely blocked in emotional expression. They frequently denied their dependency by overcompensating with an outward facade of independence, self-assurance, and self-control. Their attitude towards work and responsibility varied from an attempt to negate their dependence, both by accepting far more responsibility than they could handle and by overwork, to a manifestation of their dependency and inadequacy by avoidance of all responsibility and reliance upon others for guidance. They avoided closeness, were aware of strong unexpressible angry feelings, reacted oversensitively to the slightest criticism or rejection, and tended to court others' favor, allowing themselves to be imposed upon. The patients also appeared to deal with their tensions defensively by varying degrees of overactivity. Ludwig agreed with others in stating that the single most important precipitating factor was the loss of, or separation from, important key figures upon whom these patients depended for support.

A clinical study of 33 patients concluded that patients learned to discharge aggression through muscle activity in ego syntonic channels, for example, hard work, sports, gardening, and to relieve their guilt over this aggression by serving others (Johnson *et al.,* 1947). Arthritic females tended to reject the feminine role, a rejection which was manifested by their being head of the house, by making decisions, and by a predilection for the masculine posture in sexual relationships. The competitive relation with men served as a discharge for hostile feelings, while the excessive masochism served both as a discharge of hostility, allowing the arthritic woman to express her anger in an acceptable fashion, and as a denial of dependent demands.

A number of investigations prior to those of Moos and Solomon utilized control groups. Rorschach test and interview data on 73 arthritic patients and matched hypertensive patients were compared (Booth and Klopfer, 1936; Booth, 1937). Arthritics were predominantly introverted, righteous, obstinate, strict and rigid in moral matters, eager to confirm to accepted social standards, and unrelenting and unforgiving. They showed poor sexual adjustment, were hypersensitive, and had an inordinate need to be dominant and controlling. Booth also observed that arthritics were restless and showed aimless muscular activities. He concluded that "the more closely one studies these patients, the more conviction grows upon one that the arthritic process is not merely frequently, but always, the expression of a personality conflict."

The Minnesota Multiphasic Personality Inventory (MMPI) was utilized in two comparable studies of a total of 125 male arthritics and 175 controls (Cohen, 1949; Wiener, 1952). Findings indicated that arthritics overreacted to their disease and showed symptoms of emotional disturbances. The arthritics obtained higher scores than nondisabled controls on the "neurotic" scales of the MMPI; they had an unusual number of elevated scores; however, they generally obtained more normal scores than did a second group of neurotic patients.

A study of 29 male rheumatoid arthritic patients and 29 matched neurotic controls indicated that arthritics tended to turn hostility inward, that they were not as concerned as controls with obstacles that might provoke aggression, that they were more inclined to seek solutions to frustrating problems and not as inclined to be defensive, and that they attempted to conform to conventional modes of behavior (Mueller and Lefkovits, 1956). The Rorschach data indicated that the arthritics had unresolved conflicts in the area of parental authority, that they operated on a level of defective personality integration, that they showed defective emotional responsiveness, and that they lacked emotional maturity and were constricted. The authors concluded that the arthritics were not significantly different from the neurotic controls. A further investigation by the same group had similar findings and concluded that arthritics tend to repress or suppress negative feelings more than controls (Mueller *et al.,* 1961).

Two well-controlled studies agreed on several findings (Cleveland and Fisher, 1954, 1960). In both, arthritics reported an intensive interest and participation in sports, athletics, and hunting and fishing and, contrastingly, an interest in household activities, especially cooking. They also emphasized the inconsistent nature of things and tended to show an excess of exhibitionistic and voyeuristic fantasies. Value was placed on the act of looking and being seen, and in most cases this impulse was denied and inhibited. Overtly, the arthritic appeared to be calm, composed, and optimistic, rarely if ever expressing or even consciously feeling anger. He boasted of never fighting or getting angry, although he admitted that a "smart alec or braggart" or "loud mouth guy" could get him angry. The arthritics complained of social shyness and inadequacy, tended to shun the limelight, and desired to be "just average and not stand out at all." They also complained of inability to say the right things at the right time and were concerned about their looks, their clothes, and the impressions they made on others. The arthritics tended to describe their parents similarly. Mother was seen as a hardworking, efficient, self-sacrificing "Christian" woman, who would give anyone anything and go without herself. She was also a compulsively clean and efficient housekeeper. However, she was the source of considerable frustration, since she tended to be a very strict disciplinarian. Father was perceived as being hardworking, honest, friendly, easy going and good natured, but inconsistent. "He was quiet, but watch out!" Father was either physically absent from home, beginning early in the patient's life, or he was psychologically weak. Cleveland and Fisher (1954) concluded that rheumatoid arthritics were psychiatrically sick and suggested that rheumatoid arthritis may be a defense against regression and personality disintegration.

With the siblings of patients as controls, 18 sib–patient pairs were studied (Cormier *et al.,* 1957). Activity and impulsiveness, interest in games and sports, and competitive and aggressive fantasies had been dominant in rheumatoid arthritics. The sibs were quiet, shy, reserved, and conforming, recalling that they had been jealous of their more active, now arthritic, sibs and that they had shown less energy in athletics. Both groups described their parents as strict. The arthritics, however, were apt to regard parental demands as excessive and to react to them with impulsive defiance; whereas, their sibs either uncomplainingly accepted similar demands or by-passed them unprovocatively. The sibs became disinhibited in adulthood and developed poise and self-confidence. Outbursts of rage tended to be more common and more violent in the arthritics than in the controls. However, the controls could "forget it," while the arthritics were harassed by guilt and remorse, a need for self-punishment, and a fear that they had inflicted great harm on the object of aggression. The arthritics tried to be punctual, tidy, and perfectionistic. They emphasized financial security and showed self-sacrificing and forgiving attitudes.

An extensive and careful psychosomatic study of patients with rheumatoid arthritis, primarily utilizing interviews, was conducted in Finland on 102 consecutive female outpatients (Rimón, 1969). Aggression tests were controlled by comparison with other medical patients. Rimón had only two patients with a history of psychotic symptoms, these not occurring in parallel with rheumatoid symptoms, thus agreeing with previous observations of the rarity of coincidence of schizophrenia and rheumatoid disease (Nissen and Spencer, 1936; Gregg, 1939; Trevathan and Tatum, 1954; Pilkington, 1956; Rothermilch and Philips, 1963). Overt neurotic symptoms, excluding depressive ones, were manifested relatively infrequently. Other psychosomatic conditions, particularly hyperthyroidism (which may be associated with immunologic disturbance), were relatively common. In evaluating the role of life stress in the onset of the rheumatic process, interestingly, Rimón's research provided evidence for two types of rheumatoid arthritis (analogous to the process and reactive forms of schizophrenia). "In the first one, the disease begins suddenly and the symptoms appear distinct and even fierce. The onset of the disease is most often associated with a significant psychodynamic conflict situation, and a hereditary predisposition for rheumatoid arthritis is obviously lacking. In the other type, the onset of the disease is slow and the progression of the symptoms retarded. A correlation to an actual psychodynamic conflict situation is absent; whereas, a hereditary predisposition for rheumatoid arthritis does exist, judging by the relatively great number of other affected members of the family." Rimón's "nonconflict group" did not differ from a series of ordinary medical patients in direct expression of agression. Those patients with an insidious onset of disease had no obvious inability to discharge aggressive impulses and to become conscious of aggressive tendencies.

A group of patients with documented rheumatoid arthritis was studied extensively—medically, psychiatrically, and socially—by Shochet et al. (1969). This group of patients was found to be specifically vulnerable to separation, real or threatened. Onset or exacerbation of symptoms of rheumatoid arthritis was temporally related to a major life crisis involving a separation in this group of patients. In contrast, Hendrie et al. (1971) found no evidence of life change events occurring more often in a group of patients suffering from early polyarthritis than in a control group; however, the arthritic patients with elevated immunoglobulin levels did tend to have increased life change scores.

A psychoanalytic study of two patients with rheumatoid arthritis discussed the mechanism of fusion with the bad internalized significant persons or family network, and the correlation of such fusion was conflictual motility of affected muscle groups or afflicted joints (Lefer, 1972). Somatization becomes an appeal to significant others. In one patient, disease symptoms served an existential defense, "I hurt, therefore, I exist." In both patients, there were simultaneous appeals for relief and to be taken care of, to be dependent without danger. Somatization served the purpose of achieving touch, a warped form of intimacy, along with the hope that relief would come from the "good" mother. Isacaroff's discussion of Lefer's paper suggested that the patient struggled to resolve an uncertainty in his or her link with the symbiotic mother, the symptom providing a solution by decreasing the space in which the body can move and the emotional distance between the now solicitous mothering person and the desexualized infantile symbiotically fused parent. The symptom becomes necessary to reduce the uncertainty in the link with the mother and the unbearable anxiety that this uncertainty arouses. [Like Alexander (1950), I have a resistance to the symbolic interpretation of symptoms in psychosomatic disease in contrast to the validity of such interpretation in conversion reactions, preferring to consider the effects of affects on physiological processes underlying the disease state.]

The significance of psychological factors in the pathogenesis of rheumatoid arthritis is particularly emphasized by the study of Meyerowitz *et al,* (1968) of monozygotic twins discordant for rheumatoid arthritis. In their critical review of previous reports of arthritis in twins in the world literature, they found that in 20 monozygotic twins there were only three instances with concordance for rheumatoid arthritis. Their study of 8 monozygotic twins discordant for the disease showed no consistent differential patterns of development or health deviations preceding the occurrence of the disease. However, detailed psychosocial data obtained from 4 out of the 5 adult twin sets revealed that in all of the 4 affected twins a period of psychological stress preceded the onset of disease. Similar finding of psychological stress was clearly demonstrated in two of the three younger sets of twins but was not seen in the third set of children. In all cases, there was no comparable experience of stress for the unaffected sister. In addition, there was a personality trend toward great involvement in physical activity in both twin sisters of all sets.

WELL-CONTROLLED STUDIES OF RHEUMATOID ARTHRITIS

Moos and I attempted to overcome some of the severe methodological problems limiting the generalizability of results of prior studies in a series of investigations by means of: (*a*) utilizing carefully matched control groups; (*b*) testing the assumption that similar underlying personality characteristics may manifest themselves in different and/or opposite ways; (*c*) utilizing different assessment methods and comparing their results; and (*d*) combining observations of investigators of different theoretical orientations to attempt to "balance bias" (Moos and Solomon, 1965a,b). Sixteen female patients with rheumatoid arthritis classified as definite or classical by American Rheumatism Association criteria were compared with their closest aged, healthy sisters providing an automatic control for age, sex, parents' occupational status, and many other background factors. We gleaned 140 statements from the literature, each suggested by at least one author to be descriptive of patients with rheumatoid arthritis. Three raters then independently rated these statements into personality trait dimensions to eliminate overlap and redundancy. Fifteen bipolar scales (e.g., dependency versus denial of dependence, hyperindependence) emerged. If arthritics have underlying characteristics which may be manifested in opposite ways (as, for example, through the defense mechanism of reaction formation), they should show higher inter- or intra-individual variability than controls; so that differences might be reflected either in mean differences or variability differences on any of the scales. These personality trait dimensions were measured in three independent ways: (a) by regular and rationally constructed scales for the MMPI; (b) by ratings made independently by two raters for a recorded 45-minute semi-structured interview; and (c) by a specially constructed personality test. Two raters categorized all 556 MMPI items as relevant to one of the dimensions. Raters scored interviews on a five-point scale on the dimensions and achieved very high inter-rater reliability. Since some personality characteristics of arthritics might manifest themselves in a situation-specific manner, that is, arthritics may be overly dependent in some situations or with some people but overly independent in other situations or with other people, our Affective Reaction Inventory (ARI) comprised a number of situations, such as "when I have a lot of things to do," "when I meet a group of new people," "when I buy a big item," and several items under each situation relevant to one of the personality trait dimensions.

Our results on the MMPI scales showed patients were significantly higher on scales measuring perfectionism, compliance and subservience, nervousness and restlessness, reserve and introversion, depression, and sensitivity (to anger). Interview rating results were largely in agreement with MMPI data. The ARI significantly differentiated patients in only two personality trait dimensions, the masochism and self-sacrifice and the bound and repressed affect dimensions. However, a comparison between patients and siblings revealed 26 cases in which a personality characteristic manifested itself significantly in one specific situation. For example, patients scored significantly lower than siblings on the response "I feel at ease" in the situation "when I am with someone I like." On the other hand, siblings scored high on the response "I tend to think of radical solutions" to the situation "when things go wrong." In regard to inter-individual variability, patients showed a greater number of extreme scores on 15 of the reaction dimensions on the ratings.

All the interviews covered the following areas: descriptions of self, sibling, mother, father, current and/or former husband; expression of anger; ability to manifest dependent behavior; extent of present and previous physical activity; and events at the time of onset of symptoms. In addition, a short psychodrama was conducted. Each subject was told she had purchased a steam iron and found it defective. The interviewer played an unreasonable, hostile store complaint manager and tried to elicit anger, defiance and assertiveness in the subject by refusing to accept the iron, blaming her for damage, requesting money for repairs, etc. Each of the ten different content areas were transferred on to separate tapes, for example, all patients' self-descriptions recorded on one tape. Recordings were analyzed by an independent judge utilizing word counts of frequency of relevant material.

Vast differences in self-descriptive adjectives utilized by the two groups were clear. The patients generally described themselves as nervous, tense, worried, struggling, depressed, moody, highly strung, and easily upset. Their siblings generally described themselves as liking people; as active and constantly busy; as easy to get acquainted with; as good, hard, productive workers; and as enjoying life in a generally unruffled manner. Thus, the patients saw themselves as far more "pathologic" than the siblings saw themselves. Actual counts of adjectives and descriptive phrases used by the two groups indicated, further, that the patients put more emphasis on their emotional sensitivity, that is, on being shy, inhibited, and hard to get to know; whereas, the siblings put more emphasis on being optimistic and easy going. Both groups seemed to have strong needs to see themselves as hardworking, productive, energetic, constantly busy individuals who successfully completed a large variety of tasks and continually saw progress in their lives. The siblings could, in fact, accomplish many of these goals, while the patients, in general, could not. These descriptions were in agreement with test results, which showed the patients to be higher on a variety of test scales measuring clinical symptomatology.

There are two other important findings relative to the patient's and siblings' descriptions of each other. First, the siblings showed greater freedom to express criticism. Second, the siblings tended to utilize negatively toned descriptive phrases in describing what the patients were like as children, that is, before the onset of arthritis. For example, phrases such as "poor little girl," "always felt inferior," "was told she was homely," was "sickly and inactive," "was shy, worried, and lazy," etc., were generally used by the sibling in describing the patient as a child. They were hardly ever used in the patients' descriptions of what their siblings were like as children.

The patients and siblings tended to agree on their descriptions of their mothers. The mothers were described in very positive terms, such as "she worked very hard," "she was never cross," "she was very easy going," "nothing ever bothered her," "she took everything in her stride," "she was sweet," "she'd do anything for anyone to help them." This picture of the mothers was in close agreement with that given by Cleveland and Fisher's (1954) male arthritic patients. Interestingly, some patients did call their mothers intolerant, cold, unexpressive, overly submissive, impatient, and strict, while the siblings of these patients made essentially no critical comments about these same mothers. These differences suggest that the patients may have been more aware of and possibly more exposed to and/or bothered by their mothers' "negative" traits and perhaps by what they perceived to be their mothers' inconsistency and rejection of them.

In general, fathers were described as representing one of two extremes.

Some were seen as completely irresponsible, unreliable, unambitious, unreasonable, high-tempered, strict, and overly dominating. For example, one father was described as habitually drunk, as continually beating his wife, as burning the bed when his wife would not sleep with him, and as trying to "get fresh with me, his own daughter." Other fathers were described as easy going, gentle, determined, smart, hardworking, affectionate, lenient, wonderful, kind, good-natured, tolerant, yielding. These rather stereotypic descriptions would suggest that neither the patients nor the siblings viewed their fathers very realistically.

Both patients and siblings tended to perceive both parents as being rather strict in discipline. The patients, however, viewed their fathers as stricter than the siblings viewed them. There was no evidence that the patients reacted to this discipline any more defiantly than their siblings. In those homes in which the parents were described as more lenient, the patients stated that they felt they knew what the boundaries were and never dared cross them. For example, one patient stated that her father "was not strict and never hit us, he didn't have to." The patients were, then, bothered more by the rejection they perceived from their mothers and the strictness they perceived from their fathers.

The patients' and siblings' descriptions of their spouses and their marriages showed striking differences. Almost all siblings tended to describe their marriages as reasonably happy and generally satisfactory, although with some problems. The patients, on the other hand, tended to describe their marriages in one of two extreme ways. Patients stated that their husbands were "so good to me, it's pathetic;" "marvelous, very easy going, calm, and relaxed;" or, in contrast, "irresponsible, alcoholic, completely ununderstanding;" "mean, used to torture me."

An even more noteworthy difference between the two groups was in their descriptions of the handling of disagreements between themselves and their husbands. There were no siblings who stated that they did not have any fights with their husbands, while 13 of the 16 patients so stated. Even those patients who had described very poor marriages still stated that they never argued with their husbands. These patients were martyrlike and masochistic in the extreme in relation to their husbands. For example, one patient described grotesque beatings she received from her husband. He stretched her mouth, would choke her and hold the bedcovers over her head, would make her sit and watch him bowl for hours on end. She stated that she kept all her feelings inside and never complained. "You can't blame him; he had a mean father." The siblings, as stated, mentioned that they did have arguments and disagreements with their husbands. In addition, they tended to react to situations more quickly and defiantly. For example, one sibling, who had had an alcoholic husband, told with some glee how she managed to get him to endorse a $900 check, had given him $30 in cash, and had then left, never to see him again.

The patients and siblings, as might be expected, also showed differences in their answers to: "Tell me the last time you got angry." Almost all siblings either stated that they expressed their anger or provided at least one recent example of when they had expressed anger. Only two patients directly stated that they expressed angry feelings. There were no patient–sibling pairs in which the patient stated that she expressed anger more freely than the sibling. The siblings were apt to get angry at their husbands and children if provoked; the patients tended almost never to admit anger towards people who played significant roles in their lives. When patients did give examples of getting angry, these were far more remote in time than the examples given by the siblings. In addition, almost all patients made statements about feeling hurt, getting upset, or feeling bad when they were in situations which might, according to outside observers, be termed anger-provoking. The siblings did not mention these feelings nearly as often.

Examples convey the flavor of the patients' anger. One patient stated that the last time she had got slightly annoyed (not angry) was when she had a disagreement with a lady friend about what baseball team was playing in town. She found that she was wrong and stated that she felt very bad in that she had probably annoyed her friend and hurt her feelings. Another patient mentioned a "serious" disagreement with her husband. When pressed for details, she stated that one night he had said that she was henpecking him. This caused her to leave the house immediately, drive away, park the car, and think. This incident had occurred 2 years previously, and, since the patient remembered even the exact words her husband had spoken, it can be safely surmised that she was particularly sensitive to his anger.

During the psychodrama, the interviewer attempted, by various techniques such as raising objections and questioning the honesty, trustworthiness, or sense of fair play of the subject, to induce some anger and assertiveness in each subject. The psychodrama was used in order to give a "real-life" estimate of possible differences between the two groups in their tendency to express anger. Analysis of these data strongly supported earlier results. There were no patients who expressed more anger in this situation than did their siblings, and there were only two patients who were more assertive than their siblings. For example, many of the siblings stated that they would complain to the store manager, to the Better Business Bureau, to the company which had made the iron, or to a small claims court. This ability to threaten the mediation of a "higher authority" was part of what was labeled an assertive handling of the problem and was much more prevalent in the siblings than in the patients.

There was no evidence of a difference in dependency between the patients and their siblings. Almost every subject in the two groups described herself as being highly independent. The subjects made statements such as "I cooperate with others but never rely on them;" "I don't think I ever relied on anyone;" "I have never in the past asked anyone for favors." In addition, the patients were only able to accept help if others strongly wished to give it and directly offered it. Patients felt pride in not asking others for favors and accepted favors only with an expressed fear of being obligated. On the other hand, patients frequently commented on how they derived pleasure from helping others.

Both groups were asked about the extent of their physical activity in childhood and at present. There were no differences in the amount of physical activity mentioned by the two groups; hence, the oftenmade hypothesis that rheumatoid arthritic patients involved themselves in more activity before their illness was not confirmed by these data. This negative finding seems related to the control group since both patients and sisters had shown considerable interest in sports. The patients had a certain keenness, delight, and pleasure in discussing their past and present activity; whereas, the siblings seemed to be much more matter-of-fact in their descriptions.

Previous data on traumatic events in relation to onset of arthritis indicated that when large groups of matched patients and controls were questioned, there were no differences in the number of such events mentioned by the two groups (Empire Rheumatism Council, 1950). Though uncontrolled for similar events in the lives of controls, almost every patient of ours did link the development of her arthritis with some acute or chronic stress situation. One patient talked of having to move from one town to another against her strong wishes; another talked of a traumatic experience associated with surgery; a third developed arthritis during a year in which her father had a stroke, her brother-in-law passed away, her mother-in-law, for whom she did not care, came to live with her, and her house caught fire; still another spoke about taking care of her mentally ill husband for 3 years.

A large-scale MMPI study compared 49 female rheumatoid arthritic patients and 53 of their healthy female family members by our rationally derived scales, the regular 3 validation and 9 clinical scales, and 113 published special scales (Moos and Solomon, 1964a). Statistical significance was evaluated by determining the percentage of MMPI scales that would show "significant" differences between the groups on the basis of chance alone. Far more scales than would occur by chance showed significant differences between arthritics and family members and comprised scales reflecting: (a) physical symptoms; (b) depression, apathy, and lack of motivation; (c) other general "neurotic" symptoms such as anxiety, masochism, self-alienation, and overcompliance; (d) psychological rigidity; and (e) similarity to the other psychosomatic conditions.

To summarize, our studies differed from previous ones in that there were no significant differences between patients and controls in dependency; both patients and siblings described themselves as being very independent though patients had somewhat more difficulty in accepting help from others. Both patients and siblings, likewise, had shown interest and earlier participation in sports, but patients spoke of their interest with great keenness and delight in physical activity, possibly as the result of the restriction of their disease. Evidence for at least some patients does suggest, however, that decreases in the amount of physical activity to which a patient had been accustomed may have *preceded* the development of arthritis, for example, abandonment of participation in competitive sport because of the responsibility of family or advancing age. Observers but not patients themselves considered the patients more duty-oriented and conscientious. The clearest and most consistent finding related to the masochism, self-sacrifice, and denial of hostility shown by arthritic patients. Although patients and siblings agreed reasonably closely in the descriptions of their parents, the patients were bothered more by the rejection they perceived from their mothers and the strictness they perceived from their fathers. The patients tended to describe their marriages either as extremely good or extremely bad; whereas, the siblings tended to describe their marriages as average and reasonably happy. The patients' unhappy marriages lasted for a considerable length of time, partially because the patients were almost completely unassertive and very strongly masochistic and self-sacrificing in relation to their husbands. The findings, in agreement with those of Cobb *et al.* (1959), suggest that patients will endure uncomfortable stressful situations longer than their siblings. It is possible, then, that chronic long-term stress, rather than simple discreet stress situations, may relate closely to later development of rheumatoid arthritis in at least some cases. As mentioned, practically every patient did link the development of her arthritis with environmental stress, and it seemed that more acute short-term stresses were not present. The arthritic patients' inability to express anger may make some situations more stressful to them than these same situations would be to other people. Similar situations may be differentially stressful to different individuals because of their particular personality characteristics.

COURSE OF DISEASE

Moos and I (1964b) attempted to correlate psychological variables with course of rheumatoid arthritis. Patients with relatively slow disease progression scored higher on scales reflecting compliance–subservience, perfectionism, denial of hostility, capacity for social responsibility and social status; whereas, those with relatively rapid disease progression scored higher on scales reflecting physical malfunctioning, general maladjustment, judged anxiety, judged manifest hostility, and imperturbability. We suggested that patients whose disease was progressing most rapidly were experiencing feelings of ego disorganization with concomitant increase in anxiety and depression and decrease in the ability to continue former modes of psychological adaptation and coping. Our data were similar to those of Klopfer (1957) in regard to cancer and of Grinker and Robbins (1954) in the case of multiple sclerosis. We suggested that a "vicious cycle" may occur in which a high degree of energy

involved in ego defensiveness and rapid progression of disease initially re-
enforce each other in the case of those diseases associated with immunologic
deficiency states. We also compared a group of female patients with
rheumatoid arthritis whose stage of progression of illness was less than the
class of functional incapacity with a second group in whom the stage of progression was greater or equal to the class of functional incapacity. The patients with greater functional incapacity scored significantly higher on MMPI
scales reflecting (a) physical symptoms; (b) depression, apathy, and lack of
motivation; (c) general "neurotic" symptoms such as lack of ego strength,
alienation, isolation from self and others, anxiety, and hostility; (d) general
"psychotic" symptoms; (e) problems of uncontrolled impulses; and (f) particular personality traits, such as prejudice, ethnocentrism, and dependency.

We found results similar to those between patients with slowly progressing
and rapidly progressing disease and between patients with relatively great and
relatively little incapacity between those patients who responded well in contrast to those who responded poorly to medical management of their disease
(Moos & Solomon, 1965c; Solomon & Moos, 1965b). Patients who responded
well to treatment seemed to be maintaining relatively intact their habitual
modes of coping with their own impulses and with their environment. Conflicting feelings were not breaking through to consciousness. These patients
were maintaining an interest in other people and in life events, and their image
of and respect for themselves had not suffered greatly. Our findings, again,
are similar to those described for the immunologically-resisted infectious disease, tuberculosis, about which Wittkower, et al. (1955) stated, "Sometimes it
may be safer to assess the patient's prognosis on the basis of his personality
and emotional conflicts than on the basis of the shadow on his film."

JUVENILE RHEUMATOID ARTHRITIS

The role of personality, emotions, and stress in juvenile rheumatoid arthritis is much less well studied than in the adult disease, and there are few
studies. Cleveland (1965) found that arthritic children are unusually expressive
in physical and muscle action and score significantly higher on tests emphasizing motor skills than on verbal tests, in contrast to asthmatic children, raising
the suggestion that prolonged immobilization is particularly traumatic
psychologically to such children. A detailed survey of 88 children with
juvenile rheumatoid arthritis was conducted in an attempt to elucidate
characteristics that might participate in the etiologic mechanism (Henoch et
al., 1978). Comparison data were obtained from a random pediatric population. There was a marked preponderance of children whose parents were un-
married as a result of divorce, separation, and death in the arthritic group,
and adoption occurred three times more frequently in the juvenile rheumatoid
arthritic population as in the comparison group. Fifty-one percent of these

events (divorce, separation, death, or adoption) occurred near the onset of the disease. Heisel (1972) reported that children who develop juvenile rheumatoid arthritis tend to have recently experienced a cluster of changes in their world, higher in amount and intensity than the average child and pointed to "specific trigger" events, particularly object loss and hospitalization. In an extensive (and well-done) study, Rimón et al. (1977) found that 39% (21 of 54) patients had suffered from an emotional disturbance (primarily depression) prior to the investigation, and manifest psychopathology was observed in 31%. In addition, a personality profile marked by features similar to those reported in many adults, was found in 58%: shyness, unresponsiveness, passivity, submissiveness, aloofness, feelings of inferiority, and inability to express emotions or to establish contact with fellow patients. However, no uniform pattern of distorted family relationships was observed. In only 37% of patients could an emotionally important conflict be correlated with onset of illness. Like Rimón's study of adults (1969), the nonconflict group had a high percentage of relatives with rheumatoid illness, suggesting greater genetic loading in a multicausal disease in those less emotionally disturbed.

PSYCHOLOGICAL FACTORS IN OTHER AUTOIMMUNE DISEASES

Psychosomatic studies of other diseases with autoimmune features reveal findings similar to ours and others' studies of patients with rheumatoid arthritis. Engel's (1953) classical review and study of psychological processes in ulcerative colitis, a disease often associated with anti-colon antibodies, refers to obsessive–compulsive character traits of neatness, indecision, conscientiousness, worrying, rigid morality, and conformity. Engel's colitis patients, likewise, generally had difficulty directly expressing hostility, were concerned with appearance and others' opinions, and had significant conflicts over dependency. Colitis patients' mothers were controlling and had a propensity to assume the role of a martyr, again as arthritics' mothers have been described (Cleveland and Fisher, 1954; Alexander, 1950). The hyperthyroidism and exophthalmos of Graves' disease result from the action of long-acting thyroid stimulator (LATS), a unique antithyroid autoantibody with physiological activity (Kriss, 1968). Mandelbrote and Wittkower (1955) state about female Graves' disease patients, "Hidden behind their bustling activities and their constant emphasis on independence and self-sufficiency lie the same outdated needs for maternal love. . ." These authors found *chronic* stress generally preceded onset of hyperthyroidism. Bereavement as a documented factor in precipitation of childhood Graves' disease has been postulated to trigger immunosuppression in genetically predisposed individuals, leading to activity of an unsuppressed "forbidden clone" of antithyroid T lymphocytes and their "cooperation" in production of thyroid stimulating immunoglobulin (TSI) by B lymphocytes (Morillo and Gardner, 1979).

Stress, especially loss of a significant relationship or fear of loss of love, can be documented as preceding the onset of systemic lupus erythematosus, a serious disease associated with a variety of antinuclear globulins (McClary, *et al.* 1955). These authors' lupus patients showed compulsive traits and an unusual need for activity and independence, interpreted as a defensive denial of guilt-provoking wishes for maternal affection. Childhood emotional deprivation and stress prior to onset of illness were more common in a group of women with systemic lupus erythematosus than in a group of matched controls with accidental hemorrhage in pregnancy (Otto and MacKay, 1967).

Grinker and Robbins (1954) state about patients with multiple sclerosis, which some feel may be an immune disease analogous to experimental allergic encephalomyelitis, "The multiple sclerotics seem to have an excessive need for love and affection, which was not gratified in childhood. The resulting frustration evokes anger which must be repressed in order to preserve whatever gratification was available. As a result, the external personality is happy-go-lucky with a paramount desire to please and be appreciated." Autoerythrocyte sensitization is a chronic purpuric state in women manifested by production of painful, spontaneous ecchymoses. These women demonstrate hysterical and masochistic traits, and the data suggest that the illness serves the psychological purpose of expiating guilt resulting from aggressive impulses (Agle *et al.,* 1969).

PREDICTION

I feel that the ability to be convincing in regard to psychosomatic hypotheses will come not so much from correlative studies as so far described but from predictive ones and from clear elucidation of underlying pathogenic mechanisms that lead from experience through the central nervous system to tissue alteration. In an attempt to overcome the objection that observed personality traits might be induced by the disease or, when reported as existing prior to disease might represent retrospective distortions, I and Moos (1965a) attempted to correlate personality variables with a physiological variable, rheumatoid factor, that may be predisposing towards rheumatoid disease (Lawrence, 1963). Rheumatoid factor is a macromolecular anti-γ-globulin autoantibody that itself is a γ-globulin (IgM). We utilized the MMPI, analyzing 12 basic and 66 special scales in a group of relatives of rheumatoid patients deemed physically healthy on the basis of medical history, physical examinations, and X-rays. Twenty-one FII-(rheumatoid factor) positive female relatives were compared with 21 FII-negative female relatives.

The responses of the subjects on 16 of the 88 MMPI scales showed statistically significant differences between the two groups. The FII-positive relatives scored significantly higher on scales reflecting inhibition of aggression (impulse control), concern about the social desirability of actions and about socioeconomic status, and ego strength (indicative of capacity for successful psychological defense, coping, mastery, and integration). They also scored higher on an ulcer scale, the items of which reflect compliance, shyness, conscientiousness, religiosity, and moralism.

The FII-*negative* relatives scored higher on the standard psychasthenia scale, essentially indicative of the obsessive–compulsive syndrome consisting of rumination and rituals, abnormal fears, worrying, difficulties in concentrating, guilt feelings, excessive vacillation in making decisions, excessively high personal standards, self-critical feelings, and aloofness. Interestingly, the FII-negative relatives had more somatic complaints; showed more psychoneuroticism and less ego mastery, with defective inhibition of impulses; and tended more readily to admit psychiatric symptoms, to lack self-acceptance, and to feel both self and social alienation. Self-concept and ideal self are seen as relatively disparate in the FII-negative group. The FII-negative group also tended more frequently to dissimulate, to attempt deliberately to appear less healthy. This group more often demonstrated evidence of failure of psychological defenses, as reflected in scores on the judged-anxiety scale and inner-maladjustment scale, indices of emotional illness. Consistent with these elevations, the FII-negative group had higher dependency scores. Their relative elevation on the ethnocentrism scale implies rigidity and inflexibility of emotional attitudes, which may be related to poor prognosis in psychotherapy. It should be recalled that the ego strength scale, the criterion for the development of which was response to psychotherapy, was higher in the FII-positive group. The FII-negative group also scored higher on the paranoia scale, similar to general psychiatric cases, which, as might be expected, contains a great number of unfavorable items.

Both scale score and specific item differences showed that apparently healthy relatives of rheumatoid arthritic patients who had rheumatoid factor in their sera tended to have well-functioning psychological defenses and to be essentially psychiatrically asymptomatic. On the other hand, psychoneurosis and even more serious mental disturbances with failure of psychic homeostasis—anxiety, alienation, lack of control, fear, guilt, low self-esteem—were relatively much more common in those relatives lacking rheumatoid factor. A reasonable hypothesis based upon these data would seem to be that, given a genetic or constitutional predisposition to rheumatoid disease, individuals with significant emotional conflict and psychological distress go on to the development of disease. Thus, individuals with rheumatoid factor but without manifest rheumatoid disease must be in good psychological equilibrium; if they were not, they might be expected to become physically ill.

Although the presence of rheumatoid factor in a healthy individual seems to be related to well-functioning psychological defenses, it seems that the *kind* of adaptations of FII-positive relatives are similar to those in persons with rheumatoid arthritis, but that they are working better, either as a result of greater ego strength or of less environmental stress. The inhibition of aggression, concern about appearances, and similarity to other psychosomatic groups seen in the FII-positive relatives have been found in patients with rheumatoid arthritis when compared with a group of healthy relatives without regard to their FII status. Thus, a propensity to formation of rheumatoid factor might be linked to psychological mechanisms but still needs to be coupled with some degree of emotional decompensation to lead to disease. The possible physiological mechanism for emotional influence on production of rheumatoid factor, especially if not tied to the concept of psychological distress, which relates to dysfunction of the immunologic system, is unclear. Genetic or constitutional factors might be integrated with a psychological theory by the assumptions that the biologic *capacity* for production of rheumatoid factor is present in some or all individuals; that actual rheumatoid factor production is triggered in some cases by the physiological consequences of certain types of psychological conditions and is accompanied by *disease* in the presence of other or more intense psychological factors.

In a small pilot study, suggestive but not statistically significant, I found that football players (who might be expected to have a high incidence of "autoimmune-prone personalities"), who showed elevations on "neurotic" scales of the MMPI before the football season, developed low titers of rheumatoid factor after the stress of close losses to teams with whom there was keen rivalry. Goodman *et al.* (1963) found that emotional stress heightens the tendency to produce thyroid autoantibodies.

In patients with existing disease, Wolfe (1970) compared preoperative predictions of motivation and potential cooperation in surgical rehabilitation of rheumatoid arthritis based upon global personality evaluations derived from psychological testing and clinical interviews with 6-month postoperative ratings of outcome of orthopedic surgery. He obtained a significant correlation between the psychological predictions and the postoperative ratings. His work particularly suggested that tolerance to pain influenced rehabilitation. Moldofsky and Chester (1970) reported significant correlations between pain, measured both objectively by a pressure dolorimeter and subjectively, and mood patterns in rheumatoid arthritic patients. They found that half their patients fell into a "synchronous" state group in whom the pain and mood correlations were positive and significant (e.g., anxiety decreases, pain lessens). The other half were placed in a "paradoxical" state category as there was a significant inverse relationship between mood and pain (e.g., hopelessness increases, pain decreases). The authors found that in their followup studies, the synchronous group fared better than the paradoxical group.

SEX INCIDENCE AND PERSONALITY
FACTORS: PREGNANCY

Rheumatoid arthritis, like other autoimmune diseases such as systemic lupus erythematosus, thyroiditis, and Graves' disease, occurs more commonly in females. Some autoantibodies are more common in symptom-free females than males (Goodman *et al.*, 1963). I raised the question whether disease at times emerges when psychological defenses fail. In the context of the personality trait structure described for patients who develop autoimmune diseases, the possibility presents itself that males are better able in our current cultural context to ward off anxiety and depression by physical activities, busyness, and hyperindependence, and that females, whose social role traditionally involves the need for greater submissiveness and allows for less mobility, are less able successfully to employ such defenses. Also, the apparently crucial role of the mother of the patient with autoimmune disease may have greater impact on the female child, for whom mother is not only the source of nurturance but is a subsequent figure for identification. We might expect that, if the social roles of women shift in the context of the women's liberation movement and social evolution, the incidence of rheumatoid arthritis in women might drop, just as the incidence of peptic ulcer and hypertension in women with executive positions appears to have risen.

The sort of psychological defenses we describe are prone to failure in old age. Autoantibodies, like clinical depression, are more commonly found in the elderly (Goodman *et al.*, 1963).

Case Illustration: A woman Army officer in her mid-thirties appeared for treatment of a clinically significant depressive reaction. She had been the only woman active in major international sports car races, but she had wrecked her Maserati. She had not been able to perform nearly as well in a lesser substitute car. She was an avid sky diver. She prided herself on her perfectionism and independence. I felt that if anyone was likely to develop an autoimmune disease, it was she. I then took a medical history. Two years previously she had a documented episode of idiopathic thrombocytopenic purpura. I sent serum for determination of antinuclear antibodies, which were present in significant titer. Three months later she came down with frank systemic lupus erythematosus.

Rheumatoid arthritis and other autoimmune diseases are often ameliorated in the course of pregnancy, though progesterone and placental extracts of various kinds have not been effective in treatment of arthritis (Landsbury, 1953). In my clinical experience, the meaning and attitude toward pregnancy on the part of the patient determines whether exacerbation or remission of autoimmune disease ensues. Some patients with autoimmune disease appear for symbolic reasons to be gratified by the state of pregnancy, though there is conflict after the baby is born.

Case Illustration: Mrs. Z, a young woman with mild rheumatoid arthritis, was fed up with her husband's irresponsibility and, with a great deal of difficulty, resolved to leave him, only to learn she was pregnant. Severe exacerbation of disease ensued. After the baby was born, her husband, who was delighted with the child, appeared to mature remarkably. Disease went into remission. For evidently psychodynamic reasons, the usual pattern of remission during pregnancy and exacerbation following delivery was reversed.

PSYCHOLOGICAL APPROACHES TO TREATMENT

In a personal communication (1962), Charles A. Janeway told of a patient with severe disseminated lupus erythematosus who had the distinction of being the only such patient of his who at that time had recovered in spite of renal involvement (in remission for 6 years off corticosteroids), which remission he attributed to "curing herself" by "spending a summer unloading all her deepseated concealed hostility toward her father on him." A former president of the American Rheumatism Association, Loring Swaim (1962), came to the conclusion from many years of practice that emotional factors are crucial in the etiology of rheumatoid arthritis and attributed a number of remarkable remissions and "cures" to Divine intervention as a result of faith. His case material lends itself to interpretation that God serves the patient as a powerful, forgiving, protective transference figure allowing the patient to abandon somatic symptoms of psychogenic origin. Such an approach would particularly be expected to be applicable to the individual with difficulty in expressing hostility, proneness to guilt, and strong dependency needs. Dr. Swaim found that the first attack of arthritis was almost always preceded by unhappy events and long periods of sustained emotional strain. The emotions found most frequently were chronic bitterness and resentment. It is of note that Razi, a Persian physician, treated a patient suffering from rheumatoid arthritis with a direct psychotherapeutic technique more than 1000 years ago (Shafii, 1973). He related the patient's arthritic condition to his inability to experience and express aggression.

Moos *et al.* (1965) suggested that psychologically oriented techniques, based on an understanding of the psychodynamics of patients with rheumatoid arthritis, would be potentially useful in the rehabilitation of individuals with rheumatoid disease.

SUMMARY AND CONCLUSION

A considerable number of studies indicate that personality factors seem to predispose to the development of rheumatoid arthritis and other autoimmune diseases and that stress events and/or decompensation of psychological defenses and adaptations are related to onset of disease. Moos and I found that, in comparison with their healthy sisters, female patients with rheumatoid arthritis show more masochism, self-sacrifice, denial of hostility, compliance-subservience, depression, and sensitivity to anger and are described as always having been nervous, tense, worried, highly strung, moody individuals. Course of disease appears related to integrity of psychological defenses; patients with emotional decompensation are more likely to have rapidly progressing disease, to be more incapacitated, and to respond more poorly to medical treatment. Physically healthy relatives of rheumatoid patients with rheumatoid factor in their sera are psychologically more healthy than those relatives lacking this autoantibody, implying that a combination of physical predisposition and psychological decompensation leads to manifest disease. Personality data similar to those in rheumatoid arthritis have been reported for patients with other autoimmune diseases. Physiologically, autoimmunity appears to be related to relative immunologic incompetence. There is evidence that stress may be immunosuppressive. There is also experimental evidence for regulation of immune response by the hypothalamus. Thus, central nervous system-mediated alteration in immunologic responsivity might represent the pathogenic link among stress events, emotions, and diseases associated with immunologic dysfunction. Psychotherapeutic intervention may have some role in the treatment of immunologically mediated diseases.

REFERENCES

Agle, D. P., Ratnoff, O., and Wasman, M. (1969). Conversion reactions in auto-erythrocyte sensitization. *Arch. Gen. Psychiatry* **20**, 438–447.

Alexander, F. (1950). "Psychosomatic Medicine." Norton, New York.

Allison, A. C., Denman, A. M., and Barnes, R. D. (1971). Cooperating and controlling functions of thymus-derived lymphocytes in relation to autoimmunity. *Lancet,* 135–140.

Booth, G. C., (1937). Personality and chronic arthritis. *J. Nerv. Ment. Dis.* **85**, 637–662.

Booth, G. C., and Klopfer, B. (1936). Personality studies in chronic arthritis. *Rorschach Res. Exch.* **1**, 40–51.

Cleveland, S. E. (1965). Psychological factors in juvenile rheumatoid arthritis. *Arthritis Rheum.* **8**, 1152–1158.

Cleveland, S. E., and Fisher, S. (1954). Behavior and unconscious fantasies of patients with rheumatoid arthritis. *Psychosom. Med.* **16**, 327–333.

Cleveland, S. E., and Fisher, S. (1960). A comparison of psychological characteristics and phsyiological reactivity in ulcer and rheumatoid arthritic groups. I. Psychological measures. *Psychosom. Med.* **22**, 283–289.

Cobb, S., Miller, M., and Wieland, M. (1959). On the relationship between divorce and rheumatoid arthritis. *Arthritis Rheum.* **2**, 414–418.

Cohen, D. (1949). Psychological concomitants of chronic illness: A study of emotional correlates of pulmonary tuberculosis, peptic ulcer, the arthritides, and cardiac disease. Doctoral dissertation, University of Pittsburgh, Pittsburgh, Pennsylvania.

Cormier, B. M., Wittkower, E. D., Marcotte V., and Forget, F. (1957). Psychological aspects of rheumatoid arthritis. *Can. Med. Assoc. J.* **77**, 533–541.

Day, G. (1951). The psychosomatic approach to pulmonary tuberculosis. *Lancet,* 1025–1028.

Ellman, P., and Mitchell, S. D. (1936). The psychological aspects of chronic rheumatic joint disease. In "Reports on Chronic Rheumatic Diseases" (C. W. Buckley, ed.). Macmillan, New York.

Empire Rheumatism Council (1950). A controlled investigation into the aetiology and clinical features of rheumatoid arthritis. Br. Med. J. 1, 799-805.

Engel, G. L. (1953). Studies of ulcerative colitis. III. The nature of the psychologic processes. AM. J. Med. 19, 231-256.

Fudenberg, H. H. (1968). Are autoimmune diseases immunologic deficiency states? Hosp. Pract. 3, 43-53.

Goodman, M., Rosenblatt, M., Gottlieb, J. S., Miller, J., and Chen, C. H. (1963). Effect of age, sex and schizophrenia on autoantibody production. Arch. Gen. Psychiatry 8, 518-526.

Gregg, D. (1939). The paucity of arthritis among psychotic patients. Am. J. Psychiatry 95, 853-858.

Grinker, R. R., Jr., and Robbins, F. P. (1954). "Psychosomatic Case Book." Blakiston, New York.

Habel, K. (1963). Immunologic aspects of oncogenesis by polyoma virus. In "Conceptual Advances in Immunology and Oncology." Harper (Hoeber), New York.

Halliday, J. L. (1942). Psychological aspects of rheumatoid arthritis. Proc. R. Soc. Med. 35, 455-457.

Heisel, J. S. (1972). Life changes as etiologic factors in juvenile rheumatoid arthritis. J. Psychiatr. Res. 16, 411-420.

Hendrie, H. C., Paraskevas, F., Baragar, F. D., and Adamson, J. D. (1971). Stress, immunoglobulin levels and immunological processes. J. Psychosom. Res. 15, 337-342.

Henoch, M. J., Batson, J. W., and Baum, J. (1978). Psychosocial factors in juvenile rheumatoid arthritis. Arthritis Rheum. 21, 299-233.

Janeway, C. A. (1962). Personal communication to W. C. Kuzell, Jan. 8.

Johnson, A., Shapiro, L., and Alexander, F. (1947). Preliminary report on a psychosomatic study of rheumatoid arthritis. Psychosom. Med. 9, 295-300.

Klopfer, B. (1957). Psychological variables in human cancer. J. Proj. Techniques 21, 331-340.

Kriss, J. P. (1968). The long-acting thyroid stimulator. Calif. Med. 109, 202-213.

Landsbury, J. (1953). Pregnancy and rheumatoid arthritis. Bull. Rheum. Dis. 4, 38-39.

Lawrence, J. S. (1963). Epidemiology of rheumatoid arthritis. Arthritis Rheum. 6, 166-171.

Lefer, J. (1972). Fusion and rheumatoid arthritis. Contemp. Psychoanal. 9, 63-78.

Ludwig, A. O. (1955). Psychiatric considerations in rheumatoid arthritis. Med. Clin. North Am. 39, 447-458.

McClary, A. R., Meyer, E., and Weitzman, D. J. (1955). Observations on role of mechanism of depression in some patients with disseminated lupus erythematosus. Psychosom. Med. 17, 311-321.

MacKay, I. R. (1964). A survey of autoimmunity. Postgrad. Med. 35, 7-15.

Mandelbrote, B. M., and Wittkower, E. D. (1955). Emotional factors in Graves' disease. Psychosom. Med. 17, 109-117.

Meyerowitz, S., Jacox, R. F., and Hess, D. W. (1968). Monozygotic twins discordant for rheumatoid arthritis: A genetic, clinical and psychological study of 8 sets. Arthritis Rheum. 11, 1-21.

Moldofsky, H., and Chester, W. J. (1970). Pain and mood patterns in patients with rheumatoid arthritis. Psychosom. Med. 32, 309-317.

Moos, R. H. (1963). Personality factors associated with rheumatoid arthritis: A review. J. Chronic Dis. 17, 41-55.

Moos, R. H., and Solomon, G. F. (1964a). Minnesota Multiphasic Personality Inventory response patterns in patients with rheumatoid arthritis. J. Psychosom. Res. 8, 17-23.

Moos, R. H., and Solomon, G. F. (1964b). Personality correlates of the rapidity of progression of rheumatoid arthritis. Ann. Rheum. Dis. 23, 145-151.

Moos, R. H., and Solomon, G. F. (1965a). Psychologic comparisons between women with rheumatoid arthritis and their nonarthritic sisters. I. Personality test and interview rating data. *Psychosom. Med.* **27**, 135–149.

Moos, R. H., and Solomon, G. F. (1965b). Psychologic comparisons between women with rheumatoid arthritis and their nonarthritic sisters. II. Content analysis of interviews. *Psychosom. Med.* **27**, 150–164.

Moos, R. H., and Solomon, G. F. (1965c). Personality correlates of the disease of functional incapacity of patients with physical disease. *J. Chronic Dis.* **18**, 1019–1038.

Moos, R. H., Solomon, G. F., and Lieberman, E. (1965). Psychological orientations in the treatment of rheumatoid arthritis. *Am. J. Occup. Ther.* **14**, 153–159.

Morillo, E., and Gardner, L. I. (1979). Bereavement as an antecedent factor in thyrotoxicosis of childhood: Four case studies with survey of possible metabolic pathways. *Psychosom. Med.* **41**, 545–555.

Mueller, A. D., and Lefkovitz, A. M.(1956). Personality structure and dynamics of patients with rheumatoid arthritis. *J. Clin. Psychol.* **12**, 143–146.

Mueller, A. D., Bryant, J. E., and Marshall, M. L. (1961). Some psychosocial factors in patients with rheumatoid arthritis. *Arthritis Rheum.* **4**, 275–282.

Nissen, H. A., and Spencer, K. A. (1936). The psychogenic problem (endocrinal and metabolic) in chronic arthritis. *N. Engl. J. Med.* **214**, 576–581.

Otto, R., and MacKay, I. R. (1967). Psychosocial and emotional disturbance in systemic lupus erythematosus. *Med. J. Aust.* **2**, 488–493.

Paterson, P. Y., Jacobs, A. F., and Coia, E. M. (1965). Complement-fixing antibrain antibodies and allergic encephalomyelitis. II. Further studies concerning their protective role. *Ann. N.Y. Acad. Sci.* **124**, 292–298.

Pilkington, T. L. (1956). The coincidence of rheumatoid arthritis and schizophrenia. *J. Nerv. Ment. Dis.* **124**, 604–606.

Reinherz, E. L., Rubinstein, A., Geha, R. S., Strelkauskas, A. J., Rosen, F. S., and Schlossman, S. F. (1979). Abnormalities of immunoregulatory T- cells in disorders of immune function. *N. Engl. J. Med.* **301**, 1018–1022.

Rimón, R. (1969). A psychosomatic approach to rheumatoid arthritis: A clinical study of 100 female patients. *Acta Rheum. Scand., Suppl.* **13**, 1–154.

Rimón, R., Belmaker, R. H., and Ebstein, R. (1977). Psychosomatic aspects of juvenile rheumatoid arthritis. *Scand. J. Rheumatol.* **6**, 1–10.

Robinson, C. E. (1957). Emotional factors in rheumatoid arthritis. *Can. Med. Assoc. J.* **77**, 344–345.

Rogers, M. P., Dubey, D., and Reich, P. (1979). The influence of the psyche and the brain on immunity and disease susceptibility: A critical review. *Psychosom. Med.* **41**, 147–164.

Rothermilch, N. O., and Philips, V. K. (1963). Rheumatoid arthritis in criminal and mentally ill populations. *Arthritis Rheum.* **6**, 639–640.

Salk, J. (1962). Biological basis of disease and behavior. *Perspect. Biol. Med.* **5**, 198–206.

Sampter, M., and Alexander, H. L., eds. (1965). "Immunological Diseases." Little Brown, Boston, Massachusetts.

Shafii, M. (1973). Psychotherapuetic treatment for rheumatoid arthritis. *Arch. Gen. Psychiatry* **29**, 85–87.

Shochet, B. R., Lisansky, E. T., Schubart, A. F., Fiocco, V., Kurland, S., and Pope, M. (1969). A medical psychiatric study of patients with rheumatoid arthritis. *Psychosomatics* **10**, 271–279.

Solomon, G. F., and Moos, R. H. (1964). Emotions, immunity and disease: A speculative theoretical integration. *Arch. Gen. Psychiatry* **11**, 657–674.

Solomon, G. F., and Moos, R. H. (1965a). The relationship of personality to the presence of rheumatoid factor in asymptomatic relatives of patients with rheumatoid arthritis. *Psychosom. Med.* **27**, 350–360.

Solomon, G. F., and Moos, R. H. (1965b). Psychologic aspects of response to treatment in rheumatoid arthritis. *GP* **114**, 113–119.

Solomon, G. F., and Amkraut, A. A. (1981). Psychoneuroendocrinological effects on the immune response. *Ann. Rev. Microbiol.* **35,** 155–184.
Solomon, G. F., Amkraut, A. A., and Rubin, R. (1979). Stress and psycho-immunological response. *In* "Mind and Cancer Prognosis" Cancer (B. A. Stoll, ed.). Wiley, London, England.
Swaim, L. T. (1962). "Arthritis, Medicine and Spiritual Laws: Power Beyond Science." Chilton Co., Philadelphia, Pennsylvania.
Trevathan, R. D., and Tatum, J. C. (1954). Rarity of occurrence of psychosis and rheumatoid arthritis in individual patients. *J. Nerv. Ment. Dis.* **120,** 83–84.
Wiener, D. (1952). Personality characteristics of selected disability groups. *Genet. Psychol. Monogr.* **45,** 175–255.
Wittkower, E. D., Durost, H. B., and Laing, W.A.R. (1955). A psychosomatic study of the course of pulmonary tuberculosis. *Amer. Rev. Tuberc. Pulm. Dis.* **71,** 201–219.
Wolfe, B. B. (1970). "Experimental Pain Parameters as Predictive for Rehabilitation of the Disabled Chronic Patient," Final Rep., SRS Grant No. RD 1733-P.

PART II

Psychosocial Factors, Stress,
and Immune Processes

Stress and Immunologic Competence: Studies in Animals[1]

ANDREW A. MONJAN

Life is an adventure in a world where nothing is static; where unpredictable and ill-understood events constitute dangers that must be overcome, often blindly and at great cost; where man himself, like the sorcerer's apprentice, has set in motion forces that are potentially destructive and may someday escape his control. Every manifestation of existence is a response to stimuli and challenges, each of which constitutes a threat if not adequately dealt with. The very process of living is a continual interplay between the individual and his environment, often taking the form of a struggle resulting in injury or disease.

[RENE DUBOS, *Mirage of Health*]

INTRODUCTION

It has long been appreciated that states of stress induced by environmental and psychosocial factors can have deleterious effects upon the general health and well-being of individuals. However, it was not until the now classic studies of Hans Selye (1936a,b, 1937, 1946; Selye and Collip, 1936) that the physiological manifestations of these states were delineated and exposed to scientific investigation. Selye found that in response to a wide variety of stressors, the body reacted with a characteristic syndrome: adrenal enlargement, thymicolymphatic involution, catabolism of tissues, and gastrointestinal ulcers. This initial response he termed the "alarm reaction." Continued exposure to the stressor resulted in an enhanced state of recovery, the "stage of resistance," with a diminution or disappearance of the changes manifested during the alarm reaction. Following longer exposure, resistance was decreased and the pathology of the alarm reaction irreversibly reestablished, leading eventually to death. This triphasic response to a stressor, Selye labeled the "General Adaptation Syndrome" (GAS). Whereas the state of stress is usually construed as being deleterious to health, Selye also coined the

[1] Supported in part by USPHS grants HD 08490 and AI 15626.

185

term "eustress" to indicate that some tonic level of stress is required for well being; a similar pattern, documented for a number of physiological and psychological parameters, comes under the general rubric of arousal theory, that is, low or high levels of activity are maladaptive (Broadbent, 1971). Whatever the specific arguments against Selye's model, it is unquestionable that the heuristic value of these observations was immense (e.g., Selye, 1955, 1975).

One of the more intriguing aspects of these data are the findings that a diverse array of stimuli, acting through the brain, can induce a similar constellation of neuroendocrinological events in addition to the specific responses pertaining to those stimuli. Among the organ systems affected by these perturbations is the immune system. It is becoming clear that host immune defenses are dependent, not only upon specific immunologic mechanisms, but also upon the milieu in which these processes take place; an internal microenvironment modified by many nonspecific factors. The brain, intermediate between the environment and the immune response, modulates the ability of the organism to invoke adequate immunologic defenses against various pathogens.

The last two decades have seen a phenomenal increase of knowledge concerning both brain–endocrine interactions and immunology such that it would not be inappropriate to label earlier work as ancient history. Thus, it is timely to reassess the relationship between stress and immunologic competence in the light of these newer findings, a task which reflects the resurgence of interest in stress and disease (this volume as well as reviews by LaBarba, 1970; Amkraut and Solomon, 1974; Stein et al., 1976; Fox, 1978; Rogers et al., 1979).

The determination of a state of stress, as an independent variable, is difficult and likely to mire one in a semantic morass. This issue will be sidestepped initially but will be considered later in this chapter. Immunologic competence, as a dependent variable, has been defined in a variety of ways, from susceptibility to disease to responsiveness of cells in vitro. The following review will illustrate the sundry approaches for exploring the role of stress in the modulation of immunologic competence.

STRESS AND SUSCEPTIBILITY

Stress and Infection

Psychosomatic medicine has long been interested in the interaction of emotions, stress, and the susceptibility to infection. For example, recurrent herpes simplex sores have been reported not only as being precipitated by emotional factors (Heilig and Hoff, 1928; Schneck, 1947) but have also been treated by psychotherapy (Blank and Brody, 1950). A strong association between severe emotional conflicts prior to the onset of clinical tuberculosis has also been noted (Breur, 1935; Benjamin et al., 1948; Berle, 1948; Day, 1951; Shultz, 1952). Although there is a suggestion of a genetic contribution to resistance to TB (Lewis and Loomis, 1928), one of the first uses of animals to study the relationship between emotional patterns and susceptibility to acute tuberculosis was done by Tobach and Bloch (1955). They used strains of rats and mice that varied in degree of "emotionality," and found that the most "emotional" strains had the shortest mean survival times to a standard dose of intravenously administered bacilli. They later (Tobach and Bloch, 1958) used crowding as a stressor (Bullough, 1952; Christian, 1955) to study the outcome of acute tuberculosis infection in mice. Their data indicated that the stress of crowding (living in groups of 20 before and after infection) significantly reduced survival time by almost 2 days.

Utilizing adrenal hypertrophy as a measure of stress, Teodoru and Shwartzman (1956) varied several environmental factors and showed that incidence of paralytic polio in hamsters after intracerebral (i.c.) inoculation of the virus was positively correlated with adrenal size, and thence, presumably endocrine reactivity. However, adaptation to the stressor could abrogate this effect. For example, maintaining the ambient temperature at 5°C after inoculation of the polio virus increased the incidence of paralysis. Prior exposure to cold, on the other hand, decreased this enhancement of susceptibility in proportion to the preinfection exposure period although chronic adrenal hypertrophy was still present.

Rasmussen and colleagues conducted a series of experiments with various stressors interacting with virus challenge which indicated that stress-induced thymicolymphatic involution increased the susceptibility of mice to these agents. Rasmussen et al. (1957) utilized a shock-avoidance paradigm (shuttlebox) or confinement of mice administered daily for 4 weeks prior to, 2 weeks prior to and 2 weeks after, or 1 day prior to an intraperitoneal (i.p.) injection of herpes simplex virus at a dose which was fatal to 50–60% of control mice. They found an enhancement of susceptibility to the infection, as manifested by increased death rate and decreased survival times, when the mice were exposed to the stressors from 2 to 4 weeks, but not 1 day, prior to challenge. Marsh and Rasmussen (1959, 1960), by subjecting mice to these same stress situations, produced adrenocortical hypertrophy, decreases in circulating leukocyte counts, and reduction of thymus and spleen weights coincident with the continued exposure to the stressors. The avoidance task has been used to enhance the effects in mice of Coxsackie B-2 virus (Johnsson et al., 1963; Friedman et al., 1965) and poliomyelitis virus (Johnsson and Rasmussen, 1965). Thus, it appears that impaired lymphoreticular function induced by these stressors produces a state of reduced resistance to the clinical effects of these viruses.

Jensen and Rasmussen (1963) determined that exposure of mice to a high intensity sound (800 Hz at 123 db) for 3 hr per day for 3 days caused a leukopenia during the stress period and a transient leukocytosis following termination of the sound. They found no weight changes in spleen or thymus although there was a progressive hypertrophy of the adrenal glands. Intranasal inoculation with vesicular stomatitis virus (VSV) showed a similar biphasic response, that is, mice infected just before sound onset were more

susceptible while those injected just after sound offset were more resistant to
death than were the controls. Exposure of mice to this sound stressor after inoculation with polyoma virus increased the incidence of tumors (Chang and
Rasmussen, 1964) while suppressing slightly the progress of Rauscher virus
leukemia (Jensen and Rasmussen, 1970). No direct evidence has been
presented that, in this stress paradigm, there was a decrease of immune function. In fact, neutralizing antibody titers to VSV were unaffected by stressors,
although there appeared to be a reduction in interferon production (Yamada
et al., 1964; Chang and Rasmussen, 1965).

Other types of stressors have been used to demonstrate increased susceptibility to infection under the state of stress. Fighting of mice, produced by
grouping animals after growth in isolation, followed by inoculation with
Trichinella spiralis resulted in larger numbers of worms and larvae in the
grouped as compared to mice maintained in isolation (Davis and Read, 1958).
Similarly, chickens introduced into new pecking orders showed an increased
incidence of Marek's disease (Gross, 1972). Crowding has been reported to
reactivate a rabies virus infection in a guinea pig 8 months after inoculation
(Soave, 1964). Gravidity appears to increase the susceptibility of mice (Knox,
1950; Dalldorf and Gifford, 1954) and humans (Weinstein *et al.,* 1951) to viral
diseases.

The general conclusion that can be drawn from these studies is that "stress"
can act through the hypophyseal–adrenal axis to increase susceptibility to infectious agents. However, there are exceptions to this generality; variations in
host, agent, and criteria utilized may affect the conclusions reached. Duration
of stress and host species can indicate an avoidance-stress related decrease
(Marsh *et al.,* 1963), increase, or no change in susceptibility to poliomyelitis
(Johnsson and Rasmussen, 1965). Periodic paired light–shock presentations
can increase susceptibility of mice to Coxsackie B-2 virus infection, while the
same paradigm can increase mean survival time but not affect overall mortality to *Plasmodium berghei* in mice (Friedman *et al.,* 1969, 1973). On the other
hand, depending upon mouse strain (Friedman and Glasgow, 1973) group-
housed mice are more susceptible to *P. berghei* than are animals individually
housed (Plaut *et al.,* 1971), an effect voided by splenectomy (Plaut *et al.,*
1969). Polyoma virus infection of neonatal mice followed by sound or
avoidance learning stress increased the incidence of tumors in susceptible inbred strains of mice (Chang and Rasmussen, 1964). However, these stressors
had no significant effects on overall tumor incidence or survival times and
mortality following the infection of Swiss–Webster mice (Rasmussen *et al.,*
1963). On the other hand, Swiss–Webster mice, when infected with Rauscher
murine leukemia virus at 6–8 weeks of age and after 1 week of avoidance conditioning with daily sessions continuing throughout the experiment, exhibited
significantly lower death rates than their unstressed controls (Jensen, 1968).
In contrast, protection of susceptible mice from the usual stressors of the
animal colonies decreased the incidence of mouse mammary tumors (Riley,

1975). Incidence of tumors induced by Moloney murine sarcoma virus was increased by partial body restraint of mice, a stress sufficient to produce marked atrophy of the thymus (Seifter *et al.*, 1973).

Obviously, the dynamics of tumor formation and the chronicity of the disease permit obfuscation of the relevant parameters. It appears that acute stress in association with an acute infection does induce in the host a state of lowered resistance to disease. When either the exposure to the stressor and/or the pathological process is chronic, then the direction of the outcome of the infection is difficult to predict. More information is required as to the physiological state of the host. Additional reviews on this problem are available (e.g., Dubos, 1959; Friedman and Glasgow, 1966; Bahnson, 1969).

Corticosteroids and Infections

A primary assumption in the majority of the preceding reports was that the stress-induced increase in disease susceptibility was due to the immunosuppressive effects of the adrenal corticosteroids: cortisol, corticosterone, and cortisone. None of these studies made direct assessments of these hormones, but relied upon indirect measures such as involution of the thymicolymphatic organs, lymphocytopenia, and adrenal hypertrophy. Supporting the role of the adrenocortical hormones in the modification of disease were a series of observations that large and nonphysiological doses of exogenously applied corticosteriods enhanced the course of viral infections in animal hosts (Schwartzman, 1950; Kilbourne and Horsfall, 1951a; Giron and Allen, 1970; Giron *et al.*, 1971, 1973).

One of the most dramatic examples of disease enhancement by these hormones involves Coxsackie virus infection of mice. Coxsackie B-2 viruses are extremely lethal to neonatal mice but rapidly lose their virulence in older animals. A single subcutaneous injection of cortisone prior to inoculation with a normally avirulent dose of virus, however, can induce 100% mortality in adult mice (Kilbourne and Horsfall, 1951b; Sulkin *et al.*, 1952; Boring *et al.*, 1955). It is of interest, and a point to be developed later, that growth hormone, which appears to counteract the metabolic effects of cortisone, can significantly decrease the susceptibility of neonatal mice to Coxsackie B-2 virus (Behbehani *et al.*, 1962).

Endogenous levels of corticosteroids in mice, as well as in man, exhibit a diurnal cycle with maxima occurring just prior to the usual initiation of gross body activity (Halberg *et al.*, 1959). Interestingly, the daily periodicity of corticosterone levels in mice correlate well with the rhythm of susceptibility to *E. coli* endotoxin (Halberg *et al.*, 1960) and pneumococcal infection (Feigin *et al.*, 1969). Thus, not only do high levels of exogenously administered corticosteroids decrease resistance to manifestation of disease, but so do normally elevated endogenous levels.

Just what the mechanisms of action of these steroids are is not clear. In addition to the possible anti-inflammatory and immunosuppressive effects, there appear to be associated decreases in interferon synthesis (Rytel and Kilbourne, 1966; Giron *et al.,* 1971) at high but not at physiological levels of corticosteroids (Solomon *et al.,* 1967), impairments of the normal intracellular mechanisms for uptake and elimination of bacteria by phagocytic cells (Baardsen, 1976; Christie *et al.,* 1977), inhibition of incorporation of viral genes into cellular genomes (Gupta and Rapp, 1977), and interference with the healing of injured tissues (Dale and Petersdorf, 1973). Further reviews may be found in Shwartzman (1953) and Kass and Finland (1953, 1958).

Stress and Immunity

The acute alarm reaction described by Selye strongly suggests a corresponding decrease of immunoreactivity. Involution of thymicolymphoreticular organs involved in the generation of immunologically reactive cells, and the role of the adrenal glands for the production of stress-induced leukocytopenia (Elmadjian and Pincus, 1945) support this premise.

Mice, exposed to the avoidance learning or high-intensity sound stress paradigms, were more resistant to passive anaphylaxis (Rasmussen *et al.,* 1959; Treadwell *et al.,* 1959; Jensen and Rasmussen, 1963), and had slightly increased (but not significant) mean survival times of skin allografts (Wistar and Hildemann, 1960).

A body of evidence has accumulated which shows that experiences early in life can affect various physiological and behavioral parameters later in life. The stress of short periods of handling prior to the weaning of mice has been reported as significantly shortening survival times to a transplanted lymphoid leukemia between ages 45 and 55 days (Levine and Cohen, 1959). Similar early preweaning experience of rats enhanced mortality due to transplantation of Walker 256 carcinosarcoma (Ader and Friedman, 1964, 1965b), while postweaning handling significantly reduced adrenal sizes and lengthened survival times of rats to this tumor (Newton *et al.,* 1962). Ader and Friedman (1965a) have shown that the response to the tumor transplant is a function of type of early manipulation, age at manipulation, and the dependent measures utilized.

These preceding studies indirectly assessed the alteration of the immune response by the outcome of the introduction of foreign antigens into the stressed host. Solomon and co-workers (1968) used the stress of preweaning handling and then determined the antibody response to flagellin inoculated at 9 weeks of age. There was a slight, but significant, increase in antibody levels to primary and secondary immunization of the handled over the unhandled control rats. On the other hand, overcrowding of adult rats was found to reduce both the primary and secondary antibody responses to the salmonella flagellin whereas low-voltage shock proved to be ineffective (Solomon, 1969). A similar shock paradigm during the preweaning period was found to be ineffectual in modifying a later challenge with the Walker carcinosarcoma tumor (Ader and Friedman, 1965b). Chronic intermittent environmental stress (noise, lights, aperiodic vertical movement) over a 30-day period following initial immunization of monkeys with bovine serum albumin resulted in a transient elevation in serum cortisol levels over controls, during the first 2 weeks and significantly lower precipitating antibodies during the fifth and sixth weeks after the initial challenge (Hill et al., 1967). Immunization of monkeys with Vibrio cholerae polysaccharide coincident with a diverse pattern of irritating stressors resulted in a retardation of antibodies correlated with an increase in serum cortisol levels (Felsenfeld et al., 1966).

Crowding (Christian and Williamson, 1958) and high intensity sound stress (Smith et al., 1960; Funk and Jensen, 1967) have reduced granuloma formation (an inflammatory response) to subcutaneously implanted cotton pellets in mice. Thus, not only can the humoral limbs of the immune response be affected by stress, but so can the cellular component, or cell-mediated immunity (CMI). The stress of capture of Rocky Mountain bighorn sheep was studied by determining the blastogenic effect of phytohemagglutinin (PHA), a mitogen specific for thymus-derived lymphoid cells, upon their peripheral lymphocytes (Hudson, 1973). Over a 2-month postcapture period, there was a marked reduction in PHA-stimulated blast transformation during the first 20 days in captivity. Sera from these animals had no effect upon lymphocytes from an established ewe. Similar alterations in responses to PHA were serendipitously observed in mice exposed to the stress of new building construction, that is, loud noise and water deprivation (Folch and Waksman, 1974). A period of 1–3 weeks passed before normal responses from splenic lymphocytes could be obtained. The effect was mimicked by a single injection of hydrocortisone acetate.

Trauma, in the forms of surgical stress and burn wounds, has been reported as altering immunologic competence. Saba and DiLuzio (1969) found that surgical stress in rats depressed intravasculaphagocytosis, while primary and secondary antibody levels against sheep red blood cells (SRBC) were found to be transiently enhanced following a similar surgical manipulation of rats (Kinnaert et al., 1978, 1979). The confounding variable of anesthetic has been noted by these workers as well as by others (Wingard et al., 1967). Severe burn injury has also been found to be immunosuppressive (Munster and Artz, 1974) reflected by the increased susceptibility of rats, following a 30% third-degree scald burn, to mortality from pseudomonas infection (McEuen et al., 1976), and accelerated growth of Ehrlich ascites tumor in similarly treated mice (Munster et al., 1977). Since there was a transient 1-week depression of the graft-versus-host (GVH) response elicited from splenic lymphocytes from adrenalectomized scalded rats (Munster *et al.,* 1972), it has been proposed that this posttraumatic suppression of cell-mediated immunity is the consequence of the activation of a suppressor-cell population (Munster, 1976).

IMMUNOLOGIC MECHANISMS

The immunologic response to foreign antigens can manifest itself in several ways. Prior to the 1960s, the principal measures were for antibody (involved in immediate-type hypersensitivity and the humoral limb of the immune response) and the local inflammatory skin reactions (involved in delayed-typed hypersensitivity (DTH) and the cellular limb of the immune response). The effector cells for these two responses were recognized as plasma cells (the antibody producing cells), and macrophages (the inflammatory cells). Lymphocytes had been recognized as necessary for the production of these effects but not until the last two decades has the dissection of lymphocyte function taken place.

T and B Cells

It is now known that all lymphocytes arise from a common hematopoietic stem cell pool in the fetal liver and bone marrow. A portion of the lymphocytes are exported to the thymus where, under the influence of factors, for example, hormones endogenous and exogenous to the thymus (Wolstenholme and Knight, 1970) and macrophage products (Unanue, 1978; Diamantstein *et al.,* 1979), they undergo developmental steps which change functional properties as well as cell surface markers. Relatively immature cells, found in great number in the cortical thymic areas, possess high densities of the alloantigen Thy-1 or θ as well as the mouse lymphocyte cell surface differentiation antigens Ly-1, 2, 3, and 5 (Goldschneider and Barton, 1976). By the time these lymphocytes reach the thymic medullary areas, the densities of these membrane glycoproteins have diminished and the cells gain or increase their ability to respond to various mitogens and antigens. These thymus-derived lymphocytes (T cells) bearing the Thy-1 antigen marker are then distributed to the various peripheral lymphoid organs (Table 1). Another class of lymphocytes mature within the bone marrow and carry immunoglobulin (Ig) molecules on their membranes. These bone-marrow-derived lymphocytes (B cells) are also distributed peripherally (Table 1).

In addition, there are lymphocytes which carry little or not yet identified surface markers (null cells), and of which relatively little is known. Emerging within this group are the natural killer (NK) cells which may account for as much as 50% of the bone marrow lymphocyte population. These cells are unique in their ability to lyse transformed cells *in vitro,* without primary sen-

TABLE 1
Percentage of Distribution of T and B Lymphocytes in Mouse[a]

	Thymus	Lymph nodes	Spleen	Blood	Bone marrow
T cells	>99	70	40	40	<1
B cells	<1	20	40	40	20

[a] Adapted from Playfair, 1971; Goldschneider and Barton, 1976.

sitization, suggesting that their *in vivo* role may be tumor surveillance (Welsh, 1978).

In the processes of maturation from stem cells to immature to mature lymphocytes and passage from central to peripheral lymphoid organs, the T and B cells have been shown to be influenced by their hemopoietic microenvironments. A number of humoral factors, some clearly modulated by states of stress, can alter this internal milieu and alter normal developmental patterns. An understanding of how these perturbations effect the expression of immunologic function will require a more basic understanding of the cellular mechanisms of the immune system.

Cellular Interactions and the Immune Response

The last two decades have witnessed profound and monumental advances in our knowledge of immunologic processes. Fundamental to the understanding of these mechanisms is the collaboration between the B cells, T cells, and macrophages in response to most antigenic challenges (Playfair, 1971; Golub, 1977). Furthermore, it has become clear that each of these classes of lymphocytes themselves are heterogeneous and contain various subsets which can be identified by function and/or surface markers (Goldschneider and Barton, 1976; Cantor and Boyse, 1977; Golub, 1977; Snell, 1978). These cells interact by direct contact or release of soluble factors which affect other lymphocytes or macrophages within the local environment.

Recent years have seen many changes in the details of the various pathways in the immunologic process, such that present models may be rapidly outdated. With this caveat, we can consider one current murine model (Cantor and Gershon, 1979) which associates function of lymphocyte subsets with characteristic cell-surface glycoproteins related to the major histocompatibility complex (MHC). The cells are categorized as subsuming either inducer, regulatory, or effector function.

The initial response to most foreign antigens, such as viruses, is phagocytosis by macrophages which then process the antigen. This step appears to associate the foreign material with glycoproteins expressed by genes within the I-region of the MHC. The macrophage "signals" and/or activates lymphocytes by the release of soluble factors which potentiate the interaction between the antigen and I-region determinant protein complex on the macrophage cell surface and the inducer T cell (Benacerraf and Germain, 1979).

When activated by the antigen presented on macrophages or other cells, the inducer cells (T cells bearing Ly-1 and Ia glycoproteins), are genetically programmed to induce and "help" effector cells perform their functions, hence the term T-helper (T_H) cells. Antigen activation of T_H cells results in a clonal expansion of these cells, as evidenced in the mixed lymphocyte reaction (MLR), and in their secretion of lymphokines to modulate other lymphocytes which serve regulatory and effector functions.

Regulatory cells (T_E) appear to be a functionally heterogeneous set of T cells that bear the Ly-1,2,3 phenotype. One subset presumably represents a precursor pool that gives rise to the more mature Ly-1 and Ly-2,3 cells. A second subset bearing, in addition, the surface antigen Qa-1 seems to provide a feedback inhibition upon a class of inducer cells which also carry the Qa-1 marker. The inhibition is related to the number of these Ly-1, Qa-1 positive cells, which account for about 60% of all Ly-1 cells. Thus, while the Ly-1 inducer cells (T_H) activate B cells toward antibody formation, there is a proportional feedback inhibition upon these cells regulated by the Ly-1,2,3, Qa-1$^+$ cells which in turn are mediated by the Ly-1, Qa-1$^+$ cells. A similar circuitry has been proposed by Benacerraf and Germain (1979).

The effector cells form the efferent limb of the immune response. Macrophages, activated by a variety of lymphokines presumably secreted by a T_{DTH} cell with phenotype, Ly-1$^+$, Ia$^-$ (Snell, 1978), gather at the site of antigen and phagocytize pathogens either nonspecifically or specifically. The latter is the consequence of macrophage cell membranes being "armed" with antibodies which bind them to antigens and initiate an interiorization of this antigen–antibody complex leading to its digestion within a lysosome. The effector macrophages differ from those involved in antigen presentation to the T_H cells in that the latter macrophages bear the Ia surface glycoproteins (Unanue, 1979).

Cytotoxic T cells (T_c) are the effectors of cell-mediated lysis (CML) *in vitro*. In the absence of complement, this Ly-2,3 set causes lysis of target cells bearing antigens, such as viruses, against which they have been primed, or alloantigens at the K or D loci of the MHC. It is presumed that T_c cells also partake, *in vivo,* in the GVH and DTH reactions.

Another subset of T cells (T_s), with the Ly-2,3, I–J phenotype, act to suppress T_H activity. Suppressor cells are typically antigen-specific and serve to regulate immunologic reactivity, thereby preventing excess tissue damage.

Antibody production is the only function of the plasma cell, an end stage of B cell development. The primary antibody response to an antigen is principally of the IgM class with an admixture of IgG while rechallenge results in production exclusively of the IgG class.

Antigenic memory, a hallmark of the immune system, apparently lies within the antigen-sensitized cells, be they Ly-1, Ly-2,3, or B cells. An amnestic response is characterized by the more rapid and intense reaction upon representation of the pathogenic challenge. A continued effector cell activity implies continued presence of the antigen while the absence of antigen results in a decrease of these primed cells within the host.

This model of immunologic functioning stresses the precise manner in which cells signal and interact within the system (Figure 1). There is a maintenance of homeostasis until perturbation occurs either by antigen presentation or by physiological changes altering the responsiveness of one or more of the subsets. Restoration of the system results either in an enhanced level of functioning (immunity) or lower levels of responsiveness (suppression). At least within murine systems, cell surface markers of varying densities are available which correlate with many of the lymphocyte functions (Table 2). These markers can be detected by specific antisera. The potential exists, therefore, to measure stress-induced changes in immunologic competence not only by effector cell output but also by alterations in the subsets that regulate these activities. Considering the complexity of the cellular cooperation in generating any effector response, it would be difficult to dissect the site of such a stress-evoked lesion accurately without the use of these markers.

MODULATION OF IMMUNOLOGIC COMPETENCE

It is clear from the preceding text that various exogenous and endogenous manipulations that we associate with states of stress produce changes in immunologic response. It is also clear that these changes may be the result of altering cellular interactions regulating the effector cells as well as, or instead of, actions upon the end stage cells themselves. Similarly, the physiologically active components of the stress response appear to be varied and able to produce differing effects upon the immune system. Obviously, then, neither stress nor the immune response can be treated as unitary factors.

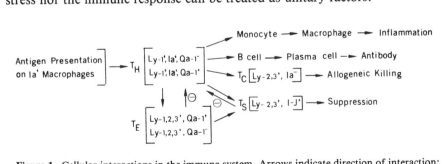

Figure 1. Cellular interactions in the immune system. Arrows indicate direction of interaction; ⊖ indicates an inhibitory interaction. Adapted from Cantor and Gershon (1979).

TABLE 2
Association between Murine Lymphocyte Markers and Function[a]

Cell type	Cell surface markers	Function
T cells		
	TL	Early differention alloantigens expressed only on surface of cortical thymocytes from some species of mice.
	Thy-1 (θ)	Antigen present on all lymphocytes processed through thymus; seen on thymic medullary cells.
T_E	Thy-1, Ly-1,2,3	Short-lived cells appearing early in ontogeny and accounting for approximately 50% of peripheral T cells; probably involved in GVH, but most important as a precursor cell for cytotoxic killer cells.
T_H	Thy-1, Ly-1, Ia	Long-lived cells appearing later in ontogeny and accounting for approximately 33% of peripheral T cells; necessary as "helper" for generating (a) antibody by B cell (for T-dependent antigens); (b) cytoxic killer cells; (c) DTH; (d) suppressor cells; primarily responsible for MLR by responding to MHC I-region differences, and a major contributer to the mitotic activity, although not directly contributing to cytotoxic activity.
T_c	Thy-1, Ly-2,3	Long-lived cells appearing later in ontogeny and accounting for 5–10% of peripheral T cells, but 50–75% of splenic prekiller, and almost all lymph node prekiller and killer activities; effector cell for *in vitro* CML and presumably *in vivo* GVH and DTH; responds to allogeneic stimulation by K and D antigens.
T_s	Thy-1, Ly-2,3 I-J	Long-lived cells appearing early in ontogeny and accounting for 5–10% of peripheral T cells (along with T_c) but most abundant in spleen; suppresses both antibody and allotypic and antigen-specific cellular responses; as with T_c, responds to K and D alloantigens.

TABLE 2 (*Cont.*)

Cell type	Cell surface markers	Function
B cells		
B₁	Ig, BLA, Th-B	Short-lived immature or precursor B cells; IgM most common Ig, species-specific B lymphocyte antigen (BLA) on B cells at all stages of development, Th-B shared by cortical lymphocytes and B lymphocytes with surface density greater in younger animals.
B₂	Ig, Ly-4.2, β, Ia, BLA, C, Fc	Long-lived mature, and memory cells, which represent most of the peripheral B cells; Ly-4.2, β, and Ia are associated with the MHC.
Plasma cells	Ig, Ly-4.2, BLA, PC-1, MSPCA	Long-lived antibody-secreting cells; plasma cell antigen (PC-1) and mouse-specific plasma cell antigen (MSPCA) are distinct antigens.
Null cells		
NK	None, although very low concentrations of Thy-1 and Fc have been reported	Derived from bone marrow, appear late in ontogeny and are found in spleen, lymph nodes, peritoneum, and peripheral blood; lyse transformed cells, *in vitro*; maybe involved in tumor surveillance and regulation of immune system.

[a]Adapted from Goldschneider and Barton (1976), Cantor and Boyse (1977), Golub (1977), and Snell (1978).

Corticosteroids

An underlying assumption of most stress studies is that the action on the immune response is a suppression consequent to the stress-induced release of the adrenal glucocorticosteroids. There is, indeed, no question that these steroids are secreted with acute stress and that they act upon components of the immune response [see recent reviews such as Clamen (1972, 1975), Zurier and Weissman (1973) or the older classic of Kass and Finland (1953)]. One must note that neither species of animal (e.g., Claman *et al.*, 1971) nor species of lymphoid cell (e.g., Lee, 1977; Papiernik and Bach, 1977) have equal sensitivity to the corticosteroids. Mouse, rat, hamster, and rabbit are steroid sensitive, whilst guinea pig, ferret, monkey, and man are relatively resistant. Neither are all of these steroids equally represented in each species nor are they all equally effective. Primates primarily circulate cortisol while rodents circulate corticosterone. The biologic activity of cortisol upon the lymphoreticular system is much greater than that of corticosterone (Medawar and Sparrow, 1956).

Administration of corticosteroids, *in vivo,* induces in man and guinea pig a lymphocytopenia which depletes a larger proportion of the circulating T than B lymphocytes (Fauci, 1975b). On the other hand, murine splenic lymphocytes exhibit the opposite effect; the proportion of B cells reduced is greater than that of T cells (Dumont and Barrois, 1977). The decrease in lymphocytes may be due to a steroid-mediated lymphocytolysis, but more likely to redistribution and trapping of lymphocytes (Zatz, 1976) or to a reduction of cellular proliferation (Hofert and White, 1968).

In man, cortisol in high doses reduces total serum IgG concentrations but does not significantly alter the ability to mount a primary or secondary response to an antigenic challenge, thus suggesting that the hormone inhibits the production of antibody by previously committed plasma cells (Butler and Rossen, 1973), probably from a pool located in bone marrow rather than spleen (McMillan *et al.,* 1976). In mice, a transitory increase in plasma corticosterone, induced by injection of adrenocorticotropic hormone, is correlated with a depression in the ability of splenic lymphocytes to be stimulated *in vitro* to produce antibody against SRBC, that is, a decrease in plaque-forming cells (PFC); this effect does not occur in the absence of the adrenal glands (Gisler and Schenkel-Helliger, 1971).

The functional heterogeneity of lymphocytes appears to be reflected in their sensitivity to action of adrenal corticosteroids (Claman, 1972; Fauci, 1976); this is particularly applicable to thymus-derived lymphocytes (Bach *et al.,* 1975; Stutman and Shen, 1977). Thymic involution associated with elevation of these steroids results from a depletion of the small short-lived thymocytes within the cortical follicles but not within the medullary regions. Cortisone acts on immature uncommitted lymphocytes (Ly-1,2,3) and not on the immunoreactive antigen-primed corticosteroid-resistant effector lymphocytes (Ly-2,3). Hydrocorticosterone treatment of mice prior to or after immunization with an allogeneic mastocytoma decreased the ability to generate cytotoxic T cells against those targets whereas there was an enhancement of the graft-versus-host reaction (Fernandes *et al.,* 1975; Babu and Sabbadini, 1977). Cortisone-resistant murine T cells have also been shown able to take part in antibody-dependent cell-mediated cytotoxicity (Lamon *et al.,* 1978) and in certain infections (Zinkernagel and Doherty, 1975). Mitogen-activated blastogenesis of mouse lymphoid cells is depressed with heightened corticosteroid levels (Monjan and Collector, 1977) as is that of man (Webel and Ritts, 1977). With age, there is a reduction in the proportion of cortisone-sensitive lymphocytes, suggesting that the immune system of older animals has more antigen-primed cells (Popp, 1977). The populations of cells affected by cortisone may be either the naive precursor or the activated helper cells (Ly-1). Addition, *in vivo,* of educated T cells, activated monocytes, 2-mercaptoethanol, or cell-free supernatants from cultures of normal activated lymphocytes can restore the immunologic responsiveness of lymphoid cells pretreated with cortisone *in vivo* or *in vitro* (Vann, 1974; Mishell *et al.,* 1977; Lee, 1977).

High levels of cortisol decrease synthesis of DNA and DNA-dependent RNA (Hofert and White, 1968; Cohen and Gershon, 1975) and have general anti-inflammatory effects (Claman, 1975). However, it now appears that lower levels (0.1–1.0 μM) are necessary for the induction of the immune response (Ambrose, 1964, 1970; Cooper *et al.,* 1979). Our data support these findings and identify some confounding variables.

Splenic lymphocytes from mice were cultured with optimal concentrations of the mitogens concanavalin A (ConA), a T-cell mitogen, or *Escherichia coli* lipopolysaccharide (LPS), a B-cell mitogen, in the presence of various concentrations of hydrocortisone sodium succinate (Solu-Cortef) for a 72-hr period which terminated a 4-hr pulse of 1 μCi of tritiated thymidine (6 Ci/mM specific activity) to determine the effect of this steroid (cortisol) upon the mitogen-activated lymphocyte blastogenesis. Low levels of cortisol, 0.1–10 ng/ml, enhanced the thymidine incorporation, due to the mitogen stimulation, up to tenfold in lymphocytes from BALB/c male mice (Figure 2). Inhibition of the blastogenic response occurred at doses greater than 10 μg/ml.

On the other hand, a similar experiment using C57BL/6 mice failed to demonstrate the low dose enhancement of ConA stimulation but did show the inhibitory effects of hydrocortisone at concentrations greater than 10 μg/ml (Figure 3). Lymphocytes from female mice were affected at lower doses of the steroid, a significant difference from males occurring at 100 ng/ml.

Both of these experiments have been replicated several times, showing, furthermore, that the hydrocortisone exerts its effects during the induction phase of the response to the mitogen. That is, addition of the corticosteroid after 24 hr of exposure to ConA attenuates the steroid effect while addition after 48 hr totally eliminates it.

This strain-mediated difference to the low dose cortisol enhancement of thymidine uptake was also found in a MLR system (in collaboration with Dr. E. Johnson). Male BALB/c splenic lymphocytes were cultured with irradiated (2000 rad from a ^{60}Co source) male C57BL/6 stimulator lymphocytes for 5 days as were the normal C57BL/6 responder cells with inactivated BALB/c lymphocytes. The proliferative responses to the respective alloantigens were assessed by incorporation of a 4-hr pulse of 1 μCi of tritiated thymidine before harvest. Aliquots of these one-way MLR were conducted in varying concentrations of hydrocortisone for the 5-day period, which was established as the optimal duration. The BALB/c cells' thymidine incorporation was up to sevenfold greater in the presence of low concentrations of hydrocortisone than in its absence (Figure 4). No low dose effect was seen using C57BL/6 responder cells. Cortisol-induced suppression of the MLR for both strains was found at concentrations of 10 ng/ml or greater. This thousandfold increase in sensitivity to the inhibitory effects of the steroid as compared to the previously

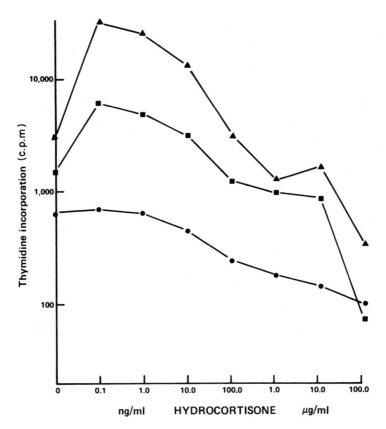

Figure 2. Hydrocortisone enhancement of mitogen-induced blastogenesis. BALB/c splenic lymphocytes (4 × 10⁵ cells/0.25 ml) were cultured for 72 hr with optimal concentrations of ConA (2.0 μg/ml) (▲-▲) or LPS (6.2 μg/ml) (■-■) in the presence of varying concentrations of hydrocortisone. No stimulatory effects were seen in the absence of mitogen (● - ●). Points are medians of triplicate determinations.

presented mitogen data presumably reflects the more massive activation of lymphocytes by the mitogens.

The experiments done in our laboratories used a culture medium consisting of RPMI-1640 plus 10% heat-inactivated fetal calf serum. If $5 \times 10^{-5} M$ of 2-mercaptoethanol (2-ME), a reducing agent commonly used to enhance lymphocyte function *in vitro,* was added to the media, then all concentrations of hydrocortisone suppressed the BALB/c thymidine incorporation in the mitogen as well as in the MLR assays. The site of action of 2-ME on the lymphocyte is not known; it is thought to enhance macrophage function (Rosenstreich and Mizel, 1978).

These data confirm that corticosteroids at physiological doses can enhance lymphocyte reactivity, thus permitting this hormone to modulate the cellular responsiveness up as well as down. Since T_H cells are the primary contributor

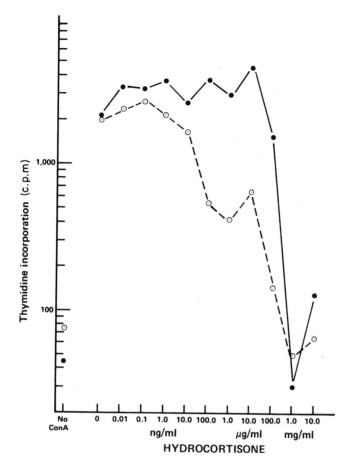

Figure 3. Response of C57BL/6J lymphocytes to ConA in the presence of hydrocortisone. Splenic lymphocytes from male (●–●) or female (○---○) C57BL/6J (2−4 × 10⁵ cells/0.25 ml) were cultured for 72 hr with an optimal concentration ConA (4.0 μg/ml) in the presence of varying concentrations of hydrocortisone. Values are the means from 2 pools of 2 spleens per pool with triplicate determinations per pool.

to the MLR, it would appear that they represent one subset of T cells responsive to this modulation. The strain and sex differences deserve further exploration before explanations can be offered. Corticosteroid responsiveness has been shown to vary with mouse strain (Treiman and Levine, 1969) with C57BL/6 relatively resistant to hydrocortisone-induced thymic atrophy *in vivo* (Tyan, 1979). In addition, female mice were found to be significantly more sensitive to that thymic atrophy.

The glucocorticosteroids can also affect monocyte and macrophage populations and functions. Decrease in plasma corticosterone levels in mice significantly increased blood monocyte numbers as well as the intensity of DTH reactions (Van Dijk *et al.*, 1976). High levels of cortisone markedly

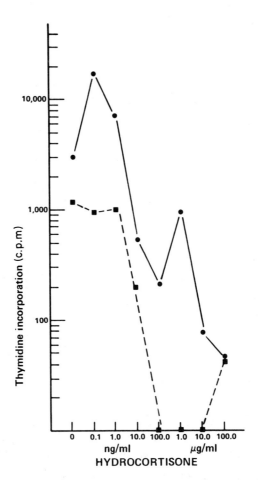

Figure 4. Mixed lymphocyte reaction as a function of strain and hydrocortisone concentration. Thymidine incorporation of BALB/cJ splenic lymphocytes responding to allogeneic stimulation by irradiated C57BL/6J lymphocytes (● - ●) or of C57BL/6J cells responding to allogeneic stimulation by irradiated BALB/cJ lymphocytes (■-■). 4 × 10⁵ responder cells were cultured with 1 × 10⁵ stimulators in 0.2 ml for 5 days, the last 4 hr of which were with [³H]thymidine. Points are the means of quintriplicate aliquots from a splenic cell pool from 10 male mice per pool. The stimulation values represent the difference between the heterologous (e.g., BALB/c versus C57BL/6) and the homologous (e.g., BALB/c versus BALB/c) mixtures.

reduce the phagocytic abilities of mouse liver phagocytes (Gotjamanos, 1970), induce monocytopenia (Fauci, 1975a), impair the cytotoxic effector function of guinea pig alveolar macrophages (Hunninghake and Fauci, 1977), and suppress the induction of cytotoxic murine macrophages by macrophage arming factor (Dimitriu, 1976). Furthermore, stress inhibits the ability of rabbit alveolar macrophages to degrade ingested microorganisms without altering the process of ingestion (Lockard *et al.*, 1973).

In summary, glucocorticosteroids at large doses (*a*) reduce antibody formation and suppress cell-mediated immunity; (b) alter migration patterns of lymphocytes; (c) depress blastogenesis of precursor cells by lysis or cellular alterations; (d) interfere with phagocytosis and intracellular digestion by stabilization of lysosomal membranes; and (e) prevent lymphokines from activating macrophages. At low doses, these corticosteroids may enhance the inductive phase of lymphocyte reactions.

Other Humors

Corticosteroids are not the only hormones influenced by stressors impinging upon the organism. It is obvious that in order that environmental and psychosocial factors affect the body's immunologic defenses they must pass through the individual's sensorium to enter the central nervous system (CNS). Within the brain these afferent impulses are modified by the personal history of the organism. Thus, similar inputs may evoke different responses. The neural region most likely involved as the final control center is the hypothalamus in its role as the "head ganglion" of the autonomic nervous system.

The hypothalamus maintains control over the pituitary gland via neural and humoral pathways. The former projects to the posterior lobe, which secretes the hormones vasopressin and oxytocin. The latter influences the anterior pituitary by the passage of releasing factors through the hypothalamo-hypophyseal portal system. Among the variety of hormones secreted by the anterior hypophysis are adrenal corticotrophic hormone (ACTH) and somatotrophic hormone (STH), both of which have been shown to modulate the immune response nonspecifically. The hypothalamus, through its sympathetic efferents, has a neural connection with the medulla of the adrenal gland. Cholinergic discharges from the postganglionic neurons stimulate the chromaffin cells of the adrenal medulla to discharge the catecholamines, norepinephrine and epinephrine. In addition, the enzymatic step from norepinephrine to epinephrine is also regulated by the corticosteroids released from the adrenal cortex (Wurtman and Axelrod, 1966). Hormonal regulation occurs through a feedback loop to the pituitary gland and possibly to brain nuclei containing receptors for the glucocorticosteroids (general reviews are available, e.g., Fessel, 1962; Solomon and Moos, 1964; Kopin, 1976; Rees, 1976; Stein et al., 1976).

Lesion studies have indicated that immune mechanisms may be modified by interruption of neural pathways. In guinea pigs, protection from anaphylaxis was provided by lesions in the tuberal portion of the hypothalamus (Filipp and Szentiványi, 1955, 1958; Szentiványi and Filipp, 1958; Szentiványi and Székely, 1958), and in the midbrain reticular formation (Freedman and Fenichel, 1958). Stein and colleagues (1976) have found that lesions of the anterior basal hypothalamus reduce the severity of the anaphylactic response in sensitized guinea pigs as well as reducing DTH and antibody titers to the relevant antigens. Under stress, rats with premammillary area lesions did not manifest adrenal hypertrophy (Ahren, 1961), indicating a deficit in the production of ACTH. Hypophysectomy or adrenalectomy counter the immunosuppressive effects of anterior hypothalamic lesions in the rat (Tyrey and Nalbandov, 1972), suggesting that this region exerts an inhibitory control over the pituitary. Janković and Isaković (1973) placed electrolytic lesions in a number of brain regions prior to immunization of rat foot pads with bovine serum albumin. Only destruction of the anterior hypothalamic nuclei and midbrain reticular formation produced significant decreases in the immunologic assays: antibody formation, Arthus and DTH skin reactions, up to 30 days after immunization. Associated with these changes were involution of the thymicolymphoreticular organs (Isaković and Janković, 1973). They proposed that the anterior hypothalamus, via STH and ACTH releasing factors, influence the adenohypophysis to secrete STH and ACTH, while the posterior hypothalamus, through the dorsolateral fasciculus of Schutz and the postganglionic synpathetic fibers, stimulate the adrenal medulla to secrete norepinephrine. These hormones, they suggested, act on the lymphocyte by binding to adenyl cyclase and activating the cyclic 3', 5'-adenosine monophosphate system. The search for the stress-induced ACTH-releasing factor(s), such as vasopressin (VP), vasotocin, and/or hypothalamic and posterior pituitary peptides, is still under way (Saffran and Schally, 1977).

In contrast to the ablation studies, chronic stimulation of lateral and dorsomedial hypothalamus induced elevation of circulating Ig levels (Fessel and Forsyth, 1963). Neurons within the nucleus ventramedialis hypothalami, but not anterior nuclei, significantly increased their firing rates following immunization with SRBC (Besedovsky et al., 1977). Iontophoretic administration of cortisol to neurons in the medial aspect of the ventralmedial nucleus suppressed firing of these cells, indicating the possibility of an inhibitory circuit (Mandelbrod et al., 1973), although it has also been proposed that serotonin is involved in the negative feedback control of release of adrenal corticosteroids (Ulrich et al., 1975). The neuroendocrine cells within this tuberal region of the hypothalamus stimulate the median eminence and posterior pituitary (Hayward and Jennings, 1973), as well as the anterior lobe to secrete ACTH (Lang et al., 1976). Cells that contain glucocorticosteroid-binding proteins can be found in the amygdala and hippocampus (McEwen et al., 1972) but it appears that only cells within the mediobasal hypothalamus are responsive to these steroids (BenBarak et al., 1977).

Kawakami et al. (1971) have studied the electrophysical changes in rabbit brain manifested by the repeated stress of immobilization. Their data indicate that the arcuate and posterior hypothalamic nuclei and the midbrain reticular formation respond to stress tonically, while neurons within the preoptic ventromedial and anterior hypothalamus, and amygdala and dorsal hippocampus are phasic responders. Furthermore, they found that ACTH production was facilitated by the amygdala and hippocampus under "no-stress" but inhibited by these areas under "stress" states. Under stress, the hypothalamic nuclei facilitated ACTH secretion, but only the arcuate nucleus continued to so function after repeated exposures. These effects were stress-specific. These very interesting results fit well with the model of gonadotropin secretion proposed by Gorski (1970), which places phasic control within the preoptic nuclei and tonic or basal secretion modulated by more caudally placed arcuate nucleus. In addition to the neuroendocrine mechanisms, Stein *et al.* (1976) have suggested that damage to the anterior hypothalamic nuclei interferes with its parasympathetic pathways and the vagal stimulation of histamine-induced bronchoconstriction which may explain the protection offered by hypothalamic and midbrain reticular formation lesions on anaphylaxis.

The relationship between stress and brain catecholamines is less clear. While peripheral levels of norepinephrine and epinephrine are usually elevated in response to various stressors and glucocorticoids, the effects within the CNS are more equivocal (Németh, 1973; Stone, 1975; Thoenen and Otten, 1978). Stress-related brain catecholamine levels and/or turnover rates have been found to be increased, decreased, or not affected, depending upon species, stressor, or investigator. The major controversy lies in the catecholaminergic control of hypothalamic nuclei under states of stress or of glucocorticosteroids. However, there are sufficient data to indicate that there are areas of the CNS where catecholamine activity is altered in response to stress, for example, the amygdala (Winson and Gerlach, 1971) and arcuate nucleus of the hypothalamus (Palkovits *et al.,* 1975).

Secretion of STH by the anterior pituitary is also under the control of releasing factors transported through the hypothalamus–hypophyseal portal system: somatotropin-releasing factor stimulates STH secretion from the somatotrophs (acidiphilic STH-containing anterior pituitary cells) and somatostatin inhibits this release. Destruction of the ventromedial nucleus of the hypothalamus results in an accumulation of secretory granules in the somatotrophs while loss of the dorsomedial nucleus produces a decrease in the number of secretory granules per cell (Nakayama *et al.,* 1974). Thus, ventromedial neurons appear to signal release and dorsomedial neurons signal inhibition of STH secretion; large medial hypothalamic lesions encompassing these two areas do not alter the levels of circulating STH. Exposure of rats to ether stress, while decreasing serum STH in normal and sham-operates, did not affect levels in those animals with the large lesions (Dunn and Arimura, 1974). Furthermore, the stress induced elevations of corticosterone in all but the rats with the hypothalamic destruction. It appears that, in rodents, there is an overlap of the neuronal regions which modulate STH and ACTH secretion, and that the hormones act in mutual antagonism under states of stress. In man, the relationship is less clear. The stress of pneumoencephalography has increased both plasma ACTH and STH (Allen *et al.,* 1974); the stress of venipuncture and catheterization tends to increase STH levels, although in a minority of individuals, and considerably less frequently than those experiencing increases in serum cortisol (Brown and Heninger, 1976). In man, it appears that stress-induced STH secretion is more related to anxiety and perceived stress (Abplanalp et al., 1977).

It has been shown that an intact pituitary is necessary for the recovery from ACTH-stimulated depression of antibody production, in vitro, following stressor (ACTH), in vivo. A hypophysectomized mouse would not regain normal immune responsiveness unless the administration of ACTH was preceded by receipt of STH (Gisler and Schenkel-Hulliger, 1971; Gisler, 1974). This hormone, whose circulating levels are modified by states of stress, is thymicotropic and necessary for the transformation of thymocytes into immunocompetent cells (Pierpaoli and Sorkin, 1968; Pierpaoli et al., 1970). Rat thymic lymphocytes have membrane receptors for STH which are apparently not species-specific. In vitro stimulation of rat thymocytes with rat, bovine, or human STH results in an increased uptake of uridine into RNA and the hormone can be localized on lymphocyte membrane with immunoelectron-microscopy (Arrenbrecht, 1974; Pandian et al., 1975).

In addition to ACTH and STH, other anterior pituitary hormones appear to be affected by stress (Blizard et al., 1977; Dohler et al., 1977): luteinizing (LH), follicle stimulating (FSH), and thyroid stimulating (TSH) hormones, prolactin, and also triiodothyronine (T_3) from the thyroid gland. Acute stress generally results in an increase of their secretion while chronic stress may result in a decrease in plasma levels due, apparently, to an inhibition of release from, rather than an impairment of synthesis by the pituitary (Knigge et al., 1959; Du Ruisseau et al., 1977, 1979).

A new class of hormones released by the pituitary are the endorphins. ACTH and β-lipotropic hormone (β-LPH) have a common 31,000 molecular weight peptide precursor, "big ACTH;" β-endorphin is cleaved from β-LPH and is homologous with the amino acid sequence 61–91 of β-LPH (Orth and Nicholson, 1977; Snyder and Childers, 1979). The endorphins have obtained their notoriety as morphinelike peptides endogenous to the body; they may function as neuromodulators. Stress-induced secretion of ACTH is associated with concomitant increases in β-endorphin plasma levels, both apparently released from the same pituitary cells (Rossier et al., 1977; Krieger and Liotta, 1979). Synthesis and release of β-endorphin, as with ACTH, is inhibited by glucocorticosteroids (Simantov, 1979).

We can no longer consider that the glucocorticoids are the only immunoreactive hormones released during states of stress. Many other humors are secreted and the pattern varies as a function of stress duration, stress intensity, stress quality, and behavioral and physiological history of the organism. Which of these hormones modulate immunoreactivity and by what mechanisms remain to be established, but it is clear that factors other than the adrenal corticosteroids affect lymphocyte reactivity (Monjan and Collector, 1977; Peters and Kelly, 1977; Saxena and Talivar, 1977; Newman et al., 1979).

Cyclic Nucleotides

With the notable exception of the steroids, the site of action of hormones is a plasma membrane receptor of the target cell. The transfer of information from receptor to the appropriate intracellular sites is controlled by the "second messenger system" of the cyclic nucleotides. The cyclic nucleotides, adenosine and guanosine 3′, 5′-cyclic monophosphates (cAMP and cGMP, respectively) are ubiquitous components of most cells. They are of prime importance in cellular metabolism and mediate cell function under the influence of various humors in the extracellular environment (Robison *et al.*, 1971a). Thus, it is not surprising that lymphocyte function is also modulated by this mechanism (Braun *et al.*, 1974; Wedner *et al.*, 1975).

The cAMP system has been the more studied of the two cyclic nucleotides, due to the at least tenfold lower tissue levels of cGMP (on the order of 10^{-8} *M*) (Robison *et al.*, 1971b). Both nucleotides are derived from their respective precursor molecules, adenosine triphosphate or guanosine triphosphate, by the loss of two phosphate groups through the action of the plasma membrane enzymes adenylate cyclase (AC) or guanyl cyclase (GC). Both cAMP and cGMP activate a variety of protein kinases which, in turn, initiate a series of phosphorylations modulating a number of cellular functions, primarily secretory. Inactivation of both cyclic nucleotides is by one or more phosphodiesterases catalyzing the hydrolysis to 5′-AMP or 5′-GMP. The sequence of events from hormone (first messenger) activation of cell receptor and membrane enzyme (AC or GC) to the physiological response of the cell through the modulation of the cyclic nucleotide (second messenger) results in a biochemical amplification of the hormonal stimulus. Furthermore, nonhumoral events, such as influx of calcium into the cell, can regulate the phosphorylase kinase activity initiated by the cyclic nucleotide-induced activation of protein kinases.

Activation of adenylate cyclase by β-adrenergic catecholamines, hormones, E prostaglandins, histamine, and high concentrations of mitogenic lectins serve to increase cellular levels of cAMP and inhibit lymphocyte effector function (Bourne *et al.*, 1974; Watson, 1976; Coffey *et al.*, 1977; Morgan *et al.*, 1977; Gallin *et al.*, 1978). Intracellular cGMP levels can be enhanced by lower concentrations of these mitogens as well as by cholinergic stimuli (Hadden *et al.*, 1970, 1974; Strom *et al.*, 1973a,b, 1974; Schreiner and Unanue, 1975; Galant *et al.*, 1976; Coffey *et al.*, 1977) concomitant with increased immunologic function. Parathyroid hormone (PTH), vasopressin, STH, and cortisol, at the appropriate doses, stimulate DNA synthesis in lymphocytes by the modulation of cAMP and/or cGMP (Whitfield *et al.*, 1969, 1970a,b; Hadden *et al.*, 1970). The site(s) of action of these hormones is (are) unknown, but may involve control of Ca^{2+} influx which in turn elevates cytoplasmic cGMP which leads to stimulation of AC causing a pre-S-phase increase in cAMP (MacManus and Whitfield, 1970).

While high levels of AC stimulators (e.g., 10^{-3} M dibutyryl cAMP) inhibit, lower levels (e.g., 10^{-6} M) increase lymphocyte proliferation (MacManus *et al.*, 1974; Watson, 1974; Morgan *et al.*, 1977). On the other hand, mitogenic stimulation of lymphocytes with PHA or ConA does not alter endogenous cAMP but is associated with augmentation of cGMP levels (Novogrodsky and Katcholski, 1970; Hadden *et al.*, 1974). Rather than immune reactivity being related to absolute levels of one or the other of these nucleotides, Watson has eloquently argued that it is the intracellular ratio of cAMP to cGMP that controls the proliferative response to antigen or mitogen (Watson, 1974, 1975a,b, 1976).

Murine lymphocyte subpopulations vary as to their basal cAMP levels as well as to the sensitivity of their ACs to be stimulated by isoproterenol or prostaglandin E. The immature thymocytes are the most sensitive to β-adrenergic stimulation while the peripheral T cells (spleen, lymph node, or blood) are the more resistant. Basal levels of cAMP follow the opposite pattern, being lowest in the thymic cells and highest in the blood-borne cells (Bach, 1975). Histamine receptors, on the other hand, appear upon the more mature splenic T cells but not on the thymocytes or B cells (Roszkowski *et al.*, 1977). They developed on T cells of C57BL/6 mice, increasing in density up to a peak 18 days after challenge with alloantigens or P815 mastocytoma cells; maximum cytolysis, *in vitro*, occurred 12 days after immunization (Plaut *et al.*, 1975). Changes in splenic lymphocytes also occurred following immunization; basal cAMP levels were elevated, isoproterenol (10^{-5} to 10^{-3} M) failed to stimulate cAMP, and isoproterenol (10^{-5} to 10^{-4} M) stimulated thymidine uptake in cultures of immune cells while inhibiting it in normal splenocytes. These effects, in guinea pigs, were limited to a period of around 3 days after immunization with typhoid vaccine (Sandberg *et al.*, 1978).

It is likely that the differing responsiveness of lymphocytes to cAMP activation reflects differing densities of surface β-adrenergic receptors. Using Sepharose beads to which were bound histamine, or isoproterenol, or norepinephrine, or E and F prostaglandins, Melmon *et al.* (1974a,b,c, 1976) passed murine (BALB/c) splenic lymphocytes from SRBC immunized mice through columns of the insolubilized hormones and found reduction (on the order of 50%) of plaque forming cells, *in vitro*, in all of the cell preparations except those reacted with norepinephrine or the F prostaglandins. This indicates that a substantial number of antigen-primed B cells exhibited membrane receptors for one or more of the hormones. Cells from similarly primed C57BL/6, in contrast, evidence no reduction in PFCs and were not retained in any of the columns.

Shearer *et al.* (1972, 1974) transferred immune splenic lymphocytes, which had been passed through the biogenic amine–Sepharose columns, into syngeneic irradiated (BALB/c × C57BL/6) F_1 mice along with antigen (SRBC). Recipient spleens were assayed for PFCs and a two- to fivefold increase in numbers was found when compared with the unfiltered cell transfers. Furthermore, when C57BL/6 mice were used in this system, they, too, had enhanced PFC responses. The regulatory cell population containing the amine receptor site, when eluted from the columns and added to filtered cells on transfer to the recipients, suppressed the number of antibody-forming cells consequently produced.

From the data presented, it is clear that lymphocytes have membrane receptors for a variety of hormones that act to modulate cellular proliferation and immunoreactivity. The list may grow longer as more humors are tried. Common to many or all (steroids being enigmatic) is the second messenger system of the cyclic nucleotides (Melmon and Insel, 1977). It is not unlikely that stress-induced hormonal secretions produce alterations in cAMP and cGMP levels in the lymphoreticular cells. The expression of appropriate receptor sites on these cells appear to change with maturation and antigenic history, thus altering their responsiveness to the stress-mediated internal milieu. Both brain and immune system are modified by the individual's history. The immunologic expression of stress reflects not only things present but also events past.

STRESS AND INTERACTING VARIABLES

A recurrent problem that plagues all stress research is the definition of stress, both theoretical and operational. As with many terms that occur in science as well as in common usage, the concept of psychological and physiological stress has many surplus meanings. Selye defined stress as "the state manifested by a specific syndrome which consists of all the non-specifically induced changes within a biologic system" (Selye, 1956, p. 54); other theoreticians have utilized definitions to best fit their constructs (see Moss, 1973, for a review of the more prominent of the stress models). As is most often the case, it is assumed that the experimental situation to which the organism is exposed is stressful because of the "disturbing quality of the stimulus" (Fox, 1978, p. 47), which alters the ongoing homeostatic state. This approach lacks the experimental rigor usually applied to the assessment of the outcome measures.

A number of studies have defined stressors as those stimuli which produce physiological changes associated with acute stress, for example, activation of the hypophyseal–adrenalcortical axis, thymicolymphatic involution, changes in heart rate, and other autonomic functions. Often ignored, however, is the patterning of other hormones, such as STH, epinephrine, norepinephrine, neuropeptides, vasopressin, which may reflect qualitative and quantitative differences of the stressors (Mason, 1975; Cohen, 1977). Nonetheless, the utilization of an independent physiological verification, based upon some stress model, is necessary, especially in animal studies.

Clearly, stress as an independent variable requires an operational definition incorporating some independent criterion for validation. This is especially needed when dealing with interacting variables such as the temporal relationships of stress, history of stress, age, genetics, and sex. These factors can all influence the hormonal milieu experienced by the immune system and, thereby, effect the characteristics of the immunologic response generated to the antigenic challenge.

Temporal Relationships

Most studies of stress and immunologic competence deal with the immunosuppressive effects of acute exposure to stressors. Chronic stress, on the other hand, may enhance immunologic function. For example, rats stressed by overcrowding for 1 week prior to immunization to a nonreplicating flagellar antigen had significantly lower antibody levels than did the uncrowded animals (Solomon, 1969), while splenic lymphocytes from rats crowded for 5 weeks prior to immunization with human thyroglobulin had increased *in vitro* incorporation of [^{3}H] thymidine when stimulated with that antigen (Joasoo and McKenzie, 1976). Rashkis (1952) delayed the onset of mortality following injection of Swiss albino mice with ascites tumor by subjecting them to forced swimming for 17 days prior to and continuing for 14 days after infection. Only after cessation of the stress did their mortality pattern approach that of the nonstressed tumor controls.

Acuteness and chronicity are temporal parameters of the stress state that may vary as a function of the properties of the stressor. They reflect the relationship between stress-onset and antigenic challenge. The importance of this timing has been seen in a number of studies reviewed earlier. A clear demonstration of this was shown when Amkraut and Solomon (1972) found that exposure to a stressor (random electric shock) for only the 3 days prior to injection of female BALB/c mice with Moloney murine sarcoma virus developed smaller lesions than did unshocked controls. Three days of the intermittent shock initiated on day of infection, on the other hand, enhanced tumor development.

We have shown that exposure to a chronic stressor produces similar changes in immunologic reactivity (Monjan and Collector, 1977). The basic paradigm used in these experiments was to present daily high intensity intermittent sound (115 db broad band noise for 5 sec once a minute for 3 hr starting at midnight) to inbred mice. After various periods of stress, the *in vitro* responses of lymphoid cells were assessed. Our data indicate that there are both short- and long-term alterations in lymphocyte reactivity. Acutely, there was a depression of immunologic function associated with circulating adrenal glucocorticosteroids. Chronically, there was an enhancement of function. The assays of immunologic reactivity, one nonspecific and the other specific, showed the same temporal pattern of hypo- and hyper-responsiveness. Both B- and T-cell activities appeared to be affected similarly; B-cell function reflected by LPS stimulation, and T-cell function both by ConA stimulation and by the specific lysis of target cells *in vitro* following immunization *in vivo*.

While the acute effect was correlated with steroid elevation, the potentiation of the immune response during the chronic phase was associated with basal corticosteroid levels. The enhanced response may have been due simply to an enrichment of the splenic cell preparations with corticosteroid-resistant lymphocytes which are a more highly immunocompetent and reactive subpopulation than are the corticosteroid-sensitive cells (Cohen and Gershon, 1975).

To test for circulating stimulating factors in the serum, new groups of C57BL/6 mice (4 per cage) were exposed to the stress paradigm. After various durations of stress, the mice and their normally housed controls were killed by decapitation between 0900 and 1000. The trunkal blood and splenic lymphocytes for each group were pooled. The cells from the stressed mice were cultured *in vitro* for 3 days in RPMI-1640 + 10% heat-inactivated FCS and graded doses of the mitogen ConA or LPS with or without the addition of 1% normal mouse serum. The cells from the normal controls were similarly incubated but with or without the addition of 1% stressed mouse serum. The incorporation of 1% normal mouse serum into the medium of RPMI-1640 + 10% FCS was found to be neither inhibitory nor mitogenic for normal lymphocytes.

As before, acute (less than 2 weeks) exposures to this auditory stressor resulted in a depression of thymidine incorporation of the mitogen–stimulated lymphocytes as compared with control values. Longer stress durations produced enhancement of blastogenic activity (Figure 5, upper curves). The presence of 1% normal mouse serum did not alter these results. Splenic lymphocytes from the normal control mice which were exposed to sera from the stressed mice exhibited a similar, although less marked, pattern of mitogen reactivity (Figure 5, lower curves), which appears to be shifted temporally to precede the pattern just described for the cells from these same stressed animals. The suppression of normal cells by sera from 35-day stressed cells was not due to corticosterone but, instead, to a substance with molecular weight between 18,000 and 30,000. It has been shown by others that stress alters lymphocyte trafficking patterns as well as increasing the density of corticosteroid-resistant cells. Our data indicate that stress-induced alterations in immunoreactivity also may result from circulating humoral factors.

Analogous modulation by stress has been reported by Sklar and Anisman (1979). They found that a single session of 60 inescapable 6-sec 150 μA shocks significantly increased tumor size and decreased survival time of DBA/2J mice injected with syngeneic P815 tumor cells.[2] However, 10 daily shock sessions resulted in mean tumor areas significantly less than and sur-

[2] A similar result occurred when DBA/2J mice injected with P815 cells were exposed to the acute sound–stress paradigm previously described (A. A. Monjan and M. I. Collector, unpublished data).

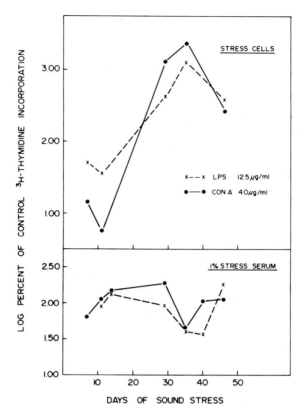

Figure 5. Effect of sound stress upon lymphocyte responsiveness to mitogens and the transference of this effect to normal lymphocytes by serum. Splenic lymphocytes from male C57BL/6J mice exposed to sound stress for varying durations of time were incubated with optimal concentrations of ConA (4.0 μg/ml) ($\bullet$-$\bullet$) or LPS (12.5 μg/ml) ($\times$--$\times$) for 72 hr with [³H]thymidine during the last 4 hr. Normal C57BL/6J splenocytes were similarly cultured with ConA ($\bullet$-$\bullet$) or LPS ($\times$--$\times$) but had, in addition, 1% serum from the stressed mice. Values are the median of triplicate aliquots from pools consisting of lymphocytes from 4 spleens per pool.

vival times approximating those of controls. Furthermore, they observed that exposure to a single shock session with opportunity for the mice to escape the shock did not lead to pathological consequences any different than the no-shock controls. Thus, these data show not only the depression and enhancement of immunological mechanisms in the control of tumor development associated with acute and chronic stress, but, in addition, show that control over the stressor can abrogate its immunosuppressive properties.

History

One major source of variability in studies of stress is attributable to unaccounted for concurrent or prior stressors. These can occur either as shifts in basal levels due to events common to groups of animals but differing between groups, or as variations in the interpretation of stimuli as stressors due to differences in experiential histories of individuals.

Animal housing conditions can have potent effects upon immunologic responsiveness. Aside from rare occurrences, such as new building construction (Folch and Waksman, 1974), mice maintained in conventional facilities may have fivefold higher corticosterone levels and greater incidence of mammary tumors than mice raised in restricted and protected quarters (Riley and Spackman, 1977a; Riley, 1975). Concurrent infections, such as with lactic dehydrogenase virus, can also alter immunoreactivity (Riley and Spackman, 1977b).

The situation becomes more complex when we consider the prior experience of the organism upon which a stressor is superimposed. A striking example was found when we collected blood by retro-orbital bleeding for corticosteroid determination of our sound-stressed mice. The whole process from bleeding and cervical dislocation to removal of spleen took no more than 3 min. Yet, the effects of the acute stress of retro-orbital bleeding on lymphocytes was still evident as long as 3 days in culture. This was reflected as an almost tenfold increase in [³H]thymidine uptake of the splenic lymphocytes when compared to those from unbled normal mice. The effect upon the sound-stressed mice was even more marked and dependent upon the animals' stress histories (Figure 6). In the absence of mitogen, the DNA synthetic activity of mice stressed with sound for up to 8 days was over 3 times that of the controls; longer exposure decreased this blastogenic potential. Mitogen stimulation with LPS or ConA produced a similar pattern of enhancement, a pattern totally different from that seen in the absence of the trauma of retro-orbital bleeding.

Age

Immunologic competence changes with age, developing through early life and lapsing into a gradual decay after the onset of sexual maturity (Makinodan and Yunis, 1977; Makinodan, 1978). While both humoral and cellular components of the immune response decline, it appears that the principal change involves diminished T-cell function (Menon et al., 1974; Walters and Claman, 1975; Haaijman and Hijmans, 1978) without apparent reduction in T or B cell numbers (Perkins et al., 1975). What the mechanisms for this immunologic senescence are [e.g., enhancement in suppressor cell functions (Singhal et al., 1978) or thymic involution (Kay, 1978)] remain to be determined.

There is a suggestion, however, of an interdependence between age, immunity, and the neuroendocrine system (Fabris et al., 1972; Pierpaoli et al., 1977; Denckla, 1978). Whether stress, through its effect upon the various hormonal systems, can alter immunologic function in an age-specific manner is an open question. Cortisone administered to fetal and neonatal rats can pro-

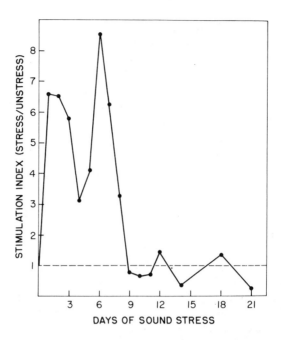

Figure 6. Interaction of two stressors upon thymidine uptake of unstimulated lymphocytes. The incorporation of a 4-hr pulse [³H]thymidine, after 68 hr in culture without mitogen, of splenic lymphocytes from male C57BL/6J mice to varying durations of sound stress, relative to control (no sound stress) levels, following the acute stress of retro-orbital bleeding appears to be dependent upon the sound stress history. Control counts were 2982 c.p.m., or about tenfold higher than usually found without retro-orbital bleeding. Points are the mean indices of 2 mice.

duce a transitory depletion of lymphocytes in thymicolymphatic structures (Fein *et al.*, 1974). As reviewed earlier, stressors early in life can alter susceptibility to a variety of pathogens. However, this effect is unpredictable and dependent upon a variety of experimental conditions (Friedman *et al.*, 1969). In light of current advances in our knowledge of neuroendocrinology and immunology, it would appear worthwhile to reinvestigate this area using endocrinologic and immunologic dependent variables.

Genetics

In addition to the species differences in corticosteroid secretion and sensitivity noted earlier in this review, there also appear to be marked strain differences to both hormonal responses to stress as well as lymphocyte responses to hormones. For example, rats bred selectively for high and low defecation scores in the open field (the Maudsley reactive and nonreactive rat strains) differ in central and peripheral norepinephrine concentrations and rates of metabolism (Slater *et al.*, 1977). Strains of rats selected for genetic predispositions to develop hypertension differ from normotensive rats in their catecholamine metabolism in response to stress (Lamprecht *et al.,* 1974; McCarty and Kopin, 1978). It is becoming apparent, as discussed earlier, that lymphocyte reactivity can come under hormonal control and that there are differences in membrane receptor sensitivity with strain and with cell type. Furthermore, susceptibility to disease and control of immune responsiveness have been associated with genetic differences in the major histocompatibility complex (McDevitt and Bodmer, 1972; McDevitt *et al.,*1972; Gasser and Silvers, 1974).

Sex

The importance of sex as a variable in stress or immunologic studies has not been well established but may prove to be significant. Female rodents have larger adrenal glands than do the males. The adrenal cortex produces androgens similar in function and structure to estrogen and testosterone. In response to stress, the anterior pituitary may secrete the gonadotropins FSH and LH. Whether the associaton between the onset of thymic involution and of sexual maturity is causal or fortuitous remains to be determined.

Preliminary data from our laboratory indicate that corticosterone levels in response to housing at moderately low ambient temperatures (12°C) are more elevated and variable in female C57BL/6 mice than in males (A. A. Monjan and R. B. Guchhait, unpublished observations). Paradoxically, the lymphocytes from these females do not appear to evidence the same degree of suppression to mitogen-induced blastogenesis as do the cells from the male mice. Obviously, the humoral milieu in males is different from that in females. It may develop that the interaction between stress and immunologic reactivity is modified by this difference.

RETROSPECT AND PROSPECT

Stress has long been known to affect our general well-being. It is part of our common experience that under states of psychological or environmental distress, we appear to be more prone to illness. The data in this review amply show that a variety of manipulations regarded as stressful, psychosocial or physical, can modify the immunologic mechanisms of the host and alter the course of infection and disease. Unfortunately, no clear model relating stress to immunologic competence has been developed.
* Why is this so? The early studies, influenced by Selye's description of the alarm reaction, assumed a model of adrenal glucocorticosteroid-induced immunosuppression as resulting from exposure to stressors. Stress was defined, essentially, as that environmental configuration which lead to adrenal hypertrophy. Immunologic competence, as the dependent variable, was reflected by

increases in susceptibility to disease. In general, this model worked with acute stressors and infectious agents, but it became less predictive as the stressors became less acute and the disease processes more chronic.

A further assumption, reflecting the state of immunologic knowledge, was that stress increased susceptibility to disease by a corticosteroid-mediated suppression of antibody production. Unfortunately, only the administration of high levels of exogenous steroids was able unequivocally to generate that type of data. Using nonpharmacologic stressors, depression of antibody titers, when found, tended to be slight and not reliably replicable between studies.

More recent experiments find, based upon current immunologic techniques, that it is the cellular, rather than the humoral, limb of the immune response that is most affected by states of stress. The T-cell population has been shown to be composed of a heterogeneous assembly of functional subgroups which are, in addition, differentially sensitive not only to the adrenal glucocorticosteroids but also to a number of other hormones.

Coincident with basic advances in our understanding of immunologic functioning has been a corresponding enlargement in our knowledge of the neuroendocrine systems. This has been due, in large part, to the development of very sensitive assay methods. It is now clear that stress is associated not only with a single hypophyseal–adrenal axis but evokes, instead, a multihumoral response. As the neural pathways which oversee the endocrine systems are elucidated, it becomes more evident that the patterning of the release of hormones is dependent upon both the experiential history of the individual and the current internal milieu. The animal of this decade appears not to reestablish a prior homeostatic level after perturbation but enters into a new stochastic balance.

Future models of stress and immunologic competence must concern themselves with the three components: stress, host, and immunity. The state of stress will have to be more carefully defined and validated. The temporal relation between the stressful event and the antigenic stimulation of the immune system can influence the immunologic response due to the variations in the microenvironment of the lymphoreticular organs. In similar fashion, the acuteness or chronicity of the stressor will establish different hormonal patterns, as will adaptation to the state of stress. Individual histories will determine whether a particular stimulus is stressful, as well as modifying responses to those stimuli. Not to be overlooked is the question of "normal" basal levels of the neurohumoral factors which can modulate the lymphoid cells.

In addition to the qualitative and quantitative properties of the stressor being integrated within the CNS of the host, genetic predispositions must also be incorporated into the stress model. Species differences have always been recognized as limiting the generalizability of any set of experimental data. However, it is now evident that interstrain genetic heterogeneity enters into both the neuroendocrine and immune systems. Inconsistencies between studies may be rectified by understanding this potential source of variance.

Immunologic competence can now be dissected based upon functional and antigenic markers for the various cellular subsets. The final outcome, resistance or disease, can be altered at many points in the interaction between antigen, macrophages, T cells, and B cells. It is likely that the final common site of action for the varied stress-induced humors may be the activation of lymphocyte and macrophage cyclic nucleotide systems.

It has been said that neuroscientists and immunologists agree that the important functions end at the thymus, they just disagree on the direction of approach. The future directions of research in stress and immunologic competence will bridge that small gap and permit the cross-fertilization of these disciplines to produce new growths in the understanding of how the whole organism functions.

REFERENCES

Abplanalp, J. M., Livingstone, L., Rose, R. M., and Sandwisch, D. (1977). Cortisol and growth hormone responses to psychological stress during the menstrual cycle. *Psychosom. Med.* **39**, 158–177.

Ader, R., and Friedman, S. B. (1964). Social factors affecting emotionality and resistance to disease in animals. IV. Differential housing, emotionality and Walker-256 carcinosarcoma in the rat. *Psychol. Rep.* **15**, 535–541.

Ader, R., and Friedman, S. B. (1965a). Differential early experiences and susceptibility to transplanted tumor in the rat. *J. Comp. Physiol. Psychol.* **59**, 361–364.

Ader, R., and Friedman, S. B. (1965b). Social factors affecting emotionality and resistance to disease in animals. V. Early separation from the mother and response to a transplanted tumor in the rat. *Psychosom. Med.* **27**, 119–122.

Ahren, C. (1961). The effect of hypothalamic lesions as acute and chronic stress reaction. *Acta Pathol. Microbiol. Scand.* **55**, Suppl. 144, 145–149.

Allen, J. P., Kendall, J. W., McGilvra, R., Lamorena, T. L., and Castro, A. (1974). Adrenocorticotrophic and growth hormone secretion. *Arch. Neurol. Chicago* **31**, 325–328.

Ambrose, C. T. (1964). The requirement for hydrocortisone in antibody-forming tissue cultured in serum-free medium. *J. Exp. Med.* **119**, 1027–1049.

Ambrose, C. T. (1970). The essential role of corticosteroids in the induction of the immune response *in vitro*. *In* "Hormones and the Immune Response" (G. E. W. Wolstenholme and J. Knight, eds.), pp. 100–116. Churchill, London.

Amkraut, A. A., and Solomon, G. F. (1972). Stress and murine sarcoma virus (Moloney) induced tumors. *Cancer Res.* **32**, 1428–1433.

Amkraut, A. A., and Solomon, G. F. (1974). From the symbolic stimulus to the pathophysiologic response: Immune mechanisms. *Int. J. Psychiat. Med.* **5**, 541–563.

Arrenbrecht, S. (1974). Specific binding of growth hormone to thymocytes. *Nature (London)* **252**, 255–257.

Baardsen, A. (1976). Influence of hydrocortisone on uptake and elimination of ^{32}P-labelled *E. coli* by rat polymorphonuclear neutrophils (PMN) *in vitro*. *Acta Pathol. Microbiol. Scand. Sect. C* **84**, 131–134.

Babu, U. M., and Sabbadini, E. (1977). Regulation of cell-mediated cytotoxicity. *J. Immunol.* **119**, 781–785.

Bach, J. F., Duval, D., Dardenne, M., Solomon, J. C., Tursz, T., and Fournier, C. (1975). The effects of steroids on T cells. *Transplant. Proc.* **7,** 25–30.

Bach, M. A. (1975). Differences in cyclic AMP changes after stimulation by prostaglandins and isoproterenol in lymphocyte subpopulations. *J. Clin. Invest.* **55,** 1074–1081.

Bahnson, C. B., ed. (1969). Second conference on psychophysiological aspects of cancer. *Ann. N.Y. Acad. Sci.* **164,** 307–634.

Behbehani, A. M., Sulkin, S. E., and Wallis, C. (1962). Factors influencing susceptibility of mice to Coxsackie virus infection. *J. Infect. Dis.* **110,** 147–154.

Benacerraf, B., and Germain, R. N. (1979). Specific suppressor responses to antigens under I region control. *Fed. Proc. Fed. Am. Soc. Exp. Biol.* **38,** 2052–2057.

BenBarak, Y., Gutnick, M. J., and Feldman, S. (1977). Iontophoretically applied corticosteroids do not affect the firing of hippocampal neurons. *Neuroendocrinology* **23,** 248–256.

Benjamin, J. D., Coleman, J. V., and Hornbein, R. (1948). A study of personality in pulmonary tuberculosis. *Am. J. Orthopsychiatry* **18,** 704–707.

Berle, B. (1948). Emotional factors and tuberculosis. *Psychosom. Med.* **10,** 366–372.

Besedovsky, H., Sorkin, E., Felix, D., and Hass, H. (1977). Hypothalamic changes during the immune response. *Eur. J. Immunol.* **7,** 323–325.

Blank, H., and Brody, M. W. (1950). Recurrent herpes simplex. A psychiatric and laboratory study. *Psychosom. Med.* **12,** 254–260.

Blizard, D. A., Slater, J., Liang, B., and Shenkman, L. (1977). Serum prolactin and hypothalamic dopamine in rat strains selectively bred for differences in susceptibility to stress. *Neuroendocrinology* **23,** 297–305.

Boring, W. D., Angevine, D. M., and Walker, D. L. (1955). Factors influencing host–virus interactions. *J. Exp. Med.* **102,** 753–766.

Bourne, H. R., Lichtenstein, L. M., Melmon, K. L., Henney, C. S., Weinstein, Y., and Shearer, G. M. (1974). Modulation of inflammation and immunity by cyclic AMP. *Science* **184,** 19–28.

Braun, W., Lichtenstein, L. M., and Parker, C. W., eds. (1974). "Cyclic AMP, Cell Growth, and the Immune Response." Springer-Verlag, Berlin and New York.

Breur, M. J. (1935). The psychic element in the etiology of tuberculosis. *Am. Rev. Tuberc.* **31,** 233–239.

Broadbent, D. E. (1971). "Decision and Stress." Academic Press, New York.

Brown, W. A., and Heninger, G. (1976). Stress-induced growth hormone release: Psychologic and physiologic correlates. *Psychosom. Med.* **38,** 145–147.

Bullough, W. S. (1952). Stress and epidermal mitotic activity. I. The effects of the adrenal hormones. *J. Endocrinol.* **8,** 265–274.

Butler, W. T., and Rossen, R. D. (1973). Effects of corticosteroids on immunity in man. *J. Clin. Invest.* **52,** 2629–2640.

Cantor, H., and Boyse, E. (1977). Regulation of the immune response by T-cell subclasses. *Contemp. Top. Immunobiol.* **6,** 47–67.

Cantor, H., and Gershon, R. K. (1979). Immunological circuits: Cellular composition. *Fed. Proc., Fed. Am. Soc. Exp. Biol.* **38,** 2058–2064.

Chang, S. S., and Rasmussen, A. F., Jr. (1964). Effect of stress as susceptibility of mice to polyoma virus infection. *Bacteriol. Proc.* **64,** 134.

Chang, S. S., and Rasmussen, A. F., Jr. (1965). Stress-induced suppression of interferon production in virus-infected mice. *Nature (London)* **205,** 623–624.

Christian, J. J. (1955). Effect of population size on the weights of the reproductive organs of white mice. *Am. J. Physiol.* **181,** 477–480.

Christian, J. J., and Williamson, H. O. (1958). Effect of crowding an experimental granuloma formation in mice. *Proc. Soc. Exp. Biol. Med.* **99,** 385–387.

Christie, K. E., Kjøsen, B., and Solberg, C. O. (1977). Influence of hydrocortisone on granulocyte function and glucose metabolism. *Acta Pathol. Microbiol. Scand., Sect. C* **85,** 284–288.

Claman, H. N. (1972). Corticosteroids and lymphoid cells. *N. Engl. J. Med.* **287**, 388–397.

Claman, H. N. (1975). How corticosteroids work. *J. Allergy Clin. Immunol.* **55**, 145–151.

Claman, H. N., Moorhead, J. W., and Benner, W. H. (1971). Corticosteroids and lymphoid cells *in vitro*. I. Hydrocortisone lysis of human, guinea pig, and mouse thymus cells. *J. Lab. Clin. Med.* **78**, 499–507.

Coffey, R. G., Hadden, E. M., and Hadden, J. W. (1977). Evidence for cyclic GMP and calcium mediation of lymphocyte activation by mitogens. *J. Immunol.* **119**, 1387–1394.

Cohen, P., and Gershon, R. K. (1975). The role of cortisone-sensitive thymocytes in DNA synthetic responses to antigen. *Ann. N.Y. Acad. Sci.* **249**, 451–461.

Cohen, S. I. (1977). Some implications of current neuropeptide studies for clinical psychophysiology of the future. *In* "Neuropeptide Influences on the Brain and Behavior" (L. H. Miller, C. A. Sandman, and A. J. Kastin, eds.), pp. 269–291. Raven, New York.

Cooper, D. A., Duckett, M., Petts, V., and Penny, R. (1979). Corticosteroid enhancement of immunoglobulin synthesis by pokeweed mitogen-stimulated human lymphocytes. *Clin. Exp. Immunol.* **37**, 145–151.

Dale, D. C., and Petersdorf, R. G. (1973). Corticosteroids and infectious diseases. *Med. Clin. North Am.* **57**, 1277–1287.

Dalldorf, G., and Gifford, R. (1954). Susceptibility of gravid mice to Coxsackie virus infection. *J. Exp. Med.* **99**, 21–27.

Davis, D. E., and Read, C. P. (1958). Effect of behavior on development of resistance in Trichinosis. *Proc. Soc. Exp. Biol. Med.* **99**, 269–272.

Day, G. (1951). The psychosomatic approach to pulmonary tuberculosis. *Lancet* **1**, 1025–1028.

Denckla, W. D. (1978). Interactions between age and the neuroendocrine and immune systems. *Fed. Proc., Fed. Am. Soc. Exp. Biol.* **37**, 1263–1267.

Diamantstein, T., Handschumacker, R. E., Oppenheim, J. J., Rosenstreich, D. L., Unanue, E. R., Waksman, B. H., and Wood, D. D. (1979). Nonspecific "Lymphocytes Activating" factors produced by macrophages. *J. Immunol.* **22**, 2633–2635.

Dimitriu, A. (1976). Suppression of macrophage arming by corticosteroids. *Cell. Immunol.* **21**, 79–87.

Dohler, K. D., Gartner, K., von zur Muhlen, A., and Dohler, U. (1977). Activation of anterior pituitary, thyroid and adrenal gland in rats after disturbance stress. *Acta Endocrinol. Copenhagen* **86**, 489–497.

Dubos, R. (1959). "Mirage of Health." Doubleday, New York.

Dumont, F., and Barrois, R. (1977). Electrokinetic properties and mitogen responsiveness of mouse splenic B and T lymphocytes following hydrocortisone treatment. *Int. Arch. Allergy Appl. Immunol.* **53**, 293–302.

Dunn, J., and Arimura, A. (1974). Serum growth hormone levels following ablation of medial hypothalamus. *Neuroendocrinology* **15**, 189–199.

Du Ruisseau, P., Taché, Y., Selye, H., Ducharme, J. R., and Collu, R. (1977). Effects of chronic stress on pituitary hormone release induced by combined hemi-extirpation of the thyroid, adrenal and ovary in rats. *Neuroendocrinology* **24**, 169–182.

Du Ruisseau, P., Taché, Y., Brazeau, P., and Collu, R. (1979). Effects of chronic immobilization stress on pituitary hormone secretion, on hypothalamic factor levels and on pituitary responsiveness to LHRH and TRH in female rats. *Neuroendocrinology* **29**, 90–99.

Elmadjian, F., and Pincus, G. (1945). The adrenal cortex and the lymphocytopenia of stress. *Endocrinology* **37**, 47–49.

Fabris, N., Pierpaoli, W., and Sorkin, E. (1972). Lymphocytes, hormones and aging. *Nature (London)* **240**, 557–559.

Fauci, A. S. (1975a). Corticosteroids and circulating lymphocytes. *Transplant. Proc.* **7**, 37–40.

Fauci, A. S. (1975b). Mechanisms of corticosteroid action on lymphocyte subpopulations. I. Redistribution of circulating T and B lymphocytes to the bone marrow. *Immunology* **28**, 669–680.

Fauci, A. S. (1976). Mechanisms of corticosteroid action on lymphocyte subpopulations. *Clin. Exp. Immunol.* **24**, 54–62.

Feigin, R. D., San Joaquin, V. H., Haymond, M. W., and Wyatt, R. G. (1969). Daily periodicity of susceptibility of mice to pneumococcal infection. *Nature (London)* **224**, 379–380.

Fein, A., Ornoy, A., and Nebel, L. (1974). Effects of cortisone on the fetal and neonatal thymolymphatic organs in rats. *J. Anat.* **117**, 223–237.

Felsenseld, O., Hill, C. W., and Green, W. E. (1966). Response of *Cercepitheaus aethiops* to *Cholera vibrio* lipopolysaccharide and psychological stress. *Trans. R. Soc. Trop. Med. Hyg.* **60**, 514–518.

Fernandes, G., Yunis, E. J., and Good, R. A. (1975). Depression of cytotoxic T cell subpopulation in mice by hydrocortisone treatment. *Clin. Immunol. Immunopathol.* **4**, 304–313.

Fessel, W. J. (1962). Mental stress, blood proteins, and the hypothalamus. *Arch. Gen. Psychiatry* **7**, 427–435.

Fessel, W. J., and Forsyth, R. P. (1963). Hypothalamic role in control of gamma globulin levels. *Arthritis Rheum.* **6**, 771–772.

Filipp, G., and Szentiványi, A. (1955). Anaphylaxis and the nervous system. *Q. Rev. Allergy* **9**, 1–2.

Filipp, G., and Szentiványi, A. (1958). Anaphylaxis and the nervous system. III. *Ann. Allergy* **16**, 306–311.

Folch, H., and Waksman, B. H. (1974). The splenic suppressor cell. *J. Immunol.* **113**, 127–139.

Fox, B. H. (1978). Premorbid psychological factors as related to cancer incidence. *J. Behav. Med.* **1**, 45–133.

Freedman, D. X., and Fenichel, G. (1958). Effect of midbrain lesion on experimental allergy. *Arch. Neurol. Psychiatry* **79**, 164–169.

Friedman, S. B., and Glasgow, L. A. (1966). Psychologic factors and resistance to infectious disease. *Pediatr. Clin. North Am.* **13**, 315–335.

Friedman, S. B., and Glasgow, L. A. (1973). Interaction of mouse strain and differential housing upon resistance to *Plasmodium berghei*. *J. Parasitol.* **59**, 851–854.

Friedman, S. B., Ader, R., and Glasgow, L. A. (1965). Effects of psychological stress in adult mice inoculated with Coxsackie B viruses. *Psychosom. Med.* **27**, 361–368.

Friedman, S. B., Glasgow, L. A., and Ader, R. (1969). Psychological factors modifying host resistance to experimental infections. *Ann. N.Y. Acad. Sci.* **164**, 381–392.

Friedman, S. B., Ader, R., and Grota, L. J. (1973). Protective effect of noxious stimulation in mice infected with rodent malaria. *Psychosom. Med.* **35**, 535–537.

Funk, G. A., and Jensen, M. M. (1967). Influence of stress on granuloma formation. *Proc. Soc. Exp. Biol. Med.* **124**, 653–655.

Galant, S. P., Landak, R. L., and Eaton, L. (1976). Enhancement of early human E rosette formation by cholinergic stimuli. *J. Immunol.* **117**, 48–51.

Gallin, J. I., Sandler, J. A., Clyman, R. I., Manganiello, V. C., and Vaughan, M. (1978). Agents that increase cyclic AMP inhibit accumulation of cGMP and depress human monocyte locomotion. *J. Immunol.* **120**, 492–496.

Gasser, D. L., and Silvers, W. K. (1974). Genetic determinants of immunological responsiveness. *Adv. Immunol.* **18**, 1–66.

Giron, D. J., and Allen, P. T. (1970). Effect of estrogen and other steroids on MM virus infection in mice. *Infect. Immun.* **2**, 426–430.

Giron, D. J., Allen, P. T., Pindak, F. F., and Schmidt, J. P. (1971). Inhibition by estrone of the antiviral protection and interferon elicited by interferon inducers in mice. *Infect. Immun.* **3**, 318–322.

Giron, D. J., Allen, P. T., Pindak, F. F., and Schmidt, J. P. (1973). Further studies on the influence of steroids on viral infection in mice. *Infect. Immun.* **8**, 151–155.

Gisler, R. H. (1974). Stress and the hormonal regulation of the immune response in mice. *Psychother. Psychosom.* **23**, 197–208.

Gisler, R. H., and Schenkel-Hulliger, L. (1971). Hormonal regulation of the immune response.

II. Influence of pituitary and adrenal activity on immune responsiveness *in vitro*. *Cell. Immunol.* **2,** 646–657.

Goldschneider, I., and Barton, R. W. (1976). Development and differentiation of lymphocytes. *In* "The Cell Surface in Animal Embryogenesis and Development" (G. Piste and G. L. Nicolson, eds.), pp. 599–695. Elsevier/North-Holland Biomedical Press, Amsterdam.

Golub, E. S. (1977). "The Cellular Basis of the Immune Response." Sinauer Assoc., Sunderland, Massachusetts.

Gorski, R. A. (1970). Localization of hypothalamic regulation of anterior pituitary function. *Am. J. Anat.* **129,** 219–222.

Gotjamanos, T. (1970). Alterations in reticuloendothelial organ structure and function following cortisone administration to mice. *RES, J. Reticuloendothel. Soc.* **8,** 421–433.

Gross, W. B. (1972). Effect of social stress on occurrence of Marek's disease in chickens. *Am. J. Vet. Res.* **33,** 2275–2279.

Gupta, P., and Rapp, F. (1977). Effect of hormones on herpes simplex virus type-2-induced transformation. *Nature (London)* **267,** 254–255.

Haaijman, J. J., and Hijmans, W. (1978). Influence of age on the immunological activity and capacity of the CBA mouse. *Mech. Ageing Dev.* **7,** 375–398.

Hadden, J. W., Hadden, E. M., and Middleton, E. (1970). Lymphocyte blast transformation. I. Demonstration of adrenergic receptors in human peripheral lymphocytes. *Cell. Immunol.* **1,** 583–595.

Hadden, J. W., Hadden, E., and Goldberg, N. D. (1974). Cyclic GMP and cyclic AMP in lymphocyte metabolism and proliferation. *In* "Cyclic AMP Cell Growth, and the Immune Response" (W. Braun, L. M. Lichtenstein, and C. W. Parker, eds.), pp. 237–246. Springer-Verlag, Berlin and New York.

Halberg, F., Peterson, R. E., and Silber, R. H. (1959). Phase relations of 24-hour periodicities in blood corticosterone, mitoses in cortical adrenal parenchyma, and total body activity. *Endocrinology* **64,** 222–230.

Halberg, F., Johnson, E. A., Brown, B. W., and Bittner, J. J. (1960). Susceptibility rhythm to *E. coli* endotoxin and bioassay. *Proc. Soc. Exp. Biol. Med.* **103,** 142–144.

Hayward, J. N., and Jennings, D. P. (1973). Influence of sleep-waking and nociceptor-induced behavior on the activity of surpraoptic neuron in the hypothalamus of the monkey. *Brain Res.* **57,** 461–466.

Heilig, R., and Hoff, H. (1928). Ueber psychogenen Enstehung des Herpes labialis. *Med. Klin. Munich* **24,** 1472–1473.

Hill, C. W., Greer, W. E., and Felsenfeld, O. (1967). Psychological stress, early response to foreign protein, and blood cortisol in vervets. *Psychosom. Med.* **29,** 279–283.

Hofert, J. F., and White, A. (1968). Effect of a single injection of cortisol on the incorporation of ^{3}H-thymidine and ^{3}H-deoxycytidine into lymphatic tissue DNA of adrenalectomized rats. *Endocrinology* **82,** 767–776.

Hudson, R. J. (1973). Stress and *in vitro* lymphocyte stimulation by phytohemagglutinin in Rocky Mountain bighorn sheep. *Can. J. Zool.* **51,** 479–482.

Hunninghake, G. W., and Fauci, A. S. (1977). Immunologic reactivity of the lung. *J. Immunol.* **118,** 146–150.

Isaković, K., and Janković, B. D. (1973). Neuro-endocrine correlates of immune response. *Int. Arch. Allergy Appl. Immunol.* **45,** 373–384.

Janković, B. D., and Isaković, K. (1973). Neuro-endocrine correlates of immune response. *Int. Arch. Allergy Appl. Immunol.* **45,** 360–372.

Jensen, M. M. (1968). The influence of stress on murine leukemia virus infection. *Proc. Soc. Exp. Biol. Med.* **127,** 610–614.

Jensen, M. M., and Rasmussen, A. F., Jr. (1963). Stress and susceptibility to viral infection. I. Response of adrenals, liver, thymus, spleen and peripheral leukocyte counts to sound stress. *J. Immunol.* **90,** 17–20.

Jensen, M. M., and Rasmussen, A. F., Jr. (1970). Audiogenic stress and susceptibility to infection. *In* "Physiological Effects of Noise" (B. L. Welch and A. S. Welch, eds.), pp. 7–19. Plenum, New York.

Joasoo, A., and McKenzie, J. M. (1976). Stress and the immune response in rats. *Int. Arch. Allergy Appl. Immunol.* **50,** 659–663.

Johnsson, T., and Rasmussen, A. F., Jr. (1965). Emotional stress and susceptibility to poliomyelitis virus infection in mice. *Arch. Gesamte Virusforsch.* **18,** 393–396.

Johnsson, T., Lavender, J. F., Hultin, F., and Rasmussen, A. F., Jr. (1963). The influence of avoidance-learning stress on resistance to Coxsackie B virus in mice. *J. Immunol.* **91,** 569–575.

Kass, E. H., and Finland, M. (1953). Adrenocortical hormones in infection and immunity. *Annu. Rev. Microbiol.* **7,** 361–388.

Kass, E. H., and Finland, M. (1958). Corticosteroids and infections. *Adv. Intern. Med.* **9,** 45–80.

Kawakami, M., Seto, K., Kimura, F., and Yanase, M. (1971). Brain mechanisms involved in adaptation to the immobilization stress. *Gunma Symp. Endocrinol.* **8,** 171–195.

Kay, M. M. B. (1978). Effect of age on T cell differentiation. *Fed. Proc., Fed. Am. Soc. Exp. Biol.* **37,** 1241–1244.

Kilbourne, E. D., and Horsfall, F. L., Jr. (1951a). Increased virus in eggs injected with cortisone. *Proc. Soc. Exp. Biol. Med.* **76,** 116–188.

Kilbourne, E. D., and Horsfall, F. L., Jr. (1951b). Lethal injection with Coxsackie virus of adult mice given cortisone. *Proc. Soc. Exp. Biol. Med.* **77,** 135–138.

Kinnaert, P., Mahieu, A., and Van Geertruyden, N. (1978). Stimulation of antibody synthesis induced by surgical trauma in rats. *Clin. Exp. Immunol.* **32,** 243–252.

Kinnaert, P., Mahieu, A., and Van Geertruyden, N. (1979). Stimulation of antibody synthesis induced by surgical trauma in rats. Revised statistical analysis. *Clin. Exp. Immunol.* **37,** 174–175.

Knigge, K. M., Penrod, C. H., and Schindler, W. J. (1959). *In vitro* and *in vivo* adrenal corticosteroid secretion following stress. *Am. J. Physiol.* **196,** 579–582.

Knox, A. W. (1950). Infection and immunity in offspring of mice inoculated during gestation with murine poliomyelitis virus. *Proc. Soc. Exp. Biol. Med.* **74,** 792–796.

Kopin, I. J. (1976). Catecholamines, adrenal hormones, and stress. *Hosp. Pract.* **11,** 49–55.

Krieger, D. T., and Liotta, A. S. (1979). Pituitary hormones in brain, where, how, and why? *Science* **205,** 366–372.

LaBarba, R. C. (1970). Experiential and environmental factors in cancer. A review of research in animals. *Psychosom. Med.* **32,** 259–276.

Lamon, E. W., Williams, B. R., Fuson, E. W., Whitten, H. D., and Walia, H. S. (1978). Murine T cells that lyse antibody-sensitized target cells. *J. Immunol.* **120,** 244–248.

Lamprecht, F., Eichelman, B. S., Williams, R. B., Wooten, G. F., and Kopin, I. J. (1974). Serum dopamine-beta-hydroxylase (DBH) activity and blood pressure response of rat strains to shock-induced fighting. *Psychosom. Med.* **36,** 298–303.

Lang, R. W., Voigt, K. H., Fehm, H. L., and Pfeiffer, E. F. (1976). Localization of corticotropin releasing activity in the rat hypothalamus. *Neurosci. Lett.* **2,** 19–22.

Lee, K. C. (1977). Cortisone as a proble for cell interactions in the generation of cytotoxic T cells. *J. Immunol.* **119,** 1836–1845.

Levine, S., and Cohen, C. (1959). Differential survival to leukemia as a function of infantile stimulation in DBA/2 mice. *Proc. Soc. Exp. Biol. Med.* **102,** 53–54.

Lewis, P. A., and Loomis, D. (1928). Allergic irritability; capacity of guinea pigs to produce antibodies as affected by inheritance and as related to familial resistance to tuberculosis. *J. Exp. Med.* **47,** 437–448.

Lockhard, V. G., Grogan, J. B., and Brunson, J. G. (1973). Alterations in the bactericidal ability of rabbit alveolar macrophages as a result of tumbling stress. *Am. J. Pathol.* **70,** 57–62.

McCarty, R., and Kopin, I. (1978). Alterations in plasma catecholamines and behavior during acute stress in spontaneously hypertensive and Wistar-Kyoto normotensive rats. *Life Sci.* **22,** 997–1006.

McDevitt, H. O., and Bodmer, W. F. (1972). Histocompatibility antigens, immune responses and susceptibility to disease. *Am. J. Med.* **52**, 1-8.

McDevitt, H. O., Deak, B. D., Schreffler, D. C., Klein, J., Stimpfling, J. H., and Snell, G. D. (1972). Genetic control of the immune responses. Mapping of the Ir-1 locus. *J. Exp. Med.* **135**, 1259-1278.

McEuen, D. D., Blair, P., Delbene, V. E., and Eurenius, K. (1976). Correlation between pseudomonas burn wound infection and granulocyte antibacterial activity. *Infect. Immun.* **13**, 1360-1362.

McEwen, B. S., Magnus, C., and Wallach, G. (1972). Soluble corticosterone-binding macromolecules extracted from rat brain. *Endocrinology* **90**, 217-226.

MacManus, J. P., and Whitfield, J. F. (1970). Inhibition by thyrocalcitonin of the mitogenic actions of parathyroid hormone and cyclic adenosine $3',5'$-monophosphate on rat thymocytes. *Endocrinology* **86**, 934-939.

MacManus, J. P., Whitfield, J. F., and Rixan, R. H. (1974). Control of normal cell proliferation *in vivo* and *in vitro* by agents that use cyclic AMP as their mediator. *In* "Cyclic AMP, Cell Growth, and the Immune Response" (W. Braun, L. M. Lichtenstein, and C. W. Parker, eds.), pp. 302-316. Springer-Verlag, Berlin and New York.

McMillan, R., Longmire, R., and Yelenosky, R. (1976). The effects of corticosteroids on human IgG synthesis. *J. Immunol.* **116**, 1592-1595.

Makinodan, T. (1978). Mechanism of senescence of immune response. *Fed. Proc., Fed. Am. Soc. Exp. Biol.* **37**, 1239-1269.

Makinodan, T., and Yunis, E., eds. (1977). "Immunology and Aging." Plenum, New York.

Mandelbrod, I., Feldman, S., and Werman, R. (1973). Effects of microelectrophoretically administered cortisol on single cell activity in the tuberal hypothalamus of the rat. *Isr. J. Med. Sci.* **9**, 1058-1061.

Marsh, J. T., and Rasmussen, A. F., Jr. (1959). Effects of exposure to fear producing stressors on mouse organ weights and leukocyte counts. *Fed. Proc., Fed. Am. Soc. Exp. Biol.* **18**, 583.

Marsh, J. T., and Rasmussen, A. F., Jr. (1960). Response of adrenals, thymus, spleen and leukocytes to shuttle box and confinement stress. *Proc. Soc. Exp. Biol. Med.* **104**, 180-183.

Marsh, J. T., Lavender, J. F., Chang, S. S., and Rasmussen, A. F., Jr. (1963). Poliomyelitis in monkeys: Decreased susceptibility after avoidance stress. *Science* **140**, 1414-1415.

Mason, J. W. (1975). A historical view of the stress field. *J. Hum. Stress* **1**, 22-36.

Medawar, P. B., and Sparrow, E. R. (1956). The effects of adrenocortical hormones, adrenocorticotrophic hormone and pregnancy on skin transplantation immunity in mice. *J. Endocrinol.* **14**, 240-256.

Melmon, K. L., and Insel, P. A. (1977). Inflammatory and immune responses: Cell individuality amidst ubiquitous hormonal signals. *Johns Hopkins Med. J.* **141**, 15-22.

Melmon, K. L., Weinstein, Y., Bourne, H. R., Shearer, G., Poon, T., Krasny, L., and Segal, S. (1976). Isolation of cells with specific receptors for amines: Opportunities and problems. *In* "Cell Membrane Receptors for Viruses, Antigens and Antibodies, Polypeptide Hormones, and Small Molecules" (R. F. Beers and E. G. Bassett, eds.), pp. 117-133. Raven, New York.

Melmon, K. L., Weinstein, Y., Shearer, G. M., and Bourne, H. R. (1974a). Leukocyte separation on the basis of their receptors for biogenic amines and prostaglandins: Relation of the receptor to antibody formation. *In* "Cyclic AMP, Cell Growth, and the Immune Response" (W. Braun, L. M. Lichtenstein, and C. W. Parker, eds.), pp. 114-134. Springer-Verlag, Berlin and New York.

Melmon, K. L., Bourne, H. R., Weinstein, Y., Shearer, G. M., Kram, J., and Bauminger, S. (1974b). Hemolytic plaque formation by leukocytes *in vitro*. Control by vasoactive hormones. *J. Clin. Invest.* **53**, 13-21.

Melmon, K. L., Weinstein, Y., Shearer, G. M., Bourne, H. R., and Bauminger, S. (1974c). Separation of specific antibody forming mouse cells by their adherence to insolubilized endogenous hormones. *J. Clin. Invest.* **53**, 22-30.

Menon, M., Jaroslow, B. N., and Koesteres, R. (1974). The decline of cell-mediated immunity in aging mice. *J. Gerontol.* **29**, 499–505.

Mishell, R. I., Lucas, A., and Mishell, B. B. (1977). The role of activated accessory cells in preventing immunosuppression by hydrocortisone. *J. Immunol.* **119**, 118–122.

Monjan, A. A., and Collector, M. I. (1977). Stress-induced modulation of the immune response. *Science* **196**, 307–308.

Morgan, J. I., Hall, A. K., and Perris, A. D. (1977). The ionic dependence and steroid blockade of cyclic nucleotide-induced mitogenesis in isolated rat thymic lymphocytes. *J. Cyclic Nucleotide Res.* **3**, 303–314.

Moss, G. E. (1973). "Illness, Immunity, and Social Interaction." Wiley, New York.

Munster, A. M. (1976). Post-traumatic immunosuppression is due to activation of suppressor T cells. *Lancet* **1**, 1329–1330.

Munster, A. M., and Artz, C. P. (1974). A neglected aspect of trauma pathophysiology: The immunologic response to injury. *South. Med. J.* **67**, 935–940.

Munster, A. M., Eurenius, K., Mortenson, R. F., and Mason, A. D., Jr. (1972). Ability of splenic lymphocytes from injured rats to induce a graft-versus-host reaction. *Transplantation* **14**, 106–108.

Munster, A. M., Gale, G. R., and Hunt, H. H. (1977). Accelerated tumor growth following experimental burns. *J. Trauma* **17**, 373–375.

Nakayama, I., Nickerson, P. A., Bernardis, L. L., and Matsuo, T. (1974). Fine structural studies of rat adenohypophysis. Effects of exogenous growth hormone and hypothalamic lesions on somatotrophs. *Acta Pathol. Jpn.* **24**, 569–594.

Németh, S. (1973). "Hormones, Metabolism and Stress." Slovak Acad. Sci., Bratislavia.

Newman, B. R., Byers, V. S., Levin, A. S., and German, D. F. (1979). Variability of lymphocyte functions mediated by serum factors. *J. Clin. Lab. Immunol.* **2**, 151–154.

Newton, G., Bly, C. G., and McCrary, C. (1962). Effects of early experience on the response to transplanted tumor. *J. Nerv. Ment. Dis.* **134**, 522–527.

Novogrodsky, A., and Katcholski, E. (1970). Effect of phytohemagglutinin and prostaglandins on cyclic AMP synthesis in rat lymph node lymphocytes. *Biochim. Biophys. Acta* **215**, 291–296.

Orth, D. H., and Nicholson, W. E. (1977). Different molecular forms of ACTH. *Ann. N.Y. Acad. Sci.* **297**, 27–46.

Palkovits, M., Kobayashi, R. M., Kizer, J. S., Jacobowitz, D. M., and Kopin, I. J. (1975). Effects of stress on catecholamines and tyrosine hydroxylase activity of individual hypothalamic nuclei. *Neuroendocrinology* **18**, 144–153.

Pandian, M. R., Gupta, P. D., Talwar, G. P., and Avrameas, S. (1975). Presence of "receptors" for growth hormone on membranes of rat thymocytes. *Acta Endocrinol. Copenhagen* **78**, 781–790.

Papiernik, M., and Bach, J. F. (1977). Thymocyte subpopulation in young and adult mice. II. Study of steroid-resistant populations by means of a specific heteroantiserum. *Eur. J. Immunol.* **7**, 800–803.

Perkins, E. H., Peterson, W. J., Gottlieb, C. F., Halsall, M. K., Cacherio, L. H., and Makinodan, T. (1975). The late effects of selected immunosuppressents on immunocompetence, disease incidence and mean life-span. I. Humoral immune activity. *Mech. Ageing Dev.* **4**, 231–239.

Peters, L. J., and Kelly, H. (1977). Effect of stress on tumor transplantation. *Cancer* **39**, 1482–1488.

Pierpaoli, W., and Sorkin, E. (1968). Hormones and immunologic capacity. *J. Immunol.* **101**, 1036–1043.

Pierpaoli, W., Fabris, N., and Sorkin, E. (1970). Developmental hormones and immunological maturation. *In* "Hormones and the Immune Response" (G. E. W. Wolstenholme and J. Knight, eds.), pp. 126–143. Churchill, London.

Pierpaoli, W., Kopp, H. G., Müller, J., and Keller, M. (1977). Interdependence between neuroendocrine programming and generation of immune recognition in ontogeny. *Cell. Immunol.* **29**, 16–27.

Plaut, M., Lichtenstein, L. M., and Henny, C. S. (1975). Properties of a subpopulation of T cells bearing histamine receptors. *J. Clin. Invest.* **55**, 856–874.

Plaut, S. M., Ader, R., Friedman, S. B., and Ritterson, A. L. (1969). Social factors and resistance to malaria in the mouse: Effects of group versus individual housing on resistance to *Plasmodium berghei* infection. *Psychosom. Med.* **31**, 536–552.

Plaut, S. M., Friedman, S. B., and Grota, L. J. (1971). *Plasmodium berghei:* Resistance to infection in group and individually housed mice. *Exp. Parasitol.* **29**, 47–52.

Playfair, J. H. L. (1971). Cell cooperation in the immune response. *Clin. Exp. Immunol.* **8**, 839–856.

Popp, D. M. (1977). Qualitative changes in immunocompetent cells with age: Reduced sensitivity to cortisone acetate. *Mech. Ageing Dev.* **6**, 355–362.

Rashkis, H. A. (1952). Systemic stress as inhibitor of experimental tumors in swiss mice. *Science* **116**, 169–171.

Rasmussen, A. F., Jr., Marsh, J. T., and Brill, N. Q. (1957). Increased susceptibility to herpes simplex in mice subjected to avoidance-learning stress or restraint. *Proc. Soc. Exp. Biol. Med.* **96**, 183–189.

Rasmussen, A. F., Jr., Spencer, E. S., and Marsh, J. T. (1959). Decrease in susceptibility of mice to passive anaphylaxis following avoidance-learning stress. *Proc. Soc. Exp. Biol. Med.* **100**, 878–879.

Rasmussen, A. F., Jr., Hildeman, W. H., and Sellers, M. I. (1963). Malignancy of polyoma virus in relation to stress. *J. Natl. Cancer Inst.* **30**, 101–112.

Rees, W. L. (1976). Stress, distress and disease. *Br. J. Psychiatry* **128**, 3–18.

Riley, V. (1975). Mouse mammary tumors: Alteration of incidence as apparent function of stress. *Science* **189**, 465–467.

Riley, V., and Spackman, D. (1977a). Housing stress. *Lab. Anim.* **6**, 16–21.

Riley, V., and Spackman, D. (1977b). Modifying effects of a benign virus on the malignant process and the role of physiological stress on tumor incidence. *Fogarty Int. Cent. Proc.* **28**, 319–336.

Robison, G. A., Butcher, R. W., and Sutherland, E. W. (1971a). "Cyclic AMP." Academic Press, New York.

Robison, G. A., Nahas, G. G., and Triner, L. eds. (1971b). Cyclic AMP and cell function. *Ann. N.Y. Acad. Sci.* **185**, 1–556.

Rogers, M. P., Dubey, D., and Reich, P. (1979). The influence of the psyche and the brain on immunity and disease susceptibility: A critical review. *Psychosom. Med.* **41**, 147–164.

Rosenstreich, D. L., and Mizel, S. B. (1978). The participation of macrophages and macrophage cell lines in the activation of T lymphocytes by mitogens. *Immunol. Rev.* **40**, 102–135.

Rossier, J., French, E. D., Rivier, C., Ling, N., Guillemin, R., and Bloom, F. E. (1977). Footshock induced stress increases β-endorphin level in blood but not brain. *Nature (London)* **270**, 618–620.

Roszkowksi, W., Plaut, M., and Lichtenstein, L. M. (1977). Selective display of histamine receptors on lymphocytes. *Science* **195**, 683–685.

Rytel, M. W., and Kilbourne, E. F. (1966). The influence of cortisone on experimental viral infection. *J. Exp. Med.* **123**, 767–775.

Saba, T. M., and DiLuzio, N. R. (1969). Surgical stress and reticuloendothelial function. *Surgery* **65**, 802–807.

Saffran, M., and Schally, A. V. (1977). The status of the corticotropin releasing factor (CRF). *Neuroendocrinology* **24**, 359–379.

Sandberg, G., Ernström, U., Nordlind, K., and Fredholm, B. B. (1978). Effect of immunization on the cyclic AMP level and ^{3}H-thymidine incorporation in cultured lymphoid cells. *Int. Arch. Allergy Appl. Immunol.* **56**, 449–456.

Saxena, R. K., and Talivar, G. R. (1977). An anterior pituitary factor stimulates thymidine incorporation in isolated thymocytes. *Nature (London)* **268**, 57–58.

Schneck, J. M. (1947). The psychological components in a case of herpes simplex. *Psychosom. Med.* **9**, 62–64.

Schreiner, G. F., and Unanue, E. R. (1975). The modulation of spontaneous and anti-Ig-stimulated motility of lymphocytes by cyclic nucleotides and adrenergic and cholinergic agents. *J. Immunol.* **114**, 802–808.

Shwartzman, G. (1950). Enhancing effect of cortisone upon poliomyelitis infection (strain MEFI) in hamsters and mice. *Proc. Soc. Exp. Biol. Med.* **75**, 835–838.

Shwartzman, G. ed. (1953). "The Effect of ACTH and Cortisone Upon Infection and Resistance." Columbia Univ. Press, New York.

Seifter, E., Rettura, G., Zisblatt, M., Levenson, S. M., Levine, N., Davidson, A., and Seifter, J. (1973). Enhancement of tumor development in physically-stressed mice incubated with an oncogenic virus. *Experientia* **29**, 1379–1382.

Selye, H. (1936a). A syndrome produced by diverse nocuous agents. *Nature (London)* **138**, 32.

Selye, H. (1936b). Thymus and adrenals in the response of the organism to injuries and intoxications. *Br. J. Exp. Pathol.* **17**, 234–248.

Selye, H. (1937). Studies on adaptation. *Endocrinology* **21**, 169–188.

Selye, H. (1946). The general adaptation syndrome and the diseases of adaptation. *J. Clin. Endocrinol.* **6**, 117–230.

Selye, H. (1955). Stress and disease. *Science* **122**, 625–631.

Selye, H. (1956). "The Stress of Life." McGraw-Hill, New York.

Selye, H. (1975). "Stress in Health and Disease." Butterworth, London.

Selye, H., and Collip, J. B. (1936). Fundamental factors in the interpretation of stimuli influencing endocrine glands. *Endocrinology* **20**, 667–672.

Shearer, G. M., Melmon, K. L., Weinstein, Y., and Sela, M. (1972). Regulation of antibody responses by cells expressing histamine receptors. *J. Exp. Med.* **136**, 1302–1307.

Shearer, G. M., Weinstein, Y., Melmon, K. L., and Bourne, H. R. (1974). Separation of leukocytes by their amine receptors: Subsequent immunologic functions. *In* "Cyclic AMP, Cell Growth, and the Immune Response" (W. Braun, L. M. Lichtenstein, and C. W. Parker, eds.), pp. 135–146. Springer-Verlag, Berlin and New York.

Shultz, I. T. (1952). The emotions of the tubercular: A review and an analysis. *J. Abnorm. Psychol.* **37**, 260–263.

Simantov, R. (1979). Glucocorticoids inhibit endorphin synthesis by pituitary cells. *Nature (London)* **280**, 684–685.

Singhal, S. K., Roder, J. C., and Duive, A. K. (1978). Suppressor cells in immunosenescence. *Fed. Proc., Fed. Am. Soc. Exp. Biol.* **37**, 1245–1252.

Sklar, L. S., and Anisman, H. (1979). Stress and coping factors influence tumor growth. *Science* **205**, 513–515.

Slater, J., Blizard, D. A., and Pohorecky, L. A. (1977). Central and peripheral norepinephrine metabolism in rat strains selectively bred for differences in response to stress. *Pharmacol., Biochem. Behav.* **6**, 511–520.

Smith, L. M., Molomat, N., and Gottfried, B. (1960). Effect of subconvulsive audiogenic stress in mice on turpentine-induced inflammation. *Proc. Soc. Exp. Biol. Med.* **103**, 370–372.

Snell, G. D. (1978). T cells, T cell recognition structures, and the major histocompatibility complex. *Immunol. Rev.* **38**, 3–69.

Snyder, S. H., and Childers, S. R. (1979). Opiate receptors and opioids peptides. *Annu. Rev. Neurosci.* **2**, 35–64.

Soave, O. A. (1964). Reactivation of rabies virus in a guinea pig due to the stress of crowding. *Am. J. Vet. Res.* **25**, 268–269.

Solomon, G. F. (1969). Stress and antibody response in rats. *Int. Arch. Allergy Appl. Immunol.* **35**, 97–104.

Solomon, G. F., and Moos, R. H. (1964). Emotions, immunity and disease: A speculative theoretical integration. *Arch. Gen. Psychiatry* **11**, 657–674.

Solomon, G. F., Merigan, T. C., and Levine, S. (1967). Variation in adrenal cortical hormones within physiologic ranges, stress and interferon production in mice. *Proc. Soc. Exp. Biol. Med.* **126**, 74–79.

Solomon, G. F., Levine, S., and Kraft, J. K. (1968). Early experience and immunity. *Nature (London)* **220**, 821–822.

Stein, M., Schiavi, R. C., and Camerino, M. (1976). Influence of brain and behavior on the immune system. *Science* **191**, 435–440.

Stone, E. A. (1975). Stress and catecholamines. *In* "Catecholamines and Behavior" (A. J. Friedhoff, ed.), pp. 31–72. Plenum, New York.

Strom, T. B., Carpenter, C. B., Garvoy, M. R., Austen, K. F., Merrill, J. P., and Kalmer, M. (1973a). The modulating influence of cyclic nucleotide upon lymphocyte-mediated cytotoxicity. *J. Exp. Med.* **138**, 381–393.

Strom, T. B., Deisseroth, A., Morgan-Roth, J., Carpenter, C. B., and Merrill, J. P. (1973b). Regulatory role of the cyclic nucleotides in alloimmune lymphocyte-mediated cytotoxicity. Effect of imidazole. *Transplant. Proc.* **5**, 425–427.

Strom, T. B., Deisseroth, A., Morganroth, J., Carpenter, C. B., and Merrill, J. P. (1974). Modulation of cytotoxic T lymphocyte function by cyclic 3′, 5′-mononucleotides. *In* "Cyclic AMP, Cell Growth, and the Immune Response" (W. Braun, L. M. Lichtenstein, and C. W. Parker, eds.), pp. 209–221. Springer-Verlag, Berlin and New York.

Stutman, O., and Shen, F. W. (1977). Post-thymic and precursor cells are sensitive to steroids and belong to the Ly-1, 2, 3⁺ subset. *Fed. Proc., Fed. Am. Soc. Exp. Biol.* **36**, 1301.

Sulkin, S. E., Wallis, H. C., and Donaldson, P. (1952). Differentiation of Coxsackie viruses by altering susceptibility of mice with cortisone. *J. Infect. Dis.* **91**, 290–296.

Szentiványi, A., and Filipp, G. (1958). Anaphylaxis and the nervous system. II. *Ann. Allergy* **16**, 143–151.

Szentiványi, A., and Székely, J. (1958). Anaphylaxis and the nervous system. IV. *Ann. Allergy* **16**, 389–392.

Teodoru, C. V., and Shwartzman, G. (1956). Endocrine factors in pathogenesis of experimental poliomyelitis in hamsters: Role of inoculating and environmental stress. *Proc. Soc. Exp. Biol. Med.* **91**, 181–187.

Thoenen, H., and Otten, U. (1978). Role of adrenocortical hormones in the modulation of synthesis and degradation of enzymes involved in the formation of catecholamines. *In* "Frontiers in Neuroendocrinology" (W. F. Ganong and L. Martini, eds.), pp. 163–184. Raven, New York.

Tobach, E., and Bloch, H. (1955). A study of the relationship between behavior and susceptibility to tuberculosis in rats and mice. *Adv. Tuberc. Res.* **6**, 62–89.

Tobach, E., and Bloch, H. (1958). Effect of stress by crowding prior to and following tuberculous infection. *Am. J. Physiol.* **187**, 399–402.

Treadwell, P. E., Wistar, R., Rasmussen, A. F., Jr., and Marsh, J. T. (1959). The effect of acute stress on the susceptibility of mice to passive anaphylaxis. *Fed. Proc., Fed. Am. Soc. Exp. Biol.* **18**, 602.

Treiman, D. M., and Levine, S. (1969). Plasma corticosteroid response to stress in four species of wild mice. *Endocrinology* **84**, 676–680.

Tyan, M. L. (1979). Genetic control of hydrocortisone-induced thymus atrophy. *Immunogenetics* **8**, 177–181.

Tyrey, I., and Nalbandov, A. B. (1972). Influence of anterior hypothalamic lesions on circulating antibody titers in the rat. *Am. J. Physiol.* **222**, 179–185.

Ulrich, R., Yuwiler, A., and Geller, E. (1975). Effects of hydrocortisone on biogenic amine levels in the hypothalamus. *Neuroendocrinology* **19**, 259–268.

Unanue, E. R. (1978). The regulation of lymphocyte functions by the macrophages. *Immunol. Rev.* **40**, 227–255.

Unanue, E. R. (1979). The macrophage as a regulator of lymphocyte function. *Hosp. Pract.* **14**, 61–74.

Van Dijk, H., Testerink, J., and Novrdegraff, E. (1976). Stimulation of the immune response against SRBC by reduction of corticosterone plasma levels: Mediation by mononuclear phagocytes. *Cell. Immunol.* **25**, 8–14.

Vann, D. C. (1974). Restoration of the *in vitro* antibody response of cortisone-treated spleen cells by T cells or soluble factors. *Cell. Immunol.* **11**, 11–18.

Walters, C. S., and Claman, H. N. (1975). Age-related changes in cell-mediated immunity in BALB/c mice. *J. Immunol.* **115**, 1438–1443.

Watson, J. (1974). The nature of the signals required for the induction of antibody synthesis. *In* "The Immune System: Genes, Receptors, Signals" (E. E. Sercarz, A. R. Williamson, and C. F. Fox, eds.), pp. 511–532. Academic Press, New York.

Watson, J. (1975a). Cyclic nucleotides as intracellular mediators of B cell activation. *Transplant. Rev.* **23**, 223–249.

Watson, J. (1975b). The influence of intracellular levels of cyclic nucleotides on cell proliferation and the induction of antibody synthesis. *J. Exp. Med.* **141**, 97–111.

Watson, J. (1976). The involvement of cyclic nucleotide metabolism in the initiation of lymphocyte proliferation induced by mitogens. *J. Immunol.* **117**, 1656–1663.

Webel, M. L., and Ritts, R. E., Jr. (1977). The effects of corticosteroid concentrations on lymphocyte blastogenesis. *Cell. Immunol.* **32**, 287–292.

Wedner, H. J., Bloom, F. E., and Parker, C. W. (1975). The role of cyclic nucleotides in lymphocyte activation. *In* "Immune Recognition" (A. S. Rosenthal, ed.), pp. 337–357. Academic Press, New York.

Weinstein, L., Aycock, W. L., and Feemster, R. F. (1951). The relation of sex, pregnancy and menstruation to susceptibility in poliomyelitis. *N. Engl. J. Med.* **245**, 54–58.

Welsh, R. M., Jr. (1978). Mouse natural killer cells: Induction specificity, and function. *J. Immunol.* **121**, 1631–1635.

Whitfield, J. F., Perris, A. D., and Yondale, T. (1969). The calcium-mediated promotion of mitotic activity in rat thymocyte populations by growth hormone, neurohormones, parathyroid hormone and prolactin. *J. Cell. Physiol.* **73**, 203–212.

Whitfield, J. F., MacManus, J. P., and Rixon, R. H. (1970a). The possible mediation by cyclic AMP of parathyroid hormone-induced stimulation of mitotic activity and deoxyribonucleic acid synthesis in rat thymic lymphocytes. *J. Cell. Physiol.* **75**, 213–224.

Whitfield, J. F., MacManus, J. P., and Rixon, R. H. (1970b). Cyclic AMP-mediated stimulation of thymocyte proliferation by low concentrations of cortisol. *Proc. Soc. Exp. Biol. Med.* **134**, 1170–1174.

Wingard, D. W., Lang, R., and Humphrey, L. J. (1967). Effect of anesthesia on immunity. *J. Surg. Res.* **7**, 430–432.

Winson, J., and Gerlach, J. C. (1971). Stressor-induced release of substances from the rat amygdala detected by the push–pull cannula. *Nature (London)* **230**, 251–253.

Wistar, R. T., and Hildemann, W. H. (1960). Effect of stress on skin transplantation immunity in mice. *Science* **131**, 159–160.

Wolstenholme, G. E. W., and Knight, J. eds. (1970). "Hormones and the Immune Response." Churchill, London.

Wurtman, R. J., and Axelrod, J. (1966). Control of enzymatic synthesis of adrenaline in the adrenal medulla by adrenal cortical steroids. *J. Biol. Chem.* **241**, 2301–2305.

Yamada, A., Jensen, M. M., and Rasmussen, A. F., Jr. (1964). Stress and susceptibility to viral infections. III. Antibody response and viral retention during avoidance learning stress. *Proc. Soc. Exp. Biol. Med.* **116**, 677–680.

Zatz, M. M. (1976). Effects of cortisone on lymphocyte homing. *In* "Lymphocytes and Their Cell Membranes" (M. Schlesinger, ed.), pp. 140–147. Academic Press, New York.

Zinkernagel, R. M., and Doherty, P. C. (1975). H-2 compatibility requirement for T-cell mediated lysis of target cells infected with lymphocytic choriomeningitis virus. Different cytotoxic T-cell specificities are associated with structures coded for in H-2K or H-2D. *J. Exp. Med.* **141**, 1427–1436.

Zurier, R. B., and Weissmann, G. (1973). Anti-immunologic and anti-inflammatory effects of steroid therapy. *Med. Clin. North Am.* **57**, 1295–1307.

Stress and Immunologic Competence: Studies in Man

JAN PALMBLAD

INTRODUCTION

Since ancient times, man has recognized an important connection between the mind and the body, and vice versa, as exemplified in the Roman proverb *Mens sana in corpore sano*. Although these links would seem rather obvious, it has not been possible until recently to demonstrate, in a scientific way, that man's susceptibility to many diseases may be influenced by major or complex alterations of life. In this respect, much interest has been given, for example, to the frequency of onset of myocardial infarction occurring after obvious life change, such as divorce or bereavement (Jenkins, 1976).

During the last 2 decades the rapidly expanding interest in immunology, together with improved methods of assessing immunologic functions, has made it possible to probe the probability that life change in humans is related to susceptibility to infectious agents and autoimmune disorders. In particular it has been hypothesized that exposure to various stress-eliciting situations would be accompanied by a decrease in host defense. Data and interpretations come from epidemiological and experimental studies linking incidence and severity of infections and/or measurements of variables reflecting host defense to estimations of life changes, feelings, or other psychological ratings. There is also much animal experimentation. This review will focus on such studies in human beings, where the interrelations of stress, infectious diseases,

229

and host defenses have been investigated. Neoplastic and autoimmune disorders are the subjects of other chapters in this book.

IMMUNOLOGIC COMPETENCE

There is no intention to give the reader a full description of the human immune system here, since excellent reviews are available elsewhere. However, it might be pertinent to discuss how assays, referred to later, might be performed and their results usually interpreted.

Immunologic competence could briefly be explained as the capacity to identify and reject material foreign to the particular individual, whereas material furnished with markers of self are accepted. This is accomplished by means of a complex system including many cellular and humoral factors, as described in Table 1. Thus, according to this very simplified definition, infections are due to deficient recognition or mobilization of appropriate defense systems against the invader. Similarly, autoimmune disorders would be the consequence of a failure to recognize markers of self and an attack on a host's own tissues.

Granulocytes

Polymorphonuclear (PMN) granulocytes mature in the bone marrow, from which they are released to the bloodstream, where they spend approximately 6

TABLE 1
Host Defense against Microorganisms

Phagocytes
  Neutrophils
    Adherence, chemotaxis, engulfment, bactericidal action
  Monocytes-macrophages
    Phagocytosis, antigen presentation to lymphocytes, cytotoxic action

Lymphocytes
  T cells
    Cytotoxic action
  B cells
    Antibody production
  Other subpopulations
    T helper, T suppressor, Natural killer cells

Humoral immunity
  Antibodies (IgG, IgM, IgA, etc.)

Miscellaneous
  Serum complement factors
  Interferon

hr. By adhering to and emigrating between the endothelial cells of the blood vessels they reach the tissues, where their duties are performed.

Adherence to endothelial cells can be imitated *in vitro* by the adherence of PMNs in heparinized blood to nylon fibers or to glass beads. Tests utilizing nylon fibers are easily performed and it has been shown that this adherence also reflects the ability to adhere to endothelial cells *in vivo*. Decreased adherence to nylon fibers *in vitro* has been shown to correlate with decreased accumulation of PMNs in infected tissues and increased severity of infections.

PMN *migration* into tissues can be observed by means of a skin window or by migration *in vitro* in Boyden chambers or under agarose, gelled in Petri dishes. Impaired directed migration (chemotaxis) towards various chemo-attractants is accompanied by slower or decreased accumulation of PMNs at infected sites. Clinically, the consequence is an increased frequency and/or severity of infections in congenital as well as acquired disorders (Gallin and Quie, 1977).

After *attachment* of the microbe to the PMN surface, the former is engulfed. The rate of *engulfment* can be easily measured by microscopy after *in vitro* incubation of bacteria with PMNs either as the proportion of PMNs engaged in engulfment or as the number of ingested particles. More sophisticated methods employ the measurement of ingested radiolabeled bacteria or artificial particles. The subsequent *killing* of the microbes is usually calculated by a quantitative bacterial culturing technique, after incubating PMNs with a known quantity of living bacteria. The killing is dependent on the generation of extremely cell-damaging oxygen radicals and release of several lysosomal enzymes and cationic proteins.

As described in the preceding paragraphs on adherence and chemotaxis, disorders of uptake and killing are accompanied by an increased tendency to acquire infections. Disorders of the uptake and killing steps have been described in a large number of congenital as well as acquired pathologic conditions as a consequence of some underlying disease. Indeed, the plethora of diseases associated with defective phagocytosis suggests that any process of sufficient severity might result in a phagocytic impairment. Patients with such defects usually exhibit an increased susceptibility to bacteria and fungi, but not viruses. Most studies also suggest that the results of *in vitro* measurements reflect rather well the propensity to become infected, that is, the more profound the defect, the more pronounced the risk. However, although most such studies have been performed prospectively, there are some conflicting data leaving us uncertain whether there really is a correlation between degrees of impairment of killing and susceptibility.

Usually, these tests possess a reasonably high methodological accuracy, with a low day-to-day variability. This is an advantage if they are used repeatedly in the same individual, for example, in studying changes after exposure to a stressor. Thus they reflect an important part of the defense against microbes and they are often well suited to studies of stress and host defense.

Monocytes

The peripheral blood monocyte, which eventually becomes the tissue-bound macrophage, belongs to the same bone marrow "family" as the PMN. Monocytes are able to migrate in response to chemotactic stimuli and to phagocytize. However, their importance to local defense in the tissues seems to be less than that of the PMNs. Instead, they scrutinize the circulating blood entering the reticuloendothelial system in, inter alia, the liver and spleen. The phagocytic ability of monocytes can be measured by the rate of disappearance of radiolabeled albumin from peripheral blood.

In addition to this direct antimicrobial function, the monocytes have an important role to play in specific immunity by *cooperating with lymphocytes.* Monocytes are probably able to prepare and present antigens to lymphocytes. Hence, many mitogens or bacterial products employed in assays measuring the stimulability of lymphocytes, by assessing the incorporation of new DNA, are dependent on this processing of macrophoges–monocytes.

Another important clinical measurement of immunologic competence is the induction of *delayed skin hypersensitivity,* that is the skin induration 48–72 hr after an intracutaneous administration of various bacterial products [streptokinase–streptordenase, mumps antigen, purified protein derivate (PPD) of tubercle bacilli]. This induration is partly composed of macrophages, partly of lymphocytes.

Finally, macrophages might be "activated" by lymphocytes, thereby increasing their killing and destroying of adjacent cells, whatever kind they might be. This *cytoxic* activity can be measured as the release of ^{51}Cr from tagged erythrocytes, which are incubated with isolated monocytes.

Many *in vitro* tests of monocyte–macrophage functions are impaired by the low concentration of peripheral blood monocytes. A large volume of blood is needed to separate appropriate cell quantities. Further, the paucity of studies employing *in vitro* monocyte assays leaves us with some uncertainty whether the results reflect a clinically relevant host defense variable. On the other hand, delayed hypersensitivity skin tests have been widely used. They are an easily obtainable source of information, and it seems likely that they reflect clinically important aspects of host defense. Despite their simplicity, their usefulness is limited because repeated testing in man has been shown to lead either to tolerance and diminished skin response or immunization and enhanced size of induration.

Lymphocytes

Lymphocytes are of many kinds. In man, they originate from the bone marrow (B lymphocytes), or the thymus (T lymphocytes). The B lymphocytes are the basis of the antibody-producing system, whereas T cells form the bulk of peripheral blood lymphocytes engaged in surveillance for example. In addition to these two main categories, there are probably many other subclasses, including K and O lymphocytes and the natural killer cell, which morphologically resembles a traditional lymphocyte, but lacks other characteristic signs. Another subset of lymphocytes are the T helper and suppressor cells, which, as the name implies, might influence the activity of lymphocyte DNA synthesis and antibody production.

B lymphocytes can be distinguished by their surface-bound immunoglobulin (Ig), which can be made visible under the microscope by the attachment of fluorescent antibodies to human immunoglobulins. Sheep erythrocytes will gather as a rosette around T lymphocytes when appropriately incubated together. Thus, according to the demonstration of various surface markers, subclasses of blood lymphocytes can be quantified.

Purified peripheral blood lymphocytes will start to divide, when incubated *in vitro* with a variety of mitogens and bacterial products. In a cell culture system, this can be measured as the incorporation of the tritiated amino acid thymidine, which is required for DNA replication. Most mitogens, such as phytohemagglutinin and concanavalin A, will engage T lymphocytes, whereas certain lipopolysaccharides and doses of pokeweed mitogen selectively stimulate B cells.

Lymphocyte cytotoxicity, or the ability of sensitized lymphocytes to attach to and kill certain target cells, can be measured as the release of a marker substance, such as ^{51}Cr, from the target cell. This test is commonly used in tumor immunity research.

A relatively newly developed test measures natural killer cells. Although morphological lymphocytes, natural killer cells have no Ig receptors on the surface and will not form rosettes. They will spontaneously kill their target cells, for example, selected tumor cells. Killing occurs without the addition of antibodies or other substances to the system.

With so many available assays, the clinical significance of the individual results has been increasingly difficult to understand. A single system measures only a small part of the immune apparatus, and nothing else.

Therefore, many investigators have now resorted to performing a battery of immunologic tests, where both *in vitro* and *in vivo* measures are made. By combining the individual results, a broader evaluation of immunocompetence is obtained. However, there seems to be no doubt that a marked impairment of a single variable, such as DNA synthesis, or a broad but not so marked impairment of many variables, would mean an increased susceptibility of the host to many microorganisms. Patients with acquired or genetically transmitted immune deficiency will often contract infections caused by viruses and other intracellular organisms, for example, tuberculosis, Pneumocystis carinii, and Listeria.

A drawback of many of the tests of cell-mediated immunity is the relatively high degree of assay variability. The day-to-day variation for a single subject can be so great that it is difficult to assess whether there is a real change in immune function over time or if fluctuations are due solely to technical factors. These question are especially important when the tests are used in studies of stress and immunity.

Immunoglobulins

Following challenge B lymphocytes or their cellular successors, the plasma cells will produce antibodies, that is, immunoglobulins of classes IgG, IgM, IgA, and others. Plasma immunoglobulin levels are usually measured by immunochemical methods or by radial diffusion.

The production of antibodies in response to various antigens is often measured in clinical practice. The specific titer of antibodies to antigens—new or familiar to the host—might be measured *in vitro* by their complement binding or hemagglutinating capacity.

The clinical relevance of very low plasma levels of antibodies has been clearly documented, for example, susceptibility to infection with capsulated bacteria such as *Klebsiella* or *Pneumococcus*. However, the relevance of small changes within the normal range still remains to be determined. Such changes might just be the result of technical variations of the assay, as described for assays of cell-mediated immunity, or they could be the result of extraneous influences on the individual. However, since the plasma levels of immunoglobulins usually are rather stable in response to what are regarded as severe changes (such as total starvation for 10 days), it is not likely that many commonly encountered everyday stressors will affect immunoglobulin levels in such a way that proneness to infection is radically increased. Less is known, however, about naturally occurring changes of local production of antibodies in the mucous membranes in airways.

PSYCHOSOCIAL FACTORS AFFECTING IMMUNOLOGIC COMPETENCE

In addition to stress, a number of physiological and pharmacological factors are capable of altering immunologic function. Many of these factors are normal aspects of our daily lives and are often characterized as psychosocial in nature. They tend to occur in combination, often in a complex fashion, and either precede or are coexistent with stress of psychosocial origin. Although they are regarded mainly as "noise" in the present context, they could, in fact, also be considered stressors in their own right. Thus they often create important methodological problems, especially when we are trying to interpret data obtained from other stressor exposure studies with regard to possible mediating mechanisms. Appropriate controls must be included in stressor studies and considerable care must be taken to measure and/or control these extraneous changes and factors that are seldom described in published reports.

Among these factors, the influence of age and nutrition will be briefly discussed.

Age

Aging obviously is part of our daily life and has a considerable impact on immune functions. More specifically, the serum levels of immunoglobulins and auto-antibodies as well as the *in vitro* reactivity of lymphocytes are age dependent.

1. The *newborn,* and in particular the premature child, has not yet fully developed its immune apparatus (for a review, see Miller, 1977). Defects have been noted in many variables. For instance, many serum complement components belonging to both the classical and alternative pathways, as well as serum IgM concentrations, are lower than in adults; IgM levels do not reach adult levels until the child is 2–3 years old (Strunk *et al.,* 1979). There is only a little information about cell-mediated immunity, such as lymphocyte stimulability. An increased suppressor T-cell activity has been noted, which might be involved in the impaired antibody synthesis and a diminished delayed skin hypersensitivity (Morito *et al.,* 1979). Granulocyte functions, such as uptake of bacteria and their killing, are usually intact, although in premature children defects have been noted. Granulocyte chemotaxis might be deficient. Similarly, opsonization of bacteria is usually decreased in premature children, most probably because immunoglobulin and serum complement levels have not attained normal levels (Miller, 1977; Mills *et al.,* 1979). Briefly, in studies performed in these first years of life it is conceivable that aging, by itself, might affect the variables studied, and consequently, appropriate controls must be included for comparison.

2. *Senescence* is also accompanied by changes in the immune apparatus. It is well known that an involution of the thymus occurs in the elderly, affecting the epithelial part of the gland responsible for the maturation of active T lymphocytes. Many hypotheses have been advanced in which immune system defects have been ascribed a central role in normal aging (Buckley and Roseman, 1976). These defects not only predispose to infectious and autoimmune diseases and malignancies, but also accelerate other degenerative diseases (Yunis *et al.,* 1976). Studies of aging humans and laboratory animals have demonstrated changes in various cell-mediated and humoral immune reactions (for reviews, see Makinodan, 1976; Palmblad and Haak, 1978), and it has been suggested that mortality is higher in old people with decreased thymus-dependent functions (Roberts-Thomson *et al.,* 1974). It may be

speculated, then, that these reactions may be of value as predictors of health, and also of prognosis when treating malignant disease in the elderly.

Thus, normal aging is followed not only by quantitative but also qualitative decreases mainly of cell-mediated immune reactions, such as the numbers of peripheral blood T lymphocyte counts and spontaneous and mitogen-stimulated DNA synthesis. All these changes could be reflected in any study extending over a considerable time on subjects over 60 years of age. Examples of this could be the effects of bereavement on immune functions, and other situations that occur more often in elderly people.

Nutrition

Food is a prerequisite for life, besides conferring pleasure. However, too much or too little food injures health and may menace life. Also changes in eating habits, both compulsive overeating and loss of appetite, accompany more or less regularly changes of life and stress-eliciting events.

Although the consequences for health of under- and overnutrition differ considerably, these two extremes of inadequate food intake (malnutrition), do have some features in common. One of them is an increased incidence of infectious diseases compared with a normally fed population. This increased morbidity and its causes have been investigated thoroughly in some of the extreme cases, that is, in starving people (especially in developing countries) and in patients suffering from anorexia nervosa and diseases where undernutrition is a prominent concomitance. An increased morbidity in infections has also been demonstrated at the other extreme (in obesity), where, however, it, and the host defense, have attracted far less attention. Hence, too much and too little food have effects on host defense and the causes for changes in eating habits often have a psychosocial background. Because of this complex and important relationship, some pertinent data will be reviewed.

CHRONIC AND ACUTE UNDERNUTRITION

Throughout history, man has recognized an association between famine and pestilence. Several studies have shown that infections occur more often and may be more severe in chronically undernourished groups (for reviews, see Scrimshaw *et al.,* 1968; Suskind, 1977). Because of this often noted coincidence, it has been suggested that undernutrition predisposes to infections, although the evidence is in no way conclusive. Several other concomitant environmental factors may have contributed to an increased susceptibility, for example, overcrowding, poor hygiene, increased psychosocial stress, and increased exposure to infectious agents. All of these contribute to the difficulties of identifying cause–effect relationships (cf. Murray and Murray, 1977). It also exemplifies how psychosocial factors must be taken into account in research mainly focused on other topics.

In this complex situation, common in chronically undernourished subjects in developing countries, depression of several variables generally assumed to be of importance for host defense has been reported repeatedly (e.g., Suskind, 1977). However, it is equally difficult to determine to what extent it is the undernutrition which has caused the impairment in these responses, and to what extent other environmental factors and concomitant diseases, such as infections, have contributed. In some studies attempts have been made to overcome these problems by evaluating the positive effect of food administration. However, even in the latter situation, which commonly occurs in connection with hospitalization, environmental factors are changed in addition to the dietary regimen. These "extraneous" changes, rarely measured and controlled, might well have profound effects on the variables under study.

Another strategy is determining the impact of chronic undernutrition on host defense is to study patients with anorexia nervosa, where energy intake is greatly reduced. While infections are rather common in chronic undernutrition in the developing countries, nothing definite is known about infections in anorexia nervosa. The sparse available evidence indicates that infections in general are uncommon and viral diseases even rare, although paronychia and staphylococcal skin infections may be frequent. Moreover, severe infections might be the cause of death (Theander, 1970; Warren and Wiele, 1973). Several studies have also demonstrated various alterations of host defense in anorectic patients. For example, blood polymorphonuclear (PMN) granulocyte glucose oxidation, adherence, and bactericidal capacity may be decreased (Kjösen et al., 1975; Gotch et al., 1975; Palmblad et al., 1977c). Further, Kim and Michael (1975) and Palmblad et al. (1979) described changes in the serum complement system, mainly depressions of factors C1, C2, C3, C1s inactivator, B, and total hemolytic complement, whereas C4 was normal.

The clinical significance of the reduced host defense variables is not clear. All available information, however, points to a certain risk of acquiring infections which, while it may be relatively low, could increase if other precipitating factors (e.g., trauma) supervene.

Since these above-mentioned research strategies still leave us uncertain whether undernutrition really is accompanied by an impaired host defense and, in order to study possible causal relationships between food deprivation and host defense, experimental models can be used. Apart from animal systems (Good et al., 1976), one might resort to exposing healthy human volunteers to total or subtotal energy deprivation for shorter or longer periods of time.

This has been accomplished in a series of studies in which the effects of short-term total, or long-term subtotal food deprivation on variables reflecting host defense and endocrine systems have been studied.

During exposure of healthy normal weight human volunteers to 10 days of total energy deprivation (Kjellberg *et al.,* 1977) the following results were noted: a depression of serum levels of several acute phase reactants, such as complement factor C3, haptoglobin, orosomucoid, and transferrin, and the plasma levels of iron: depressions of the DNA synthesis of blood lymphocytes, and the bacteridical capacity and the alkaline phosphatase activity of blood neutrophils. Refeeding of starving subjects enhanced serum levels of specific antibodies to flagellin whereas no reductions occurred during starvation. No effect of the exposure was noted on serum levels of IgG, IgM, IgA, IgE, C4, haptoglobin, the interferon producing capacity and subpopulations of blood lymphocytes, the iron saturation index of serum transferrin, and skin delayed hypersensitivity to PPD and mumps antigen (Palmblad, 1976; Holm and Palmblad, 1976; Palmblad *et al.,* 1977b).

Taken together, total food deprivation for 10 days was accompanied by changes in many variables reflecting host defense. In an attempt to determine whether these changes were the result of energy deprivation per se or other factors occurring simultaneously (e.g., hormonal changes and emotional responses to the exposure), a battery of pituitary, adrenomedullary and adrenocortical hormone tests was used as well as assessments of feelings and intellectual and psychomotor performance. Serum growth hormone and cortisol concentrations and urinary output of adrenalin and noradrenalin rose during starvation, whereas serum thyroid hormone levels fell (Palmblad *et al.,* 1977d). The reported feelings of "stress," "fatigue," "anxiety," as well as intellectual performance were comparable with those of a concomitant normally eating control group participating in all other activities except food deprivation (J. Palmblad, unpublished observations). Moreover, none of the endocrine changes were significantly correlated with changes in host defense variables. Hence, it is most probable that in this study energy deprivation directly impaired host defense and this effect was probably not mediated via any of those endocrine pathways often mentioned in this context.

The question of whether a reduction of food intake for one or several months also affects host defense has been studied in obese subjects participating in a weight reducing dietary regimen or after a small bowel shunt operation. No changes of neutrophil functions were found after a weight reduction of 10% of body weight after 1 month with a 600 kcal/day diet (Palmblad *et al.,* 1979b). However, if food intake was reduced because of abdominal discomfort after a small bowel shunt operation (which also induced a malabsorption and a weight loss of approximately 35 kg), neutrophil bactericidal capacity was instead enhanced (Palmblad *et al.,* 1980). The cause for this reaction—which at first glimpse seems paradoxical—is unknown.

In conclusion, undereating will probably decrease a previously normal host resistance if energy intake is substantially restricted or prolonged. If, however, diseases are present in the fasting or food intake restricted individuals, responses might be different, as exemplified in a recent study of total fasting in rheumatoid arthritis patients for 7 days. Instead of the decreased granulocyte function noted previously in healthy subjects, an increased bactericidal capacity was found (Udén et al., 1980).

OBESITY

Obesity and being overweight are prevalent in affluent countries. They are generally regarded as a result of overeating, decreased energy utilization, and similar psychosocial factors. A positive correlation has been demonstrated between the degree of obesity and overweight and an increase in mortality, although obesity may not be directly responsible (Mann, 1974). Many diseases are overrepresented in the obese, including atherosclerotic heart disease, diabetes mellitus, and gallstones.

Although most interest has been paid to the possible connection between obesity and the above-mentioned disorders, other diseases may be of importance, too, for both mortality and morbidity. One of these is infections. Such an associaton has not attracted any general attention, although it has been demonstrated in a number of studies (for reviews, see Palmblad, 1977; Palmblad et al., 1977a).

The prevalence of infectious diseases as a cause of death is increased in subjects rated as overweight. Similarly, morbidity in infectious diseases is elevated, as in the case of postoperative infections. Additional evidence comes from experimental infections in obese dogs, where an increased morbidity and a more severe course of infections were found (Fiser et al., 1972a,b). The mechanisms behind the increased infectious morbidity and mortality are essentially unknown but some hypotheses have been presented. It has been suggested that the increased incidence of postoperative infections is due to local factors, such as low blood supply to the adipose tissue and restricted pulmonary function.

Obesity in humans is also accompanied by a decreased neutrophil bactericidal capacity and glucose oxidation and enhanced adherence (Kjösen et al., 1975; Palmblad et al., 1977a), whereas various cell-mediated and humoral immunity reactions are normal (Hallberg et al., 1976). Also, obesity in animals may be associated with an increased frequency of autoimmune phenomena (Wick et al., 1974) and food reduction may retard the development of autoimmune diseases (Good et al., 1976).

Some investigations concerning the possible influence of other metabolic factors might help to explain why alterations in host defense may occur in obesity and, since they include factors which obviously are of psychosocial nature, they will be briefly reviewed.

First, some data have been presented on the effects of protein intake on host defense. An increased intake of dairy proteins, especially, was associated with increased mortality in lymphomas (Cunningham, 1976); decreased intake was associated with decreases in the occurrence of certain animal tumors, in mortality/morbidity in viral diseases, and in resistance to bacteria (Good et *al.,* 1976). Hence, these studies suggest an association between changes in protein intake and host defense.

Second, there may be other factors in food (be it protein-rich or not) which could be responsible for the increased susceptibility. One such factor might be lipids. It has been suggested that they influence host defense, for example, high-fat diets may decrease and low-fat diets increase it (earlier studies are reviewed in Scrimshaw *et al.,* 1968; Fiser *et al.,* 1972a,b). Further, other studies have shown that the addition of cholesterol and free fatty acids (FFA) decreases phagocytosis (Dianzani *et al.,* 1976; Hawley and Gordon, 1976) and that hyperlipidemia, mainly hypercholesterolemia, impairs antibody formation and reduces lymphocyte proliferation (Fiser *et al.,* 1972b; Waddell *et al.,* 1976). Since serum lipid abnormalities are commonly found in obesity, it is possible that lipids are involved in the reduced resistance to infectious agents in obesity.

In conclusion, infections may be more prevalent in the obese, and it is not clear which host defense variables are altered, although hyperlipidemia has received special attention.

Miscellaneous

Among the many factors suspected of influencing immune variables in relation to stress, the influence of drugs and alcohol must be considered. Subjects experiencing a radical life change, such as death of spouse, loss of job, or infidelity, are at high risk to coping by taking alcohol, tranquilizers, or analgesics. The intake of such substances is often difficult to measure or control. Still they could influence many immunologic variables under study, giving rise to erroneous conclusions regarding mechanisms associated with stress.

Variables such as circadian rhythms and endocrine factors are discussed elsewhere in this volume.

STRESS AND IMMUNOLOGIC COMPETENCE

"Stress"

Definitions of stress are confused by differing conceptions. For the purpose of the present chapter, stress is mainly used in Selye's sense, as defined by Levi (1972). Briefly, any physiological, psychological, or behaviorial responses within the organism elicited by evocative agents are called stress. The evocative stimuli are accordingly called stressors. Whether stress is a stereotypical response will not be discussed here (cf. Mason, 1975; Selye,

1975). Moreover, stressors might be of a mainly psychological nature—which is the primary subject of this review—or of a more physical nature. The latter are not excluded from this discussion because it is often difficult to separate these events from each other in the few studies on stressed humans. An excellent example of this complex interaction is the influence of changes in eating habits (i.e. malnutrition), as discussed previously. Rogers *et al.* (1979) have discussed these and other factors and pitfalls.

Stress and Immunologic Competence—Studies in Humans

The hypothesis that psychosocial stimuli, eliciting a stress response, may affect resistance to infections and immunologic mechanisms rests mainly on experimental studies on animals subjected to various stressors. Although these studies provide a useful basis for speculation, very little is known about human resistance to infectious agents and immunologic reactions after various stressor exposures. Also the mechanisms in these responses are unclear. What is known will be reviewed here, starting with studies of an epidemiologic character, followed by those examining a particular group of individuals at risk, and ending with experimental stressor studies.

EPIDEMIOLOGIC STUDIES LINKING STRESS TO INFECTIONS

The assumption that stressful events may increase a person's susceptibility to or aggravate the course of infectious diseases has been based to a large extent on speculation and anecdotes. It is only recently that some statistical evidence has been presented of a positive association between the degree of exposure to psychosocial stressors and morbidity in various diseases, including infections (Rahe, 1972; Jacobs *et al.*, 1969).

In a study of patients with tuberculosis, Holmes *et al.* (1957) found that disintegration of precarious psychosocial adjustment invariably occurred in the 2-year period preceding the onset or relapse of disease.

Meyer and Haggerty (1962) found that, during the course of 1 year, the factors that seemed to play an important role in determining whether a given person acquired a streptococcal respiratory tract infection were inter alia acute or chronic family stress, as evidenced by interviews and diaries. Streptococcal acquisition and illness, as well as nonstreptococcal respiratory tract infections, were about four times as likely to be preceded as to be followed by acute stress.

Jacobs *et al.* (1969, 1970) reported that life situations characterized by failure, unresolved role crisis and social isolation in students were frequently associated with respiratory infections. The more incapacitating the disorder, the more likely situations of life stress would be reported as having occurred during the year preceding the seeking of treatment for the infections.

Greenfield *et al.* (1959) showed that recovery from infectious mononucleosis (using hematological data as criteria) was delayed in subjects showing low ego-strength.

These studies have shown a positive relation between what has been regarded as stress-eliciting moments and certain personality types and infections. However, negative studies have also appeared. Luborsky *et al.* (1976)
could not document life changes and changes of feelings and mood prior to
the appearance of herpes simplex infections and upper respiratory tract infections.

In conclusion, it is difficult to assess whether stress really has been an important contributing factor in disease due to infectious agents; so few studies
are available and most of them are retrospective, which always increases the
methodological difficulties and possible bias. Indeed, if it was not for the
other kinds of studies that are available, the present epidemiologic material
would not allow any conclusions regarding the relationship between stress and
infection.

CLINICAL STUDIES

The characteristic feature of the clinical studies that have been reported is
that a group of selected subjects is followed for a period of time during which
changes in measures of host defense and psychosocial factors are related to
one another.

Bartrop *et al.* (1977) investigated the effect of bereavement on cell-mediated
and humoral immune functions and also on endocrine reactions. They found
that the mean T-lymphocyte response to phytohemagglutinin and concanavalin A was reduced approximately 8 weeks after the bereavement (Figure 1).
There were no differences in blood T- and B-cell numbers, serum immunoglobulin levels, presence of delayed hypersensitivity or autoantibodies.
Moreover, there was no alteration of the serum concentrations of any of those
hormones most often mentioned as being the mediators of stress-associated
immune reactions (e.g., thyroid, adrenocortical, and pituitary hormones).
This is one of the first prospective studies on healthy humans demonstrating a
reduction of immune reactions under conditions that most of us would find
stressful for a long period of time. The stress response to this life change was,
however, not measurable by hormonal alterations, and we do not know the
severity of the grief reactions. Similarly, it seems important to document
weight loss or gain due to changes in eating habits following the bereavement.
The mechanisms within the immune response are also unknown, both with
regard to possible impairment of the macrophage–lymphocyte interaction,
suppressor lymphocyte activity and/or whether hormonal, dietary, or other
reactions were mediators of the effects. Finally, we would like to know if
diseases occurred later and, if so, if they could be related to the immune reactions. Questions of this kind will be essential in future studies.

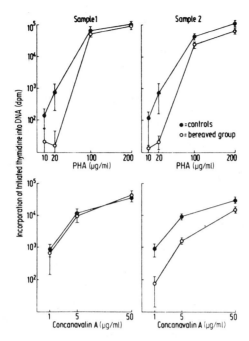

Figure 1. The influence of bereavement on lymphocyte stimulability after challenge with phytohemagglutinin (PHA) and concanavalin A *in vitro*. Geometric mean values (± S.E.M.) in control and bereaved groups. Sample 1 was obtained shortly after and sample 2 about 8 weeks after bereavement. From Bartrop, R. W., Lazarus, L., Luckhurst, E., Kiloh, L. G., and Penny, R. Depressed lymphocyte function after bereavement. *Lancet* 1977, I, 834–836. Reprinted by permission.

The influences of psychosocial factors on cell-mediated and humoral immune functions were investigated by Locke *et al.* (1978), whose research strategy differed from that of Bartrop *et al.* (1977). Repeated determinations of natural killer cell activity (NKCA) were made in healthy human subjects and found to be related to a combination of life change stress (LCS) and psychiatric symptoms during the previous year. When LCS was graded "high" or "low," no apparent influence on the NKCA was observed. However, by also taking into account the self-reported psychiatric symptoms occurring during the same time, significant interactions were noted. Thus, NKCA was highest for those subjects reporting fewest symptoms despite high levels of LCS, and lowest for those subjects reporting most symptoms (e.g., anxiety and depression) together with high levels of LCS. Low NKCA was not related to coexisting somatic illness–which certainly could be a serious pitfall—but, rather with type of personality. The conclusion was that the ability to cope with feelings aroused by changes in life events is a determinant of NKCA, but these reactions must be protracted, at least for 1 year.

This well-controlled study does not report whether any diseases followed the establishment of the natural killer cell activity, and, in particular, a low NKCA. Neither were the possible mechanisms investigated (e.g., hormonal and dietary changes). It is suggested that this measure of cell-mediated immunity is more responsive to the influence of sustained stress than short-term stress.

In a study reported by Greene et al. (1978), a statistically significant correlation was found between stress (here defined as life change units combined with a high vigor score on a profile of mood state) and lymphocyte cytotoxicity. When stress increased, as a result of unsuccessful coping mechanisms, lymphocyte cytotoxicity decreased. We are awaiting the full report to be able to interpret these findings.

In a similar study, Roessler et al. (1979) followed subjects vaccinated against influenza for changes in antibody titers and related these to measurements of ego-strength and life events. The study was carried out double blindly since placebo vaccinations were also performed. Six months after the initial immunization it was found that the combination of high measures of ego-strength and low life events were related to high antibody titers. Again the full report is awaited with interest.

Canter et al. (1972) reported that hypersensitive reactions—and some of them were of an objective character—to an immunization procedure occurred more frequently in subjects rated as "vulnerable" according to standard questionnaries on personality.

To summarize, all these studies have found that life changes and/or emotions evoked by life changes occurring for a rather prolonged period were associated with depression of one, or, less frequently, two or more immune reactions. Both the mechanisms and the clinical significance of these observations are unknown.

In contrast to these observations on healthy subjects, other studies have been carried out on patients suffering from various diseases. Liedman and Prilipko (1972) described that, in comparison with controls, schizophrenic patients receiving no pharmacological treatment showed a higher spontaneous activation of lymphocytes which could not be enhanced any further by the addition of a mitogen. Bock et al. (1971) found higher serum concentrations of some acute phase proteins and lower IgA in patients with acute psychotic symptoms. Hendrie et al. (1971) found that patients with rheumatoid arthritis with elevated immunoglobulin levels tended also to have increased life change scores.

Wright et al. (1975) compared neutrophil phagocytosis and killing in newborn infants which were either healthy or "stressed." By "stressed" the authors meant suffering from a variety of mild to moderately severe conditions such as infections or respiratory distress and Caesarian section. The "stressed" children exhibited impaired neutrophil function to a significantly higher degree than the healthy infants. Although the term "stressed" was used in an undefined and vague way it is interesting to note that virtually all of the conditions studied conferred a certain risk for an impaired neutrophil anti-bacterial activity. This could be interpreted as a demonstration of the stereo-typical, nonspecific response to many stimulus situations as suggested by Selye. However, the investigators could not show a relationship between their assessment of the severity of the condition and the degree of impairment of neutrophil function.

EXPERIMENTAL STUDIES

This third approach to the study of whether stress affects immune com-petence in man has utilized the exposure of healthy volunteers to various stress-eliciting situations. By doing so, it has been possible to concentrate the exposure and define it under well-controlled conditions. Also, this approach usually provides an opportunity to see what happens after the exposure. This is important since it has been claimed from animal studies that stress inter alia may have a biphasic influence on immune competence (Solomon et al., 1967; Monjan and Collector, 1977).

Depression in the T-lymphocyte response to mitogens was found in astro-nauts during the first 3 days after return to earth (Kimzey et al., 1976), whereas serum concentrations of immunoglobulins and the C3 complement factor were unaffected (Fischer et al., 1972; Kimzey et al., 1976). Lymphocyte stimulability was slightly decreased prior to launching, possibly due to an-ticipation, which is perhaps more interesting than decreases found after the flight when it is difficult to partial out the effects of expectation and the more physical effects of splashdown.

In four different experiments, Palmblad et al. (1976, 1979c,d) investigated the effects of sleep deprivation on immune competence, hormonal concentra-tions and reported feelings in healthy volunteers.

Sleep deprivation is undoubtedly a distressing, taxing experience and in-creases the organism's need for energy. Accordingly, behavioral, metabolic, and endocrine responses have received most attention (Naitoh, 1976). Beside these rather obvious changes, sleep deprivation also affects the function of several other organs, including the defense against infectious agents. In a first study (Palmblad et al., 1976), blood neutrophil granulocytes exhibited a decreased ability to phagocytize Staphylococcus aureus during sleep depriva-tion, and blood lymphocytes showed an increased interferon production. After the exposure neutrophil phagocytosis was even higher than before (Figure 2).

In the second study (Palmblad et al., 1979d), it was found that the PHA-induced DNA synthesis of blood lymphocytes was reduced after a 48-hr period of sleep deprivation, although DNA synthesis remained within the nor-mal range of PHA-reactivity. Five days after the vigil, it had returned to pre-exposure levels (Figure 3). Neutrophil adherence and the stainable activity of

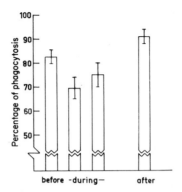

Figure 2. During a 72-hr vigil the rate of phagocytosis of neutrophils decreased, but was enhanced after the exposure. From Palmblad *et al.* (1976).

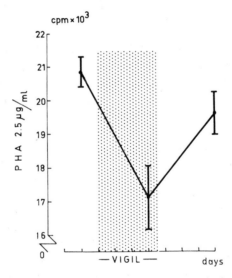

Figure 3. Lymphocyte stimulability to PHA before, during and after a 48–hr vigil. From Palmblad *et al.* (1979d).

alkaline phosphatase were unaltered. Taken together, both lymphocyte and granulocyte functions may be reduced during sleep deprivation.

These findings could indicate a diminished host defense during a phase when proper sleep is not achieved, a condition that is associated with irregular work hours, for example, in the medical and military professions and in conventional industrial shift work.

However, a few days after termination of such an exposure the function of these cells is probably restored or even enhanced, since the lymphocyte reactivity depressions had then regressed and interferon production and possibly phagocytosis were enhanced.

In both studies measurements were made of perceived "stress," "anxiety," etc., as well as adrenomedullary, adrenocortical, and pituitary hormones (Palmblad *et al.*, 1976, 1979e; Åkerstedt *et al.*, 1980). Briefly, thyroid hormonal activity was increased as was shown previously by Levi (1972), whereas serum cortisol together with urinary catecholamine output was increased in the first study, but decreased in the second. Because these disparate hormonal reactions were accompanied by a uniform immune response type, it is suggested that it is not likely that such hormones are important mediators.

Another study was concerned with acute phase reactants (Palmblad *et al.*, 1979c). The erythrocyte sedimentation rate (ESR) is one of the most common measures for screening in clinical medicine. A rise in ESR is usually taken to signify some ongoing pathological process in the body, but does not convey any specific information about the nature of the process. It is generally assumed that the ESR reaction may involve several rather diverse mechanisms, for example, increased serum concentrations of fibrinogen and γ-globulins. A decreased ESR is likewise associated with a variety of situations, including an increased concentration of serum corticosteroids. The occurrence of ESR changes in diverse conditions raised the question whether the ESR also would react as part of the stress response in the Selye (1975) sense. Stress is generally accompanied by sympathotonic reactions and by an increase in lipolysis and, thereby, conceivably in ESR. If this is so, ESR rises should occur in response not only to physical stressors such as infections and inflammation but also to stimuli of a more psychological character. This hypothesis was confirmed in two separate experiments, where it was found that the ESR rose in both studies (Figures 4 and 5). The rises were statistically significant.

The results would imply that a rise or an increased level of ESR in a patient could not only be due to well-known "conventional" causes but may also occur in response to various environmental influences, including psychosocial factors. In this sense, ESR reactions resemble others such as serum iron, protein bound iodine, serum cholesterol, triglycerides and free fatty acids, electrocardiograms and others (for results and discussion, see Levi, 1972). It follows that environmental factors such as those in our studies (e.g., leading to sleep deprivation, apprehension, and fatigue) should be taken into account when interpreting laboratory data in clinical practice.

Another interesting demonstration of the influence of mind on immune functions concerns hypnosis and delayed hypersensitivity. By subjecting volunteers to hypnosis, Black *et al.* (1963) found that the characteristic edema and erythema did not appear after intradermal administration of tuberculin, although skin biopsies exhibited the expected appearance. In fact, the usual accumulation of cells was found, but evidently production of vasoactive substances or the reaction of blood vessels to them were inhibited.

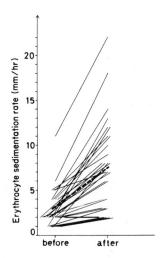

Figure 4. The ESR and stress, Study I. The subjects, 31 army officers, were deprived of all sleep for 75 hr. The exposure to stressor included, inter alia, performance on a specially designed shooting range, where an authentic battle noise was amplified to 95 dB-C. Blood samples were obtained a week prior to the experiment ("before") and its end ("after"). The ESR rose from 2.8 ± .4 mm to 7.5 ± .9 mm (mean ± S.E.M.).

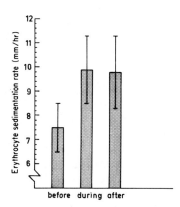

Figure 5. The ESR and stress, Study II. The 32 officers were exposed to sleep deprivation and other stressors as described in Figure 4. Blood samples were drawn on the day before the vigil started ("before"), 30 hr after the start ("during"), and immediately after the end ("after"). The ESR rose from 7.5 ± 1.1 mm to 9.8 ± 1.4 mm ("during") and remained at 9.8 ± 1.5 mm on "after" (mean ± S.E.M.).

Conclusions

So far the evidence for a link between mind and immunity in man rests only on approximately a dozen well-controlled studies. There are of course many studies on this topic not mentioned here. Most of them concern the occurrence or course of disease, in which immunity conceivably plays an undefined role.

Moreover, with few exceptions these studies have been retrospective and, consequently, their results difficult to interpret, particularly with regard to the fact that the psychological symptoms might be caused by the disease or have been colored by it, rather than being a factor in its development.

Although it is not possible to draw any definite conclusions concerning conditions in man, the present pioneering studies should be given credit for indicating the possibility and for raising important questions, the answers to which will be sought in forthcoming investigations.

To summarize, the least well-documented evidence concerns the key question—is stress followed by disease because immunity is altered? Similarly, no data have been presented concerning the opposite question—could stress enhance immunity and resistance? Apart from autoimmune and neoplastic conditions reviewed elsewhere in this volume, the manifestation of infectious disease reflects one of the best criteria for a decreased host defense and immunity. Infections of a rather trivial nature, such as common colds, seem to be more prevalent following a year of maladaptive behavior. Similarly, recovery from some viral disease may be delayed in unhappy subjects. Apart from the early studies on tuberculosis and streptococcal diseases we know nothing at all about more severe diseases such as pneumonias and septicemias or trivial bacterial ones such as boils. In the latter it is probably less likely that maladaptive behavior is also associated with altered social contacts and increased exposure to infectious agents. Accordingly, more attention should be given to such conditions in the future. Indeed, cold sores—an example of an endogenous, recurrent infection where extraneous exposure to the agents is unimportant—were not more prevalent in "stressed" subjects. As discussed later, it is essential for future research to reassess the stress–infection hypothesis, as well as the influence of stress on the course of various immunologic disorders.

Another line of research has consisted of relating stress to a variety of measures of immunity *in vitro*. There are at present, only those five studies reviewed above and conducted on healthy people demonstrating that bereavement or other life changes, together with their psychological concomitant reactions, are accompanied by rather slowly appearing cell-mediated or humoral immune depressions. Usually only one or a few variables have been examined. In addition, psychotic patients and diseased newborn children might show impairments or changes of host defense.

As discussed in the section describing the assays of immunity, it must be borne in mind that, for example, a decreased response of lymphocytes to mitogens after stressor exposure of the host may just suggest a shift of cell subpopulations in peripheral blood being due either to the influence of helper, suppressor or other lymphocytes, or homing of the previously reacting cell to, for example, lymph nodes, where, in fact, it has taken its place in the first line of defense.

We must also look for an answer to the question of whether observed changes are harmful to the host, or whether they are beneficial. Although immunosuppression is generally assumed to be harmful for healthy subjects (whereas it may be beneficial in certain diseases!), available studies in this particular area report no details on morbidity and mortality following a demonstration of immunosuppression. Furthermore, since only one variable has been followed in some studies it is not feasible to assess host defense adequately, considering the many complex and only partly known interactions among its components.

Experimentally introduced stressors in human studies have generally demonstrated that cell-mediated immune functions may be depressed, but that some enhancements may occur (*vide supra*). As with the clinical studies, no data are available on the possible propensity to acquire infections exhibited by the subjects. From one point of view, this is satisfying since it would have been highly unethical to subject volunteers to potentially harmful situations. In fact, one of the major problems inherent in experimental studies of this kind is the lack of reality of the stimulus situation. In contrast to animal studies that might be designed rather drastically, we can overcome part of this drawback in human studies by simply asking the participants about their feelings. We might then relate the behavioral responses to immune changes, assuming that the assays used are sufficiently sensitive so that changes are not masked by background methodological noise. However, it is seldom feasible to perform an experimental, well-controlled study over a sufficiently prolonged period to allow for many cell-mediated immune reactions to occur.

This type of experiment provides an opportunity to elucidate mechanisms. In many studies of psychosocial stress, endocrine reactions have been shown to play a prominent role in relating stressor to disease or precursor of disease. Since many of these hormones affect immunity, there has been an interest in relating stress-induced immune changes to endocrine reactions. However, immunosuppression has been found regardless of concomitant enhancements, depressions, or indifferent serum concentrations of, for instance, cortisol, suggesting that, in man, the hormonal and immune systems might react independently but sometimes simultaneously.

Finally, experimental studies present the best available opportunity to assess hypotheses regarding the influence of different phases of the stress reaction on immune functions. One of the prevalent concepts is that stress is generally immunosuppressive. Conflicting data exist. Monjan and Collector (1977, 1980) and Solomon et al. (1967) have called attention to the fact that exposures of animals to stressors were associated with an initial depression of investigated immune functions, which was followed by immunostimulation. When animal and human studies are reviewed in detail with regard to the timing of the stressor exposure in relation to measurements of host defense, it is found that an increased morbidity and mortality in experimental infections or depressions of immune functions occur if the microorganism or antigen is administered prior to or during the stressor exposure (Palmblad et al., 1976; Chang and Rasmusen, 1965; Hill et al., 1967; Solomon et al., 1967; Rasmusen, 1969; Jensen, 1969; Solomon, 1969; Schildt, 1970; Kimzey et al.,

EXPERIMENTAL INFECTIONS

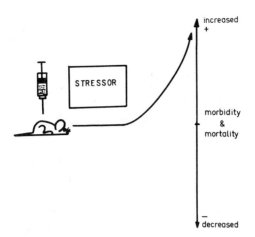

Figure 6. When a stressor exposure follows administration of microorganisms or antigens, many investigators have found an increased morbidity/mortality rate.

CELL-MEDIATED IMMUNITY

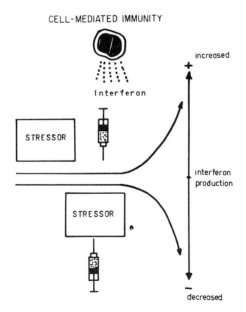

Figure 7. As depicted in Figure 6, when stressor and antigen exposures occur simultaneously, a decrease in interferon production was noted; when stressor exposure precedes antigen, induction of interferon production was enhanced.

EXPERIMENTAL INFECTIONS

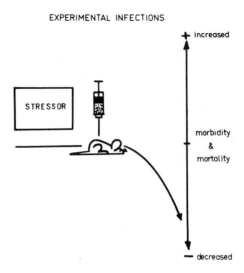

Figure 8. When stressor exposure precedes administration of microorganisms (or antigens), it is hypothesized that an increased resistance could occur.

1976; Bartrop *et al.*, 1977; Figures 6 and 7). On the other hand, an increased resistance may be found if stressor exposure precedes the antigen administration or determinations of immune functions (Palmblad *et al.*, 1976; Solomon *et al.*, 1967; Palmblad, 1979, Figures 7 and 8). Based on present evidence, the following hypothesis is suggested: Stressor exposure may depress host defense as long as it prevails, or at least for the initial phase of more chronic stress. Thereafter, a period of enhanced resistance may follow. Future research is certainly needed to assess this hypothesis, especially in clinical situations.

SUGGESTIONS FOR FUTURE RESEARCH

The assumption that stressful events may increase a person's susceptibility to or aggravate the course of infectious disease and other disorders depending on an intact immune system still needs confirmation, as emphasized in the previous sections.

First, it is important to assess whether stress really influences the immune system in a broader sense than shown hitherto, that is, that it does affect several important mechanisms, not only one or two isolated *in vitro* variables. Second, it is essential to show that these alterations of immunologic reactivity also confer an increased risk of acquiring disease. When planning studies we should not forget that it might be equally worthwhile to investigate the possibility that stress might also increase host defense—at least under certain circumstances. Consequently, the absence of disease could be a valuable piece of evidence. When these phenomena have been established, we can begin to deal with questions concerning mechanisms, for example, whether hormonal responses are the mediators and could predict future illness.

One way of demonstrating both basic parts of the chain would be to follow healthy individuals who are assessed for psychosocial changes and subsequent feelings, immune reactions, and incidence and severity of appropriate diseases. Evidently, it will not be feasible in the forseeable future to undertake such a large study because thousands of human beings should be followed repeatedly with all these measures in order to obtain sufficient numbers of responders in each category.

The general approach just described might be utilized if we followed, instead of healthy humans, subjects already running a certain risk of acquiring infections or other appropriate disorders. These subjects could for example, be afflicted with congenital inborn errors of immunity such as chronic granulomatous disease, agammaglobulinemia, and similar conditions, which are more or less rare. Similarly, it would be worthwhile to explore the possibility of examining patients with various disorders, who are being treated with standardized pharmacotherapeutic regimens which include immuno- and myelosuppressive drugs. By rendering these patients susceptible to infection because of treatment for disease, we could also follow them for feelings concerning the future, ability to cope, and simultaneous measurements of occurring infection and immune function.

Another line of research has already been exploited with apparent success. It comprises assessments of all the above mentioned measures in a healthy population facing an epidemiologic outbreak of contagious disease, such as influenza. In addition, the response and protection afforded by active immunizations could be included and examined in their own right.

Finally, since ethical considerations prohibit experimental induction of disease in humans subjected to various stressors, a way out of this dilemma might be to perform antistress experiments. By eliminating naturally occurring exposures to environmental stressors in one group but not in another we could collect data relevant to our hypotheses (Levi, 1979). Such experiments might even be performed in a dose–response manner, which would further strengthen the case.

By undertaking studies of the feasibility of any one of these or other lines of research, it will eventually be established whether, and, if so, in which way stress affects immune competence in humans.

ACKNOWLEDGMENTS

This review was supported by a grant from the National Swedish Defence Research Institute. Professors A. Kagan and L. Engstedt contributed valuable criticism, which is gratefully acknowledged.

REFERENCES

Akerstedt, T., Palmblad, J., de la Torre, B., Manana, R., and Gillberg, M. (1980). Adrenocortical and gonadal reactions during sleep deprivation. *Sleep* **3**, 23–30.

Bartrop, R. W., Lazarus, L., Luckhurst, E., Kiloh, L. G., and Penny, R. (1977). Depressed lymphocyte function after bereavement. *Lancet* **1**, 834–836.

Black, S., Humphrey, J. H., and Niven, J. S. (1963). Inhibition of Mantoux reaction by direct suggestion under hypnosis. *Br. Med. J.* **6**, 1649–1652.

Bock, E., Weeke, B., and Rafaelsen, O. J. (1971). Serum proteins in acutely psychotic patients. *J. Psychiatr. Res.* **9**, 1–9.

Buckley, C. E., and Roseman, J. M. (1976). Immunity and survival. *J. Am. Geriatr. Soc.* **24**, 241–248.

Canter, A., Cluff, L. E., and Imboden, J. B. (1972). Hypersensitive reactions to immunization, inoculations and antecedent psychological vulnerability. *J. Psychosom. Res.* **16**, 99–101.

Chang, S. S., and Rasmussen, A. F. (1965). Stress-induced suppression of interferon production in virus-infected mice. *Nature (London)* **205**, 623–625.

Cunningham, A. S. (1976). Lymphomas and animal-protein consumption. *Lancet* **2**, 1184–1186.

Dianzani, M. U., Torrielli, M. V., Canuto, R. A., Garcea, R., and Feo, F. (1976). The influence of enrichment with cholesterol on the phagocytic activity. *J. Pathol.* **118**, 193–199.

Fisher, C. L., Gill, C., Daniels, J. C., Cobb, E. K., Berry, C. A., and Ritzman, S. E. (1972). Effects of the space flight environment on man's immune system. *Aerosp. Med.* **43**, 856–859.

Fiser, R. H., Rollins, J. B., and Beisel, W. R. (1972a). Decreased resistance against infectious canine hepatitis in dogs fed a high fat ration. *Am. J. Vet. Res.* **33**, 713–719.

Fiser, R. H., Denniston, J. C., Kaplan, J., McGann, V. G., and Beisel, W. R. (1972b). Hypercholesterolemia and altered immunity in Rhesus monkeys. *Fed. Proc., Fed. Am. Soc. Exp. Biol.* **31**, 727.

Gallin, J. I., and Quie, P. G. (1977). "Neutrophil Chemotaxis." Raven, New York.

Good, R. A., Fernandez, G., Yunis, E. J., Cooper, W. C., Jose, D. C., Cramer, R. T., and Hansen, M. A. (1976). Nutritional deficiency, immunologic function and disease. *Am. J. Pathol.* **84**, 599–614.

Gotch, F. M., Spry, C. J. F., Mowat, A. G., Beeson, P. B., and MacLennan, I. C. M. (1975). Reversible granulocyte killing defect in anorexia nervosa. *Clin. Exp. Immunol.* **21**, 244–249.

Greene, W. A., Bets, R. F., and Ochitill, H. N. (1978). Psychosocial factors and immunity: Preliminary report. *Psychosom. Med.* **40**, 87 (abstr.).

Greenfield, N. S., Roessler, R., and Crosley, A. P. (1959). Ego strength and length of recovery from infectious mononucleosis. *J. Nerv. Ment. Dis.* **128**, 125–128.

Hallberg, D., Nilsson, B., and Backman, L. (1976). Immunological function in patients operated on with small intestinal shunts for morbid obesity. *Scand. J. Gastroenterol.* **11**, 41–48.

Hawley, H. P., and Gordon, G. B. (1976). The effect of long-chain free fatty acids on neutrophil function and structure. *Lab. Invest.* **34**, 216–222.

Hendrie, H. C., Paraskevas, F., Baragar, F. D., and Adamsom, J. D. (1971). Stress, immunoglobulin levels and early polyarthritis. *J. Psychosom. Res.* **15**, 337–342.

Hill, C. W., Greer, W. E., and Felsenfeld, O. (1967). Psychosocial stress early response to foreign proteins, and blood cortisol in vervets. *Psychosom. Med.* **29**, 279–283.

Holm. G., and Palmblad, J. (1976). Acute energy deprivation in man: Effect on cell-mediated immunological reactions. *Clin. Exp. Immunol.* **25**, 207–211.

Holmes, T. H., Hawkins, N. G., Bowerman, C. E., Clarke, E. R., and Joffe, J. R. (1957). Psychosocial and psychophysiologic studies of tuberculosis. *Psychosom. Med.* **19**, 134–143.

Jacobs, M. A., Spilken, A., and Normal, M. (1969). Relationship of life change, maladaptive aggression and upper respiratory infection in male college students. *Psychosom. Med.* **31**, 33–42.

Jacobs, M. A., Spilken, A., Norman, M. M., and Andersson, L. S. (1970). Life stress and respiratory illness. *Psychosom. Med.* **32**, 233–242.

Jenkins, C. D. (1976). Recent evidence supporting psychologic and social risk factors for coronary disease. *N. Engl. J. Med.* **294**, 987-994, 1033-1038.

Jensen, M. M. (1969). The influence of vasoactive amines on interferon production in mice. *Proc. Soc. Exp. Biol. Med.* **130**, 34-39.

Kim, Y., and Michael, A. E. (1975). Hypocomplementemia in anorexia nervosa. *J. Pediatr.* **87**, 582-585.

Kimzey, S. L., Johnson, P. C., Ritzman, S. E., and Mengel, C. E. (1976). Hematology and immunology studies: The second manned sky lab mission. *Aviat. Space Environ. Med.* **47**, 383-390.

Kjellberg, J., Levi, L., Palmblad J., Paulsson, L., Theorell, T., and Yensen, R. (1977). Energy deprivation in man—methodological problems and possibilities. *Acta Med. Scand.* **201**, 9-13.

Kjösen, B., Bassoe, H. H., and Myking, O. (1975). The glucose oxidation in isolated leukocytes from female patients suffering from overweight or anorexia nervosa. *Scand. J. Clin. Lab. Invest.* **35**, 447-454.

Levi, L. (1972). Stress and distress in response to psychosocial stimuli. *Acta Med. Scand., Suppl.* **528**.

Levi, L. (1979). Psychosocial factors in preventive medicine. *In* "Healthy People—The Surgeon General's Report on Health Promotion and Disease Prevention" (D. Hamburg, E. O. Nightingale, and V. Kalmar, eds.), U. S. Dept. of Health, Education and Welfare, Washington, D.C. pp. 207-252.

Liedeman, R. R., and Prilipko, L. L. (1972). The spontaneous activation of lymphocytes in schizophrenic patients *in vitro* revealed by a micro fluoremetric method. *J. Psychiatr. Res.* **9**, 155-161.

Locke, S. E., Hurst, M. W., Williams, R. M., and Heisel, I. S. (1978). The influence of psychosocial factors on human cell-mediated immune function. Presented at the meetings of the American Psychosomatic Society, Washington, D.C.

Luborsky, L., Mintz, J., Brightman, V. J., and Katcher, A. H. (1976). Herpes simplex and moods, a longitudinal study. *J. Psychosom. Res.* **20**, 543-548.

Makinodan, T. (1976). Immunobiology of aging. *J. Am. Geriatr. Soc.* **24**, 249-252.

Mann, G. V. (1974). The influence of obesity on health. *N. Engl. J. Med.* **291**, 178-85, 226-232.

Mason, J. W. (1975). A historical view of the stress field. *J. Hum. Stress* **1**, 6-12, 22-36.

Meyer, R. J., and Haggerty, R. J. (1962). Streptococcal infections in families: Factors altering individual susceptibility. *J. Pediatr.* **29**, 539-549.

Miller, M. E. (1977). Host defense in the human neonate. *Pediatr. Clin. North Am.* **25**, 413-423.

Mills, E. L., Thompson, T., Björkstén, B., Filipovich, B. S., and Quie, P. G. (1979). The chemiluminescence response and bactericidal activity of PMN neutrophils from newborns and their mothers. *J. Pediatr.* **63**, 429-34.

Monjan, A. A., and Collector, M. I. (1977). Stress-induced modulation of the immune response. *Science,* **196**, 307-308.

Monjan, A. A., and Collector, M. I. (1980). Noise as a stressor in the laboratory rodent: Modulation of lymphocyte reactivity. *Cancer Res.* (in press).

Morito, T., Bankhurst, A. D., and Williams, R.C. (1979). Studies of human cord blood and adult lymphocyte interactions with *in vitro* immunoglobulin production. *J. Clin. Invest.* **64**, 990-995.

Murray, M. J., and Murray, A. B. (1977). Starvation suppression and refeeding activation of infection. *Lancet* **1**, 123-126.

Naitoh, P. (1976). Sleep deprivation in human subjects. *Waking Sleeping* **1**, 53-60.

Palmblad, J. (1976). Fasting in man: Effect on PMN granulocyte function, plasma iron and serum transferrin. *Scand. J. Haematol.* **17**, 217-226.

Palmblad, J. (1977). Malnutrition and host defense—a study on the effects of starvation, anorexia nervosa and obesity on humoral and cell-mediated immunological mechanisms and polymorphonuclear granulocyte reactions and their relationship to some metabolic and endocrine functions. Thesis, Stockholm.

Palmblad, J. (1979). Activation of the bactericidal capacity of blood granulocytes after surgery. *Scand. J. Haematol.* **23**, 10–16.

Palmblad, J. and Haak, A. (1978). Ageing does not change blood granulocyte bactericidal capacity and levels of complement factors 3 and 4. *Gerontology* **24**, 381–385.

Palmblad, J., Cantell, K., Strander H., Fröberg, J., Karlsson, C. -G., Levi, L., Granström, M., and Unger, P. (1976). Stressor exposure and immunological response in man: Interferon-producing capacity and phagocytosis. *J. Psychosom. Res.* **20**, 193–199.

Palmblad, J., Hallberg, D., and Rössner, S. (1977a). Obesity, plasma lipids and polymorphonuclear (PMN) granulocyte functions. *Scand, J. Haematol.* **19**. 293–303.

Palmblad, J., Cantell, K., Holm, G., Norberg, R., Strander, H., and Sundblad, L. (1977b). Acute energy deprivation in man: Effect on serum immunoglobin, antibody response, complement factors 3 and 4, acute phase reactants and interferon producing capacity of blood lymphocytes. *Clin. Exp. Immunol.* **30**, 50–55.

Palmblad, J., Fohlin, L., and Lundström, M. (1977c). Anorexia nervosa and polymorphonuclear (PMN) granulocyte reactions. *Scand. J. Haematol.* **19**, 334–342.

Palmblad, J., Levi, L., Burger, A., Melander, A., Westgren, U., von Schenck, H., and Skude, G. (1977d). Effects of total energy withdrawal (fasting) on the levels of growth hormone thyrotropin, cortisol, adrenaline, noradrenaline, T_4, T_3, and rT_3 in healthy males. *Acta Med. Scand.* **201**, 15–22.

Palmblad, J., Fohlin, L., and Norberg, R. (1979a). Plasma levels of complement factors 3 and 4. orosomucoid and opsonic functions in anorexia nervosa. *Acta Paediatr. Scand.* **68**, 617–618.

Palmblad, J., Rössner, S., and Udén A. M. (1979b). Granulocyte functions during treatment of obesity. *Int. J. Obes.* **3**, 119–122.

Palmblad, J., Karlsson, C. G., Levi, L., and Lidberg (1979c). The erythrocyte sedimentation rate and stress. *Acta Med. Scand.* **205**, 517–520.

Palmblad, J., Petrini, B., Wasserman, J., and Åkerstedt, T. (1979d). Lymphocyte and granulocyte reactions during sleep deprivation. *Psychosom. Med.* **41**, 273–278.

Palmblad, J., Åkerstedt, T., Fröberg, J., Melander, A., Schenck, H. (1979e). Thyroid reactions during sleep deprivation. *Acta Endocrinol. (Copenhagen)* **90**, 233–239.

Palmblad, J., Hallberg, D., and Engstedt, L. (1980). Polymorphonuclear function after small intestinal shunt operation for morbid obesity. *Br. J. Haematol.* **44**, 101–108.

Rahe, R. H. (1972). Subject's recent life changes and near-future illness susceptibility. *Psychosom. Med.* **8**, 2–19.

Rasmussen, A. F. (1969). Emotions and immunity. *Ann. N.Y. Acad. Sci.* **164**, 458–462.

Roberts-Thomson, I. C., Whittingham, S., Youngchaiyud, U., and Mackay, I. R. (1974). Ageing, immune response and mortality. *Lancet* **2**, 368–370.

Roessler, R., Cabe, T. R., Lester, J. W., and Couch, R. B. (1979). Ego strength, life events, and antibody titers. Presented at the Meetings of the *American Psychosomatic Society,* Dallas, Texas.

Rogers, M., Trentham, D., McCune, J., Ginsberg, B., Reich, P., and David, J. (1979). Abrogation of type II collagen-induced arthritis in rats by psychological stress. *Clin. Res.* **27**, 513A.

Schildt, B. E. (1970). Fluctuation of the RES after thermal and mechanical trauma in mice. *Acta Chir. Scand.* **136**, 359–64.

Scrimshaw, N. S., Taylor, C. E., and Gordon, J. E. (1968). "Interactions of nutrition and infection." World Health Organization, Geneva.

Selye, H. (1975). Confusion and controversy in the Stress-field. *J. Hum. Stress,* **1**, 37–44.

Solomon, G. F. (1969). Stress and antibody response in rats. *Int. Arch. Allergy Appl. Immunol.* **35**, 97–104.

Solomon, G. F., Merigan, T. C., and Levine, S. (1967). Variations in adrenal cortical hormones within physiological ranges, stress and interferon production in mice. *Proc. Soc. Exp. Biol. Med.* **126**, 74–79.

Strunk, R. C., Fenton, L. J., and Gaines, J. A. (1979). Alternative pathway of complement activation in fullterm and premature infants. *J. Pediatr. Res.* **13**, 641–643.

Suskind, R. (1977). "Malnutrition and the Immune Response." Raven, New York.

Theander, S. (1970). Anorexia nervosa. *Acta Psychiatr. Scand., Suppl.* **214**.

Udén, A. M., Trang, L., Venizelos, N., and Palmblad, J. (1980). Neutrophil functions and clinical performance after total fasting in patients with rheumatoid arthritis. Int. Symp. of Infections in the Immunocomised Host, Veldhofen, the Netherlands, 1980, Abstracts, p. 55.

Waddell, C. C., Taunton, O. D., and Twomey, J. J. (1976). Inhibition of lymphoproliferation by hyperlipoproteinemic plasma. *J. Clin. Invest.* **58**, 950–54.

Warren, M. P., and Wiele, R. L. (1973). Clinical and metabolic features of anorexia nervosa. *Am. J. Obstet. Gynecol.* **117**, 435–449.

Wick, G., Sundich, R. S., and Albini, B. (1974). The obese strain of chickens. *Clin. Immunol. Immunopathol.* **3**, 272–300.

Wright, W. C., Ank, B. J., Herbert, J., and Stiehm, E. R. (1975). Decreased bactericidal activity of leukocytes of stressed new born infants. *J. Pediatr.* **56**, 579–584.

Yunis, E. J., Fernandes, G., and Greenberg, L. J. (1976). Tumor immunology, autoimmunity and aging. *J. Am. Geriatr. Soc.* **24**, 253–263.

Immunologic Abnormalities in Mental Illness

GEORGE FREEMAN SOLOMON

INTRODUCTION

A variety of immunologic abnormalities has been reported in conjunction with mental illness, particularly schizophrenia. These findings include abnormalities in levels of immunoglobulins; abnormal heterophile antibodies; the presence of autoantibodies to a variety of self components, including the presence of antibrain antibodies; deficient immune responsivity; and morphologic and functional abnormalities of immunologically competent cells. Other portions of this book document the relationship of experiential events to immune functions, the role of the central nervous system in regulation of immunity, and the presence of emotional factors in diseases associated with immunologic dysfunction. There is a philosophical attractiveness in linking the immune and central nervous systems: Both relate the organism to the outside world; both serve functions of defense and adaptation; both result in illness when operating inappropriately or overdefensively; and both have the property of memory and "learning" from experience. If there is a close relationship between the central nervous system and immune function and if stress and emotional distress are related to immune responsivity, it would seem to follow that the presence of a profound emotional disturbance, such as psychosis, particularly of schizophrenic nature, would be associated with

259

alterations in immune function. However, the significance of immune abnormalities in the etiology or pathogenesis of mental illness remains most unclear.

IMMUNOGLOBULINS IN PSYCHIATRIC PATIENTS

Fessel and Grunbaum (1961), in early work similar to that of several European investigators (Cepulic *et al.*, 1954; Milhaud *et al.*, 1959; Pospisilova and Janik, 1958), reported a significant elevation of γ-globulin levels in various groups of chronically psychotic state hospital patients. Fessel reported elevation of 19S ultracentrifugal class macroglobulins (now known to be IgM antibody) in acute functional mental illness (Fessel, 1962b), but this finding was not confirmed in a group of drug-free schizophrenic patients (Bishop *et al.*, 1966; Kuruvilla *et al.*, 1973), nor was it correlated with illness in monozygotic twins discordant for schizophrenia (Stabenau *et al.*, 1968). Qualitative, as well as quantitative, disturbances in electrophoretic serum patterns in schizophrenic patients, some of whom were drug free, have been described, including: splitting of alpha$_2$-globulin, a density line superimposed on the gamma region, an abnormally shaped globulin curve (Fessel and Grunbaum, 1961), and an increase in alpha$_1$ (Grunbaum *et al.*, 1964), alpha$_2$ (Donnini *et al.*, 1962; Pospisilova and Janik, 1958; Hippius *et al.*, 1958) and/or beta globulin (Kopeloff and Fischell, 1963; Sapira, 1964; Grunbaum *et al.*, 1964; Pospisilova and Janik, 1958), including correlation of globulin abnormalities with specific psychotic symptoms in some studies.

In our first work on the subject (Solomon *et al.*, 1966), we found a slight positive correlation between the severity of general psychotic symptoms and 19S macroglobulin levels in chronic schizophrenic patients. The administration of very low doses of an antimetabolite drug, chlorambucil, which lowers macroglobulin, led neither to clinical improvement nor to significant changes of γ-globulin or macroglobulin. Our next work (Solomon *et al.*, 1969) found that levels of IgA and IgM were significantly elevated in a group of 73 male psychiatric inpatients. Among the 49 schizophrenic patients, there were no significant differences between process–reactive, paranoid–nonparanoid, and active–remission categories in immunoglobulin levels, nor were there differences between schizophrenic and nonschizophrenic patients. Significant differences were not found on the basis of duration of hospitalization, chronicity of illness, severity of symptoms, or the receiving of phenothiazine drugs. We felt that this work provided further evidence that psychiatric disorders are associated with immunologic abnormalities, but that it cast a doubt upon the specificity of dysglobulinemias for schizophrenia. In our last work on immunoglobulins (Amkraut *et al.*, 1973), we found that IgA and IgM levels all were significantly elevated in a population of 80 male psychiatric inpatients suffering from acute schizophrenic reactions, none of whom had received any medication within a month, compared to normal controls. Patients with levels of both IgG and IgA below the median were significantly more likely to show clinical improvement during the course of hospitalization than those in whom either or both immunoglobulin levels were above the median, whether treated with chlorpromazine or drug-free.

In contrast to our work, Strahilevitz and Davis (1970) found elevations only in IgA, not IgM and IgG, in schizophrenic patients compared to non-schizophrenic patients or healthy blood donors. Strahilevitz' group subsequently found: (a) significantly higher mean serum levels of IgA in schizophrenic women than in control women and in schizophrenic blacks than in either schizophrenic whites or black controls; (b) higher IgD in schizophrenic blacks than in schizophrenic whites; (c) higher IgM in controls than in nonschizophrenic patients; and (d) higher IgG in schizophrenics whose urine was positive for phenothiazines than in schizophrenics whose urine was negative. High serum levels of IgG were associated with no or mild hallucinations and low levels with moderate or severe hallucinations. High serum levels of IgG, either drug induced or not drug induced, seemed to be associated with low or absent hallucinations. The authors speculated that IgG antibody may act as a "protective antibody" against hallucinations, analogous to the role of protective antibodies in experimental allergic encephalomyelitis. In another study, Hendrie et al. (1972) found elevation of IgM in female psychiatric inpatients but did not find that this elevation was related to the diagnosis of schizophrenia, all patients having had no psychotropic medication for the 6 months prior. Conflicts in findings concerning immunoglobulin levels are illustrated by the observation of significant elevations of IgM in female patients but not in males and the fact that this finding was related to psychiatric illness in hospitalized patients rather than to schizophrenia, per se. These authors also found an apparent relationship between severe disorganizing levels of anxiety and increased IgA levels. To add to the confusion, Bock et al. (1971) in comparing acutely ill psychiatric patients, about half of whom were schizophrenic, found that IgA was *decreased* in borderline psychotic patients and, in other work, that IgM also was decreased (Bock, 1978). In a sophisticated study relating immunoglobulin levels in 76 schizophrenic patients to psychopathology and to prognosis, Pulkkinen (1977) found the highest IgM concentration in withdrawn schizophrenics and the lowest in paranoid patients. Present age had a positive correlation and rural birth a negative correlation to IgA concentrations! Higher IgA and IgM values than average at the beginning of treatment predicted a shorter hospital stay, in contrast to our findings of lower IgG and IgA being correlated with clinical improvement. Torrey (1977) found that analysis of cerebrospinal fluid (CSF) immunoglobulins appeared to be better than the analysis of serum immunoglobulins for distinguishing psychiatric patients from controls. First admission schizophrenics had significantly elevated CSF levels of IgA. Serial CSF levels of IgG were inversely correlated with clinical condition in some patients and appeared to be independent of serum levels. Torrey's work is compatible with older findings that elevated CSF γ-globulin levels in some mental hospital patients disappeared more frequently in those whose clinical condition improved, although elevation of CSF γ-globulin did not appear specific to schizophrenia (Hunter et al., 1969). Studies reporting elevated levels of IgA and/or IgM indirectly support an autoimmune hypothesis of schizophrenia in that other clinical conditions most often associated with such elevations fall into the category of autoimmune diseases, for example, rheumatoid arthritis and systemic lupus erythematosus (Vaughn, 1965).

HETEROPHILE ANTIBODIES IN SCHIZOPHRENIA

Frohman et al. (1960, 1961) reported a biochemical assay which could detect a difference between the plasma of some schizophrenic patients and that of normal volunteers based on the incubation of chicken erythrocytes with plasma. High terminal ratios of lactate to pyruvate (L/P) were associated with schizophrenia. The responsible substance was felt to be an antibody (Ryan et al., 1966). However, the work was not confirmed in controlled studies of other workers by the same or alternative techniques (Ryan et al., 1968). Turner and Chipps (1966) described a heterophile hemolysin active against rabbit erythrocytes present in the sera of schizophrenic patients contrasted to normals, but the presence of this hemolysin (or an agglutinin) was not confirmed in subsequent work by the same or other investigators (Lang and Corvin, 1969). In spite of lack of confirmation by other workers, the Layfayette Clinic group continued to study the heterophile phenomenon and identified the serum protein responsible for the abnormal L/P ratio as an α_2 globulin (Frohman, 1968). Since this substance, subsequently characterized biochemically and biophysically and claimed to affect animal behavior when injected into the brain, turned out (if existing) not to be an antibody, it will not be discussed further here.

AUTOANTIBODIES IN PSYCHIATRIC PATIENTS

An increased incidence of a variety of autoantibodies, other than those directed against brain constituents, has been reported in conjunction with schizophrenia and other psychiatric illnesses. By means of the FII latex agglutination test, Fessel (1961) showed an increased incidence of rheumatoid factor, an anti-γ-globulin autoantibody (now known to be an IgM anti-IgG) in the sera of psychotic state hospital patients. Soviet workers also found human antiglobulins in the sera of schizophrenic patients (Burian et al., 1964). These findings are of particular interest because a number of studies, including some very careful ones, have documented an extremely low or absent coincidence of rheumatoid arthritis and schizophrenia (Funkenstein, 1950; Rothermich and

Philips, 1963). (In my experience the only psychotic patients with rheumatoid arthritis have suffered from an organic brain syndrome, an affective disorder or a paranoid state.) Perhaps the antiglobulin in schizophrenia is different from that in rheumatoid arthritis (S. Cobb, personal communication, 1961). This view is supported by our finding that healthy relatives of patients with rheumatoid arthritis who have rheumatoid factor in their sera are emotionally healthy as well, as if the presence of the antiglobulin *and* emotional distress or decompensation lead to overt rheumatoid disease. Possibly relevant to the peculiar relationship between rheumatoid arthritis and schizophrenia is Taylor's (1978) postulate that different aberrations of tryptophan metabolism underlie both diseases.

Antinuclear factor (ANF) incidence is also reportedly increased in schizophrenia (Fessel, 1961). This may be related to the high incidence (an average of 22% in reviewed reports) of psychosis in conjunction with systemic lupus erythematosis (SLE), an autoimmune disease associated with antinuclear acid antibodies (Fessel and Solomon, 1960). Psychosis in SLE may be clinically indistinguishable from schizophrenia and, like epilepsy, can be a presenting symptom of the disease. An increased incidence of antinuclear antibody, but not of antibody to thyroid, gastric, muscle, or mitochondrial antigens, was found in mentally ill and mentally deficient hospitalized psychiatric patients (Mellsop *et al.,* 1973). In a double blind study, von Brauchitsch (1972) found elevated ANF only in psychotic patients whose conditions were characterized by depression. Deberdt *et al.* (1976) suggested that the (30%) proportion of patients newly admitted to psychiatric hospitals for depression who were found to be positive for ANF might be suffering from a distinctive disease. Soviet workers report antithymic antibodies in schizophrenic patients (Luria and Domashneva, 1974; Domashneva and Maznina, 1976). The involvement of antibodies to common antigens of thymic lymphocytes and brain neurons is suggested (Golub, 1972; Vartanian, 1968).

ANTIPSYCHOTIC DRUGS AND IMMUNOLOGIC ABNORMALITIES

Although some studies took place in drug-free patients and in other studies there was an attempt to tease out drug effects, the role of antipsychotic medication must be considered, particularly in evaluating reports of dysglobulinemias and autoantibodies in psychiatric patients. Chlorpromazine (Quismorio *et al.,* 1972; Alarcón-Segovia *et al.,* 1973) and other antipsychotic drugs (Gallien *et al.,* 1975), including lithium (Presley *et al.,* 1976), have been reported to induce antinuclear antibodies. Appearance of antibodies to single-stranded DNA, native DNA nucleoprotein, IgG (rheumatoid factor), erythrocyte membrane, and coagulation factor in patients treated with chlorpromazine is suggested by studies of Zarrabi *et al.* (1979). Patients who had undergone long-term treatment with chlorpromazine also showed elevations of serum IgM (as well as prolongation of thromboplastin time caused by a circulating inhibitor similar to that seen with SLE). The percentage of T cells was below normal in a significant proportion of patients treated with chlorpromazine. (T-cell lymphopenia occurs in SLE.) The possibility that the therapeutic effect of chlorpromazine might be immunologically mediated, however, is negated by the absence of immunologic abnormalities found by these authors in patients treated with other antipsychotic drugs.

ANTIBRAIN ANTIBODIES IN SCHIZOPHRENIA

An autoimmune hypothesis of schizophrenia is attractive in that, like schizophrenia, autoimmune diseases appear to be related to genetic, personality, and stress factors (Solomon, 1970). A clearly defined autoimmune disease, systemic lupus erythematosis, can be associated with a schizophreniform psychosis that remits when the disease is brought under control, as by the use of immunosuppresant drugs. Stress, especially loss of a significant relationship or fear of loss of love, often can be documented as preceding the onset of SLE (McClary et al., 1955). Could schizophrenia be a psychosomatic disease of the brain? Burch (1964) postulated an autoimmune origin for schizophrenia on theoretical grounds from a study of the age- and sex-specific rates of first admission to mental hospitals. Fessel sought antibrain activity in the sera of schizophrenic patients by utilizing sheep brain, which may or may not share antigens with human brain. By means of a latex agglutination technique, he found that 28% of sera of acutely disturbed psychiatric patients had antibrain activity, compared to a rate of 15% in chronically psychotic patients' sera and 10% in blood donor controls' (Fessel, 1962a). Utilizing a hemagglutination technique, he subsequently found brain-coated red cells agglutinated with 31% of state hospital patients' sera compared with 6.4% of blood donors' sera, with 27% of sera having abnormal ultracentrifugal protein patterns, and with 17% of sera of patients with connective tissue diseases (likely to be autoimmune) (Fessel, 1963). Kuznetsova and Semenov (1961), using a complement fixation technique, found that the sera of neuropsychiatric patients reacted with antigens from brain but not from other tissues. Nazarov (1962) found skin hypersensitivity to various brain antigens in mental patients, particularly schizophrenics. Vartanian and co-workers (1978) found that serum from 35 of 50 schizophrenics reacted with an antigen derived from brains of normal individuals who died in accidents. Other Soviet researchers (Kolyaskina and Kushnir, 1969) correlated prevalence of antibrain antibodies with "malignancy" of the disease, found the highest incidence (28%) in "nuclear" schizophrenics, and pointed out a significant increase in discovery of antibrain antibodies (10.3% to 62.2%) by repeated investigations. They found that 20% of siblings and 10% of parents of schizophrenics showed antibrain antibodies. Complement fixation revealed anticerebral antibodies in a significant percentage of schizophrenic patients, more frequently in those with severe disease and more commonly in relatives of schizophrenics than in controls (Gosheva et al., 1969). In more recent Soviet work, existence of antibrain antibodies in schizophrenic patients was determined by complex formation reaction and passive hemagglutination, the former revealing antibodies early in the course of the disease, and the latter later but only for a relatively short time (Glebov and Zil'bersheteyn, 1975). Late in the illness complement-fixing antibodies decreased, and there was no increased incidence to be observed during remissions of the disease. Experimental stress in animals and humans appeared to induce antibrain antibody activity in a significant proportion of subjects, according to Davidova et al. (1966).

The greatest impetus to the concept of schizophrenia as an autoimmune disease has arisen from the controversial work of Robert Heath and co-workers at Tulane University. In 1956–1957, Heath described a protein fraction obtained from the sera of schizophrenic patients he named "taraxein," which he claimed was capable of inducing psychotic behavior when administered to human volunteers (Heath et al., 1957). When administered to monkeys, taraxein induced focal electroencephalographic changes in the septal region as determined by implanted electrodes, along with "catatonic" behavioral manifestations (Heath et al., 1967a). Heath concluded that schizophrenia is a specific biologic disease since sera from patients with other psychoses lacked this factor (Heath and Krupp, 1968). Although first rejecting the idea that this alleged substance was a γ-globulin or an antibody (personal communication, 1959), Heath and Krupp (1968) subsequently characterized taraxein as an IgG immunoglobulin. To confirm the immunologic nature of this specific disorder, Heath and co-workers prepared sheep antibodies to specific parts of monkey and human brain and found that fractions of antisera against monkey septal and caudate areas induced EEG spiking and slow waves in homologous brain sites and concomitant catatonic behavior analogous to the effects of taraxel (Heath and Krupp, 1967; Heath, 1970; Heath et al., 1967b).

Moreover, fluorescent antibody studies (using fluorescein-tagged antisheep γ-globulin) showed antibrain fractions administered intraventricularly had attached to neural cell nuclei of the septal region and caudate nucleus of recipient monkeys, the EEG's and behavior of which had been altered by the injections. Heath also found that such binding occurred with cells from specific areas of the brains only of schizophrenic patients. He finally identified the target substrate as the cytoplasm of satellite glial cells (Heath, 1969). Heath came to the conclusion that the septal-basal-caudate region of the brain contained a unique antigen, an antibody against which is responsible for schizophrenic symptoms on an autoimmune basis.

A full critique of Heath's work is beyond the scope of this paper, although obvious questions come to mind including the ability of a globulin to cross the blood–brain barrier, cross reactivity of antibodies from different species, and claims of antigenic differences in human brains between schizophrenics and normals in spite of absence of histological differences. Difficulty or impossibility in repeating Heath's work, which is of profound implication if valid, has occurred (generally explained away by Heath as resulting from technical errors). Heath, himself, appears not to have continued the work. (This author on a personal visit in 1967 was not convinced of the accuracy of the reported observations.) In careful work in an excellent immunologic laboratory in Australia, Whittingham et al. (1968) using immunofluorescence were unable to confirm Heath's findings by incubating 3 brains from patients with schizophrenia with sera from 53 patients with chronic schizophrenia and from 53 normal controls. Logan and Deodhar (1970) also were unable to confirm the Heath findings and found no evidence of fixed or circulating antibrain antibodies in schizophrenics. Using both direct and indirect immunofluorescent techniques on brain tissue obtained at autopsy from nonpsychotic as well as from schizophrenic patients, Boehme, et al. (1973) found no evidence of attachment of immunoglobulin to nuclei of brain cells but did find nonspecific cytoplasmic immunofluorescence in both psychotic and nonpsychotic patients.

After much disillusionment, the autoimmune hypothesis of schizophrenia has received new impetus from the A. E. Bennet Award in Biological Psychiatry-winning work of Miron Baron and co-workers at Albert Einstein College of Medicine. They utilized the modern technique of radioimmunofixation, with fresh brain tissue obtained at autopsy from the septal regions of a schizophrenic's and a normal's brains (Baron et al., 1977). Schizophrenic individuals tended to have higher levels of brain serum affinity than depressives and normal controls. The binding substance appeared to be globulin, but its autoantibody nature was only suggested. Brain–serum affinity also distinguished relatives of schizophrenic probands from normal controls and was more common in relatives of probands with such affinity than without, suggesting that brain–serum affinity might represent a genetic marker for schizophrenia. Serum activity against other tissue components was found more commonly in sera from schizophrenic patients than normals, supporting earlier work on autoimmunity by less sophisticated techniques. It is of note that the specific areas of the brain (septal) purported by Heath to be the site of autoimmune fixation by antibrain antibodies and by Baron as the site of brain–serum affinity have been implicated as those areas of the brain in which a functional overactivity of dopamine neurotransmission may be important in schizophrenia (Stevens, 1973). To tie an autoimmune hypothesis to the dopamine hypothesis of schizophrenia, it has been suggested that autoantibody might act by disrupting synaptic receptor sites (Garey et al., 1974, or by altering neuronal permeability for neurotransmitters (Gottlieb et al., 1970).

HLA ANTIGENS

That there may be genetic factors in schizophrenia reflected in a differing antigenic constitution, which itself might predispose to autoimmunity, is suggested by findings of a preponderance of a few of the very many histocompatibility locus antigens in schizophrenic patients. Such preponderance has been demonstrated to be predisposing to multiple sclerosis, a likely autoimmune disease with psychosomatic aspects (Solomon, 1970; Jersild, 1978). Jersild (1976) reviewed seven studies worldwide and, combining data, found a significantly more common incidence of HLA antigens A28 and 35 in schizophrenics. However, Crowe and co-workers (1979) were not able to document such an association from their own work or review except for an association between AW26 and hebephrenic subtype. Both positive and negative correlations with specific HLA antigens were found in patients with bipolar affective illness (Shapiro et al., 1976). It is now known (in the mouse) that specific genes control immune response and that these genes are in the same region of the chromosome as genes for the major histocompatibility antigens (Notkins, 1979). As has been postulated in the case of diabetes, genetically controlled differences in the immune response may affect the development or manifestations of schizophrenia, possibly by directly affecting the development of autoimmunity or by doing so via altered susceptibility and/or response to viral infection.

IMMUNE RESPONSIVITY IN SCHIZOPHRENIA

If schizophrenia be autoimmune, it might be expected that there be an association with immunologic deficiency in terms of diminished responsivity to exogenous antigens (Fudenberg, 1968). Molholm (1942) found diminished sensitivity to foreign protein (guinea pig serum) as determined by skin test (and controlled by histamine wheal) in schizophrenic patients. Vaughan and co-workers (1949) found a lessened ability of schizophrenic patients to develop high antibody titers after hyperimmunization with pertussis vaccine relative to controls. Quite contrary findings were reported by Friedman et al. (1967) who found higher antibody titers to cholera vaccine in schizophrenics than in normals or depressed patients. Hyporeactivity to a variety of antigens as determined by skin tests, again controlled against histamine wheal, was reported in schizophrenics by Certcov (1969). However, histamine wheal formation, itself, (histamine is released by mast cells as a result of antigen–antibody reactions) was found to be smaller in chronic schizophrenic patients than in normals, acute schizophrenics or nonschizophrenics. Such diminished cutaneous response to intradermal histamine has been reported in at least a dozen studies of schizophrenic patients over the past 50 years, but has not been replicated in drug-free patients in other studies (Simpson and Kline,

1961; Rausher *et al.*, 1980). Chronic schizophrenics, especially catatonics, showed a lowered immune response to tularemia vaccine (Matveets *et al.*, 1957). However, no difference in antibody titer or skin test reactivity after diphtheria toxoid immunization was found by Hussar *et al.* (1971). Likewise, we found no lowered secondary immune response to tetanus toxoid in schizophrenic patients (Solomon *et al.*, 1970). Kerbikov (1961), utilizing immunization with a variety of antigens, concluded that immune reactivity is decreased only in certain forms of schizophrenia, such as catatonia, but may be normal or even increased in other mentally ill patients with some influence of increasing titer by treatment with drugs or insulin. The effects of phenothiazine drugs on antibody synthesis are unclear, some authors reporting a decrease (Saunders and Muchmore, 1964) and others an increase (Kocsár *et al.*, 1958). We found no effect (Solomon *et al.*, 1970), and in unpublished work (1978) found that levels of chlorprozine equivalent to therapeutic serum levels have no effect on stimulation of lymphocytes *in vitro* by phytohemagglutinin (PHA).

SCHIZOPHRENIA AS AN ALLERGIC REACTION

Old suggestions and interest in the possibility that schizophrenia may be a disease of hypersensitivity (analogous to asthma, for example) have been reawakened in recent years. Obviously, the relative lack of permeability of the blood–brain barrier to peripherally synthesized antibody poses a theoretical objection to this reasoning. [Relevantly, the Feingold theory of sensitivity to artificial food additives in hyperkinetic children does not postulate an immune mechanism (Feingold, 1975).] The work of Dohan, begun in 1966, on gluten hypersensitivity in schizophrenia, like that which occurs in coeliac disease (a chronic intestinal disorder with malabsorbtion), has stimulated much interest. There are reported abnormalities of amine metabolism in both schizophrenia and coeliac disease (Lancaster-Smith and Strickland, 1970). There is some suggestion that there is a greater than chance association of the two diseases (Dohan, 1969 a, b). Dohan *et al.* (1969) reported good therapeutic effects of a milk-and-cereal-free diet on schizophrenic patients in exacerbation. Singh and Kay (1976) reported that schizophrenics maintained on a cereal- and milk-free diet with concomitant treatment with neuroleptics showed interruption or reversal of therapeutic progress when given a gluten challenge in a blind design, with resumption of improvement when gluten was removed. This work could not be replicated by Rice *et al.* (1978). In a good quality immunologic investigation by Ashkenezi *et al.* (1979), production of leukocyte migration inhibition factor (MIF) (a "lymphokine" intermediate in immune response) by cultured peripheral blood leukocytes in response to challenge with gluten fractions was studied in hospitalized psychiatric patients and compared with the reaction in normals and in children and adolescents with coeliac disease. The schizophrenic and other psychiatric patients (without difference) could be divided about equally into two groups, those responding in the MIF test similarly to coeliac patients and those responding as normals. (Interestingly, the psychotic patients' leukocytes responded poorly to PHA stimulation, suggesting immune deficiency.) The psychotic patients, however, had no evidence of malabsorbtion. Hekkins (1978) found that, in contrast to coeliac patients, only 2 of 20 schizophrenics had antibodies to gliadin. Klee *et al.* (1978) reported the presence of an endorphinlike substance and opioid antagonists in wheat gluten, and the Ashkenezi group found that half the psychiatric patients absorbed such polypeptides, leading to sensitization of lymphocytes. A relationship between gluten hypersensitivity and lowered immune responsivity is suggested by Faulk and Cockrell (1978), who point out that secretory immunity (IgA) serves to bind antigen in the gut, the failure of which could prevent absorbtion. Hemmings (1978) claims that large breakdown products of dietary proteins (such as gliadin), not only amino acids, can be absorbed from the gut and can pass the blood–brain barrier.

VIRUSES AND SCHIZOPHRENIA

New knowledge that the central nervous degenerative disease, kuru, among cannibals of New Guinea, Jacob–Creutzfeld disease, scrapie in sheep, and transmissable encephalopathy in minks are due to "slow" viruses led Torrey and Peterson (1976) to hypothesize that schizophrenia may have a viral etiology. Their argument was based on rather tenuous indirect clinical, epidemiologic, and laboratory evidence, including immunoglobulin data to which we have referred and their own finding of elevated cerebrospinal fluid (CSF) IgG in 6 of 30 schizophrenic patients. Such patterns of isolated CSF IgG elevations are seen over the variable course of multiple sclerosis and early in subacute sclerosing panencephalitis caused by measles virus. These authors, however, found no increase in antibodies to a number of common viruses in a group of schizophrenic patients. Serum and CSF antibodies to measles, rubella, and herpes simplex type 1 viruses, the latter analyzed by techniques including sophisticated radioimmunoassay, were not found to be elevated among schizophrenic patients (Rimón *et al.*, 1978, 1979). Negative findings of antibody to virus, however, do not necessarily exclude slow or latent virus infection, since in Jacob–Creutzfeld disease and kuru immunologic response to the known etiologic agents has never been demonstrated (Scully *et al.*, 1977). Tyrrell *et al.* (1979) reported a "viruslike agent" with a cytopathic effect on tissue culture in the CSF of 18 of 47 schizophrenic patients, as well as 8 of 11 patients with multiple sclerosis or Huntington's chorea. It is noteworthy, in view of other reports of abnormalities of serum immunoglobulin levels reviewed here, that the same research group found elevated serum IgA levels in those schizophrenic patients with the viruslike agent, but not in those without (Crow *et al.*, 1979). Could a relatively deficient immune system allow CNS invasion by virus (Dwyer, 1979)? Could such immunosuppression be stress-induced (Solomon *et al.*, 1979)?

ABNORMAL LEUKOCYTES IN SCHIZOPHRENIA

The presence of abnormal immunologic reactivity in schizophrenia might be expected to be reflected in the morphology of immunologically competent cells, lymphocytes and/or in their functions under *in vitro* conditions. [Immunocompetent cells are divided into two major types—T (thymus-derived) and B (bursal equivalent but bone marrow-derived in mammals) cells. B cells give rise to five antibody producing cell populations. T cells, of which there are a number of subgroups, have a variety of functions including cell-mediated immunity, "helping" B cells, suppressing response to antigen, and giving rise to humoral factors, "lymphokines," that modulate the immune response.]

The work on morphologic abnormalities of lymphocytes in schizophrenia was given real impetus by W. J. Fessel, an internist who pioneered in investigations of immunologic abnormalities in mental illness and with whose early work this author was associated, and Motoe Hirata-Hibi, a pathologist. Prior to their work, Kamp (1962), Vanderkamp (1962), Pennington (1963), and Hollister and Kosek (1962) had described differences in the nuclei of some lymphocytes of schizophrenic patients compared to normal samples. Erban (1965) noted rapid development of nuclear pyknosis in some lymphocytes of schizophrenic patients maintained in artificial medium (Kerbikov, 1961). More recently, Fischer and Mala (1971) made observations similar to those of Erban's child and adolescent schizophrenics, reflecting, he felt, a decreased ability of those leukocytes to utilize oxygen. In their first paper, Fessel and Hirata-Hibi (1963) found abnormal leukocytes of three types in the peripheral blood of most schizophrenic patients. The majority of these abnormal cells did not correspond to the so-called "stress lymphocytes" of Frank and Dougherty (1953). (Abnormalities did not seem related to the use or amount of psychotropic medication.) In a blind study of coded pairs of slides from 50 schizophrenic patients and 50 controls, 49 were correctly diagnosed. Extending their work from peripheral blood to bone marrow of schizophrenic patients, Hirata-Hibi and Fessel (1964) again found abnormalities of lymphocytes consisting of strong basophilic cytoplasm with a prominent perinuclear clear zone, containing small vacuoles, a faintly lamellar structure or both; an indented or lobulated nucleus, and variably fine or course chromatin structure, often heterogeneously within the same nucleus. Dividing abnormal lymphocytes into "stress lymphocytes" and "P lymphocytes," thought to be specific to schizophrenia, Fessel *et al.* (1965) studied normal families, schizophrenic patients' families, stressed families of youthful offenders, and prisoners about to appear before a parole board. The families of "process" schizophrenics (insidious, gradual onset of disease, poor premorbid history, and little or no apparent precipitating stress) but not of reactive schizophrenics had 30 times as many P lymphocytes and stressed families 5 times as many as did normal families. Stressed prisoners had significant increases in stress lymphocytes. They concluded that their work favored a genetic hypothesis of schizophrenia.

Fessel and Hirata–Hibi's work was essentially confirmed in chronic schizophrenics and in family members by Sethi et al. (1973) and by Fowle (1968) in schizophrenic children. A histochemical study of schizophrenic patients prior to institution of drug treatment showed a distinct increased concentration and abnormal distributions of nucleohistones, attributed to an increase in arginine-rich histones (Stefanis and Issidorides, 1976). This leukocyte finding, however, was made in neutrophils rather than in lymphocytes. Pharmacotherapy exerted a normalizing effect on nucleohistone distribution pattern.

Soviet workers (Gosheva et al., 1969) noted spontaneous blast transformation of cultured lymphocytes from schizophrenics and a peculiar relationship, consisting of plasmatic bridges, existing between schizophrenics' lymphocytes and embryonal brain cells cultured together. Cultured lymphocytes from schizophrenics showed a "high level of cell physiological activity," as determined by a variety of (hard-to-evaluate) techniques (Liedemann, 1976). To test the functional state of untreated schizophrenic patients' peripheral blood lymphocytes, T cell mitogens phytohemagglutinin (PHA) and concanavalin A (conA) were added in tissue culture by Liedeman and Prilipko (1978). The peripheral blood of schizophrenics was found to be characterized by the presence of functionally nonactive lymphocytes, which do not respond to T mitogens, but at the same time are physiologically active as determined by adhesive characteristics, RNA synthesizing, and ultrastructural properties. Similar findings, as well as the ability of the serum of schizophrenic patients to inhibit PHA stimulation of lymphocytes of normals, were reported by Vartanian et al. (1978). Such inhibition occurs with phenothiazines and nonphenothiazine antipsychotic drugs (Baker et al., 1977), but Soviet workers claimed such effects in drug-free patients.

DISCUSSION

I have attempted a comprehensive review of the rather extensive literature suggesting a variety of immunologic abnormalities in mental illness. Some studies claim specificity of these disturbances for schizophrenia, for types or phases of the illness. Investigators vary widely in both behavioral and immunologic sophistication and credibility. (Clearly, it is far beyond the scope of this chapter to offer methodological critiques of specific work.) The reader reasonably may feel confused at this point. Trends are not clear. Some studies, including those on elevated immunoglobulin levels and on presence of heterophile antibodies, suggest hyperreactivity of the immune system. Others, such as some on response to immunization and the large number on increased autoimmune reactions in schizophrenia point, on the contrary, to relative immunologic incompetence. Although theoretically attractive for its potential to integrate genetic and stress factors, the work on schizophrenia as a specific autoimmune disease, with antibrain antibodies playing a pathogenic role, is not convincing. Perhaps most impressive is work on structural and functional abnormalities of lymphocytes in schizophrenic patients, an area that certainly deserves further investigation. That some disturbances in immunologic function can and do occur in conjunction with mental illnesses and are not mere artifacts of medication or institutional effects seems highly likely from the evidence at hand and should not be surprising in view of experimental evidence of central nervous system effects on immunity. The known effects of neuroendocrines on immune response and newer evidence of receptor sites for neuroendocrines and neurotransmitters on lymphocytes and macrophages increases the likelihood of immune abnormalities in conjunction with mental conditions that alter the balance of such substances (Solomon et al., 1979). We have seen from work described elsewhere in this book that the central nervous system may directly regulate immune response (perhaps in part, I speculate, through control of thymic hormones). The nature of specific immunologic disturbances in mental illness needs considerable clarification. Any etiologic role for those immunologic disturbances present in schizophrenia and possibly in other mental illnesses remains quite unproved and rather doubtful but certainly should not be dismissed as a possibility at this point. Far more likely is that both behavioral and immunologic dysfunctions are manifested as a result of whatever environmental, genetic, functional, and organic factors underlie mental illness.

REFERENCES

Alarcón-Segovia, D., Fishbein, E., Centina, J. A., Rais, R. J., and Barrera, E. (1973). Antigenic specificity of chlorpromazine-induced antinuclear antibodies. Clin. Exp. Immunol. 15, 543–548.

Amkraut, A., Solomon, G. F., Allansmith, M., McClellan, B., and Rappaport, M. (1973). Immunoglobulins and improvement in acute schizophrenic reactions. Arch. Gen. Psychiatry 28, 673–677.

Ashkenazi, A., Krasilowsky, D., Levin, S., Idar, D., Kalian, M., Or, A., Ginat, Y., and Halperin, B. (1979). Immunologic reaction of psychotic patients to fractions of gluten. Am. J. Psychiatry 136, 1306–1309.

Baker, G. A., Santalo, R., and Blumenstein, J. (1977). Effect of psychotropic agents upon the blastogenic response of human T lymphocytes. Biol. Psychiatry 12, 159–168.

Baron, M., Stern, M., Anair, R., and Witz, I. P. (1977). Tissue-binding factor in schizophrenic sera: A clinical and genetic study. Biol. Psychiatry 12, 199–212.

Bishop, M. P., Hollister, L. E., Gallant, D. M., and Heath, R. G. (1966). Ultracentrifugal serum proteins in schizophrenia. *Arch. Gen. Psychiatry* **15**, 337-340.

Bock, E. (1978). Plasma and CSF proteins in schizophrenia. *In* "Neurochemical and Immunologic Components in Schizophrenia" (D. Bergsma and A. L. Goldstein, eds.), pp. 283-295. Alan R. Liss, Inc., New York.

Bock, E., Weeke, B., and Rafaelsen, O. J. (1971). Serum proteins in acutely psychotic patients. *J. Psychiatr. Res.* **9**, 1-9.

Boehme, D. H., Cottrell, J. C., Dohan, F. C., and Hillegass, L. M. (1973). Fluorescent antibody studies of immunoglobulin binding by brain tissues. *Arch. Gen. Psychiatry* **28**, 202-207.

Burch, P. R. J. (1964). Schizophrenia: Some new aetiological considerations. *Br. J. Psychiatry* **110**, 818-824.

Burian, L., Kubikova, A., and Krejeova, O. (1964). Human antiglobulins in the serum of schizophrenic patients. *Cesk. Psychiatr.* **60**, 26-29.

Cépulic, P., Doman, V., and Ruzdie, I. (1954). Aenderungen im Verhaltnis der Serumwisse bei Schizophrenie. *Neuropsihijatrija* **2**, 213-220.

Certcov, D. (1969). Immunity and mental illness: A study of the immediate and delayed skin response to a series of various antigens. *Ann. Med. Psychol.* **127**, 733-742.

Crow, T. J., Ferrier, I. N., Johnstone, E. C., MacMillan, J. F., Owens, D. G. C., Parry, R. P., and Tyrell, D. A. J. (1979). Characteristics of patients with schizophrenia or neurological disorder and virus-like agent in cerebrospinal fluid. *Lancet*, April 21, 842-844.

Crowe, R. R., Thompson, J. S., Flink, R., and Weinberger, B. (1979). HLC antigens and schizophrenia. *Arch. Gen. Psychiatry* **36**, 231-233.

Davidova, I. B., Minsker, E. I., and Orlovskaja, D. D. (1966). Effect of blood serum of schizophrenic patients on the content of catecholamines in brain tissue of animals. *Vopr. Med. Khim*, **2**, 150-154.

Deberdt, R., Van Hooren, J., Biesbrouck, M., and Amery, W. (1976). Antinuclear factor-positive mental depression: A single disease entity? *Biol. Psychiatry* **11**, 69-74.

Dohan, F. C. (1966). Cereals and schizophrenia: Data and hypothesis. *Acta Psychiatr. Scand.* **42**, 125-152.

Dohan, F. C. (1969a). Is coeliac disease a clue to the pathogenesis of schizophrenia? *Ment. Hyg.* **53**, 525-529.

Dohan, F. C. (1969b). Schizophrenia: Possible relationship to cereal grains and ceoliac disease. *In* "Schizophrenia, Current Concepts and Research" (D. V. Siva Sankar, ed.), pp. 539-551. P. J. D., Ltd., Westbury, New York.

Dohan, F. C., Grasberger, J. C., and Lowell, F. M. (1969). Relapsed schizophrenics: More rapid improvement on a milk- and cereal-free diet. *Br. J. Psychiatry* **115**, 595-596.

Domashneva, I. V., and Maznina, T. P. (1976). Clinical-immunological correlations in the study of antithymic antibodies in schizophrenia. *Zh. Nevropatol. Psikhiatr. im S. S. Korsakova* **76**, 78-81.

Donnini, L. (1962). Ricerche sulla funzionalita epatica in schizofrenici prima e dopo trattamento con cloropromazina. *Fegato* **8**, 155-169.

Dwyer, S. D. (1979). Virus-like particles in C. S. F. in schizophrenia. *Lancet,* June 2, 1184-1185.

Erban, L. (1965). Viability changes of white blood cells in patients with schizophrenic reaction. *J. Psychiatr. Res.* **3**, 73-77.

Faulk, W. P., and Cockrell, J. R. (1978). Nutrition and immunity: Possible new approaches to research in schizophrenia. *In* "The Biological Basis of Schizophrenia" (G. Hemmings and W. A. Hemmings, eds.), pp. 231-238. University Park Press, Baltimore, Maryland.

Feingold, B. (1975). "Why Your Child is Hyperactive." Random House, New York.

Fessel, W. J. (1961). Disturbed serum proteins in chronic psychosis. *Arch. Gen. Psychiatry* **4**, 154-159.

Fessel, W. J. (1962a). Autoimmunity and mental illness: Preliminary report. *Arch Gen. Psychiatry* **6**, 320-323.

Fessel, W. J. (1962b). Macroglobulin elevations in functional mental illness. *Nature (London)* **193**, 1005.

Fessel, W. J. (1963). "Antibrain" factors in psychiatric patients' sera. I. Further studies with hemagglutination technique. *Arch. Gen. Psychiatry* **8**, 614–621.

Fessel, W. J., and Grunbaum, B. W. (1961). Electrophoretic and analytical ultracentrifuge studies in sera of psychotic patients: Elevation of gamma globulins and macroglobulins and splitting of alpha₂ globulins. *Ann. Intern. Med.* **54**, 1134–1145.

Fessel, W. J., and Hirata-Hibi, M. (1963). Abnormal leukocytes in schizophrenia. *Arch. Gen. Psychiatry* **9**, 91–103.

Fessel, W. J., and Solomon, G. F. (1960). Psychosis and systemic lupus erythematosus. A review of the literature and case reports. *Calif. Med.* **92**, 266–270.

Fessel, W. J., Hirata-Hibi, M., and Shapiro, I. M. (1965). Genetic and stress factors affecting the abnormal lymphocyte in schizophrenia. *J. Psychiatr. Res.* **3**, 275–283.

Fischer, J., and Mala, E. (1971). Pycnotic changes in leukocytes in the group of children and adolescent schizophrenics. *Cesk. Psychiatr.* **67**, 193–200.

Fowle, A. M. (1968). Atypical leukocyte pattern of schizophrenic children. *Arch. Gen. Psychiatry* **18**, 666–680.

Frank, J. A., and Dougherty, T. F. (1953). Evaluation of susceptibility to stress stimuli determined by "stress" lymphocytes. *Fed. Proc., Fed. Am. Soc. Exp. Biol.* **12**, 45–46.

Friedman, S. B., Cohen, J., and Iker, H. (1967). Antibody response to cholera vaccine. *Arch. Gen. Psychiatry* **16**, 312–315.

Frohman, C. (1968). Studies on the plasma factors in schizophrenia. *In* "Mind as a Tissue" (C. Rupp, ed.), pp. 181–195. Harper, New York.

Frohman, C. E., Czajkowski, N. P., Luby, E. D., Gottlieb, J. S., and Senf, R. (1960). Further evidence of a plasma factor in schizophrenia. *Arch. Gen. Psychiatry* **2**, 263–267.

Frohman, C. E., Tourney, G., Beckett, P. G. S., Lees, H., Latham, L. K., and Gottlieb, J. S. (1961). Biochemical identification of schizophrenia. *Arch. Gen. Psychiatry* **4**, 404–412.

Fudenberg, H. H. (1968). Are autoimmune diseases immunologic deficiency states? *Hosp. Pract.* **3**, 43–53.

Funkenstein, D. H. (1950). Psychophysiological relationship of asthma and urticaria to mental illness. *Psychosom. Med.* **12**, 377–385.

Gallien, M., Schnetzler, J. P., and Morin, M. (1975). Anticorps antinucléaires et lupus induits par les phénothiazines chez six cents malades hôspitalisés. *Ann. Med. Psychol.* **1**, 237–248.

Garey, R. E., Heath, R. G., and Harper, J. W. (1974). Focal electroencephalographic changes induced by anti-septal antibodies. *Biol. Psychiatry* **8**, 75–88.

Glebov, V. S., and Zil'bersheteyn, A. A. (1975). A comparative study of the reactions of complement fixation and hemagglutinin for elucidating antibrain antibodies in the blood serum of schizophrenic patients. *Zh. Nevropatol. Psikhiatr. im. S. S. Korsakova* **75**, 82–87.

Golub, E. S. (1972). The distribution of brain-associated antigen cross-reactive with mouse in the brain of other species. *J. Immunol.* **109**, 168–170.

Gosheva, A. E., Domashneva, I. V., Kobrinsky, G. D., Kolyaskina, G. I., Kushner, S. G., and Podozerova, N. P. (1969). A study into immunological reactions of delayed type in schizophrenic patients. *News, Sci. Acad. Med., USSR* **4**, 70–75.

Gottlieb, J. S., Frohman, C. E., and Beckett, P. S. (1970). The current status of the alpha₂ globulin in schizophrenia. *In* "Biochemistry, Schizophrenia and Affective Illnesses" (H. E. Himwich, ed.), pp. 153–170. Williams & Wilkins, Baltimore, Maryland.

Grunbaum, B. W., Forrest, F. M., and Kirk, P. L. (1964). The serum proteins in the alcoholic and mentally ill treated with chlorpromazine. *Proc. Soc. Exp. Biol. Med.* **117**, 195–198.

Heath, R. G. (1969). Schizophrenia: Evidence of a pathologic immune mechanism. *Proc. Am. Psychopathol. Assoc.* **58**, 234–236.

Heath, R. G. (1970). An antibrain globulin in schizophrenia. *In* "Biochemistry, Schizophrenia and Affective Illnesses" (H. W. Himwich, ed.), pp. 171–197. Williams & Wilkins, Baltimore, Maryland.

Heath, R. G., and Krupp, I. M. (1967). Schizophrenia as an immunologic disorder. I. Demonstration of antibrain globulins by fluorescent antibody techniques. *Arch. Gen. Psychiatry* **16**, 1–9.

Heath, R. G., and Krupp, I. M. (1968). Schizophrenia as a specific biologic disease. *Am. J. Psychiatry* **124**, 37–42.

Heath, R. G., Martens, S., Leach, B. E., Cohen, M., and Angel, C. (1957). Effect on behavior in humans with the administration of taraxein. *Am. J. Psychiatry* **114**, 14–24.

Heath, R. G., Krupp, I. M., and Byers, L. W. (1967a). Schizophrenia as an immunologic disorder. II. Effects of serum protein fractions on brain function. *Arch. Gen. Psychiatry* **16**, 10–23.

Heath, R. G., Krupp, I. M., Byers, L. W., and Liljekvist, J. I. (1967b). Schizophrenia as an immunologic disorder. III. Effects of antimonkey and antihuman brain antibody on brain function. *Arch. Gen. Psychiatry* **16**, 24–33.

Hekkens, W. T. J. M. (1978). Antibodies to gliadin in serum of normals, coeliac patients and schizophrenics. *In* "The Biological Basis of Schizophrenia" (G. Hemmings and W. A. Hemmings, eds.), pp. 259–261. University Park Press, Baltimore, Maryland.

Hemmings, W. A. (1978). The absorption of large breakdown products of dietary proteins into the body tissue including brain. *In* "The Biological Basis of Schizophrenia" (G. Hemmings and W. A. Hemmings, eds.), pp. 239–257. University Park Press, Baltimore, Maryland.

Hendrie, H. C. Paraskevas, F., and Varsamis, J. (1972). Gamma globulin levels in psychiatric patients. *Can. Psychiatr. Assoc. J.* **17**, 93–97.

Hippius, H., Kanig, K., and Selbach, A. (1958). Das Serumeiweissbild bei Psychosen vor und während der Pharmakotherapy. *Klin. Wochenschr.* **36**, 530–535.

Hirata-Hibi, M., and Fessel, W. J. (1964). The bone marrow in schizophrenia. *Arch. Gen. Psychiatry,* **10**, 414–419.

Hunter, R., Jones, M., and Malleson, A. (1969). Abnormal cerebrospinal fluid total protein and gamma globulin levels in 256 patients admitted to a psychiatric unit. *J. Neurol. Sci.* **9**, 11–38.

Hussar, A. E., Cradle, J. L., and Beiser, S. M. (1971). A study of the immunologic and allergic responsiveness of chronic schizophrenics. *Br. J. Psychiatry* **118**, 91–92.

Jersild, C. (1976). *Lect., 1st Int. Symp. Immunol. Components Schizophrenia,* Galveston, Texas.

Jersild, C. (1978). The HLA system and multiple sclerosis. *In* "Neurochemical and Immunologic Components in Schizophrenia" (D. Bergsma and A. L. Goldstein, eds.), pp. 123–170. Alan R. Liss, Inc., New York.

Kamp, H. V. (1962). Nuclear changes in the white blood cells of patients with schizophrenic reaction. A preliminary report. *J. Neuropsychiatry* **4**, 1–3.

Kerbikov, O. V. (1961). Immunological reactivity in schizophrenia as influenced by some modern drugs. *Ann. N.Y. Acad. Sci.* **92**, 1098–1104.

Klee, W. A., Ziondrou, C., and Streaty, R. A. (1978). Exorphins, peptides with opioid activity isolated from wheat gluten, and their possible role in the etiology of schizophrenia. *In* "Endorphins in Mental Health Research" (E. Usdin, ed.), Macmillan, New York.

Kocsár, L., Szilágyi, T., Veress, O., and Bán, A. (1958). Effect of chlorpromazine on immune body formation. *Acta Physiol. Acad. Sci. Hung.* **13, 14**, 163–166.

Kolyaskina, G. I., and Kushnir, S. G. (1969). Concerning some regularities in the appearance of antibrain antibodies in the blood serum of schizophrenic patients. *Zh. Nevropatol. Psikhiatr. im. S. S. Korsakova* **69**, 1679–1682.

Kopeloff, L. M., and Fischell, E. (1963). Serum levels of bactericidin and globulin in schizophrenia. *Arch. Gen. Psychiatry* **9**, 524–528.

Kuruvilla, K., Ansari, S. A., and Sridhara Rama Roa, B. S. (1973). Serum proteins in schizophrenics. *Indian J. Psychiatry* **15**, 382–385.

Kuznetsova, M. I., and Semenov, S. F. (1961). Detection of anti-brain antibodies in the blood serum of patients with neuropsychiatric diseases. *Zh. Nevropatol. Psikhiatr. im. S. S. Korsakova* **61**, 869–874.

Lancaster-Smith, M. J., and Strickland, I. (1970). Coeliac disease and schizophrenia. *Lancet,* Nov. 21, 1090–1091.

Lang, R. W., and Corvin, A. (1969). Rabbit erythrocyte hemagglutinins in schizophrenia. *Arch. Gen. Psychiatry* **21**, 665–672.

Liedemann, R. R. (1976). Some traits of the functional state of lymphocytes in cultures of the peripheral blood of schizophrenic patients. *Zh. Nevropatol. Psikhiatr. im. S. S. Korsakova* **76**, 81–85.

Liedemann, R. R., and Prilipko, L. L. (1978). The behavior of T lymphocytes in schizophrenia. *In* "Neurochemical and Immunologic Components in Schizophrenia" (D. Bergsma and A. L. Goldstein, eds.), pp. 365–377. Alan R. Liss, Inc., New York.

Logan, D. G., and Deodhar, S. D. (1970). Schizophrenia, an immunologic disorder? *J. Am. Med. Assoc.* **212**, 1703–1704.

Luria, E. A., and Domashneva, I. V. (1974). Antibodies to thymocytes in sera of patients with schizophrenia. *Proc. Natl. Acad. Sci. U.S.A.* **71**, 235–236.

McClary, A. R., Meyer, E., and Weitzman, D. J. (1955). Observations on role of mechanism of depression in some patients with disseminated lupus erythematosus. *Psychosom. Med.* **17**, 311–321.

Matveets, L. S., Olsuf'ev, N. G., Il'inskii, Yu.A., and Zharikov, N. M. (1957). Immunological reactivity in persons suffering from derangement of the central nervous system to tularaemia vaccination. *Zh. Mikrobiol. Epidemiol. Immunobiol.* **9**, 1263–1268.

Mellsop, G., Whittingham, S., and Ungar, B. (1973). Schizophrenia and autoimmune serological reactions. *Arch. Gen. Psychiatry,* **28**, 194–196.

Milhaud, F., Chatagnon, C., Sandor, M., and Sandor, G. (1959). Une enquete humorale chez les psychopates: Analyse statistique des résultats obtenu, *Ann. Inst. Pasteur, Paris* **96**, 114–116.

Molholm, H. B. (1942). Hyposensitivity to foreign protein in schizophrenic patients. *Psychiatr. Q.* **16**, 570–571.

Nazarov, K. N. (1962). Specific brain antigens and autosensitization to them in various mental disorders. *Zh. Nevropatol. Psikhiatr. im. S. S. Korsakova* **62**, T375–T378.

Notkins, A. L. (1979). The causes of diabetes. *Sci. Am.* **241**, 62–73.

Pennington, V. M. (1963). A study to determine possible differences in the formed blood elements of normal and schizophrenic subjects. *J. Neuropsychiatry* **5**, 21–28.

Pospisilova, U., and Janik, A. (1958). Relation of blood serum protein fractions to clinical picture in psychoses and psychotic states, determined by paper electrophoresis. *Rev. Czech. Med.* **4**, 29–39.

Presley, A. P., Kahn, A., and Williamson, N. (1976). Antinuclear antibodies in patients on lithium carbonate. *Br. Med. J.* **2**, 280–281.

Pulkkinen, E. (1977). Immunoglobulins, psychopathology and prognosis in schizophrenia. *Acta Psychiatr. Scand.* **56**, 173–182.

Quismorio, F. P., Bjarnason, D. F., Dubois, E. L., and Friou, G. J. (1972). Chlorpromazine-induced antinuclear antibodies (ANA). *Arthritis Rheum.* **15**, 451.

Rausher, F. P., Nasrallah, H. A., and Wyatt, R. J. (1980). Cutaneous histamine response in schizophrenia. *J. Clin. Psychiatry* **41**, 44–50.

Rice, J. R., Ham, C. H., and Gore, W. E. (1978). Another look at gluten in schizophrenia. *Am. J. Psychiatry* **135**, 1417–1418.

Rimón R., Nishmi, M., and Halonen, P. (1978). Serum and CSF antibody levels to herpes simplex type 1, measles and rubella viruses in patients with schizophrenia. *Ann. Clin. Res.* **10**, 291–293.

Rimón, R., Halonen, P., Puhakkla, P., Laitinen, L., Marttila, R., and Salmela, L. (1979). Immunoglobulin G antibodies to herpes simplex type 1 virus detected by radioimmunoassay in serum and cerebrospinal fluid of patients with schizophrenia. *J. Clin. Psychiatry* **40**, 241–243.

Rothermich, N. O., and Philips, V. K. (1963). Rheumatoid arthritis in criminal and mentally ill populations. *Arthritis Rheum.* **6**, 639–640.

Ryan, J. W., Brown, J. D., and Durell, J. (1966). Antibodies affecting metabolism of chicken erythrocytes: Examination of schizophrenic and other subjects. *Science* 151, 1408-1410.

Ryan, J. W., Brown, J. D., and Durell, J. (1968). Concordance between two methods of assaying the plasma affects on chicken erythrocyte metabolism. *J. Psychiatr. Res.* 6, 45-49.

Ryan, J. W., Steinberg, H. R., Green, R., Brown, J. D., and Durell, J. (1968). Controlled study of effects of plasma of schizophrenic and nonschizophrenic psychiatric patients on chicken erythrocytes. *J. Psychiatr. Res.* 6, 33-43.

Sapira, J. D. (1964). Immunoelectrophoresis of the serum of psychotic patients. *Arch. Gen. Psychiatry* 10, 196-198.

Saunders, J. C., and Muchmore, E. (1964). Phenothiazine effect on human antibody synthesis. *Br. J. Psychiatry* 110, 84-89.

Scully, R. E., Galdabini, J. J., and McNeely, B. U. (1977). Case records of the Massachusetts General Hospital, Case 43. *N. Engl. J. Med.* 277, 930-937.

Sethi, N., Sethi, B. B., and Kumar, R. A. J. (1973). A family study of atypical lymphocytes in schizophrenia. *Indian J. Psychiatry* 15, 267-271.

Shapiro, R. W., Bock, E., Rafaelsen, O. J., Ryder, L. P., and Svejgaard, A. (1976). Histocompatibility antigens and manic depressive disorders. *Arch. Gen. Psychiatry* 33, 823-825.

Simpson, G. M., and Kline, N. S. (1961). Histamine wheal formation and mental illness. *J. Nerv. Ment. Dis.* 133, 19-24.

Singh, M. M., and Kay, S. R. (1976). Wheat gluten as a pathogenic factor in schizophrenia. *Science* 191, 401-402.

Solomon, G. F. (1970). Psychophysiological aspects of rheumatoid arthritis and autoimmune disease. *In* "Modern Trends in Psychosomatic Medicine" (O. W. Hill, ed.), pp. 189-216. Butterworth, London.

Solomon, G. F., Moos, R. H., Fessel, W. J., and Morgan, E. E. (1966). Globulins and behavior in schizophrenia. *Int. J. Neuropsychiatry* 2, 20-26.

Solomon, G. F., Allansmith, M., McClellan, B., and Amkraut, A. (1969). Immunoglobulins in psychiatric patients. *Arch. Gen. Psychiatry* 20, 272-277.

Solomon, G. F., Rubbo, S., and Batchelder, E. (1970). Secondary immune response to tetanus toxoid in psychiatric patients. *J. Psychiatr. Res.* 7, 201-207.

Solomon, G. F., Amkraut, A. A., and Rubin, R. T. (1979). Stress and psychoimmunological response. *In* "Mind and Cancer Prognosis" (B. A. Stoll, ed.), pp. 73-84, Wiley, New York.

Stabenau, J. R., Pollin, W., and Mosher, L. (1968). Serum macroglobulin (S19) in families of monozygotic twins discordant for schizophrenia. *Am. J. Psychiatry* 125, 147-150.

Stefanis, C. N., and Issidorides, M. R. (1976). Histochemical changes in the blood cells of schizophrenic patients under pimozide treatment. *Biol. Psychiatry* 11, 53-68.

Stevens, J. R. (1973). An anatomy of schizophrenia? *Arch. Gen. Psychiatry* 29, 177-189.

Strahilevitz, M., and Davis, S. D. (1970). Increased IgA in schizophrenic patients (ltr. to ed.). *Lancet,* Aug. 15, 370.

Taylor, W. M. (1978). Schizophrenia, rheumatoid arthritis tryptophan metabolism. *J. Clin. Psychiatry* 39, 499-503.

Torrey, E. F. (1977). CSF better than serum in study of immunology in mental patients. *Clin. Psychiatr. News* 5.

Torrey, E. F., and Peterson, M. R. (1976). The viral hypothesis of schizophrenia. *Schizophr. Bull.* 2, 136-146.

Turner, W. J., and Chipps, H. I. (1966). A heterophil hemolysin in human blood. *Arch. Gen. Psychiatry* 15, 373-377.

Tyrell, D. A. J., Parry, R. P., Crow, T. J., Johnstone, E., and Ferrier, I. N. (1979). Possible virus in schizophrenia and some neurological disorders. *Lancet,* 1, 839-841.

Vanderkamp H. and Daly, R. (1962). Nuclear changes in the white blood cells of patients with schizophrenic reaction. *J. Neuropsychiat.* 4, 1-3.

Vartanian, M. E. (1968). Biochemical and immunological changes in schizophrenia and their relation to inheritance. *Proc. World Congr. Psychiatry, 4th, 1966* p. 3030.

Vartanian, M. E., Kolyaskina, G. I., Lozovsky, D. V., Burbaeva, G. Sh., and Ignatov, S. A. (1978). Aspects of humoral and cellular immunity in schizophrenia. *In* "Neurochemical and Immunologic Components In Schizophrenia" (D. Bergsma and A. L. Goldstein, eds.), pp. 339–364, Alan R. Liss, Inc., New York.

Vaughan, W. T., Jr., Sullivan, J. C., and Elmadjian, F. (1949). Immunity and schizophrenia. Psychosom. Med. **2**, 327–333.

Vaughn, J. H. (1965). Diseases with immunological features. *In* "Immunological Diseases" (M. Samter and H. L. Alexander, eds.), Little, Brown, Boston, Massachusetts.

von Brauchitsch, H. (1972). Antinuclear factor in psychiatric disorders. *Am. J. Psychiatry* **128**, 1552–1554.

Whittingham, S., Mackay, I. R., Jones, I. H., and Davies, B. (1968). Absence of brain antibodies in patients with schizophrenia. *Br. Med. J.* **1**, 347–348.

Zarrabi, M. H., Zucker, S., Miller, F., Derman, R. M., Romano, G. S., Hartnett, J. A., and Varma, A. O. (1979). Immunologic and coagulation disorders in chlorpromazine-treated patients. *Ann. Intern. Med.* **91**, 194–199.

PART **III**

Conditioning Effects

Conditioned Immunopharmacologic Responses[1]

ROBERT ADER
NICHOLAS COHEN

INTRODUCTION

In this chapter, we will describe studies which suggest that behavioral conditioning techniques may be used to modify immune responses. Thus far, our studies have been primarily concerned with the conditioned suppression of antibody responses resulting from the prior association of a neutral stimulus with the effects of drugs which suppress immunologic reactivity. These studies are preliminary in the sense that neither we nor others have yet determined those experimental conditions that may be optimal for demonstrating the effects of conditioning or the extent to which different components of immune function may be influenced by conditioning. Consequently, the available data are, as yet, insufficient to suggest the mechanisms that might mediate conditioned alterations in immune responses. These studies must also be considered

[1] Preparation of this chapter was supported by a USPHS Research Scientist Award (K05–MH–06318) from the National Institute of Mental Health (RA). The research described was supported by the above award and a Research Career Development Award (K04–AI–70736) from the National Institute of Allergy and Infectious Diseases (NC) and by consecutive research grants from the W. T. Grant Foundation, the National Institute of Child Health and Human Development (HD–09977), and the National Institute of Neurological and Communicative Diseases and Stroke (NS–15071).

PSYCHONEUROIMMUNOLOGY

preliminary in the sense that they implicate central nervous system processes in the regulation of immune responses. While this entire volume addresses such relationships, this concept is far from a generally accepted premise in immunology. Our studies are, nevertheless, a logical extension of a rapidly growing interest and literature on the conditioning of physiological responses and the conditioning of pharmacologic effects.

Historically, the conditioning of physiological responses dates from the work of Pavlov (1928). The classical paradigm involves the selection of a stimulus (e.g., food) which unconditionally elicits a response (e.g., salivation). Food, then, is the unconditioned stimulus (US) for salivation, an unconditioned response (UR). By repeatedly pairing a neutral stimulus (one that does not unconditionally elicit salivation) with an unconditioned stimulus, that neutral stimulus will subsequently come to evoke salivation even when the neutral stimulus is presented without the US. The neutral stimulus has become a conditioned stimulus (CS) for salivation, and salivation in response to the CS is designated as a conditioned response (CR), even though the salivation elicited by the CS may not be qualitatively or quantitatively identical to the unconditioned salivary response. Similarly, if an external stimulus such as a light or a tone (the CS) is repeatedly paired with an electric shock that unconditionally evokes a flexion of the stimulated leg, a conditioned leg flexion will eventually occur in response to the CS alone.

In contrast to classical or Pavlovian conditioning where there is a predictable contingency established between the stimulus events, instrumental or operant conditioning involves the reward or reinforcement of whatever response or approximation of the desired response occurs to some specified stimulus or signal. For example, a hungry rat may be rewarded with food for turning left in a maze, or a thirsty animal may be reinforced with water when, in the presence of an auditory stimulus, it eventually depresses a lever in its cage. Each such reinforcement strengthens or increases the probability of occurrence of the immediately preceding response, a response which is instrumental in procuring the reward.

Classical and instrumental conditioning paradigms may be used to alter physiological states. The interest in visceral and autonomic conditioning and the physiological concomitants of the acquisition and performance of conditioned responses has received a great deal of attention over the past 15–20 years. Previously, the majority of such research had been confined to physiology laboratories in the Soviet Union (Razran, 1961). A revival of interest in the area, however, was stimulated by the studies of Neal Miller and his colleagues (e.g., Miller, 1969; DiCara, 1970) who showed that autonomic responses, previously thought to be involuntary, were subject to instrumental as well as classical conditioning. Most of this work, for technologic and methodologic reasons, however, has been confined to cardiovascular responses. Other visceral responses involving, for example, the gastrointestinal system, have received some attention, and endocrine responses are only now being studied. Recently, research has also been addressed to the conditioning of a variety of pharmacologic responses (Siegel, 1977a). Indeed, evidence is accumulating that the response (tolerance) to opiates, for example, may be a conditioned response (Siegel, 1977b). These studies, too, derive from observations made by Pavlov (1928).

A relatively new and particularly effective technique for establishing a conditioned response has come to be known as taste aversion learning (e.g., Garcia *et al.*, 1974) and there is now a large literature on the subject (Riley and Baril, 1976). In this passive avoidance paradigm, consumption of a distinctively flavored drinking solution is paired with an injection of a pharmacologic agent. One might, for example, provide water-deprived rats with a novel drinking solution of sodium saccharin (the CS) for a period of, say, 15 minutes. Immediately, (or at some interval) thereafter, these same animals would be injected with a drug such as lithium chloride (LiCl), an unconditioned stimulus for gastrointestinal upset (nausea, diarrhea). Other conditioned stimuli (e.g., coffee, tea, or sucrose, almond, or garlic-flavored water) and other unconditioned stimuli (e.g., apomorphine, d-amphetamine, ethanol, or cyclophosphamide) are equally effective. The appetitive response to the flavored solution is, in effect, punished by the aversive effects of the injection of toxin. The association between the novel taste of the flavored solution and the aversive effects of the drug evidently occurs upon the *single* pairing of these events since the organism will subsequently avoid consumption of that flavored solution on the very next occasion of its presentation—even when the effects of the drug have long since disappeared. In addition to the ease and rapidity with which the association is established, the illness-induced taste aversion is retained over long periods of time (e.g., 3 months). A distinctive feature of this conditioning paradigm is the long (several hours) interval between presentation of the CS and the presentation of the US that can be tolerated by the animal in associating these stimuli. Given the survival value of forming relationships between gustatory cues and gastrointestinal consequences, it is not surprising that the effects of this conditioning paradigm are so highly reproducible.

For reasons which are not immediately relevant, we were studying the effects of varying the volume of a distinctively flavored CS solution on the acquisition and extinction of a conditioned taste aversion. Intraperitoneal (i.p.) injections of cyclophosphamide (50 mg/kg) were administered 30 min after rats drank 1, 5, or 10 ml of a 0.1% sodium saccharin solution. As expected, the magnitude of the conditioned response (reduction in subsequent saccharin consumption) and its resistance to extinction measured at 3-day intervals were directly related to the volume of saccharin consumed on the single conditioning trial. Unexpectedly, however, some of the *conditioned* animals died during the course of extinction trials—trials on which the CS, saccharin, was provided but animals were *not* injected with cyclophosphamide. Moreover, the first animals that died came from the group that received the largest volume of the saccharin solution on the conditioning trial. This suggested that mortality rate might be directly related to the magnitude of the CS. The potential significance of this serendipitous observation was not immediately apparent, and the experiment was (prematurely) concluded.

Cyclophosphamide (CY) was used to induce the taste aversion simply because previous studies (Wilcoxon *et al.*, 1971; Wright *et al.*, 1971) had documented its effectiveness as an unconditioned stimulus. The dosage used, however, was well below the LD_{50} for adult animals and only a single injection of the drug was administered. The fact that CY is an immunosuppressive drug, however, suggested an hypothesis, consistent with principles of conditioning, that could provide an explanation for the mortality *and* for the possibility that mortality was related to the amount of saccharin that had been used as the CS rather than to the direct effects of CY. Because one would expect (and, indeed, one observes) a greater magnitude of conditioning and a greater resistance to extinction from increasing the level of a CS, it was possible that the taste aversion conditioned by pairing saccharin with CY resulted in the conditioning of the immunosuppressive effects of the drug, that is, a conditioned immunosuppressive response. Conditioned animals that were subsequently presented with saccharin might have reacted with a conditioned response that reproduced, in whole or in part, a suppression of immunologic reactivity. If so, the repeated immunosuppression that occurred in response to the CS during the course of extinction might have increased the susceptibility of these animals to latent pathogens in the laboratory environment.

Based on this speculative analysis, an experiment was designed to examine the possibility of conditioned immunosuppression (Ader and Cohen, 1975).

CONDITIONED IMMUNOSUPPRESSION: INITIAL STUDIES

The basic design of the studies to be described below is essentially the same, so the protocol for our initial experiment will be described in some detail.

Charles River (CD) male rats, approximately 3-month-old, were individually housed in stainless steel suspended cages under a 12-hr light–dark cycle (light beginning at 5 A.M.) and provided with food and water *ad libitum*. During a period of adaptation the daily provision of plain tap water was gradually reduced until all animals were provided with and consumed their total daily allotment during a single 15-min period (between 9 and 10 A.M.). This regimen was maintained throughout the experiments. The first 5 days under this restricted 15-min drinking schedule provided baseline data on fluid consumption.

On the day of conditioning (Day 0), animals were randomly assigned to conditioned, nonconditioned, and placebo groups. During their 15-min drinking period, conditioned animals received a 0.1% solution of sodium saccharin in tap water, the CS, and 30 min later were injected i.p. with CY[2] (50 mg/kg

---

[2] Cyclophosphamide was generously supplied by the Mead Johnson Research Center, Evansville, Indiana.

in a volume of 1.5 ml/kg), the US. Noncondiitoned animals were provided with plain tap water and 30 min later were injected with CY. Placebo animals received plain water and were injected with an equal volume of vehicle. On the following 2 days all animals were given plain water during their 15-min drinking period.

Three days after conditioning, all animals were injected i.p. with antigen, 2 ml/kg of a 1% thrice-washed suspension of sheep red blood cells (SRBC; approximately 3×10^8 cells/ml). Thirty minutes later, randomly selected subgroups of conditioned and nonconditioned animals were provided with either the saccharin solution or plain water and then received an injection of CY or saline. The basic protocol is outlined in Table 1.

Conditioned animals were divided into three basic subgroups. Group CS, the critical experimental group, received a single drinking bottle containing the saccharin solution, and drinking was followed by a saline injection. In the first experiment there were actually three such experimental groups: One subgroup was provided with saccharin on Day 3, the day on which antigen was introduced; one subgroup received saccharin on Day 6; and one subgroup received saccharin on Days 3 and 6. The two additional subgroups of conditioned animals were essentially control groups. One of these (Group US) received plain water followed by an injection of CY. These animals were used to define the unconditioned immunosuppressive effects of CY treatment. The other subgroup (Group CS_0) received plain water followed by an injection of saline. These animals constituted a control for the prior effects of conditioning, per se.

The basic protocol also included nonconditioned animals (Group NC) and a placebo (P) group. As described in the preceding paragraph, NC animals received plain water and an injection of CY on the conditioning day (Day 0). Subgroups of these animals were subsequently provided with the saccharin drinking solution and injected with saline whenever the corresponding CS groups received saccharin and i.p. injections as a control for the effects of these treatments. Placebo animals remained unmanipulated and received plain water during the 15-min drinking periods.

On Day 9 (6 days after injection with SRBC), all animals were sacrificed. Trunk blood was collected for the hemagglutinating antibody assay. Serum from each rat was heat inactivated (56°C for 30 min) and divided into aliquots, some of which were stored at $-70°C$ while others were refrigerated and assayed for hemagglutinating antibody activity within 24 hr of collection. Titrations were performed according to standard procedures in microtiter trays and hemagglutination was assessed under a microscope. Titers were recorded as reciprocals of the endpoint dilutions and expressed as powers of the base$_2$.

The appropriate drinking solutions and injections of CY or saline were indicated on coded data sheets. Also, all laboratory procedures were conducted without knowledge of the group to which an animal belonged.

TABLE 1
Experimental Protocol

| | | Days after conditioning | | | | | | |
| | | 0 | 3 | 6 | | Days after antigen | | 9 |
Group	Adaptation	Cond. Day	Sub group	0 (Antigen)	1-2	3	4-5	6
Conditioned	H_2O	SAC + CY	US	H_2O + CY	H_2O	H_2O	H_2O	Sample
				H_2O	H_2O	H_2O + CY	H_2O	Sample
			CS_0	H_2O + Sal	H_2O	H_2O	H_2O	Sample
				H_2O	H_2O	H_2O + Sal	H_2O	Sample
			CS_1	SAC + Sal	H_2O	H_2O	H_2O	Sample
				H_2O	H_2O	SAC + Sal	H_2O	Sample
			CS_2	SAC + Sal	H_2O	SAC	H_2O	Sample
Nonconditioned	H_2O	H_2O + CY	NC	SAC + Sal	H_2O	H_2O	H_2O	Sample
				H_2O	H_2O	SAC + Sal	H_2O	Sample
Placebo	H_2O	H_2O + P	P	H_2O	H_2O	H_2O	H_2O	Sample

Behaviorally, the results of this initial experiment were the same as those of several previous studies (e.g., Peck and Ader, 1974; Wilcoxon *et al.,* 1971; Wright *et al.,* 1971) showing that CY is an effective stimulus for inducing a conditioned taste aversion. In other words, when CY is administered 30 min after consumption of a novel, distinctively flavored drinking solution, there is a clear aversion to that same drinking solution when it is subsequently presented (Figure 1). Conditioned animals provided with saccharin on Day 3, Day 6, or Days 3 and 6 displayed a significantly reduced intake on just those days.

With regard to antibody responses, the pattern of results illustrated in Figure 2 was expected or predicted by the hypothesis that immunosuppression could be influenced by conditioning processes. Sera from placebo-treated animals were expected to show relatively high hemagglutinating antibody titers. Sera from nonconditioned animals (provided with saccharin when injected with antigen) were also expected to be high titered. However, since

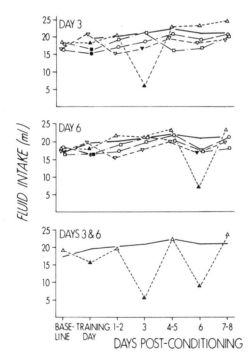

Figure 1. Mean intake of plain water (open symbols) and saccharin (closed symbols) for placebo (—) and nonconditioned (▼) animals, and for conditioned animals that received saccharin (▲), cyclophosphamide (□), or neither (0) on Day 3, Day 6, or Days 3 and 6 after conditioning. As a point of reference, placebo-treated animals are shown in each panel. From "Behaviorally conditioned immunosuppression" by Ader, R. and Cohen, N., *Psychosomatic Medicine,* 1975, **37**, 333–340. Copyright 1975 by Elsevier North-Holland, Inc. Reprinted by permission.

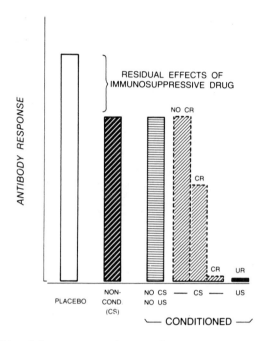

Figure 2. Conditioned immunosuppression: Predicted pattern of differences in hemagglutinating antibody titer.

Group NC had been treated with CY 3 days before SRBC, it was anticipated that the titers from NC animals might be somewhat lower than those of placebo-treated animals because of the residual effects of the drug (Santos and Owens, 1964; Makinodan *et al.,* 1970). Conditioned animals that were not again presented with the conditioned or unconditioned stimuli (Group CS_0) were also expected to show relatively high antibody levels. Like Group NC, however, these animals also received CY 3 days before SRBC and were therefore expected to have titers which were lower than those in placebo-treated animals but equivalent to NC animals. Conditioned animals that were injected with CY at the time that antigen was introduced were expected to show a minimal antibody response to SRBC. The critical experimental groups, those that were reexposed to the CS rather than the US, could show an antibody response that did not differ from Groups NC and CS_0, they could show a complete suppression of antibody production as was expected from Group US, or, more reasonably and as hypothesized, they could show some diminution of the antibody response.

The actual data are shown in Figure 3. Conditioned animals that were exposed to saccharin on Day 3 or Day 6 did not differ and were collapsed into a single group that received one (CS_1) in contrast to two (CS_2) exposures to saccharin, the conditioned stimulus. The comparable control groups, which also did not differ, were similarly combined. The pattern of observed results was

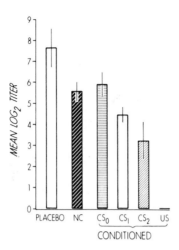

Figure 3. Hemagglutinating antibody titers (mean ± s.e.) obtained 6 days after i.p. injection of SRBC. NC, nonconditioned animals provided with saccharin on Day 0 (day of antigen) or Day 3; CS_0, conditioned animals that did not receive saccharin following antigen treatment; CS_1, conditioned animals reexposed to saccharin on Day 0 or Day 3; CS_2, conditioned animals reexposed to saccharin on Days 0 *and* 3; US, conditioned animals injected with cyclophosphamide following antigenic stimulation. From "Behaviorally conditioned immunosuppression" by Ader, R. and Cohen, N., *Psychosomatic Medicine,* 1975, **37,** 333–340. Copyright 1975 by Elsevier North-Holland, Inc. Reprinted by permission.

as we had predicted. Placebo animals showed the highest antibody titers and, as expected, treatment with CY just after injection of SRBC (Group US) suppressed antibody production. There were no differences between the non-conditioned animals and the subgroup of conditioned animals that was *not* reexposed to the CS (Group CS_0), and both groups had lower titers than placebo-treated animals. This difference presumably reflects the residual effects of CY administered 3 days before antigen. Consequently, it is the NC and CS_0 groups that represent the relevant control conditions against which to assess the effects of conditioning (i.e., the antibody response of conditioned animals that are reexposed to the CS). Conditioned animals that experienced either one or two exposures to saccharin following antigenic stimulation showed an attenuated antibody response which was significantly different from both the NC and CS_0 groups. These initial results, then, supported the supposition that the association of saccharin with CY enabled saccharin to elicit a conditioned immunosuppressive response.

Some of the procedures used in this initial study were theoretically and empirically less than optimal for attempting to document a conditioned immunosuppressive response. These methodological issues will be discussed in the next section. Nevertheless, replications of this experiment have yielded comparable results in support of the phenomenon. Rogers *et al.* (1976) followed our procedures quite closely except for the inclusion of an additional

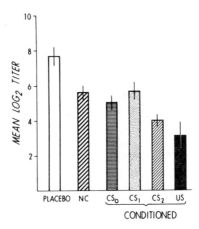

Figure 4. Effects of conditioning on hemagglutinating antibody titer. Group designations are the same as in Figure 3. Data redrawn from "Behaviorally conditioned immunosuppression: Replication of a recent study" by Rogers, M. P. *et al. Psychosomatic Medicine,* 1976, **38,** 447–451. Copyright 1975 by Elsevier North-Holland, Inc. Redrawn by permission.

NC group that was not exposed to saccharin at any time, and they used an assay procedure purported to be more sensitive. Their findings are shown in Figure 4. There were no immunosuppressive effects of a single reexposure to the CS in conditioned animals, but two reexposures to the saccharin drinking solution significantly attenuated the antibody response of conditioned animals. Essentially the same results (Figure 5) were obtained by Wayner *et al.*

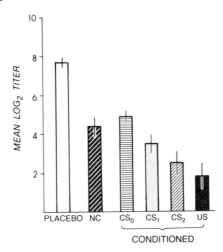

Figure 5. Effects of conditioning on hemagglutinating antibody titer. Group designations are the same as in Figure 3. Data redrawn from "Effects of taste aversion conditioning on the primary antibody response to sheep red blood cells and *Brucella abortus* in the albino rat" by Wayner, E. A. *et al. Physiology and Behavior,* 1978, **21,** 995–1000. Copyright 1978 by Pergamon Press. Redrawn by permission.

(1978)[3]. Smaller (but statistically significant) differences were also found by M. King (1979).

Referring back to Figure 1, it will be noticed that there is no evidence of extinction of the aversion to saccharin as a result of two unreinforced exposures to the CS. In the studies by Rogers *et al.* and Wayner *et al.*, however, two unreinforced CS trials did decrease the taste aversion. Both groups of investigators note the fact that, although the behavioral response appears to be showing extinction, the greater attenuation of antibody titer occurs after two postconditioning exposures to the CS. It would be premature, however, to assume that the behavioral and immune responses are necessarily independent, even temporally. Wayner *et al.* (1978) included a group of conditioned animals that were reexposed to the CS on three occasions. Antibody titers in this group did not differ from those in Groups NC or CS_0, although it should be pointed out that no control samples were actually available on Day 12 when their CS_3 group was sacrificed.

VARIATIONS IN THE EXPERIMENTAL PARADIGM AND METHODOLOGIC ISSUES

Effects of Time of Sampling

Hemagglutinating antibody titer was measured 6 days after stimulation with SRBC in these first studies; we had established that the peak production of total serum antibody was detectable at about this time with the dose of antigen that was being used. However, measuring antibody titer 6 days after antigen was not necessarily the optimal time for observing a *conditioned* suppression of immunologic reactivity. In an effort to describe more fully the effects of conditioning, then, a study was conducted in which hemagglutinating antibody was measured 4, 6, 8, and 10 days after the coincidental injection of antigen and reexposure of conditioned animals to the CS. The protocol for this experiment was precisely the same as our original study except that all conditioned animals were reexposed to the CS only once, 30 min after an injection of SRBC introduced 3 days after conditioning.

As can be seen in Figure 6, circulating levels of antibody are low in all animals 4 days after the introduction of antigen. Six days after stimulation with SRBC, the antibody titer in conditioned rats reexposed to the CS is significantly lower than the titers in nonconditioned animals and in conditioned rats that were not reexposed to the CS. These 6-day results reaffirm the conditioned attenuation of antibody production described above. There are no differences among the groups when antibody titers are sampled 8 and 10

---

[3] In the report by Wayner *et al.* (1978) the SRBC suspension is given as 0.1%. In fact, however, a 1.0% solution was used (E. A. Wayner, personal communication, 1979).

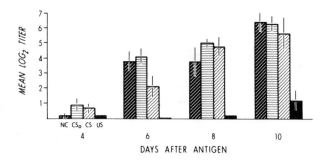

Figure 6. Effects of conditioning on hemagglutination titers (mean ± s.e.) measured 4,6,8, and 10 days after treatment with SRBC. Group designations are the same as in Figure 3.

days following this immunogenic stimulation. It would appear, then, that the qualitative effects of conditioning are not an inhibition of antibody production, but, rather, a transient delay in the complex of events which culminate in the appearance of antibody in the serum. The failure to observe an attenuated antibody response when conditioned animals exposed to three unreinforced CS presentations are sampled on Day 12 (9 days after antigenic stimulation) (Wayner *et al.*, 1978) may not, therefore, result from extinction of the behavioral response. It might only reflect the "catching" up that appears to characterize the production of antibody that has been delayed by the specific effects of the CS introduced at some critical time in the developing response of the conditioned animal.

Effects of Fluid Deprivation

Conditioned animals that are subsequently provided with a single drinking bottle containing the distinctively flavored solution previously paired with CY consume a minimal amount of that solution. That is, they are well-conditioned animals that are displaying the taste aversion. Since antigen is injected on the day that conditioned animals are also reexposed to the CS, it could be hypothesized that the attenuation in antibody titer somehow results from the administration of antigen to animals that are in a relatively water-deprived state or, perhaps, in an altered state determined by some interaction between deprivation and the immunosuppressive effects of CY.

An alternative means of assessing the acquisition of a taste aversion involves the use of a preference testing procedure. Rather than provide the animal with a single drinking bottle containing the distinctively flavored drinking solution used as the CS, the animal is provided with two bottles, one containing the solution previously paired with the immunosuppressive drug and one containing plain tap water. With respect to the conditioned avoidance response, the preference procedure is actually the more sensitive technique (Dragoin *et al.,* 1971).

One study was conducted in which half the animals in each group were tested under the "forced choice" or single-bottle procedure and half were tested with a "preference" or choice procedure. As expected, there were no differences in fluid consumption or antibody titers within relevant subgroups of control animals tested under the two procedures, so these subgroups were combined. Both testing procedures confirmed the acquisition of an aversion to the saccharin solution paired with 50 mg/kg CY. Of primary interest, though, was the behavior of Group CS when tested under the preference procedure. For these animals, the intake of saccharin was only 15 and 25% of the total fluid consumed on the two test days that followed conditioning as compared to an 80 and 94% preference for saccharin in nonconditioned animals. However, as can be seen in Figure 7, the *total* fluid intake of conditioned animals reexposed to the CS was the same as that for all the other groups on the day that antigen was injected and on the test given 3 days later.

While the CS animals that were given no choice of drinking solution consumed relatively small amounts of saccharin, the total fluid intake of the animals that were provided with plain water in addition to the saccharin solution was not less than that consumed by controls. Both CS groups, however, showed a diminution of hemagglutinating antibody titer (Figure 8). It should be noted, though, that the CS animals in this experiment that were tested under the single-bottle procedure differed significantly from only one of the two relevant control groups. Using the preference procedure we have also observed a conditioned suppression of the humoral response to a thymus-independent antigen in mice (Cohen *et al.,* 1979). These data will be described in the section entitled "Generalizability of Conditioned Immunosuppression."

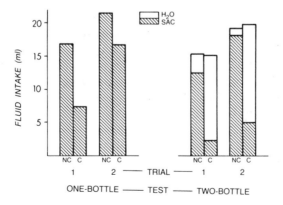

Figure 7. Mean consumption of saccharin in the one-bottle, forced choice testing procedure, or saccharin and plain water in the two-bottle, preference testing procedure in conditioned (C) and nonconditioned (NC) rats.

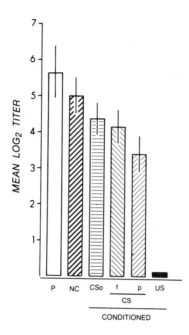

Figure 8. Mean (± s.e.) hemagglutinating antibody titers in placebo (P), nonconditioned (NC), and in conditioned animals injected with CY at the time of antigen exposure (US), provided with plain water (CS₀), or provided with the CS solution (CS) under "forced choice" (f) or "preference" (p) testing procedures.

Effects of a Change in the Conditioned Stimulus

The nature of the CS paired with immunosuppressive treatment does not appear to be a relevant variable. We have used sucrose, and E. A. Wayner (personal communication) has used a mild citric acid solution as the CS. A conditioned suppression of antibody titer was observed in both instances. Similarly, the nature of the immunosuppressive drug does not yet appear to be critical, although we have preliminary data on only one other agent, methotrexate (see section on Methotrexate).

Effects of Dose of Cyclophosphamide

In an effort to magnify the effects of conditioning, two experiments were conducted in which we varied the dose of the US. In one study the dose of CY was *decreased* from 50 to 25 mg/kg, but two conditioning trials were imposed. The first pairing of saccharin consumption with an i.p. injection of CY occurred 7 days before antigenic stimulation and the second trial on which saccharin was introduced by pipette (conditioned rats will not voluntarily consume saccharin previously paired with CY) was imposed 4 days before the injection of SRBC. Irrespective of the differential treatment conditions, all animals that received two i.p. injections of CY showed a markedly depressed antibody response. Since mean hemagglutination titers varied between 1.1 and 2.4 log units, no group differences could be discerned. It would appear that the immunosuppressive effects of CY are cumulative and therefore such an experimental protocol obviated any discrimination between conditioned and nonconditioned animals.

In a second study, the dose of CY was increased to 75 mg/kg and we injected either 8×10^7 or 8×10^8 SRBC in an effort to stimulate antibody production in the face of the higher dose of CY. The design of this experiment was essentially the same as our original study. An i.p. injection of 75 mg/kg CY immediately followed a 15-min drinking period during which rats were provided with the novel saccharin solution. Three days later, randomly selected subgroups were inoculated with SRBC and subgroups of conditioned animals were provided with the saccharin solution (Group CS), plain water (Group CS_0), or plain water plus an i.p. injection of CY (Group US); nonconditioned animals were provided with saccharin (Group NC). Half the animals in each group were sacrificed 6 days after antigen and half were sampled on Day 8.

The effect of 75 mg/kg CY is shown in Figure 9. The two concentrations of

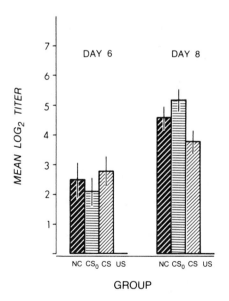

Figure 9. Effects of conditioning with 75 mg/kg CY as the US on hemagglutinating antibody titers measured 6 and 8 days after the introduction of SRBC. Group designations are the same as in Figure 3.

antigen yielded essentially the same antibody titers and have been combined, yielding Ns of 20–22 per group. Six days after antigen, all animals were relatively low titered (excluding the US group, 36% of the rats showed no detectable antibody response) and no group differences were apparent. Eight days after antigen, there was a moderate antibody response and there were group differences. Conditioned animals reexposed to the CS on the day on which SRBC were introduced had antibody titers that were significantly lower than those in both control groups.

These data are reminiscent of those previously described in Figure 6, except that the increased dose of CY appears to be reflected in a shift in the kinetics of the antibody response. The higher dose of CY further attenuates antibody production. Titers are low 6 days after antigen administration but are continuing to rise and eventually achieve the same approximate level seen when animals are pretreated with 50 mg/kg CY. As in the case of the lower dose of CY, when antibody levels are relatively low (shortly after antigenic stimulation) one can not discriminate among the experimental treatments; at a moderate level of serum antibody, a conditioned immunosuppressive response is again observed. Increasing the effectiveness of the US by simply increasing the dose of CY, however, was not successful in magnifying the conditioned immunosuppressive response. These data suggest, nevertheless, that there is a relationship between the immunosuppressive effects of CY, the concentration of antigen, sample time, and, perhaps, other variables such as the interval between CY pretreatment and antigenic stimulation or the circadian rhythmicity in the effects of CY (Cardoso et al., 1978; Haus et al., 1974), and that a complete parametric analysis of this relationship, together with systematic variation of the conditioning paradigm itself, might yet prove fruitful in yielding a combination of variables that would be optimal for the purposes of studying conditioned immunosuppressive effects.

Residual Effects of Cyclophosphamide

That the interval between pretreatment with CY and antigenic stimulation is a potentially critical variable is suggested by the literature (e.g., Mackenzie et al., 1978; Makinodan et al., 1970; Rollinghoff et al., 1977; Santos and Owens, 1964) as well as by our own data. As can be seen in Figures 3–5, for example, the difference between placebo-treated animals and the two control groups (nonconditioned animals and conditioned animals that are not reexposed to the CS) is as great as the difference between the NC or CS_0 groups and the experimental group, (conditioned animals that are reexposed to the CS). The reduced antibody level in Groups NC and CS_0 is, presumably, a reflection of the residual effects of CY administered 3 days before the introduction of antigen. It became necessary, therefore, to define the residual effects of CY if it was to be used effectively in a conditioning paradigm.

To this end, data that were available from placebo-treated animals and controls that were part of the same experiment were collated. These were animals that had been injected with 50 or 75 mg/kg CY at varying times before injection with 3×10^8 SRBC.

The residual effects of a single i.p. injection of CY are shown in Figure 10. Antibody production in rats is almost totally inhibited when CY and SRBC are injected on the same day (at approximately the same time.) When CY is injected before animals are exposed to the antigen, there is a dose-related at-

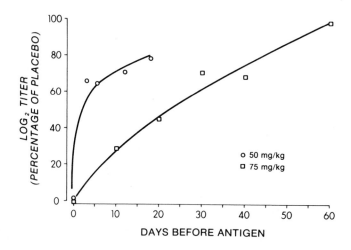

Figure 10. Residual immunosuppressive effects of cyclophosphamide in male rats. The mean values plotted are based on mean hemagglutinating antibody titers determined 6 days after exposure to SRBC from 2 to 17 groups relative to their respective (same experiment) placebo-treated control groups. From "Adrenal involvement in conditioned immunosuppression" by Ader, R. et al. *International Journal of Immunopharmacology*, 1979, **1**, 141-145. Copyright 1979 by Pergamon Press. Reprinted by permission.

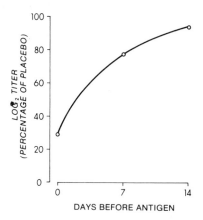

Figure 11. Residual immunosuppressive effects of CY in the mouse.

tenuation of antibody production. In the case of the 75 mg/kg dose, for example, the residual effects are discernable even when CY is injected 6 weeks before immunogenic stimulation. Similar effects were observed in mice (Figure 11). It seems clear, then, that one of the factors that may be contributing to the small differences between experimental and control groups is the mild suppression of antibody production seen in control relative to placebo-treated animals which, in turn, could be acting to mask the effects of conditioning.

Environmental Variables

A critical examination of our experimental paradigm has suggested that there may be other environmental as well as procedural variables that might be acting to reduce or mask the effects of conditioning. In our initial studies, for example, one group of conditioned animals (Group US) was injected with CY at the time that antigen was administered, a necessary treatment to define the unconditioned effects of the drug being used. To control for this experimental intervention, animals from all other groups were given an i.p. injection of saline at the same time. Is it necessary or desirable, however, to provide a placebo injection to the remaining animals? It has long been recognized (e.g., Dolin et al., 1960; Hutton et al., 1970; Pavlov, 1928; Siegel, 1975) that in such psychopharmacologic research, the injection procedure can and does act as a conditioned stimulus—and in our paradigm the immunosuppressive effects of CY have been associated with an i.p. injection for *all* animals. The administration of an i.p. injection to animals in Groups CS_0 and NC at the time that antigen is introduced may, therefore, constitute a CS for immunosuppression. If this is so, the differences that have been observed thus far may reflect differences between animals exposed to quantitative differences in the CS (i.e., differences between "well" conditioned and "not so well" conditioned animals) rather than differences between animals that are or are not reexposed to the CS when antigen is introduced.

Another extraneous factor that has existed in all but our most recent experiments is the manner in which the several groups have been housed, namely, in the same experimental colony room. Other experiments in our laboratory have indicated that when taste aversion is assessed under a preference or two-bottle testing procedure, conditioned animals consume plain water without necessarily first drinking from the randomly positioned bottle containing the CS solution. There would appear to be recognition of the presence of saccharin, the CS, in one of the bottles without the necessity for consuming any measurable amount. Presumably, the animal's choice is based on an olfactory discrimination. There is evidence that a poison-induced avoidance response can be established on the basis of an association involving an olfactory CS (Domjan, 1973; Lorden et al., 1970; Lovett et al., 1968;

Supak *et al.*, 1971; Taukulis, 1974). The presence of olfactory cues could be influencing our data in several ways. For example, "nonconditioned" animals might actually be weakly conditioned animals, or the presence of saccharin in the common experimental room (e.g., between successive CS presentations after the administration of antigen) might contribute to extinction of the behavioral and immunosuppressive responses.

Two experiments were conducted to examine the potential influence of olfactory cues in the conditioning of a taste aversion (Ader, 1977). In one experiment, the presence of the CS solution (saccharin) in the environment of conditioned animals during the interval between conditioning and testing resulted in an attenuation of the aversion (i.e., facilitated extinction of the conditioned response). In a second experiment, the consumption of *plain water* by conditioned animals was reduced to the level of the consumption of saccharin in conditioned animals when the rats that were provided with plain water were tested in the presence of animals that were provided with saccharin. It is on the basis of such data that our routine protocol now requires that different groups of animals be maintained in separate colony rooms.

ADRENAL INVOLVEMENT IN CONDITIONED IMMUNOSUPPRESSION

Although the relationship between corticosteroids and immunologic reactivity is not entirely clear (Parillo and Fauci, 1979), high circulating levels of adrenocortical steroids are immunosuppressive (Claman, 1972; Parillo and Fauci, 1979). Since an increase in adrenal activity is intimately associated with "stress," it could be postulated that the attenuated antibody response consistently observed in conditioned animals is the direct reflection of a nonspecific "stress" response induced by the conditioning procedures. Such an hypothesis would be consistent with the prevalent explanation proffered to account for the effects of emotional states or experimentally manipulated socioenvironmental factors on immunologic reactivity. Even here, though, all of the available data are not easily subsumed by such an hypothesis. Gisler *et al.* (1971), for example, found that spleen cell suspensions obtained 6–24 hr after mice were exposed to stressful stimulation showed a suppression of *in vitro* reactivity and that such "stress" effects could be reproduced by injections of ACTH (Gisler and Schenkel-Hulliger, 1971). Solomon *et al.* (1979), however, reports that neither they nor Gisler were able to suppress *in vivo* responses by such hormone administration. Several investigators (e.g., Rasmussen *et al.*, 1959; Treadwell and Rasmussen, 1961) have presented data implicating adrenal changes in resistance to anaphylactic shock. Because of the literature indicating that "crowded" mice have higher levels of adrenocortical activity, Treadwell and Rasmussen (1961) also examined the anaphylactic response in group- and individually-housed animals. Under the lower of two challenge doses, what these authors referred to as the "incidental stress of isolation" resulted in increased resistance to anaphylaxis. Also, Amkraut *et al.* (1973) observed that a limited feeding regimen could suppress a graft-versus-host response in rats. However, further studies on adrenalectomized or ACTH-treated hosts indicated that the effects of restricted feeding could not be attributed to changes in corticosteroid levels. A fuller treatment of this complicated issue is given in the earlier chapter by Monjan.

Whatever the explanation of the above data may be, these studies involved more sustained environmental stimulation than occurs in the conditioning paradigm. Nevertheless, it could be hypothesized that the phenomenon of conditioned immunosuppression is a "stress" (i.e., adrenocortically) mediated response. If, however, we assume that the depressed immune responses that occur in response to ("stressful") environmental or physiological stimulation are, in fact, the result of increases in circulating levels of glucocorticoids, it does not necessarily follow that the phenomenon of conditioned immunosuppression *is* an adrenocortically mediated effect. Such observations would indicate only that elevations in steroid level *might* account for such an effect (i.e., such a possibility has not been excluded). More direct evidence in the form of experiments designed to examine the effects of an absence of adrenal activity or the action of steroids would be required.

If an elevated steroid level can be invoked to account for the observations of conditioned immunosuppression, it is most likely to be the result of a *conditioned* elevation in steroid level. It is, after all, the conditioned animals *that were reexposed to the CS* that displayed the attenuation in antibody titer. We had speculated (Ader and Cohen, 1975) that the conditioning of a taste aversion might result in a concomitant conditioning of an elevation in steroid level and, indeed, it has been shown possible to condition an adrenocortical response in the taste aversion paradigm (Ader, 1976; Rigter, 1975).

In an initial attempt to evaluate the possibility that an elevation in adrenocortical steroids might be responsible for the attenuation of antibody titer in conditioned animals, an experiment was conducted in which LiCl, rather than CY, was used as the unconditioned stimulus (Ader and Cohen, 1975). Like CY, LiCl has noxious gastrointestinal effects sufficient to induce a conditioned taste aversion. It is also an effective stimulus for conditioning a concomitant elevation in steroid level (Ader, 1976). However, LiCl is not immunosuppressive (Ader, 1976; A. L. Duigan and I. G. Otterness, personal communication, 1979; E. A. Wayner, personal communication, 1979). Behaviorally, LiCl induced an aversion to a saccharin drinking solution which was indistinguishable from the aversion induced by CY, but the pairing of saccharin and LiCl did not effect an attenuation of antibody titer when conditioned animals were subsequently injected with antigen and reexposed to the saccharin (Figure 12).

Since the animals conditioned with LiCl consume no more fluid than

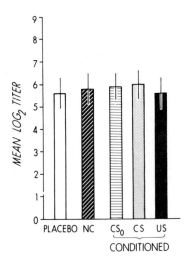

Figure 12. Mean (± s.e.) hemagglutination titers measured 6 days after SRBC exposure in animals conditioned with LiCl as the US. Group designations are the same as in Figure 3. From "Behaviorally conditioned immunosuppression" by Ader, R. and Cohen, N. *Psychosomatic Medicine,* 1975, **37,** 333–340. Copyright 1975 by Elsevier North-Holland, Inc. Reprinted by permission.

animals conditioned with CY when such groups are reexposed to the CS, these findings, incidentally, also bear on the question of whether a relative state of dehydration coincidental with antigenic stimulation might have accounted for the attenuated antibody response. Similar to the study described previously in which a preference testing procedure was used, fluid intake does not appear to be a critical factor. These results, then, provide no support for the hypothesis of an adrenal mediation of the conditioned suppression of an antibody response. However, the possibility remains that there is some special synergistic relation between a conditionally elevated steroid level and the residual immunosuppressive effects of CY (see Figure 10). Two additional experiments were therefore conducted to assure a high circulating level of steroid at the time of antigen administration (Ader *et al.,* 1979).

On the day of conditioning, conditioned Fischer (CD-F) rats were provided with a 0.1% solution of sodium saccharin during their 15-min drinking period and immediately thereafter were injected i.p. with 50 mg/kg CY. Nonconditioned rats were given plain water and then injected with CY. In the first experiment, LiCl was used to elicit an endogenous elevation in steroid level. Three days after conditioning, when all animals were injected with SRBC, one additional subgroup of *conditioned* animals was added to the standard protocol. These animals received plain water followed by an i.p. injection of 150 mg/kg LiCl. An additional subgroup of nonconditioned animals was also provided with plain water and injected with LiCl, a drug which dramatically elevates plasma corticosterone level (Ader, 1976; Jacobs, 1978). In a second study, the potential interaction between high steroid level and the residual effects of CY was examined by exogenous administration of steroid. An additional subgroup of animals previously conditioned with CY was injected with 1 mg/kg corticosterone rather than being presented with the conditioned stimulus.

Hemagglutinating antibody titers measured 6 days after injection of SRBC when LiCl was used instead of saccharin, the CS, are shown in Figure 13. The antibody titer in Group CS was significantly lower than that in nonconditioned animals but, in this instance, it was not significantly lower than that in Group CS_0. Conditioned animals reexposed to the CS had titers that were also significantly lower than the titers in the conditioned animals that received an injection of LiCl instead of reexposure to saccharin. These latter animals did not differ from either of the control groups.

Similar results (Figure 14) were obtained when conditioned animals were injected with corticosterone instead of being reexposed to the CS. Conditioned animals that were again subjected to the CS had hemagglutinating antibody titers that were significantly lower than the titers of both control groups. There was only a slight (nonsignificant) attenuation of antibody titer in conditioned animals injected with steroid.

Besides eliciting an adrenocortical response, LiCl would have caused certain

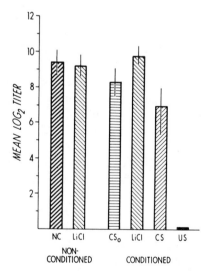

Figure 13. Hemagglutination titers (mean ± s.e.) obtained 6 days after injection of SRBC. Nonconditioned animals were injected with saline after consumption of saccharin (NC) or injected with LiCl after consumption of water (LiCl); conditioned animals were provided with water and injected with saline (CS_0), LiCl (LiCl), or CY (US), or were provided with saccharin and injected with saline (CS). Treatments occurred on the day animals were injected with antigen. From "Adrenal involvement in conditioned immunosuppression" by Ader, R. *et al., International Journal of Immunopharmacology,* 1979, **1,** 141–145. Copyright 1979 by Pergamon Press. Reprinted by permission.

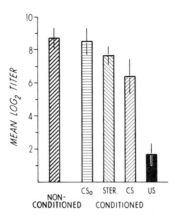

Figure 14. Hemagglutination titers (mean ± s.e.) obtained 6 days after SRBC exposure in nonconditioned animals provided with saccharin and injected with saline (NC); conditioned animals provided with water and injected with saline (CS_0), corticosterone (STER), or CY (US), or provided with saccharin and injected with saline (CS). Treatments occurred on the day animals were injected with antigen. From "Adrenal involvement in conditioned immunosuppression" by Ader, R. *et al. International Journal of Immunopharmacology*, 1979, **1**, 141–145. Copyright 1979 by Pergamon Press. Reprinted by permission.

noxious gastrointestinal effects. These effects may not be identical to the noxious effects of CY, but the effects of LiCl could be viewed as an approximation of the total stimulus complex to which the animals were initially exposed and conditioned. Even so, neither the LiCl-induced stimulation of an adrenocortical response (plus its noxious gastrointestinal effects) nor the exogenous administration of corticosterone superimposed upon the residual immunosuppressive effects of CY acted to suppress antibody production to any significant extent. Based on the same reasoning, E. A. Wayner (personal communication) also conducted a study in which conditioned animals were injected with physiological levels of corticosterone and she, too, observed no attenuation of the antibody response.

As reported above, one can observe a conditioned depression of antibody production even when a preference procedure is used to control for total fluid consumption in the conditioned taste aversion paradigm. Although there is a demonstrable taste aversion, there is no elevation in steroid level when animals are tested with the preference procedure, that is, when the total fluid intake of conditioned animals is as high as it is in controls (Smotherman *et al.,* 1976; E. A. Wayner, personal communication, 1979). By inference, then, these earlier data provide the additional information that conditioned immunosuppression is observable in the absence of an elevated steroid level.

That an elevation in steroid level may be immunosuppressive under certain therapeutic regimens or that even a transient elevation in the level of circulating steroids may be sufficient to attenuate antibody production in response to minimally effective immunogenic stimulation (Amkraut and

Solomon, 1974) is not at issue. Under the experimental conditions imposed in these experiments, there is no compelling evidence that comparable effects can be achieved simply by elevating steroid levels. One might speculate, however, that, *in vivo,* the defense reactions of the organism are hierarchically organized such that only those resources sufficient to combat the prevailing challenge are initiated in the interest of conserving defensive energies and minimizing homeostatic disturbances. Consequently, stimuli that are qualitatively and/or quantitatively more threatening to the survival of the organism might be relatively insensitive to perturbations initiated by external events. Depending upon a variety of environmental circumstances and depending upon factors such as the magnitude, duration and, perhaps, the timing of the response, then, an elevation in circulating steroids may be sufficient to attenuate the response to a relatively mild antigenic stimulus and be insufficient to modify the immune response to a more potent challenge. Be that as it may, our several experiments, taken together, provide no evidence in support of the hypothesis that the attenuation in antibody production seen in conditioned animals reexposed to the CS at the time of antigenic stimulation is mediated by an elevation in adrenocortical steroids.

GENERALIZABILITY OF CONDITIONED IMMUNOSUPPRESSION

To establish the generalizability of the phenomenon of conditioned immunosuppression, it becomes necessary to determine if the effects of conditioning can be observed with immunosuppressive drugs other than cyclophosphamide, antigens other than sheep erythrocytes, or cell-mediated as well as antibody-mediated responses. In addition to a concern with the generalizability of the phenomenon, several such studies were conducted because of their potential for directing attention to underlying mechanisms and in an effort to identify an experimental model that might be particularly sensitive to the effects of conditioning.

Methotrexate as an Unconditioned Immunosuppressive Stimulus

Based on its known immunosuppressive properties, its use in chemotherapeutic regimens, and the available literature, preliminary studies were undertaken with methotrexate (MTX). Since the literature on MTX is focused upon its use in a prolonged regimen of chemotherapy rather than upon the immunosuppressive effects induced by a single administration, we first established the dose of a single injection of MTX that would be effective in inducing a taste aversion. Single doses of 15, 20, or, particularly, 25 mg/kg were mildly effective in inducing a taste aversion, but did not result in any suppression of antibody titer when the drug was administered on the same day as the antigen

(SRBC). Rats injected with 25 mg/kg MTX 1, 2, 3, or 4 days after being injected with SRBC revealed that a single injection of MTX was maximally effective in suppressing antibody titer only if administered 2 or 3 days after antigen. Increasing the dose to 50 mg/kg MTX was immunosuppressive when administered 2, 3, and 4 days after antigen. These preliminary data, then, indicated that (a) a single injection of MTX *before* the administration of antigen (i.e., at the time of conditioning) would not be likely to have residual effects on antibody production that would attenuate the conditioning phenomenon, and (b) if MTX, itself, were only effective when administered 2, 3 or, perhaps, 4 days *after* antigen (depending upon the dose), a CS previously associated with the effects of MTX was most likely to be effective presented at these times. The fact that these doses of MTX did not have residual effects (or residual effects approximating those of CY) also would permit the design of experiments involving more than a single conditioning trial. It should be noted, though, that subsequent data indicated that even at 50 mg/kg, a single CS–US pairing using MTX is not as effective as CY in inducing a taste aversion, and multiple trials with 50 mg/kg MTX result in as much as a 25% mortality.

Initial conditioning studies with MTX using a single CS–US trial or using two or three such presentations, yielded equivocal data; the CS group had the lowest antibody titers, but the differences were not necessarily statistically significant in comparison with all the control conditions. For example, in one study using 50 mg/kg MTX, rats received three conditioning trials at intervals of 7–10 days. An additional control group (Group CS_R) received noncontingent CS and US presentations, that is, they received the same number of MTX injections and the same number of saccharin presentations as Group CS, but the stimuli were not paired. There was no evidence of immunosuppression in Group CS_R and, in fact, the antibody level in Group CS was significantly lower than that in Group CS_R. Group CS did not, however, differ significantly from either of the other individual control groups although they had significantly lower titers than the combined controls (Groups NC and CS_0). It should be emphasized that these are preliminary data in the sense that these initial conditioning studies were conducted before we had complete data on the optimal or appropriate conditions for presenting the CS to animals conditioned with MTX and on the housing of animals in conditioning studies (see section on "Environmental Variables"). It would appear, however, that MTX has some advantages that make it an immunosuppressive drug appropriate for future studies of conditioning.

Effects of Conditioning on the Antibody Response to a T-Cell-Independent Antigen

As described previously, Wayner *et al.* (1978) were able to replicate the phenomenon of conditioned immunosuppression using SRBC and an experimental protocol which was essentially the same as ours. Using this protocol, Wayner and her colleagues also examined conditioned immunosuppression using *Brucella abortus* (1 mg/kg), a T-cell-independent antigen. In this instance, however, there were no differences among the several treatment groups. To conclude that the effects of conditioning on a primary humoral antibody response are therefore limited to some influence on T lymphocytes, however, would be premature; there appear to be too many potentially interacting variables that could influence the effects of conditioning (e.g., species and strain, residual effects of CY on T-cell-dependent and independent responses, dose of antigen, kinetics of antibody production in the two systems, time of sampling). In an effort to increase the generalizability of the effects of conditioning and to delineate the effects of conditioning, we, too, have conducted experiments with a T-cell-independent antigen (Cohen *et al.*, 1979). These studies were carried out in mice stimulated with the hapten 2,4,6-trinitrophenyl coupled to the thymus-independent carrier, lipopolysaccharide (TNP–LPS).

In the first study, BDF_1 male mice were treated in a manner essentially similar to the rats of previous experiments. Water intake was gradually reduced to a 30-min drinking period at the same time each day. On the training day, the conditioned groups were provided with a 0.15% sodium saccharin solution which was followed immediately by an i.p. injection of 200 mg/kg CY. Nonconditioned mice were injected with CY after consuming plain water. However, these NC animals were exposed to saccharin 5 days later, a flavored drinking solution that was *not* paired with CY. Placebo animals received plain water and an injection of saline. In an attempt to reduce the residual effects of CY, antigen was not introduced until 2 weeks after conditioning. Based on a prior analysis of the kinetics of the antibody response to different doses of TNP–LPS, all animals were injected i.p. with 50 μg TNP–LPS in a volume of 0.2 ml per mouse and blood samples were collected 6 days after the introduction of antigen. A CS group was reexposed to saccharin and given an i.p. injection of saline on the day that antigen was injected and, again, 2 days later. Group CS_0 received no further exposure to saccharin and Group CS received only an injection of CY at the time of antigenic stimulation. Nonconditioned animals were reexposed to saccharin according to the same schedule as Group CS, and placebo animals received only antigen. While 200 mg/kg is not an especially high dose of CY for the mouse, it was sufficient to induce an aversion to the subsequent presentation of the saccharin drinking solution. Conditioned animals consumed 34% less saccharin than nonconditioned animals on the test day that first occurred 14 days after conditioning.

In a second experiment, the dose of CY was increased to 300 mg/kg and an attempt was made to increase the saliency of the conditioned stimulus. In this instance, the saccharin solution was introduced by pipette and the mice were immediately thereafter injected with LiCl (200 mg/kg). When Groups CS and NC were subsequently reexposed to the CS, they received both the saccharin drinking solution (in a *preference* testing procedure) plus the LiCl (125 mg/kg). The dose of LiCl was reduced because of the high mortality that was initially observed and due, presumably, to the combination of LiCl and CY paired on the day of conditioning. In all other respects, this second experiment followed the paradigm described for the first experiment with TNP–LPS.

The results of these two experiments are shown in Table 2. It may be noted, first, that the anti-TNP antibody titers in the first experiment (measured by passive hemagglutination) are higher than in the second. We assume that this reflects the lower dose of CY that was used in the first experiment. At the same time, it could reflect adrenocortical activation by LiCl. Also, with the higher dose of CY there appears to be some residual effects of the immunosuppressive treatment even after the 2-week interval between conditioning and the introduction of antigen (which might also account for the variability among animals in Experiment 2 which is considerably larger than in Experiment 1).

In the first experiment, total hemagglutinating antibody titer in Group CS is significantly lower than in either Group NC or Group CS_0. In Experiment 2, CS animals have the lowest antibody titers but only the difference between Groups CS and NC is statistically significant. By using a CS with internal as well as external sensory effects, then, we were only partially successful in magnifying the effects of conditioning. Relative to nonconditioned animals, conditioned animals showed a nearly 50% attenuation in antibody production, one of the largest differences observed thus far. Conditioned animals reexposed to the CS did not differ significantly, however, from conditioned animals that were not reexposed to the CS. The antibody titer in Group CS was approximately 27% lower than the titer in Groups CS_0, a difference which corresponds to previously observed differences, but the exceptionally high variability, due to any one or combination of factors that were novel in this experiment, preclude any definitive conclusions. Taken together with the small but significant differences obtained in the first experiment, though, it would appear that a conditioned suppression of the immune response to a T-cell-independent antigen can be observed in the mouse. It should also be remarked that the humoral response to T-independent antigens is relatively insensitive to corticosteroids (e.g., Mantzouranis and Borel, 1979) and that a preference testing procedure which would obviate differences in levels of circulating corticosteroids was used in the second of these experiments.

As is well known, antibody production in response to SRBC, for example, involves a complex series of interactions among macrophages and subsets of T and B cells (Claman and Chaperon, 1969; Opitz et al., 1978). Thus, the observations of conditioned suppression of the response to xenogeneic erythrocytes described in the preceding paragraph could have resulted from effects on any or all of these cell populations. Our finding that conditioning can also result in an attenuation of the antibody response to TNP–LPS, a T-cell-independent antigen, suggests the possibility that conditioned immunosuppression might

TABLE 2

Effects of Conditioning in BDF$_1$ Mice on the Antibody Response to a Challenge with TNP-LPS [Mean ±s.e.m. (N) Antibody Titer][a]

Experiment	Conditioned stimulus	CY (mg/kg)	Group				
			P	NC	CS$_0$	CS	US
1	SAC	200	6.68 ± .35(19)	6.78 ± .16(23)	6.29 ± .15(24)	5.76 ± .27(25)	2.53 ± .30(15)
2	SAC + LiCl	300	5.00 ± .17(15)	4.50 ± .38(8)	3.14 ± .94(7)	2.28 ± .84(7)	0.0 (2)

[a] Anti-TNP antibody titers determined by passive hemagglutination (Kettman and Dutton, 1970; Rittenberg and Pratt, 1969) and recorded as reciprocals of endpoint dilutions expressed as powers of the base$_2$. From "Conditioned suppression of a Thymus-independent antibody response" by Cohen, N. *et al.*, *Psychosomatic Medicine*, 1979, **41**, 487–491. Copyright 1979 by Elsevier North-Holland, Inc. Reprinted by permission.

involve a direct effect on lymphocytes of the B-cell lineage. Whatever the mechanisms, the present results, using a T-cell-independent rather than a T-cell-dependent antigen, and mice rather than rats, essentially replicate and extend previous observations of conditioned immunosuppression.

Effects of Conditioning on a Graft-Versus-Host Response

The generality of conditioned immunosuppression would be further extended if it could be shown to apply to a cell-mediated response as well as a humoral response. In this regard, Whitehouse et al. (1973) reported that multiple low doses of CY were effective in suppressing a popliteal graft-versus-host (GvH) response if administered on the day that splenic lymphocytes were injected and on the succeeding 2 days. Such a protocol seemed amenable to a conditioning paradigm that, incidentally, might also enable us to reinforce the previously conditioned response. That is, if injections of low doses of CY on *3* successive days were required to suppress the GvH response, it might be possible to reinforce the previously conditioned response with a *single* low dose of CY that was not, in itself, sufficient to attenuate the GvH reaction to any significant extent. We could, in effect, introduce a "reminder" of the previous conditioning (cf. Campbell and Jaynes, 1966; Campbell and Spear, 1972).

The design of this conditioning study (Bovbjerg et al., 1981) was basically the same as the studies already described although specific procedures had to be modified. Based on pilot observations, rats were conditioned by pairing consumption of a 0.15% saccharin solution with an i.p. injection of 50 mg/kg CY *48 days* before testing. Recipient animals, female Lewis × Brown Norwegian hybrids (LBN) were initially divided into conditioned, nonconditioned, and placebo groups. On Day 0, all animals were injected subdurally into the plantar surface of a hind footpad with a suspension of splenic leukocytes (2×10^7 spleen cells/footpad) obtained from female Lewis (L) donors. The experimental group of previously conditioned rats (Group CS_r) was treated as follows: On Day 0 they were reexposed to the CS and injected i.p. with saline; on Day 1 they were reexposed to the CS and injected with 10 mg/kg CY; on Day 2 they were reexposed to the CS and injected with saline. Another group of conditioned animals (Group CS_0) was not reexposed to the CS but was injected with 10 mg/kg CY on Day 1. Conditioned animals in Group US were not reexposed to the CS, but were injected with CY on Days 0, 1, and 2. Like Groups CS_r, nonconditioned animals (Group NC_r) were provided with the saccharin drinking solution on Days 0, 1, and 2, and were injected with 10 mg/kg CY on Day 1. Placebo animals were also provided with saccharin on Days 0, 1, and 2 but received no injections. All groups were tested using the two-bottle, "preference" procedure. Popliteal lymph nodes (which drain the injection site) were harvested and weighed 5 days after inoculation with the cellular graft.

Referring to Figure 15, it can be seen that the administration of 10 mg/kg CY on Days 0, 1, and 2 (Group US) markedly suppressed the GvH response relative to untreated controls (Group P), replicating the findings of Whitehouse *et al.* (1973). A single injection of CY at this low dose effected some attenuation of the response: Group NC_r did not differ from Group P, but Group CS_0 animals showed less of a node weight response than untreated controls. Groups NC_r and CS_0 did not differ; both of these treated control groups that received the *single* injection of CY had a greater GvH response than animals that received three injections of CY (Group US). It is of particular interest that conditioned animals that were reexposed to the CS in addition to receiving a *single* injection of CY did not differ from animals in Group US. Moreover, there was an attenuation of the GvH response in Group CS_r. In terms of absolute values, the stimulated lymph nodes harvested from rats in Group CS_r weighed significantly less than those from NC_r and CS_0 animals. In terms of the *change* in node weight (injected node weight–contralateral node weight), CS_r animals differed significantly from Group NC_r but not from Group CS_0.

We have not yet examined the possibility that the conditioned suppression of this GvH response is the result of an elevation in steroid levels. Amkraut *et*

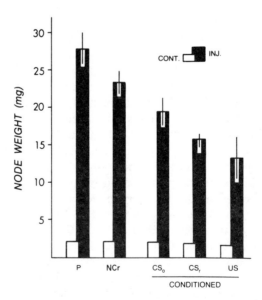

Figure 15. Popliteal lymph node weights determined 5 days after inoculation with splenic lymphocytes. Values for injected and contralateral footpads are given for placebo-treated (P) rats; for nonconditioned (NC_r) animals exposed to a single low dose of CY administered 1 day after the cellular graft; and for conditioned animals given a single low dose of CY and provided with plain water (CS_0), conditioned animals given a single low dose of CY and reexposed to the CS on Days 0, 1, and 2 after the cellular graft (CS_r), and conditioned animals given 3 low dose injections of CY (on Days 0, 1, and 2) and provided with plain water (US).

al. (1973) reported that their restricted feeding regimen resulted in suppression of a GvH response that could not be attributed to changes in corticosteroid levels. Other data (e.g., Cohen and Claman, 1971), however, indicate that steroids can suppress a GvH response. Differences in regimens of exogenously administered hydrocortisone and the endogenous release of corticosterone (the primary steroid in the rat and mouse), species differences, and differences in the measurements obtained in different models of cellular immunity make extrapolations between studies difficult. It should be recalled, though, that the use of a preference testing procedure in our study would have obviated major elevations or differences in steroid levels among the several groups, so that the hypothesis of a direct adrenocortical mediation becomes tenuous, at best. Again, then, we are not yet able to specify the mechanisms by which conditioning could alter a GvH response. Nonetheless, the conditioned suppression of a cell-mediated response provides still further evidence of the generalizability of the effects of conditioning on immune responses.

THE CONDITIONING PARADIGM: A REANALYSIS

Thus far, the conditioning of an immunosuppressive response would appear to be a highly reproducible phenomenon. As a matter of fact, it is the reliability of the phenomenon rather than the magnitude of the effect that is compelling. The magnitude of the conditioned suppression of antibody titer is relatively small—in our experiments and in the experiments of others. In one and/or another experiment we have changed the CS, changed the US, varied the dose of immunosuppressive drug, varied the number of conditioning trials and the number of reexposures to the CS, reduced the possibility that control animals were being exposed to some part of the original CS, lengthened the interval between conditioning and antigenic stimulation to reduce the residual effects of immunosuppressive treatment, controlled for fluid consumption, and sampled for antibody titer at various times after antigenic stimulation. The basic phenomenon obtains under all of these circumstances but, despite the "improvements" in methodology, we have been unable to magnify the effects of conditioning. The effect is consistent, independently verifiable, but small. Of course, the magnitude of an effect has no necessary bearing on its biologic significance. Nonetheless, the effect is too small to form the basis of additional questions that relate to conditioning processes (e.g., extinction of the conditioned response) or to the mechanisms that may be mediating the effect. If such issues are to be addressed efficiently, it behooves us to establish the conditions that may be optimal for studying the impact of conditioning in modulating immune responses. An initial question, then, is: Why are the effects so small?

It is possible that hemagglutinating antibody titer measured several days after superimposition of the CS is not sufficiently sensitive to yield larger effects. Circulating antibody is, after all, the result of a complex chain of events, and the effects of conditioning are, presumably, acting on one or more of these earlier events that culminate in the production of antibody. One may also speculate that the effects of reexposure to the conditioned stimulus could differentially influence different populations of lymphocytes and/or influence them in a differential fashion (proliferation, differentiation, etc.). Since CY, itself, can have such diverse effects (e.g., Hunninghake and Fauci, 1976; Turk and Poulter, 1972), it would not be unreasonable to suppose that the CS might also have multiple effects, the additive or, at least, ultimate effect of which is the resultant attenuation in antibody titer. The inhibition of suppressor cell activity, for example, could act to dilute the effects of a conditioned immunosuppressive stimulus. This, in turn, raises additional issues of the critical nature of the timing of CS presentations in relation to the nature and dose of antigen and the kinetics of the corresponding immunobiologic response (interacting with the several host factors that might contribute to immunologic reactivity). These are all relevant variables and reasonable possibilities to account for the small but consistent effects that have been observed thus far. Clearly, it will require considerable research to unravel the relative contribution of these several factors.

There is, in addition, a parallel approach to the question of why conditioned immunosuppressive effects are small. It is based, not on the operations of the immune system, but on an analysis of the conditioning paradigm, itself. Moreover, this analysis may constitute the most parsimonious explanation of all. Quite simply, it is proposed that the effects of conditioning in suppressing antibody titer are small because the conditioning is so effective.

The organism is, in a sense, prewired to respond to the introduction of antigen with a variety of defense mechanisms including the production of antibody. In effect, then, we are asking if the animal will, on the basis of a symbolic stimulus, exhibit an inhibition or decrease in its natural adaptive response. The observations that have been made thus far suggest that principles of conditioning may be applied to the modulation of immune responses. It is not unreasonable, therefore, to think of the entire experimental system in terms of conditioning processes. In conditioning terms, an antigen constitutes an unconditioned stimulus for the production of antibody, that is, antibody production is unconditionally elicited by antigenic stimulation. We first pair a neutral stimulus with the immunosuppressive effects of a pharmacologic agent, and the neutral stimulus presumably becomes a conditioned stimulus for immunosuppression. When, in our experimental situation, we present a CS for immunosuppression coincidentally with the introduction of antigen, we are, in effect, pairing a *CS* for suppression of immunologic reactivity with a *US* for activation of an immune response. By pairing a *CS for suppression* with a *US for activation* of some of *the same responses,* we are presenting conflicting stimuli having opposite but *unequal* effects. There would be no grounds for assuming that the CS would be the prepotent stimulus—that a CS would override the effects of a stimulus which, by definition, will unconditionally elicit the response in question. It would be comparable to presenting an established CS for extension of the leg together with a US for leg flexion. The response would undoubtedly be leg flexion, modified on the order of fractions of a second, perhaps, but modified nonetheless.

Our observations of conditioned immunosuppression are quite consistent with this analysis. We do not see total inhibition of antibody production. Rather, there is a transient attenuation of the response, reflecting, perhaps, some interference with or delay of the processes involved in the production of antibody that may be attributed to the effects of the conditioned stimulus. In a situation in which an inhibition of antibody production would be teleologically maladaptive and operationally incompatible with the effects of a unconditioned stimulus, we are still able to observe a small but consistent effect of conditioning. This, we submit, attests to the effectiveness of the conditioning paradigm.

If this analysis is correct, there are experimental situations that should yield larger conditioning effects than the attempt to suppress antibody production. One such situation would utilize a system in which immunosuppression is in the biologic best interests of the organism (the spontaneous development of autoimmune disease in NZB × NZW F_1 mice represents a model that we are currently studying). Also, in keeping with the above analysis, potentiation of immunologic reactivity should be more amenable to the effects of conditioning than suppression of reactivity. According to this analysis, conditioned enhancement of an immune response is not simply the converse of conditioned suppression. Many of the variables mentioned above would still be of parametric concern in terms of developing an optimal conditioning paradigm. However, given the necessity of introducing antigenic stimulation, the superimposition of a conditioned stimulus for a potentiated response would be consistent with the biologic defense reactions of the organism and might facilitate or augment immunologic reactivity as measured by the dose of antigen required to detect a response or the magnitude or rate of response.

SUMMARY

It was hypothesized that the pairing of a neutral stimulus with the immunosuppressive effects of a pharmacologic agent could enable that neutral stimulus to exert a suppressive effect on the immune response to antigenic stimulation (i.e., that the immunosuppressive effect of a pharmacologic agent could be conditioned). Using an illness-induced taste aversion conditioning paradigm, consumption of a novel distinctively flavored drinking solution, saccharin, was paired with an injection of an immunosuppressive drug, cyclophosphamide. When subsequently injected with sheep erythrocytes, conditioned animals reexposed to the saccharin drinking solution showed an attenuated antibody response. Since no such attenuation of antibody titer was found in nonconditioned animals or in conditioned animals that were not reexposed to the saccharin drinking solution, these results were interpreted to reflect a conditioned immunosuppressive response in the experimental group.

These original observations (Ader and Cohen, 1975) have been confirmed in our laboratory on several occasions and under a variety of experimental circumstances, only some of which have been reported previously (Ader *et al.,* 1979; Bovbjerg *et al.,* 1980; Cohen *et al.,* 1979). More importantly, perhaps, our experimental observations have since been replicated by others (Rogers *et al.,* 1976; Wayner *et al.,* 1978; M. G. King, personal communication, 1979). The research to date has concentrated on two basic issues: The evolution of an optimal paradigm for the study of conditioned immunosuppression (predicated on an implicit acceptance of the phenomenon) and the hypothesis that the effects of conditioning in depressing immunologic reactivity are an indirect result of a stress-induced elevation in adrenocortical steroids (predicated on an implicit rejection of the phenomenon).

It cannot be said that we have, as yet, developed an "optimal" conditioning paradigm or immunologic model within which to pursue the study of conditioned immunopharmacologic responses in terms of either conditioning processes or the neuroendocrine–immunologic mechanisms mediating conditioned immunosuppression. The effects of conditioning in modulating a primary humoral antibody response have been relatively small. The conditioned immunosuppressive effect appears to be transient, but it can be observed with the use of different drinking solutions, and preliminary data suggest that it can be observed with an immunosuppressive drug other than cyclophosphamide. In experiments conducted to control for the reduced fluid consumption that characterizes successful taste aversion conditioning, a preference testing procedure was introduced. Under conditions where there are no differences in fluid intake (or relative deprivation state), the effects of conditioning still occur. We have established the residual immunosuppressive effects of cyclophosphamide in the doses used in these experiments and, accordingly, increased the interval between conditioning and exposure to antigenic stimulation. Also, we have introduced procedural modifications to reduce the influence of environmental cues that we have presumed or documented to be potential conditioned stimuli for the control groups. None of these changes in the experimental protocol, however, has altered the basic pattern of the results. A conditioned immunosuppressive response can be observed in the mouse as well as in different strains of rat, in animals exposed to a thymus-independent as well as a thymus-dependent antigen, and in the case of a cell-mediated as well as an antibody-mediated response. Although we have not been able to increase the magnitude of the effect, the consistency of our results is compelling; the phenomenon of conditioned immunosuppression appears to have some generalizability across species, antigens and responses, and is independently reproducible.

High levels of circulating glucocorticoids can be immunosuppressive under certain circumstances. It was hypothesized, therefore, that the effects of our conditioning procedures were to elevate steroid levels and thereby attenuate antibody production. More reasonably, it was hypothesized that the conditioning of a taste aversion resulted in the concomitant conditioning of an elevation in steroid levels which, in turn, resulted in the attenuation of antibody titer in conditioned animals reexposed to the conditioned stimulus. Several experiments were undertaken to examine this possibility. A conditioning study with LiCl (which is not immunosuppressive but would cause a conditioned elevation in steroid levels) failed to result in an attenuation of antibody titer. Studies in which animals conditioned with cyclophosphamide were subsequently injected with LiCl or with corticosterone instead of being reexposed to the conditioned stimulus also failed to affect the antibody response. Even the superimposition of an exogenously elevated steroid level on the residual immunosuppressive effects of cyclophosphamide, then, was ineffective in attenuating the immune response. Conversely, animals tested for taste aversion with a preference procedure show conditioned immunosuppression but do not show an elevation in steroid level. Our results, taken together, provide no support for the hypothesis of an adrenocortical mediation of conditioned immunosuppression.

If the effects of conditioning in modifying immunologic reactivity can not be accounted for on the basis of an experimentally elevated level of circulating steroid, how can the phenomenon of conditioned immunosuppression be explained? At this juncture, any attempt to provide an analysis of the underlying mechanisms would be premature and highly speculative. Our observations are based on a very limited sampling of immune processes and, however consistent the available data, the magnitude of the conditioned immunosuppressive effect is relatively small. As was pointed out, the magnitude of the effect could be the result of a number of interacting factors. Broadly speaking, we assume, initially at least, that the effects of conditioning are mediated via neuroendocrine changes that have the potential to influence afferent, central, and/or efferent immune processes. To begin to examine these, however, would seem to be predicated upon an "optimal" experimental paradigm, that is, an experimental model that results in larger effects of conditioning than have been observed thus far, and one that might be sensitive to systematic variations in the conditioning paradigm. Such a model might be uncovered empirically. We have, however, become preoccupied with the recurrent problem of why the effects of conditioned immunosuppression are small. This had led us to reanalyze our experimental paradigm and to conclude that not only is our current experimental situation less than optimal, but it may be extraordinarily inefficient.

In the reanalysis of our paradigm from the perspective of a conditioning situation that applies to the immunologic as well as the behavioral stimulus and response, antigenic stimulation is defined as an unconditioned stimulus, a stimulus that unconditionally elicits antibody production (the unconditioned response). When we introduce a stimulus previously paired with an immunosuppressive drug at the time of exposure to antigenic stimulation, we are pairing a conditioned stimulus for suppression of immunologic reactivity with an unconditioned stimulus for the initiation of an immune response. These stimuli elicit incompatible responses. By definition, however, the result will be elicitation of the unconditioned response, albeit an unconditioned response which has, to some extent, been modified by the coincidental presentation of the conditioned stimulus for suppression of reactivity. Such an analysis is consistent with the available data which provide evidence of a small, transient attenuation in the production of antibody in conditioned animals that are reexposed to the conditioned stimulus. Under the circumstances, then, it is surprising that the conditioned stimulus exerts any effects at all, and it would appear that we are able to observe a small effect only because the conditioning paradigm is so potent. Viewed in this way, the effects that we and others have observed become more understandable. More importantly, this analysis of the situation suggests alternative strategies that may prove fruitful for pursuing studies of conditioned immunobiologic effects.

The application of conditioning techniques to the study of immunobiologic processes can be viewed as an extension of one of the more significant frontiers in the behavioral sciences, namely, the conditioning of visceral and autonomic responses and the conditioning of pharmacologic effects. Together with the wide ranging observations reported elsewhere in this volume, the results obtained thus far with regard to the conditioning of immune responses further substantiate the notion of an intimate relationship between the central nervous system and the immune system. Methodologically, the application of conditioning techniques provides a means for studying this relationship in the intact organism. Clinically, an elaboration of this phenomenon could lead to new regimens of chemotherapy. Conceptually, the capacity of conditioning to suppress or facilitate immune responses raises innumerable issues with respect to the normal operation and modifiability of the immune system and could lead to very basic studies of the mediation of individual differences in the body's natural armamentarium for adaptation and survival along lines that are currently poorly understood or almost totally unrecognized. Finally, in a field that already recognizes the potential of psychophysiological interactions in determining disease susceptibility, the conditioning of immune processes suggests a mechanism that may be involved in the complex pathogenesis of psychosomatic phenomena and bears eloquent witness to the principle of a very basic integration of biologic and psychological function.

ACKNOWLEDGMENT

The collaboration of Lee J. Grota, Nicola Green, and Dana Bovbjerg in one or another of these studies and the able assistance of Sumico Nagai and Wendy Makrides is gratefully acknowledged.

REFERENCES

Ader, R. (1976). Conditioned adrenocortical steroid elevations in the rat. *J. Comp. Physiol. Psychol.* **90**, 1156–1163.

Ader, R. (1977). A note on the role of olfaction in taste aversion learning. *Bull. Psychon. Soc.* **10**, 402–404.

Ader, R., and Cohen, N. (1975). Behaviorally conditioned immunosuppression. *Psychosom. Med.* **37**, 333–340.

Ader, R., Cohen, N., and Grota, L. J. (1979). Adrenal involvement in conditioned immunosuppression. *Int. J. Immunopharmacol.* **1**, 141–145.

Amkraut, A. A., and Solomon, G. F. (1974). From the symbolic stimulus to the pathophysiologic response: Immune mechanisms. *Int. J. Psychiatr. Med.* **5**, 541–563.

Amkraut, A. A., Solomon, G. F., Kasper, P., and Purdue, P. (1973). Stress and hormonal intervention in the graft-versus-host response. *In* "Microenvironmental Aspects of Immunity" (B. D. Jankovic and K. Isaković, eds.), pp. 667–674. Plenum, New York.

Bovbjerg, D. H., Cohen, N., and Ader, R. (1980). Conditioned suppression of a cellular immune response. *Psychosom. Med.* **42**, 73.

Campbell, B. A., and Jaynes, J. (1966). Reinstatement. *Psychol. Rev.* **73**, 478–480.

Campbell, B. A., and Spear, N. E. (1972). Ontogeny of memory. *Psychol. Rev.* **79**, 215–236.

Cardoso, S. S., Avery, T., Venditti, J. M., and Goldin, A. (1978). Circadian dependence of host and tumor responses to cyclophosphamide in mice. *Eur. J. Cancer* **14**, 949–954.

Claman, H. N. (1972). Corticosteroids and lymphoid cells. *N. Engl. J. Med.* **287**, 388–397.

Claman, H. N., and Chaperon, E. A. (1969). Immunological complementation between thymus and marrow cells—a model for the two-cell theory of immunocompetence. *Transplant. Rev.* **1**, 92–113.

Cohen, J. J., and Claman, H. N. (1971). Hydrocortisone resistance of activated initiator cells in graft-versus-host reactions. *Nature (London)* **229**, 274–275.

Cohen, N., Ader, R., Green, N., and Bovbjerg, D. (1979). Conditioned suppression of a thymus independent antibody response. *Psychosom. Med.* **41**, 487–491.

DiCara, L. V. (1970). Learning in the autonomic nervous system. *Sci. Am.* **222**, 31–39.

Dolin, A. O., Krylov, V. N., Luk'ianenko, V. I., and Flerov, B. A. (1960). New experimental data on the conditioned reflex production and suppression of immune and allergic reactions. *Zh. Vyssh. Nervn. Deyat. im. I. P. Pavlova* **10**, 832–841.

Domjan, M. (1973). Role of ingestion in odor-toxicosis learning in the rat. *J. Comp. Physiol. Psychol.* **84**, 507–521.

Dragoin, W. B., McCleary, G. E., and McCleary, P. (1971). A comparison of two methods of measuring conditioned taste aversions. *Behav. Res. Methods & Instrum.* **3**, 309–310.

Garcia, J., Hankins, W. G., and Rusiniak, K. W. (1974). Behavioral regulation of the milieu interne in man and rat. *Science* **185**, 824–831.

Gisler, R. H., and Schenkel-Hulliger, L. (1971). Hormonal regulation of the immune response. II. Influence of pituitary and adrenal activity on immune responsiveness *in vitro*. *Cell. Immunol.* **2**, 646–657.

Gisler, R. H., Bussard, A. E., Mazie, J. C., and Hess, R. (1971). Hormonal regulation of the immune response. I. Induction of an immune response *in vitro* with lymphoid cells from mice exposed to acute systemic stress. *Cell. Immunol.* **2**, 634–645.

Haus, E., Fernandes, G., Kuhl, J. F. W., Yunis, E. J., Lee, J. D., and Halberg, F. (1974). Murine circadian susceptibility rhythm to cyclophosphamide. *Chronobiologia* **1**, 270–277.

Hunninghake, G. W., and Fauci, A. S. (1976). Divergent effects of cyclophosphamide administration on mononuclear killer cells: Quantitative depletion of cell numbers versus qualitative suppression of functional capabilities. *J. Immunol.* **117**, 337–342.

Hutton, R. A., Woods, S. C., and Makous, W. L. (1970). Conditioned hyperglycemia: Pseudoconditioning controls. *J. Comp. Physiol. Psychol.* **71**, 198–201.

Jacobs, J. J. (1978). Effect of lithium chloride on adrenocortical function in the rat. *Proc. Soc. Exp. Biol. Med.* **157**, 163–167.

Kettman, J., and Dutton, R. W. (1970). An *in vitro* primary immune response to 2,4,6-trinitrophenyl substituted erythrocytes: Responses against carrier and hapten. *J. Immunol.* **104**, 1558–1561.

Lorden, J. F., Kenfield, M., and Braun, J. J. (1970). Response suppression to odors paired with toxicosis. *Learn. Motiv.* **1**, 391–400.

Lovett, D., Goodchild, P., and Booth, D. A. (1968). Depression of intake of nutrient by association of its odor with effects of insulin. *Psychon. Sci.* **11**, 27–28.

Mackenzie, A. R., Pick, C. R., Sibley, P. R., and White, B. P. (1978). Suppression of rat adjuvant disease by cyclophosphamide pretreatment: Evidence for an antibody-mediated component in the pathogenesis of the disease. *Clin. Exp. Immunol.* **32**, 86–96.

Makinodan, T., Santos, G. W., and Quinn, R. P. (1970). Immunosuppressive drugs. *Pharmacol. Rev.* **22**, 198–247.

Mantzouranis, E., and Borel, Y. (1979). Different effects of cortisone on the humoral immune response to T-dependent and T-independent antigens. *Cell. Immunol.* **43**, 202–208.

Miller, N. E. (1969). Learning of visceral and glandular responses. *Science* **163**, 434–445.

Opitz, H. G., Lemke, H., and Hewlett, G. (1978). Activation of T cells by a macrophage of 2-mercaptoethanol activated serum factor is essential for induction of a primary immune response to heterologous red cells *in vitro*. *Immunol. Rev.* **40**, 53–77.

Parillo, J. E., and Fauci, A. S. (1979). Mechanisms of glucocorticoid action on immune processes. *Annu. Rev. Pharmacol. Toxicol.* **19**, 179–201.

Pavlov, I. P. (1928). "Lectures on Conditioned Reflexes." Liveright, New York.

Peck, J. H., and Ader, R. (1974). Illness-induced taste aversion under states of deprivation and satiation. *Anim. Learn. Behav.* **2**, 6–8.

Rasmussen, A. F., Jr., Spencer, E. S., and Marsh, J. T. (1959). Decrease in susceptibility of mice to passive anaphylaxis following avoidance-learning stress. *Proc. Soc. Exp. Biol. Med.* **100**, 878–879.

Razran, G. (1961). The observable unconscious and the inferable conscious in current Soviet psychophysiology: Interoceptive conditioning, semantic conditioning, and the orienting reflex. *Psychol. Rev.* **68**, 81–147.

Rigter, H. (1975). Plasma corticosterone levels as an index of $ACTH_{4-10}$-induced attenuation of amnesia. *Behav. Biol.* **15**, 207–211.

Riley, A. L., and Baril, L. L. (1976). Conditioned taste aversions: A bibliography. *Anim. Learn. Behav.* **4**, Suppl. 1–13.

Rittenberg, M. B., and Pratt, K. L. (1969). Anti-trinitrophenyl (TNP) plaque assay: Primary response of BALB/c mice to soluble and particulate immunogens. *Proc. Soc. Exp. Biol. Med.* **132**, 575.

Rogers, M. P., Reich, P., Strom, T. B., and Carpenter, C. B. (1976). Behaviorally conditioned immunosuppression: Replication of a recent study. *Psychosom. Med.* **38**, 447–452.

Rollinghoff, M., Starzinski-Powitz, A., Pfizenmaier, K., and Wagner, H. (1977). Cyclophosphamide-sensitive T lymphocytes suppress the *in vivo* generation of antigen-specific cytotoxic T lymphocytes. *J. Exp. Med.* **145**, 455–459.

Santos, G. W., and Owens, H. A., Jr. (1964). A comparison of selected cytotoxic agents on the primary agglutinin response in rats injected with sheep erythrocytes. *Bull. Johns Hopkins Hosp.* **114**, 384–401.

Siegel, S. (1975). Conditioned insulin effects. *J. Comp. Physiol. Psychol.* **89**, 189–199.

Siegel, S. (1977a). Learning and psychopharmacology. *In* "Psychopharmacology in the Practice of Medicine" (M. E. Jarvik, ed.), pp. 61–70. Appleton, New York.

Siegel, S (1977b). Morphine tolerance acquisition as an associative process. *J. Exp. Psychol.: Anim. Behav. Proc.* **3**, 1–13.

Smotherman, W. P., Hennessy, J. W., and Levine, S. (1976). Plasma corticosterone levels during recovery from LiCl produced taste aversions. *Behav. Biol.* **16**, 401–412.

Solomon, G. F., Amkraut, A. A., and Rubin, R. T. (1979). Stress and psychoimmunological response. *In* "Mind and Cancer Prognosis" (B. A. Stoll, ed.), pp. 73–84. Wiley, New York.

Supak, T., Macrides, F., and Chorover, S. (1971). The bait-shyness effect extended to olfactory discrimination. *Commun. Behav. Biol.* **5,** 321–324.

Taukulis, H. K. (1974). Odor aversions produced over long CS–US delays. *Behav. Biol.* **10,** 505–510.

Treadwell, P. E., and Rasmussen, A. F., Jr. (1961). Role of the adrenals in stress-induced resistance to anaphylactic shock. *J. Immunol.* **87,** 492–497.

Turk, J. L., and Poulter, L. W. (1972). Selective depletion of lymphoid tissue by cyclophosphamide. *Clin. Exp. Immunol.* **10,** 285–296.

Wayner, E. A., Flannery, G. R., and Singer, G. (1978). The effects of taste aversion conditioning on the primary antibody response to sheep red blood cells and *Brucella abortus* in the albino rat. *Physiol. Behav.* **21,** 995–1000.

Whitehouse, M. W., Levy, L., and Beck, F. J. (1973). Effect of cyclophosphamide on a local graft-versus-host reaction in the rat: Influence of sex, disease and different dosage regimens. *Agents Actions* **3,** 53–60.

Wilcoxon, H. C., Dragoin, W. B., and Kral, P. A. (1971). Illness-induced taste aversions in rats and quail: Relative salience of visual and gustatory cues. *Science* **171,** 826–828.

Wright, W. E., Foshee, D. P., and McCleary, G. E. (1971). Comparison of taste aversion with various delays and cyclophosphamide dose levels. *Psychon. Sci.* **22,** 55–56.

A Historical Account of Conditioned Immunobiologic Responses[1]

ROBERT ADER

INTRODUCTION

As described in the chapter "Conditioned Immunopharmacologic Responses" by Ader and Cohen, the hypothesis of a behaviorally conditioned suppression of immunologic reactivity (Ader and Cohen, 1975) evolved from an attempt to explain certain serendipitous observations. At that time, we were unaware that attempts to condition immune responses had been initiated by Russian investigators 50 years ago (Metal'nikov and Chorine, 1926). We were also unaware of some early clinical observations cited by Smith and Salinger (1933): Osler, for example, described the case of a patient who experienced an asthmatic attack when presented with an artificial rose, and Hill (1930) observed that a picture of a hay field could evoke a hay fever attack in very sensitive subjects. Additional clinical and experimental examples are provided by Dekker *et al.* (1957) and by Ottenberg *et al.* (1958).

Indeed, it turns out that there is a reasonably large literature purporting to document the conditioning of nonspecific and immunologically specific

[1] Preparation of this review was supported by a Research Scientist Award (K5-MH-06318) from the National Institute of Mental Health and by a Research Grant (NS-15071) from the National Institute of Neurological, Communicative Diseases and Stroke (USPHS).

321

defense reactions. This literature played a central role in the sometimes heated controversies that developed within the Soviet Union with respect to theoretical formulations regarding the mechanisms of antibody formation—formulations which were, perhaps, appropriate to their time and to the underdeveloped state of theory in immunology. Soviet investigators started from the position that immunologic phenomena were essentially physiological phenomena, and were therefore regulated by the central nervous system (CNS). Besides their work on conditioning, then, Soviet investigators studied the possibility of direct antigenic stimulation of the nervous system, pharmacologic and neurophysiological interventions and their effects on immune responses, and, behaviorally, the differences in immunologic reactivity between animals that were characterized as being of different nervous system "types." A review of all this material would constitute a volume in itself. Whatever the shortcomings of these early studies, the possibility that the CNS plays a role in immunogenesis or that neuroendocrine mechanisms contribute to the regulation of immune responses remains a tenable hypothesis that has not received due attention. That the mechanisms by which the nervous system may exercise some regulatory role in the modulation of immune processes remain unknown, may only reflect the commonly held view that the immune system is an autonomous defense agency and that little systematic research on the interaction between the CNS and the immune system has been undertaken.

Experiments on conditioning represent one approach to the study of CNS processes in the regulation of immune responses. The present chapter will confine itself to this literature. Being more a historical report than a synthesizing review, the material is organized chronologically. Russian studies of conditioned "immunobiologic" responses range from investigations of nonspecific cellular defense reactions (e.g., changes in leukocytes) involved, for example, in the phagocytosis of foreign material, to responses such as phagocytosis which are not specific for a given antigen but are evoked by immunogenic stimuli, and to specific immunologic responses such as the production of antibody. To impose an organization on the early work in this field, however, would imply an orderliness or systematization which does not characterize these efforts. By today's standards, most of the studies to be described constitute little more than preliminary observations. They are poorly designed and fail to provide important procedural details. Moreover, the results are inadequately portrayed and/or analyzed. I have tried not to interrupt this narration too frequently by pointing out the inadequacies of individual studies; the reader will have little difficulty in recognizing them. When possible, I have, in several instances (and for illustrative purposes), constructed tables, replotted figures, and even applied statistical analyses to reported data. Despite the methodological flaws, the preponderance of data indicates that a variety of immunobiologic responses are, indeed, subject to the influence of conditioning processes. The main purpose of this chapter, then, is to describe the historical perspective for modern studies of conditioned immunobiologic responses for the insights it might provide for future research.

CONDITIONED IMMUNOBIOLOGIC RESPONSES

Progressing directly from Pavlov's experiments on the conditioning of salivary responses, Metal'nikov and Chorine (1926) attempted to apply Pavlov's methods to the study of immunity. It had already been observed that injecting antigenic material into the peritoneum of guinea pigs elicits a typical reaction that includes a nonspecific defense response as well as the formation and secretion of antibodies. Metal'nikov and Chorine examined the possibility of creating a conditioned response by repeating such injections and associating them with external stimuli. For this initial series of observations, each guinea pig received intraperitoneal (i.p.) injections of a small dose of tapioca, *Bacillus anthracis,* or staphylococcus filtrate. These unconditioned stimuli (US) were always associated with external stimulation, the conditioned stimulus (CS)—scratching a single area of the skin, or heat applied to the same area of the skin. The CS-US pairings occurred once daily for a period of 18-25 days. After a 12-15-day rest period to allow the peritoneal exudate to return to normal, the CS was presented several times without the US.

Under normal conditions, the peritoneal exudate contains mostly mononuclear leukocytes. In response to the injection of foreign material, there was a rapid increase in polynucleated cells which decreased after 1 or 2 days. In one guinea pig it was observed that polynucleated cells comprised 90% of the peritoneal exudate 5 hr after an i.p. injection of a tapioca emulsion. This same animal received 21 CS-US pairings and 13 days later was presented only with the CS. In this instance, polynucleated cells increased from 0.6 to 62% by 5 hr after the CS presentations. Observations of two other animals yielded similar results. The reaction to the CS was weaker and more transient than the unconditioned response to the i.p. injections of foreign material, but it was clearly demonstrable.

Metal'nikov and Chorine then asked if conditioned stimuli could be used to combat infection. Two guinea pigs received 12 daily CS-US pairings involving scratching the skin and the i.p. injection of a staphylococcus filtrate. Ten days later, the CS was presented alone several times. On the next day, these two experimental animals, and an additional guinea pig that had not experienced the CS-US pairings, were injected i.p. with a lethal dose of a culture of *Vibrio cholera.* The control animal died; the two experimental animals survived. In two other experiments, an additional control was introduced. The same protocol was followed except that one of the experimental guinea pigs was not reexposed to the CS just before being injected with the *Vibrio* culture. In this instance, only the experimental animal that was reexposed to the CS survived or survived longer than the experimental animal that did not receive the CS or the animal that had not experienced the prior CS-US pairings.

In a subsequent study (Metal'nikov and Chorine, 1928), antibody titer was measured in rabbits. In one population of three animals, the application of heat to an ear or scratching of a flank was followed by an i.p. injection of 2 cc of an emulsion of *Vibrio cholera.* Daily CS-US pairings occurred for 12-15 days. Three weeks later (when antibody titers were still relatively high), two animals (rabbits 92 and 93) were exposed to the CS alone three times in 24 hr. Antibody titers rose in these animals, reaching a maximum in 5–6 days. Rabbit 96 was not reexposed to the CS and showed no change in titer. Two months later, the CS was presented again to rabbits 93 and 96 while No. 92 remained as the control. Agglutinating titers rose in animals 93 and 96 and showed no change in No. 92. Although the actual data reported indicate that the change in titer in those animals that were reexposed to the CS was quite small in every instance, the repeated determinations of antibody titer in those instances when the CS was not presented never exceeded the pre-CS level. Somewhat larger increases in antibody titers were observed when two additional rabbits were subjected to 23 CS–US pairings of the sound of a trumpet followed by the intravenous administration of *V. cholera* and tested 18 days later following the sound of the trumpet, alone. It was on the basis of such data that Metal'nikov and Chorine concluded that conditioned responses can play an important role in immunity, confirming their notion that the central nervous system is involved in immune reactions.[2]

Because of the novelty and importance of this phenomenon, several experiments were undertaken to confirm these initial observations. Vygodchikov and Barykini (1927), for example, applied a heated plate to the stomach of guinea pigs. This was followed immediately by the i.p. injection of 2 cc of a bouillon solution. Experimental animals received 21 such CS–US trials, a 12-day rest period, and were then reexposed to the CS alone; control animals received only the i.p. injections of bouillon and were tested with another injection of bouillon. Peritoneal exudate was sampled 0.5, 2, 5, and 24 hr after the test stimulation. Although 41 guinea pigs were used in this study, data are provided for only one experimental and one control animal. It is reported, however, that the results were the same in all animals: An increase in polynucleated cells in conditioned animals reexposed to the CS as well as in animals injected with the bouillon solution.

A study by Nicolau and Antinescu-Dimitriu (1929a) was designed to replicate the study reported by Metal-nikov and Chorine (1928). These investigators used 15 rabbits: 5 received a heat stimulus, 5 received a scratching stimulus, and 5 received an auditory stimulus for a period of 2 min, followed by an i.p. injection of a cholera culture. The CS–US pairings were presented daily for 3 weeks and were followed by a 3-week rest period. Hemagglutinating antibody titers were then determined before and for several days after the presentation of the CS to 4 of the 5 animals in each subgroup; one animal in each subgroup remained unmanipulated. Experimental animals subjected to the thermal and tactual stimulation showed an elevation in antibody titer rela-

---

[2] Luk'ianenko (1961) refers to (but does not reference) more than 15 papers published by Metal'nikov and his colleagues demonstrating the effects of conditioning on cellular reactions and the regulation of agglutinins and hemolysins. I have been informed by Dr. N. Herbert Spector that most of this material can be found in Metal'nikov's book (1934).

tive to either their pre-CS baseline or to the level shown by the two control animals. No change was observed in the animals that had experienced the auditory stimulation. The magnitude of the effect in the other two groups, however, provided confirmation of the results obtained by Metal'nikov and Chorine.

A second study (Nicolau and Antinescu-Dimitriu, 1929b) was designed to replicate the increase in leukocytes that Metal'nikov and Chorine had recorded in response to conditioned stimuli. Five guinea pigs received CS–US pairings consisting of a heat stimulus followed by an i.p. injection of a tapioca emulsion and 5 other animals received a scratch stimulus followed by an i.p. injection of some other antigenic stimulus. The CS–US pairings occurred daily for a period of 3 weeks and were followed by a 3-week rest period. Four of 5 animals in each group were then presented with the CS alone, and samples of peritoneal exudate were examined before the CS was presented and 3–6 and 24 hr later. In addition, peritoneal exudate was examined from (an unspecified number of) "normal" guinea pigs that had been injected with the *same* antigenic substances. As expected, there was an increase in the percentage of polynucleated cells. However, almost identical results were found in the controls. It was concluded, therefore, that these modifications in the peritoneal exudate were localized and irritative in nature and probably resulted from the repeated abdominal punctures rather than from the CS presentation. If, however, we infer from the authors' description that the "normal" population received the same number and distribution of i.p. injections associated with the administration of the emulsions that were experienced by the experimental animals, it would be reasonable to assume—and would be consistent with the observations of Pavlov (1928) and others (Dolin *et al.*, 1960; Hutton *et al.*, 1970; Siegel, 1975)—that the abdominal punctures constituted a conditioned stimulus for the "normal" population.

This same issue was addressed by Podkopaeff and Saatchian (1929). Unable to understand how or where the central nervous system could be influenced by the coincidental occurrence of external stimulation and the injection of foreign material, these authors also attempted to replicate the observations of Metal'nikov and Chorine. Although their methods were basically the same, the studies were carried out " . . . with all the precautions and controls which are used in the work with conditioned reflexes." Observations on 14 rabbits were always conducted " . . . in the same room, by the same persons and at the same time of day." The CS–US pairings (20-sec bell plus a killed staphylococcus culture) occurred daily for 15–18 days and were followed by a 10-day rest period. Peritoneal fluid was examined before conditioning (to establish the unconditioned cellular response as well as the normal content of the exudate) and at the end of the rest period (at which time the peritoneal fluid was normal). On the subsequent test day, each animal received 5 CS presentations and the cellular elements of the peritoneal fluid were counted after 1.5, 3, 24, 48, and 72 hr. The authors provide data from only a single conditioned animal, but claim to have confirmed the data reported by Metal'nikov and Chorine. They considered, however, that a significant factor might have been the simple mechanical irritation of the skin necessitated by the injection of the staphylococcus culture. No data are reported in this regard, but the authors comment that special control experiments indicated that mechanical irritation of the abdominal cavity caused by needle puncture produces changes in the cellular constituents of peritoneal fluid which are different from those induced by foreign substances.

Although the number of animals was, again, small, an additional control condition was introduced by Polettini (1929). Conditioned rabbits ($N = 4$) experienced 11 trials on which an auditory stimulus was followed by an injection of saline or killed typhus bacilli on alternate days. Nonconditioned animals ($N = 2$) received only the immunogenic stimulation. After a 30-day interval, serum agglutinins to typhus bacillus were titrated. Two days later, 2 of the conditioned rabbits and the 2 nonconditioned rabbits were subjected to the auditory stimulus alone, while the remaining 2 conditioned animals received no stimulation. Repeated measurement of agglutinin titers showed a 2–3-fold elevation over the pre-test level in the two conditioned animals that were reexposed to the CS but no change in titer in either of the other groups.

Zeitlenok (1930) examined the effects of conditioning on susceptibility to anaphylactic shock. Experimental piglets were scratched on the side and injected subcutaneously with .01–.05 ml of normal horse serum on 10 successive days. Control animals received only the horse serum. Six days later, the conditioned animals were reexposed to the CS. Control animals were divided into subgroups: one received another injection of horse serum, one was subjected to the scratching stimulation, and one subgroup remained unstimulated. Five hr later, all animals were injected subdurally with a large dose of horse serum. The control animals preinjected with serum exhibited only a mild anaphylaxis and all survived the test stimulation. Conditioned animals reexposed to the CS prior to the test stimulus also showed only a mild anaphylactic reaction which 7 of 9 animals survived. Control animals that received either no stimulation or only the scratching stimulus showed a severe shock reaction and 5 of the 9 died.

Another attempt to verify the observations of Metal'nikov and Chorine was undertaken by Ostravskaya (1930). Ostravskaya's report, like so much of the literature of this time, lacks adequate detail concerning many of the procedures. It is, nonetheless, a significant paper because of the inclusion of control conditions conspicuously absent in the experiments conducted by Metal'nikov and Chorine, and because a sufficiently large number of animals were tested to permit a reconstruction of the groups and a statistical analysis of the data. This information is given in Table 1.

In an initial population of 43 guinea pigs, a conditioned stimulus, presented for 3–5 min, was followed by an i.p. injection of antigen once daily for 3 weeks. After a rest period of 10–15 days, the CS was presented alone. Peri-

TABLE 1

Conditioned Increase in Polynucleated Cells in the Peritoneal Exudate of Guinea Pigs[a]

Treatment	N	Number of trials	Rest period	Test stimulation	Results (Positive reactions)		
					Number	%	Stat.
Heat, scratching, or electrical stimulation *plus* antigen	43	21	10–15 days	Heat, scratching, or electrical stimulation	29	67.4	
Heat, scratching, or electrical stimulation, only	36	Unspecified	Unspecified	Heat, scratching, or electrical stimulation	8		$X^2 = 15.8$ $p < 0.01$
Antigen only	8	15	Unspecified	Heat	2	22.7	

[a] Data derived from Ostravskaya (1930).

toneal exudate was examined at different times before and after the administration of antigen as well as before and after the presentation of the CS on the test day. A majority of these animals (67%) showed a conditioned response (i.e., an increase in the percentage of polynucleated cells in the peritoneal exudate).

Ostravskaya then asked if the heat stimulation or the scratching of the skin or the electrical stimulation of an ear which were used as conditioned stimuli were, in fact, "neutral" stimuli. To answer this question, 36 nonimmunized guinea pigs were subjected to these stimuli alone, and an additional 8 animals received repeated injections of antigen without experiencing any of these stimuli. As can be seen in Table 1, 8 of the 36 nonimmunized animals gave a positive response to the external stimuli, and 2 of the 8 animals that were repeatedly injected with antigen responded to the heat stimulus. As a group, then, 23% of these "control" animals showed a change in leukocytes in response to the "neutral" stimulus. The difference between the number of "conditioned" and "nonconditioned" animals that showed a cellular response to external stimulation, however, was highly significant.

In a second study with rabbits (Ostravskaya, 1930), immunization with killed typhoid vaccine was associated with an auditory or heat stimulus on 21 daily trials. When antibody titers returned to normal, the CS was applied without injection of antigen. Eleven of 12 animals showed an elevation in antibody titer in response to the CS. This experiment, too, involved "nonconditioned" controls previously immunized with typhoid vaccine. Whether these animals were subjected to the external stimuli that served as the CS for the conditioned group is not clear, but 9 of the 11 rabbits showed an elevation in antibody titer which was described as being less "stable" than that seen in conditioned animals. The data from only 3 conditioned and 2 nonconditioned animals are presented, but if these are representative, it does appear that the magnitude and duration of the response in conditioned animals is greater than that in the controls.

Other studies, ranging from fortuitous observations (Kanarevskaya, 1945) to the measurement of cellular and humoral responses (Diacono, 1933; Smith and Salinger, 1933), provide further confirmation of the potential impact of conditioning on the modulation of immunologic reactivity. Not all of these early studies, however, yielded positive conditioning effects (Friedberger and Gurwitz, 1931; Kopeloff et al., 1933, 1935).

In the study by Kopeloff et al. (1935), for example, the CS consisted of electrical stimulation applied to a shaved ear in conjunction with an auditory stimulus presented for 30 sec. The US was an intravenous injection of pneumococcus Type III vaccine. Eight rabbits received one CS–US trial per day for 16 days; one control animal received only irregular presentations of the vaccine. After a 34-day interval, the CS was presented in conjunction with an injection of saline. Blood samples obtained before and after the test stimulation showed no change in immunologic reactivity in the conditioned animals.

With minor variations in procedure, a second experiment also failed to elicit conditioned alterations in response.

These early studies on the application of conditioning techniques to the study of immunobiologic responses stimulated a great deal of interest and attention, at least within the Soviet Union. The implications and, indeed, the underlying premise was quite consistent with the predominant view that all physiological processes were regulated by the central nervous system. Nevertheless, the data on conditioning were viewed with appropriate skepticism, especially since there were no known mechanisms that might account for such phenomena. According to reviews prepared by Zdrodovskii (1951, 1953), there were considerable data to implicate the CNS in the regulation of immunogenesis. Fluctuations in immunologic activity were inferred to be a function of CNS processes as evidenced, for example, by changes in reactivity as a function of age, that is, the capacity to produce antibody after immunization was a function of maturation within the CNS. Other indirect evidence was based on observations of climatic effects, the relative inertia seen in hibernating animals, and differences in reactivity in animals characterized as being of different nervous system "types."[3] More direct evidence for neural regulation of immunologic reactivity was indicated by studies on the depression and potentiation of immune responses effected by pharmacologically induced suppression or activation of the central or autonomic nervous system.

With respect to the conditioning of immune responses, Zdrodovskii was more cautious. There appeared to be little question or contradiction with regard to the conditioning of leukocytic responses, these being a stereotyped defense mechanism of the organism. But, insofar as the production of antibodies was concerned, the available data were not considered sufficient to draw any definitive conclusions. The possibility was not denied, but was considered questionable or, at least, difficult to resolve since the production of antibody was a new response to the presence of each new antigenic stimulus. Studies on conditioning, however, implied to Soviet investigators that antigenic stimulation was transmitted via neural pathways to the brain and that the production of antibody was the direct result of central nervous system activity. Zhukov-Verezhnikov (1952), for example, took the findings of Metal'nikov, Pododkopaeff, Vygodchikov, and others as evidence that immune responses (including the production of specific antibodies) were subject to conditioning influences and that it was only the CNS that could initiate and control selective mechanisms of specific immunity. Reading further, it may be assumed (with some mixture of justification and generosity) that Zhukov-Verezhnikov was alluding to the regulatory function of CNS processes which

[3] Evidently, there is considerable literature on the relationship between behavior (Pavlovian typology) and immunologic reactivity which is of relevance but beyond the scope of this review. Although I have made no systematic search, the interested reader may wish to consult the following references: Amiantova (1961), Evseev (1957), Kriachko and Guonbis (1958), Krylov and Malinovskii (1961), and Pletsityi (1957b).

can, via conditioning, facilitate the action of mechanisms selectively acting in the adaptive interests of the organism. That is, conditioning plays a role in initiating those CNS processes responsible for the regulation of defense mechanisms—including immune responses. Zdrodovskii (1953) makes the point (largely ignored in the controversy that later developed) that the failure to document the neural transmission of antigenic stimuli does not preclude a CNS involvement or effects of conditioning in immunogenesis. Further, he speculates on how the CNS and the immune system may complement each other and suggests that, if conditioning is applicable to the production of the antibody, it would most likely be evident in the case of a secondary rather than a primary response.

Dolin and Krylov (1952) attribute the 20-year hiatus in experimentation in this area to acceptance of the attitude expressed by Zdrodovskii and others (e.g., Zil'ber, 1958; unreferenced) that the data obtained by Metal'nikov and the other early investigators could not be confirmed authoritatively. Indeed, the phenomenon was supposedly refuted by investigators who tried to repeat the conditioning experiments. Dolin and Krylov do cite some of the negative data which had been published up to that time and, in a rather cavalier fashion, discount the meaningfulness of the results, considering the manner in which the experiments were conducted. The study by Kopeloff et al. (1935), for example, was rejected on procedural grounds which, in fact, would also apply to studies that obtained positive results. The study by Friedberger and Gurwitz (1931) was discounted because the authors found no differences based on statistics (group means), and ignored the evident conditioning that occurred in individual animals. While one can not cite such data (e.g., Friedberger and Gurwitz, 1931) as supporting evidence, they do not, as Dolin and Krylov argue, refute the possibility of conditioning within the immune system.

Dolin and Krylov also acknowledge the shortcomings of many of the early studies. They refer specifically to procedural imprecision, the variety of conditioned stimuli, and the interaction among stimuli intended to be and those accidently associated with the immune response, the "neutrality" of conditioned stimuli, and the temporal relationship between a brief CS and the effects and duration of the US. Based on their prior observations of the effects of conditioning on other complex physiological states, Dolin and Krylov undertook a series of experiments on the conditioning of immune responses which, for all the additional sophistication introduced (particularly in their later studies), still suffered from the lack of some controls.

In their first experiment, Dolin and Krylov (1952) used confinement in a special box as the CS. Vaccine of a 24-hr culture of Gärtner's paratyphoid (B. enteritis Gärtneri) in gradually increasing doses was used as the US. To ensure coincidence between the CS and US, the US was introduced, first, after 30 min, then in gradual steps, after 3 hr of exposure to the CS where the animal remained for 3 hr after treatment with the vaccine. Experimental rabbits

($N = 5$) were subjected to 12 CS–US trials in a period of a month. There were 5 controls, but their treatment protocol was not specified and the data they provided were not presented. After a 1-month rest period, the experimental animals were reexposed to the CS and injected with saline rather than the vaccine. Based on blood samples obtained before and after each conditioning and test session, there was a consistent elevation in agglutinin titer in response to the saline injected under the environmental circumstances that defined the CS. In some cases, the conditioned elevation in titer was higher than the unconditioned response to the last injection of vaccine. These data were corroborated by Doroshkevich (1954) in a similar study in which rabbits were injected with a vaccine of paratyphoid B bacteria after each of 20 intranasal administrations of different concentrations of saline (Figure 1).

In previous studies conducted by Dolin, it had been noted that when, for example, a dog was repeatedly injected with saline and then given milk to drink under precisely the same conditions every day, the eventual substitution of an injection of morphine in a dose that is toxic to unstimulated animals did not have toxic effects in animals previously conditioned with the saline. In other experiments, pilocarpine was repeatedly administered and elicited salivation. When atropine, which has the opposite effect on salivation, was subsequently administered, it, too, caused a salivary response. This phenomenon is referred to in terms of the formation of a "dynamic cortical stereotype." This is a highly reliable and stereotyped response to the relationship among stimuli and is evidently capable of modifying the organism's response to a variety of pharmacologic and toxic agents. These observations prompted Dolin and Krylov (1952) to examine the effects of such a conditioned dynamic stereotype

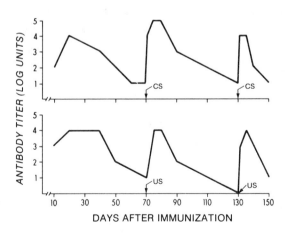

Figure 1. Conditioned elevation in antibody titer in rabbits. After 20 CS–US pairings (intranasal administration of saline followed by injection of paratyphoid B bacteria), animals were given a rest period and then reexposed to either the CS (top panel) or the US (lower panel), alone. Data redrawn from Doroshkevich (1954).

on the response to immunogenic stimulation. In their second study, rabbits were repeatedly and systematically injected with saline. When the Gärtner paratyphoid vaccine was eventually substituted for saline, conditioned animals failed to show an immune response within the following 7 days. Controls that were not previously treated with saline showed a rise in agglutinin titer to the bacterial antigen within 3–4 days.

Analogous results were obtained in a final study in which rabbits were injected subcutaneously with a mixture of horse, sheep, and guinea pig serum (1 cc of each). Four such injections were given at 5–6-day intervals and precipitin titers were measured after each session. After a final 5-day interval, only one of the previously used sera was injected (1 cc of serum and 2 cc of saline). Irrespective of which single serum was injected, the response evoked was immunologically identical to the response elicited when the 3-serum mixture was administered. The possible cross reactivity of these different sera, however, was not discussed.

A particularly interesting study was conducted by Zeitlenok and Bychkova (1954) in that control groups similar to those used by Ader and Cohen (1975) were introduced. Thirty albino rats were subjected to a 5-min tactile stimulus and either simultaneously or subsequently injected intraperitoneally with influenza Type A virus. The CS–US pairing occurred daily for 10 days. Ten control (NC) animals received only the injections of virus material. After 1–1.5 months, antibody titers had decreased and samples obtained over 2–3 consecutive days were assayed to establish a stable baseline. Of the 30 conditioned animals, 24 were then reexposed to the tactile stimulation or the CS plus an i.p. injection of saline (Group CS). Six of the conditioned animals remained unstimulated (Group CS_0). Of the previously nonconditioned animals, 6 animals were subjected to the tactile stimulation (Group NC) and 4 animals were again injected with virus (Group US). Daily blood samples were taken from all animals over the next 10–12 days. When antibody titers had again stabilized at a sufficiently low level, the test procedure was repeated for a second and, then, a third time.

Control animals reinjected with influenza virus showed the expected increase in antibody titer. Nonconditioned animals exposed to the tactile stimulation and conditioned animals that were not reexposed to the CS showed no change in antibody titer. However, 17 of the 24 animals in Group CS (the previously conditioned animals that were reexposed to the CS) displayed an increase in titer. The change was less consistent, less pronounced, and developed more slowly than it did in Group US, but the change in Group CS was statistically significant relative to the controls (Groups CS_0 and NC; $X^2 = 16.1, p < .01$). Based on the tabulated data, it was possible to determine the magnitude of the response by arbitrarily selecting the maximal titer in the final 3 samples and comparing it to the titer determined 2–3 days before the test stimulation. These data are shown in Figure 2.

Like Dolin and Krylov, Zeitlenok and Bychkova (1954) also sought to take

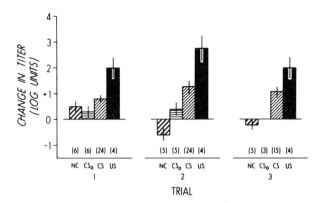

Figure 2. Maximal (mean ± s.e.) change in antibody titers in nonconditioned animals exposed to the CS (NC) or to virus (US), and in conditioned animals that remained unstimulated (CS_0) or were reexposed to the CS (CS). Numbers in parentheses indicate the number of animals available for samples. Data derived from Zeitlenok and Bychkova (1954).

advantage of a conditioned dynamic stereotype in modifying an immunologic response. In their experiment, 20 rats received daily subcutaneous injections of pilocarpine (3–4 mg/kg) followed immediately by i.p. injections of influenza Type A virus for a period of 15 days. Twenty control animals received only injections of virus. Antibody levels were determined as in their previous experiments and when titers had decreased, the test session was introduced. Conditioned animals were reexposed to the CS (pilocarpine) while controls were divided into groups that received pilocarpine, or virus, or no stimulation. Relative to controls, conditioned animals reexposed to the CS showed an increase in the titer of antiinfluenza antibodies. Comparable results were obtained in a replication conducted with rabbits.

Several interesting studies (see Vygodchikov, 1955; Zdrodovskii, 1953) suggested that at least some immune responses could be prevented or attenuated by depression of the CNS (e.g., by narcosis) and, conversely, CNS activation could facilitate or magnify immunologic responses, particularly anamnestic responses. These studies are beyond the scope of this review. A related study on conditioning, however, was conducted by Bereznykh (1955). In a preliminary experiment it was noted that when acetylcholine chloride was injected subcutaneously throughout the course of immunization, the subsequent administration of acetylcholine caused an elevation in antibody titer (to an unspecified antigen). Since it was evidently possible, under some experimental conditions, to evoke an immune response in previously immunized animals by acetylcholine in animals that had not previously been treated with acetylcholine (Klimentova and Uchitel', 1950), the additional question of the neutrality of the CS must be addressed.

In another study, Bereznykh (1955) treated rabbits with increasing doses of a Flexner dysentery vaccine. Seven trials were administered at 3-day intervals.

Four animals received subcutaneous injections of acetylcholine chloride 10 min before and 24 hr after each presentation of the US; 4 additional animals were injected with saline on the same schedule. When antibody titers fell to the original (baseline) level, the effects of the two conditioned stimuli were examined. Of the 4 animals treated with acetylcholine chloride, 2 were injected with saline and 2 were injected with acetylcholine. Similarly, 2 of the animals originally treated with saline were injected with saline and 2 were injected with acetylcholine. Although the actual data are not presented, it is reported that agglutinin titers rose sharply in rabbits that were conditioned with acetylcholine and tested with acetylcholine and in animals conditioned with saline and tested with saline. Titers remained low, however, in animals for which the CS had been switched. Evidently, there was evidence of a conditioned response independent of any nonspecific stimulatory effects of acetylcholine chloride, per se.

The renewed interest in experimentation on conditioned immunobiologic responses prompted Zdrodovskii (1956) to devote a section of an address on the then current status of theoretical immunology in the Soviet Union to the studies of conditioning. According to Zdrodovskii's analysis, only a relatively few studies had yielded positive results; most of the studies reporting positive results lacked appropriate controls, and several studies yielded negative results, including those conducted by Klimentova and by Shumakova (in Zdrodovskii's laboratory). Interestingly, some of these same "negative" studies are cited by other writers (e.g., Vygodchikov, 1955) as illustrating positive effects, some are subject to the same methodological criticisms that apply to some of the positive results, and some open up new issues.

Klimentova (1955) studied rabbits that had previously been repeatedly immunized with typhoid vaccine (or, in another experiment, with diptheria toxoid). For these animals, small doses of typhoid vaccine were used as the unconditioned stimuli and diptheria anatoxin was used as the CS. Twelve CS–US trials were administered over a 33-day period and, after a 30-day interval, the CS was presented alone. There was essentially no change in antibody titer in the experimental animals whereas animals that received only the injection of typhoid vaccine showed an elevation in titer in response to another injection of the vaccine. These data, which purportedly confirmed previous observations, were taken as evidence of the inability to condition a change in antibody titer.

In one of the published studies by Shumakova (1958), rabbits were placed into a box containing camphor vapor for 1 hr, then removed and injected 4 times (0.05 ml/injection) with diptheria toxoid, and then returned to the experimental box for an additional 5 hr. Control animals received only the antigenic stimulation. Twelve such treatments were administered over 33 days and, after a 30-day interval, conditioned and nonconditioned animals were reexposed to the CS. Both groups showed an increase in antibody titer. A second experiment was conducted with guinea pigs and yielded similar results.

As Shumakova points out, the results indicate that the CS was *not* neutral with respect to its effects on immunologic reactivity under these experimental conditions. How the complex of stimuli which constituted the CS could have altered the physiologic status of the animals to influence the production of antibody in both experimental and control animals, is not known. Zdrodovskii (1958) postulates that it is the hypothalamic–pituitary–adrenal system weakly controlled by the cerebral cortex that serves some regulatory function in the formation of antibodies. How the altered physiological state of the animal might have been further modified by the repeated exposure to the CS in the conditioned group, and how the process of extinction might have differentially affected the response to the CS in conditioned and nonconditioned animals are other interesting questions that were not addressed. Be that as it may, if the CS, for whatever reason, has an effect on the response in question and if appropriate control conditions are not included, the study can not necessarily be interpreted as meaningful with respect to the phenomenon of conditioning. There is, too, the further question of what may actually constitute the CS for nonconditioned animals (Krylov, 1958). That is, the elevation in antibody titer seen in nonconditioned animals (with or without exposure to the stimulation that defines the CS for conditioned animals) may be elicited by the environmental cues (room, experimenter, preparation, injection, etc.) that actually constitute a part of the complex of stimuli that define the CS for both conditioned and nonconditioned subjects. Thus, while the data of Shumakova, for example, may not provide any unequivocal evidence of conditioning effects, they clearly do not contradict the possibility of a conditioned immune response.

Other negative data are presumably to be derived from the studies of Rihá (1955) and Kuskova (1955). Rihá was able to confirm the conditioning of a leukocytic reaction, but failed to observe a conditioned elevation in antibody titer in response to a CS that had been repeatedly associated with the introduction of *Salmonella paratyphus* B vaccine which eventually and persistently led to a *suppression* of antibody during the course of the conditioning trials. Kuskova (1955) immunized rabbits intravenously with a bacterial antigen on 10 trials given at 4-day intervals. Conditioned rabbits were subjected to a variety of stimuli (physical restraint, tying different limbs, and/or covering all or part of the head) for periods which progressed from 30 min to 6 hr. The US was introduced after 30 min, which was subsequently extended to 3 hr, after CS stimulation began. One month later, conditioned animals were reexposed to the CS and injected with saline; control animals that previously received only vaccine were tested with vaccine or with saline, but were not exposed to the stimuli that comprised the CS for the conditioned group. As expected, control animals injected with saline showed no change and controls injected with vaccine showed an increase in antibody titer. Of the 12 conditioned rabbits, 3 showed no change in antibody titer while 9 showed a 2–4-fold *decrease*. Although the control groups demanded by Zdrodovskii for an unequivocal documentation of conditioning are not present in these data, he nevertheless interprets them as a refutation of the conditioning phenomena. Furthermore, the data prompt one to ask what might actually have been the subject of conditioning in this study.

This question of a conditioned suppression of an antibody response within the context of such experimental circumstances was raised by Krylov (1956) in a paper prepared as a rejoinder to the presentations of Zdrodovskii, Klimentova, and Shumakova. Krylov reviews, first, a study from Zdrodovskii's laboratory in which the daily administration of diptheria toxoid was paired with the simultaneous placement of monkeys into a dark chamber for 2 hr, during which time the concentration of CO_2 reached 6%. After the session, the monkeys were given a piece of sugar. Twenty-five such trials were administered. When subsequently placed into the experimental chamber, conditioned animals did not show an increase, but a decrease in antibody titer. Like Kuskova (1955), only the failure to induce a conditioned *elevation* in antibody was discussed; there was no discussion or explanation of the decreased response. Krylov's analysis of the situation was that it illustrates the inhibitory effects of antigenic overstimulation. This phenomenon was described by Zdrodovskii, himself, as well as others (Vygodchikov, 1955), and, as a matter of fact, would seem to characterize the data reported by Rihá (1955). Further, Krylov points out that previous data on dogs indicate the difficulty of establishing conditioning effects in a dark chamber. Krylov argues that these data actually provide confirmation and extension of the effects of conditioning by demonstrating the capacity to condition inhibition of a response and by doing so in a different species and with a different antigenic stimulus. The negative experiments on rabbits are criticized on the grounds of the supramaximal kind of stimulation used as the CS and, in the case of the use of diptherial toxoid as a CS with typhoid vaccine as the US (Klimentova, 1955), Krylov argues that the CS was not neutral after having been repeatedly presented. Moreover, it would be expected that in a population of animals previously immunized with the typhoid vaccine, the experimental reintroduction of small doses of that same vaccine would, initially, have elicited an elevation in antibody titer but, after being paired repeatedly with the stronger diptheria anatoxin, a new dynamic stereotype would have developed: a decrease in the titer to the typhoid and an increased response to the anatoxin. Editorially speaking, the lack of unequivocal data on these points leaves one with the impression that Krylov had prepared a highly speculative and overzealous response to Zdrodovskii's overstated and ill-conceived critique of the possibility of conditioned immunobiologic effects.

A more reasoned analysis of the controversy that had obviously grown up around the issue of the extent of central nervous system involvement in immune processes, in general, and the issue of conditioning, in particular, was provided by Vygodchikov (1955). While recognizing the rapid advances that were being made in immunology, Vygodchikov bemoaned the reductionistic approach that failed to consider the total organism within which immunologic processes were taking place. Early studies involved a simple analogy of immunologic phenomena to a physiologic phenomena and generated several interesting demonstrations for which there were no readily available explanations. These studies were based on the premise that, whatever the outcome, immune processes were subject to general physiological laws and, as a result, were regulated by the central nervous system. There followed a period during which a great deal was being learned about immunology, but few investigators were studying infectious and immunologic processes from a physiological point of view. One problem, of course, was that the physiological approach required that immunologists reject the familiar conceptualization of the autonomy of the immune system.[4] For the most part, immunology ignored the host within which defense reactions occurred. This was not idiosyncratic to Soviet investigators—nor is it an overstatement of the situation that exists in 1981.

There were, by 1955, abundant data indicating that the nervous system regulates the activity of various responses directed toward the neutralization, destruction, and elimination of the toxic effects of foreign substances. With respect to resistance to disease, then, the primary role of the CNS is in regulating normal physiological activity aimed at the restoration of homeostasis. Therefore, Vygodchikov argued, greater attention should be directed to the role of these physiological mechanisms in the regulation of those processes which influence immune responses and protect the organism from disease.

Like most authors, Vygodchikov considered the effects of conditioning on cellular reactions to have been conclusively demonstrated. Similarly, there was evidence that another defense mechanism, phagocytosis, was influenced by the CNS (probably the autonomic nervous system) and that phagocytosis, too, was subject to modification by conditioning. Vygodchikov cites a paper by Golovkova (1947) who reported the conditioning of a 23% increase in phagocytosis. He was evidently not yet aware of a paper by Pel'ts (1955) which had just appeared. Pel'ts reported that an electric current applied to the skin of dogs or rabbits influenced the phagocytic activity of leukocytes and the development of antibodies. He therefore proceeded to examine the conditioning of phagocytosis.

Pel'ts' experiments were conducted on dogs treated at the same time of day and under constant environmental circumstances. The CS was a bell, the orienting response to which was extinguished before initiating conditioning trials. The US consisted of either strong or weak electric shock applied to the hind legs of the animal for 10 or 1 min, respectively. Phagocytic activity was measured before stimulation, after the CS, and after the US. Initially, the CS presented alone did not affect phagocytic activity. Strong electric shock

---

[4] Unfortunately, this meant, for some, (the unnecessary) acceptance of the theory that the central nervous system was primarily responsible for the initiation of antibody production. There was no middle ground—and no influential advocate of a constructive rapprochement of these seemingly incompatible views.

caused a lowering of phagocytic activity and, after 98, 102, and 120 CS–US trials in the three dogs tested, the CS, alone, also resulted in a decrease in phagocytosis. Electric shock of relatively low intensity and/or of short duration yielded a more complicated biphasic response pattern. Initially, low level electric shock, alone, increased phagocytosis, but an elevation occurred in response to repeated stimulation. The same pattern apparently occurred in response to successive CS–US trials, and this pattern, slightly delayed, also occurred in response to the CS. Although it is difficult to reconstruct the procedural details, Figure 3 represents an attempt to describe the temporal changes effected by conditioning and a series of unreinforced presentations of the CS (extinction) based on the tabled data provided by Pel'ts. The pattern of response to the US and to the CS may be similar, in principle to the stress-induced modulation of immunologic reactivity described by Monjan and Collector (1976).

Conditioned changes in phagocytosis had also been observed by Strutsov-skaya (1953) who studied children with scarlet fever. Fourteen children, 5–8 years old, were studied during recovery from the disease (when treatment had been discontinued). Each child was injected intramuscularly with 3 cc of γ-globulin. A phagocytic index was determined before and 3 hr after injections administered on 4 consecutive days. On Day 5, the children were injected with saline. In contrast to controls who received daily injections of saline and showed no change in the phagocytic index, the γ-globulin injections caused an increase in phagocytosis over the course of 4 conditioning trials and an increase in the phagocytic index when the children were only injected with saline.

In discussing the effects of conditioning on antibody responses, Vygod-chikov (1955) refers (without specific citation) to investigators who believed

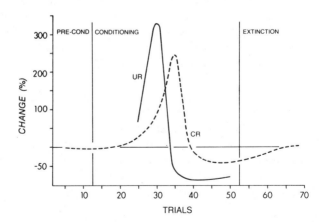

Figure 3. Kinetics of the unconditioned (UR) and conditioned (CR) phagocytic response to repeated electric shock stimulation in dogs. Values are expressed as the percentage change from the prestimulus level. Data derived from Pel'ts (1955).

that a primary formation of specific antibodies could be elicited by reflex, (i.e., without contact with an antigen) an hypothesis which he rejects. This does not, of course, negate the potential role of the CNS in the regulation of processes responsible for the initiation and/or the modulation of immunologic defense mechanisms. Vygodchikov cites some of the conflicting reports, but also notes the methodological problems involved and the critical nature of the conditioned and unconditioned stimuli that have been used. He also cites an unreferenced study from his own laboratory (Vygodchikov and Voskresenskii) which "succeeded in showing that conditioned reflex formations causing an increased production of antitoxin in the blood of preliminarily immunized rabbits requires a prolonged influence by the unconditioned stimulus in multiple combinations with the conditioned stimulus. This is achieved by immunization of animals with adsorbed antitoxins in which the specific antigen has the role of unconditioned stimulus and the nonspecific components of the adsorbed antitoxins constitute the conditioned stimulus. Under these conditions (these investigators) observed a regular and very clear rise in the production of antitoxins by conditioning."

There followed in 1957, another series of more or less vitriolic discussions of the opposing views regarding the role of the CNS in immune processes (Gordienko, 1957; Pletsityi, 1957a). The following paraphrases Vygodchikov's (1957) summary of these meetings and statements: The most detailed discussions centered around the nervous system in immunity to infectious disease and with hypotheses about mechanisms of immune processes. Considerable data have been amassed to justify the conclusion that the nervous system plays an important role in immunologic phenomena and attention can now be directed to defining the degree to which and the concrete form in which the central nervous system influences immune responses. It is on these issues that differences of opinion have developed, particularly with respect to the effects of conditioning. In this regard, it can be said that the influence of conditioning in the mechanisms of natural immunity (e.g., cellular responses, phagocytosis, and the like) had been unequivocally demonstrated. The question of a conditioned elicitation of antibody production, however, has not been resolved.

These same issues receive prominent attention in Zil'ber's (1958) then current book on the *Foundations of Immunology*. As summarized in a review of this volume by Vasil'yev (1959), the central questions were : (*a*) Is antigenic stimulation transmitted by nerve fibers, and (*b*) Can antibody production be stimulated by conditioned reflex? Despite Zil'ber's general position that the CNS is primarily responsible for the control of all the body's defense mechanisms, he accepts only the conditioned reproduction of nonspecific cellular responses. He categorically rejects the data and the assertions of neural transmission of antigenic stimulation and, therefore, the possibility of the conditioned stimulation of antibody formation. Vygodchikov (1957) does not accept the hypothesis of a *de novo* conditioned stimulation of antibody production, but does not make this issue a central feature of his argument. He does point out the differences between the results obtained in different laboratories which seems to depend upon the choice and adequacy of CS and US and the temporal relationship between the CS and US. Vygodchikov does not (by implication) equate the effects or importance of conditioning in the modulation of immunologic reactivity with the hypothesis of the reflex production of antibody. Further, while recognizing the importance of antibody formation, he does not consider it appropriate to concentrate solely on this one feature of immunity in assessing the role of CNS processes. His conclusion: Studies designed to clarify the role of neuroendocrine factors in the regulation of immune processes and more refined studies of the conditioning of immune responses are needed.

Studies designed to document conditioning effects continued, although they did not contribute to a resolution of the theoretical issues involved. Sakanjan and Kostanjan (1957) began their study with rabbits that had been immunized with paratyphoid vaccine on four occasions at 10-day intervals. Ten days after the last immunization one group of 4 rabbits received injections of saline and vaccine while 4 others received only injections of vaccine for 15 consecutive days. During this time agglutinin titers rose. During the next 25 days the rabbits in the first group received only saline injections and titers decreased, while animals in the second group continued to receive the vaccine and titers increased. During the next 70 days, animals in Group I were injected with vaccine and animals in Group II were injected with saline. Agglutinin titers in the Group I animals given vaccine decreased whereas agglutinin titers in the Group II animals given saline began to rise.

In a second experiment (Sakanjan and Kostanjan, 1957) rabbits were injected with paratyphoid vaccine or with saline plus vaccine daily for 20 days. Thereafter, animals given the repeated injections of vaccine were subdivided into groups that received saline (Group I), vaccine (Group II), a needle prick only (Group III), or no stimulation (Group IV); animals that had received saline plus vaccine were treated with saline, alone (Group V). Agglutinin titers decreased in Groups III and IV, and increased in the remaining animals. These several groups can be reconstituted into groups that, again, correspond generally to the treatments imposed by Ader and Cohen (1975). Groups I and V ($N = 8$) would meet the criterion of conditioned animals reexposed to the CS (Group CS), Groups III and IV ($N = 6$) correspond to conditioned animals that were not reexposed to the CS (Group CS_0), while Group II ($N = 5$) consists of conditioned animals reexposed to the US (Group US). Combining the groups in this way (Figure 4), it is clear conditioned animals reexposed to the CS respond with antibody titers that are comparable to those of animals treated with the US.

Positive results were also obtained by Savchuk (1958), although the details of his experiments are difficult to reconstruct from the available summary. Evidently, rabbits were immunized with 3 doses of paratyphoid vaccine (on 3 different occasions). For the 5 days following treatment with vaccine, condi-

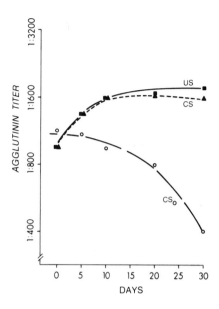

Figure 4. Agglutinin titers in conditioned rabbits that were not reexposed to the CS (CS$_0$), those that were reexposed to the CS(CS), and those that were reexposed to paratyphoid vaccine (US). Data derived from Sakanjan and Kostanjan (1957).

tioned animals were injected with solutions of caffeine, sodium bromide, or garlic (stimulants previously found to stimulate antibody production) and exposed to an auditory stimulus plus an injection of distilled water. Two trials per day were administered. One control group received only injections of vaccine, a second control group was given only distilled water, and a third was given only one of the stimulants following each dose of vaccine. When conditioned animals were injected with vaccine and reexposed to the CS, alone (i.e., without the accompanying stimulant), agglutinin titer was higher than in controls given only vaccine or vaccine plus distilled water, and did not differ from the animals given vaccine plus one of the stimulating agents (the US for an elevated titer). Again, the data are suggestive although the control groups did not consist of previously conditioned animals and there were no nonconditioned animals that were subjected to the stimulation that defined the CS.

In a study designed in reaction to previous criticism, Luk'ianenko (1959) first adapted 4 monkeys *(Papio hamadryas)* to chair restraint. The experiment was conducted under constant conditions (e.g., by the same experimenters, at the same time of day, for a constant period of time, with a constant site of injection for the administration of antigen and a constant site for the collection of blood samples). The US was a paratyphoid vaccine (a strain of *Salmonella enteritidis*) administered to each animal in gradually increasing doses; the CS consisted of the complex of stimuli associated with chair restraint and treatment which lasted for 2 hr. After 30 min in the chair, blood samples were taken to estimate initial agglutinin titer. Ten min later, a subcutaneous injection of antigen was administered and the animals remained under restraint for an additional 80 min. Six such trials were administered over the course of 5 weeks. The animals remained unmanipulated for the next 5 weeks except for periodic blood sampling. The 2 experimental monkeys were then reexposed to the CS and injected with saline rather than vaccine while the 2 controls were injected with saline but were not subjected to the experimental conditions that defined the CS.

The results (Figure 5) showed a gradual increase in antibody titer during the course of the conditioning trials in all animals. This was followed by a decrease in titers during the rest period. Experimental animals injected with saline during reexposure to the CS then showed an increase in antibody titer whereas control animals injected with saline outside the experimental situation showed no change in antibody titer.

By administering 6 CS-US trials over a 5-week period, Luk'ianenko claimed to have obviated the problem of an immunologic refractory period that could result from overstimulation with antigenic stimuli at brief intervals. He recognized, however, that he was unable to assess independently the immunogenic effects of his CS per se (he had no nonconditioned group). These were considered very improbable since (a) the monkeys were adapted to the restraining chair before the experiments began, (b) by the time the experiments began the animals were behaving quietly which probably excluded any influence of hormonal factors, and (c) chair restraint caused only a very slight increase in antidysentery agglutinins which were present in all these monkeys. These data, then, were viewed as confirmation of a nervous system regulation

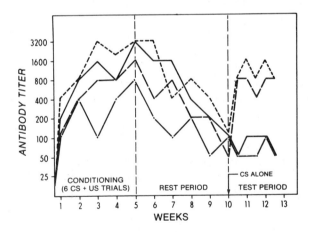

Figure 5. Antibody titers in 4 conditioned monkeys, 2 of which were eventually reexposed to the CS (broken lines) and 2 of which served as unstimulated controls (solid lines). Data redrawn from Luk'ianenko (1959).

of an antibody response and a contradiction of the "negative" data cited by Zdrodovskii (1956).

A rather lengthy and diverse series of experiments are described in the paper by Dolin *et al.* (1960). These studies are characterized by an emphasis on the careful repetition of precisely controlled environmental stimulation in an effort to create a stereotypical response in the experimental animals. Creation of a "dynamic stereotype," referred to above, involves the establishment of a reproducible response to the relationship between stimuli. Thus, a stereotype was created in rabbits in response to repeated injections of two stimuli differing in immunologic activity. Specifically, injection of Gärtner vaccine was followed 4 days later by an injection of homologous serum. Four days later the vaccine was again presented and 4 days after that the rabbits were again injected with rabbit serum. This unvarying sequence of events was repeated (for an unspecified period of time) until the stereotype was consolidated, that is, until the conditioned response was established so that there was a reproduction of the reaction to the succession of stimuli even when rabbit serum, for example, was substituted for a scheduled injection of vaccine. That is, the substitution of rabbit serum for vaccine elicits a response which approximates the response to the vaccine, and the substitution of vaccine for homologous serum fails to elicit the characteristic response to vaccine but, rather, evokes the typical response to homologous serum.

In another study, guinea pigs received daily injections of saline under stereotypical conditions. After 16 days the animals were injected with horse serum (1 ml of a 1:100 dilution), and, for the next 10 days, were again injected with saline. Precipitin titers for the protein stimulus injected on Day 17 were measured on Day 26. Of the 15 experimental (saline-treated) guinea pigs, 8 showed no precipitin reaction and 7 showed low titers of 1:10–1:20. Of the 10 control animals previously injected only with horse serum, 8 showed a reaction and 6 of these had precipitin titers of 1:40–1:80. In a subsequent experiment, rabbits were injected with saline once daily for 60 days. The injection of saline was then replaced by an injection of *Escherichia coli* (2×10^9 cells). Reaction to the *E. coli* was completely inhibited in all 7 experimental animals whereas an antibody response was seen in the 3 controls. The experimental animals continued to receive injections of saline for an additional 21 days and both experimental and control animals received two further injections of antigen during this period. Four of the 7 experimental animals remained areactive to the antigenic stimulus; the other 3 had titers ranging from 1:25 to 1:50. The 3 control animals had titers ranging from 1:800 to 1:1600. Thus, a conditioned dynamic stereotype could be applied to the attenuation of the reaction to an antigenic stimulus. In these experiments, the choice of the species of animal and the use of threshold doses of antigen were dictated by the intent to examine the effects of conditioning under circumstances that were as close to physiological as possible.

An additional control condition was introduced in a study in which rabbits were protected against a lethal dose of tetanus toxin by the conditioning of a dynamic stereotype. Experimental animals received daily injections of magnesium sulfate under identical conditions. After 26 injections, a lethal dose of tetanus toxin instead of magnesium sulfate was injected. One control group was simply injected with the tetanus toxin. A second control group also experienced the repeated injections of magnesium sulfate, but under conditions that were purposely altered from day to day in order to prevent the formation of a dynamic stereotype. Two of the 4 experimental animals survived and 2 died after a mean of 249 hr. The 3 unstimulated controls died after a mean of 90 hr, and the 3 animals in the "random" control group died after a mean of 128 hr.

In one of several experiments on analphylactic reactions, Dolin and his colleagues subjected 15 guinea pigs to a series of 15 standardized injections of saline followed by a sensitizing dose of protein (1 ml of a 1:100 dilution). The experimental animals were subjected to an additional 25 injections of saline and then injected with a provocative dose of protein (1 ml of 40–80% horse serum) under precisely the same conditions. There were 10 control animals: 5 served as "clean" controls to evaluate the anaphylactic response in experimentally naive animals, and 5 received the daily injections of saline under conditions which varied daily with respect to the experimental setting, time of day, site of injection, and procedure for holding the animal.

The results of this experiment are shown in Table 2. Responses to the provocative dose of horse serum varied from a loss of orienting and alimentary responses, through slight and moderate degrees of shock, to death which occurred in 2 of the 15 experimental animals and 4 of the 10 controls. The distribution of responses shown in Table 2 would yield a statistically significant difference between the experimental and control groups ($p < .005$).

Similar results were obtained in a study on the role of conditioning in the suppression of anaphylactic shock using a model of passive anaphylaxis (Dolin et al., 1960). Twenty guinea pigs were passively sensitized with rabbit

TABLE 2
Conditioned Suppression of the Anaphylactic Response[a]

Group	Anaphylactic reaction				
	0	+	+ +	+ + +	+ + + +
Experimental					
Periodic stimulation ($N = 15$)	5	5	3		2
Control					
Aperiodic stimulation ($N = 5$)			1	3	1
No stimulation ($N = 5$)				2	3

[a] Data derived from Dolin et al. (1960).

antiequine serum (dilution of 1:10,000) following the repeated injection of saline over a period of 70 days. Twenty control animals were so sensitized without the preliminary elaboration of a conditioned dynamic stereotype to saline injections. Twenty-four hr later, all animals were given an intracardiac injection of a provocative dose of horse serum. Twelve of the 20 experimental animals survived while the remaining 8 died after 8–16 hr. Seventeen of the 20 controls died after 2–5 min. This difference in mortality was highly significant ($X^2 = 6.83, p < .01$).

As a natural component of immunity, Dolin and his colleagues also examined the effects of conditioning on changes in complement titer. Experimental guinea pigs received daily injections of saline. On Day 16, the animals received a sensitizing dose of horse serum diluted 1:100. After 25 additional saline injections, the animals were given an injection of horse serum diluted 1:1 in place of saline. Whereas all 10 control animals showed a reduction in the level of complement, complement titers declined in only 2 of 15 experimental animals. The absolute complement titers plotted by the authors would yield a significant difference between the experimental and control groups ($t = 9.10$, $p < .001$).

Evidently, conditioning procedures can be used to modify complement levels when sensitized animals are treated with provocative doses of foreign protein which elicit subacute or chronic shock. Such findings, which the authors indicate are consistent with results obtained in (unreferenced) experiments in Zil'ber's laboratory on the control of lysozymes via conditioning, are taken as evidence that the CNS can play a role in natural immunity. The results obtained by Dolin and his colleagues (1960) are also purported to be consistent with the observations described in several additional (unreferenced or unavailable) reports indicating that the unconditioned effects of antigenic and toxic stimuli (e.g., tetanus toxemia, foot and mouth disease) on leukocyte reactions, phagocytosis, and antibody responses can be modified by conditioning. With respect to the latter, a concurrently published study by Il'enko and Kovaleva (1960) measured antibody titers in response to influenza virus. Experimental rats were placed into an inhalation chamber where they were subjected to a sprayed suspension of virus. The CS was defined as the closed experimental chamber, the noise and vibration of the chamber, and all the other stimuli attendant upon this treatment. Control animals were also immunized, but they were treated with nasal drops outside the chamber. After 32 CS-US trials, and an interval of 1 month (when antibody titers measured by agglutination–inhibition tests were decreasing), experimental and control rats were placed into the inhalation chamber and sprayed with normal saline. This stimulation had no effect on the 7 control rats; antibody titers remained constant or continued to decline. In contrast, reexposure to the CS resulted in a substantial increase in antibody titer in 7 of the 12 experimental animals ($p < .05$).

SUMMARY

The most recent review of the impact of conditioning in the regulation of immunobiologic responses was prepared by Luk'ianenko (1961) and serves as an appropriate summary of the literature cited above.

With respect to the conditioned regulation of cellular reactions, the available data confirm the original observations of Metal'nikov and Chorine (1926). Conditioned changes in leukocyte reactions were reported by Vygodchikov and Barykini (1927), Nicolau and Antinescu-Dimitriu (1929b), Podkopaeff and Saatchian (1929), Ostravskaya (1930), Rihá (1955), and others (Benatato, 1955; Diacono, 1933; Ul'yanov, 1953). Luk'ianenko (1961) also cites earlier studies by Makukhin (1911) and Voronov and Riskin (1925) in which conditioned leukocyte reactions were observed; evidently, these observations were not appreciated or recognized as conditioned responses at that time.

Another nonspecific immune defense mechanism consists of the phagocytosis of foreign protein. Luk'ianenko views phagocytosis as a bridge between nonspecific and specific immunobiologic reactions and this process, too, appears to be subject to conditioning effects (Golovkova, 1947; Hadnagy and Kovats, 1954; Kazarov, 1958; Pel'ts, 1955; Strutsovskaya, 1953).

Relatively little attention has been devoted to nonspecific humoral factors in immunity. Experiments have demonstrated, though, conditioned changes in complement (Berezhnaya, 1956; Dolin et al., 1960; Reidler, 1956) and in the activity of lysozyme (Gasanov, 1953). It is assumed that the nonspecific cellular and humoral parameters of immune defense reactions are mediated via hypothalamic–pituitary–adrenocortical mechanisms and that the demonstrated effects of conditioning emphasize the role of the cerebral cortex (cf. Ader, 1976).

Metal'nikov and Chorine (1928) were also the first to study the possible influence of conditioning on specific factors of acquired immunity. The repeated association of a presumably neutral stimulus with an antigenic stimulus resulted in an increase in the titer of specific agglutinins when the CS was presented alone. These observations were replicated by Nicolau and Antinescu–Dimitriu (1929a) and were subsequently confirmed under a variety of experimental circumstances, with a variety of antigenic (bacterial, cellular, viral, anatoxic) stimuli in different species (Luk'ianenko, 1961, and literature cited above). Because of the diversity of conditions used and the lack of systematic studies, it is difficult to abstract any general relationship among the several parameters of the conditioning process. It is possible, though, to at least comment on some of the more prominent issues.

The nature of the antigenic stimulus is, almost certainly, a relevant parameter. Qualitatively, Il'enko and Kovaleva (1960) reported more rapid acquisition of a conditioned response to sheep erythrocytes than to influenza virus. Also, although the magnitude of the effects of conditioning in modulating antibody responses is typically small, there is considerable variability that may be due as much to the nature of the antigen and the route of inoculation as to any of the other procedural differences among experiments. Quantitatively, a consideration of the dose of antigen, the interval between antigenic stimuli, and/or the frequency of antigenic stimulation (Dolin et al., 1960; Luk'ian-endo, 1959; Vygodchikov, 1955) would also be relevant parameters that could facilitate, mask, or inhibit conditioning effects.

Similarly, the nature and strength of the CS would appear to be a relevant variable. Nicolau and Antinescu-Dimitriu (1929a), for example, observed no effects using an auditory CS in contrast to the positive effects of thermal and tactile stimuli. Comparable results were obtained by Mustardy, Kiss, and Karady (1959, cited by Luk'ianenko, 1961). Extrapolating from recent studies on the conditioning of taste aversions and the relatedness of gustatory stimuli to gastrointestinal stimuli (e.g., Garcia et al., 1974; Rozin and Kalat, 1971; Wilcoxon et al., 1971) it seems reasonable to assume that interoceptive conditioned responses would be facilitated by the use of conditioned stimuli which influence proximal relative to distal receptors. The point is made by Peshkovskii (cited by Luk'ianenko, 1961) who claimed that it was essential to use conditioned stimuli that were naturally related to the infectious (or immunogenic) stimulus. The point is reinforced in the study by Vygodchikov (1955) who defined his CS as the nonspecific components of the adsorbed toxoid used as the US.

It is not possible to characterize the rate of acquisition of a conditioned immunobiologic response in consideration of the variables mentioned above, the individual and species differences that have been observed, and a myriad of other interacting procedural variables. Conditioned responses have been observed after as few as 6 CS–US pairings, but no systematic analyses are available. This issue, though, raises more general procedural problems in all such studies; namely, the duration of the immune response to antigenic stimulation and, consequently, the coincidence of the CS and US, the interval between CS–US trials, and the interval between conditioning and test (extinction) trials, and the quantitatively altered response to the repetition of an antigenic stimulus—all of which may be relevant to the association of CS and US and the qualitative and quantitative nature of the conditioned response. Luk'ianenko (1961) considers that many of the discrepancies in the literature may be related to such procedural issues.

Finally, Luk'ianenko (1961) addressed the problem of the mechanisms that could be mediating conditioned immunobiologic responses. For many immunologists, this issue was linked to the issue and the possibility of neural transmission of antigenic stimulation and the conditioned stimulation of antibody production de novo. The controversies that emerged (cf. Gordienko, 1957; Krylov, 1956; Pletsityi, 1957a; Vygodchikov, 1957; Zdrodovskii, 1956) were, in part, a reflection of the state of theory regarding the mechanism of antibody production that were being considered in the 1950s. These issues are beyond the scope and immediate focus of the present review. It seems, though, that the hypothesis of direct reflex stimulation of antibody production provided the premature and restrictive framework which directed these early studies of conditioning. As a result, studies of conditioning effects and the implied role of the CNS in regulating immune responses were narrowly conceived. And, when the underlying concepts were questioned, the experimental data became suspect, as well.

Even today it would be premature to speculate on the mechanisms of conditioned immunobiologic effects until we have a clearer picture of the cellular interactions resulting in synthesis and production of antibodies on the one hand, and the neuroendocrine factors that are clearly capable of modulating such defensive responses on the other. It would certainly be premature to assert that the phenomenon of a conditioned modification of antibody responses contradicts or is even inconsistent with what is currently known about the synthesis of antibodies. Current approaches to understanding the underlying immunologic (biochemical) mechanisms have not directed appropriate attention to concomitant neuroendocrine function and the conditioned regulation of immune responses which implicates the CNS in immunogenesis, therefore, can not be summarily dismissed.

As Luk'ianenko (1961) summarizes the results up to that time, the available data provide sufficient evidence of the likelihood that conditioning procedures can alter the threshold of sensitivity of the organism to antigenic stimuli and modulate the level of immunologic reactivity, thereby establishing a role for the CNS in the regulation of immune processes. Therefore, and consistent with modern thinking regarding the inseparable nature of psychobiological processes, the presence of antigenic stimulation is a necessary factor for the initiation of antibody production, but it is not sufficient in itself for defining or assuring the complex chain of events that determine immunogenesis and the defense of the organism that it serves under *in vivo* conditions (i.e., under conditions found by the behaving individual in the real world). The critical nature of such a perspective has been elaborated elsewhere (e.g., Ader, 1980; Engel, 1977; Weiner, 1978).

It seems premature and restrictive to predicate a specific role for the CNS in regulating immune processes based on or limited by what incomplete knowledge of the operation of the immune system currently exists or is generally accepted. From the data reviewed above, it is not unreasonable to suggest that conditioning, for example, can act to alter the functional activity of the immune system at any of several (undetermined) levels or stages in the development of a protective response. Moreover, other recent data obtained by Besedovsky and Sorkin (1977), Korneva and Klimenko (1976), Korneva et al. (1978), and others (e.g., Spector, 1980; Spector and Korneva, this volume) suggest that the possibility that some information provided by antigenic stimulation and/or immune responses is transmitted to the CNS is not to be dismissed. And this is particularly true in view of recent studies suggesting some neural innervation of lymphoid tissue (Bulloch and Moore, 1980; Reilly *et al.,* 1979; Besedovsky and Sorkin and Hall and Goldstein, this volume). It seems reasonable, therefore, to speculate that the immune system and the central nervous system are complementary and operate in concert to increase the adaptive capacity of the individual.

ACKNOWLEDGMENTS

I am particularly indebted to Samuel Corson and his associates, Roland Dartau and Justina Epp, and to Leonid Margolin, Robert Berkow, Sumico Nagai, and Deborah Ader for translations of Russian, French, and German literature. I also wish to thank N. Herbert Spector, Nicholas Cohen, Lee Grota, Norman Braveman, and Dana Bovbjerg for their critical comments on a preliminary draft of this review.

REFERENCES

Ader, R. (1976). Conditioned adrenocortical steroid elevations in the rat. *J. Comp. Physiol. Psychol.* **90,** 1156–1163.

Ader, R. (1980). Animal models in the study of brain, behavior and bodily disease. *In* "Brain, Behavior, and Bodily Disease" (H. Weiner, M. Hofer, and A. J. Stunkard, eds.), pp. 11–26, Raven Press, New York.

Ader, R., and Cohen, N. (1975). Behaviorally conditioned immunosuppression. *Psychosom. Med.* **37,** 333–340

Amiantova, L. D. (1961). Stability of reactions of organism to antigenic stimulation. *Dokl. Akad. Nauk SSSR* **136,** 153–155.

Benetato, G. (1955). Le mécanisme nerveux central de la réaction leucocytaire et phagocytaire. *J. Physiol. (Paris)* **47,** 391–403.

Berezhnaya, N. M. (1956). *In* "Principles of immunity" (Proc. Sci. Conf.), Vol. 3, p. 185.

Bereznykh, D. V. (1955). On the question of conditioned reflex restoration of immunogenesis. *Byull. Eksp. Biol. Med.* **40,** 49–52.

Besedovsky, H., and Sorkin, E. (1977). Network of immune–neuroendocrine interactions. *Clin. Exp. Immunol.* **27,** 1–12.

Bulloch, K., and Moore, R. Y. (1980). Nucleus ambiguus projections to the thymus gland: Possible pathways for regulation of the immune response and the neuroendocrine network. *Anat. Rec.* **196,** 25A.

Dekker, E., Pelser, H. E., and Groen, J. J. (1957). Conditioning as a cause of asthmatic attacks. *J. Psychosom. Res.* **2,** 84–98.

Diacono, H. (1933). Le phénomène hémolytique: Contribution à l'étude de l'hémolyse. XI. Réflexes conditionnels et hémolyse. *Arch. Inst. Pasteur Tunis* **22,** 376–385.

Dolin, A. O., and Krylov, V. N. (1952). The role of the cerebral cortex in immune reactions of the organism. *Zh. Vyssh. Nervn. Deyat. im. I. P. Pavlova* **2,** 547–560.

Dolin, A. O., Krylov, V. N., Luk'ianenko, V. I., and Flerov, B. A. (1960). New experimental data on the conditioned reflex reproduction and suppression of immune and allergic reactions. *Zh. Vyssh. Nervn. Deyat. im. I. P. Pavlova* **10,** 832–841.

Doroshkevich, A. A. (1954). Origination of immunological reactions from the effect of a conditioned stimulant. *Zh. Vyssh. Nervn. Deyat. im. I. P. Pavlova* **4,** 108–115.

Engel, G. (1977). The need for a new medical model: A challenge for biomedicine. *Science* **196,** 129–136.

Evseev, V. A. (1957). The influence of typological characteristics of the nervous system of animals upon the production of tetanus antitoxin. *Zh. Mikrobiol. Epidemiol. Immunobiol.* **38,** 1008-1012.

Friedberger, V. E., and Gurwitz, I. (1931). Sind bedingte reflexe im sinne von Pawlow befähigt, die Bildung von Immunantikorpern anzuregen? Ein Beitrag zur Frage der Bildung spezifischer Antikorper. *Z. Immuntataetsforsch. Exp. Ther.* **72,** 173-179.

Garcia, J., Hankins, W. G., and Rusiniak, K. W. (1974). Behavioral regulation of the milieu interne in man and rat. *Science* **185,** 823-831.

Gasonov, G. T. (1953). Experimental data on the study of the effect and excretion of lysozyme (unpublished dissertation).

Golovkova, I. N. (1947). The influence of nociceptive and conditioned reflex stimulation on phagocytic capability or leukocytes in the organism. *Byull. Eksp. Biol. Med.* **24,** 268-270.

Gordienko, A. N. (1957). A few words regarding the reflex agency in immunogenesis. *Zh. Mikrobiol. Epidemiol. Immunobiol.* **28,** 138-142.

Hadnagy, C. S., and Kovats, I. (1954). Die Rolle der Hirnrinde bei den Veranderungen der Fähigkeit des Serums zur Stimulation der Phagozytose. *Acta Physiol. Acad. Sci. Hung.* **5,** 325-330.

Hill, L. E. (1930). "Philosophy of a Biologist," Arnold, London.

Hutton, R. A., Woods, S. C., and Makous, W. L. (1970). Conditioned hyperglycemia: Pseudoconditioning controls. *J. Comp. Physiol. Psychol.* **71,** 198-201.

Il'enko, V. I., and Kovaleva, G. A. (1960). The conditioned reflex regulation of immunological reactions. *Zh. Mikrobiol. Epidemiol. Immunobiol.* **31,** 108-113.

Kanarevskaya, A. A. (1945). Conditioned reflex anaphylactic shock. *Byull. Eksp. Biol. Med.* **20,** 32-34.

Kazarov, A. P. (1958). The influence of conditioned and unconditioned stimuli on the number of leukocytes in the blood and their phagocytic ability. *Izv. Akad. Nauk Arm. SSR, Biol. Nauki* **13,** 11-19.

Klimentova, A. A. (1955). The significance of conditioned reflexes in the development of specific agglutinins. *Zh. Mikrobiol. Epidemiol. Immunobiol.* **26,** 80-84.

Klimentova, A. A., and Uchitel', I Ya. (1950). *In* "Problems of Reactivity in the Theory of Infection and Immunity," pp. 197-198. Medgiz, Moscow.

Kopeloff, L. M., Kopeloff, N., and Raney, M. (1933). The nervous system and antibody production. *Psychiatr. Q.* **7,** 84-106.

Kopeloff, L. M., Kopeloff, N., and Posselt, E. (1935). Agglutinins and the conditioned reflex. *J. Immunol.* **29,** 359-366.

Korneva, E. A., and Klimenko, V. M. (1976). Neuronale Hypothalomusktivität und Homëostatische Reactionen. *Ergebn. Exp. Med.* **23,** 373-382.

Korneva, E. A., Klimenko, V. M., and Schinek, A. K. (1978). "Neurohumoral Basis of Immune Homeostasis." Nauka, Leningrad.

Kriachko, L. I., and Guonbis, G. Ia. (1958). On the connection of the cellular immunity reaction and the general course of experimental staphylococcal intoxication with the typological characteristics of the nervous system in dogs. *Zh. Mikrobiol. Epidemiol. Immunobiol.* **29,** 356-363.

Krylov, V. N. (1956). On the possibility of a conditioned reflex regulation of immune reactions. *Zh. Mikrobiol. Epidemiol. Immunobiol.* **27,** 97-101.

Krylov, V. N. (1958). The methodological basis of the study of the role of the higher parts of the central nervous system in the production of specific antibodies. *Zh. Mikrobiol. Epidemiol. Immunobiol.* **29,** 810-815.

Krylov, V. N., and Malinovskii, O. V. (1961). The link between individual features of immunogenesis and typological features of the nervous system in rabbits. (Experimental investigation.) I. Pattern of formation of agglutinins in relation to the functional mobility of nervous processes. *Zh. Mikrobiol. Epidemiol. Immunobiol.* **32,** 10-14.

Kuskova, V. F. (1955). On the question concerning the role of the cerebral cortex in immuno-genesis. *Byull. Eksp. Biol. Med.* **12**, 40–42.

Luk'ianenko, V. I. (1959). The conditioned reflex regulation of immunologic reactions *Zh. Mikrobiol. Epidemiol. Immunobiol.* **30**, 53–59.

Luk'ianenko, V. I. (1961). The problem of conditioned reflex regulation of immunobiologic reactions. *Usp. Sovrem. Biol.* **51**, 170–187.

Makukhin, I. I. (1911). Leukocytosis (unpublished dissertation).

Metal'nikov, S. (1934). "Rôle de système nerveux et des facteurs biologiques et psychiques dans l'immunité." Masson, Paris.

Metal'nikov, S., and Chorine, V. (1926). Rôle des réflexes conditionnels dans l'immunité. *Ann. Inst. Pasteur, Paris* **40**, 893–900.

Metal'nikov, S., and Chorine, V. (1928). Rôle des réflexes conditionnels dans la formation des anticorps. *C. R. Seances Soc. Biol. Ses Fil.* **99**, 142–145.

Monjan, A. A., and Collector, M. I. (1976). Stress-induced modulation of the immune response. *Science* **196**, 307–308.

Nicolau, I., and Antinescu-Dimitriu, O. (1929a). Rôle des réflexes conditionnels dans la formation des anticorps. *C. R. Seances Soc. Biol. Ses Fil.* **102**, 133–134.

Nicolau, I., and Antinescu-Dimitriu, O. (1929b). L'influence des réflexes conditionnels sur l'exsudat peritonéal. *C. R. Seances Soc. Biol. Ses Fil.* **102**, 144–145.

Ostravskaya, O. A. (1930). Le réflex conditionnel et les réactions de l'immunité. *Ann. Inst. Pasteur, Paris* **44**, 340–345.

Ottenberg, P., Stein, M., Lewis, J., and Hamilton, C. (1958). Learned asthma in the guinea pig. *Psychosom. Med.* **20**, 395–400.

Pavlov, I. P. (1928). "Lectures on Conditioned Reflexes." Liveright, New York.

Pel'ts, D. G. (1955). The role of the cerebral cortex in the modification of phagocytic activity of blood leukocytes of animals from the application of electrocutaneous stimuli. *Byull. Eksp. Biol. Med.* **40**, 55–58.

Pletsityi, D. F. (1957a). The role of the nervous system in resistance to infectious diseases. *Zh. Mikrobiol. Epidemiol. Immunobiol.* **28**, 131–137.

Pletsityi, D. F. (1957b). Types of nervous system, immunological reactivity and resistance. *Zh. Mikrobiol. Epidemiol. Immunobiol.* **28**, 1564–1571.

Podkopaeff, N. A., and Saatchian, R. L. (1929). Conditioned reflexes for immunity. I. Conditioned reflexes in rabbits for cellular reaction of peritoneal fluid. *Bull. Battle Creek Sanit. Hosp. Clinic* **24**, 375–378.

Polettini, B. (1929). Importance des réflexes dit conditionnels sur certaines phénomènes immunitaires. *Boll. Sez. Ital. Soc. Int. Microbiol.* **1**, 84–87.

Reidler, M. M. (1956). The effect of a complex conditioned and unconditioned (nocioceptive) stimulus on antibody formation in the blood under normal conditions and after extirpation of the cerebellum. *Fiziol. Zh. SSSR im. I. M. Sechenova* **42**, 398–405.

Reilly, F. D., McCuskey, P. A., Miller, M. L., McCuskey, R. S., and Meineke, H. A. (1979). Innervation of the periarteriolar lymphatic sheath of the spleen. *Tissue & Cell* **11**, 121–126.

Rihá, I. (1955). A contribution to the question of conditioned reflex formation of antibodies. *Folia Biol. (Prague)* **1**, 139–143.

Rozin, P., and Kalat, J. W. (1971). Specific hungers and poison avoidance as adaptive specializations of learning. *Psychol. Rev.* **78**, 459–486.

Sakanjan, S., and Kostanjan, A. (1957). The role of the cerebral cortex in the formation of post-vaccination immunity. *Izv. Akad. Nauk. Arm. SSR, Biol. S-kh. Nauki* **12**, 9–16.

Savchuk, O. Ye. (1958). The reflex mechanism of the formation of antibodies. *Zh. Mikrobiol. Epidemiol. Immunobiol.* **29**, 304–305.

Shumakova, G. V. (1958). The effect of conditioned reflex stimulation on the production of diptherial antitoxin. *Zh. Mikrobiol. Epidemiol. Immunobiol.* **29**, 121.

Smith, G. H., and Salinger, R. (1933). Hypersensitiveness and the conditioned reflex. *Yale J. Biol. Med.* 5, 387–402.

Siegel, S. (1975). Conditioned insulin effects. *J. Comp. Physiol. Psychol.* **89**, 189–199.

Spector, N. H. (1980). The hypothalamus in health and disease: Old and new concepts. In "Handbook of the Hypothalamus" (P. J. Morgane and J. Panskepp, eds.) Dekker, New York.

Strutsovskaya, A. L. (1953). An experiment on the formation of conditioned phagocytic reactions in children. *Zh. Vyssh. Nervn. Deyat. im. I. P. Pavlova* 3, 238–246.

Ul'yanov, M. I. (1953). On the question of cortical regulation of the leukocyte composition of peripheral blood. *Klin. Med.* 31, 52–56.

Vasil'yev, N. V. (1959). Review of L. A. Zilber, "Foundations of Immunology." Medgiz, Moscow, 1958. *Zh. Mikrobiol. Epidemiol. Immunobiol.* 30, 151–154.

Vornov, A., and Riskin, I. (1925). On leukocytosis in normal subjects and dogs. *Russ. Klin.* 3, 484–512.

Vygodchikov, G. V. (1955). Certain controversial questions in the theory of immunity. *Zh. Mikrobiol. Epidemiol. Immunobiol.* 26, 5–14.

Vygodchikov, G. V. (1957). Results of a discussion on the basic problems of the study of immunity. *Zh. Mikrobiol. Epidemiol. Immunobiol.* 28, 623–628.

Vygodchikov, G. V., and Barykini, O. (1927). The conditioned reflex and protective cell reactions. *J. Biol. Med. Exp.* 6, 538–541.

Weiner, H. (1978). The illusion of simplicity: The medical model revisited. *Am. J. Psychiatry* 135, Suppl., 27–33.

Wilcoxon, H. C., Dragoin, W. B., and Kral, P. A. (1971). Illness-induced aversions in rats and quail: Relative salience of visual and gustatory cues. *Science* 171, 826–828.

Zdrodovskii, P. F. (1951). Physiological reorganization of immunology. *Zh. Mikrobiol. Epidemiol. Immunobiol.* 22, 3–15.

Zdrodovskii, P. F. (1953). Soviet immunology and its tasks. *Zh. Mikrobiol. Epidemiol. Immunobiol.* 24, 6–13.

Zdrodovskii, P. F. (1956). Current status of theoretical immunology and its immediate tasks. *Vestn. Akad. Med. Nauk SSSR* 11, 43–57.

Zdrodovskii, P. F. (1958). Problems of infectious pathology and immunology. *Vestn. Akad. Med. Nauk SSSR* 13, 19–37.

Zeitlenok, N. A. (1930). Conditioned reflexes to biological reactions. *Zh. Eksp. Biol. Med.* 13, 99–102.

Zeitlenok, N. A., and Bychkova, E. N. (1954). On the study of the role of higher nervous activity in infection and immunity. *Zh Vyssh. Nervn. Deyat. im. I. P. Pavlova* 4, 267–281.

Zhukov-Verezhnikov, N. N. (1952). The ideas of I. P. Pavlov on causes of diseases and experimental therapy as the basis of microbiology and immunology. *Zh. Vyssh. Nervn. Deyat. im. I. P. Pavlova* 2, 9–19.

Zil'ber, L. A. (1958). "Foundations of Immunology." Medgiz, Moscow.

PART **IV**

Neuroendocrine Influences

Hormonal Influences on Immunologic and Related Phenomena

JOHAN AHLQVIST

INTRODUCTION

Background

The majority of patients suffering from various types of autoimmune disease are female, and most of these diseases have peculiar age distributions which seem to be related to periods characterized by physiological endocrine alterations. Such links prompted me some years ago to discontinue temporarily my own histological research work and review relevant studies of endocrine influences on immune responses and inflammation (Ahlqvist, 1976). The present paper constitutes a summary of that review plus the results of recent studies which have provided information about the mechanisms that may be involved. These include data indicating that the major histocompatibility complex is linked not only to immunologic phenomena but also to endocrine and metabolic events. I crave the patience of those readers who may find some of the expressions and terms used unfamiliar, since one of the purposes of this review is to try to convince at least some readers that their field of interest may be intimately linked to that of their neighbors.

355

Mechanisms in Immune Reactions and Inflammation

Thymus-dependent lymphocytes, or T cells, participate in the defense against viral and some other infectious diseases and in the rejection of grafts and certain neoplasms. If introduced into an organism unable to kill them, they may also activate other lymphoid cells, inducing a graft-versus-host reaction. Activated T cells produce a number of lymphokines, mediators that, among other effects, may activate macrophages. Activated T helper cells induce B cells to produce immunoglobulins, and macrophages are important in this cooperation. Beneficial and harmful effects of antibodies and antigen–antibody complexes are, to a large extent, mediated by activation of the complement cascade. The cytotoxic effects of nonsensitized killer cells on target cells coated with antibody might be an important mechanism in organ-specific autoimmune diseases. On contact with antigen, reaginic IgE antibodies attached to mast cells, for example, may release histamine and other mediators of acute hypersensitivity reactions. Some thymic cells suppress the production of immunologic effectors. Data on these mechanisms are found in all textbooks on immunology, but I will deal in some detail with a few findings which may be important for the understanding of the effects of hormones on immunologic and allied phenomena.

CELL SURFACE GLYCOPROTEINS, THE MAJOR HISTOCOMPATIBILITY SYSTEM AND IMMUNE RESPONSES

The carbohydrate-containing NH_2 terminal parts of different glycoproteins protrude from the surface of cells. Such hydrophilic parts constitute the antigenic fractions proper of the molecules coded for by the major histocompatibility system (MHS) and of various differentiation antigens (Katz, 1977; Crumpton et al., 1978; Andersson and Gahmberg, 1979). Hydrophobic parts of such molecules cross the lipid bilayer of the cellular wall, the COOH terminal ends being located on the cytoplasmic side of the wall, and extend to the interior of the cell the effects of factors that act on the cell surfaces (Gahmberg, 1977). All cell surface proteins may be such glycoproteins (Gahmberg, 1977; Andersson and Gahmberg, 1979).

Classical Histocompatibility, Ia, and Other Glycoprotein Antigens. The genes of the MHS are located on chromosome 6 in man (*HLA*) and on chromosome 17 in mice (*H-2*). The classical major histocompatibility antigens are coded for by the *HLA-B, HLA-C,* and *HLA-A* loci in man and by the *H-2K* and *H-2D* loci in mice. These heavy glycoprotein molecules are associated with a lighter β_2-microglobulin molecule which is coded for by another chromosome. A part of the heavy molecules and β_2-microglobulin closely resemble immunoglobulin (IgG) heavy chains (Terhorst *et al.*, 1977; Wiman *et al.*, 1979). Also, haptoglobin (cf. Terhorst *et al.*, 1977) and C-reactive protein, the latter of which appears to be of considerable importance in infection and inflammation, resemble immunoglobulin heavy chains (Osmand *et al.*, 1977). These and some other proteins may have a related evolution. These classical histocompatibility antigens are expressed on most cells of the body with the exception of erythrocytes and placental cells (Goodfellow *et al.*, 1976).

Different immune-associated (*Ia*) antigens are coded for by *I* region subloci of the *H-2* complex in mice and by the *HLA-D/DR* region in man. They are not associated with β_2-microglobulin (Crumpton *et al.*, 1978). These antigens are expressed on a limited number of cell types such as epidermal cells, various endodermal cells, sperm, B cells and macrophages, but in very low amounts or not at all on resting T cells (Katz, 1977; Crumpton *et al.*, 1978; Forsum *et al.*, 1979). They are also found on some endothelial cells (Häyry *et al.*, 1980b). In mouse skin, the *Ia*-positive cells, however, are the phagocytic Langerhans' cells and not the epithelial cells proper (Rowden *et al.*, 1978); it has not been proved conclusively that the positive cells in the thymus (Forsum *et al.*, 1979) are epithelial cells proper.

A number of glycoprotein antigens (*TL, LY, θ* or *Thy-1, G_{IX}*) in different combinations are expressed on developing or neoplastic and to some extent on mature mouse T cells. Some of these molecules are coded for by genes close to the *H-2* complex, some by other genes, and the G_{IX} antigen constitutes the expression of incorporated viral genome. Three of the *Ly* antigens (1,2,3) are expressed on immature cortisone-sensitive thymocytes and peripheral T cells in newborn mice. Later, many T cells lack (have lost ?) some of these antigens and *Ly-1* positive cells have helper functions whereas *Ly-2,3* positive cells have suppressor effects (Katz, 1977) and are thus associated with immunologic functions.

Self-Recognition and Immunity. It has been recognized (cf. Zinkernagel *et al.*, 1978b) that effective immune responses to thymus-dependent antigens require the recognition by a T cell, not only of the antigenic determinants of the antigen proper, but of cell surface molecules coded for by the major histocompatibility complex. Some of the numerous problems reviewed (Katz, 1977) may have been resolved by the finding that mouse prethymic cells in the thymus appear to develop recognition structures for histocompatibility antigens on the fixed cells of the thymus in which these thymocytes mature (Zinkernagel *et al.*, 1978a). Later, in peripheral tissues, cooperation between mature T cells and other cells (e.g., in T–B cooperation) requires the recognition by the T cell of *I* region products of these other cells, whereas direct T cell killing requires, in addition, the recognition of at least one *K* or *D* region product (Zinkernagel *et al.*, 1978b). Effective immune responses thus depend on the kind of information the thymocytes have acquired in the thymus. The quantity of, for example, *Ia* antigens on some cells appears to be influenced by certain hormones (see sections "Gonadal and Adrenal Steroids" and "The Pituitary Gland"). Does the same apply to fixed thymic cells?

On B cells, surface immunoglobulins function as antigen receptors. The T cell receptor for a certain antigen shares antigenic determinants with the immunoglobulins to the same antigen in the same animal; such unique antigenic determinants are termed idiotypic and, in conformity with the network theory of Jerne (1973), have been shown to moderate immune responses (e.g., Aguet *et al.*, 1978). Classical histocompatibility antigens may also function as antigen receptors (Helenius *et al.*, 1978; Wiman *et al.*, 1979).

Recognition of different histocompatibility gene products during thymocyte differentiation may determine the functional class (cytotoxic, helper, etc.) of various T cell populations (Munro and Waldman, 1978). Thymocytes with one high affinity or two low affinity receptors for self may possibly become inactivated in the thymus (Janeway *et al.*, 1976); in a way this constitutes a return to the hypothesis of Burnet regarding the elimination of forbidden (autoreactive T cell) clones during ontogeny. Circulating soluble histocompatibility molecules may block weak T cell receptors and prevent them from offering immunologic help (Cohen and Wekerle, 1977). Activation of T cells induces specific changes in the surface glycoprotein pattern (Andersson and Gahmberg, 1979).

The few examples cited above indicate that immunologic reactions are intimately associated with cell surface glycoproteins coded for by the MHS and other genes. I have stressed these findings since endocrinologic mechanisms are also linked at many levels to the MHS.

THYMIC HORMONES

A number of thymic polypeptide hormones have been described (e.g., White, 1975). It is generally assumed that they are produced by the thymic epithelial cells, but, theoretically, they might also be produced by amine-containing APUD cells since these cells (see section on "Biogenic Amines") often produce peptide hormones, too. Such thymic hormones have been found to influence thymocyte maturation and to stimulate a number of T cell functions, including suppressor effects (Bach *et al.*, 1977; Goldstein *et al.*, 1978). The level of one of these factors correlates with age and with thymic epithelial abnormalities; the level is low in systemic lupus erythematosus, but rather high in rheumatoid arthritis (Bach *et al.*, 1977). It is, however, difficult to believe that these hormones could be substitutes for the above receptors that develop on thymocytes in the thymus.

RELATIONSHIP BETWEEN IMMUNOLOGIC
AND OTHER MECHANISMS

There are close links between the allegedly separate mechanisms of coagulation, inflammation, and immunologic reactions. Figure 1 shows some of the

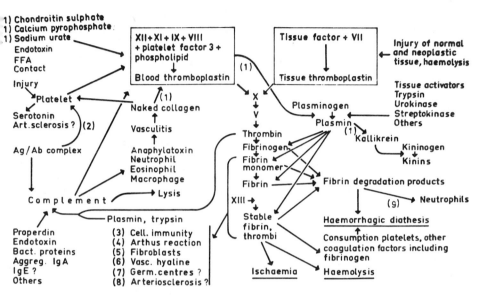

Figure 1. The sequences in coagulation are shown in the center of the figure. On the left are listed some activators of intrinsic, and on the right those of extrinsic, coagulation, including immunologic mechanisms. The links marked (1) have been reviewed by Ratnoff (1971). Classically, complement is activated by antigen–antibody complexes, by the alternate complement pathway (bottom left), and by proteolytic activators such as thrombin and plasmin. Complement may also have beneficial effects by removing immune complexes (e.g., Editorial, 1979). Plasmin-generated fibrin degradation products (9) are chemotactic for neutrophils (Stecher, 1975). Terminal coagulation events also influence (3) cellular immunity (Colvin *et al.*, 1973; Edwards and Rickles, 1978), possibly the (4) Arthus reaction, (5) fibroblastic proliferation, (6) vascular degenerative phenomena, (7) possibly the function of germinal centers (Ahlqvist *et al.*, 1974), and (8) the development of arteriosclerosis. Further references are stated in the monograph (Ahlqvist, 1976) from which the Figure is taken. The novel fibrinogen–fibrin associated protein fibronectin may be of importance in cellular interactions (Gahmberg, 1977; Stenman and Vaheri, 1978). The stimulation of B cells by one proteolytic enzyme, trypsin (Vischer, 1974), may be shared by plasmin, and the proteolytic stimulation of B cells might be due to lysis of cell surface fibronectin (Gahmberg, 1977); this would fit the presence of thin fibrinogen threads in mitotically active germinal centers (Ahlqvist *et al.*, 1974). Links between coagulation and inflammation have recently been reviewed by Zimmerman *et al.* (1977). Antibodies to fibrinogen split products are found in an astonishingly large proportion of healthy adults (Plow and Edgington, 1975), thus possibly explaining those by no means rare types of immune complex-like vasculitis in which a thrombotic diathesis rather than circulating immune complexes appear to be involved (cf. Ahlqvist, 1976). The clinical importance of these links may be underrated by orthodox immunologists. From Ahlqvist (1976), reprinted by permission.

frequently overlooked links; references are given in the legend. In addition to the "proteolytic twins" (Konttinen, 1968), thrombin and plasmin, kallikrein, collagenases, lysosomal proteases, elastase, complement components (C1s, C42, alternative pathway factors), a factor induced by malignant cells (Stroud, 1974), and intracellular enzymes of importance in immunologic reactions (Kaliner and Austen, 1974) also belong to a phylogenetically old group of serine proteases which show some substrate and inhibitor overlap (Stroud, 1974). Such links strongly suggest that immunologic mechanisms should not be regarded as separate from other protective and pathogenetic ones. This will serve as my excuse for including data on the influences of hormones not only on immunoglobulins and lymphocytes but also on the mechanisms depicted in Figure 1.

INFLUENCES OF DIFFERENT HORMONES

It is assumed that the reader is generally familiar with the basics of the regulation of production and secretion and with the effects and metabolism of hormones. Under the heading "Some Endocrine Aspects," I shall mention aspects seldom considered in studies of endocrine influences on immunologic reactions.

Gonadal and Adrenal steroids

SOME ENDOCRINE ASPECTS

General Influences of Gonadal Hormones. Testicular organization and the ensuing testosterone production are due to the (usually Y chromosome-induced) expression of the *H–Y* histocompatibility antigen (Ohno, 1978). The male phenotype is determined by androgens, mainly testosterone, and girls are girls because they lack the male level of testosterone production not only in pubertal–adult life, but also the peaks found in boys during fetal and postnatal periods (Forest *et al.,* 1976). These early testosterone peaks in males thereafter extinguish the hypothalamic cycling center responsible for periodicity in females (Forest *et al.,* 1976), alter certain brain functions (De Moor *et al.,* 1973; Kolata, 1979), increase certain hepatic steroid hydroxylases, and also appear to influence hepatic sulfatases and the level of hepatic cytochrome P–450 (De Moor *et al.,* 1973). An adult female can therefore not be turned into a male by castration and androgen administration.

In both sexes, puberty begins with an increased adrenal production of weak androgens at about the age of 6 (Forest *et al.,* 1976). For several years after menarche, an astonishing number of the menstrual cycles remain anovulatory (Apter and Vihko, 1977). Menopause is often accompanied by relative hyperestrogenism and androgen excess. Prolactin decreases progesterone production during the luteal phase (Seppälä, 1978). The menstrual cycle is also accompanied by alterations in the level of a number of other hormones.

Effective Plasma Levels. The plasma level of the weak adrenal androgen dehydroepiandrosterone, which circulates mainly as a sulfate, is higher than that of any other hormonally active steroid. Most steroids are bound to albumin, and some of them are also bound to specific carrier proteins. Only the free steroid fractions are thought to be hormonally effective. The pioneer studies of Westphal (1971) are still regarded as valid: a large part of cortisol is bound to a cortisol-binding globulin (CBG, transcortin) which is a glycoprotein. Displacement of cortisol from CBG by progesterone might be of importance during luteal phases with a comparatively low cortisol level. Estrogens and thyroxine (increase) and a number of endocrine manipulations alter the CBG level and the level of the globulin (sex hormone-binding, SHBG) which binds testosterone and estradiol is increased by estrogens. Dehydroepiandrosterone sulfate may displace testosterone from this molecule. Also, α-fetoprotein effectively binds estrone and estradiol (Raynaud *et al.*, 1971; cf. Keller *et al.*, 1976) and the α-acid glycoprotein or orosomucoid is a potent progesterone binder (Westphal, 1971; see section on "Relationship between MHS and Endocrinology in Man"). The plasma binding of many synthetic steroids is quite dissimilar to that of endogenous ones, and the displacement of other steroids from their proper carriers and receptors may explain some of the side-effects of synthetic ones (Jänne *et al.*, 1978).

Mechanisms of Steroid Effects. Most steroids are thought to exert important influences on cells after binding to specific cytosol proteins, transfer to the nucleus and interaction with the genome, resulting in the synthesis of RNA and proteins (Thompson and Lippman, 1974; Mayer and Rosen, 1977; Jänne *et al.*, 1978). Lack of receptors often results in unresponsiveness. Receptor levels are by no means constant, and, for example, estrogens increase the progesterone cytosol receptor level whereas progesterone decreases it (Jänne *et al.*, 1978). Steroids may bind to a wrong receptor; thus androgens may block dexamethasone receptors (Mayer and Rosen, 1977) and the androgenic effect of certain progestins may be due to binding to androgen receptors (Jänne *et al.*, 1978). Although the main effects of glucocorticoids are not mediated by cyclic adenosine-3',5'-monophosphate (cAMP), they may enhance the effects of hormones and mediators, the influences of which are mediated by cAMP (Thompson and Lippman, 1974; Lee and Reed, 1977). It has been suggested (Singhal and Tsang, 1975) that testosterone induces the formation of adenyl cyclase. Thus, lack of some effect of a hormone may be due to lack of the receptor or of a proper amplification system; both might be induced by small amounts of other hormones.

Very little attention is generally paid to questions regarding the peripheral interconversion of steroids, conjugation of steroids with hydrophilic molecules, and steroid metabolism. Steroid conjugates escape detection in many routine determinations, yet, for example, the estrogen sulfates are hormonally active whereas steroid glucuronides usually appear immediately before excretion (Ahlqvist, 1976). Sulfated and free natural estrogens appear to have metabolic effects that are different from those of synthetic estrogens and organic esters of otherwise physiological estrogens (Adlercreutz et al., 1980). Some steroid metabolites are pyrogenic and their formation is decreased by thyroid hormones (Ahlqvist, 1976).

LYMPHATIC ORGANS

Gonadectomy. Many reviews (Dougherty, 1952; Grégoire and Duchateau, 1956; Ahlqvist, 1976) indicate that gonadectomy in experimental animals of both sexes increases the size of the thymus. Neither the time of onset nor the rate of involution seems to be altered and thus gonadal hormones appear not to be solely responsible for the involution. Gonadectomy also counteracts thymic involution induced by stress and fasting (Dougherty, 1952). In rats, orchidectomy performed 49 days before (but not after) induction of thymic involution by X-rays seems to stimulate the epithelium, and the number of large cortical thymocytes is secondarily increased (Grégoire and Duchateau, 1956). Also, large thymi have been observed in cases of human hypogonadism (Ahlqvist, 1976).

Estrogens. According to all the studies reviewed (Dougherty, 1952; Ahlqvist, 1976), comparatively large doses of estrogens induce thymic involution in rats and mice. To some extent, the alterations resemble those induced by glucocorticoids, and part of the effect many be mediated by the adrenals. It has not been conclusively determined, however, whether the effect of the three main physiological estrogens on the lymphatic organs parallels their effects on gonadal targets (Ahlqvist, 1976).

Three early investigators found that estrogens induce pathological proliferation of the rat thymic epithelium (Ahlqvist, 1976), and to my knowledge no other steroid has been found to have such an effect. Estrogen receptors have recently been described in the rat thymus (Reichman and Villee, 1978; Grossman et al., 1979a); they were not present in thymocytes and were thought to be epithelial (Grossman et al., 1979a). In estrogen-, progesterone-, and prolactin-treated guinea pigs and mice, the expression of *Ia* antigens on mammary gland epithelial cells was considerably increased (Klareskog et al., in press), and it would be extremely important to know whether they have a similar effect on the thymus.

Spontaneous C-type RNA virus-linked lymphoma and leukemia are common in AKR and other mouse strains with the *H–2ᵏ* haplotype (Iványi, 1978). The tumors often start in the thymus and the incidence is higher in females than in males. Estrogens rank high among the inducers of these tumors, and castration of male mice increases the incidence, whereas testosterone in females is protective (Hirsch and Black, 1974; see section "Endocrine Features in Autoimmune Diseases"). The tumor cells express the G_{IX} antigen on their surface (Iványi, 1978). In AKR/0 mice, tumor development is preceded by cortical depletion of small thymocytes and epithelial hyperplasia (Ahlqvist, 1976), but I have no information about epithelial estrogen receptors in mice thymi.

Progestins. Progesterone has not been found to be thymolytic even when used in large doses, whereas some synthetic progestins decrease thymic size (Ahlqvist, 1976), possibly because they may have androgenic (Jänne *et al.,* 1978) and glucocorticoid (DiSorbo *et al.,* 1977) effects. Murine thymocytes and peripheral T cells contain an enzyme that metabolizes progesterone to 20 α-dihydroprogesterone (Weinstein, 1977).

Androgens. Testosterone decreases thymic size to some extent (Ahlqvist, 1976). Testosterone propionate was found to damage the rat thymic epithelium and appeared to affect lympho–epithelial interaction in the thymic cortex (Grégoire and Duchateau, 1956). Other researchers have suspected that testosterone increases bone marrow differentiation along the erythrocyte line, decreasing the thymic lymphopoiesis (Frey-Wettstein and Craddock, 1970).

Testosterone did not induce thymocyte metabolic alterations resembling those due to cortisol (cf. Munck *et al.,* 1972). Rat thymus high affinity cytosol receptors for dihydrotestosterone also bind testosterone, which is converted into dihydrotestosterone, androstendione, androstandiol, and estradiol (Grossman *et al.,* 1978). The studies of Grégoire in the 1940s (Grégoire and Duchateau, 1956) led me to suspect that these receptors may also be present on epithelial cells. This suspicion is confirmed by a recently published report (Grossman *et al.,* 1979b). The expression of guinea pig mammary epithelial cell *Ia* antigens that had been increased by female sex hormones and prolactin could be reversed by testosterone (Klareskog *et al.,* in press), might it have a similar effect on the thymus? In patients with myasthenia gravis, the presence of thymic germinal centers is associated with low levels of the sulfates of dehydroepiandrosterone and androsterone (see section "Myasthenia Gravis"). Thus, it might be worthwhile to pay attention to the relationship between weak androgens and the thymus.

Adrenalectomy. This operation increases thymic size (Dougherty, 1952). Adrenalectomy seems to stimulate the mitotic index in both epithelial cells and thymocytes after X-ray-induced involution in rats (Grégoire and Duchateau, 1956). The presence of large thymi in some autoimmune diseases was earlier suspected to be due to gonadal and/or adrenal hypofunction (Ahlqvist, 1976).

Glucocorticoids. The acute involution of the rodent thymus after stress is generally ascribed to glucocorticoids (Dougherty, 1952). In many experiments rat thymus size was inversely correlated with plasma levels of unbound corticosterone (Westphal, 1971), the main glucocorticoid in rodents. AKR (*H–2^k*) mice with a high incidence of the previously mentioned lymphomas have large thymi, a strong thymic sensitivity to cortisone, and a relative unresponsiveness of the thymus to adrenalectomy and ACTH (Metcalf, 1960; cf. Gorbalenia *et al.*, 1977), indicating that corticosterone production may be *H–2* associated.

Cortisol-induced thymocytolysis seems to involve binding of the glucocorticoid to a cytosol receptor, transfer to the nucleus, and rapid synthesis of a protein that inhibits the uptake of glucose (Munck *et al.*, 1972), or an enhanced uptake of Ca^{2+} into the cell (Kaiser and Edelman, 1977). Interestingly, a cortisol-binding globulin-like receptor has also been described in human lymphocytes (Werthamer *et al.*, 1973).

In rabbits, cortisone acetate induces a germinal center lymphoid cell depletion which was suspected to be due to a decreased influx of B cells (van den Broek, 1971). Hellman-type reaction centers ("germinal" centers with exudative phenomena) have been observed in experimental immune responses, in stressed animals and after the administration of endotoxin and glucocorticoids (Ahlqvist, 1976), and glucocorticoids might play an important role in the development of these lesions that also occur in man.

Mineralocorticoids. I have not come across studies that would indicate that mineralocorticoids have clear thymolytic effects in rodents, but there is one as yet unverified report indicating that desoxycorticosterone acetate and aldosterone may slightly increase the size of the thymus and lymph nodes (Selye and Bois, 1955). Rat thymocytes bind desoxycorticosterone as well as corticosterone but the former induces no cortisol-like metabolic alterations (cf. Munck *et al.*, 1972).

PLASMA ALTERATIONS

Sex- and Age-Related Alterations. According to Stiehm and Fudenberg (1966), plasma immunoglobulin levels increase gradually during childhood, but, judging from their tabulated data, there may have been a decrease in the IgM and IgG levels in the 12–16 year age group. Serum IgM, IgG, and IgA levels in healthy subjects vary with age, sex, and race (Buckley and Dorsey, 1971), but it is not known to what extent they are regulated by sex steroids (cf. Kaslow and Masi, 1978).

Preceding ovulation, plasma fibrinogen, plasminogen, and fibrinolysis inhibitors increase slightly and there is a new peak about 5 days before menstruation. In anovulatory women, the pattern is irregular, with slightly elevated fibrinogen levels, and the alterations correlate with the excretion of estrogens in the urine (Phillips *et al.,* 1961).

Oral Contraceptives; Sex Steroids. An oral contraceptive used for 6 months induces decreases (e.g., orosomucoid, haptoglobin) or increases (e.g., plasminogen, α_1-antitrypsin, thyroxin-binding globulin, ceruloplasmin) in a number of plasma proteins but no change in immunoglobulin level; cortisol level increases (Laurell *et al.,* 1968). The alterations resemble those in pregnancy (Ganrot, 1972). Estrogens and 17α-alkylated anabolic steroids (in contrast to the corresponding nonalkylated ones) and a testosterone ester induce significant alterations in the levels of, for example, some acute phase proteins and the sex hormone-, cortisol-, and thyroxin-binding globulins; estrogens increase the C-reactive protein, fibrinogen, and plasminogen levels (Barbosa *et al.,* 1971a). Some synthetic progestins increase the plasminogen level without influencing fibrinogen level (Barbosa *et al.,* 1971b). A number of these proteins bear a resemblance to *HLA* antigens. Autoantibodies have been described in women who develop arthritic symptoms from oral contraceptives (Ahlqvist, 1976), but not in those who remain symptomless (Ahlqvist, 1976; Keller *et al.,* 1977).

In both males and females, estrogens were found to increase the level of a pregnancy zone protein which has been claimed to be immunosuppressive (Svendsen *et al.,* 1978). Oral contraceptives do not significantly increase the level of α-fetoprotein (Chayvialle *et al.,* 1977), whereas a considerable rise was noted in the level of a protein considered to be a carrier of vasopressin and oxytocin (Robinson, 1974).

Many oral contraceptives induce a slightly hypercoagulable state; the alterations induced by sulfated estrogens appear less pronounced (Phillips *et al.,* 1961; von Kaulla *et al.,* 1975). There is a vast literature on the increased incidence of thromboembolism in women on oral contraceptives, but some of the statistical evidence has been claimed to be inconclusive (Goldzieher and Dozier, 1975). Other data suggest that the type of contraceptive used may be important (Masi, 1976).

Anabolic steroids appear to enhance fibrinolysis (Nilsson, 1974; Ahlqvist, 1976; Cunliffe, 1976), but I have no information about the possible effects of weak adrenal androgens in this respect.

Glucocorticoids. I shall not review the vast literature on the effects of glucocorticoids on plasma proteins. The possibility of an enhanced immunoglobulin turnover under the influence of glucocorticoids should also be taken into consideration (Ahlqvist, 1976). Somewhat unexpectedly, these hormones are considered to suppress fibrinolytic activity (Konttinen, 1968; Nilsson, 1974), and suppression of plasminogen activator secretion from macrophages (Werb, 1978) may be involved.

PERIPHERAL LYMPHOCYTES

Sex and Age. The spontaneous and the PHA- and PPD-induced uptake of thymidine is relatively high in newborns, and the means (except for PPD) are higher in male infants (Lanning, 1978). In children 2–5 years old, the uptake is low. Thereafter, it gradually increases to reach a peak at 13 years. At 16 years, there is, in general, a drop which is more pronounced in boys. In adults, the uptake is higher, but in elderly people the response to PHA and PPD decreases. It was suspected (Lanning, 1978) that the fluctuations, (e.g., those around puberty) are linked to the output of sex steroids. The data may indicate a stimulatory effect of moderate in contrast to very low plasma steroid levels. Unfortunately, the alterations were not correlated with pubertal development, menstrual cyclic events, or onset of the climacterium. Preliminary data indicate decreased PHA responses in women during ovulation (Bjune, 1979).

According to one report there is a loss of demonstrable *HLA* antigens on the surface of human lymphocytes during menstruation and supposed ovulation (Májský and Jakoubkova, 1976). This observation might be of a considerable importance but so far I have not seen reports confirming the findings (see section on "Relationship between MHS, Immune Responses, and Endocrinology").

Oral Contraceptives, Other Hormones, and Pregnancy. Some early studies (Ahlqvist, 1976) indicated decreased PHA responses in users of oral contraceptives. A slight decrease in PHA reactivity seemed to correlate directly with the duration of use and inversely with the progestagenic potency of the compound drug; the decreasing effect seemed to persist for some months and may have been mediated by some serum factor (Keller *et al.*, 1977). The plasma pregnancy zone protein mentioned above might have been involved.

Lymphocyte reactions to PHA and, in some studies, to other mitogens during pregnancy have been studied by many groups (Ahlqvist, 1976; Petrucco *et al.*, 1976; Tomoda *et al.*, 1976; Poskitt *et al.*, 1977). Decreased responses have generally been reported. The clearest inhibitions were found in the early studies (Ahlqvist, 1976), in which comparatively high concentrations of maternal sera were used in the incubation media.

The influence of estrogens, progestins, androgens, cortisol, and human placental lactogen and chorionic gonadotropin on human lymphocyte reactions *in vitro* are included in several studies (Petrucco *et al.*, 1976; Tomoda *et al.*, 1976; Mendelsohn *et al.*, 1977; Mori *et al.*, 1977; Poskitt *et al.*, 1977; Wyle and Kent, 1977; Siiteri *et al.*, 1977). The results are somewhat conflicting and many authors note large individual variations in the response. The clinical significance of many of these studies is doubtful since most authors used incubation media with very low plasma concentrations, thus disregarding the steroid-binding plasma globulins. The incubation medium of Mori *et al.*

(1977) contained 20% autologous plasma, and estradiol, estrone, estriol, testosterone, dehydroepiandrosterone, androstendion, and 17α-hydroxyprogesterone were found to have a very weak (if any) influence on PHA-induced transformation. Progesterone and 20α-dihydroprogesterone decreased the response but only in concentrations so high that they were regarded as unphysiological, with the possible exception of the placental surface. Siiteri *et al.* (1977) had observed that similar concentrations decreased the mixed lymphocyte reaction.

Phytohemagglutinin was reported to induce a two- to threefold increase in the number of dexamethasone binding sites in human lymphocytes (Neifeld *et al.*, 1977), but no estrogen-, androgen-, or progestin-binding sites were detected in unstimulated or PHA-stimulated lymphocytes. Members of this research group had previously reported a lack of glucocorticoid receptors in leukemic cells obtained from patients unresponsive to certain combinations of drugs. Murine and human lymphoma cells may have a greater than normal capacity to oxidize cortisol to the less potent cortisone (Ahlqvist, 1976). In 1953, cortisone was found to reverse the increase in rat lymphocyte size induced by adrenalectomy, and comparable observations had been made in human Addison's disease (Ahlqvist, 1976).

IMMUNE RESPONSES

Gonadal Influences. In almost all the studies reviewed (Ahlqvist, 1976), experimental gonadectomies in both sexes and estrogens and androgens were found to influence antibody responses. Females of many species, including human, are generally stronger antibody responders than males. Male gonadectomy increases antibody responses to female levels; endocrine interventions may influence antibody responses to thymus-independent and thymus-dependent antigens differently; and the class of immunoglobulins formed may be influenced by gonadectomy (Ahlqvist, 1976). The type and dose of estrogen, androgen, and of progestin (Vecchi *et al.*, 1976; Kenny and Diamond, 1977) used is important. The magnitude and direction of the effects of some endocrine interventions may be altered by adult thymectomy. Thus, the data are consistent with influences on the thymus. But, at least with regard to estrogens, we also have to consider direct effects on antigen-primed cells cultivated *in vitro,* low estrogen concentrations increasing and higher ones decreasing the number of antibody-forming cells (Kenny *et al.*, 1976). Also, in one strain of mice, androgens may promote the function of suppressor cells, while estrogens favor the development of helper T cells (see section on "Autoimmune Diseases").

The survival of weakly incompatible grafts (Graff *et al.*, 1969) and of strongly incompatible grafts in recipients treated with antithymocyte sera (Kongshavn and Bliss, 1970) is shorter in female than in male mice. Orchidectomy appears to shorten graft survival more than adrenalectomy (Graff *et al.*,

1969). The literature (Ahlqvist, 1976) contains both failures and moderate successes in attempts to prolong graft survival time with estrogens; the number of reported successes with progestins (Ahlqvist, 1976; Pettirossi *et al.,* 1976; Siiteri *et al.,* 1977) seem to outnumber the reports of failures (Ahlqvist, 1976; Vecchi *et al.,* 1976). Failures with progesterone may be due to the use of oily vehicles (Munroe, 1971); successes with some synthetic progestins may be due to their androgenic (Jänne *et al.,* 1978) or glucocorticoid (DiSorbo *et al.,* 1977) properties. The successes with progestins probably do not involve macrophages since progesterone blocks activity-inhibiting glucocorticoid receptors in these cells (Werb, 1978).

Immunologists working with sex hormones should also pay attention to the induction of progesterone receptors by estrogens. The increase in mouse ear thickness after sensitization with picryl chloride is decreased in estrogen-primed (dose-independent) mice in a dose-dependent fashion by progesterone (Carter, 1976). In similarly treated animals there was a remarkable growth *in utero* of xenografts (Moriyama and Sugawa, 1972) and of allografts (Watnick and Russo, 1968). Might the influence of hormones in this (possibly) preferential recipient site also be reflected in other organs?

The data reviewed above clearly indicate that gonadal factors can influence immune responses. With regard to the magnitude and, in some instances, the direction of the effects, many of the results appear to be contradictory. Thus, estradiol propionate increases hemolysin responses in C57BL ($H-2^b$) mice, while it had the opposite effect in C3H ($H-2^k$) mice (Stern and Davidson, 1955). Like immune responsiveness in general, the effect of gonadal hormones on immune responses also seems to be associated with the histocompatibility haplotypes of the animal strains used. By now, sufficient data are probably available to allow a mapping of these links in mice.

Adrenal Influences. There are reports indicating that adrenalectomy may enhance antibody formation and susceptibility to anaphylaxis and Arthus reaction in rodents (Ahlqvist, 1976). Also, glucocorticoids suppress antibody formation provided that they are administered before antigen challenge (van den Broek, 1971; Ahlqvist, 1976). In man, the usual doses of corticosteroids probably do not influence antibody formation (Frick, 1976).

The effect of glucocorticoids on cell-mediated responses has been regarded as small or negligible (Gabrielson and Good, 1967; van den Broek, 1971; Ahlqvist, 1976). After treatment with glucocorticoids, monocytes–macrophages fail, however, to respond to the macrophage-inhibiting factor and to become activated and Werb (1978) described inhibitory glucocorticoid receptors in macrophages of different species, including man; progesterone blocked the receptor. Increase in this cell fraction in fine-needle biopsies from human renal allografts heralded acute rejection better than increases in the other cell types studied, and large doses of glucocorticoids administered for brief periods were suspected of preventing rejection by influencing these cells

(Häyry *et al.*, 1980a). These observations correspond to findings in cortisone-treated mice in which an unresponsiveness to alloantigens could be restored by peritoneal macrophages, the unresponsiveness not being due to a lack of cytotoxic T cell precursors or of helper cells (Lee, 1977).

Gluco- and mineralocorticoids may also have effects less widely known than those described above. For example, skin allograft rejection in nude athymic mice may require the presence of neonatal thymus or of adult thymus and cortisol (Pierpaoli and Sorkin, 1973). Also, adrenalectomy has been claimed to prolong the survival of skin allografts in rats, an effect counteracted by implants of corticosterone and desoxycorticosterone. The enhancing effect of thyroxine on graft rejection in thyroidectomized animals appeared to require a functioning adrenal (Comsa, 1977). Antigen-primed rabbit lymph node cells do not give a proper secondary antibody response when restimulated *in vitro* unless cortisol, corticosterone, aldosterone, or some other steroids (not sex steroids) are present in low levels in the incubating media (Ambrose, 1970). Such data indicate that proper immune responses require low levels of gluco- and mineralocorticoids.

SOME DISEASES IN HUMANS

Oral contraceptives are suspected of being associated with an increased incidence of thrombotic events, viral disease, hypertension, pleurisy, duodenal ulcer, Crohn's disease, ulcerative colitis, gall bladder disease, erythema multiforme, erythema nodosum (Royal College of General Practitioners, 1974), genital moniliasis, photosensitivity, telangiectasis, herpes gestationis, alopecia, erythema nodosum, purpura, lupus erythematosus (Jelinek, 1970) and "idiopathic" pulmonary hypertension (Masi, 1976), but with a decreased incidence of rheumatoid arthritis (Royal College of General Practitioners, 1978).

The most common cyclic complaint in menstruating women is premenstrual tension, and women with premenstrual tension and psychic symptoms have high estrogen/progesterone ratios (Bäckström and Carstensen, 1974). In 1947, Zondek and Bromberg reported that in 73 of 116 women with premenstrual tension and other cyclic and menopausal complaints (such as migraine, urticaria, asthma, angioneurotic edema, and fever) there were delayed cutaneous hypersensitivity reactions to different estrogens and, in some cases, to other steroids as well. They also mentioned positive passive cutaneous transfer reactions. This track has since been followed by only a few gynecologists. Sulfated estrogens might possibly be less toxic. Immunoglobulins may bind steroids, but the mechanisms involved in the "endocrine allergy" have not been properly investigated (Ahlqvist, 1976).

Numerous mechanisms (e.g., Thompson and Lippman, 1974) may contribute to the suppressing effects of glucocorticoids on inflammation, resistance to infection, symptoms in autoimmune diseases, and on granulation tissue proliferation in man. To do justice to this vast literature, however, is beyond the scope of this review.

Findings indicating that mineralocorticoids may enhance graft rejection were mentioned above. Before the present immunologic era, Selye and numerous other investigators (Selye, 1950; Selye and Heuser, 1956) found that mineralocorticoids are prophlogistic (i.e., enhance inflammatory reactions). These experimental lesions resemble, to a great extent, the clinical vasculitic, arthritic, and other lesions now suspected of having an autoimmune pathogenesis (Ahlqvist, 1976). In mice, an arteritis belonging to this group of lesions was dependent on a functioning thymus (Svendsen, 1978). I suspect that prophlogisticity (in Selye's sense) and immune reactions may have common denominators.

Arterial hypertension is an important etiologic factor in the polyarteritis nodosa group of vasculitis (Alarcón-Segovia, 1977). Also, in the immune complex group of vasculitis, factors such as increased hydrostatic pressure and permeability may be important (Carter, 1973; Ahlqvist, 1976). Systemic sclerosis is mentioned in most textbooks on immunology, but plasma renin involved in the regulation of mineralocorticoids has also been considered to be a pathogenetic factor (Gavras et al., 1977).

Biogenic Amines and Other Transmitters

SOME ENDOCRINE ASPECTS

Catecholamines and other biogenic amines are produced by amine precursor uptake and decarboxylation (APUD) cells which also produce a number of polypeptide hormones (Pearse, 1969). The latter include several (e.g., ACTH, enkephalin, somatostatin) that are produced both in the gut wall and other peripheral tissues and in the brain (Rehfeld, 1979).

THYMUS AND THYMOCYTES

The expression of the θ-antigen on mouse embryo thymic stem cells *in vitro* is increased by isoproterenol and by histamine but not by phenylepinephrine, indicating that substances that tend to increase intracellular levels of cAMP enhance the maturation of thymic stem cells (Singh and Owen, 1976). Cyclic AMP and agonists increasing the intracellular levels of cAMP mimic a thymic hormone by inducing expression of the θ-antigen on mouse spleen and bone marrow cells (Bach et al., 1977). During maturation of mouse thymocytes, their cAMP response to histamine increases while that to isoproterenol decreases (Roszkowski et al., 1977). Thus, certain biogenic amines induce the expression of thymocyte surface antigens (see section "Mechanisms in Immune Reactions and Inflammation"), concomitantly altering the response of these cells to other biogenic amines.

Varicose adrenergic nerves are intimately associated with epithelial Hassal's corpuscles in some mammals. APUD cells have been described in the thymus of chickens and rats (Ahlqvist, 1976), and in view of the general properties of APUD cells, it is possible that these may produce some of the thymic polypeptide hormones. Given that there are acetylcholine receptors on thymic epithelial cells (see section "Myasthenia Gravis"), the morphology and function of the thymus appears to be under both adrenergic and cholinergic control.

IMMUNOLOGIC AND INFLAMMATORY REACTIONS

A number of reviews (Bourne et al., 1974; Kaliner and Austen, 1974; Ahlqvist, 1976; Frick, 1976; Roszkowski et al., 1977; Strom et al., 1977) indicate that a huge number of peripheral immunologic and inflammatory reactions are moderated by increases in the levels of cAMP or the cAMP/cGMP ratio in lymphoid cells, mast cells, neutrophils and other cells, and vice versa. Thus, the effects are opposite to those on thymocyte maturation.

The basic mechanisms are depicted in Figure 2. Briefly, epinephrine, histamine, and the prostaglandins E_1 and E_2 (but not PGF_2), via their cor-

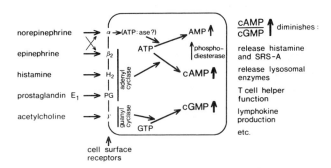

Figure 2. The influence of certain amines, acetylcholine (ACh), and the prostaglandins on immunologic and inflammatory effector cells. Decreases in the level of cAMP or in the cAMP/cGMP ratio enhance a number of immunologic and inflammatory reactions. β-Receptor blockers are propranolol and dichloro-isoproterenol, and butoxamine which more specifically blocks β_2-receptors (Frick, 1976). Blockers of α-receptors include phenoxybenzamine, dibenamine, phentolamine, tolazoline, and ergot alkaloids; phenothiazines, chlorpromazine and haloperidol to some extent have similar properties. Effects mediated by ACh receptors are diminished by physostigmine, organophosphates, the muscarinic atropine, scopolamine and a number of synthetic compounds. H_2-receptor effects are antagonized by buriamide and metiamide, and H_1-receptor effects responsible for histamine-mediated smooth muscle reactions are diminished by phenothiaziness and diphenhydramine. Quite a number of these drugs also influence psychic behavior.

responding cell surface receptors, activate adenyl cyclase, which increases the formation of cAMP from adenosine triphosphate (ATP). Intracellular phosphodiestererase converts cAMP into AMP; this is inhibited by theophylline, theobromine, and caffeine. Stimulation of α-receptors may decrease intracellular levels of cAMP, possibly by increasing the conversion of ATP to AMP by ATPase. Epinephrine has a stronger effect on β-receptors than norepinephrine, and acetylcholine increases the formation of cGMP from GTP. Certain blockers of the above effects are mentioned in the Figure legend. For details and exceptions please consult the above mentioned reviews.

These mechanisms are involved in modulating the effects of some mitogens on lymphoid cells, the strength of mixed lymphocyte reactions, B cell activation and antibody formation, T cell helper functions, antibody-mediated killer cell cytotoxicity, release of lysosomal enzymes from neutrophils, mast cell histamine release, release of the slow reacting substance of anaphylaxis and the eosinophil chemotactic factor, and platelet aggregation (e.g., Strom et al., 1977). Studies on isolated human and animal tissues have yielded corroborating results.

Histamine released from mast cells may moderate the response of other effector cells, and has been regarded as one of the self-regulatory mechanisms in inflammation and immune reactions (Bourne et al., 1974). The influence of some agonists on effector cells is time-dependent and rather short-lived (e.g., Higgins and David, 1976) which may be due to the formation of a complex between agonist–receptor and adenyl cyclase and a decrease in the number of available receptors (Mukherjee and Lefkowitz, 1976; cf. Lesniak and Roth, 1976).

Cortisol, some mineralocorticoids, and estradiol potentiate the cAMP-increasing effect of isoproterenol and PGE_1 (Lee and Reed, 1977), and testosterone has been suggested to increase the formation of adenyl cyclase (Singhal and Tsang, 1975).

Doubts about such mechanisms have also been expressed (e.g., Berenbaum et al., 1976). Some of the discrepancies may be explained by the occurrence of adenyl cyclase in different subcellular fractions. Early transient increases of cAMP generated by an intramembranous fraction of adenyl cyclase that induces phosphorylation of membrane proteins might even mediate the effects of lymphocyte mitogens, for example, while the later inhibitory increase of cAMP, possibly mediated by microsomal adenyl cyclase, is the one that is stimulated by adrenergic agonists, PGE_1, and theophylline (Parker, 1976).

It has just been reported that norepinephrine and interferon have similar effects on myocardial contraction rates, and both have antiviral effects (Blalock and Stanton, 1980). This may agree with the general effects of norepinephrine (Figure 2) and with the suggestion that certain β-adrenergic antagonists may be worth a trial in the treatment of malignant tumors (Ahlqvist, 1976).

HUMAN AND EXPERIMENTAL DISEASES

The experimental findings described in the preceding paragraphs correspond to the effects of biogenic amines and their antagonists in allergic diseases, and they bridge part of the gap between the concepts of extrinsic and intrinsic asthma bronchiale. The cAMP response to β-adrenergic agonists is decreased in lymphocytes from patients with asthma bronchiale (Lee *et al.*, 1977) and atopic eczema (Busse and Lee, 1976), indicating a metabolic defect in these patients. In chronic lymphatic leukemia, the cAMP response to different catecholamines and prostaglandins is blunted (Polgar *et al.*, 1977). The reviews mentioned above provide references to other studies indicating that these mechanisms operate *in vivo*.

Arterial hypertension is pathogenetically important in the periarteritis nodosa group and a similar vasculitis may be seen in methamphetamine abusers (Alarcón-Segovia, 1977). Vasculites due to sudden increases in blood pressure may morphologically resemble inflammations usually considered to be induced by immunologic mechanisms (Ahlqvist, 1976). In addition, increased intravascular hydrostatic pressure and vascular permeability influenced by catecholamines are important in the pathogenesis of different immune complex vasculites (Carter, 1973); fibrin deposition is an important feature in most vascular inflammations (Figure 1); and catecholamines and indoleamines (Konttinen, 1968; Nilsson, 1974) and the prostaglandins and thromboxanes (Vapaatalo and Parantainen, 1978) are involved in coagulation and thrombocyte function. Vascular smooth muscle from patients with scleroderma appears to be hyperresponsive to 5-hydroxytryptamine, and other studies reviewed indicate that a fibrosis-inducing effect of this amine is potentiated by norepinephrine (Winkelmann *et al.*, 1976). These amines combined with ceruloplasmin may render fibrin resistant to fibrinolysis (Ahlqvist, 1976).

These data indicate that biogenic amines may be of the utmost importance in diseases suspected of having an immunologic pathogenesis. Might the sex differences in catecholamine responses during stress (Frankenhaeuser *et al.*, 1978) contribute to sex differences in the incidence of autoimmune diseases (see section "Rheumatoid Arthritis") and other diseases associated with immune reactions?

The Thyroid Gland

SOME ENDOCRINE ASPECTS

The thyroid output of thyroxine (T_4) and triiodothyronine (T_3) is increased by pituitary thyrotropin (TSH) under the influence of a hypothalamic releasing hormone (TRH) which also releases prolactin. T_4 and T_3 exert a negative feedback on the pituitary and possibly also on the hypothalamus. Thyroxine is bound to prealbumin and to a specific carrier glycoprotein (TBG) from which it may be displaced by some psychotropic drugs (Bondy and Rosenberg, 1974), whereas T_3 is less firmly bound to protein. T_4 has been considered a prohormone for T_3. Estrogens increase whereas androgens decrease the TBG level and the response to TRH is stronger in women than in men. Catecholamines and 5-hydroxytryptamine may increase the secretion of thyroid hormones, and adrenergic nerves are intimately associated with thyroid follicular epithelium (Ahlqvist, 1976). TSH has additional metabolic effects that are not connected with the thyroid (Doniach, 1978).

LYMPHATIC ORGANS

There are species differences in the sensitivity of lymphatic organs to thyroid hormones. Early experiments indicate that in many species the weight of the thymus, and also of other lymphatic organs, is slightly decreased by thyroidectomy and/or thyrostatic drugs. A moderate hyperthyroidism slightly increases thymic size or potentiates the effects of adrenalectomy and gonadectomy, whereas in mice and guinea pigs large doses of T_4 induce thymic involution (Ahlqvist, 1976). After X-ray-induced involution of the guinea pig thymus, moderate doses of T_4 stimulate regeneration of the organ. Thyroxine treatment does not seem to affect the thymic epithelium or the medulla, whereas cortical thymocytes histologically appear stimulated (Grégoire and Duchateau, 1956). Such early observations agree with the recent finding that T_4 increases thymic thymidine uptake and the number of peripheral θ-positive T cells in C3H/He mice (Aoki et al., 1976).

Moderate doses of thyroxine induced in guinea pig lymph nodes significant differentiation waves of large lymphocytes (in areas which today would be regarded as thymus-dependent) and of plasma cells in medullary cords, although no antigens proper had been administered (Ernström, 1963). Such studies indicate direct stimulatory effects of thyroid hormones on lymphoid cells which may be explained by the nuclear T_3 receptors described in human lymphocytes (Ahlqvist, 1976).

Thymic hyperplasia with germinal centers and a generalized lymphatic hyperplasia is common in Graves' disease (cf. Grégoire and Duchateau, 1956; Aoki et al., 1976; Ahlqvist, 1976). Graves' disease and Hashimoto's thyroiditis are regarded as autoimmune diseases; in both there occur antibodies to thyroid epithelium. In the former, antibodies which stimulate cell function by acting on TSH receptors predominate, whereas in cases of thyroiditis with hypofunction there may be TSH receptor blocking antibodies (Doniach, 1977). In Graves' disease, oligomenorrhea is rather common and idiopathic Addison's disease may occur. The lymphatic hyperplasia is generally regarded as a purely immunologic phenomenon. Earlier, the hyperplasia was suspected to be due to an increased output of thyroid hormones or the coexistence of adrenal and gonadal dysfunction (cf. Grégoire and Duchateau, 1956). Aoki *et al.* (1976) observed an increase in peripheral T cell counts in patients with Graves' disease and a decrease in counts after treatment with radioiodine. Might the old concepts in part still be valid?

IMMUNE RESPONSES AND INFLAMMATION

In newborn and young rats, thyroidectomy decreases the number of splenic PHA-responding cells and of cells producing antibody to sheep red blood cells (Fabris, 1973). In intact C3H/He mice, thyroxine enhances the rejection of Ehrlich carcinoma cells (Aoki *et al.*, 1976). In Snell pituitary dwarf mice 7 days and 3 months old, thyroxine increases the hemagglutinin response to sheep red blood cells (Okouchi, 1976). In female C57BL ($H-2^b$) mice immunized with sheep red blood cells, increased numbers of splenic antibody-producing cells are found in T_3 and, curiously, the same response is seen in propyl thiouracil-treated mice, but serum antibodies are increased only in the group treated with TSH (Panoussopoulos *et al.*, 1976). The authors speculated about an influence mediated by lymphocytic TSH receptors.

A pituitary substance decreasing the peripheral sensitivity to thyroid hormones was thought to prolong the survival of xenografts in old rats since survival time was shortened to the level of young rats by hypophysectomy and thyroxine (Bilder and Denckla, 1977). A slightly prolonged allograft rejection time in thyroidectomized rats was also reported to be restored by thyroxine, provided the animals had a functioning thymus (Comsa, 1977). Some of the preceding experiments may require confirmation. In guinea pigs, depressed thyroid function increases resistance not only to anaphylactic shock but also to histamine and acetylcholine (Ahlqvist, 1976); thus, the effect need not be directly immunologic.

Plasma T_4 level is correlated with the level of free sulfate, and administration of the hormone increases the sulfate level (Tallgren, 1980). If the level of free sulfate is also correlated with the level of sulfated steroids, one could expect thyroid hormone balance to influence the peripheral effects of and adverse reactions to many steriods (see section "Gonadal and Adrenal Steroids"). In myxedema, the androsterone (5α-H)/etiocholanolone (5β-H) ratio is decreased but is reversed by thyroid hormone administration, and androsterone overcomes the hypercholesterolemia in myxedema (Gallagher *et al.*, 1960). In view of the "pyrogenic" properties of 5β-H steroids but not of their sulfate esters (Kappas and Palmer, 1967), it has been suspected that the not too infrequently "associated" hypothyreosis might be of pathogenetic significance in diseases regarded as autoimmune and especially in primary biliary cirrhosis (see section on "Primary Biliary Cirrhosis").

Calcium and Phosphate

Plasma calcium levels regulate the secretion of parathyroid hormone and of calcitonin. The latter is derived from thyroid parafollicular APUD cells. Phosphate deprivation increases the plasma calcium level.

In the rat, thymic cAMP-dependent mitotic activity and thymic size have been claimed to be correlated with the plasma calcium level and a circadian rhythm in the mitotic index also appears to be correlated with calcium level (Hunt and Perris, 1974). Certain estrogens appear to inhibit this effect (Morgan et al., 1976). On the other hand, rat glucocorticoid-induced thymocytolysis seems to be dependent on calcium, and an ionophore which moves calcium ions into the cells has a similar effect (Kaiser and Edelman, 1977). Neither parathormone nor calcitonin increases the expression of the θ-antigen on mouse embryo thymocytes in vitro (Singh and Owen, 1976).

Pig lymphocyte PHA transformation requires calcium, and the calcium ion level has been found both to enhance and to diminish immune responses to sheep red blood cells, the direction of the effect being dependent on the phase of the immune response at which the calcium level is altered (Ahlqvist, 1976; Swierenga et al., 1976).

Other reports describe correlations between low plasma phosphate levels and decreased phagocytosis by neutrophils (Craddock et al., 1974), joint symptoms in cattle, and multiple sclerosis (Ahlqvist, 1976). Oral phosphate is also reported to correct visual field defects in multiple sclerosis (Becker et al., 1974), to decrease growth hormone levels (Ahlqvist, 1976; Ditzel, 1975), and, possibly, to enhance fibrinolysis. In contrast, calcium ions may decrease lysis of fibrin(ogen) (Ahlqvist, 1976).

In addition to its influence on membrane stability, neuromuscular excitability, and the effects of hormones requiring the generation of cAMP, calcium ions participate in blood coagulation and other enzymatic mechanisms of importance in immunologic reactions. The effects on cellular contact (e.g., Gahmberg, 1977) might explain the influence on immune responses requiring T–B cooperation, but I am not qualified to judge to what extent minor physiological alterations may influence these events. Certain calcium salts have well-known beneficial effects on allergic manifestations.

The important influence of calcium ions and calmodulin on numerous mechanisms associated with immunologic and inflammatory reactions has been reviewed by Cheung (1980).

Insulin

I shall not deal with the extremely interesting relationship between the regulation of pancreatic insulin secretion and other hormones, nor with the glucagon, gastrin, or corticotropin in the endocrine pancreas (Rehfeld, 1979).

Early morphological studies did not indicate that insulin exerted any clear influence on the thymus or other lymphatic organs (Ahlqvist, 1976). In contrast to glucagon, insulin did not increase the expression of the θ-antigen on mouse embryo thymocytes (Singh and Owen, 1976).

The decreased number of PHA-responsive lymphocytes in poorly controlled (in contrast to well-controlled) insulin-requiring diabetes is thought to be due to a secondary metabolic effect (Ahlqvist, 1976). The low number of sheep red blood cell rosette-forming T lymphocytes in juvenile-onset diabetes was found, however, to be corrected by the addition of insulin (Cattaneo *et al.*, 1977).

Although no insulin receptors could be demonstrated on normal unstimulated lymphocytes, high affinity receptors have been found on lymphocytes stimulated by some mitogens and on a continuous cell line, and the increase induced by PHA is dramatic. The receptors described on unstimulated lymphocytes by some investigators might be due to contamination with other cells, notably macrophages (Cuatrecasas, 1974). Some early reports show prolonged graft survivals and decreased susceptibility to allergic reactions in experimental diabetes (Ahlqvist, 1976). Insulin augments lymphocyte-mediated cytotoxicity in rats and the effect is hypothesized to be mediated by a rise in cGMP (cf. Strom *et al.*, 1977). Might these mechanisms be involved in the susceptibility to infections in poorly controlled diabetes?

In juvenile-onset, insulin-requiring diabetes there is an increased incidence of *HLA* allotypes *B8, B18, Bw15, Dw3,* and *Dw4* (Svejgaard and Ryder, 1977). At least one *HLA*-linked type of this disease is regarded as autoimmune, and islet cell autoimmunity may be combined with a predisposition to islet cell damage by viral or other agents (Irvine, 1977). It is also of interest that the onset of diabetes shows peaks at menarche and menopause and at the same periods in men (Ezrin *et al.*, 1973).

Management of diabetes with insulin often results in the development of antibodies to the hormone, but sulfated insulin is less immunoreactive (Ezrin *et al.*, 1973).

Vascular lesions in diabetics involve the exudation of plasma proteins (Ahlqvist, 1976) but, in spite of the insulin–antibody complexes probably present in many cases, these lesions lack proper vasculitic features. Might this be due to lack of activation of complement or of fibrinolysis (cf. Figure 1)?

The Pituitary Gland

SOME ENDOCRINE ASPECTS

In the present section, I shall deal mainly with somatotropin, or growth hormone (GH), and prolactin. The secretion of GH from the pituitary mediated by a GH-releasing factor (GHRF), seems by and large to be enhanced by dopamine, norepinephrine, and 5-hydroxytryptamine, while it is generally decreased by α-blockers and somatostatin, β-blockers having the opposite effect. The increased GH secretion during sleep is not influenced by adrenergic blockers, whereas imipramine may have such an effect. The secretion of prolactin is decreased by an inhibitory factor (PIF) which appears to be dopamine, while it is increased by chlorpromazine, reserpine, the false neurotransmitter α-methyldopa, and 5-hydroxytryptamine. Thyrotropin (TSH), itself, appears to exert a negative feedback on the hypothalamic TSH-RF. L-DOPA and the serotonin precursor, 5-hydroxytryptophan, decrease TSH secretion. The output of corticotropin is also influenced by biogenic amines (Frohman, 1975). TSH-RF also releases prolactin, which, in turn, inhibits the formation of progesterone in the corpus luteum (Seppälä, 1978). Moreover, prolactin may influence the production of adrenal androgens in man (Vermeulen and Ando, 1978; Parker et al., 1978). The morning plasma level of GH is higher in women than in men, and is increased by estrogens but decreased by corticosteroids which also appear to decrease the peripheral metabolic effect of GH. Estrogens appear to be responsible for the higher female than male GH levels. Estrogens increase the secretion of prolactin, but sulfated estrogens may be less effective in this respect (Ahlqvist, 1976). Thyroid hormones may increase production of somatomedin or the sulfation factor which mediates many effects of GH, and also other pertinent data are discussed in a volume on GH, prolactin, placental lactogen, and related peptides (Pecile and Müller, 1976).

Pineal melatonin (see section "Primary Biliary Cirrhosis") may be antigonadotropic also in humans (Ahlqvist, 1976).

THE THYMUS

Growth hormone increases the weight of the thymus after hypophysectomy, and, in spite of earlier doubts (Dougherty, 1952), it seems that the effect on the thymus is stronger than that on other organs (Ahlqvist, 1976). This effect was observed in neonatal but not in adult Snell pituitary dwarf mice (Okouchi, 1976); in rats, the effect may require mineralocorticoids (Selye and Bois, 1955). Antisera to GH have been found to decrease thymic size in mice, and neonatal thymectomy to induce degranulation of pituitary acidophils (Pierpaoli et al., 1971). It has been claimed that GH stimulates rat thymocyte mitosis in vitro and influences thymic glucose metabolism (Ahlqvist, 1976). Moreover, rat thymocyte uridine incorporation has been recommended as an assay for the biologic activity of human GH, and the cells binding GH appear to be cortical thymocytes (Talwar et al., 1975). Murine and bovine thymocytes, in contrast to lymph node cells, appear to have specific GH receptors operating at physiological hormone levels (Arrenbrecht, 1974). The slight decrease in rat thymic epithelial cell volume induced by hypophysectomy appears to be reversed by GH. Surprisingly, corticotropin clearly appears to decrease the thymic epithelial cell volume in adrenalectomized rats (Morel *et al.*, 1977).

Prolactin receptors could not be demonstrated on postnatal murine thymocytes (Arrenbrecht, 1974), although the hormone appears to increase the expression of the θ-antigen on murine embryonic thymocytes *in vitro* (Singh and Owen, 1976). An extract with a strong prolactin activity failed to keep the rat thymus small during the postpartum period (Grégoire and Duchateau, 1956). The immunologic significance of prolactin may prove to be considerable if the report of its *Ia* surface antigen-increasing effect on murine and guinea pig mammary epithelium (Klareskog *et al.*, in press) is valid and if this hormone has a similar effect on, for example, thymic, salivary duct, and biliary epithelia. Prolactin is suspected to be responsible for the homing of lymphoid cells to the mammary gland (Klareskog *et al.*, in press). Might it have a similar effect in the thymus and in diseases such as Sjögren's syndrome and primary biliary cirrhosis?

Thyrotropin and a neurohypophyseal extract increased the number of rat thymic cells containing biogenic amines (Ahlqvist, 1976).

IMMUNE RESPONSES

Some investigators have shown that immune responses, usually to sheep red blood cells, are low in pituitary dwarf mice and in hypophysectomized rodents. Growth hormone, though, increases the response, especially if supplemented with thyroxine (a somatomedin effect?) (Ahlqvist, 1976). These early observations are supported by more recent work (Okouchi, 1976).

Allograft studies (Pierpaoli and Sorkin, 1973; Comsa, 1977; Bilder and Denckla, 1977) indicate such complicated relationships between GH, the thymus and thymic extracts, corticotropin, adrenal steroids, thyroid hormones, TSH, and other factors that I am unable to give a coherent summary of the findings and conclusions at this time. It has been claimed that prolactin (Ahlqvist, 1976) and TSH (Pannousopoulos *et al.*, 1976) have direct immunostimulatory effects. A Swiss group (Pierpaoli; Besedovski and Sorkin, this volume) presents data which indicate that immune responses are dependent on early secretion of different pituitary hormones and that the thymus plays a role in programing neuroendocrine functions. These relationships are extremely complicated and some of the findings may require confirmation. In addition to the mechanisms discussed by the above authors, it might be worthwhile to consider thyroid influences on steroid-binding globulins (Westphal, 1971) and hepatic somatomedin production and the direct effects of biogenic amines on immune responses (see section "Biogenic Amines"). Experimental data on the influence of central nervous system lesions on immune responses (e.g., Janković *et al.*, 1978) should also be considered in this context.

INFLAMMATORY REACTIONS

Selye (1950; Selye and Heuser, 1956; Ahlqvist, 1976) regarded GH as a prophlogistic hormone that enhanced a large number of different experimental vasculitic, arthritic, carditic, and other inflammatory reactions, prevented tuberculosis in cortisone-treated rats, and turned monilial foci into proper granulomas.

The sequelae of treatment with estradiol benzoate and follicle stimulating hormone in the rat (Perry, 1955) were remarkable: an initial lymphatic hyperplasia was followed by a tumorlike proliferation in the pituitary, and 4–12 months after the treatment there was a pronounced vasculitis described as periarteritis nodosa. The pituitary tumors induced by estrogens have growth-promoting, mammotropic, and sometimes corticotropic effects in rats (Ahlqvist, 1976). I have not come across studies on GH in users of oral contraceptives, but hyperprolactinemia is not uncommon (Seppälä, 1978). Further studies would be required to determine whether there are links between prophlogisticity in Selye's sense and immune responses.

In dogs, GH increases the fibrinogen level and the erythrocyte sedimentation rate (E.S.R.) and induces a neutrophilic reaction. Furthermore, in rats, it increases hepatic fibrinogen synthesis in 3 hours without altering the production of albumin (Ahlqvist, 1976). Increased plasma GH responses have only recently been found in certain diseases thought to be autoimmune (section on "Endocrine Features in Autoimmune Diseases"), but I have found no studies on prolactin in this group of diseases.

Pregnancy, an Immunologic Paradox?

A mother generally does not reject her fetoplacental F_1 hybrid graft until labor. For three reasons the role of immunosuppression in this state (Ahlqvist, 1976; Editorial 1977; Section "Gonadal and Adrenal Steroids") may have been overemphasized. First, the expression of histocompatibility antigens on early embryonic (Håkanson et al., 1975) and placental (Goodfellow et al., 1976) surfaces may be negligible. Second, the concentration of some steroids, especially progesterone, and of some other substances is much higher close to the placental surface than elsewhere in the maternal circulation. Among the latter, for example, is α-fetoprotein which binds estradiol (Keller et al., 1976); also, chorionic gonadotropin which may not be as important (e.g., Pattillo et al., 1976) as suggested earlier (Ahlqvist, 1976). Third, the estrogen-primed, progesterone-induced uterine decidua may be a preferential site for the survival of grafts (see section "Gonadal and Adrenal Steroids"; Bernard et al., 1978).

The preceding paragraph does not imply that pregnancy is not of interest in this context, since the course of many autoimmune diseases is fundamentally altered during this state (see section on "Endocrine Features in Autoimmune

Diseases''). This may involve some of the above substances that are present in the maternal circulation in concentrations higher than in nonpregnant subjects but lower than at the placental surface. Fetally derived histocompatibility antigen molecules circulating in the mother might play some role. The possible role of the pregnancy zone protein (see section "Gonadal and Adrenal Steroids") in rheumatoid arthritis has been discussed, but there are clinically normal pregnancies with low plasma levels of this protein (C.-B. Laurell, personal communication). In 1976, I erroneously stressed decreased size of the thymus during pregnancy, suspecting a lack of thymotropic factors, especially of GH. Theoretically, placental lactogen interfering with GH receptors (Pernitcheva-Rostaing and Morin, 1976; Lesniak *et al.*, 1977) might be involved. The rat thymus may, however, be of normal size during pregnancy, the decrease in size after parturition being correlated with a decreased corticosteroid-binding globulin level (Westphal, 1971). According to a very recent report (Beck-Nielsen *et al.*, 1979), the number of insulin receptors on monocytes is decreased in pregnant women. A similar effect of pregnancy on lymphocytes might be immunosuppressive.

The effect of pregnancy on autoimmune diseases might also be due to hormonal effects on mechanisms other than purely immunologic ones (see Figure 1). Plasma protein levels, for example, undergo considerable alterations (Ganrot, 1972), and a large number of maternal steroids have unknown effects on relevant mechanisms (Ahlqvist, 1976). Also, the plasma levels of many steroid sulfates are increased (Ahlqvist, 1976) and may parallel the increases in free sulfate and T_4 concentrations (Tallgren, 1980; Section "The Thyroid Gland"). Considerably more attention should be paid to the relationships between pregnancy, inflammatory reactions, and the activity of many immunologic, inflammatory, and other diseases.

Concluding Comments

Almost all the hormones dealt with here have been shown to influence immunologic and allied phenomena. With few exceptions, the mechanisms involved have not been clarified. I shall comment on a few examples, the elucidation of which may be most important.

Gonadectomy and adrenalectomy in both sexes remove moderating influences on thymic size. Immune responses are, in general, stronger in females, and the prevalence of autoimmune diseases is higher in this sex. The suggestion that androgens promote thymic suppressor functions and estrogens enhance helper functions in certain mice (see section on "Systemic Lupus Erythematosus") may be an oversimplification. There are estrogen and androgen receptors in the rat thymus, and the former, at least, are epithelial. Estrogens have been found to induce thymocyte depletion and late epithelial (pathological) proliferation, while androgens have been suggested to induce primary degenerative alterations in the epithelium. Might sex steroids and prolactin alter in the thymus, as in the mammary gland, the expression of *Ia* antigens, thus explaining protracted effects of sex steroids on immune responses? Is there, in some autoimmune diseases, lack of a moderating influence by adrenal weak androgens on the thymus? Is part of the estrogen effect mediated by growth hormone? Do mineralocorticoids stimulate the thymus and immunologic reactions? Rodent thymic glucocorticoid receptors are thymocytic (and epithelial?); the lytic receptors may be less important in adult man.

High concentrations of progesterone may have immunosuppressive effects, but blocking of macrophage glucocorticoid receptors might also be important. These receptors might explain immunosuppressive effects of glucocorticoids. Do (weak?) androgens increase the level of certain complement components in man, too (see section on the "Major Histocompatibility System")? Biogenic amines and other transmitters influence immunologic and inflammatory reactions at many levels. In peripheral tissues, such reactions are generally enhanced by α-adrenergic and cholinergic stimuli, while β-adrenergic stimuli have opposite effects. These influences are mediated by cyclic nucleotides. In this respect the stronger male than female catecholamine responses during stress are interesting (see section on "Biogenic Amines").

The stimulating effect of thyroid hormones on lymphatic organs and immunologic reactions may be due to direct effects on lymphocytes. The net effect of alterations in the plasma calcium level remains to be elucidated. Insulin might be needed by transformed lymphocytes in order to permit them to exert their effects.

Most hormones influence the secretion and effects of other hormones. Estrogens, for instance, enhance the secretion of growth hormone and prolactin, induce progesterone receptors, increase the levels of three specific hormone-binding globulins and, in addition, increase the level of certain acute phase proteins and appear to induce a slightly hypercoagulable state. In these and other respects, there may be considerable differences between the generally stronger effects of certain synthetic estrogens (and of organic esters of natural estrogens?) and the effects of free natural estrogens and their sulfate esters. Progesterone and androgens influence the metabolism of other steroids in the liver. Progesterone secretion by the corpus luteum is decreased by prolactin, etc. One oversimplifies by writing about estrogens, androgens, and progestins collectively.

The pattern is far from clear. I suggest that it might be worthwhile to start by studying the influence of the interrelated functions of the gonads, the adrenal gland (including the production of weak androgens), the thyroid, amine-producing cells, and the pituitary on "immune functions." Furthermore, the results of such studies (and of studies on the effects of many drugs) will probably be ambiguous unless they are related to the genetic background (*HLA* and other traits) of the subjects. Such studies may provide us with therapeutic tools that are more physiological than the ones presently used in diseases associated with immunologic phenomena.

ENDOCRINE FEATURES IN SOME AUTOIMMUNE DISEASES

In this section I shall review data demonstrating endocrine disturbances in certain diseases associated with autoimmunity. For the sake of brevity, I shall not comment on the possible pathogenetic significance of most findings and I request the reader, by turning to the corresponding parts of the Section "Influences of Different Hormones," to draw such conclusions her- or himself. Relevant data will also be cited in the last two Sections.

Rheumatoid Arthritis

The *HLA* allotypes *A2, B27,* and *Dw4* (Svejgaard and Ryder, 1977) and *DRw4* (Stastny, 1978) are increased in adult rheumatoid arthritis (RA). The overall female/male (F/M) sex ratio is 3.2/1, but in a rheumatoid factor-positive young adult onset group it was 6.8/1 (Josipovic *et al.,* 1977). The menarche of women who later developed RA may have been delayed by about 2 years compared to the mean in a Finnish population (K. Sievers, preliminary, unpublished data). Preceding his introduction of the effects of cortisone, Hench (1949) stated that "any theory on the aetiology of rheumatoid arthritis must take into account the powerful ameliorating influence of jaundice and pregnancy." The influence of pregnancy has been confirmed by Persellin (1977) who suspected (erroneously? Section "Pregnancy. An Immunologic Paradox") the pregnancy zone protein to be involved.

Microscopically, there are considerable similarities between the synovitis in RA and the synovial alterations occurring in most other clinical entities associated with arthritis. In RA acute phase protein reactions and the E.S.R. seem to correlate better with local clinical synovitic activity than immunological parameters (Ahlqvist, 1981). Attention should be paid to mechanical and rheological (induced by, for instance, fibrinogen) factors, genetic differences in the production and effects of vasoactive amines, prostaglandins, and of kinins, and to local complement activation by factors other than immunological ones as possible causes of synovial exudation. I also suspect that the local metabolic alterations (induced by exudation) may be important mediators of inflammatory cell reactions (Ahlqvist, 1981). Proteolytic activation of B cells (Figure 1) might also be involved. Active RA, in my experience, is almost invariably associated with synovial fibrinous exudates, but immune reactions to fibrinogen-fibrin split products (Figure 1) do not seem to have evoked the interest of many rheumatologists.

Endocrine mechanisms may be involved. The excretion of androsterone, dehydroepiandrosterone, and etiocholanolone is decreased in female RA patients (Masi *et al.*, 1977), and there are scattered reports on beneficial influences of androgens, progesterone (Ahlqvist, 1976), and oral contraceptives (see section "Gonadal and Adrenal Steroids"). The excretion of 17-hydroxycorticosteroids is decreased in female RA patients with a high E.S.R. (Pekkarinen and Kalliomäki, 1958). Thyroidectomy frequently aggravates RA (Kalliola *et al.*, 1957). In attempts to elucidate the significance of reported alterations in the metabolism of catecholamines (Igari *et al.*, 1977; Kudintseva, 1977) and amino acids (Kalliomäki *et al.*, 1966; Gerber, 1975), it might be worthwhile to consider also the low incidence of RA in schizophrenia (Horrobin, 1977) and the sex differences in catecholamine responses to stress (see section on "Biogenic Amines").

Chronic Active Hepatitis and Primary Biliary Cirrhosis

There is an increased prevalence of *HLA* allotypes *A1, B8,* and *Dw3* in autoimmune chronic active hepatitis (CAH) (Svejgaard and Ryder, 1977), whereas no such links have been found between primary biliary cirrhosis (PBC) and the *HLA* system (Sherlock, 1976). There are, however, cases with clinical, morphological, and serological features of both diseases (Ahlqvist, 1979). Both CAH and PBC are more common in females than in males and PBC favors older age groups. Any theory on the etiology of these diseases must, therefore, take into account their peculiar age and sex distributions (Sherlock, 1976). Amenorrhea and virilization as well as abnormally elevated GH responses are common in CAH (Ahlqvist, 1976, 1979). Could the patients suffer from some acquired adrenal hyperplasia (AAH) in spite of the fact that (one type of ?) AAH, in contrast to the congenital form of the disease, does not appear to be associated with *HLA* (New *et al.*, 1979; Dupont *et al.*, 1978)? May there (as in RA) be decreased production of adrenal androgens, the virilization being due to increased peripheral formation of dihydrotestosterone? Amenorrhea and synthetic estrogens may unfavorably influence the clinical activity of CAH, whereas pregnancy frequently has the opposite effect (Ahlqvist, 1979). Also, the not uncommon hypothyreosis might be of a pathogenetic significance, especially in PBC (Section "The Thyroid Gland"). Lesions similiar to those in CAH have been induced by α-methyldopa and isoniazid. Both drugs, as well as 17α-substituted synthetic estrogens, may be turned (by cytochrome P-450 generated superoxide anions) into toxic covalently binding metabolites which might also function as haptens (Ahlqvist, 1979; cf. Dybing *et al.*, 1976).

I suspect that endocrine aberrations, possibly mediated in part by alterations in the bile (decreased formation of well-hydroxylated, nontoxic bile acids?), may influence the clinical activity of these diseases (Ahlqvist, 1976, 1979). Monohydroxylated lithocholic acid in rabbits induces a cirrhosis

(Holsti, 1956) that resembles CAH (Ahlqvist, 1979), and the diminished output of bile and of taurocholic acid induced by adrenalectomy and the restoration of bile flow by glucocorticoids (Telkkä *et al.*, 1964) are not inconsistent with this hypothesis. Consistent with the skin hyperpigmentation, a deficiency of pineal melatonin formation, by inducing a decreased formation of prostaglandin E_1, has been claimed to be of pathogenetic significance in PBC (Cunnane *et al.*, 1979).

My suspicion that endocrine factors may activate CAH and PBC has recently been summarized in periodicals (Ahlqvist 1980a,b) more easily accessible than my small monograph (Ahlqvist, 1979).

Systemic Lupus Erythematosus

Systemic lupus erythematosus (SLE) is characterized to a large extent by autoantibodies to different nuclear components and by vascular lesions regarded to be of the immune complex type. Thymic epithelial hyperplasia is common and there may be thymic germinal centers. The incidence of lymphomas is high. The level of a thymic hormone is low (Bach *et al.*, 1977), and a number of complement deficiencies are associated with SLE (Lachmann and Hobart, 1978).

There is an increased incidence of *HLA-B5* and *B8* in Caucasians suffering from the disease (Svejgaard and Ryder, 1977). Haplotypes involving complement deficiences may also be involved. The F/M incidence ratio is age-dependent: 0–4 years, 1.4/1; 5–9, 2.3/1; 10–14, 5.8/1; and 15–19, 5.4/1. In adult clinical cases, the mean ratio is 5.9/1 with a peak at 30–39 years of 8.1/1. In patients over 60 years of age, the ratio is only 2.2/1 (Masi and Kaslow, 1978). (Please compare these data with the endocrine alterations at puberty described in Section "Gonadal and Adrenal Steroids"). The direction of the influence of pregnancy may be more unpredictable than in RA (Ahlqvist, 1976), but post-partum exacerbations are common (Zurier, 1975). Oral contraceptives may increase the incidence of disease. The luteinizing hormone-releasing factor induces an excessive increase of luteinizing hormone, whereas the increase of follicle-stimulating hormone corresponds to the response in controls (Yozai, 1976). One monozygotic twin who underwent oophorectomy escaped the disease in contrast to her sister, and there may be an increased prevalence of SLE in Klinefelter's syndrome (Masi and Kaslow, 1978). Klinefelter patients usually have high urinary gonadotropin but low plasma testosterone levels. In view of the complement deficiencies associated with SLE-like disease (Lachmann and Hobart, 1978) and of the influence of androgens on complement levels in mice (see section on Major Histocompatibility System), it would be interesting to gather data on complement levels in Klinefelter patients suffering from SLE. In contrast to the controls, two patients with both diseases metabolized a greater proportion of labeled estradiol

into estriol than into 2-hydroxyesterone (Stern *et al.,* 1977), and similar observations have been made in female SLE patients (Lahita *et al.,* 1979). I have
not come across studies on the excretion of adrenal androgens in females with
this disease. It is well known that α-methyldopa and isoniazid may also induce
SLE-like disease (cf. CAH, above).

New Zealand black (NZB) and NZB/NZW F_1 hybrids develop a disease
very much resembling SLE. The animals harbor a C-type virus. At birth the
animals appear immunologically hyperactive; later they produce a number of
autoantibodies, show decreased suppressor T cell functions, and levels of a
thymic hormone are low. Subsequently, the anti-DNA antibodies switch from
IgM to IgG and the animals get hemolytic anemia and glomerulonephritis; in
old age they tend to develop lymphomas. The disease develops at an earlier
age in females than in males (Talal, 1977) but the onset of hemolytic disease is
delayed in actively breeding females (Ahlqvist, 1976). An antiestrogen prolongs survival (Duvic *et al.,* 1978), and it was reported (Roubinian *et al.,* 1978)
that prepubertal castration hastens the development of the disease in male
mice, an effect which is augmented by estradiol. Prepubertal castration of
females does not clearly decrease mortality, while estradiol accelerates the
development of disease. In castrated females, dihydrotestosterone decreases
mortality and the same effect is observed in older males about to develop active disease. Neonatal thymectomy accelerates the disease in males. It is
suspected that androgens promote the function of suppressor cells, whereas
estrogens favor the development of helper T cells (Roubinian *et al.,* 1978).
The final explanation may be more complicated, and I regret that I have no
information about the effect of hormones on mortality after thymectomy or
of adrenal weak androgens on the disease.

The endocrinology of this spontaneous disease in mice was discussed at a recent conference (Talal, 1979). None of the contributors, however seem to have
considered fully the effects of steroid hormones on the thymic epithelium
(Ahlqvist, 1976; Section "Gonadal and Adrenal Steroids") or on complement
levels (see section on "Major Histocompatibility System").

Myasthenia Gravis (MG)

In Caucasians with myasthenia gravis (MG), the overall prevalence of
HLA-A1, B8, and *Dw3* is increased (Svejgaard and Ryder, 1977). *HLA-B8* is
significantly increased only in females with onset of the disease before the age
of 35 (Pirskanen, 1976). In this group, aggravation of symptoms often seemed
to be preceded by psychic stress, infection, menarche, puerperium, or the use
of oral contraceptives (R. Pirskanen, personal communication). Antibodies to
acetylcholine (ACh) receptors have been described in MG (Mittag *et al.,* 1976)
and probably are pathogenetically important (Grob, 1976). ACh receptors occur not only on skeletal muscle but also on thymic epithelial (Engel *et al.,*

1977) and myoid (Kao and Drachman, 1977) cells. Antibodies to ACh receptors have also been found in the cerebrospinal fluid (Lefvert and Pirskanen, 1977). In patients with MG and thymic hyperplasia with germinal centers, plasma levels of the sulfates of dehydroepiandrosterone and androsterone are low (cf. RA and SLE) and, curiously, the levels tend to decrease further after thymectomy (Papatestas *et al.*, 1977). These findings, combined with those on adrenal androgens in RA and the not uncommon occurrence of thymic germinal centers in other autoimmune diseases, raise interesting questions concerning the relationship between adrenal androgens and other steroids and the thymus. Unfortunately, relevant data are not presently available.

Other Diseases and Comments

Links between endocrine function and disease activity also exist in other autoimmune diseases. Relevant findings in thyroid autoimmunity, multiple sclerosis and systemic sclerosis have been discussed in preceding sections.

I suspect that fundamental but practical problems in clinical autoimmunity cannot be solved unless immunologic disturbances are considered side by side with the established metabolic, endocrinologic, psychological, and genetic factors and with the mechanisms depicted in Figure 1. It would require a target-centered teamwork of a kind that I have not yet seen.

RELATIONSHIPS BETWEEN THE MAJOR HISTOCOMPATIBILITY SYSTEM, IMMUNE RESPONSES, METABOLIC EVENTS INCLUDING NEUROTRANSMITTER EFFECTS, AND ENDOCRINOLOGY

Research leading to the discovery and molecular analysis of the histocompatibility antigens was initiated to reveal the laws underlying the long recognized failure of man to accept tissue grafts from his fellow man, including most of his own kin. There gradually evolved from this a recognition of the significance of the major histocompatibility system (MHS) in immune responses to other than alloantigens and in different cellular interactions (Section "Mechanisms in Immune Reactions and Inflammation"). The fact that many of the diseases subsequently found to be linked to certain *HLA* allotypes belonged to the group called, or suspected to be, autoimmune, served to focus interest on the significance of the MHS-coded surface glycoproteins in the cellular contacts of importance in immunology. The following pages indicate that the time has come to challenge the concept that immunology is the sole link between *HLA* and disease.

The Mouse

Iványi (1978) recently reviewed his own pioneer studies and those of others on the links between the mouse MHS (*H-2*) and immunologic and other functions. A number of traits are quantitatively (and some qualitatively) influenced by the *H-2* system, that is, quantitative expression of these traits is linked to the histocompatibility haplotypes (as detected by differences in the cell surface antigens) of the mouse. To mention a few: natural killer cells, thymus, spleen, and lymph node mass, manifestation of Ly-1 on lymph node cells, splenic PHA responsiveness and the proportion of T and B cells, adjuvant effects, viral leukemogenesis, as well as the levels of total complement (C), and the Ss and Slp proteins which apparently are subclasses of C4 (cf. Dupont *et al.*, 1978). Further examples include: body mass, skeletal characteristics, tail length, mating preference of males, and expression of the male *H-Y* antigen (Section "Gonadal and Adrenal Steroids") on thymic and skin cells. Last but not least, the *H-2* system influences a number of purely endocrine parameters: testis mass, plasma testosterone binding globulin levels, the lytic effect of cortisone on thymocytes, the cytosol cortisol-binding protein, the sensitivity of gonadal targets to testosterone after castration, and the cAMP level in liver cells (Iványi, 1978). To these may be added estrogen effects on murine leukemogenesis and immune responses, and probably corticosterone production in mice (see section on "Influences of Different Hormones"), as well. I shall briefly comment on some of the findings.

In mice, the IgG response to a hapten coupled to bovine insulin is linked to *H-2* haplotypes such that *H-2^d* mice are good and *H-2^b* mice are low responders, and *H-2^k* mice are nonresponders (Kolb *et al.*, 1977). The cAMP level in the liver decreases in the order *H-2^a* and *H-2^b*, *H-2^d*, and *H-2^k* (Meruelo and Edidin, 1975). The *H-2^a* haplotype ensures a relatively higher testosterone level and testosterone-binding capacity than *H-2^b*. H-2^b homozygotes have larger vesicular glands and smaller testes and are less susceptible to viral leukemogenesis than *H-2^k* homozygotes (Iványi, 1978). The Ss protein level decreases in the order *H-2^d, H-2^b,* and *H-2^k*, being very low in the last mentioned (Shreffler and David, 1975). Generally, the level is higher in males than in females and the female levels of Ss and Slp proteins are increased by androgens, but there are no sex differences in a mutant with testicular feminization (Shreffler and David, 1975). Complement component levels thus appear to be dependent on androgen effects in adult animals. It has been suspected that some erythrocyte antigens coded for by MHS-genes in the mouse, as in man, might be complement components (Dupont *et al.*, 1978). It even seems possible that the effect of androgens on the SLE-like disease in mice (Section "Systemic Lupus Erythematosus") may be due, in part, to an increase in complement components.

In contrast to the findings with complement components, the sex differences in IgM and IgG_2 levels in one of two strains of mice with different sensitivities to androgens of gonadal targets are not altered by early gonadectomy, possibly indicating that in this respect androgens exert their influence at a very early stage of life (Cohn and Hamilton, 1976).

Thymocyte maturation (alterations in the expression of surface glycoproteins; decrease in cortisone sensitivity) in the mouse is paralleled by an increase in the cAMP response to histamine and a decrease in the response to isoproterenol (see section "Biogenic Amines").

Man

The MHS in man (*HLA*) codes for the surface glycoprotein molecules responsible for graft rejection (Section "Mechanisms in Immune Reactions") and is also involved in immune responses to other antigens (Sasazuki *et al.*, 1978).

HLA is also involved in the expression of complement components C2, C4 and factor B of the alternate pathway (Lachman and Hobart, 1978). Thus, it plays a part in the proteolytic activation of C3. The Rodgers and Chido erythrocyte blood group antigen molecules present in about 97% of the population are also coded for by this system (Dupont *et al.*, 1978). These molecules have been shown to be antigenic components of C4 and, interestingly, the lack of these components is in positive linkage disequilibrium with *B8* and with *B12, Bw35* and *B5,* respectively. This may imply that the complement system, via C4, is involved as a genetic host factor in diseases associated with these *HLA* allotypes. A *HLA-B18*/C2 deficiency/*Dw2* haplotype is associated with cases of SLE (Dupont *et al.*, 1978), and various complement deficiencies in man have been associated with SLE-like diseases (Lachmann and Hobart, 1978) and intrinsic asthma (Brostoff *et al.*, 1976). I have no information about the influence of testosterone and weaker androgens on complement levels in man.

One type of congenital adrenal hyperplasia in man is due to a defect in steroid 21-hydroxylase. This deficiency gene has been mapped close to the *HLA-B* locus (Dupont *et al.*, 1978). Acquired adrenal hyperplasia with 21-hydroxylase deficiency, however, has a different genetic background (New *et al.*, 1979).

The association between asthma and the MHS (Brostoff *et al.*, 1976; Rachelsky *et al.*, 1976) and the decreased lymphocyte cAMP responses in asthma (Lee *et al.*, 1977) might indicate links between cAMP and MHS in man as in mice, a point that might be of the utmost importance from an endocrinologic point of view.

Certain *HLA* allotypes increase the risk of development of certain autoimmune diseases. Some idiopathic inflammatory diseases, however, have not yet been found to be linked to *HLA*. These include primary biliary cirrhosis, scleroderma, Hashimoto's disease (in contrast to the closely related Graves' disease), and polymyalgia rheumatica. In addition, many diseases associated with *HLA* cannot be regarded as immunologic diseases, for example, polycystic kidney disease, retinoblastoma, idiopathic hemochromatosis, adrenocortical hyperfunction, schizophrenia, and manic–depressive disorder (Svejgaard and Ryder, 1977).

The progesterone- (Westphal, 1971) and propranolol- (Scott *et al.*, 1979) binding acute phase glycoprotein orosomucoid is synthesized by and expressed on human lymphoblasts in a *HLA*-like manner and shows a significant amino acid homology with IgG (Andersson and Gahmberg, 1980). In many respects it also resembles the cortisol-(CBG) and testosterone-(SHBG) binding glycoproteins (Westphal, 1971). Since there are CBG-like molecules in human lymphocytes (Werthamer *et al.*, 1973), might CBG and SHBG also be associated in a orosomucoid-like manner with human lymphoid cells?

The possibility that physiological variations in the levels of sex steroids influence the expression of *HLA* antigens on peripheral lymphocytes (Section "Gonadal and Adrenal Steroids") might be of some importance in cellular cooperation and the development of autoimmune diseases in females.

Pretreatment of *HLA-A1* lymphocytes with chlorpromazine, dopamine, norepinephrine, sulpyrid, propranolol, haloperidol, or apomorphine prevents or decreases the cytotoxic effect of an antiserum to *HLA-A1*. In similar fashion, the drugs also decrease the cytotoxic effect of this antiserum on *HLA-A3, A10,* and *A11* cells, antigens which crossreact with *HLA-A1*. The drugs do not have this effect on lymphocytes that do not react with the antiserum to *HLA-A1* (Scorza-Smeraldi *et al.*, 1977). The drugs also alter the PHA-induced transformation of these lymphocytes in a fashion different from that of other lymphocytes, and it is claimed that there are differences in the clinical effects of chlorpromazine parallelling the results obtained with lymphocytes *in vitro* (Bellodi *et al.*, 1977). It was also suggested that *HLA*-antigens and β-adrenergic receptors originate from a common ancestor. Similarly, *HLA-A12* has been found to decrease the amount of prednisolone required to inhibit lymphocyte transformation by PHA (Becker *et al.*, 1976).

Comments

These few examples, combined with many of the findings described in the preceding sections, prove that in the mouse, as well as in man, the MHS is closely linked to endocrine and metabolic events, and I conclude that it may be deceptive to regard the latter as separate from mechanisms in immunology and autoimmunity (cf. Svejgaard and Ryder, 1976; Dupont *et al.*, 1978). Cellular receptors for hormones other than thyroid and steroid ones are located on cell surfaces and such hormones exert their effects by inducing the formation of cyclic nucleotides. Our knowledge about the structure of these receptor molecules is limited (e.g., Barnard, 1979), but, since most cell surface proteins may resemble antigenically important glycoproteins, there is reason to suspect that immunologic, metabolic, endocrinologic, and other mechanisms may prove to be even more intimately related to each other than is suspected at present.

Autoimmune and many other diseases seem to have a multifactorial pathogenesis. If the combination of activating mechanisms is not the same in all patients it follows that a promising drug may not have the same effect in all patients suffering from "one" disease. Drug effect statistics may therefore be based on biologically false concepts, making a good clinical eye indispensable—unless, perhaps, all patients can be mapped with regard to *HLA* and numerous other genetic traits (Ahlqvist, 1980b).

CONCLUSIONS AND COMMENTS

A number of mechanisms that cannot be regarded as strictly immunologic have to be considered in diseases associated with immunologic aberrations. Almost all the hormones and transmitters dealt with above have been shown to influence immunologic reactions (Section "Influences of Different Hormones"). There are data indicating an altered endocrine homeostasis in autoimmune diseases, and some of the alterations might influence the activity of the diseases (Section "Endocrine Features of Autoimmune Diseases"). A number of not only immunologic but also of metabolic and endocrine functions are associated with the major histocompatibility system (MHS) in the mouse and in man. Associations between *HLA* and autoimmunity might be due, in part, to endocrine and metabolic mechanisms secondarily reflected in tissue damage and autoimmune aberrations. Mechanisms regarded as immunologic may be fundamentally endocrinologic (section on "Major Histocompatibility System").

The *HLA*-associated genetic background of autoimmune and other diseases should not dictate a fatalistic standpoint with regard to treatment of these diseases since many MHS-associated traits are, quantitatively, under hormonal control. The use of hormonal interventions in immunologic disease, with few exceptions, is limited to glucocorticoids and drugs mimicking or antagonizing biogenic amines and similar compounds. The major part of this review indicates that there are additional ones worth consideration.

Do prophlogisticity in Selye's sense and immune reactions (Section "Gonadal and Adrenal Steroids" and "The Pituitary Gland") have common denominators? Do the shortcomings in Selye's work derive from the circumstance that it was performed before the immunologic era and that he generalized a bit too much, failing to consider the great differences between diseases that are regarded today as autoimmune? Do the long since forgotten concepts about vagotonia and sympathicotonia now reappear as transmitter effects on immunologic and inflammatory reactions mediated by cyclic nucleotides? Decades ago, the physician considered the constitution of his patient; today he determines his *HLA* antigens. Are the fundamental mechanisms in disease so complicated that a general practitioner or a specialist with advanced knowledge of some of the mechanisms involved will never be able to give his patient the multifactorial treatment that he may require?

All the hypothalamic releasing factors, acetylcholine, different amino acids, biogenic amines, prostaglandins, most steroids, various peptides such as somatostatin, angiotensin, thyrotropin (Barchas *et al.*, 1978) and "proopiocortin" fragments (Krieger and Liotta, 1979) are mentioned among the substances that are certain or possible neurotransmitters. Cyclic nucleotides mediate transmitter effects in the brain. In mice, lithium chloride in doses corresponding to those used in mania induce a considerable involution of the thymus (Pérez-Cruet and Dancey, 1977). In view of these facts and of the data reviewed on the influences of hormones on immunologic and inflammatory mechanisms, the links between *HLA* and metabolic and mental disease, and the well-known psychic effects of corticosteroids, thyroid hormones, progesterone, and different amines and their blockers, I think that I am justified in stating that a denial of the possibility of close links between mental state and immunologic reactions ought to be regarded as scientific suicide. I have reviewed mechanisms which may explain how disturbed mental health and stress could influence, via the endocrine system, the course of "organic" diseases associated with immune reactions. I shall leave it to others to answer the question of whether the concept of psychosomatic disease should be extended.

ACKNOWLEDGMENTS

Leif C. Andersson and Sykkö Pesonen checked parts of my text on immunologic and endocrinologic data, respectively. Robert von Essen and Leif G. Tallgren have spontaneously sent me copies of relevant papers. Elvi Kaukokallio corrected my English, and Raili Korpela typed the manuscript. Medica Pharmaceuticals Co., Ltd. helped me in the computerized bibliographic search. My knowledge of endocrinology and of coagulation originally stems from textbooks (Bondy and Rosenberg, 1974; Ezrin *et al.*, 1973; Konttinen, 1968; Nilsson, 1974) that have not been quoted to the extent that they deserve. To all of you, as well as to many colleagues at this and other hospitals with whom I have had stimulating discussions, I extend my sincere thanks.

REFERENCES

Adlercreutz, H., Lillienberg, L., and Svanborg, A. (1979). Effect of sequential estrogen-progestin therapy on the plasma level of estrogens and lipids in postmenopausal women. *Acta Endocrinol. (Copenhagen)* **92**, 319–329.
Aguet, M., Andersson, L. C., Andersson, R., Wight, E., Binz, H., and Wigzell, H. (1978). Induction of specific immune unresponsiveness with purified mixed leucocyte culture-activated

T lymphoblasts as autoimmunogen. II. An analysis of the effects measured at the cellular and serological levels. *J. Exp. Med.* **147**, 50–62.

Ahlqvist, J. (1976). Endocrine influences on lymphatic organs, immune responses, inflammation and autoimmunity. *Acta Endocrinol. (Copenhagen), Suppl.* **206** and Almqvist & Wiksell International, Stockholm.

Ahlqvist, J. (1979). "Can Endocrine Factors Influence Pathogenetic Mechanisms in Chronic Active Hepatitis and Primary Biliary Cirrhosis? A Speculative Review." Academic Book Store (Distrib.), Helsinki.

Ahlqvist, J. (1980a). Can endocrine factors influence pathogenetic mechanisms in chronic active hepatitis (CAH) and primary biliary cirrhosis (PBC)? A hypothesis. *Hepato-gastroenterologica* **27**, 64–67.

Ahlqvist, J. (1980b). Primary biliary cirrhosis and graft-versus-host disease. *Lancet* **2**, 207.

Ahlqvist, J. (1981). On the pathogenesis of rheumatoid synovitis. Comments after the plenary lectures at the XVIII Nordic Rheumatology Congress. *Scand. J. Rheumatol.* **10**, 156–158.

Ahlqvist, J., Räsänen, J. A., Antoniades, K., and Wallgren, G. R. (1974). On the morphology of lymph node immune responses and fibrin, IgM, IgG, and IgA in lymphatic tissues. *Ann. Clin. Res.* **6**, 50–64.

Alarcón-Segovia, D. (1977). The necrotizing vasculitides. A new pathogenetic classification. *Med. Clin. North Am.* **61**, 241–260.

Ambrose, C. T. (1970). The essential role of corticosteroids in the induction of the immune response *in vitro*. In "Hormones and the Immune Response" (G. E. W. Wolstenholme and J. Knight, eds.), pp. 100–116. Churchill, London.

Andersson, L. C., and Gahmberg, C. G. (1979). Surface glycoproteins of resting and activated human T lymphocytes. *Mol. Biol. Biochem.* **27**, 117–131.

Aoki, N., Wakisaka, G., and Nagata, I. (1976). Effects of thyroxine on T-cell counts and tumor rejection in mice. *Acta Endocrinol. (Copenhagen)* **81**, 104–109.

Apter, D., and Vihko, R. (1977). Serum pregnenolone, progesterone, 17-hydroxyprogesterone, testosterone and 5α-dihydrotestosterone during female puberty. *J. Clin. Endocrinol. Metab.* **45**, 1039–1048.

Arrenbrecht, S. (1974). Specific binding of growth hormone to thymocytes. *Nature (London)* **252**, 255–257.

Bach, J. F., Bach, M. A., Carnaud, C., Dardenne, M., and Monier, J. C. (1977). Thymic hormones and autoimmunity. In "Autoimmunity: Genetic, Immunologic, Virologic and Clinical Aspects" (N. Talal, ed.), pp. 207–230. Academic Press, New York.

Bäckström, T., and Carstensen, H. (1974). Estrogen and progesterone in plasma in relation to premenstrual tension. *J. Steroid Biochem.* **5**, 257–260.

Barbosa, J., Seal, U. S., and Doe, R. P. (1971a). Effects of anabolic steroids on hormone-binding proteins, serum cortisol and serum nonprotein-bound cortisol. *J. Clin. Endocrinol. Metab.* **32**, 232–240.

Barbosa, J., Seal, U. S., and Doe, R. P. (1971b). Effects of steroids on plasma proteins–progestational agents. *J. Clin. Endocrinol. Metab.* **32**, 547–554.

Barchas, J. D., Akil, H., Elliot, G. R., Holman, R. B., and Watson, S. J. (1978). Behavioral neurochemistry: Neuroregulators and behavioral states. *Science* **200**, 964–973.

Barnard, E. A. (1979). Visualization and counting of receptors at the light and electron microscope level. In "The Receptors. A Comprehensive Treatise". (R. D. O'Brien, ed.), Vol. 1, pp. 247–310. Plenum, New York.

Becker, B., Shier, D. H., Palmberg, P. F., and Waltman, S. R. (1976). HLA antigens and corticosteroid response. *Science* **194**, 1427–1428.

Becker, F. O., Michael, J. A., and Davis, F. A. (1974). Acute effects of oral phosphate on visual function in multiple sclerosis. *Neurology* **24**, 601–607.

Beck-Nielsen, H., Kühl, C., Pedersen, O., Bjerre-Christensen, C., Nielsen, T. T., and Klebe, J. G. (1979). Decreased insulin binding to monocytes from normal pregnant women. *J. Clin. Endocrinol. Metab.* **49**, 810–814.

Bellodi, L., Smeraldi, R. S., Negri, F., Resele, L., Sacchetti, E., and Smeraldi, E. (1977). Histocompatibility antigens and effects of neuroactive drugs on phytohaemagglutinin stimulation of lymphocytes *in vitro*. *Arzneim.-Forsch.* **27**, 144–146.

Berenbaum, M. C., Purves, E. C., and Allison, I. E. (1976). Intercellular immunological controls and modulation of cyclic AMP levels. Some doubts. *Immunology* **30**, 815–823.

Bernard, O., Scheid, M. P., Ripoche, M. -A., and Bennett, D. (1978). Immunological studies of mouse decidual cells. I. Membrane markers of decidual cells in the days after implantation. *J. Exp. Med.* **148**, 580–589.

Bilder, G. E., and Denckla, W. D. (1977). Restoration of ability to reject xenografts and clear carbon after hypophysectomy of adult rats. *Mech. Ageing Dev.* **6**, 153–163.

Bjune, G. (1979). *In vitro* lymphocyte responses to PHA show covariation with the menstrual cycle. X. *Scand. Congr. Immunol.* Abstract 51.

Blalock, J. E., and Stanton, J. D. (1980). Common pathways of interferon and hormonal actions. *Nature* **283**, 406–408.

Bondy, P. K., and Rosenberg, L. E., eds. (1974). "Duncan's Diseases of Metabolism," 7th ed. Saunders, Philadelphia, Pennsylvania.

Bourne, H. R., Lichtenstein, L. M., Melmon, K. L., Henney, C. S., Weinstein, Y. S., and Shearer, G. M. (1974). Modulation of inflammation and immunity by cyclic AMP. *Science* **184**, 19–28.

van den Broek, A. A. (1971). Immune suppression and histophysiology of the immune response. PhD. Thesis, University of Groningen.

Brostoff, J., Mowbray, J. F., Kapoor, A., and Hollowell, S. J. (1976). 80% of patients with intrinsic asthma are homozygous for HLA W6. Is intrinsic asthma a recessive disease? *Lancet* **2**, 872–873.

Buckley, C. E., and Dorsey, F. C. (1971). Serum immunoglobulin levels throughout the life-span of healthy man. *Ann. Intern. Med.* **75**, 673–682.

Busse, W. W., and Lee, T. -P. (1976). Decreased adrenergic responses in lymphocytes and granulocytes in atopic excema. *J. Allergy Clin. Immunol.* **58**, 566–596.

Carter, J. (1976). The effect of progesterone, oestradiol and HCG on cell-mediated immunity in mice. *J. Reprod. Fertil.* **46**, 211–216.

Carter, P. (1973). Immune complex disease. *Ann. Rheum. Dis.* **32**, 265–271.

Cattaneo, R., Saibene, V., Margonato, A., and Pozza, G. (1977). *In vitro* effect of insulin on peripheral T-lymphocyte E-rosette function from normal and diabetic subjects. *Boll. Ist. Sieroter. Milan.* **56**, 139–143.

Chayvialle, J. A., Courpron, P., Mikaelian, S., and Lambert, R. (1977). Serum alpha-fetoprotein concentration in adult patients under corticoid, estroprogestative and androgen therapy. *Digestion* **15**, 223–226.

Cheung, W. Y. (1980). Calmodulin plays a pivotal role in cellular regulation. *Science* **207**, 19–27.

Cohen, J. R., and Wekerle, H. (1977). Autoimmunity, self-recognition, and blocking factors. *In* "Autoimmunity: Genetic, Immunologic, Virologic and Clinical Aspects" (N. Talal, ed.), pp. 231–265. Academic Press, New York.

Cohn, D. A., and Hamilton, J. B. (1976). Sensitivity to androgen and the immune response: Immunoglobulin levels in two strains of mice, one with high and one with low target organ responses to androgen. *RES, J. Reticuloendothel. Soc.* **20**, 1–10.

Colvin, R. B., Johnson, R. A., Mihm, M. C., and Dvorak, H. F. (1973). Role of the clotting system in cell-mediated hypersensitivity. I. Fibrin deposition in delayed skin reactions in man. *J. Exp. Med.* **138**, 686–698.

Comsa, J. (1977). Influences hormonales sur les fonctions immunitaires. *Pediatrie* **32**, 439–446.

Craddock, P. R., Yawata, Y., Vansanten, L., Gilberstadt, S., Silvis, S., and Jacob, H. S. (1974). Acquired phagocyte dysfunction. A complication of hypophosphatemia of parenteral hyperalimentation. *N. Engl. J. Med.* **290**, 1403–1407.

Crumpton, M. J., Snary, D., Walsh, F. S., Barnstable, C. J., Goodfellow, P. N., Jones, E. A., and Bodmer, W. F. (1978). Molecular structure of the gene products of the human HLA system: Isolation and characterization of HLA-A,-B,-C and Ia antigens. *Proc. R. Soc. London, Ser. B.* **202**, 117-158.

Cuatrecasas, P. (1974). Membrane Receptors. *Annu. Rev. Biochem.* **43**, 169-214.

Cunliffe, W. J. (1976). Fibrinolysis and vasculitis. *Clin. Exp. Dermatol.* **1**, 1-16.

Cunnane, S. C., Manku, M. S., and Horrobin, D. F. (1979). The pineal and regulation of fibrosis: Pinealectomy as a model of primary biliary cirrhosis: Roles of melatonin and prostaglandins in fibrosis and regulation of T lymphocytes. *Med. Hypothesis* **5**, 403-414.

De Moor, P., Verhoeven, G., and Heyns, W. (1973). Permanent effects of foetal and neonatal testosterone secretion on steroid metabolism and binding. *Differentiation* **1**, 241-253.

DiSorbo, D., Rosen, F., McParland, R. P., and Milholland, R. J. (1977). Glucocorticoid activity of various progesterone analogs: Correlation between specific binding in thymus and liver and biologic activity. *Ann. N.Y. Acad. Sci.* **286**, 355-366.

Ditzel, J. (1975). The problem of tissue oxygenation in diabetes mellitus. III. The "three-in-one concept" for the development of diabetic microangiopathy and a rational approach to its prophylaxis. *Acta Med. Scand. Suppl.* **578**, 69-83.

Doniach, D. (1977). Autoantibodies to thyrotropin (TSH) receptors on thyroid epithelium and other tissues. *In* "Autoimmunity: Genetic, Immunologic, Virologic and Clinical Aspects" (N. Talal, ed.), pp. 621-642. Academic Press, New York.

Dougherty, T. F. (1952). Effect of hormones on lymphatic tissue. *Physiol. Rev.* **32**, 379-401.

Dupont, B., O'Neill, G. J., Yang, S. Y., Pollack, M. S., and Levine, L. S. (1978). Genetic linkage of disease-genes to HLA. *In* "Genetic Control of Autoimmune Disease" (N. R. Rose, P. E. Bigazzi, and N. L. Warner, eds.), pp. 15-25. Am. Elsevier, New York.

Duvic, M., Steinberg, A. D., and Klassen, L. W. (1978). Effect of the anti-estrogen, nafoxidine, on NZB/W autoimmune disease. *Arthritis Rheum.* **21**, 414-417.

Dybing, E., Nelson, S. D., Mitchell, J. R. Sasame, H. A., and Gilette, J. R. (1976). Oxidation of α-methyldopa and other catechols by cytochrome P-450-generated superoxide anion: Possible mechanism of methyldopa hepatitis. *Mol. Pharmacol.* **12**, 911-920.

Editorial (1977). Immunology of early pregnancy. *S. Afr. Med. J.* **52**, 253-254.

Editorial (1979). Immune-complex splitting. *Lancet* **1**, 592-593.

Edwards, R. L., and Rickles, F. R. (1978). Delayed hypersensitivity in man: Effects of systemic anticoagulation. *Science* **200**, 541-543.

Engel, E. K., Trotter, J. L., MacFarlin, D. E., and McIntosh, C. L. (1977). Thymic epithelial cell contains acetylcholine receptor. *Lancet* **1**, 1310-1311.

Ernström, U. (1963). Thyroxine-induced changes in cell composition of lymph node tissue, spleen and thymus. A quantitative examination on young guinea pigs. *Acta Pathol. Microbiol. Scand.* **59**, 145-155.

Ezrin, C., Godden, J. O., Volpé, R., and Wilson, R., eds. (1973). "Systematic Endocrinology." Harper & Row, Hagerstown, Maryland.

Fabris, N. (1973). Immunodepression in thyroid deprived animals. *Clin. Exp. Immunol.* **15**, 601-611.

Forest, M. G., DePeretti, E., and Bertrand, J. (1976). Hypothalamic–pituitary–gonadal relationships in man from birth to puberty. *Clin. Endocrinol. (Oxford)* **5**, 551-569.

Forsum, U., Klareskog, L., and Peterson, P. A. (1979). Distribution of Ia-antigen-like molecules on nonlymphoid tissues. *Scand. J. Immunol* **9**, 343-349.

Frankenhaeuser, M., Rauste von Wright, M., Collins, A., von Wright, J., Sedvall, G., and Swahn, C. -G. (1978). Sex differences in psychoneuroendocrine reactions to examination stress. *Psychosom. Med.* **40**, 334-343.

Frey-Wettstein, M., and Craddock, C. G. (1970). Testosterone-induced depletion of thymus and marrow lymphocytes as related to lymphopoiesis and myelopoiesis. *Blood* **35**, 257-271.

Frick, O. L. (1976). Immediate hypersensitivity. *In* "Basic and Clinical Immunology" (H. H. Fudenberg, ed.), pp. 204-224. Lange Med. Publ., Los Altos, California.

Frohman, L. A. (1975). Neurotransmitters as regulators of endocrine function. *Hosp. Pract.* **10**, 54-67.

Gabrielson, A. E., and Good, R. A. (1967). Chemical suppression of adapted immunity. *Adv. Immunol.* **6**, 90–229.

Gahmberg, C. G. (1977). Cell surface proteins: Changes during cell growth and malignant transformation. *In* "Dynamic Aspects of Cell Surface Organization" (G. Poste and G. L. Nicolson, eds.), pp. 371–421. North-Holland Publ., Amsterdam.

Gallagher, T. F., Hellman, L., Bradlow, H. L., Zumoff, B., and Fukushima, D. K. (1960). The effects of thyroid hormones on the metabolism of steroids. *Ann. N.Y. Acad. Sci.* **86**, 605–611.

Ganrot, P. O. (1972). Variation of the concentration of some plasma proteins in normal adults, in pregnant women and in newborns. *Scand. J. Clin. Lab. Invest.* **29**, Suppl. 124, 83–88.

Gavras, H., Gavras, I., Cannon, P. J., Brunner, H. R., and Laragh, J. H. (1977). Is elevated plasma renin activity of prognostic importance in progressive systemic sclerosis? *Arch. Intern. Med.* **137**, 1554–1558.

Gerber, D. (1975). Decreased concentration of free histidin in serum in rheumatoid arthritis, an isolated amino acid abnormality not associated with generalized hypoaminoacidemia. *J. Rheumatism* **2**, 384–392.

Goldstein, A. L., Thurman, G. B., Low, T. L. K., Rossio, J. L., and Trivers, G. E. (1978). Hormonal influences on the reticuloendothelial system: Current status of the role of thymosin in the regulation and modulation of immunity. *RES, J. Reticuloendothel. Soc.* **23**, 253–266.

Goldzieher, J. W., and Dozier, T. S. (1975). Oral contraceptives and thromboembolism. A reassessment. *Am. J. Obstet. Gynecol.* **123**, 878–914.

Goodfellow, P. N., Barnstable, C. J., Bodmer, W. F., Snary, D., and Crumpton, M. J. (1976). Expression of HLA system antigens on placenta. *Transplantation* **22**, 595–603.

Gorbalenia, A. E., Shulga, V. A., Videlets, I. Iu., and Grutenko, E. V. (1977). Functional activity of the adrenal cortex and thymus of mice of strains AKR, C57BL/6, C3H/He and C3Hf *Probl. Endokrinol.* **23** (4), 89–93.

Graff, R. J., Lappé, M. A., and Snell, G. D. (1969). The influence of the gonads and adrenal glands on the immune response to skin grafts. *Transplantation* **7**, 105–111.

Grégoire, C., and Duchateau, G. (1956). Study on lympho-epithelial symbiosis in thymus. Reactions of the lymphatic tissue to extracts and to implants of epithelial components of thymus. *Arch. Biol.* **67**, 269–296.

Grob, D. (1976). Cause of weakness in myasthenia gravis. *N. Engl. J. Med.* **294**, 722–723.

Grossman, C. J., Nathan, P., and Sholiton, L. J. (1978). Specific androgen receptor in the thymus of the castrate male rat. *Biol. Reprod.* **18**, Suppl. 1, p48A.

Grossman, C. J., Sholiton, L. J., and Blaha, G. C. (1979a). Rat thymic estrogen receptor. II. Physiological properties. *J. Steroid Biochem* **11**, 1241–1246.

Grossman, C. J., Nathan, P., Taylor, B. B., and Sholiton, L. J. (1979b). Rat thymic dihydrotestosterone receptor: preparation, location and physicochemical properties. *Steroids* **34**, 539–553.

Håkansson, S., Heyner, S., Sundqvist, K. -G., and Bergström, S. (1975). The presence of paternal H-2 antigens on hybrid mouse blastocysts during experimental delay of implantation and the disappearance of these after onset of implantation. *Int. J. Fertil.* **20**, 137–140.

Häyry, P., von Willebrand, E., Ahonen, J., Lindström, B. L., and Eklund, B. (1980a). Use of fine needle aspiration cytology in the monitoring of the *in situ* inflammatory response of kidney allograft rejection, and the impact of glucocorticosteroids. *Transplant. Proc.* **12**, 331–334.

Häyry, P., von Willebrand, E., and Andersson, L. C. (1980b). Expression of HLA–ABC and DR locus antigens on human kidney endothelial, tubular and glomerular cells. *Scand. J. Immunol.* **11**, 303–310.

Helenius, A., Morein, B., Friers, E., Simons, K., Robinson, P., Schirmacher, V., Terhorst, C., and Strominger, J. L. (1978). Human (HLA-A and HLA-B) and murine (H-2K and H-2D) histocompatibility antigens are cell surface receptors for Semliki Forest virus. *Proc. Natl. Acad. Sci. U.S.A.* **75**, 3846–3850.

Hench, P. S. (1949). The potential reversibility of rheumatoid arthritis. *Ann. Rheum. Dis.* **8**, 90–96.

Higgins, T. J., and David, J. R. (1976). Effects of isoproterenol and aminophylline on cyclic AMP levels of guinea pig macrophages. *Cell. Immunol.* **27**, 1–10.

Hirsch, M. S., and Black, P. H. (1974). Activation of mammalian leukemia viruses. *Adv. Virus Res.* **19**, 265–313.

Holsti, P. (1956). Experimental cirrhosis of the liver in rabbits induced by gastric instillation of desiccated whole bile. *Acta Pathol. Microbiol. Scand, Suppl.* **113**.

Horrobin, D. F. (1977). Schizophrenia as a prostaglandin disease. Lancet 1, 936–937.

Hunt, N. H., and Perris, A. D. (1974). Calcium and control of circadian mitotic activity in rat bone marrow and thymus. *J. Endocrinol.* **62**, 451–462.

Igari, T., Takeda, M., Obara, K., and Ono, S. (1977). Catecholamine metabolism in the patients with rheumatoid arthritis. *Tohoku J. Exp. Med.* **122**, 9–20.

Irvine, W. J. (1977). Classification of idiopathic diabetes. *Lancet* **1**, 638–642.

Iványi, P. (1978). Some aspects of the H-2 system, the major histocompatibility system in the mouse. *Proc. R. Soc. London, Ser. B* **202**, 107–158.

Janeway, C. A., Wigzell, H., and Binz, H. (1976). Two different V_H gene products make up the T-cell receptors. *Scand. J. Immunol.* **5**, 993–1001.

Janković, B. D., Isaković, K., and Kueževic, A. (1978). Ontogeny of the immuno-neuroendocrine relationship. Changes in lymphoid tissues of chick embryos surgically decapitated at 33-38 hours of incubation. *Dev. Comp. Immunol.* **2**, 479–492.

Jänne, O., Kontula, K., Vihko, R., Feil, P. D., and Bardin, C. W. (1978). Progesterone receptor and regulation of progestin action in mammalian tissues. *Med. Biol.* **56**, 225–248.

Jelinek, J. E. (1970). Cutaneous side-effects of oral contraceptives. *Arch. Dermatol.* **101**, 181–186.

Jerne, N. K. (1973). The immune system. *Sci. Am.* **229**, 52–60.

Josipovic, D. B., Berovic, Z. M., and Masi, A. T. (1977). Marked female preponderance in rheumatoid arthritis patients with younger adult onset and positive rheumatoid factor. *Int. Cong. Rheumatol., 14th, 1977* Abstract 1116.

Kaiser, N., and Edelman, J. S. (1977). Calcium dependence of glucocorticoid-induced lymphocytolysis. *Proc. Natl. Acad. Sci. U.S.A.* **74**, 638–642.

Kaliner, M., and Austen, K. F. (1974). Cyclic nucleotides and modulation of effector systems of inflammation. *Biochem. Pharmacol.* **23**, 763–771.

Kalliola, H., Kalliomäki, J. L., and Rintala, A. (1957). Thyroidectomy and rheumatoid arthritis. *Ann. Med. Intern. Fenn.* **46**, 97–102.

Kalliomäki, J. L., Lehtonen, A., and Seppälä, P. (1966). Oral tyrosine tolerance test in rheumatoid arthritis. *Ann. Rheum. Dis.* **25**, 469–471.

Kao, I., and Drachman, D. B. (1977). Thymic muscle cells bear acetylcholine receptors: Possible relation to myasthenia gravis. *Science* **195**, 74–75.

Kappas, A., and Palmer, R. H. (1967). Novel biological properties of steroid metabolites; fever-production in man. *RES, J. Reticuloendothel. Soc.* **4**, 231–236.

Kaslow, R. A., and Masi, A. T. (1978). Age, sex, and race effects on mortality from systemic lupus erythematosus in the United States. *Arthritis Rheum.* **21**, 473–479.

Katz, D. H. (1977). "Lymphocyte Differentiation, Recognition and Regulation." Academic Press, New York.

von Kaulla, E., Droegemüller, W., and von Kaulla, K. N. (1975). Conjugated estrogens and hypercoagulability. *Am. J. Obstet. Gynecol.* **122**, 688–692.

Keller, A. J., Irvine, W. J., Jordan, J., and Loudon, N. B. (1977). Phytohemagglutinin-induced lymphocyte transformation in oral contraceptive users. *Obstet. Gynecol.* **49**, 83–91.

Keller, R. H., Calvanico, N. J., and Tomasi, T. B., Jr. (1976). Immunosuppressive properties of

AFP: Role of estrogens. *In* "Onco-Developmental Gene Expression" (W. H. Fishman and S. Sell, eds.), pp. 287–295. Academic Press, New York.

Kenny, J. F., and Diamond, M. (1977). Immunological responsiveness to *Escherichia coli* during pregnancy. *Infect. Immun.* **16,** 174–180.

Kenny, J. F., Pangburn, P. C., and Trail, G. (1976). Effect of estradiol on immune competence: *In vivo* and *in vitro* studies. *Infect. Immun.* **13,** 448–456.

Klareskog, L., Forsum, U., and Peterson, P. A. (In press). Hormonal regulation of the expression of Ia antigens on mammary gland epithelium. *Eur. J. Immunol.*

Kolata, G. B. (1979). Sex hormones and brain development. *Science* **205,** 985–987.

Kolb, H., Keck, K., Momayezi, M., Schicker, C., and Trissl, D. (1977). Ir-gene control of antibody class production. *J. Immunol.* **118,** 427–430.

Kongshavn, P. A. L., and Bliss, J. Q. (1970). Sex differences in survival of H-2 incompatible skin grafts in mice treated with antithymocyte serum. *Nature (London)* **226,** 451.

Konttinen, Y. P. (1968). "Fibrinolysis. Chemistry, Physiology, Pathology and Clinics." Star Pharmaceutical Manufacturers, Tampere, Finland.

Krieger, D. T., and Liotta, A. S. (1979). Pituitary hormones in brain: Where, how, and why? *Science* **205,** 366–372.

Kudintseva, T. Z. (1977). Concentration of catecholamines, their precursors, vanilmandelic acid and monoamine oxidase in patients with rheumatism in the active phase. *Vrach. Delo* No. 7, pp 33–35.

Lachmann, P. J., and Hobart, M. J. (1978). Complement genetics in relation to HLA. *Br. Med. Bull.* **34,** 247–252.

Lahita, R. G., Kunkel, H. G., and Fishman, J. (1979). Alterations in estrogen metabolism in systemic lupus erythematosus. *Arthritis Rheum.* **22,** 633.

Lanning, M. (1978). "Spontaneous, PPD Tuberculin and Phytohaemagglutinin (PHA)-Induced Transformation of Blood Lymphocytes in Man from Birth to Old Age." Acta Univ. Ouluensis, Oulu, Finland.

Laurell, C. -B., Kullander, S., and Thorell, J. (1968). Effect of administration of a combined estrogen–progestin contraceptive on the level of individual plasma proteins. *Scand. J. Clin. Lab. Invest.* **21,** 337–343.

Lee, K. C. (1977). Cortisone as a probe for cell interactions in the generation of cytotoxic T cells. I. Effect on helper cells, cytotoxic T cell precursors, and accessory cells. *J. Immunol.* **119,** 1836–1845.

Lee, T. -P., and Reed, C. E. (1977). Effect of steroids on the regulation of the levels of cyclic AMP in human lymphocytes. *Biochem. Biophys. Res. Commun.* **78,** 998–1004.

Lee, T. -P., Busse, W. W., and Reed, C. E. (1977). Effect of beta-adrenergic agonist, prostaglandins, and cortisol on lymphocyte levels of cyclic adenosine monophosphate and glycogen: Abnormal lymphocytic metabolism in asthma. *J. Allergy Clin. Immunol.* **59,** 408–413.

Lefvert, A. K., and Pirskanen, R. (1977). Acetylcholine-receptor antibodies in cerebrospinal fluid of patients with myasthenia gravis. *Lancet* **2,** 351–352.

Lesniak, M. A., and Roth, J. (1976). Regulation of receptor concentration by homologous hormone. Effect of human growth hormone on its receptor in IM-9 lymphocytes. *J. Biol. Chem.* **251,** 3720–3729.

Lesniak, M. A., Gorden, P., and Roth, J. (1977). Reactivity of nonprimate growth hormone and prolactin with human growth hormone receptors on cultured human lymphocytes. *J. Clin. Endocrinol. Metab.* **44,** 838–899.

Májský, A., and Jakoubkova, J. (1976). Loss of HLA antigens associated with hormonal state. *Lancet* **2,** 859.

Masi, A. T. (1976). Pulmonary hypertension and oral contraceptives. *Chest* **69,** 451–453.

Masi, A. T., and Kaslow, R. A. (1978). Sex effects in systemic lupus erythematosus. A clue to pathogenesis. *Arthritis Rheum.* **20,** 480–484.

Masi, A. T., Josipovic, D. B., and Jefferson, W. E. (1977). Decreased 11-deoxy-17-ketosteroid (11-deoxy-17-KS) excretion by rheumatoid arthritis (RA) females during baseline and adrenal stimulation conditions: A controlled study. *Int. Cong. Rheumatol., 14th, 1977* Abstract 850.

Mayer, M., and Rosen, F. (1977). Interaction of glucocorticoids and androgens with skeletal muscle. *Metab., Clin. Exp.* **26,** 937–962.

Mendelsohn, J., Multer, M. M., and Bernheim, J. L. (1977). Inhibition of human lymphocyte stimulation by steroid hormones: Cytokinetic mechanisms. *Clin. Exp. Immunol.* **27,** 127–134.

Meruelo, D., and Edidin, M. (1975). Association of mouse liver adenosine 3′, 5′-cyclic monophosphate (cyclic AMP) levels with histocompatibility-2 genotype. *Proc. Natl. Acad. Sci. U.S.A.* **72,** 2644–2648.

Metcalf, D. (1960). Adrenal cortical function in high- and low-leukemia strains of mice. *Cancer Res.* **20,** 1347–1353.

Mittag, T., Kornfeld, P., Tormay, A., and Woo, C. (1976). Detection of anti-acetylcholine receptor factors in serum and thymus from patients with myasthenia gravis. *N. Engl. J. Med.* **294,** 691–694.

Morel, G., Deschaux, P., and Fontagues, R. (1977). Caryométrie des cellules reticulaires thymiques de rat: Influènce des hormones somatotrope et corticotrope. *Experientia* **33,** 544–545.

Morgan, J. I., Bramhall, J. S., Britten, A. Z., and Perris, A. D. (1976). Calcium and oestrogen interactions upon the rat thymic lymphocyte plasma membrane. *Biochem. Biophys. Res. Commun.* **72,** 663–672.

Mori, T., Kobayashi, H., Nishimoto, H., Suzuki, A., Nishimura, T., and Mori, T. (1977). Inhibitory effect of progesterone and 20α-hydroxypregn-4-en-3-one on the phytohaemagglutinin-induced transformation of human lymphocytes. *Am. J. Obstet. Gynecol.* **127,** 151–157.

Moriyama, I., and Sugawa, T. (1972). Progesterone facilitates implantation of xenogenic cultured cells in hamster uterus. *Nature (London), New Biol.* **236,** 150–152.

Mukherjee, C., and Lefkowitz, R. J. (1976). Desensitization of β-adrenergic receptor by β-adrenergic agonists in a cell-free system: Resensitization by guanosine (5′-β,γ-imino) triphosphate and other purine nucleotides. *Proc. Natl. Acad. Sci. U.S.A.* **73,** 1494–1498.

Munck, A., Wira, C., Young, D. A., Mosher, K. M., Hallahan, C., and Bell, P. A. (1972). Glucocorticoid-receptor complexes and the earliest steps in the action of glucocorticoids on thymus cells. *J. Steroid Biochem.* **3,** 567–578.

Munro, A., and Waldmann, H. (1978). The major histocompatibility system and the immune response. *Br. Med. Bull.* **34,** 253–258.

Munroe, J. S. (1971). Progesteroids as immunosuppressive agents. *RES, J. Reticuloendothel. Soc.* **9,** 361–375.

Neifeld, J. P., Lippman, M. E., and Tonney, D. C. (1977). Steroid hormone receptors in normal human lymphocytes. Induction of glucocorticoid receptor activity by phytohemagglutinin stimulation. *J. Biol. Chem.* **252,** 2972–2977.

New, M. J., Lorenzen, F., Pang, S., Gunczler, P., Dupont, B., and Levine, S. (1979). "Acquired" adrenal hyperplasia with 21-hydroxylase deficiency is not the same disorder as congenital adrenal hyperplasia. *J. Clin. Endocrinol. Metab.* **48,** 356–359.

Nilsson, I. M. (1974). "Hemorrhagic and Thrombotic Diseases." Wiley, New York.

Ohno, S. (1978). The role of H–Y antigen in primary sex determination. *J. Am. Med. Assoc.* **239,** 217–220.

Okouchi, E. (1976). Thymus, peripheral tissue and immunological responsiveness of the pituitary dwarf mice. *J. Physiol. Soc. Jpn.* **38,** 325–335.

Osmand, A. P., Gewurtz, H., and Friedenson, B. (1977). Partial amino-acid sequences of human and rabbit C-reactive proteins: Homology with immunoglobulins and histocompatibility antigens. *Proc. Natl. Acad. Sci. U.S.A.* **74,** 1214–1218.

Panoussopoulos, D. G., Humphrey, P. A., Humphrey, L. J., and Meek, J. (1976). Effect of various thyroid states on immunity. *Surg. Forum* **27**, 138–140.

Papatestas, A. E., Mulvihill, M., Genkins, G., Kornfeld, P., Aufses, A. H., Jr., Wang, D. Y., and Bulbrook, R. D. (1977). Thymus and breast cancer—plasma androgens, thymic pathology, and peripheral lymphocytes in myasthenia gravis. *J. Natl. Cancer Inst.* **59**, 1583–1588.

Parker, C. W. (1976). Control of lymphocyte function. *N. Engl. J. Med.* **295**, 1180–1186.

Parker, L. N., Suckjoo, C., and Odell, W. D. (1978). Adrenal androgens in patients with chronic marked elevation of prolactin. *Clin. Endocrinol.* **8**, 1–5.

Pattillo, R. A., Shalaby, M. R., Hussa, R. O., Bahl, O. M. P., and Mattingly, R. F. (1976). Effect of crude and purified hCG on lymphocyte blastogenesis. *Obstet. Gynecol.* **47**, 557–561.

Pearse, A. G. E. (1969). The cytochemistry and ultrastructure of polypeptide-producing cells of the APUD series and the embryologic, physiologic and pathologic implications of this concept. *J. Histochem. Cytochem.* **17**, 303–313.

Pécile, A., and Müller, E. E., eds. (1976). "Growth Hormone and Related Peptides," Int. Congr. Ser. No. 381. Excerpta Med. Found., Amsterdam.

Pekkarinen, A., and Kalliomäki, L. (1958). On the adrenocortical reserves and on the sex difference of adrenocortical excretion in patients with rheumatoid arthritis. *Acta Endocrinol. (Copenhagen)* **28**, 417–427.

Pérez-Cruet, J., and Dancey, J. T. (1977). Thymus gland involution induced by lithium chloride. *Experientia* **33**, 646–648.

Pernitcheva-Rostaing, E., and Morin, P. (1976). Action des hormones placéntaires polypéptidiques HCG et HCS sur la transformation blastique de lymphocytes. *J. Gynecol. Obstet. Biol. Reprod.* **5**, 871–877.

Perry, J. C. (1955). Experimental induction of periarteritis nodosa in white rats. *Proc. Soc. Exp. Biol. Med.* **89**, 200–206.

Persellin, R. H. (1977). The effect of pregnancy on rheumatoid arthritis. *Bull. Rheum. Dis.* **27**, 922–926.

Petrucco, O. M., Seamark, R. F., Holmes, K., and Forbes, I. J. (1976). Changes in lymphocyte function during pregnancy. *J. Obstet. Gynaecol. Br. Common W.* **83**, 245–250.

Pettirossi, O., Sakai, A., Wechter, W. J., and Kountz, S. L. (1976). Prolongation of rat heart allograft by a synthetic progestagen (melengestrol acetate) and ara-cytidine acylates. *Transplantation* **21**, 408–411.

Phillips, L. L., Turksoy, R. N., and Southam, A. L. (1961). Influence of ovarian function on the fibrinolytic enzyme system. II. Influence of exogenous steroids. *Am. J. Obstet. Gynecol.* **82**, 1216–1220.

Pierpaoli, W., and Sorkin, E. (1973). Influence of the thymus on the development of endocrine and immune functions in ontogeny. *Adv. Exp. Med. Biol.* **29**, 651–654.

Pierpaoli, W., Fabris, N., and Sorkin, E. (1971). The effect of hormones on the development of immune capacity. *In* "Cellular Interaction in the Immune Response" (S. Cohen, G. Cudkowicz, and R. T. McCluskey, eds.), pp. 25–30. Karger, Basel.

Pirskanen, R. (1976). Genetic associations between myasthenia gravis and the HL-A system. *J. Neurol., Neurosurg. Psychiatry* **39**, 23–33.

Plow, E. F., and Edgington, T. S. (1975). Immune responses to the cleavage-associated neoantigens of fibrinogen in man. Identification and characterization of human antibodies specific to cleavage fragments. *J. Clin. Invest.* **56**, 1509–1518.

Polgar, P., Vera, J. C., and Rutenberg, A. M. (1977). An altered response to cyclic AMP stimulating hormones in intact human leukemic lymphocytes. *Proc. Soc. Exp. Biol. Med.* **154**, 493–495.

Poskitt, P. K. F., Kurt, E. A., Paul, B. B., Salvaraj, R. J., Sbarra, A. J., and Mitchell, G. W. (1977). Response to mitogen during pregnancy and the postpartum period. *Obstet. Gynecol.* **50**, 319–323.

Rachelsky, G., Terasaki, P. I., Park, M. S., Katz, R., Siegel, S., and Saito, S. (1976). Strong association between B-lymphocyte Group-2 specificity and asthma. *Lancet* 2, 1042–1044.

Ratnoff, O. D. (1971). A tangled web. The interdependence of mechanisms of blood coagulation, fibrinolysis, immunity and inflammation. *Thromb. Diath. Haemorrh., Suppl.* 45, 109–118.

Raynaud, J. -P., Mercier-Bodard, C., and Baulieu, E. E. (1971). Rat estradiol binding plasma protein (EBP). *Steroids* 18, 767–788.

Rehfeld, J. F. (1979). Gastrointestinal hormones. *Int. Rev. Physiol. Gastrointestinal Physiol. III.* 19, 291–321.

Reichman, M. E., and Villee, C. A. (1978). Estradiol binding by rat thymus cytosol. *J. Steroid Biochem.* 9, 637–641.

Robinson, A. G. (1974). Elevation of plasma neurophysin in women on oral contraceptives. *J. Clin. Invest.* 54, 209–212.

Roszkowski, W., Plaut, M., and Lichtenstein, L. M. (1977). Selective display of histamine receptors on lymphocytes. *Science* 195, 683–685.

Roubinian, J. R., Talal, N., Greenspan, J. S., Goodman, J. R., and Siiteri, P. K. (1978). Effect of castration and sex hormone treatment on survival, anti-nucleic acid antibodies, and glomerulonephritis in NZB/NZW F_1 mice. *J. Exp. Med.* 147, 1568–1581.

Rowden, G., Phillips, T. M., and Delovitch, T. L. (1978). Expression of Ia antigens by murine keratinizing epithelial Langerhans cells. *Immunogenetics* 7, 465–478.

Royal College of General Practitioners (1974). "Oral Contraceptives and Health." Pitman Medical, London.

Royal College of General Practitioners (1978). Reduction in incidence of rheumatoid arthritis associated with oral contraceptives. *Lancet* 1, 569–571.

Sasazuki, T., Kohno, Y., Iwamoto, I., and Tarimura, M. (1978). Association between a HLA haplotype and low responsiveness to tetanus toxoid in man. *Nature (London)* 272, 359–361.

Scorza-Smeraldi, R., Smeraldi, E., Fabio, G., Bellodi, L., Sacchetti, E., and Rugarli, C. (1977). Interference between anti-HLA antibodies and adrenergic receptor-binding drugs. *Tissue & Antigens* 9, 163–166.

Scott, B. J., Bradwell, A. R., Schneider, R. E., and Bishop, H. (1979). Propranolol binding to serum orosomucoid. *Lancet* 1, 930.

Selye, H., ed. (1950). "Stress." Acta Inc., Medical Publ., Montreal.

Selye, H., and Bois, P. (1955). Morphologische Studien über den Synergismus zwischen dem Somatotropen Hormon und den Mineralocorticoiden. *Virchows Arch. Pathol. Anat. Physiol.* 327, 235–251.

Selye, H., and Heuser, G., eds. (1956), "Fifth Annual Report on Stress." Acta Inc., Montreal.

Seppälä, M. (1978). Prolactin and female reproduction. *Ann. Clin. Res.* 10, 164–170.

Sherlock, S. (1976). Primary biliary cirrhosis. *Prog. Liver Dis.* 5, 559–574.

Shreffler, D. C., and David, C. S. (1975). The H-2 major histocompatibility complex and the immune response region: Genetic variation, function and organization. *Adv. Immunol.* 20, 125–195.

Siiteri, P. K., Febres, F., Clemens, L. E., Chang, R. J., Goudos, B, and Stites, D. (1977). Progesterone and maintenance of pregnancy: Is progesterone nature's immunosuppressant? *Ann. N.Y. Acad. Sci.* 286, 384–396.

Singh, U., and Owen, J. J. T. (1976). Studies on the maturation of thymus stem cells. The effects of catecholamines, histamine and peptide hormones on the expression of T cell alloantigens. *Eur. J. Immunol.* 6, 59–62.

Singhal, R. L., and Tsang, B. K. (1975). Control of cyclic $3',5'$-adenosine monophosphate metabolism in gonadal steroid-sensitive tissues. *In* "Regulation of Growth and Differentiated Function in Eukaryote Cells" (G. P. Talwar, ed.), pp. 391–419. Raven Press, New York.

Stastny, P. (1978). Association of the B-cell alloantigen DRw4 with rheumatoid arthritis. *N. Engl. J. Med.* 298, 869–871.

Stecher, V. J. (1975). The chemotaxis of selected cell types to connective tissue degradation products. *Ann. N.Y. Acad. Sci.* **256,** 177–189.

Stenman, S., and Vaheri, A. (1978). Distribution of a major connective tissue protein, fibronectin, in normal human tissues. *J. Exp. Med.* **147,** 1054–1064.

Stern, K., and Davidson, I. (1955). Effect of estrogen and cortisone on immune hemoantibodies in mice of inbred strains. *J. Immunol.* **74,** 479–484.

Stern, R., Fishman, J., Brusman, H., and Kunkel, H. G. (1977). Systemic lupus erythematosus associated with Klinefelter's syndrome. *Arthritis Rheum.* **20,** 18–22.

Stiehm, E. R., and Fudenberg, H. H. (1966). Serum levels of immune globulins in health and disease: A survey. *Pediatrics* **37,** 715–727.

Strom, T. B., Lundin, A. P., and Carpenter, C. B. (1977). The role of cyclic nucleotides in lymphocyte activation and function. *Prog. Clin. Immunol.* **3,** 115–153.

Stroud, A. M. (1974). A family of protein-cutting proteins. *Sci. Am.* **231,** 74–88.

Svejgaard, A., and Ryder, L. P. (1976). Interaction of HLA molecules with nonimmunological ligands as an explanation of HLA and disease associations. *Lancet* **2,** 547–549.

Svejgaard, A., and Ryder, L. P. (1977). Associations between HLA and disease. Notes on methodology and a report from the HLA and disease registry. *In* "HLA and Disease" (J. Dausset and A. Svejgaard, eds.), pp. 46–71. Munksgaard, Copenhagen.

Svendsen, P., Stigbrand, T., Teisner, B., Folkersen, J., Damber, M.-G., von Schoulz, B., Kemp, E., and Svehag, S.-E. (1978). Immunosuppressive effect of human pregnancy zone protein on H-2 incompatible mouse heart allografts. *Acta Pathol. Microbiol. Scand., Sect. C* **86,** 199–201.

Svendsen, U. G. (1978). The importance of the thymus for hypertension and hypertensive vascular disease in rats and mice. *Acta Pathol. Microbiol. Scand., Sect. A, Suppl.* **267.**

Swierenga, S. H., McManus, J. P., Braceland, B. M., and Youdale, T. (1976). Regulation of the primary immune response *in vivo* by parathyroid hormone. *J. Immunol.* **117,** 1608–1611.

Talal, N. (1977). Autoimmunity and lymphoid malignancy: Manifestations of immunoregulatory disequilibrium. *In* "Autoimmunity: Genetic, Immunologic, Virologic and Clinical Aspects" (N. Talal, ed.), pp. 183–202. Academic Press, New York.

Talal, N. (ed.). (1979) Sex factors, steroid hormones and the host response. *Arthritis Rheum.* **22,** 1153–1313.

Tallgren, L. G. (1980). Inorganic sulphates in relation to the serum thyroxine level and in renal failure. *Acta. Med. Scand., Suppl.* 640.

Talwar, G. P., Hanjan, S. N. S., Saxena, R. K., Pandian, M. R., Gupta, P. D., and Bhattarai, Q. B. (1975). Regulation of immunologic response by hormones. *In* "Regulation of Growth and Differentiated Function in Eukaryote Cells" (G. P. Talwar, ed.), pp. 271–281. Raven Press, New York.

Telkkä, A., Lahikainen, T., and Kuusisto, A. N. (1964). Effect of adrenalectomy on bile acids in rats. *Acta Endocrinol. (Copenhagen)* **46,** 405–408.

Terhorst, C., Robb, R., Jones, C., and Strominger, J. L. (1977). Further structural studies of the heavy chain of HLA antigens and its similarity to immunoglobulins. *Proc. Natl. Acad. Sci. U.S.A.* **74,** 4002–4006.

Thompson, E. B., and Lippman, M. E. (1974). Mechanism of action of glucocorticoids. *Metab., Clin. Exp.* **23,** 159–202.

Tomoda, Y., Fuma, M., Miwa, T., Saiki, N., and Ishizuka, N. (1976). Cell-mediated immunity in pregnant women. *Gynecol. Invest.* **7,** 280–292.

Vapaatalo, H., and Parantainen, J. (1978). Prostaglandins; Their biological and pharmacological role. *Med. Biol.* **56,** 163–183.

Vecchi, A., Tagliabue, A., Mantovani, A., Anaclerio, A., Barale, C., and Spreafico, F. (1976). Steroid contraceptive drugs and immunological reactivity in experimental animals. *Biomedicine* **24,** 231–237.

Vermeulen, A., and Ando, S. (1978). Prolactin and adrenal androgen secretion. *Clin. Endocrinol.* **8,** 295–303.

Vischer, T. L. (1974). Stimulation of mouse B lymphocytes with trypsin. *J. Immunol.* **113**, 58–62.

Watnick, A. S., and Russo, R. A. (1968). Survival of skin homografts in uteri of pregnant and progesterone–estrogen treated rats. *Proc. Soc. Exp. Biol. Med.* **128**, 1–4.

Weinstein, Y. (1977). 20α-hydroxysteroid dehydrogenase: A T lymphocyte-associated enzyme. *J. Immunol.* **119**, 1223–1229.

Werb, Z. (1978). Biochemical actions of glucocorticoids on macrophages in culture. Specific inhibition of elastase, collagenase, and plasminogen activator secretion and effects on other metabolic functions. *J. Exp. Med.* **147**, 1695–1712.

Werthamer, S., Samuels, A. J., and Amaral, L. (1973). Identification and partial purification of "transcortin"-like protein within human lymphocytes. *J. Biol. Chem.* **248**, 6398–6407.

Westphal, U. (1971). "Steroid–Protein Interactions." Springer-Verlag, Berlin and New York.

White, A. (1975). Nature and biological activities of thymus hormones: Prospects for the future. *Ann. N.Y. Acad. Sci.* **249**, 523–530.

Wiman, K., Trägårdh, L., Rask, L., and Peterson, P. A. (1979). Similarities between immunoglobulins and transplantation antigens in amino acid sequence and disulfide bond distribution. *Eur. J. Biochem.* **95**, 265–273.

Winkelmann, R. K., Goldyne, M. E., and Linscheid, R. L. (1976). Hypersensitivity of scleroderma cutaneous vascular smooth muscle to 5-hydroxytryptamine. *Br. J. Dermatol.* **95**, 51–56.

Wyle, F. A., and Kent, J. R. (1977). Immunosuppression by sex hormones. I. The effect upon PHA- and PPD-stimulated lymphocytes. *Clin. Exp. Immunol.* **27**, 407–415.

Yozai, S. (1976). Studies on secretion of gonadotrophins in patients with collagen diseases. *Folia Endocrinol. Jpn.* **52**, 138–148.

Zimmerman, T. S., Fierer, J., and Rothberger, H. (1977). Blood coagulation and the inflammatory response. *Semin. Hematol.* **14**, 391–408.

Zinkernagel, R. M., Callahan, G. N., Althage, A., Cooper, S., Klein, P. A., and Klein, J. (1978a). On the thymus in the differentiation of H–2 self-recognition by T cells: Evidence for a dual recognition? *J. Exp. Med.* **147**, 882–895.

Zinkernagel, R. M., Callahan, G. N., Althage, A., Cooper, S., Streilein, J. W., and Klein, J. (1978b). The lymphoreticular system in triggering virus plus self-specific cytotoxic T cells: Evidence for T help. *J. Exp. Med.* **147**, 897–911.

Zondek, B., and Bromberg, Y. M. (1947). Endocrine allergy. Clinical reactions of allergy to endogenous hormones and their treatment. *J. Obstet. Gynaecol. Br. Emp.* **54**, 1–19.

Zurier, R. B. (1975). Systemic lupus erythematosus and pregnancy. *Clin. Rheum. Dis.* **1**, 613–620.

Pharmacologic Control of the Hormonally Mediated Immune Response

G. J. M. MAESTRONI
W. PIERPAOLI

INTRODUCTION

The physiology of the immune response is still challenging immunologists, in spite of the fact that the categories of effector cells and their fundamental functions and interactions are apparently well known. In fact, identification of the different cell lines of the thymolymphatic and hematopoietic tissues by specific membrane markers and of their functions or, at least, of those functions that these cells show in well-defined *in vitro* models, does not provide enough information for the elucidation of the physiological mechanisms which modulate the potent homeostatic devices of the immune system.

Differentiation, proliferation, and cell cooperation are complex biologic phenomena which take place during an immune response. In general, the sequence of these events is rather rigid and repetitive for any immune response, but their amplitude and kinetics display a huge variability, producing quantitatively and qualitatively different responses to a given antigen.

The variables capable of modulating immunologic responsiveness could be schematically divided into two main categories: The first includes those well-known variables concerning antigen type, dose and modality of immunization, and age. The second covers the variables dealing with the dynamics of the immune reaction (for example, the still poorly understood and highly

405

sophisticated cell-to-cell communication or cooperation system and the even less known impact of the endocrine environment).

A convincing and natural example of hormonal modulation of immunity is pregnancy. Pregnant animals show dramatic changes in their endocrine balance and develop a kind of immune tolerance towards fetal antigens. The interaction between the changed endocrine status and the immune system is still rather obscure. However, increasing evidence supports the idea that the very peculiar hormonal milieu, both at systemic and trophoblastic levels, plays a major role in inducing that functional immune blockade that is a prerequisite to a successful pregnancy (Ahlqvist, 1976). The stress-induced derangements of immune functions are also mediated by primary hormonal alterations and constitute additional natural evidence of immune–endocrine interaction. These natural models strongly substantiate the idea that hormones regulate and/or mediate the immune response.

The many enigmas of this fascinating field and the variety of experimental approaches have been challenging an increasing number of scientists in the past few years. For example, many studies have been carried out on the role of biogenic monoamines in the immune response and it is now widely recognized that these small but widespread hormonal molecules mediate several events in the immunologic reaction (Bourne et al., 1974). Also, the effects of many hormones on various immunologic parameters have been examined and dramatic effects have been shown (Ahlqvist, 1976). Nevertheless, these approaches seem to imply, somehow, a static and rigid concept of the interactions linking the endocrine and immune systems. An integrative approach would appear more productive; a perspective in which the organism as a whole is visualized and where each part influences and is influenced by the others. In fact, previous experimental work has emphasized the relevance of hormones in the differentiation of the immune system (Pierpaoli and Sorkin, 1968; Pierpaoli et al., 1970, 1971). More recently, it has been shown that the thymus exerts a crucial endocrine action on the developing neuroendocrine system of the mouse. Absence of the thymus at the perinatal stage of the development results in permanent alteration of the endocrine environment (Pierpaoli and Sorkin, 1972; Pierpaoli and Besedowsky, 1975; Pierpaoli et al., 1976). On the basis of these findings it has been postulated that the generation of bone marrow- and thymus-derived immunocompetent cells requires a well-defined, balanced and chronologically appropriate hormonal environment at a critical early stage of embryogenesis (Pierpaoli, 1975). In fact, a recent investigation on the interdependence of neuroendocrine programming and the generation of immune recognition mechanisms, showed that the sequential, chronologically and quantitatively critical inoculation of different allogeneic hybrid cells into mice during the neonatal and perinatal period, induced an indefinite prolongation of the stage during which tolerance could be readily induced. This prolongation of the tolerogenic time in immature mice was accompanied by parallel impairment and retardation of development of the still immature adrenal and gonadal functions (Pierpaoli *et al.,* 1977). All these findings are consonant with the idea that critically timed hormonal regulation is a prerequisite for the initiation of an immune response in adults as well. Our experimental approach for challenging this idea was so formulated: Does an immune reaction induce changes in the neuroendocrine system as reflected in *early* significant alterations of the hormonal environment?

We investigated whether antigenic stimulation can evoke *rapid* neuroendocrine changes. The results were rather controversial, but they opened a new pharmacologic approach to the control of the immune response. Even if still largely empirical, this new pharmacologic intervention yielded striking results. The most significant of these are reported in the Section "Pharmacologic Approach."

EARLY HORMONAL EVENTS
AFTER ANTIGENIC STIMULATION

Experiments were designed to explore whether antigenic stimulation can directly or indirectly evoke rapid changes in the endocrine system: (*a*) an allogeneic system was utilized where the lymphocyte carried the dual function of antigenic stimulus and possible producer of "chemical mediators" to the endocrine system; (*b*) sheep red blood cell (SRBC) and ovalbumin (OV) were used to evaluate whether eventual hormonal changes following antigens injection can be evoked by stimulation with particulate (SRBC) and soluble (OV) antigens.

After intravenous (i.v.) inoculation of allogeneic lymph node cells in normal mice, the most impressive hormonal variations concerned the blood levels of luteotropic hormone (LH). The inoculation of 5×10^7 allogeneic lymph node cells from normal C57BL/6 into C3H/He mice induced a sharp increase in the level of LH 2 hr after cell injection. This increase was anticipated at 0.5 hr with a peak at 1 hr when the cells were derived from donors previously immunized to the recipient strain (Table 1).

This suggested that this polypeptide hormone might be involved in the very initiation of the immune response. A successive experiment, in which mice were injected with SRBC, apparently confirmed this finding (Pierpaoli and Maestroni, 1978a). Nevertheless, to confirm further and possibly expand upon and better interpret these early findings, 4×10^8 SRBC, 1 mg OV or 0.2 ml saline were inoculated i.v. in 3 series of 14 groups of C57BL/6 × A/J F_1 hybrid female mice. The animals were then bled 1,2,5,10,20,30,45,60, 90,120,150,180,210, and 240 min after antigen or saline injection. They were killed by exsanguination between 8 and 12.00 A.M. Animals inoculated only with saline were the control groups. Sera of single groups were pooled for hormone determinations. The hormones measured were LH, follicle stimulating hormone (FSH), thyroxin (Tx), growth hormone (GH), and corticosterone.

TABLE 1
Changes of Luteotropic Hormone (LH) Levels in Blood of C3H/He Mice Elicited
by Inoculation of Allogeneic Cells from Normal or Alloimmunized Donors

Time after inoculation (hr)	Donors			
	C3H/He	C57BL/6	C57BL/6 alloimmunized	Medium alone
0.5	74	42	240	n.d.[a]
1	31	88	250	70
2	79	250	200	39
3	31	50	110	35
4	78	32	61	54
5	72	50	58	50
6	39	61	69	59
7	46	59	50	47
8	58	80	72	50

NOTE: Groups of three 5 month-old male C3H/He mice were inoculated i.v. with 5×10^7 lymph node cells from syngeneic (C3H/He), allogeneic (C57BL/6), or allogeneic and alloimmunized (with spleen cells from C3H/He mice 6 weeks beforehand) C57BL/6 mice. The mice were exsanguinated at 0.5–8 hr after inoculation of the cells and the sera were pooled. Values of LH are expressed as nanograms per ml serum.
[a] n.d., Not determined

Contrary to what was expected, no early rise of blood LH levels could be detected. Only an impressive and clearly significant ($p < 0.01$) increase of corticosterone level was shown at 120,150,180,210, and 240 min after SRBC inoculation. No significant hormonal variation was elicited by injection of OV (Figure 1).

An interpretation of these results is problematic because the two models used contain several unknown variables. Clearly, *different* antigens can evoke *differently* timed hormonal responses; in addition, the endocrine response could as well show a circadian variability. This idea is consonant with recent findings on the influence of pineal circadian rhythmicity on the immune response (W. Pierpaoli and G. J. M. Maestroni, unpublished). These preliminary findings point out that *early* endocrine changes do, in fact, follow antigenic challenge, and they provide a basis for a pharmacologic control of the immune response. In fact, it appears reasonable to assume that a drug-mediated interference with those central neuroendocrine events presumably promoting the hormonal variations observed would affect the immune response to the antigen that triggers this complex chain of reactions.

PHARMACOLOGIC APPROACH

This intervention implies that the interaction between antigen and antigen-sensitive cells or, in other words, the antigen-stimulated immunocompetent cells, delivers to the hypothalamus–pituitary axis a kind of message to pro-

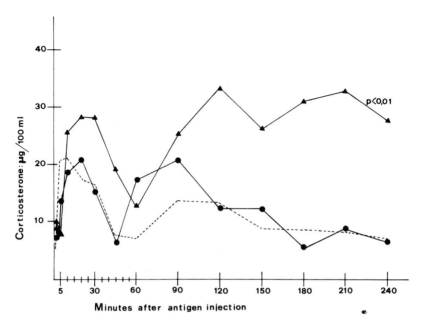

Figure 1. Early changes of corticosterone level after antigen injection in mice. Adult, C57BL/6×A/J F₁ hybrid female mice were caged in groups of 10 and the groups were divided in 3 series of 14 cages. The mice of the first series were injected with 0.2 ml of a saline suspension of 4 × 10⁸ SRBC, while 1 mg ovalbumin (OV) also dissolved in 0.2 ml of saline was injected in the animals of the second series. Finally, the control mice were inoculated only with saline (0.2 ml). The injections were done intravenously. The animals were then bled at 1, 2, 5, 10, 20, 30, 45, 60, 90, 120, 150, 180, 210, and 240 minutes after antigen and saline injections. At each time and for each series, 10 mice were sacrificed and sera were pooled for hormone determinations. SRBC ◆——◆ ; OV ●———● ; Saline - - - - - .

duce those peripheral hormonal variations apt to prompt further steps in the evolution of an immune response. A blockade or inhibition of this chain of messages at a central or peripheral level would provoke an antigen-specific blockade or suppression of the further differentiation of the antigen-stimulated cells.

For this purpose, drugs were tested which have been shown to affect synthesis and/or release of LH and adrenocorticotropin (ACTH), two main pituitary hormones.

We also considered possible hormonal effects on lymphocyte membrane at the peripheral level (blood, spleen, lymph nodes). In fact, a variety of polypeptide hormones are known to interact with specific plasma membrane receptors on target cells. This action affects intracellular concentration of two cyclic nucleotides: cyclic adenosine 3′,5′-monophosphate (cAMP) and cyclic guanosine 3′,5′-monophosphate (cGMP) that function as translators of the hormonal message. It is known that an increase in lymphocyte cAMP has a general inhibitory effect on the immune response and that early changes in cAMP occur after injection of antigens (Braun and Rega, 1972; Bourne *et al.*, 1974; Singh and Owen, 1976; Plescia *et al.*, 1975; Yamamoto and Webb, 1975). Therefore, agents known to influence cAMP levels were also considered.

The drugs were tested singly or in combination in order that they might modulate hormonal response to antigenic challenge both at peripheral and central levels.

Choice of Drugs

α- AND β-ADRENERGIC BLOCKERS

Epinephrine (E) and norepinephrine (NE) are the two main known physiological adrenergic agents. They act on cell membrane receptors which, according to their molecular structure, can be divided into α and β receptors. Many drugs are known to block adrenergic receptors, but their action shows a wide range of receptor specificity. Among the blockers with higher specificity, we chose phentolamine (PHE) as an α-blocker and propranolol (PRO) as a β-blocker.

Catecholamines (E, NE) function as hormones over long distances and as transmitters for neurons in the sympathetic nervous system over short distances (Fuxe *et al.*, 1973). Norepinephrine inhibits, by an α-adrenergic mechanism, ACTH secretion, probably by acting on the ACTH hypothalamic corticotropin releasing hormone (CRH; Ganong, 1973). Blockade of α-adrenergic receptors decreases secretion of GH, while blockade of β-adrenergic receptors is associated with a rise in GH (Mueller, 1973; Nakay and Imura, 1974). Release of LH and FSH releasing hormones (LH-RH; FSH-RH) and of prolactin inhibiting hormone (PR-IH) is linked to α-adrenergic receptors in the hypothalamus (Kamberi, 1973; Lawson and Gala, 1975). Adrenergic and dopaminergic mechanisms may also be involved in the control of thyrotropic hormone releasing hormone (TSH-RH) and melanocyte stimulating hormone inhibiting hormone (MSH-IH; Prange *et al.*, 1973). Finally, it is well known that the effect of catecholamines on lymphocyte cAMP levels is mediated by β-adrenergic receptors (Bourne *et al.*, 1974).

L-5-HYDROXYTRYPTOPHAN

L-5-Hydroxytryptophan (5HTP) is the precursor of 5-hydroxytryptamine (5HT, serotonin). Serotonin is an indoleamine that plays many very important roles as a neurotransmitter in the central nervous system. Brain serotonin seems to influence the immune response via the hypothalamo–pituitary axis. An increase of brain 5HT has been shown to be immunosuppressive (Devoino *et al.*, 1975).

Serotonin decreases the functional activity of the hypothalamo–pituitary–

thyroid system by inhibiting the TSH-RH secretion in the hypothalamus (Mess and Peter, 1975); 5HT exerts a negative control on gonadotropins (LH, FSH) and ACTH synthesis and/or release, and increases prolactin secretion (Lawson and Gala, 1975). Serotoninergic neurons are of importance in the mediation of the inhibitory feedback action of corticosterone. A combined treatment of 5HTP and monoamine oxidase inhibitors (MAOI) blocks spontaneous ovulation. Therefore, the serotoninergic neurons may exert an inhibitory action on LH-RH as well as on C-RH secretion (Fuxe *et al.*, 1974).

DOPAMINE

Dopamine (DA) is another potent neurotransmitter and is the precursor of NE and E. Dopaminergic neurons tonically inhibit prolactin secretion and stimulate LH, FSH, and ACTH synthesis and/or release (Lawson and Gala, 1975; Choudhury *et al.*, 1974). The functional relationship between 5HT and DA is still unclear, nevertheless it might be antagonistic in the regulation of gonadotropins and ACTH (Collu *et al.*, 1976).

HALOPERIDOL

Haloperidol is a butyrophenone with a powerful neuroleptic action. This drug blocks cell receptors for DA. As a consequence, haloperidol increases serum prolactin and decreases LH and FSH (Dickerman *et al.*, 1974). Haloperidol has been found to be moderately immunosuppressive (Levy and Munson, 1976).

p-CHLOROPHENYLALANINE

p-Chlorophenylalanine (PCPA) causes a profound and long lasting decrease in brain 5HT (Sanders-Bush *et al.*, 1974).

Effect of Drugs on Antibody Production

As shown in Table 2, the combination of drugs which produced the most remarkable inhibition of direct antibody forming cell (AFC) to SRBC in mice was that of 5HTP, HAL, and PHE. A repetition of the experiments with different doses of the drugs gave similar results. Therefore this combination of drugs was chosen for further experiments. The agents of this mixture were also tested singly or in pairs, but only the combination of the three drugs administered together gave a virtual blockade of the response to SRBC (Pierpaoli and Maestroni, 1978a).

The experiments reported in Table 3 show that the complete inhibition of antibody production obtained by the administration of our combination of

TABLE 2
Effect of Drugs on the Primary Immune Response to Sheep Red Blood Cells in Mice

Drug treatment	Dose per day (mg/kg b.w.)	Nucleated spleen cells[a]	AFC/10[6] spleen cells
5HTP	30	274 ± 14	204 ± 85
5HTP + PHE	30–12	239 ± 34	261 ± 104
5HTP + PRO	30–12	256 ± 49	448 ± 269
5HTP + PHE + PRO	30–12–12	236 ± 56	256 ± 114
5HTP + HAL + PHE	30–12–12	168 ± 24	48 ± 26
5HTP + HAL + PRO	30–12–12	165 ± 21	143 ± 132
5HTP + HAL + PHE + PRO	30–12–12–12	142 ± 29	148 ± 33
DA	40	200 ± 22	179 ± 30
DA + PHE	40–12	220 ± 36	302 ± 96
DA + PRO	40–12	291 ± 80	397 ± 308
DA + PHE + PRO	40–12–12	229 ± 17	410 ± 190
DA + PCPA + PHE	40–160[b]–12	199 ± 29	219 ± 140
DA + PCPA + PRO	40–160[b]–12	198 ± 9	272 ± 154
DA + PCPA + PHE + PRO	40–160[b]–12–12	242 ± 16	453 ± 191
Controls (SRBC only)	—	206 ± 30	452 ± 139

NOTE: Groups of five 4-month-old male C3H/He mice were injected intraperitoneally (i.p.) with 4×10^8 sheep red blood cells (SRBC). The number of direct antibody forming cells (AFC) was estimated 4 days later. The drugs were suspended in saline and given subcutaneously (s.c.) once a day for 4 days, starting 24 hr before antigen injection. 5HTP, L-5-Hydroxytrytophan; PHE, α-adrenergic blocker, phentolamine; PRO, β-adrenergic blocker, propranolol; HAL, Neurolepticum haloperidol; DA, Dopamine; PCPA, p-Chlorophenylalanine. From "Pharmacological control of the hormonally modulated immune response. II. Blockade of antibody production by a combination of drugs acting on neuroendocrine functions. Its prevention by gonadotropins and corticotrophin by Pierpaoli, W. and Maestroni, G. J. M., *Immunology, 34,* 419–430. Copyright 1978 by Blackwell Sci. Publ. Reprinted by permission.
[a] Total numbers of nucleated spleen cells/mouse ($\times 10^6$).
[b] PCPA, only 1 injection i.p. 24 hr before SRBC inoculation.

drugs and of an antigen is long lasting. In fact, a second injection of 4×10^8 SRBC at 12 days after the first antigen challenge evoked formation of very few IgM (direct plaques) and IgG (indirect plaques) forming cells.

This persistence of the unresponsiveness to the second injection of antigen in the blocked mice was confirmed further by the experiment shown in Figure 2. This experiment also demonstrated that the same mice, which were unresponsive to SRBC when injected a second time 67 days after the first antigen and drug administration, were perfectly able to respond to *Shigella paradysenteria* antigen (SPA) almost as efficiently as mice primed with that antigen (Figure 2). Furthermore, we could show that the drug-induced blockade of the humoral immune response can be prevented by prior administration of LH, FSH, and ACTH (Table 4). It is notable that the drug-induced inhibition of antibody formation was counteracted only when the hormones were given *before* the treatment with drugs and antigen. This might imply that these hormones are involved in the differentiation of antigen-sensitive cells to antibody-forming cells.

TABLE 3
Immunologic Unresponsiveness to Sheep Red Blood Cells (SRBC)
in Mice Induced by a Combination of Three Drugs[a]

Treatment	Primary response			Memory response		
	Number of mice	Nucleated cells/spleen ($\times 10^6$)	PFC/10^6 spleen cells	Number of mice	Nucleated cells/spleen ($\times 10^6$)	PFC/10^6 spleen cells
SRBC + drugs	16	123 ± 45	5 ± 5	16	231 ± 43	12 ± 12
SRBC	18	208 ± 43	636 ± 165	6	269 ± 32	520 ± 290

[a] Adult (4- to 5-month-old) female C3H/HeJ mice were injected intraperitoneally (i.p.) with 4×10^8 SRBC. The number of direct plaque-forming cells (PFC) was estimated 4 days after antigen injection. In some groups (memory response). 4×10^8 SRBC were reinjected at Day 12 after the first inoculation, and the number of direct PFC was measured 2 days later. One to two hours before the first antigen injection, and then once a day for 3 successive days, a mixture of three drugs was administered subcutaneously (s.c.) at the following doses: L-5-Hydroxytryptophan, 40 mg/kg body weight; haloperidol, 12 mg/kg body weight; phentolamine, 12 mg/kg body weight. The drugs were dissolved in 0.5% citric acid and incorporated into incomplete Freund's adjuvant (FIA). From "Pharmacological control of the immune response by blockade of the early hormonal changes following antigen injection," by Pierpaoli, W. and Maestroni, G. J. M., *Cellular Immunology*, 1977, 31, 355-363. Copyright 1977 by Academic Press. Reprinted by permission.

Effect of Drugs on Transplantation Immunity

The criteria for the selection of the drugs was based on our interpretation of the mechanism of action of these substances on the endocrine system, the antibody response, and on their effects when tested singly (Pierpaoli and Maestroni, 1978b).

TABLE 4
Protection from and Prevention of Drug-Induced Blockade
of Antibody Response to SRBC in Mice by Hormones[a]

Inoculation sequence	Number of mice	Nucleated cells/spleen ($\times 10^6$)	PFC/10^6 spleen cells
SRBC	10	270 ± 41	554 ± 95
Drugs–SRBC	10	130 ± 37	7 ± 5
SRBC–drugs	4	115 ± 74	49 ± 34
Drugs–hormones–SRBC–hormones	8	141 ± 25	69 ± 21
Hormones–SRBC–hormones–drugs	7	211 ± 40	386 ± 112

[a] Hormones (LH, 200 µg/day; FSH, 200 µg/day; ACTH, 5 µg/day) were injected i.p. in three aliquots on Day 0 and in two aliquots on Days 1, 2, and 3 at the given sequence. The drugs (same doses as in Table 3) were given s.c. on Day 0 and for the 3 successive days at the sequence given above. Direct plaque-forming cells (PFC) were estimated 4 days after antigen inoculation. From "Pharmacological control of the immune response by blockade of the early hormonal changes following antigen injection," by Pierpaoli, W. and Maestroni, G. J. M., *Cellular Immunology*, 1977, **31**, 355-363. Copyright 1977 by Academic Press. Reprinted by permission.

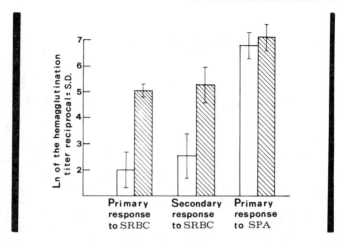

Figure 2. Antigen-specific blockade of the primary and secondary immune response to SRBC in mice by a combination of three drugs. Normal response to a second antigen. One group of ten, 3-month-old SWR female mice was injected S.C. with a saline suspension of the three drugs in combination 2hr (40 mg 5HTP, 12 mg PHE, and 12 mg HAL per kg body weight) and 15 min (80 mg 5HTP, 24 mg PHE, and 24 mg HAL per kg body weight) before injection of the antigen (0.1 ml of 20% SRBC in saline suspension i.p.). The drugs were injected again at 20, 40, and 50 hr after injection of the antigen (40 mg 5HTP, 12 mg PHE, and 12 mg HAL per kg body weight each time). One group of 6 mice was used as a control and injected only with SRBC. The mice were bled 10 days after antigen injection and serum agglutinins were measured by the direct agglutination test. The same mice were injected again with the same dose of SRBC 67 days after the first antigen injection and the serum agglutinin titer determined 3 days later. Ten days after the second injection of SRBC, the same mice were injected i.p. with 0.2 ml of *Shigella paradysenteria* antigen (SPA) and the agglutinin titer was measured 7 days later. Open columns, drug-treated; hatched columns, controls. From "Pharmacological control of the hormonally modulated immune response. II. Blockade of antibody neuroendocrine functions. Its prevention by gonadotropins and corticotrophin" by Pierpaoli, W. and Maestroni, G. J. M., *Immunology*, 1978, **34**, 419–430. Copyright 1978 by Blackwell Sci. Publ. Reprinted by permission.

The combinations of drugs are listed in Table 5 where their effect on the viability of allogeneic skin grafts is recorded. As is evident in this table, the most pronounced retardation of rejection was achieved by treating outbred mice or BALB/c mice with 5HTP, HAL, PHE, and DA. The mice treated with this mixture maintained their immune deficit even when grafted again with the same donor skin 6 months later, whereas skin from a different donor (C3H/He) was rejected normally (10–14 days). However, the transplantation immune reaction was not completely abrogated and the mice rejected their graft. Moreover, profound sedation, hypothermia, hypotonia, and diarrhea followed by constipation and loss of weight were observed in the animals treated with the most effective combination of drugs (5HTP, HAL, PHE, DA).

Effect of Combinations of Drugs on the Capacity of Mice to Reject First- and Second-Set Allogeneic Skin Grafts[a]

Combinations of drugs	Number of mice grafted		First-set graft rejection ± s.d. (days)	Second-set graft rejection after 6 months ± s.d. (days)
	Albino	BALB/c		
5HTP, HAL, PHE	18	12	22 ± 2.9	17 ± 2.3
5HTP, HAL, PRO	20		12 ± 1.5	13 ± 1.9
5HTP, IPT, HAL	6		26 ± 2	
5HTP, HAL, PHE, PRO	20		15 ± 1.8	
DA, HAL, PHE	20		18 ± 2.1	
DA, CYP, PHE	6		11 ± 1	
DA, CYP, PRO	6		10 ± 1.2	
DA, PCPA, PHE	6		11 ± 2.2	
DA, PCPA, PRO	6		9 ± 0.9	
DA, PCPA, HAL, PHE	7		15 ± 1.4	
DA, 5HTP, HAL, PHE (C20)	21	9	29 ± 5.6	23 ± 5.2 (C57BL/6 donors)
				12 ± 1.2 (C3H/He donors)
DA	8		15 ± 2.1	
5HTP	9		16 ± 1.7	
HAL	9		16 ± 0.9	
PHE	6		11 ± 1.1	
Controls untreated	5	5	12 ± 1.8	10 ± 1.2

[a] Donors of skin were young adult C57BL/6 or C57BL/6 × CBA F₁ hybrid mice. Some C3H/He donors were used to evaluate allospecificity of retardation of second-set rejection time. Recipients were adult albino outbred or BALB/c inbred male or female mice. The mice were grafted at random. The grafts were considered viable only as long as they did not show signs of rejection (induration, edema, peripheral infiltration). The schedule of injection of the various drug mixture was described previously (Pierpaoli and Maestroni, 1978). Dosage was: brain metabolites (5HTP, DA), 40 mg; receptor antagonists (PHE, PRO, CYP, HAL), 12 mg; receptor agonists (IPT), 40 mg; inhibitors of neurotransmitters synthesis (PCPA), 150 mg/kg of body weight in one single i.p. injection 12 hr before grafting. These doses are defined for each combination as dose 1. From "Pharmacological control of the hormonally modulated immune response. III. Prolongation of allogeneic skin graft rejection and prevention of runt disease by a combination of drugs acting on neuroendocrine functions," by Pierpaoli, W. and Maestroni, G. J. M., *Journal of Immunology*, 1978, **120**, 1600–1603. Copyright 1978 by Williams & Wilkins Co. Reprinted by permission.

Avoidance of Secondary Disease in Lethally Irradiated
Mice Transplanted with Allogeneic Bone Marrow

One of the main problems hindering a successful allogeneic bone marrow transplantation (BMT) is the occurrence of a secondary disease (SD) that, within a variable time, kills the transplanted recipients. The etiopathogenesis of SD is still rather obscure, but the most common view defines SD or graft-versus-host disease (GVHD) as a pathological condition of strict immunologic character (Dicke *et al.*, 1978). Although we no longer accept this interpretation of the genesis of GVHD, we adopted the immunologic concept when we tried to apply to BMT what we had learned from the effects of various drug combinations on humoral and cell-mediated immunity. In other words, we tried specifically to inhibit or block, by our drug combinations, those immune reactions believed to produce SD after allogeneic BMT. This trial resulted in the development of a method innovative in two principal respects: (*a*) the use of a combination of the three drugs (5HTP, HAL, and PHE) believed to block the initial neuroendocrine events accompanying a primary immune response, and (*b*) the administration, before irradiation, of a large number of allogeneic bone marrow cells. The basic innovation was that both procedures *preceded* supralethal total body irradiation (TBI). This system, defined as the *preconditioning* regimen, was based on the consideration that such operational procedures *preceding TBI* might be critical in creating a suitable immunologic and/or endocrinologic milieu. This situation would facilitate a proper engraftment of the foreign marrow *after TBI* (postconditioning regimen) and thus influence favorably its proliferation and maintenance, avoiding the onset of an early or late SD by conferring to the host full restoration of immune and other functions.

Figure 3 condenses the results of an experiment with all relevant controls, where donors of allogeneic bone marrow cells were 2–4-month-old C57BL/6 mice and recipients were 3–4-month-old C57BL/6 × A/J F_1 hybrid females. The mice that survived early mortality during the first 1 or 2 months after TBI, survived indefinitely and proved to be established chimeras (Pierpaoli and Maestroni, 1980). The administration of the three drugs 5HTP, HAL, and PHE, listed as C5, together with allogeneic bone marrow cells *before TBI,* allowed an indefinite survival and complete chimerism of 60–75% of the transplanted mice, while survival of the three control groups ranged from 10 to 40% (Fig. 3).

RECENT DEVELOPMENTS

We have shown that early endocrine variations concerning hormones of the adrenal and gonadal–hypophysis axis occur after antigen inoculation. The athymic nude mouse, together with the well-known impairment of immune

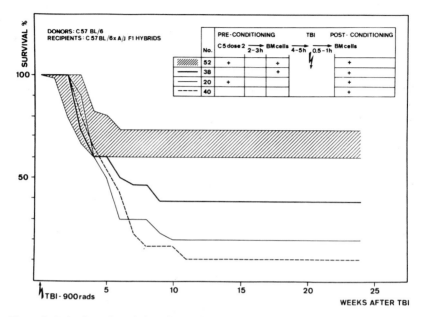

Figure 3. Induction of persisting allogeneic marrow chimerism in preconditioned and supra-lethally irradiated C57BL/6 × A/J F₁ hybrid female mice transplanted with parental C57BL/6 bone marrow. The number of bone marrow cells injected in the pre- and postconditioning stages ranged between 30 and 60 × 10⁶ per mouse in individual experiments. The cells were inoculated i.v. in 0.5 ml volume. The interval between drug administration and inoculation of BM cells in the preconditioning stage was 2–3 hr. From "The facilitation of enduring engraftment of allogeneic bone marrow and avoidance of secondary disease in mice" by Pierpaoli, W. and Maestroni, G. J. M., *Cellular Immunology*, 1980, **52**, 62–72. Copyright 1980 by Academic Press. Reprinted by permission.

functions, shows adrenal and gonadal derangements (Pierpaoli and Besedov-sky, 1975; Pierpaoli *et al.*, 1976). In recent investigations we tried to clarify whether the primary endocrine alterations consequent to thymic aplasia during ontogeny depend on *one* well-defined hormonal defect. After several experiments and ambiguous, contradictory results, we could finally identify the probable brain target for the endocrine action of the thymus. The candidate was the pineal body, a small gland that controls the circadian periodicity of the whole neuroendocrine system by cyclic release of neurohormones. One of the main messengers for the circadian hormonal variations is the pineal in-doleamine, melatonin (5-methoxy-*N*-acetyl-serotonin).

It is known that inoculation of massive amounts of newborn-derived immature T cells from normal mice into athymic nude mice does not produce per se any immune reconstitution (Pierpaoli, 1975). Most interestingly, we demonstrated that properly timed inoculation of melatonin in T-cell-transferred nude mice affords nudes the ability to reject skin allografts. At the same time, we found that nude mice have an abnormal circadian melatonin rhythm when compared to normal mice. They show a significantly lower level of melatonin during the day and normal values during the night (Pierpaoli and Maestroni, 1981). Thus, we proposed that the thymus acts as a programmer of pineal activity during ontogeny and that the circadian release of melatonin promotes, directly or indirectly, differentiation of the immature thymus-derived or processed cells to immunocompetent cells and acquisition of transplantation immunity.

A logical question emerged: Is the pineal-induced circadian variability of the endocrine environment *also* influencing immune reactivity in adult organisms?

We tried to provide a preliminary answer to this question. Experiments were designed in which acute or chronic disturbances of the circadian melatonin rhythm were induced by different methods in mice. Their immune system was then investigated morphologically and/or functionally.

Abrogation of Nocturnal Circadian Periodicity

The model was based on exposure of male and female BALB/c mice to constant environmental lighting (no dark circadian period) for several generations. The aim of this maneuver was to eradicate any circadian variation of the hormonal environment. In fact, continuous lighting leads to a functional pinealectomy (Relkin, 1976; Reiter, 1977). However, neither functional nor surgical pinealectomy abolishes circadian hormonal variations in adult animals. Other brain structures, such as the suprachiasmatic nucleus of the hypothalamus, drive the clock functions of the pineal (Klein and Moore, 1979). Furthermore, it seems that newborn rodents acquire circadian rhythms through maternal milk, regardless of the light–dark cycle (Deguchi, 1978). Thus, the mice were kept for 4 generations in a windowless room where light was constantly on. The mice of the last 2 generations (third and fourth) grew very poorly. When the mice were 1 month old, they were runty and significantly smaller than the control mice grown with a 12:12 light: dark cycle. The difference in body weight is shown in Table 6. These observations are in agreement with the findings of Nir *et al.* (1972) and Csaba *et al.* (1973) in rats. Some of the "third generation light" mice were killed and sections of thymus, spleen, lymph nodes, liver, lung, and kidney examined histologically.

Figure 4 shows thymus, spleen, and a parathymic lymph node of 1-month-old, male or female BALB/c mice kept since birth under constant environmental lighting. The grandparents of these mice were the first generation born and maintained under continuous lighting. Sections of the other organs did not show any alteration. Figure 4A shows an abnormal thymic involution. The cortex is almost depleted of lymphocytes, lymphoblasts are absent. The picture shows an alteration of the thymic structure which is different from the physiological involution of the thymus of aging mice and similar to the stress-

TABLE 6
Impaired Growth and Decreased Antibody Production of BALB/c Mice Kept for 3 and 4 Generations under Constant Environmental Lighting

Group	Number of animals	Age	Body weight (gm) (mean ± s.d.)	WBC cells/mm³ (mean ± s.d.)	% L	% PN	Hemagglutination titer reciprocal (mean ± s.d.)	
							Primary response to SRBC	Secondary response to SRBC
Third and fourth generation-"light"	16	30 days	6.4 ± 1,2	2228 ± 457	62	38	73 ± 16	1020 ± 676
Controls 12:12 light:dark	10	30 days	17.3 ± 2,4	5820 ± 1243	85	15	400 ± 148	3200 ± 1275

Male and female BALB/c mice were kept constantly under continuous lighting for 4 generations. One-month-old mice of the third and fourth generation were weighed and injected i.p. with 4×10^8 SRBC. The hemagglutination test was performed 6 days later; 15–20 days after the first antigen injection the same mice were boostered and after 3 days the hemagglutination titer evaluated. Control mice were BALB/c male or female kept in 12:12, light:dark cycle. s.d., Standard deviation; WBC, White blood cells; L, Lymphocytes; PN, Polymorphonuclear; SRBC, Sheep red blood cells.

419

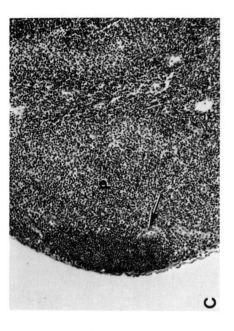

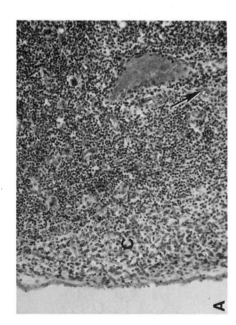

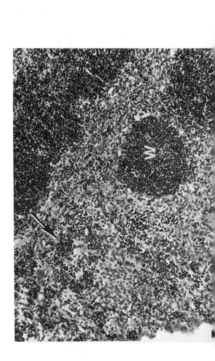

Figure 4. Consequences of constant environmental lighting on thymus and peripheral lymphatic tissues in mice. (A) Thymus. C, cortex; the arrow points to a Hassal body. × 240. Abnormal involution. The cortex is almost completely depleted of lymphocytes; the medulla contains a variable number of small lymphocytes; medium-size lymphocytes and lymphoblasts are lacking. The number of Hassal bodies seems to be increased. (B) Spleen. W, white pulp. × 180. Note the few erythropoietic plaques (arrow) in the red pulp. Lack of germinal center. The red pulp is inactive and displays only a few areas of erythropoietic activity. Granulopoiesis is absent. (C) Lymph node (parathymic). P, paracortex; the arrow indicates an oval-shaped primary follicle in the outer cortex. × 180. Only primary follicles are present in the outer cortex (B-cell dependent area). Secondary follicles are missing. The paracortex (T-cell dependent area) contains less lym-

induced morphological changes. A spleen section is shown in Figure 4B. Here major alterations are a lack of evident germinal centers and an apparent inactivity of the red pulp. The formation of germinal centers requires the presence of a subpopulation of T cells (Weissman *et al.*, 1976). It is possible that the cells absent from the thymus cortex represent such subpopulation. The apparently inactive erythro- and granulopoiesis might also depend on the lack of appropriate T cells (Cline and Golde, 1979). A lymph node is shown in Figure 4C. In the outer cortex (B-cell dependent area) only primary follicles are present, while the paracortex (T-cell dependent area) shows a reduced number of lymphocytes if compared to normal animals.

Some kind of chronic stress could be responsible for the observed histologic alterations. In fact, it is known that pinealectomy stimulates, through the CNS, adrenal and gonadal function (Relkin, 1976; Reiter, 1977). It is therefore conceivable that increased amounts of gonadal and adrenal steroids produce, among a variety of effects, those modifications of the lymphatic organs shown in Figure 4. On the other hand, the immune capacity of littermates of the mice sacrificed for histology was clearly decreased. Although preliminary and restricted to one immune parameter, the results listed in Table 6 indicate that both the primary and secondary immune responses to sheep red blood cells (SRBC) were significantly lower in the light-exposed mice than in the controls. Also noteworthy is the decreased absolute number of white blood cells (WBC) and the relative number of blood lymphocytes. Nevertheless, the same mice were able to reject a transplant of allogeneic skin within a normal time (10–14 days).

Pharmacologic Inhibition of the Melatonin Circadian Rhythm

Melatonin derives from serotonin through the action of N-acetyltransferase (NAT) and hydroxyindole-O-methyltransferase (HIOMT). Pineal NAT activation depends on the stimulation of postsynaptic β-adrenergic receptors (Oleshansky and Neff, 1978). In fact, night administration of the β-blocker propanolol (PRO) causes a reversion to daily patterns of indole metabolism (Deguchi and Axelrod, 1973). Therefore, the experimental model consisted in disturbing the circadian cyclicity of mice by evening injections of PRO. At the same time the mice were tested for their immune reactivity against SRBC or alloantigens.

Adult, C57BL/6 male mice were divided into three groups of 10 animals and caged separately. One group of mice was treated by evening inoculations (s.c.) of PRO for 7 days, starting on the day of antigen (SRBC) injection. The second group received the same treatment, but the injections of PRO were performed in the morning. The last experimental group was injected only with SRBC as a control. The primary and secondary immune response to SRBC

TABLE 7
Decrease of the Primary and Secondary Response to SRBC in C57BL/6 Mice Injected with the β-Adrenergic Blocker Propanolol

Group	Number of animals	Time of PRO treatment (30 mg/kg s.c.)	Days of treatment	Reciprocal of the hemagglutination titer ± S.D.	
				Primary response day 7	Secondary response day 18
A	10	5.00 P.M.	7 (days 0–6)	360 ± 223	208 ± 147
B	10	8.00 A.M.	7 (days 0–6)	1048 ± 660	896 ± 330
C	10	—	—	1536 ± 572	1024 ± 350

Three groups of 10 adult C57BL/6 male mice were injected i.p. with 0.2 ml of 10% SRBC (day 0). In the first two groups of mice (A, B), the immunization was performed 2 hr after a first injection of 0.5 ml of saline solution of propanolol (PRO). The dose per mouse of the β-blocker was 30 mg/kg body weight and was administered to the first group of mice (A) at 5.00 P.M. The second group (B), received the drug at 8.00 A.M. The drug was injected s.c. and the treatment was continued in both groups, in the evening and in the morning, respectively, for 7 consecutive days after antigen injection. A third group of mice (C) was only immunized with SRBC. The primary response to SRBC was evaluated on day 7, while the secondary response was measured on day 18, 3 days after reinjection of the antigen. Antibody production was estimated by the hemagglutination test.

was then evaluated by hemagglutination. Table 7 summarizes the results. Both the primary and secondary antibody production against SRBC was markedly decreased in the evening-treated (PRO) mice, while the responses of the morning-treated (PRO) mice were similar to those of the controls. These data are preliminary and more extensive investigation is clearly needed. However, these findings, together with the results listed in Table 6, support the concept of a physiological immuno-modulating function of the pineal circadian rhythm in adult organisms. On the other hand, as in the model of constant environmental lighting, mice receiving evening injections of PRO were able to reject allogeneic skin grafts within a normal time (10–14 days). This might imply that the pineal-dependent immuno-regulatory system affects humoral, but not cell-mediated immune reactions.

CONCLUSIONS AND PROSPECTS

Early Hormonal Changes After Antigen Injection

Allogeneic lymphocytes inoculated in normal C3H/He mice induced an impressive increase of LH level a few hours after injection of the cells. Different antigens (SRBC, OV) failed to evoke LH surge. A very significant increase of corticosterone level of recipient mice was the unique hormonal response at 2–4 hr after SRBC injection. These are in summary the results of the experiments described above. What is their meaning? It is very difficult to draw any conclusion. However, it seems clear that the endocrine system reacts soon after an antigenic challenge. Why and how these variations occur is still a matter of speculation. The interaction between a single hormone and the entire immune system is already, per se, very complicated. In light of our recent findings on the influence of pineal circadian rhythms on the immune response, a proper interpretation of these phenomena appears almost impossible at the present time. The circadian variability of the humoral milieu in which cells work and communicate, seems to drive and control the immuno-endocrine response (Fernandes et al., 1976). In fact, it is feasible that the kinetics, intensity, and pattern of the hormonal variation accompanying an immune response change according to the schedule of inoculation in the course of the day and in response to the nature of the antigen.

Pharmacologic Approach

An antigen-specific and long-lasting suppression of antibody production was achieved by treating mice with a combination of three drugs, 5HTP, PHE, and HAL. In order to achieve similar results in cell-mediated immunity, a fourth drug, DA, had to be added to the combination. The endocrine effect of such combinations of drugs can be inferred from the vast literature available (see choice of drugs). The probable final effect of the combination of 5HTP, PHE, and HAL on secretion of hormones at the pituitary level is summarized below.

Hormone	Effect on hormone levels
LH and FSH (LH-, FSH-RH)	Decrease
ACTH (CRF)	Decrease
TSH (TRF)	Decrease
GH (GHRF, GHIF)	No effect or slight decrease
Prolactin (PRF, PIF)	Increase

The addition of DA to the combination of the three drugs might result in a marked decrease of GH secretion by increasing the turnover of catecholamines and because of the presence of HAL.

A surge of LH and a significant increase of corticosterone were the early hormonal changes that could be detected after antigen injection (Table 1 and Figure 1). Accordingly, these are the two hormones whose synthesis and/or release should be reduced by the drug combination. Furthermore, the drug-induced suppression of the humoral immune response could be prevented by prior administration of LH, FSH, and ACTH (Table 4). This substantiates the role of these hormones in the *initiation* of the immune reaction, whatever their mechanism of action.

Therefore, it seems reasonable to assume that a primary event leading to antigen-specific immunosuppression is a drug-induced blockade of LH and ACTH at the hypothalamo–pituitary level. Of course, a direct effect on peripheral endocrine glands and a general influence on the circulatory system must also be taken into consideration. Furthermore, the drugs administered at the dosage reported showed remarkable toxic effects. It is possible that a part of the immunosuppression depends on drug toxicity rather than on specific action. These results suggest, however, that, although difficult for intrinsic reasons, a pharmacologic control of immunity by endocrine manipulations has great potential and deserves more attention.

Some Considerations

We must stress that the work on the links between hormonal circadian periodicity and the immune response is still at a preliminary stage. However, the reported data support the view that the pineal gland (i.e., the main clock of endocrine rhythms) plays a crucial role in the physiological regulation of humoral immune performance in adult organisms. It is conceivable that the circadian nonconstancy of the whole endocrine environment modulates cell differentiation and/or proliferation. It is probably by this proposed modulation that the pineal affects immune parameters because differentiation and proliferation are two important steps in any immune response. At the present time, an insistence on further speculation regarding the mechanism of action would only drive us into the kingdom of science fiction. A few points do, however, deserve some consideration. A drug-induced (PRO) or environmental (permanent light) blockade of pineal functions or, more schematically, the elimination of the nocturnal peak of melatonin would produce, among a number of other effects, a stimulation of the gonadal- and adrenal–hypophyseal axes. These endocrine axes are also those found to be reactive to antigenic challenge. A chronic disturbance of the pineal–hypothalamo–hypophyseal system is certainly reflected in a derangement of feedback mechanisms, including those involved in the immuno-endocrine response.

Finally, some more general considerations have to be made. Major homeostatic requirements oblige cells to communicate and to collaborate for the maintenance of individual integrity. Lymphoid cells are a good example of important homeostatic effectors. They possess a number of hormone receptors (only partially identified) and a distinctive ability to release substances (lymphokines) with function of humoral messengers. In other words, they appear well furnished with a complex machinery which is very sensitive and extremely reactive to many environmental variations. Therefore, the assumption that circadian endocrine variability also influences the immune response seems quite reasonable. We think that circadian hormonal periodicity is fundamental for *any* cellular activity. So, we guess that cells which live in a humoral environment cannot escape the impact of its circadian variations.

It is our conviction that highly effective pharmacologic control of the immune response can be achieved only by a knowledge of its physiological regulatory mechanisms. We consider the experiments and the data reported here as a preliminary example of a proper approach to the control of immunologic reactions. We hope that this example will be followed by less empirical experiments and we are confident that, in this way, new, powerful, immunopharmacologic tools will be devised.

ACKNOWLEDGMENTS

We are indebted to Dr. P. Groscurth for the microphotographs (Figure 4) and for his skillful histological examination.

REFERENCES

Ahlqvist, J. (1976). Endocrine influence on lymphatic organs, immune responses, inflammation and autoimmunity. *Acta Endocrinol. (Copenhagen)* **83**, Suppl. 206.
Bourne, H. R., Lichtenstein, L. M., Melmon, K. L., Henney, C. S., Weinstein, Y., and Shearer, G. M. (1974). Moderation of inflammation and immunity by cyclic AMP. *Science* **184**, 19–28.

Braun, W., and Rega, M. J. (1972). Adenyl cyclase-stimulating catecholamines as modifiers of antibody formation. *Immunol. Commun.* **1**, 523–532.

Choudhury, S. A. R., Sharpe, R. M., and Brown, P. S. (1974). The effect of pimozide, a dopamine antagonist, on pituitary gonadotrophic function in the rat. *J. Reprod. Fertil.* **39**, 275–283.

Cline, M. J., and Golde, D. W. (1979). Cellular interactions in haematopoiesis. *Nature (London)* **277**, 177–181.

Collu, R., Jeguier, J. C., and Letarte, J. (1976). L-Dopa and pituitary hormone secretion: Influence of ciproheptadine. *Horm. Metab. Res.* **7**, 96–97.

Csaba, G., Rados, I., and Wohlmuth, E. (1973). Wasting disease and tetany following neonatal pinealectomy. *Acta Med. Acad. Sci. Hung.* **29**, 231–240.

Deguchi, T. (1978). Ontogenesis of circadian rhythm of melatonin synthesis in pineal gland of rat. *J. Neural. Transm., Suppl.* **13**, 115–128.

Deguchi, T., and Axelrod, J. (1973). Control of circadian change of serotonin N-acetyltransferase in the pineal organ by the β-adrenergic receptor. *Proc. Natl. Acad. Sci. U.S.A.* **70**, 2411–2414.

Devoino, L., Eliseeva, L., Eremina, O., Idova, G., and Cheido, M. (1975). 5-Hydroxytryptophan effect on the development of the immune response: IgM and IgG antibodies and rosette formation in primary and secondary responses. *Eur. J. Immunol.* **5**, 394–399.

Dicke, K. A., Lotzava, E., Spitzer, G., and McCredie, K. B. (1978). Immunobiology of bone marrow transplantation. *Semin. Hematol.* **15**, 263–282.

Dickerman, S., Kledzik, G., and Gelato, M. (1974). Effects of haloperidol on serum and pituitary prolactin, LH and FSH, and hypothalamic PIF and LRF. *Neuroendocrinology* **15**, 10–20.

Fernandes, G., Halberg, F., Yunis, E. J., and Good, R. A. (1976). Circadian rhythmic plaque-forming cell response of spleens from mice immunized with SRBC. *J. Immunol.* **117**, 962–966.

Fuxe, K., Hoekfelt, T., Goesta, J., and Loefstroem, A. (1973). Recent morphological and functional studies on hypothalamic dopaminergic and noradrenergic mechanisms. *In* "Frontiers in Catecholamines Research" (E. Usdin and S. H. Snyder, eds.), p. 787. Pergamon, Oxford.

Fuxe, K., Schubert, J., Hoekfelt, T., and Goesta, J. (1974). Some aspect of the interrelationship between central 5-hydroxytryptamine neurons and hormones *Adv. Biochem. Psychopharmacol.* **10**, 67–74.

Ganong, W. F. (1973). Catecholamines and the secretion of renin, ACTH and growth hormone. *In* "Frontiers in Catecholamines Research" (E. Usdin and S. H. Snyder, eds.), p. 819. Pergamon, Oxford.

Kamberi, I. A. (1973). Hypothalamic catecholamines and the secretion of gonadotropins and gonadotropin releasing hormones. *In* "Frontiers in Catecholamines Research" (E. Usdin and S. H. Snyder, eds.), p. 849. Pergamon, Oxford.

Klein, D. C., and Moore, R. Y. (1979). Pineal N-acetyltransferase and hydroxyindole-O-methyltransferase: Control by the retina hypothalamic tract and the suprachiasmatic nucleus. *Brain Res.* **74**, 245–262.

Lawson, D. M., and Gala, R. R. (1975). The influence of adrenergic, dopaminergic, cholinergic and serotoninergic drugs on plasma prolactin levels in ovariectomized, estrogen treated rats. *Endocrinology* **36**, 313–318.

Levy, J. A., and Munson, A. E. (1976). Suppression of antibody mediated primary hemolytic plaque-forming cells (PFC) by haloperidol. *Fed. Proc., Fed. Am. Soc. Exp. Biol.* **35**, 333 (abstr.).

Mess, B., and Peter, L. (1975). Effect of intracerebral serotonin administration on pituitary thyroid function. *Endocrinol. Exp.* **2**, 105–113.

Mueller, E. E. (1973). Brain monoamine participation in the control of growth hormone secretion in different animal species. *In* "Frontiers in Catecholamines Research" (E. Usdin and S. H. Snyder, eds.), p. 835. Pergamon, Oxford.

Nakai, Y., and Imura, H. (1974). Effect of adrenergic blocking agents on plasma growth hormone response to L-5-hydroxytryptophan (5HTP) in man. *Endocrinol. Jpn.* **21**, 493–497.

Nir, I., Shani (Mishkinsky), J., Locker, D., and Sulman, F. G. (1972). Effect of light and pinealectomy on body weight and tibia cartilage of female rat. *Life Sci.* **12**, 41–49.

Oleshansky, M. A., and Neff, N. H. (1978). Studies on the control of pineal indole synthesis: Cyclic nucleotides, adenylate cyclase and phosphodiesterase. *J. Neural Transm., Suppl.* **13**, 81–95.

Pierpaoli, W. (1975). Inability of thymus cells from newborn donors to restore transplantation immunity in athymic mice. *Immunology* **29**, 465–468.

Pierpaoli, W., and Besedovsky, H. O. (1975). Role of the thymus in programming of neuroendocrine functions. *Clin. Exp. Immunol.* **20**, 232–338.

Pierpaoli, W., and Maestroni, G. J. M. (1977). Pharmacological control of the immune response by blockade of the early hormonal changes following antigen injection. *Cell. Immunol.* **31**, 355–363.

Pierpaoli, W., and Maestroni, G. J. M. (1978a). Pharmacological control of the hormonally modulated immune response. II. Blockade of antibody production by a combination of drugs acting on neuroendocrine functions. Its prevention by gonadotropins and corticotrophin. *Immunology* **34**, 419–430.

Pierpaoli, W., and Maestroni, G. J. M. (1978b). Pharmacological control of the hormonally modulated immune response. III. Prolongation of allogeneic skin graft rejection and prevention of runt disease by a combination of drugs acting on neuroendocrine functions. *J. Immunol.* **120**, 1600–1603.

Pierpaoli, W., and Maestroni, G. J. M. (1980). The facilitation of enduring engraftment of allogeneic bone marrow and avoidance of secondary disease in mice. *Cell. Immunol.,* **52**, 62–72.

Pierpaoli, W. and Maestroni, G. J. M. (1981). Thymus-programmed pineal circadian cyclicity promotes genesis of transplantation immunity. Symposium on Neuroimmunomodulation. *Proc. XXVIII Int. Cong.,* Budapest, 1980.

Pierpaoli, W., and Sorkin, E. (1968). Effect of gonadectomy on the peripheral lymphatic tissue of neonatally thymectomized mice. *Br. J. Exp. Pathol.* **49**, 288–293.

Pierpaoli, W., and Sorkin, E. (1972). Alterations of adrenal cortex and thyroid in mice with congenital absence of the thymus. *Nature (London), New Biol.* **238**, 282–285.

Pierpaoli, W., Fabris, N., and Sorkin, E. (1970). Developmental hormones and immunological maturation. *Ciba Found. Study Group* **36**, 126–143.

Pierpaoli, W., Fabris, N., and Sorkin, E. (1971). The effects of hormones on the development of the immune capacity. *In* "Cellular Interactions in the Immune Response" (S. Cohen, G. Cudkowicz, and R. T. McCluskey, eds.), pp. 25–30. Karger, Basel.

Pierpaoli, W., Kopp, H. G., and Bianchi, E. (1976). Interdependence of thymic and neuroendocrine functions in ontogeny. *Clin. Exp. Immunol.* **24**, 501–506.

Pierpaoli, W., Kopp, H. G., Mueller, J., and Keller, M. (1977). Interdependence between neuroendocrine programming and the generation of immune recognition in ontogeny. *Cell. Immunol.* **29**, 16–27.

Plescia, O. J., Yamamoto, I., and Shimamura, T. (1975). Cyclic AMP and immune responses: Changes in the splenic level of cyclic AMP during the response of mice to antigen. *Proc. Natl. Acad. Sci. U.S.A.* **72**, 888–891.

Prange, A. J., Wilson, I. C. J. R., Breese, G. R., Plotnikoff, N. P., Lara, P. P., and Lipton, M. A. (1973) Hypothalamic releasing hormones and catecholamines: a new interface. *In* "Frontiers in Catecholamines Research" (E. Usdin and S. H. Snyder, eds.), p. 1149. Pergamon, Oxford.

Reiter, R. S. (1977). "The Pineal." Eden Press, Montreal.

Relkin, R. (1976). "The Pineal." Eden Press, Montreal.

Sanders-Bush, E., Gallager, P. A., and Sulser, F. (1974). On the mechanism of brain 5-hydroxytryptamine depletion by *p*-chloroamphetamine and related drugs and the specificity of their action. *Adv. Biochem. Psychopharmacol.* **10**, 185–194.

Singh, U., and Owen, J. J. T. (1976). Studies on the maturation of thymus cells. The effect of catecholamines, histamine and peptide hormones on the expression of T cell alloantigens. *Eur. J. Immunol.* **6,** 59–62.

Weissman, I. L., Gutman, G. A., Friedberg, S. H., and Jerabek, L. (1976). Lymphoid tissue architecture. III. Germinal centers, T cells, and thymus-dependent vs thymus-independent antigens. *Adv. Exp. Med. Biol.* **66,** 229–237.

Yamamoto, I., and Webb, D. R. (1975). Antigen-stimulated changes in cyclic nucleotide levels in the mouse. *Proc. Natl. Acad. Sci. U.S.A.* **72,** 2320–2324.

Hypothalamic Influences
on Immune Responses

MARVIN STEIN
STEVEN J. SCHLEIFER
STEVEN E. KELLER

INTRODUCTION

The hypothalamus is at the interface between the brain and a range of critical regulatory peripheral functions. It is rich in putative neurotransmitters and neurohormones and is involved in the regulation and integration of endocrine secretion, visceral processes, and behavior.

A consideration of the relationship of the hypothalamus to immune function seems most appropriate since the hypothalamus is involved in the regulation of endocrine and neurotransmitter processes. Both of these systems participate in the modulation of humoral and cell-mediated immunity.

HYPOTHALAMUS

Anatomically the hypothalamus is a small area of the diencephalon lying on either side of the third ventricle. It is connected to the pituitary by a neurovascular stalk and to the adjacent forebrain and hindbrain by the periventricular and medial forebrain bundles. The hypothalamus can be divided anatomically and functionally into medial and lateral parts which are separated for most of its length by the descending columns of the fornix

429

(Reichlin *et al.*, 1978). The medial hypothalamus contains most of the neuronal cells concerned with pituitary function, and receptors involved in visceral regulation. The lateral hypothalamus is primarily concerned with a multineuronal and multisynaptic system which connects the limbic forebrain with the mesencephalon. Anteriorly the hypothalamus becomes part of the preoptic area without any clear distinction between the areas. The posterior hypothalamus unites with the reticular formation of the rostral midbrain and dorsally the hypothalamus joins the thalamus.

Hypothalamic neurons receive input and stimulation from multiple neural pathways and from the blood and cerebrospinal fluid. Ascending neural pathways include monoaminergic, cholinergic, and other components of the forebrain bundle. The descending neural pathways originate in olfactory and limbic structures including the septum, hippocampus, and amygdala, and terminate in the hypothalamus and preoptic area by means of the medial forebrain bundle, the fornix, and related pathways. Blood levels of hormones, glucose, electrolytes, water and CO_2 play an important role in the activity of hypothalamic neurons. Recent evidence indicates that some pituitary trophic hormones may arrive at the anterior pituitary by means of the cerebrospinal fluid in the third ventricle (Martin *et al.*, 1977; Papez, 1937). The limbic system, thus, may provide pathways whereby psychosocial processes may influence hypothalamic activity.

Endocrine effects of the hypothalamus derive from neural and neurosecretory actions on the pituitary. The neuroregulation of the posterior lobe is accomplished by direct neuronal connections resulting in the secretion of oxytocin and vasopressin. The anterior pituitary does not have a direct neural connection with the central nervous system (CNS). It has been demonstrated, however, that specific pituitary regulator substances are secreted by neurons of the hypothalamus into the portal capillary system of the median eminence and transported to the anterior pituitary. Anterior pituitary hormones regulated by the hypothalamus include adrenocorticotropin (ACTH), thyroid-stimulating hormone (TSH), growth hormone (GH), luteinizing hormone (LH), follicle stimulating hormone (FSH), and prolactin.

Several hypothalamic releasing factors have been identified and synthesized: thyrotropin-releasing hormone (TRH), luteinizing hormone-releasing hormone (LHRH), and somatostatin (growth hormone release inhibiting factor). Corticotropin releasing factor (CRF) has been identified by bioassay methods but has not been isolated in pure form as yet. Most of the hypothalamic hormones are small polypeptides. Other peptides found in the hypothalamus include the endogenous morphinelike peptides, endorphins and enkephalins. The hypothalamus has also been shown to have high concentrations of norepinephrine and other neurotransmitters (Hökfelt *et al.*, 1978).

This chapter will review the relation of the hypothalamus to humoral and cell-mediated immunity and consider neuroendocrine, neurotransmitter, and other processes which may be involved.

HYPOTHALAMIC EFFECTS ON HUMORAL IMMUNITY

Anaphylaxis, an acute hypersensitivity reaction, has been utilized to assess the effects of the CNS on immunologic phenomena. Szentivànyi and Filipp (1958) were among the first to study the role of the hypothalamus in anaphylaxis. They demonstrated that lethal anaphylactic shock in the guinea pig and in the rabbit can be prevented by bilateral focal lesions in the tuberal region of the hypothalamus. Janković and co-workers reported that hypothalamic lesions in the rat suppress the Arthus reaction, an *in vivo* measure of immediate hypersensitivity, and that electrical stimulation of the hypothalamus can enhance the Arthus phenomenon (Janković and Isaković, 1973; Janković *et al.*, 1979).

In our initial studies, Luparello *et al.* (1964) found that anterior but not posterior hypothalamic lesions inhibited development of lethal anaphylaxis in the rat. Further studies in our laboratory investigated the effect of hypothalamic lesions on guinea pig anaphylaxis (Macris *et al.*, 1970). Bilateral electrolytic lesions were placed in the anterior, median, or posterior basal hypothalamus of male Hartley strain guinea pigs (Figure 1). Anterior hypothalamic lesions damaged the anterior hypothalamic region and the suprachiasmatic nuclei, with the lesions impinging, in some animals, on the preoptic area and on the rostral portion of the ventromedial nuclei. Median hypothalamic lesions damaged the ventromedial nuclei and the arcuate nuclei. Posterior hypothalamic lesions resulted in damage to the premammillary region and to the medial mammillary nuclei. Controls included sham-operated and unoperated animals. Each group was sensitized with picryl chloride, a hapten or incomplete antigen, in Freund's adjuvant, 1 week after operation. With the use of this method of immunization, circulating antibodies to the picryl hapten were determined, and picryl-induced anaphylaxis was studied.

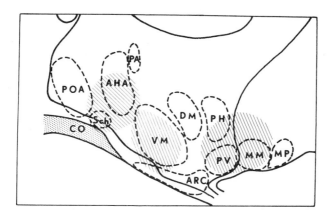

Figure 1. Sagittal diagram of guinea pig hypothalamus. Lightly shaded areas correspond to regions damaged by lesions. (Reprinted with permission from Macris *et al.* [1970].)

Significant protection against lethal anaphylaxis was found in the animals with electrolytic lesions in the anterior basal hypothalamus (Table 1). Lethal anaphylaxis occurred in 71% of control animals and in only 18% of the guinea pigs with anterior hypothalamic lesions. The median and posterior hypothalamic lesions had no significant effect on lethal anaphylaxis (Macris *et al.*, 1970).

Anterior hypothalamic lesions in the guinea pig were also found to protect against anaphylactic death with ovalbumin as the antigen (Schiavi *et al.*, 1975). Among sensitized sham-operated guinea pigs challenged with 0.25, 0.5, and 1.5 mg of ovalbumin, 17, 25, and 73% of the animals suffered anaphylactic death. In contrast, among the animals with anterior hypothalamic lesions, no deaths occurred with the two lower doses of antigen and only 36% of the animals injected with 1.5 mg of ovalbumin died.

Little is known about the mechanisms whereby hypothalamic lesions protect against anaphylaxis. Both antigen specific and nonspecific changes in the immune system as well as changes in tissue factors and target organ responsivity could explain these effects. Several investigators, using a variety of techniques, have considered the effect of lesions on the levels of circulating antibodies. Filipp and Szentiványi (1958) reported that circulating and tissue-fixed antibodies are reduced in tuber-injured guinea pigs. Korneva and Khai (1964) studied the effects of hypothalamic and other CNS lesions on antibody production in rabbits. They found that lesions in the posterior ventral hypothalamus, but not in other areas of the diencephalon, completely suppressed the production of complement-fixing antibodies to horse serum and induced a prolonged retention of the antigen in the blood. The same investigators (Korneva, 1976) provided supporting evidence for their initial finding, demonstrating that stimulation of the posterior hypothalamus resulted in

TABLE 1

Effect of Anterior Hypothalamic Lesions on Immune Processes[a]

Groups	Anaphylactic death[b]	Delayed hypersensitivity reactions		Circulating antibody titer[e]
		Picryl chloride contact[c]	Tuberculin[d]	
Nonoperated	20/27	27/29	18.2 ± 0.6	2.54 ± 0.14
Anterior sham-operated	12/18	18/20	19.1 ± 0.8	2.51 ± 0.12
Anterior hypothalamic lesions	3/17	14/20	15.7 ± 0.4	1.85 ± 0.18

[a] (From Stein *et al.* (1976). Copyright 1976 by the American Association for the Advancement of Science.)

[b] Ratio of the number of animals that died to the number tested.

[c] Ratio of animals with 4+ reaction (or more) to the number tested.

[d] Size of reaction (means ± standard error).

[e] Mean $\log_{10}$ of the reciprocal of the antibody titer.

enhanced antibody titers. Other investigators have also found changes in antibody levels with medial and posterior hypothalamic manipulations (Polyak *et al.*, 1969; Tsypin and Maltsev, 1967). In addition, posterior hypothalamic lesions in young rats were reported to be associated with subsequent depressed humoral immunity in the mature animals (Paunović *et al.*, 1976).

Studies in other laboratories have suggested that the anterior hypothalamus influences antibody production. We (Macris *et al.*, 1970) found that anterior hypothalamic lesions in the guinea pig were associated with significantly lower antibody titers to the hapten picryl chloride. Lesions in other areas of the hypothalamus did not alter antibody levels. Tyrey and Nalbandov (1972) reported that ovalbumin antibody production was depressed in rats with anterior hypothalamic lesions.

Other studies found no changes in antibody levels in animals with hypothalamic lesions. Ado and Goldstein (1973) reported that anterior, medial, and posterior hypothalamic lesions in rabbits had no effect on the titer of complement binding and hemagglutinating antibodies to ovalbumin. Thrasher *et al.* (1971) reported similar negative findings with ovalbumin in the rat. In our laboratory, we observed no difference in ovalbumin titers between sham-operated control guinea pigs and animals protected against anaphylactic death by anterior hypothalamic lesions (Schiavi *et al.*, 1975).

The variability in the findings with respect to the effect of hypothalamic lesions on antibody levels may result from the heterogeneity of the study designs. Hypothalamic lesions may affect some components of humoral immunity and only under certain conditions of sensitization and challenge. Antibody studies have utilized different animal species, a wide range of sensitizing and test doses, variable time schedules, and different antigens. For example, differences were found by our group between studies using picryl chloride antigen and those using ovalbumin. Antibody production to the hapten picryl chloride is dependent upon carrier recognition by T lymphocytes while ovalbumin does not require carrier recognition. Further research is needed to evaluate whether only some types of antibody production are altered by hypothalamic lesions and to determine if there is a relationship between lesion localization and the humoral immune response which is altered.

While it seems that the hypothalamus does influence certain aspects of antibody production, it has also been demonstrated that changes in particular classes of antibody levels are not required for the protective effect of hypothalamic lesions in anaphylaxis. In studies of passive anaphylaxis, animals are immunized by providing them with sufficient exogenous antibody to produce lethal anaphylaxis. Szentiványi and Filipp (1958) reported that guinea pigs passively sensitized with homologous as well as with heterologous (rabbit) serum were protected from anaphylactic death by hypothalamic lesions. Our group (Macris *et al.*, 1972) investigated the effect of hypothalamic lesions in guinea pigs passively immunized with heterologous (rabbit) antibody to ovalbumin. Significant protection against passive lethal anaphylaxis was found in the animals with anterior but not with posterior hypothalamic lesions. Further, in a preliminary study in which anterior hypothalamic lesions were placed in guinea pigs 1 month after sensitization, significant protection was afforded when the animals were challenged after the placement of lesions (Stein *et al.*, 1976). This protection was demonstrated in the lesioned animals at a time when no differences were found between the groups in the levels of circulating ovalbumin antibodies. These observations and those noted in the passive anaphylaxis studies suggest that the effect of anterior hypothalamic lesions may be at least partially related to other aspects of the humoral immune response or to nonimmunologic phenomena.

Several nonspecific mechanisms may be involved in the effects of the hypothalamic lesions on anaphylaxis. Lesions may interfere with antibody binding to host tissues, they may alter the content and release of mediator substances secondary to the antigen–antibody reaction, or they may diminish the responsiveness of the target tissue to the mediators. Preliminary studies suggest that anterior hypothalamic lesions may alter the release of mediators of anaphylaxis. Mathé and his co-workers found that the release of prostaglandin PGF_{2a} following anterior hypothalamic lesions was significantly reduced during ovalbumin-induced anaphylaxis in the guinea pig as compared to control, sham, and posterior lesioned animals (Mathé *et al.*, 1979).

Other studies from our laboratory have shown that anterior hypothalamic lesions do not alter tissue responsivity when ileum and skin are the target organs. Antigen-induced contraction of isolated ileum from animals actively sensitized with ovalbumin and of ileum from nonimmunized animals, passively sensitized *in vitro,* was investigated. Anterior hypothalamic lesions of size and location comparable to those providing protection against lethal anaphylaxis did not modify the anaphylactic response of ileum from actively sensitized guinea pigs or from isolated ileum passively sensitized *in vitro.*

In passive cutaneous anaphylaxis studies, serial saline dilutions of rabbit antiserum to ovalbumin were injected intradermally on the clipped backs of guinea pigs 2, 15, and 30 days after the placement of anterior hypothalamic lesions. Eighteen hours after intradermal passive sensitization, the ovalbumin antigen mixed with a dilute solution of Evans blue was injected into the jugular vein. There were no significant differences in the cutaneous anaphylactic response between the lesioned animals and the sham and non-operated controls on each of the days tested. Thrasher *et al.* (1971) similarly reported that anterior, medial, and posterior hypothalamic lesions in the rat had no effect on passive cutaneous anaphylaxis to ovalbumin 4 hr after sensitization.

The findings in these *in vivo* and *in vitro* studies do not support the hypothesis that the protective effect of anterior hypothalamic lesions in the guinea pig is due to impairment of antibody binding capacity or due to interference with the intracellular processes responsible for the release of histamine or other mediators of anaphylaxis. However, bronchial and bronchiolar smooth muscle, the primary shock organ in the guinea pig, was not utilized in the above studies. Further investigation of tissue antibody binding and mediator release in lungs from guinea pigs with anterior hypothalamic lesions is needed.

Several investigators have reported that the CNS modifies the susceptibility of animals to histamine, a primary mediator of anaphylaxis in the guinea pig (Przybylski, 1962; Whittier and Orr, 1962). Szentiványi and Székely (1958) found that lesions in the tuberal region of the guinea pig hypothalamus provided protection against lethal histamine shock. We found (Schiavi et al., 1966) that bilateral electrolytic lesions in the anterior but not the posterior medial hypothalamus of guinea pigs afforded significant protection against histamine toxicity.

Hypothalamic influences on the bronchospastic reaction may be mediated by the autonomic nervous system. The autonomic nervous system plays an important role in the mediation of the physiological changes observed during anaphylaxis (Gold, 1973; Gold et al., 1972; Koller, 1968; Mills and Widdicombe, 1970; Parker, 1973). Maslinski and Karczewski (1957) reported that electrical stimulation of the brain of guinea pigs through temporal electrodes significantly reduced the mortality of animals subjected to anaphylaxis and histamine shock. The protective effect was accompanied by a depression in the afferent and efferent activity of the vagus. Mills and Widdicombe (1970), in a study on vagotomized guinea pigs, found that a vagal reflex is partially responsible for the bronchoconstriction that occurs in anaphylaxis and that follows intravenous administration of histamine. Gold and his co-workers (1972) demonstrated that a major factor in antigen-induced bronchoconstriction in canine asthma is a cholinergic, vagally mediated reflex with an afferent component triggered by stimulation of airway receptors and an efferent limb producing airway smooth muscle contraction.

These studies indicate that suppression of vagal parasympathetic activity may protect against anaphylaxis. Damage to the region of the anterior hypothalamus, which is thought to mediate primarily parasympathetic responses, may decrease vagal bronchoconstrictor tone, resulting in the predominance of bronchial β-adrenergic receptor activity. In keeping with this hypothesis, both vagal suppression and β-adrenergic enhancement will reduce bronchospastic responses. Inhibition of vagal activity (Hexheimer, 1956; Widdicombe, 1963) or β-adrenergic stimulation (Aviado, 1970) decreases histamine-induced bronchoconstriction while blockade of β-receptors potentiates the histamine effect (McCulloch et al., 1967). Filipp (1973) has reported that propranolol and pertussis vaccine, both β-receptor blockers, diminish the protective effect of tuberal hypothalamic lesions in guinea pig anaphylaxis.

Autonomic effects may be mediated by cyclic nucleotides at the cellular level. Increased intracellular concentration of cAMP after activation of β-adrenergic receptors has been found to inhibit IgE-mediated release of histamine and other mediators of anaphylaxis from lung tissues (Orange and Austen, 1970). Further studies have demonstrated β-adrenergic, α-adrenergic, and cholinergic effects, mediated in part by cAMP and cGMP, on IgE-induced release of the mediators of anaphylaxis (Austen, 1973).

Anaphylaxis has been utilized as a model of the effect of the hypothalamus on the humoral immune response. The above review indicates that anterior hypothalamic lesions inhibit lethal anaphylactic shock in the guinea pig. The effects of hypothalamic lesions on anaphylaxis could be explained by both antigen specific and nonspecific changes in the immune system as well as by changes in tissue factors and target organ responsivity. Studies investigating the influence of hypothalamic lesions on antibody levels have been inconclusive. Several other immune components may be involved in the effects of hypothalamic lesions on the anaphylactic reaction. The lesions may interfere with antibody binding to host tissues or they may alter the content and release of histamine and other mediator substances. Hypothalamic lesions may also diminish the responsivity of the lung, the target organ in guinea pig anaphylaxis, to the pharmacologic agents liberated by the antigen–antibody reaction. The modification of target organ response may be related to changes in autonomic nervous system function. The mechanisms which may be involved in the effect of anterior hypothalamic lesions on lethal anaphylaxis in the guinea pig have not been elucidated, and a variety of aspects of the immune components involved in anaphylaxis and target organ responsivity require investigation.

Studies by Besedovsky and Sorkin (1977) have provided further evidence of a specific relationship between the hypothalamus and humoral immunity. These investigators found an increase in the firing rate of neurons of the ventromedial nuclei of the hypothalamus in rats after immunization with two different antigens. These results suggest the presence of a feedback loop between the immune response and the hypothalamus.

HYPOTHALAMIC EFFECTS ON CELL–MEDIATED IMMUNITY

The role of the hypothalamus in cell-mediated immunity has only recently become a focus of research. In 1970, we (Macris *et al.*, 1970) reported that anterior hypothalamic lesions in the guinea pig suppressed the delayed cutaneous hypersensitivity response to picryl chloride and to tuberculin. Median and posterior hypothalamic lesions did not alter the response. Janković and Isaković (1973) reported that a lesion involving a large part of the hypothalamus in the rat resulted in a decreased delayed cutaneous response to bovine serum albumin. Hypothalamic stimulation was subsequently found to enhance the delayed cutaneous hypersensitivity response (Janković *et al.*, 1979). These studies of hypothalamic effects on delayed cutaneous hypersensitivity suggest that the hypothalamus may modulate aspects of cell-mediated immunity.

The authors have recently investigated the effect of anterior hypothalamic lesions in the guinea pig on lymphocyte function utilizing *in vitro* correlates of cell-mediated immunity (Keller *et al.,* 1980). *In vitro* lymphocyte stimulation by the mitogen phytohemaglutinin (PHA) and by the antigen, tuberculin purified protein derivative (PPD), was studied after anterior hypothalamic lesions were made. Lymphocyte stimulation was conducted utilizing both whole blood and isolated lymphocytes. The number of T and B lymphocytes was also determined. In addition, the effect of anterior hypothalamic lesions on delayed cutaneous hypersensitivity was investigated. As in previous studies, bilateral electrolytic lesions were placed in the anterior hypothalamus of male Hartley strain guinea pigs. Sham-operated and unoperated animals served as controls. One week postoperatively, the guinea pigs were sensitized to tuberculin by injection of complete Freund's adjuvant. Skin reactions were elicited 32 days following sensitization by intradermal injection of PPD, and delayed cutaneous response was measured at 24 hr. The guinea pigs with anterior hypothalamic lesions had significantly smaller cutaneous tuberculin reactions (Table 2) than the nonoperated or sham-operated controls. Multiple comparison tests revealed that the tuberculin reactions of the lesioned animals were significantly smaller than both the nonoperated and the sham-operated controls and that the responses of the control groups did not differ significantly.

One week after skin tests were measured, blood was collected from each guinea pig, and aliquots of blood from each animal were used for the *in vitro* studies. No differences were found in the total number of white blood cells or in the total number of lymphocytes between the various groups. The percentage and absolute number of T and B cells were not significantly changed by the hypothalamic lesions (Table 3).

Lymphocyte function was measured by means of *in vitro* lymphocyte stimulation assays using whole blood and using isolated lymphocytes. Dose response curves were determined for the antigen PPD and for the mitogen

TABLE 2

Effect of Anterior Hypothalamic Lesions on Delayed Cutaneous Hypersensitivity[a]

Groups	Number of guinea pigs	Tuberculin reaction (mm)
Nonoperated	29	9.94 ± 0.57[b]
Sham operated	32	11.19 ± 0.54
Anterior hypothalamic lesions	25	6.24 ± 0.86

[a] (Reprinted from Keller *et al.* Values expressed as mean ± standard error. (1980).

[b] Diameter of induration 24 hr after eliciting delayed cutaneous hypersensitivity.

TABLE 3

Effect of Anterior Hypothalamic Lesions on Peripheral Blood Lymphocytes[a]

Groups	Number of guinea pigs	T Lymphocytes (Cells per ml $\times 10^{-6}$) (%)	B Lymphocytes (Cells per ml $\times 10^{-6}$) (%)
Nonoperated	29	5.81 ± 0.94 (57.8 ± 2.6)	1.81 ± 0.39 (17.7 ± 1.5)
Sham Operated	32	4.54 ± 0.66 (52.4 ± 2.7)	1.31 ± 0.17 (14.3 ± 1.2)
Anterior hypothalamic lesions	25	4.72 ± 0.73 (50.0 ± 2.6)	1.39 ± 0.26 (14.5 ± 1.7)

[a] (Reprinted from Keller *et al.* Values expressed as mean ± standard error. (1980).

PHA (a nonspecific T cell activator). The response to lymphocyte stimulation was measured by the incorporation of a radioactive precursor of DNA. All lymphocyte stimulation results were expressed as counts per minute (c.p.m.) in stimulated cultures minus the cpm in unstimulated cultures ($\triangle$ c.p.m.).

The lymphocyte stimulation data for PHA and PPD utilizing the whole blood technique are illustrated in Figure 2. An analysis of variance for repeated measures (Winer, 1962) revealed that there were significant differences among the groups for both PHA and PPD. Multiple comparison tests showed that the responses of anterior hypothalamic lesioned guinea pigs to both PHA and to PPD were significantly lower than those of the nonoperated or of the sham-operated controls. The two control groups did not differ significantly for either PHA or PPD.

The dose response curves for PHA and PPD with the isolated lymphocyte cultures are shown in Figure 3. Analysis of variance for repeated measures revealed no significant differences among the groups for PHA or for PPD.

The findings that anterior hypothalamic lesions suppress *in vitro* lym-

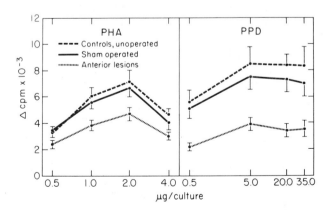

Figure 2. *In vitro* whole blood lymphocyte stimulation with PHA and with PPD in unoperated control, sham operated, and anterior hypothalamic lesioned guinea pigs. Values are expressed as $\triangle$ c.p.m. (mean ± standard error). (Reprinted with permission from Keller *et al.* (1980).

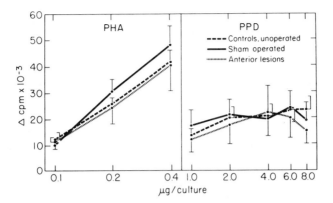

Figure 3. *In vitro* isolated lymphocyte stimulation with PHA and with PPD in unoperated control, sham operated, and anterior hypothalamic lesioned guinea pigs. Values are expressed as Δ c.p.m. (mean ± standard error). (Reprinted with permission from Keller *et al.* [1980].)

phocyte stimulation by the antigen PPD and by the mitogen PHA in whole blood cultures demonstrate that the hypothalamus can directly influence lymphocyte function. This effect does not appear to be related to a depletion of T lymphocytes. The lack of effect of anterior hypothalamic lesions on the isolated lymphocyte response to PPD further suggests that the lesions do not impair the primary acquisition of immunity to an antigen but rather modify the efferent limb of the cell-mediated immune system. The inhibition of both PHA- and PPD-induced lymphocyte stimulation in whole blood but not in isolated lymphocyte cultures in the anterior hypothalamic lesioned guinea pigs suggests that the modulating effect of anterior hypothalamic lesions may be related to humoral factors. A humoral inhibitory factor may be associated with neuroendocrine or autonomic processes since the hypothalamus is involved in the regulation of these functions (Martin *et al.*, 1977; Porter, 1962; Reichlin *et al.*, 1978).

Lymphocyte responses to mitogens and antigens have been reported to be influenced by other cells such as macrophages, monocytes, erythrocytes, and platelets (Bach and Hirschhorn, 1965; Ferguson *et al.*, 1976; Kondracki and Milgram, 1975; Rosenstreich, 1976). Lymphocyte isolation procedures remove or alter the number of such cell types. The inhibition of lymphocyte stimulation in whole blood but not in isolated lymphocyte cultures of lesioned guinea pigs could be related to changes in these cell populations.

MEDIATION OF HYPOTHALAMIC EFFECTS ON IMMUNE FUNCTION

A number of studies have examined some of the mechanisms whereby the hypothalamus may alter immune, and, in particular, lymphocyte activity. The role of the pituitary in modulating both humoral and cell-mediated immunity is demonstrated by the findings that hypophysectomy can depress both anti-body production and delayed cutaneous hypersensitivity in rats (Nagy and Berczi, 1978). The studies of Filipp and Mess (1969) suggest that the protective effect of hypothalamic lesions on anaphylaxis may be related at least in part to changes in endocrine activity. They reported that the administration of thyroxine partially restored the sensitivity to anaphylaxis of actively immunized guinea pigs with lesions in the tuberal area of the hypothalamus. They also studied the combined effect of thyroxine and metopirone, an inhibitor of adrenocortical hormone synthesis, on the anaphylactic response of sensitized guinea pigs with lesions in the tuberal region. The administration of both substances completely abolished the protective action of the lesions, suggesting that the antianaphylactic effect of hypothalamic damage is due to the combined effect of decreased thyroid function and increased adrenocortical activity. Other studies have demonstrated the role of the thyroid in enhancing immune processes in the rat, mouse, and guinea pig. It has been noted (Csaba et al., 1977; Denckla, 1978; Leger and Masson, 1947; Nilzen, 1955) that resistance to anaphylaxis is increased in thyroidectomized rats, mice, and guinea pigs. Suppression of thyroid activity inhibits local and systemic anaphylaxis, abolishes circulating precipitins, and decreases the susceptibility of the animals to exogenous histamine.

Changes in corticosteroid levels may have a major role in the mediation of the effects of the hypothalamus on immunity. Tyrey and Nalbandov (1972) found that the antibody titer depression in the rat that follows anterior hypothalamic lesions can be significantly blocked by either hypophysectomy or adrenalectomy. Corticosteroid effects on the immune system are extensive and complex and appear to vary with hormone levels. At pharmacologic doses, corticosteroids suppress immune function *in vivo* and *in vitro* while their effects at physiological doses vary (Comsa et al., 1975; Denckla, 1978; Fauci, 1975). Pharmacologic doses of corticosteroids have been shown to suppress primary and secondary antibody formation (Elliot and Sinclair, 1968; Petranyi et al., 1971), modify complement levels, protect against anaphylactic shock (Dews and Code, 1951), delay or prevent graft rejection, enhance tumor growth, control autoimmune diseases, and increase the incidence and severity of bacterial infections. Both physiological and pharmacologic doses of corticoids diminish lymphocyte stimulation by PHA *in vitro* (Berenbaum et al., 1973, 1976; Fauci, 1975; Goodwin et al., 1979). Physiological doses of corticosteroids have been reported to enhance T-cell development (Ritter, 1977) and B-cell lymphocyte stimulation by pokeweed mitogen (PWM) (Fauci et al., 1977). Physiological doses of corticoids also cause a redistribution of T cells from the circulating pool to the bone marrow (Claman, 1975; Fauci and Dale, 1975).

Aside from their direct effects on immune function, adrenocortical hormones may also alter immune phenomena such as anaphylaxis by means of their profound effects on the metabolism and actions of histamine. Corticosteroids inhibit histamine decarboxylase activity (Parrot and Laborde, 1955), tissue binding of newly formed histamine (Schayer et al., 1955), and the amount of histamine released by the tissues (Schmutzler and Freundt, 1975; Yamasaki and Yamamoto, 1963). Adrenal steroids have a protective effect against histamine toxicity in mice and rats, while findings regarding their effects on the susceptibility of guinea pigs to anaphylaxis and to exogenous histamine are contradictory (Hicks, 1969). Corticosteroid effects on histamine may influence immune function since histamine has been shown to modulate lymphocyte activity (Goodwin et al., 1979; Roszkowski et al., 1977).

A number of other hormones which are regulated by the hypothalamus influence immune processes. Growth hormone (GH) (Brown and Reichlin, 1972; Rice et al., 1978) appears to have an enhancing effect on the immune system. Gisler (1974) found that GH reversed the immunosuppressive effects of corticosteroids in the plaque-forming cell assay, a measure of humoral immunity. Growth hormone also enhances graft rejection (Comsa et al., 1975) and is required for the development of the immune system (Denckla, 1978). Sex hormones generally have an inhibitory effect on immune responses. Estrogen, testosterone, and progesterone have all been found to inhibit lymphocyte stimulation (Mendelsohn et al., 1977; Wyle and Kent, 1977). Androgens and estrogens can suppress delayed cutaneous hypersensitivity (Kappas et al., 1963) and gonadectomy in male and female guinea pigs may enhance cell-mediated immune responses (Kittas and Henry, 1979). In contrast, estrogens may increase antibody responses to antigens (Eidinger and Garrett, 1972; Thanavala et al., 1973).

Endocrine modulation of immune function may result from the interaction of hormones. As previously noted, thyroid or growth hormone and corticosteroids may have antagonistic effects on immune function (Filipp and Mess, 1969; Gisler, 1974). Denckla (1978) reported that thyroxine, together with growth hormone, restored immunocompetence to immunologically deficient animals. A study by Pierpaoli and Maestroni (1978) showed that a specific combination of LH, FSH, and ACTH inhibits a blockade of antibody production produced by an alteration in neurotransmitter function.

Temporal factors may play an important role in hypothalamic effects on immune function. Circadian rhythms have been described for humoral and cell-mediated immune processes including immediate cutaneous hypersensitivity (Reinberg et al., 1965), resistance to infection (Feigin et al., 1969) and lymphocyte stimulation by PHA (Dionigi et al., 1973). A number of studies have demonstrated that anterior hypothalamic lesions alter or abolish the pattern of corticosteroid and thyroid hormone secretion (Abe et al., 1979; Moore and Eichler, 1972; Rice et al., 1978). The effects of anterior hypothalamic lesions on immune function may therefore be mediated, in part, by alterations in hormonal circadian rhythms.

In addition to the previously described effects on target tissues, the autonomic nervous system may also be involved in the mediation of hypothalamic influences on immune activity by direct effects on immunocompetent cells. β-Adrenergic stimulation is usually immunosuppressive, whereas β-blockade enhances immune function. Isoproterenol, a β-adrenergic agonist, decreases antigen-specific cutaneous hypersensitivity (Kram *et al.*, 1975; Shereff *et al.*, 1973), inhibits T-cell rosette formation (Galant and Remo, 1975), decreases immunoglobulin production (Sherman, 1973) and inhibits mitogen-induced lymphocyte stimulation at physiological doses (Goodwin *et al.*, 1979; Smith *et al.*, 1971). Propranolol, a β-antagonist, increases immediate cutaneous hypersensitivity (Shereff *et al.*, 1973) and increases immunoglobulin production (Nakazawa *et al.*, 1977), consistent with the general finding that β-adrenergic activity inhibits immune function. In contrast to these findings, Patterson *et al.* (1976) reported that isoproterenol increases *in vitro* IgE production.

Pierpaoli and Maestroni (1978) have suggested that changes in the levels of several neurotransmitters may interact in the modulation of immune function. A combination of drugs including an α-adrenergic antagonist, a serotonin precursor, and a dopamine blocker administered together prior to exposure to an antigen was found to block the production of antibodies to the antigen completely and specifically. As previously noted, the combination of LH, FSH, and ACTH reversed the blockade.

The regulation of lymphocyte activity by hormones and catecholamines may be related to their ability to influence cellular cyclic nucleotide levels. Many studies have found that elevated cAMP levels can inhibit immune function while decreased levels enhance immune activity (Ferreira *et al.*, 1976; Galant and Remo, 1975; Schmutzler and Derwall, 1973). Recent research suggests that the control of immunocompetent cells by cAMP is complex. Watson (1975) and Ohara *et al.* (1978) have suggested that the ratio of cAMP to cGMP is important for the control of antibody synthesis, whereas the absolute concentration of cAMP is not critical. Kasahara *et al.* (1977) and Wang *et al.* (1978) found that, aside from its usual immunosuppressive effects, cAMP may be required to initiate lymphocyte responses. A biphasic cAMP pattern appears to be necessary, with an initial rise followed by a subsequent fall in cAMP levels.

SUMMARY

The hypothalamus modifies both humoral and cell-mediated immune processes. An extensive network of endocrine, autonomic, and other biologic processes may be involved in these effects. The multiple pathways linking limbic and higher cortical areas with the hypothalamus (Martin *et al.*, 1977) suggest that it may be of central importance in mediating psychosocial influences on visceral, endocrine, and immune functions. The interaction of the hypothalamus with the immune system may, in turn, alter the development, onset, and course of disease.

REFERENCES

Abe, K., Kroning, J., Greer, M. A., and Critchlow, V. (1979). Effects of destruction of the supra-chiasmatic nuclei on the circadian rhythms in plasma corticosterone, body temperature, feeding, and plasma thyrotropin. *Neuroendocrinology* **29**, 119–131.

Ado, A., and Goldstein, M. M. (1973). The primary immune response in rabbits after lesion of the different zones in the medial hypothalamus. *Ann. Allergy* **31**, 585–589.

Austen, K. F. (1973). A review of immunological, biochemical, and pharmacological factors in the release of chemical mediators from human lung. *In* "Asthma: Physiology, Immunopharmacology, and Treatment" (K. F. Austen and L. M. Lichtenstein, eds.), pp. 109–122. Academic Press, New York.

Aviado, D. M. (1970). Antiasthmatic action of sympathomimetics: A review of the literature on the bronchopulmonary effects. *J. Clin. Pharmacol.* **10**, 217–221.

Bach, F. H., and Hirschhorn, K. (1965). The *in vitro* immune response of peripheral blood lymphocytes. *Semin. Hematol.* **2**, 68.

Berenbaum, M. C., Cope, W. A., and Bundick, R. V. (1976). Synergistic effect of cortisol and prostaglandin E on the PHA response. *Clin. Exp. Immunol.* **26**, 534–541.

Berenbaum, M. C., Fluch, P. A., and Hurst, N. P. (1973). Depression of lymphocyte responses after surgical trauma. *Br. J. Exp. Pathol.* **54**, 597–607.

Besedovsky, H., and Sorkin, E. (1977). Network of immune–neuroendocrine interactions. *Clin. Exp. Immunol.* **27**, 1–12.

Brown, G. M., and Reichlin, S. (1972). Psychologic and neural regulation of growth hormone secretion. *Psychosom. Med.* **34**, 45–61.

Claman, H. N. (1975). How corticosteroids work. *J. Allergy Clin. Immunol.* **55**, 145–151.

Comsa, J., Leonhardt, H., and Schwarz, J. A. (1975). Influence of the thymus-corticotropin-growth hormone interaction on the rejection of skin allografts in the rat. *Ann. N.Y. Acad. Sci.* **249**, 387–401.

Csaba, G., Sudar, F., and Dobozy, O. (1977). Triiodothyronine receptors in lymphocytes of newborn and adult rats. *Horm. Metab. Res.* **9**, 499–501.

Denckla, W. D. (1978). Interactions between age and neuroendocrine and immune systems. *Fed. Proc. Fed. Am. Soc. Exp. Biol.* **37**, 1263–1266.

Dews, P. B., and Code, C. F. (1951). Effect of cortisone on anaphylactic shock in adrenalectomized rats. *J. Pharmacol. Exp. Ther.* **101**, 9.

Dionigi, R., Zonta, A., Albertario, F., Galeazzi, R., and Bellinzonn, G. (1973). Cyclic variation in the response of lymphocytes to phytohemagglutinin in healthy individuals. *Transplantation* **16**, 550–557.

Eidinger, D., and Garrett, T. J. (1972). Studies in the regulatory effects of the sex hormones on antibody formation and stem cell differentiation. *J. Exp. Med.* **136**, 1098–1116.

Elliot, E. V., and Sinclair, N. R. (1968). Effect of cortisone acetate on 19S and 7S haemolysin antibody: A time course study. *Immunology* **15**, 643–652.

Fauci, A. S. (1975). Corticosteroids and circulating lymphocytes. *Transplant. Proc.* **7**, 37–48.

Fauci, A. S., and Dale, D. C. (1975). The effect of hydrocortisone on the kinetics of normal human lymphocytes. *Blood* **46**, 235–243.

Fauci, A. S., Pratt, K. R., and Whalen, G. (1977). Activation of human B lymphoyctes. IV. Regulatory effects of corticosteroids on the triggering signal in the plaque-forming cell response of human peripheral blood B lymphocytes to polyclonal activation. *J. Immunol.* **119**, 598–603.

Feigin, R. D., San Joaquin, V. H., Haymond, M. W., and Wyatt, R. G. (1969). Daily periodicity of the susceptibility of mice to pneumococcal infection. *Nature, (London)* **224**, 379–380.

Ferguson, R. M., Schmidtke, J. R., and Simmons, R. L. (1976). Inhibition of mitogen-induced lymphocyte transformation by local anesthetics. *J. Immunol.* **116**, 627–634.

Ferreira, G. G., Massuda-Brascher, H. K., Javierre, M. Q, Sassine, W. A., and Lima, A. O. (1976). Rosette formation by human T and B lymphocytes in the presence of adrenergic and cholinergic drugs. *Experientia* **32**, 1594–1596.

Filipp, G. (1973). Mechanism of suppressing anaphylaxis through electrolytic lesion of the tuberal region of the hypothalamus. *Ann. Allergy* **31**, 272–278.

Filipp, G., and Mess, B. (1969). Role of the adrenocortical system in suppressing anaphylaxis after hypothalamic lesion. *Ann. Allergy* **27**, 607–610.

Filipp, G., and Szentiványi, A. (1958). Anaphylaxis and the nervous system. Part III. *Ann. Allergy* **16**, 306–311.

Galant, S. P., and Remo, R. A. (1975). β-Adrenergic inhibition of human T lymphocyte rosettes. *J. Immunol.* **114**, 512–513.

Gisler, R. H. (1974). Stress and the hormonal regulation of the immune response in mice. *Psychother. Psychosom.* **23**, 197–208.

Gold, W. M. (1973). Cholinergic pharmacology in asthma. In "Asthma: Physiology, Immunopharmacology, and Treatment" (K. F. Austen and L. M. Lichtenstein, eds.), p. 169. Academic Press, New York.

Gold, W. M., Kessler, G. F., and Yu, D.Y.C. (1972). Role of vagus nerves in experimental asthma in allergic dogs. *J. Appl. Physiol.* **33**, 719–725.

Goodwin, J. S., Messner, R. P., and Williams, R. C. Jr. (1979). Inhibitors of T-cell mitogenesis: Effect of mitogen dose. *Cell. Immunol.* **45**, 303–308.

Hexheimer, H. (1956). Bronchoconstrictor agents and their antagonists in the intact guinea pig. *Arch Int. Pharmacodyn. Ther.* **106**, 371–380.

Hicks, R. (1969). Corticosteroid modification of guinea pig anaphylaxis. *J. Pharm. Pharmacol.* **21**, 202–203.

Hökfelt, T., Elde, R., Fuxe, K., Johansson, O., Ljungdahl, A., Goldstein, M., Luft, R., Efendic, S., Terenius, L., Ganten, D., Feffcoate, S. L., Rehfeld, J., Said, S., Perez, M., de la Mora, M., Possani, L., Tapia, R., Teran, L., and Palacios, R. (1978). Aminergic and peptidergic pathways in the nervous system with special reference to the hypothalamus. *Res. Publ., Assoc. Res. Nerv. Ment. Dis.* **56**, 69–135.

Janković, B. D., and Isaković, K. (1973). Neuro-endocrine correlates of immune response. 1. Effects of brain lesions on antibody production, Arthus reactivity and delayed hypersensitivity in the rat. *Int. Arch. Allergy Appl. Immunol.* **45**, 360–372.

Janković, B. D., Jovanova, K., and Markovic, B. M. (1979). Effect of hypothalamic stimulation on the immune reactions in the rat. *Period. Biol.* **81**, 211–212.

Kappas, A., Jones, H. E. H., and Roitt, I. M. (1963). Effects of steroid sex hormones on immunological phenomena. *Nature (London)* **198**, 902.

Kasahara, K., Tanaka, S., and Hamashima, Y. (1977). Suppressed immune response to T-cell dependent antigen in chemically sympathectomized mice. *Res. Commun. Chem. Pathol. Pharmacol.* **16**, 687–694.

Keller, S. E., Stein, M., Camerino, M. S., Schleifer, S. J., and Sherman, J. (1980). Suppression of lymphocyte stimulation by anterior hypothalamic lesions in the guinea pig. *Cell Immunol.* **52**, 334–340.

Kittas, C., and Henry, L. (1979). Effect of sex hormones on the immune system of guinea-pigs and on the development of toxoplasmic lesions in non-lymphoid organs. *Clin. Exp. Immunol.* **36**, 16–23.

Koller, E. A. (1968). Atmung und Kreislauf in Anaphylaktischenasthma Bronchiale des Meerschweinchens. III. Die Lungen Veranderungen im Asthmaanfall und die Inspiratorische Reaction. *Helv. Physiol. Pharmacol. Acta* **26**, 153–17.

Kondracki, E., and Milgram, F. (1975). Cell cooperation in the lymphocyte response to mitogens and antigens. *Fed. Proc., Fed. Am. Soc. Exp. Biol.* **34**, 952.

Korneva, E. A. (1976). Neurohumoral regulation of immunological hemeostasis. *Fiziol. Chel.* **2** (3), 469–481.

Korneva, E. A., and Khai, L. M. (1964). Effect of destruction of hypothalamic areas on immunogenesis. *Fed. Proc., Fed. Am. Soc. Exp. Biol. (Trans. Supp.)* **23**, 88–92.

Kram, J., Bourne, H., Maibach, H., and Melmon, K. (1975). Cutaneous immediate hypersensitivity in man: Effects of systematically administered adrenergic drugs. *J. Allergy Clin. Immunol.* **56**, 387.

Leger, J., and Masson, G. (1947). Factors influencing an anaphylactoid reaction in the rat. *Fed. Proc., Fed. Am. Soc. Exp. Biol.* **6**, 150–151.

Luparello, T. J., Stein, M., and Park, C. D. (1964). Effect of hypothalamic lesions on rat anaphylaxis. *Am. J. Physiol.* **207**, 911–914.

McCulloch, M. W., Proctor, C., and Rand, M. J. (1967). Evidence for an adrenergic homeostatic bronchodilator reflex mechanism. *Eur. J. Pharmacol.* **2**, 214–223.

Macris, N. T., Schiavi, R. C., Camerino, M. S., and Stein, M. (1970). Effect of hypothalamic lesions on immune processes in the guinea pig. *Am. J. Physiol.* **219**, 1205–1209.

Macris, N. T., Schiavi, R. C., Camerino, M. S., and Stein, M. (1972). Effect of hypothalamus on passive anaphylaxis in the guinea pig. *Am. J. Physiol.* **222**, 1054–1057.

Martin, J. B., Reichlin, S., and Brown, G. M. (1977). "Clinical Endocrinology." Davis, Philadelphia, Pennsylvania.

Maslinski, C., and Karczewski, W. (1957). The protective influences of brain stimulation by electric currents on histamine shock in guinea pigs. *Bull. Acad. Pol. Sci.* **5**, 57–62.

Mathé, A. A., Yen, S. S., Sohn, R. J., and Kemper, T. (1979). Effect of hypothalamic lesions on anaphylactic release of PGs from guinea pig lung. *Adv. Pharmacol. Ther., Proc. Int. Congr. Pharmacol., 7th, 1978.*

Mendelsohn, J., Multer, M. M., and Bernheim, J. L. (1977). Inhibition of human lymphocyte stimulation by steroid hormones: Cytokinetic mechanisms. *Clin. Exp. Immunol.* **27**, 127–134.

Mills, J. E., and Widdicombe, J. G. (1970). Role of the vagus nerves in anaphylaxis and histamine-induced bronchoconstriction in guinea pigs. *Br. J. Pharmacol.* **39**, 724–731.

Moore, R. Y., and Eichler, V. B. (1972). Loss of a circadian adrenal corticosterone rhythm following suprachiasmatic lesions in the rats. *Brain Res.* **42**, 201–206.

Nagy, E., and Berczi, I. (1978). Immunodeficiency in hypophysectomized rats. *Acta Endocrinol. (Copenhagen)* **89**, 530–537.

Nakazawa, H., Hobday, J., Townley, R., and Chaperon, E. (1977). Effect of β-adrenergic blockade, Pertussis vaccine and Freund's adjuvant on reaginic antibody response in mice. *Int. Arch. Allergy Appl. Immunol.* **53**, 197–205.

Nilzen, A. (1955). The influence of the thyroid gland on hypersensitivity reactions in animals. *Acta Allergol.* **7**, 231–234.

Ohara, J., Kishimoto, T., and Yamamura, Y. (1978). *In vitro* immune response of human peripheral lymphocytes. 3. Effect of anti-α or anti-δ antibody on PWM-induced increase of cyclic nucleotides in human B lymphocytes. *J. Immunol.* **121**, 2058–2096.

Orange, R. P., and Austen, F. (1970). Chemical mediators of immediate hypersensitivity. *In* "Immunobiology" (R. A. Good and D. W. Fisher, eds.), pp. 115–121. Sinauer Assoc., Stamford, Connecticut.

Papez, J. W. (1937). A proposed mechanism of emotions. *Arch. Neurol. Psychiatry* **37**, 725–743.

Parker, C. W. (1973). Adrenergic responsiveness in asthma. *In* "Asthma: Physiology, Immunopharmacology, and Treatment" (K. F. Austen and L. M. Lichtenstein, eds.), pp. 185–210. Academic Press, New York.

Parrot, J. L., and Laborde, C. (1955). Inhibition d'histidine décarboxylase par la cortisone et par le salicylate de sodium. *J. Physiol., (Paris)* **53**, 441–442.

Patterson, R., Suszko, I. M., Metzger, W. J., and Roberts, M. (1976). *In vitro* production of IgE by human peripheral blood lymphocytes: Effect of choleratoxin and β-adrenergic stimulation. *J. Immunol.* **117**, 97–101.

Paunović, V. R., Petrović, S., and Janković, B. D. (1976). Influence of early postnatal hypothalamic lesions on immune responses of adult rats. *Period. Biol.* **78**, 50.

Petranyi, G., Jr., Bengzur, M., and Alfoldy, P. (1971). The effect of single large dose hydrocortisone treatment on IgM and IgG antibody production, morphological distribution of antibody producing cells and immunological memory. *Immunology* **21**, 151–158.

Pierpaoli, W., and Maestroni, G. J. M. (1978). Pharmacological control of the hormonally modulated immune response 11. Blockade of antibody production by a combination of drugs acting on neuroendocrine functions. Its prevention by gonadotrophins and corticotrophin. *Immunology* **34**, 419-430.

Polyak, A. I., Rumbesht, L. M., and Sinichkin, A. A. (1969). Antibody synthesis following electrocoagulation on the posterior hypothalamic nucleus. *Zh. Mikrobiol. Epidemiol. Immunobiol.* **46** (3), 52-56.

Porter, J. C. (1962). "Hypothalamic Peptide Hormones and Pituitary Regulation." Plenum, New York.

Przybylski, A. (1962). Effect of the removal of cortex cerebri and the quadrigeminal bodies region on histamine susceptibility of guinea pigs. *Acta Physiol. Po.* **13**, 535-541.

Reichlin, S., Baldessarini, R. J., and Martin, J. B., eds. (1978). "The Hypothalamus." Raven Press, New York.

Reinberg, A., Sidi, E., and Ghata, J. (1965). Circadian reactivity rhythms of human skin to histamine or allergen and the adrenal cycle. *J. Allergy* **36**, 273-283.

Rice, R. W., Abe, K., and Critchlow, V. (1978). Abolition of plasma growth hormone response to stress and of the circadian rhythm in pituitary–adrenal function in female rats with preoptic–anterior hypothalamic lesions. *Brain Res.* **148**, 129-141.

Ritter, M. (1977). Embryonic mouse thymocyte development enhancing effect of corticosterone at physiological levels. *Immunology 33*, 241-246.

Rosenstreich, D. L. (1976). The macrophage requirement for mitogenic activation of T-lymphocytes. *In* "Mitogens in Immunobiology" (J. J. Oppenheim and D. L. Rosenstreich, eds.), pp. 385-398. Academic Press, New York.

Roszkowski, W., Plaut, M., and Lichtenstein, L. M. (1977). Selective display of histamine receptors on lymphocytes. *Science* **195**, 683-685.

Schayer, R. W., Davis, J. K., and Smiley, R. L. (1955). Binding of histamine *in vitro* and its inhibition by cortisone. *Am. J. Physiol.* **182**, 54-56.

Schiavi, R. C., Adams, J., and Stein, M. (1966). Effect of hypothalamic lesions on histamine toxicity in the guinea pig. *Am. J. Physiol.* **211**, 1269-1273.

Schiavi, R. C., Macris, N. T., Camerino, M. S., and Stein, M. (1975). Effect of hypothalamic lesions on immediate hypersensitivity. *Am. J. Physiol.* **228**, 596-601.

Schmutzler, W., and Derwall, R. (1973). Experiments on the role of cyclic AMP in guinea pig anaphylaxis. *Int. Arch. Allergy Appl. Immunol.* **45**, 120-122.

Schmutzler, W., and Freundt, G. P. (1975). The effect of glucocorticoids and catecholamines on cyclic AMP and allergic histamine release in guinea pig lung. *Int. Arch. Allergy Appl. Immunol.* **49**, 209-212.

Shereff, R., Harwell, W., Lieberman, P., Rosenberg, E. W., and Robinson, H. (1973). Effects of beta adrenergic stimulation and blockade on immediate hypersensitivity skin test reactions. *J. Allergy Clin. Immunol.* **52**, 328-333.

Sherman, N. A., Smith, R. S., and Middleton, E., Jr. (1973). Effect of adrenergic compounds, aminophylline and hydrocortisone on *in vitro* immunoglobulin synthesis by normal human peripheral lymphocytes. *J. Allergy and Clin. Immunol.* **52**, 13-22.

Smith, J. W., Steiner, A. L., and Parker, C. W. (1971). Human lymphocyte metabolism. Effects of cyclic and non-cyclic nucleotides on stimulation by phytohemagglutinin. *J. Clin. Invest.* **50**, 442-448.

Stein, M., Schiavi, R. C., and Camerino, M. S. (1976). Influence of brain and behavior on the immune system. *Science* **191**, 435-440.

Szentivanyi, A., and Filipp, G. (1958). Anaphylaxis and the nervous system. Part II. *Ann. Allergy* **16**, 143-151.

Szentiványi, A., and Székely, J. (1958). Anaphylaxis and the nervous system. Part IV. *Ann. Allergy* **16**, 389-392.

Thanavala, Y. M., Rao, S. S., and Thakur, A. N. (1973). The effect of an oestrogenic steroid on the secondary immune response under different hormonal environments. *Acta Endocrinol. (Copenhagen)* **72**, 582-586.

Thrasher, S. G., Bernardis, L. L., and Cohen, S. (1971). The immune response in hypothalamic-lesioned and hypophysectomized rats. *Int. Arch. Allergy Appl. Immunol.* **41**, 813-820.

Tsypin, A. B., and Maltsev, V. N. (1967). The effect of hypothalamic stimulation on the serum content of normal antibodies. *Patol. Fixiol. Eksp. Ter.* **11**, 83–84.

Tyrey, L., and Nalbandov, A. V. (1972). Influence of anterior hypothalamic lesions on circulating antibody titers in the rat. *Am. J. Physiol.* **222**, 179–185.

Wang, T., Sheppard, J. R., and Foker, J. E. (1978). Rise and fall of cyclic AMP required for onset of lymphocyte DNA synthesis. *Science* **201**, 155–159.

Watson, J. (1975). The influence of intracellular levels of cyclic nucleotides on cell proliferation and the induction of antibody synthesis. *J. Exp. Med.* **141**, 97–111.

Whittier, J. R., and Orr, A. (1962). Hyperkinesia and other physiologic effects of caudate deficit in the adult albino rat. *Neurology* **12**, 529–539.

Widdicombe, J. G. (1963). Regulation of tracheobronchial smooth muscle. *Physiol. Rev.* **43**, 1–37.

Winer, B. J. (1962). "Statistical Principles in Experimental Design." McGraw-Hill, New York.

Wyle, F. A., and Kent, J. R. (1977). Immunosuppression by sex steroid hormones. *Clin. Exp. Immunol.* **27**, 407–415.

Yamasaki, H., and Yamamoto, T. (1963). Inhibitory effect of adrenal glucocorticoids on histamine release. *Jpn. J. Pharmacol.* **13**, 223–224.

Neurophysiology, Immunophysiology, and Neuroimmunomodulation

NOVERA HERBERT SPECTOR
ELENA A. KORNEVA

INTRODUCTION AND RETROSPECTIVE (NHS)

Today, most immunologists are not aware of, or choose deliberately to ignore, the central nervous system (Spector, 1980). Immunologists have their hands full studying molecular mechanisms of antigen (Ag)–antibody (Ab) interactions, the production of Ab, interferons, and anti-inflammatory substances; the ontogeny of the numerous cellular elements involved in immune responses; receptor mechanisms on lymphocytes and phagocytes; and the very complex interactions among these various cell types. They have no time nor inclination to look at higher levels of organization, that is, the direct influence of the nervous system on all of these functions.

Neurophysiologists, on the other hand, are mostly occupied with the enormously difficult task of trying to understand the functions of neurons and glia, of neuromuscular ontogeny and functions, and the almost limitless complexity of the central nervous system. Immunology is used only as a *tool* for the tracing of pathways of neurites and for the identification of receptors, on or in neural cellular elements, for neurotransmitters, drugs, hormones, and other neurally active substances.

In medical schools, teaching is organized by departments of physiology, microbiology, immunology, neurobiology, and so on. However, neither the

449

PSYCHONEUROIMMUNOLOGY

human body nor other organisms are organized by medical school divisions. These organisms are functional entities that, for the most part, do not read medical textbooks, and, by and large, do not follow the rules laid down by professors of single disciplines. We have reached a stage in the history of science, where, if we are to understand the functioning of a whole organism, its response to the challenges of invading organisms and to foreign Ag's, and we want to have a rational approach to the treatment of disease, we must begin to use, *in combination,* the tools of the physiologist, the immunologist, the virologist, the embryologist, the anatomist, and so on. Of course, this is *difficult,* but if we are to make significant progress from now on, it is *necessary.*

Physicians, scientists, and lay people have suspected, for thousands of years, that the "mind" (read: *Nervous System*) influences the "body's" condition of health and its response to disease. It was not, however, until the mid-1920s that serious and consistent attempts were made in the laboratory to pin down this elusive phenomenon. The experiments, conducted at the Pasteur Institute in Paris, were summarized by S. Metalnikov in his book, *Rôle du Système Nerveux et des Facteurs Biologiques et Psychiques dans l'Immunité* (1934). This work should be read by anyone who hopes to gain a historical perspective in this field. Among other findings, Metalnikov and his colleagues showed (as did Pavlov before him) that immune responses are common to both *invertebrates* and vertebrates (a fact forgotten or unlearned by many scientists today) and more importantly, that several immune reactions could be induced, in the absence of an Ag, by classical conditioning techniques. This was the first clear experimental evidence of neuroimmunomodulation (the influence of the central nervous system upon general immune responses). Other researchers successfully repeated and extended their experiments; still others were unable to verify them and contradicted Metalnikov's conclusions. Historical and scientific reviews of these experiments can be found in Luk'yanenko (1961), Dolin and Dolina (1972), Spector (1980), and Ader's chapter in this volume.

Today, the evidence is overwhelmingly in favor of a vital role for the central nervous system (CNS) in immunomodulation (NIM), and indeed, there is some evidence that the CNS can also initiate certain types of immune responses [neuroimmunogenesis (NIG)].

THE EVIDENCE (NHS)

For purposes of classification, the evidence for NIM and NIG can be divided roughly into three categories whose boundaries, of course, are overlapping: "psychic," neurophysiologic, and cellular–molecular. Some of the psychic factors are dealt with, in detail, elsewhere in this volume. The "psychic" evidence for NIM has accumulated from experiments in *stress, conditioning, hypnosis, biological psychiatry, psychosomatic medicine, biofeedback,* as well as *clinical observations* of changes in immune responses associated with various affective disorders.

This chapter deals more with the neurophysiologic evidence. The section below, by Professor Korneva, describes a small part of the voluminous data collected by herself and her colleagues over the past 20 years, and outlines the mechanisms by which NIM may function. This work has established the seminal position of Elena Korneva as both a pioneer scientific worker and a pioneer scientific thinker in this field.

In general, the neurophysiologic evidence can be divided according to techniques that have been used to explore these phenomena: *lesioning and stimulation of the peripheral autonomic nervous system; CNS lesioning; brain stimulation; unit recording in the brain; neuroanatomical tracing of connections; investigations of neuro-ontogeny;* and *neuroendocrine* studies.

The early experiments of Korneva and Khai (1961) dealt with effects of the sympathetic nervous system upon adrenal hormones and their subsequent effects upon immune responses. Later, Korneva and Khai focused their attention on the *hypothalamus,* in the CNS, which anatomically and functionally sits at the center of the limbic system, and which is central to the control of the autonomic nervous system. The hypothalamus also controls the pituitary which, in turn, regulates most of the other endocrine glands of the body (see below).

In many countries, other investigators made lesions in the CNS and observed changes in various aspects of immune, allergic, and inflammatory responses (e.g., Filipp *et al.,* 1952; Freedman and Fenichel, 1958; Szentiványi and Filipp, 1958; Pryzbylski, 1962; Janković and Isaković, 1973; Tyrey, 1969; Macris *et al.,* 1970; Spector *et al.,* 1974; Hall *et al.,* 1978, 1979; Spector, 1979; Cross *et al.,* 1980; Warejka and Levy, 1980; and many others. For reviews, see Stein *et al.,* 1976; Korneva *et al.,* 1978; Spector, 1980; and the chapter by Stein in this volume).

Electrical stimulation of various regions in the brain, particularly in the hypothalamus, also produced changes in phagocytosis, changes in titers of circulating Ab, and alterations of other immunologic reactions (e.g., Benetato *et al.,* 1945; Baciu, 1946, 1978; Korneva and Khai, 1967).

In 1972, V. M. Klimenko, a student of Korneva, published his doctoral dissertation on the changes in firing patterns of single neurons in the brain after peripheral injections of Ag. These experiments are described in detail in Korneva and Klimenko (1976) and summarized below. Similar studies were undertaken by Besedovsky *et al.* (1977) in Switzerland. Clearly, there are nerve cells in the hypothalamus that respond dramatically to antigenic challenges elsewhere in the body. It remains to be seen whether these are highly specific or generalized, and whether such effects are the immediate response to the Ag or secondary responses due to changes in hormonal titers or other chemical changes in the blood and cerebrospinal fluid.

It also would be important to know if the information is relayed to the central nervous system via peripheral receptors and direct neural connections. It has been known for a long time that there are nerve endings in the bone marrow, in the thymus, in the lymphatic system and in most, if not all, of the organs and tissues involved in immune responses. The function of these neural elements can only be guessed at today, but it would be surprising if they did not play a role in immunologic reactions. It is well known that the adrenal medulla is a special case of a sympathetic, postsynaptic tissue: the effects of epinephrine as well as those of the adreno*cortical* steroids upon various cellular immune reactions and upon inflammatory and allergic reations are legion.

Neurohormonal influences are discussed elsewhere in this volume. Of course, the effects of stress (see chapter in this volume by Monjan) on endocrine change have been known and studied for many years (e.g., Selye, 1950; Mason, 1974, 1975). Continuing research on thymic hormones (see Hall and Goldstein, this volume), thyroxine, ACTH, and many other hormones will undoubtedly reveal further CNS–endocrine–immune connections.

Paunović *et al.* (1976) have shown that postnatal damage to the hypothalamus in rats can influence immune responses of the adult animal. Will denervation or electrical stimulation of the thymus or bone marrow, early in life, influence the eventual production or activity of T or B lymphocytes? The development of the nervous system must be studied in connection with the development of the immune systems. This important area of neurophysiologic research is still in its infancy.

At the cellular–molecular level, receptor sites on lymphocytes and phagocytes have been identified for neurotransmitters, neurally-active polypeptides, histamines, and other substances released directly or indirectly by neural tissue, all of which are implicated in changes in inflammatory, allergic, anaphylactic, and other immunologic reactions (e.g., Baciu, 1946, 1962, 1978; Hall *et al.*, 1978, 1979; Roszkowski *et al.*, 1977; chapter by Hall in this volume).

The above is a somewhat brief and informal historical introduction to the neurophysiologic (and other) evidence for NIM. The following sections (by EAK) deal with some recent more specific and detailed evidence.

IMMUNOPHYSIOLOGY: THE PRESENT STATE AND THE PROSPECTS OF THE PROBLEM'S DEVELOPMENT (EAK)

The immune system, as one of the visceral systems of the organism, obeys the general laws applicable to the other systems of the organism.

Along with immunochemistry, immunomorphology, and immunogenetics, the past decade has seen an intensive development of immunophysiology, a scientific field whose object is the study of the organization and regulation of immunologic processes within the whole organism. Methodologically, it is characterized by a combined use of physiological and immunologic techniques of analysis, inasmuch as neither one of them taken separately can provide an answer to the questions posed by the problem: the problem is to analyze, understand, and predict the course of reactions of the whole organism and its parts to an antigenic stimulus.

The basic position from which studies are proceeding is a recognition of the fact that the genetic potencies of the lymphoid cells in the whole organism are subject to correction, that is, the intensity of immunologic processes is regulated nonspecifically by neurohumoral mechanisms.

The starting point for immunologic reactions is the action of an antigen—a genetically foreign substance. The final stage of the reactions is the formation of protective factors—cellular or humoral antibodies specific for the given antigen. Thus, in its beginning and its conclusion, the process is specific, yet in its realization, an important role is played by nonspecific reactions which, in the whole organism, are closely linked to specific mechanisms of resistance. The latter fact is determined by at least three main circumstances: (a) under natural conditions an antigen, as a rule, enters the organism not as a chemically pure protein but together with other substances producing nonspecific reactions of various kinds, such as inflammation, fever, and stimulation of chemoreceptors; the same effects may be produced by the antigen alone; (b) various nonspecific mechanisms are involved in the formation of an immune response; (c) hormonal and neural influences are of great significance in securing an immune reaction of adequate intensity.

Thus, there are nonspecific regulatory components of specific (immune) processes. Whereas the qualitative character of an immune response is determined by the properties of the antigen, the intensity is governed not only by its quality and quantity, but also by a number of other factors, including neurohumoral ones.

Studying neurohumoral factors in immune homeostasis does not differ in principle from investigating the regulation of any other neural function: it consists of a physiological analysis of the routes of inflow into the nervous system of information concerning the entry of an antigen into the organism, the study of the central links of the regulating system, and an analysis of the means by which efferent impulses are transmitted to the executant organs.

Nonetheless, specific features of the structure and function of the immune system necessitate the search for special approaches and methods that would make it possible to apply the adopted or modified techniques of physiological analysis to the solution of concrete aspects of the problem under consideration. For instance, the study of the neurophysiological correlates of the process of immunogenesis, long-lasting and multicomponent, has called for the creation of special mathematical techniques for the analysis of the data on the impulse activity of individual central nervous system neurons.

To accomplish this, we coordinate the skills of specialists in immunology, physiology, and morphology in a common effort which makes it possible to evaluate and summarize the facts accumulated as a result of studying different levels of the organization of the process of immune homeostasis regulation, from the cellular to the organismic.

It is common knowledge that the immune system is characterized by a high degree of autonomy of the processes taking place at the cellular level. This is clearly attested to by the formation of antibodies *in vitro*. However, it is hard to compare the development of processes occurring in a test tube with those in an organism whose cells, lymphoid cells included, are under the constant influence of an internal milieu which changes as a result of complex regulating effects of the nervous and endocrine systems.

The peripheral organs in the visceral sphere are generally characterized by a high degree of their own automatism (autoregulation). Suffice it to say that a perfused heart extracted from the organism continues beating, the glands under similar conditions produce their specific secretions and excreta, the intestinal loop is contracting, etc., although in all such cases the function does not correspond fully to the activity taking place within the organism. The precision and the adequacy of responding to changes in the internal and external environments are affected *in vivo*.

In this respect, the immune system is not an exception. As with organs in the visceral sphere, it possesses considerable automatism (autoregulation) which by itself does not, however, ensure optimal development of immunogenesis in the whole organism.

Some success has been attained in the experimental analysis of two fundamental aspects of immunophysiology, the complex of effects produced by the neural, endocrine, and other humoral factors on the course of immune reactions. Studies have been undertaken of the changes initiated within those systems in the course of reactions to an antigen.

Experimental studies have revealed that the intensity of immunologic reactions (production of antibodies, skin reaction of the delayed type, anaphylactic shock, etc.) depends upon the action of neurohumoral factors. It has been demonstrated that actions of the thymus, the thyroid gland, the adrenal glands, the pituitary body, and of some parts of the brain affect the intensity of the process of immunogenesis. The most effective of the central nervous system elements are the actions of the hypothalamus and limbic system (Korneva and Khai, 1961; Tsypin and Maltzev, 1967; Magaeva *et al.*, 1968; Polyak, 1969; Shatilova *et al.*, 1970; Frolov, 1974; Polyak and Zotova, 1975; Shekoyan *et al.*, 1975; Shekoyan, 1976; Korneva *et al.*, 1978; Filipp *et al.*, 1952; Kanda, 1959; Luparello *et al.*, 1964; Stein *et al.*, 1969; Filipp, 1973; Amkraut and Solomon, 1974; Stein *et al.*, 1976; Spector *et al.*, 1975).

Certain corresponding results may be obtained in the examination of patients with lesions of the endocrine glands or of the central nervous system (Chernigovskaia *et al.*, 1975; Solomon *et al.*, 1974).

According to present-day views, the maintenance of immune homeostasis is ensured by the combined action of the thymus and the bone marrow, whose cells (the so-called stem cells) migrate into the thymus and either into the Fabricius bursa analogue or directly into the peripheral lymphoid organs—the spleen and lymph nodes. The thymus is involved in the maturation of T lymphocytes, while the Fabricius bursa and, perhaps, the bone marrow itself, according to the (nonuniform) data in the literature, are involved in the development of B lymphocytes. Within the peripheral lymphoid organs, in the presence of macrophages, the T and B lymphocytes cooperate in the production of antibodies (Petrov, 1976). It has been found that the populations of T lymphocytes and B lymphocytes are not homogeneous; there are cell subpopulations with different functions. Among the B cells there are the cells producing various kinds of globulin, among the T cells there are T effectors or T killers, cells carrying antigen-binding structures on their surface, T helpers which assist in the work of B cells, and T suppressors which hinder the activity of antibody-forming cells (Petrov, 1978). The eventual effect of immune regulation depends to a great extent upon the destination of the regulating impulse. If the function of the T suppressor is inhibited, the immune response is enhanced and, vice versa (stimulation of the suppressor function inhibits the reaction to antigen).

All the organs of the immune system are provided with sympathetic and parasympathetic innervation. In addition, the blood flow delivers to these organs hormones which exert an influence on their functions based, in part, on the rate of migration of bone marrow and thymus cells (e.g., Haitov, 1977; Kozlov and Tsyrlova, 1976, 1978).

An important contribution to the study of the regulation of immune system functions has been made recently by immunologists and biochemists who described the action of hormones and neuromediators upon lymphoid cells. It has been found that lymphocytes carry, on their surface, receptors to neurotransmitters (e.g., epinephrine, norepinephrine, acetylcholine, and others). The biochemical nature of the action of those substances on the lymphoid cell also have been described: epinephrine and norepinephrine do not penetrate the cell membrane but act upon the adrenoreceptor and, through adenylcyclase and cAMP, on the metabolism of the cell, changing its functional state.

Acetylcholine acts through cholinoreceptors and on the metabolism of the cell through cGMP (Hadden *et al.*, 1975; Gordon *et al.*, 1978; Bourne *et al.*, 1974; Eskra *et al.*, 1978). This evidence suggests that neurotransmitters delivered to lymphoid cells via nerve trunks and endings can be absorbed by the lymphocyte.

Steroid hormones, on the contrary, penetrate the cell membrane to the inside of the lymphocyte, act upon the genome, and in this way regulate the level of the cells' work (Karlson, 1963; Protasova, 1975).

On the other hand, endocrine factors and the nervous system are known to affect the intensity of the immune response (Korneva *et al.*, 1978). Thus, we appear to have on hand two final links of the process. One of them is the effector—the working system, and the other is the brain–endocrine system. The modulating effects of this brain–endocrine system on the extent of the immune response is being investigated widely (e.g., Polyak, 1979; Devoino, 1979; Chebotariov, 1979). Our task now consists in finding how the process of regulation is organized, where the regulating impulses are addressed in each concrete situation, and in what temporal sequence the regulation takes place. Such is the nature of the problem as a whole.

According to the literature and the findings of our laboratory, there are three areas in the brain whose action affects the course of the immune response: the hypothalamus, the hippocampus, and the reticular formation of the midbrain. Injury or lesion or stimulation of these areas may reduce or enhance the intensity of immune responses.

There are two principal ways of investigating the mechanisms of regulation of any system: studying the effect of the regulating links on that which is regulated; and, vice versa, analyzing the operation of the regulating system in the course of development of any given form of reaction. A third step would be the analysis of neural and endocrine feedback mechanisms. Under natural conditions in the evolution of an immune response to any foreign protein, the above-named brain structures would be involved in the process by affecting the level of immunologic activity.

The available data are scarce, being accumulated in the past few years. The foundation for much research was laid by Ado (1952) who summarized the results of studying the effect of antigenic stimulation on various components of the whole reaction: respiration, blood pressure, and cardiac action.

One of the important steps in this direction was the research reporting that the number of active neurons (along the track of the electrode) in different hypothalamic structures changes during the evolution of the tuberculous process and upon administration of BCG, and that these changes are different for the phase of active immunologic changes as opposed to their exhaustion (Broun, 1969; Broun et al., 1970; Mogutov, 1972). Thus it has been demonstrated that, in the course of the development of immunologic reactions, functional changes are taking place in hypothalamic structures.

Further analysis of the changes in the patterns of operation of hypothalamic structures, based on studying the activity of individual neurons before and after immunization, has made it possible to reveal the course and the distinctive features of the variations of hypothalamic neuronal activity in the development of reactions to an antigen (Klimenko, 1972; Besedovsky and Sorkin, 1977; Korneva and Klimenko, 1979).

In the living organism, neurons of the hypothalamus continuously process incoming information of various types and sources. In turn, they control the systems for maintaining homeostasis. The background electrical activity of hypothalamic neurons is an indication of their natural functional state. Correlation of the characteristics of the unit neuronal electrical impulse activity of different hypothalamic structures, the quantitative description of the functional state of certain hypothalamic structures and of their neuronal activity in intact animals and at different time periods following the administration of an antigen, have provided a basis for determining changes in the activity of hypothalamic structures in the course of an organism's reaction to an antigen.

The determination of the degree, variations and mechanisms of the participation of different parts of the brain in the regulation of body functions, in the cerebral portions of the processes, in the autonomic sphere in particular, and of behavioral reactions, necessitates the evaluation of the state or level of activity of the brain structure under study at different stages in the evolution of the process of an immune reaction.

Not always can use be made of the traditional method of direct comparison of neuronal unit activity before and after stimulation. In particular, this method would appear to be impractical, if not impossible, in the analysis of the regulation of immunologic processes forming over a period of days or weeks. Moreover, in studying multiparameter systems, visual evaluation becomes practically impossible; ascertaining the laws which characterize the mode of operation and the bonds of different elements (links) of the system requires mathematical methods of analysis and synthesis, including the procedures of factor analysis.

For the purpose of studying changes in the operational patterns of various structures of the hypothalamus in the course of a reaction to antigenic stimulation, the background impulse electrical activity of hypothalamic cells was adapted as the reference criterion. The background activity of hypothalamic neurons appears to reflect to some extent the complexity of the neuronal organization of that structure and the continuous interaction between "the center and the periphery" which ensures the possibility of maintaining homeostasis. Hypothalamic nuclei play an important role in the series of reactions to an antigen. To study one of the links in the system of neurohumoral regulation of immune homeostasis, an analysis was made of the firing patterns of 2495 neurons of 10 hypothalamic structures of rabbits recorded before and on Day 1, 3, 6, 10, 15, 20, and 30 after the administration of antigen (Klimenko, 1975).

Hypothalamic neurons are characterized by various forms of spike activity: single, batch and group activities, and mixed forms with a considerable variability of groupings. Some of the structures under study featured a statistically definable impulse frequency—from 8.64 imp/sec for the zone incerta area to 5.79 imp/sec for the dorsomedial nucleus of the hypothalamus. The difficulties involved in the correlation of functions of individual elements and the whole in studying the activity of the nervous system may be overcome to some extent by applying statistical (integrative) methods of analysis of brain activity, by measurement of its patterns of impulse activity, and by a subsequent correlation of these patterns with other aspects of the organism's functional activities.

This approach requires a multistage machine analysis of the background

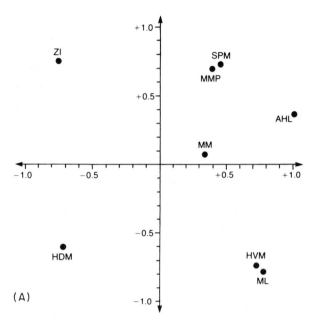

Figure 1. (A) Interrelationship among processes of reorganization of hypothalamic structures' activity in the course of immunogenesis. The position of the structures in the correlation field is determined by the degree of variations of their activity (the abscissas) and the development of their interrelation with the activities of other hypothalamic structures (the ordinates) in the process of immunogenesis. Plotted on the abscissa are the values of the coefficients of correlation among the structures' activities in the course of immunogenesis; and on the ordinate, the values of coefficients of correlation of the interrelation in the structures' activities in the course of immunogenesis. AHL = lateral hypothalamus; HDM = dorsomedial hypothalamus; HVM = ventromedial hypothalamus; ML = lateral mammillary nuclei; SPM = supramammillary nuclei; ZI = Zona incerta; MM = medial mammillary nuclei.

impulse (spike) activity of neurons before and during the course of reactions to an antigen (Klimenko and Kaplunovsky, 1972; Klimenko *et al.,* 1972). The essence of the method consists in describing the activity of certain brain structures by utilizing the data on the impulse patterns of their neurons. Subsequent comparisons of the statistically verified characteristics of the structure's activity in the absence of special impacts and after some disturbing effects, make it possible to reveal the extent, course, and direction of any functional changes in the brain areas under study during the development of a given process.

It has been mentioned that various forms of activity were encountered among the impulse patterns of the neurons before and after the administration of antigen. The plotting of histograms of interimpulse intervals has revealed their variety. The objective automatic classification of histograms by the rank correlation of their features, disclosed, in the whole mass of histograms, 52 classes with a 99.9% reliability of the similarity of histograms

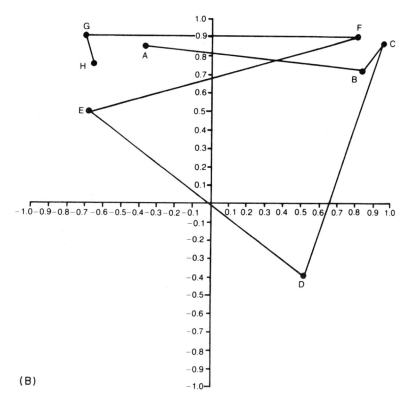

(B)

Figure 1. (B) The course of reorganization of the activity of hypothalamic structures in the course of immunogenesis before (A), and after (C–G), the administration of antigen on Day 1(B), 3(C), 10(D), 15(E), 20(F), and 30(G). Plotted on the abscissa are the coefficients of correlation of the structures' activities; and on the ordinate, the coefficients of correlation of the interrelation in the structures' activities.

within each class. This has made it possible to describe quantitatively the functional state of the hypothalamic structures under study by the type of activity of their neurons.

For each structure under consideration, the functional "spectra" of neuronal composition have been compiled, comprising the types of activity represented in the structure with a weight proportional to the quantity of each type of neuron in that specific structure.

The factor and correlational analyses of changes revealed in the patterns of action of different hypothalamic structures have shown that the process of reorganization is characterized by two principal parameters: changes in the activity of the given structure during different periods of immunogenesis and changes in its interrelationship with the activity of other hypothalamic structures (Figure 1A). These shifts have a time-organization relationship for each structure. The most distinct relationships, in terms of the character and direction of changes in the impulse activity organization, are evident in the activities of the posterior hypothalamic area (AHP), the ventromedial (NVM), lateral (AHL), mammillary (ML), and supramammillary (SPM) nuclei or areas of the hypothalamus (designations of loci according to Fivkova and Marsala, 1960).

Analysis of the reorganization of the pattern of hypothalamic activity during early periods of immunogenesis, the inductive phase, has disclosed a particular pattern. It has been found that, on Days 1–3 (Fig. 1B), concomitant reactions of the structures take place. The character of activity of each of them changes, but the relationship in the activity organization is preserved. By the sixth day, the reaction becomes peculiar to each of the structures under study and the index of the interrelation changes sharply. By the tenth day after the immunization, the indices return to the initial values and that moment corresponds to the end of antigen clearance from the organism.

Early shifts in the function of the hypothalamic structures correlate precisely with the intensive development of cellular reactions in lymphoid tissue (Days 1–3) and the commencement of antibody production (Day 6). In addition, a local lesion of the posterior hypothalamic area results in inhibition of antibody production only when the operation is performed prior to the administration of antigen, that is, the impact is registered also in the inductive phase of the process.

It is evident that the fine cellular mechanisms of immunity require reorganization of a multitude of neural and humoral influences which create the optimum conditions for reactions to foreign proteins and ensure both the adequately intensive specific immune response and nonspecific reactions of the organism.

In studying the later stages of the process, it has been found that on Day 15 of immunogenesis, a "second wave" occurs in the reorganization of the pattern of activity of hypothalamic structures, its course reminiscent of the early reaction (Days 1–3). By Days 20–30, the function of the structures under study is normalized (Fig. 1B).

The nature of the second wave observed may be surmised only with much caution. The titers of antibodies in the blood, in response to the administration of horse serum, are known to increase up to Day 15, then they begin to diminish, and by Day 25–30, as a rule, no antibodies can be discovered in the blood by the complement fixation method. The clearance of antigen ends within 10 days. The inflection point in the curve of antibody titers from maximum to reduction correlates with the time of appearance of the second wave in the reorganization of the activity pattern within hypothalamic structures.

It is likely that the appearance of the "late wave" of changes in neurophysiological characteristics is a reflection of the process of suppression of antibody synthesis by way of feedback. It may also be surmised that a certain role in the mechanism of the late-wave generation is played by antigen–antibody complex formation whose phagocytosis leads to the degranulation of cells and to the excretion of some biologically active substances.

Particular emphasis was given to control experiments. Control rabbits, unlike experimental animals, were administered a warmed autoserum that had a composition close to that of horse serum, yet was not a foreign substance. No antibodies to that serum were discovered in the animals' blood. Studies of the patterns of activity of the hypothalamic structures at different times following the administration of autoserum revealed no significant changes in their neuronal activity.

Thus, on the basis of the results obtained, it has become possible to detect in the hypothalamus the course of reorganization and to identify the complex of structures which in the process of immunogenesis are reacting most intensively and concertedly: AHP, NVM, SPM, ML.

It is significant that according to the literature on these brain areas, the lesion of AHP has the greatest effect upon the intensity of antibody production. On the one hand, this suggests differing functional significance for different structures in the course of immunogenesis and, on the other hand, shows the advantage of employing combined analyses which makes it possible to determine which brain structures are playing (different) roles in the course of the reaction to an antigen.

Studies on the course of variations of the neurophysiological correlates of immunogenesis suggest that hypothalamic structures are involved in the process of a normally developing reaction to an antigen. Thus, one of the requirements in the analysis of any regulating system, viz., the functional reorganization of its elements in the course of operation of the effector system, is satisfied.

The behavior of other parts of the brain under such conditions has not yet been investigated, but is of much interest, especially that of the limbic system.

What, then, are the mechanisms of transmission of the regulating effects of the central nervous system upon the periphery? Probably, these are endocrine and neural (sympathetic and parasympathetic) mechanisms, just as for other systems. For example, steroid hormones of the adrenal cortex are known to be extensively used for the suppression of immune reactions: in large doses they exert a suppressive effect. However, the effect of applying physiological doses is different, as shown by the results obtained in experiments *in vivo* and in tissue culture (e.g., Ambrose, 1970; Fauci *et al.*, 1977). Apparently, glucocorticoids are required for the realization of the immune response in the organism.

In order to study the effect of physiological variations of hormone level upon the course of an immune response, analyses were made of the reorganizations taking place under episodic stress (Dostoevskaia and Shkhinek, 1979). The animals were twice subjected to stress, and the course of the immune response was compared to that in unstressed animals. No effect of episodic stress upon the humoral immune response was discovered. Yet, it has been reported that under chronic stress, the intensity of the immune response undergoes a change (Stein *et al.*, 1976; Monjan and Collector, 1977).

Apparently, it would not be biologically justified for the organism to respond
with immunosuppression to every shift in the environmental situation.

The functions of the endocrine organs in the course of the reaction to
foreign proteins have not been extensively studied. These studies were mainly
on the reactions of the adrenal cortex (Shkhinek *et al.,* 1973; Besedovsky and
Sorkin, 1977).

In studying changes in the 11-oxycorticosteroid levels in blood plasma in
response to immunization, it was found that, by 2–4 hr after the administration of horse serum, there is a distinct rise in the hormone concentration in the
blood. The curve of variations in the level of corticosteroids during the first 24
hr after the administration of the serum differs reliably from that following
the administration of physiologic saline to the same animals. Within 24
hours after the injection of the serum there is, as a rule, an evident rise in corticosteroid concentration, not only as compared to the background level on
the day of immunization, but also relative to the average background on all of
the preceding days of the experiment. In most of the animals, there is a subsequent decrease in the hormone level by the eighth to tenth day after immunization (i.e., by the time of disappearance of the antigen from the blood).
(See Figure 2.)

Thus, the development of an immune reaction is accompanied, in the majority of animals, by higher 11-oxycorticosteroid concentration in the blood.

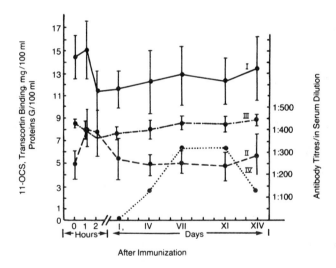

Figure 2. Fixation capacity of transcortin (I), 11-oxycorticosteroid concentration (II), total protein level (III), and intensity of immune response (IV), in rabbits immunized with typhoid bacillus
antigen. Plotted on the abscissa are hours—the Arabic numerals, and days after immunization—the Roman numerals. On the ordinate: on the left—11-oxycorticosteroid and fixation
capacity of transcortin in mg/100 ml, total protein in g/100 ml; on the right—titers of hemagglutinins in serum dilutions I:——; II:— — —; III:—•—•—•; IV:• • • • • • • •

This evidence is in agreement with the view that corticosteroids should be regarded, not only as a factor able to participate in suppressing antibody production in the organism, but also as one essential for the normal course of the process of antibody generation (Ambrose, 1970).

The course of endocrine reactions to the administration of antigen is also dependent on the character of the antigen: administration of Vi-antigen (20 ng per animal, intravenously) induces a more rapid rise in 11-oxycorticosteroid concentration than occurs in the case of horse serum, with no repeated later rise in the hormone level.

A single immunization of rabbits with Vi-antigen induces a rise in total 11-oxycorticosteroids of the blood plasma within 1 to 2 hr after the administration of antigen, and a significant drop in the fixation ability of transcortin at 2–24 hr after immunization. The latter coincides in time with the fall in the level of total plasma proteins.

These results indicate an increase in the concentration of total 11-oxycorticosteroid concentration in the inductive phase of the immune response, concomitant with a drop in the fixation ability of transcortin, which suggests the activation of glucocorticoids in that phase (Figure 2). Inasmuch as the quantity of total proteins diminishes at the same time as the fixation ability of transcortin, it is difficult to determine to what extent those changes are specific. At the same time, the amount of mineralocorticoids in the blood is changing in a way that is not characteristic of a stress reaction: aldosterone level is declining.

As a result of research on the significance of the functional state of hypothalamic structures for the realization of the adrenal cortex reaction to antigenic stimulation, it has been found that a lesion of the posterior hypothalamus intensifies the reaction, whereas a similar lesion in anterior hypothalamic nuclei results in an unchanged or diminished response. These findings demonstrate the connection between reactions of the hormonal and nervous systems in immune processes (Figure 3). That is to say, these reactions, like other stress reactions (not only to an antigen), depend on the state of the central nervous system, the hypothalamic area in particular, and appear to be mediated through those areas.

At the same time, no correlation has been found between the endocrine response level and the course of the primary immune response (Shkhinek, 1978). In studying animals with high and low immune responses, changes in the level of corticosteroids in the blood did not appear to be significantly different. Also, blocking the reaction of the adrenal cortex by the administration of dexamethasone into the ventricles of the brain was not followed by any changes in the intensity of the primary immune response.

In assessing the effect of hormones at different stages in the development of the immune response, however, it should be borne in mind that, at different periods in the evolution of immunogenesis, glucocorticoid hormones act in

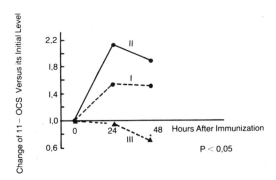

Figure 3. Changes in the level of 11-oxycorticosteroid of blood in response to the administration of horse serum in intact rabbits (I); rabbits immunized after a lesion of the posterior hypothalamus (II); and the anterior hypothalamus (III). Plotted on the abscissa are hours after immunization; and on the ordinate, changes in the 11-oxycorticosteroid concentration against the initial level (= 1.0).

various manners on different cells. Besides, the sensitivity of different cells of the population is different. It may be, for instance, that, with small doses of the hormone, it is the T suppressors that are mainly inhibited (Cohen and Gershon, 1975; Valueva and Chebotariov, 1977); with large doses of hormone, all the lymphocytes involved in the immune response might be suppressed. Thus, one of the tasks of further research is the study of the mechanisms of endocrine regulation of the functions of different cellular subpopulations and of their role in the organization of the immune response.

With the discovery of adrenoreceptors on lymphocytes, the role of the sympathetic nervous system in the regulation of immunologic processes has been clarified and some idea has been gained as to the route by which sympathetic activation may reach lymphoid cells. Of particular importance in this connection is a consideration of the mechanisms regulating the immune process at the level of the functional element of the organ (Chernukh, 1976), that is, the complex of lymphoid and stromal cells supplied with blood by a common minute vessel and having a common sympathetic and parasympathetic innervation. This is so because changes in the composition of the microenvironment of lymphocytes, including those attending the secretion of epinephrine at the sympathetic fiber endings, affect the functional state of lymphoid cells provided with receptors to epinephrine and norepinephrine.

The most frequently used approach is the pharmacologic analysis of the regulation of these functions by means of substances acting upon the mediator systems—acetylcholine, norepinephrine, and epinephrine. According to the findings of many authors, summarized by Frolov (1974) and Kozlov (1973), the autonomic nervous system is involved in the regulation of immunologic reactions. Studies of the immune response by the rosette-formation reaction, which in different experimental procedures indicates the number of cells either carrying antigen receptors or those involved in the immune response and antibody production (Guschin, 1976), have shown that the use of substances having a M-cholinomimetic action—arecoline and pilocarpine—induces a rise in the number of cells involved in the immune response. The N-cholinomimetic substance, nicotine, increases the number of cells carrying the receptors and, to a lesser extent, affects their differentiation. The opposite effect is produced by benzohexamethonium and pediphen, substances having a N-cholinoblocking effect (Figure 4). These substances also differ in their effect on the index of differentiation of cells involved in the organization of the immune response (Guschin, 1975). These results are a proof of the fact that neurotransmitters can participate in the regulation of immune reactions and in the transmission of impulses from the central regulation apparatus to the effector organs.

Research in this field has revealed experimentally a number of new neurotropic agents which, being adrenoblockers, are accumulated mainly in the hypothalamus and exert a suppressing effect on antibody production (Marat, 1975). Those preparations—pyrroxane and butyroxane—have proved fairly

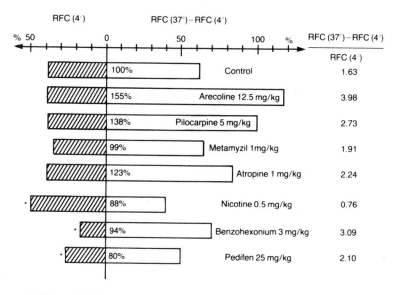

Figure 4. Effect of cholinomimetic and cholinoblocking drugs on the number of rosette-forming cells (RFC) in the spleens of SVA mice on the sixth day after immunization with ram erythrocytes (SRBC's). Figures in the columns indicate changes in the total number of antibody-forming cells (AFC) as percentages of control values. The shaded part of each column indicates the percentage of the RFC at 4°C in the total number of antibody-forming cells (% of young forms of AFC). The unshaded part of each column indicates the percentage of RFC observed additionally at 37°C (without surface Ig-receptors-% of mature AFC). ($p < .05$.)

effective in the treatment of some diseases, for example, in dermatology, in some types of transplanation, and in certain allergic conditions (Shulgina *et al.*, 1973, 1977; Burikina and Krilov, 1975).

The great volume of knowledge accumulated in the past few years in the field of regulation of immune homeostasis has required, naturally, the development of concepts which help to assimilate the sum total of the information obtained.

The complex of available facts suggests that, in evolutionally highly developed animals, there is a system of neurohumoral modulation of the reaction to an antigen.

Schematically, that system is represented in Figure 5, indicating the experimentally verified and possible levels of the system, as well as the routes of regulation of immune homeostasis. These are at the subcellular and cellular levels, and at the levels of the organ, the system, and the organism.

A noteworthy feature is the presence in the immune system of a special cellular regulation channel. Inasmuch as the switch-over from the neurohumoral forms of modulation to the cellular form is carried out at the level of the bone marrow and the thymus gland, studies of the functions of these organs under conditions of neural, hormonal, and other humoral changes appear to be particularly promising. Unfortunately, research in this field has been very scanty.

Present-day views on the regulation of immune homeostasis are based on findings accumulated by different specialists, and take into account the distinctive features of the organization of the process. As pointed out above, the specificity of immunologic reactions is shaped at the level of the interaction between antigens and cells of the lymphoid series. Even at that level there are mechanisms of regulation and autoregulation. The effects of the nervous and hormonal systems are of a modulating character: they change the intensity of immunogenesis within certain limits. The links of a regulating system

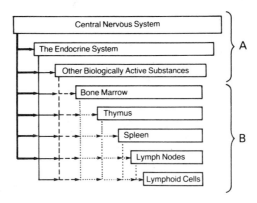

Figure 5. Possible levels and pathways in the regulation of immune homeostasis.

become involved in a process that is governed by intrinsic laws or specific conditions; they may be rigid or flexible (Bechtereva, 1971).

It should be pointed out that the regulating system's organization is complex and hierarchical. The proposed scheme of the regulation of immune homeostasis in the whole organism may be used as a plan for further immunophysiological studies. The immediate tasks and the main focus of such studies in immunophysiology center around an analysis of the mechanisms of the regulation of immune homeostasis at different levels of its integration (Figure 5). Such analyses serve as a basis for our current investigations, and will yield clues to an understanding of the regulation of the intensity of immunologic reactions.

PROSPECTIVE (NHS)

Despite all the impressive evidence listed above, most of the experimental work in neuroimmunomodulation (NIM) lies ahead.

In the realm of *basic* research:

1. The *CNS substrates* for NIM must be more clearly demonstrated and the efferent pathways traced out—in vertebrates (including man) and in invertebrates.

2. The *innervation* of the organs and tissues of the organs of the immune system (bone marrow, thymus, lymphatics, spleen, the entire reticuloendothelial system, etc.) must be studied from a physiological point of view. Although a little is known about their anatomy, almost nothing is known about their afferent and efferent *functional* roles.

3. The *chemical* mediators of NIM must be examined in much more detail: hormones; cybernins; inflammatory and anti-inflammatory agents; neurotransmitters; neuromodulators; the neurally active polypeptides, and so on.

4. At the *cellular* level, the receptor sites for all of these chemical mediators must be found on and within the membrane: on various categories of blast cells, lymphocytes, phagocytes, smooth muscle cells, ganglion cells, and Schwann cells.

5. The role of the CNS in modulating the production of *interferon* (IFN) and other antiviral substances should be explored in detail. In at least one instance, it has been shown that there is a significant positive correlation between the early increase in blood IFN and the eventual rise of circulating antibodies (Ab) in response to a single injection of virus (Spector *et al.,* 1977). NIM has been repeatedly demonstrated for changes in Ab titers, and it is entirely reasonable to expect that similar experimental demonstrations can be made for NIM of IFN production. In view of the fact that IFN is host-species-specific but not species-specific for the invading virus, the enormous clinical significance of NIM in this area is self-evident.

6. The *ontogeny* of all of these reactions should be examined with a view to

understanding CNS effects upon the development of individual immunocompetence.

7. The *chronobiology* of NIM needs to be worked out with respect to
changes as functions of ultradian, circadian, circlunar, annual, and lifetime
rhythms.

8. *Feedback* loops, both neural and chemical, must be studied in the whole
animal, in order to put all of this information into a useful perspective and to
understand the functioning of the whole organism.

All of these studies will require close collaboration among neurobiologists,
immunologists, endocrinologists, virologists and specialists from other
disciplines.

In the *clinical* sphere, we will have to begin replacing old wives' tales and
other anecdotal material from psychiatrists, professors of medicine, and
novelists, with some hard data.

What mechanisms are involved in the "spontaneous" remission of
cancer? . . . in the various individual sensitivities to virus, bacteria, parasites,
and assorted other antigens? . . . in autoimmune diseases? . . . in different
responses to pharmacologic agents? . . . in individual differences in nutritional requirements for healthy functioning of the nervous and immune
systems?

Among other benefits from such inquiries will be the great reduction in incidence of iatrogenic and nosocomial diseases. Many physicians who fail to
understand a set of symptoms and signs prescribe tranquilizers, dismiss the
problem (and the patient) by labeling the patient a "crock," or by labeling the
disease "psychosomatic." This leaves the drug company richer and the patient sicker. To these practitioners, "psychosomatic" does not mean what the
term originally was designed to describe (i.e., the *unity* of "psyche" and
"soma"). To them, the term means: having "psychological" and therefore illusory character. While the prescription of "uppers" or "downers"
represents an unconscious acknowledgment by the physician of CNS influences upon "somatic" problems, the mechanisms of NIM are unfortunately not so simple that a drug can correct any disease.

Some immunologists have taken this author to task with the
query: "Why do you say that the nervous system controls the immune system
. . . why don't you say that the immune system controls the nervous system?"
The answer is obvious, and future research will make it clear: they control
each other.

ACKNOWLEDGMENTS

We thank I. Auston of the National Library of Medicine (NIH) for volunteering her time for
the correction and verification of many of the Russian references. Not all were traceable;
therefore, the responsibility for any remaining errors is not Ms. Auston's. We thank also D.

Lonsdale for her patience in typing and retyping large portions of the manuscript, and David Spector, Nick Hall, Don Dwyer and Carol Gertz for their helpful suggestions and corrections of the manuscript.

REFERENCES[1]

Ado, A. D. (1952). "Antigens as Extraordinary Irritants of the Nervous System." Moscow.

Ambrose, C. T. (1970). The essential role of corticosteriods in the induction of the immune response *in vitro*. In *"Hormones and the Immune Response"* (G. E. W. Wolstenholme and Julie Knight, Eds.), *Ciba Found. Study Group* **36**, 100–116.

Amkraut, A., and Solomon, G. F. (1974). From the symbolic stimulus to the pathophysiologic response: Immune mechanisms. *Int. J. Psychiatry Med.* **5**(4), 542–563.

Baciu, I. (1946). The role of the central nervous system in the induction of the phagocytic reaction. Doctoral Dissertation, Institute of Physiology and Medical Physics, University of Cluj (in Romanian, English translation available).

Baciu, I. (1962). La régulation nerveuse et humorale de l'erythropoiese. *J. Physiol. (Paris)* **54**, 441–458.

Baciu, I. (1978). La physiologie du système phagocytaire. *Arch. Union Med. Balk.* **16**(3,4), 473–476.

Bechtereva, N. P. (1971). "Neurophysiological Aspects of Human Mental Activity." Meditsina, (Moscow).

Benetato, F., Sovailescu, L., and Baciu, I. (1945). Sistemul nervos central si functiunea de aparare. Mecanismul nervos central al activitatii fagocitare (contributuni experimentale). *Ardealul Med.* **2**, 49–52 (Romanian).

Besedovsky, H., and Sorkin, E. (1977). Network of immune–neuroendocrine interactions. *Clin. Exp. Immunol.* **27**(1), 1–12.

Besedovsky, H., Sorkin, E., Felix, D., and Haas, H. (1977). Hypothalamic changes during the immune response. *Eur. J. Immunol.* **7**(5), 323–325.

Bourne, H. R., Lichtenstein, L. M., Melmon, K. L., Henney, C. S., Weinstein, Y., and Shearer, G. M. (1974). Modulation of inflammation and immunity by cyclic AMP. *Science* **184**, 19–28.

Broun, G. V. (1969). "Characteristics of the Functional State of Some Hypothalamic Structures in Experimental Tuberculosis." Avtoref. diss. kand, Leningrad.

Broun, G. V., Mogutov, S. S., and Kan, G. G. (1970). The role of some hypothalamic structures in the regulation of immune processes after immunization by vaccine BCG. *Byull. Eksp. Biol. Med.* **70**(7), 74–78.

Burikina, G. N., and Krilov, S. S. (1975). The disturbances of hypothalamo–hypophysial system in pathogenesis of allergic dermatitis and the possibilities of medicinal therapy. *In* "First All-Union Symposium, Neurohumoral and Pharmacological Correction of Immunological Reactions in the Clinic and Experiments," pp. 7–8. Leningrad.

Chebotariov, V. F. (1979). "Endocrinal Regulation of Immunogenesis." Kiev.

Chernigovskaia, N. V., Korneva, E. A., Konovalov, G. V., and Khai, L. M. (1975). Mesodiencephalic brain structures in the pathogenesis of demyelinization diseases of the nervous system. *In* "Demyelinization Diseases of the Nervous System in the Clinic and in Experiments," pp. 226–334. Minsk.

Chernukh, A. M. (1976). Functional element–organ–organism. "Mechanisms of alteration, resistance, adaptation and compensation." *In* "Proceedings of the Second All-Union Conference of Pathophysiologists." Vol. 1, pp. 13–17. Tashkent.

[1] References in Russian journals are in Russian language unless otherwise indicated. Some have English abstracts. Titles have been translated herein to English.

Cohen, P., and Gershon, R. K. (1975). The role of cortisone-sensitive thymocytes in DNA synthetic responses to antigen. *Ann. N.Y. Acad. Sci.* **249**, 451–461.

Cross, R. J., Markesbery, W. R., Brooks, W. H., and Roszman, T. L. (1980). The acute effect of hypothalamic lesions on the immune response. *Fed. Proc., Fed. Am. Soc. Exp. Biol.* **39**(3), 1162 (abstr.).

Devoino, L. V. (1979). Serotoninergic system of raphe nucleus of the midbrain in immune reaction regulation. *Vyssch. Funkzii Mozga Norme Pathol.*

Dolin, A. O., and Dolina, C. A. (1972). "Pathology of Higher Nervous Functions (in Russian). Vysshaya Shkola, Moscow.

Dostoevskaia, L. P., and Shkhinek, E. K. (1981). Episodic stress and immune reactions. (In press.)

Eskra, J. D., Stevens, J. S., and Carty, T. J. (1978). B_2-adrenergic receptors in thymocytes. *Fed. Proc., Fed. Am. Soc. Exp. Biol.* **37**(3), 687 (abstr.).

Fauci, A. S., Pratt, K. R., and Whalen, G. (1977). Activation of human B lymphocytes. IV. Regulatory effects of corticosteroids on the triggering signal in the plaque-forming cell response of human peripheral blood B lymphocytes to polyclonal activation. *J. Immunol.* **119**(2), 598–603.

Filipp, G. (1973). Mechanism of suppressing anaphylaxis through electrolytic lesion of the tuberal region of the hypothalamus. *Ann. Allergy* **31**(6), 272–278.

Filipp, G., Szentiványi, A., and Mess, B. (1952). Anaphylaxis and the nervous system. *Acta Med. Acad. Sci. Hung.* **3**(2), 163–173.

Fivkova, E., and Marsala, J. (1960). A Stereotaxic Atlas of the Brains of the Cat, Rabbit and Rat. (Prague).

Freedman, D. X., and Fenichel, D. (1958). Effect of midbrain lesion on experimental allergy. *Arch. Neurol. Psychiatry* **79**, 164–169.

Frolov, E. P. (1974). "Neurohumoral Mechanisms of Regulation of Immunological Processes." Meditsina, Moscow.

Gordon, M. A., Cohen, J. J., and Wilson, I. B. (1978). Muscarinic cholinergic receptors in murine lymphocytes: Demonstration by direct binding. *Proc. Natl. Acad. Sci. U.S.A.* **75**(6), 2902–2904.

Guschin, G. V. (1975). The immune rosette-formation in inbred mice treated by some neurotropic drugs. *In* "Neurohumoral and Pharmacological Correction of Immune Reactions in the Clinic and Experiment," pp. 16–17. Leningrad.

Guschin, G. V. (1976). Participation of antibodies synthesized *in vitro* in rosette-formation. *Byull. Eksp. Biol. Med.* **82**(9), 1090–1092.

Hadden, J. W., Johnson, E. M., Hadden, E. M., Coffey, R. G., and Johnson, L. D. (1975). Cyclic GMP and lymphocyte activation. *In* "Immune Recognition" (A. S. Rosenthal, ed.), pp. 359–389. Academic Press, New York.

Haitov, R. M. (1977). Migration of "T" and "B" lymphocytes. *Obshch. Vopr. Patol.* pp. 35–60.

Hall, N. R., Lewis, J. K., Schimpff, R. D., Smith, R. T., Trescot, A. M., Gray, H. E., Wenzel, S. E., Abraham, W. C., and Zornetzer, S. F. (1978). Effects of diencephalic and brainstem lesions on haemopoietic stem cells. *Soc. Neurosci. Abstr.* **4**, 20.

Hall, N. R., Lewis, J. K., Smith, R. T., and Zornetzer, S. F. (1979). Effects of the locus coeruleus and anterior hypothalamic brain lesions on antibody formation in mice. *Soc. Neurosci. Abstr.* **5**, 511.

Janković, B. D., and Isaković, K. (1973). Neuro-endocrine correlates of immune response. I. Effects of brain lesions on antibody production, Arthus reactivity and delayed hypersensitivity in the rat. *Int. Arch. Allergy Appl. Neurol.* **45**, 360–372.

Kanda, R. (1959). Studies of the regulation centre on promotion of antibody II. On the migration and relation of normal precipitin antibody and leucocyte in the peripheral blood by electric stimuli in the hypothalamus of rabbit. *Jpn. J. Bacteriol.* **14**(6), 542–545.

Karlson, P. (1963). New concepts on the mode of action of hormones. *Perspect. Biol. Med.* **6**(2), 203–214.

Klimenko, V. M. (1972). The study of some neuronal mechanisms of hypothalamic regulation of immune reactions in rabbits. Avtoref. kand. diss., Institute for Experimental Medicine, Acad. Med. Sci. USSR Leningrad.

Klimenko, V. M. (1975). The dynamics of neuronal activity reconstruction during the last periods of immunogenesis. Tesisy Dokl., Leningrad.

Klimenko, V. M., and Kaplunovsky, A. S. (1972). A statistical investigation of the (unit electrical) impulse activity of the neurons of the rabbit hypothalamic areas. Fiziol. Zh. SSSR im. I. M. Sechenova 58(10), 1484–1493.

Klimenko, V. M., Kaplunovsky, A. S., and Neroslavsky, I. A. (1972). Automatic classification of multiparametric experimental data. Fiziol. Zh. SSSR im. I. M. Sechenova 58(4), 599–602.

Korneva, E. A., and Khai, L. M. (1961). Participation of the sympatho-adrenal system and some parts of the hypothalamus in the regulation of immunogenesis. In "First Conference on the Physiology of the Autonomic Nervous System and the Cerebellum," pp. 107–108. Erevan.

Korneva, E. A., and Khai, L. M. (1967). Effect of the stimulation of different structures of the mesencephalon on the course of immunological reactions. Fiziol. Zh. SSSR im I. M. Sechenova 53(1), 42–27 (Russian).

Korneva, E. A., and Klimenko, V. M. (1976). Neuronale Hypothalamusaktivität und Homöostatische Reaktionen. Ergebn. exp. Med. 23, 373–382.

Korneva, E. A., and Klimenko, V. M. (1979). The use of factor analysis for studying hypothalamic functions. Automedica 3, 47–56.

Korneva, E. A., Klimenko, V. M., and Shkhinek, E. K., (1978). "Neurohumoral Maintenance of Immune Homeostasis." Nauka, Leningrad. (English translation of this book in preparation: U. of Chicago Press)

Kozlov, V. K. (1973). "Anaphylaxis and the Vegetative Nervous System." Meditsina, Moscow.

Kozlov, V. A., and Tsyrlova, I. G. (1976). Effect on truncal haemopoetic elements of the bone marrow of mice hybrids (CBS X C57BL)F₁. Izv. Akad. Nauk SSSR, Ser. Biol. No. 6, pp. 914–917.

Kozlov, V. A., and Tsyrlova, I. G. (1978). Change in the proliferative activity of the polypotent haemopoetic stem cells provoked by injection of glucocorticoids and androgens. Dokl. Adad. Nauk SSSR 238(2), 501–503.

Luk'yanenko, V. I. (1961). The problem of conditioned-reflex regulation of immunologic reactions. Usp. Sovrem. Biol. 51(2), 170–187.

Luparello, T. J., Stein, M., and Park, C. D. (1964). Effect of hypothalamic lesions on rat anaphylaxis. Am. J. Physiol. 207, 911–914.

Macris, N. T., Schiavi, R. C., Camerino, M. S., and Stein, M. (1970). Effect of hypothalamic lesions on immune processes in the guinea pig. Am. J. Physiol. 219, 1205–1209.

Magaeva, S. V., Borisova, E. S., and Strukova, L. G. (1968). The analysis of some structures of the hypothalamus in the regulation of accumulation of antimicrobe antibodies in blood. Tr. Inst. Norm. Patol. Fiziol. Akad. Med. Nauk SSSR 11, 53–55.

Marat, B. A. (1975). The analysis of influences of some neurotropical pharmacological substances on the immune response. In "First All-Union Conference: Neurohumoral and Pharmacological Correction of the Immune Reaction in the Clinic and Experiments," pp. 46ff. Leningrad.

Mason, J. (1974). Specificity in the organization of neuroendocrine response profiles. In "Frontiers in Neurology and Neurosciences Research" (P. Seeman and G. Brown, eds.), pp. 68–80. Univ. of Toronto Press, Toronto.

Mason, J. (1975). Emotion as reflected in patterns of endocrine integration. In "Emotions—Their Parameters and Measurement" (L. Levi, ed.), pp. 143–181. Raven Press, New York.

Metal'nikov, S. (1934). "Role de Système Nerveux et des Facteurs Biologiques et Psychiques dans l'Immunité." Paris, Masson.

Mogutov, S. S. (1972). A study of the functional state of some parts of the nervous system after the postvaccinal reorganization of the organism following the injection of BCG vaccine. Avtoref. diss. kand., Leningrad.

Monjan, A. A., and Collector, M. I. (1977). Stress-induced modulation of the immune response. Science 196, 307–308.

Paunović, V. R., Petrović, S., and Janković, B. D. (1976). Influence of early postnatal hypothalamic lesions on immune responses of adult rats. *Period. Biol.* **78**, 50.

Petrov, R. V. (1976). "Immunology and Immunogenetics." Moscow.

Petrov, R. V. (1978). Preface to the book. "Immunology," Vol. 7, pp. 5-11. Moscow.

Polyak, A. I. (1969). Some mechanisms of regulation of immune phenomena. Avtoref. dokt. diss., Perm.

Polyak, A. I. (1979). Mechanisms of regulation of immunologic and allergic reactions. *In* "Collection of Articles: Higher Functions of Brain in Health and in Pathology" pp. 127-135. (Leningrad).

Polyak, A. I., and Zotova, V. V. (1975). Mechanisms of neurohumoral regulation of the autoimmune process in lymphoid tissue. *In* "First All-Union Conference, Neurohormonal and Pharmacological Correction of Immune Reactions in the Clinic and Experiments," pp. 53-54. Leningrad.

Protasova, T. N. (1975). "Hormonal Regulation of Fermental Activity." Meditsina, Moscow.

Pryzbylski, A. (1962). Effect of the removal of the cortex cerebri and the quadrigeminal bodies region on histamine susceptibility of guinea pigs. *Acta Physiol. Pol.* **13**, 535-541.

Roszkowski, W., Plaut, M., and Lichtenstein, L. M. (1977). Selective display of histamine receptors on lymphocytes. *Science* **195**, 683-685.

Selye, H. (1950). "The Physiology and Pathology of Exposure to Stress." Acta, Inc., Montreal.

Shatilova, N. V., Undritrov, M. I., Frolov, E. P., Lukitchova, T. I., and Vinitskaya, E. B. (1970). A study of the role of mediators in the development of allergic alteration of leucocytes during streptococcal allergy of the immediate type. *Proc. 5th Conf. Pathophysiol.,* **19** pp. 60-61.

Shekoyan, V. A. (1976). Immunogenic activity of antigen, connected with RNA and lysomal fractions of macrophages of rabbits with coagulated posterior hypothalamus. *Zh. Eksp. Klin. Med.* **16**(2), 12-16.

Shekoyan, V. A., Khasman, E. L., and Uchitel, I. Y. (1975). The effect of structures of the anterior and posterior hypothalamus on the engulfment and digestion of antigen by macrophages and on the clearance of Indian ink. *Zh. Mikrobiol., Epidemiol. Immunobiol.* No. 3, pp. 131-135.

Shkhinek, E. K. (1978). Hormones and the immune response. *In* "Neurohumoral Maintenance of Immune Homeostasis" (E. A. Korneva, V. M. Klimenko, and E. K. Shkhinek, eds.) Nauka, Leningrad.

Shkhinek, E. K., Svetkova, I. P., and Marat, B. A. (1973). Analysis of neuroendocrinal influence of the posterior hypothalamus on the pattern of specific defense reactions in rabbits. *Fiziol. Zh. SSSR im. I. M. Sechenova* **59**(2), 228-236.

Shulgina, N. S., Golubeva, N. N., Korneva, E. A., Pichtar, V. I., Savchuk, L. N., and Marat, B. A. (1973). Special features of the development of the burn process in corneas of immunosuppressed animals. *Ophthalmology* (Kiev), Vol. 3, 103-109.

Shulgina, N. S., Nikulina, N. V., Savchuck, L. N., and Pichtar, V. I. (1977). Pharmacological action of butirocsan on the reaction of incompatibility after corneal transplantation. *In* "Second Symposium on Physiology of Immune Homeostasis," pp. 141-143. Rostov-na Donu.

Solomon, G. F., Amkraut, A. A., and Kasper, P. (1974). Immunity, emotions and stress. *Ann. Clin. Res.* **6**, 313-322.

Spector, N. H. (1979). Can hypothalamic lesions change circulating antibody or interferon responses to antigens? *In* "The Pathogenesis of Allergic Processes in Experiment and in the Clinic (Festschrift for A. D. Ado) (A. M. Chernukh and V. I. Pytskii, eds.), pp. 21-37 Meditsina, Moscow (in Russian).

Spector, N. H. (1980). The central state of the hypothalamus in health and disease: Old and new concepts. *In Physiology of the Hypothalamus* "Handbook of the Hypothalamus" (P. Morgane and J. Panksepp, eds.), Vol. II, Chapter 6. Dekker, New York.

Spector, N. H., Martin, L. K., Diggs, C. L., and Koob, G. F. (1974). Hypothalamic lesions: Effects upon malaria and antibody production in rats. *Proc. Int. Union Physiol. Sci.* **26**, (abstr.).

Spector, N. H., Cannon, L. T., Diggs, C. L., Morrison, J. E., and Koob, G. F. (1975). Hypothalamic lesions: Effects on immunological responses. *Physiologist* **18**: 401 (abstr.).

Spector, N. H., Koob, G. F., and Baron, S. (1977). Hypothalamic influence upon interferon and antibody responses to Newcastle Disease Virus infection: Preliminary report. *Proc. Int. Union Physiol. Sci.* **13**, 711 (abstr.).

Stein, M., Schiavi, R. C., and Luparello, T. J. (1969). The hypothalamus and immune process. *Ann. N.Y. Acad. Sci.* **164**, 464–472.

Stein, M., Schiavi, R. C., and Camerino, M. S. (1976). Influence of brain and behavior on the immune system. *Science* **191**, 435–440.

Szentiványi, A., and Filipp, G. (1958). Anaphylaxis and the nervous system. Part II. *Ann. Allergy* **16**, 143–151.

Tsypin, A. B., and Maltzev, V. N. (1967). The effects of irritation of the hypothalamus on the concentration of normal antibodies in blood. *Patol. Fiziol.* **11**(5), 83–84.

Tyrey, L. (1969). The effect of anterior hypothalamic lesions on immunogenesis in the rat. Ph.D. Thesis, University of Illinois, Urbana.

Valueva, T. K., and Chebotariov, V. F. (1977). Thymosin, hormones of epinephrine cortex and cellular immunity. *In* "New Facts About Hormones and the Mechanisms of Their Action," pp. 313–322. Kiev.

Warejka, D. J., and Levy, N. L. (1980). Central nervous system control of the immune response: Effect of hypothalamic lesions on PHA responsiveness in rats. *Fed. Proc., Fed. Am. Soc. Exp. Biol.* **39**(3), 914 (abstr.).

Neuroendocrinology and the Immune Process[1]

DAVID MACLEAN
SEYMOUR REICHLIN

INTRODUCTION—NEUROENDOCRINE MECHANISMS AS POTENTIAL MODULATORS OF THE IMMUNE RESPONSE

The purpose of this chapter is to review the ways in which the nervous system can modulate the immune response and to outline potential neuroregulatory mechanisms that have not as yet been fully characterized (Figure 1). The best understood mechanism by which the brain can influence immune function involves hormones that are under control of the hypothalamic–pituitary axis. The hypothalamus directly controls the secretion of all known pituitary tropic hormones, including those that act indirectly through the target glands (adrenal cortex, thyroid gland, and gonads) or directly on target tissues (growth hormone (GH) and prolactin). The pituitary gland secretes a number of other factors whose effects on the immune system are unknown. Some, such as β-lipotropin and β-endorphin, are under hypothalamic control; others, such as fibroblast growth factors (Gospodarowicz, 1975) and the recently described thymocyte stimulating factor (Saxena and Talwar, 1977), by analogy with other pituitary hormones,

[1] Studies from the authors' laboratory cited in this review were supported by USPHS Grants AM 16684 and AM 07039.

475

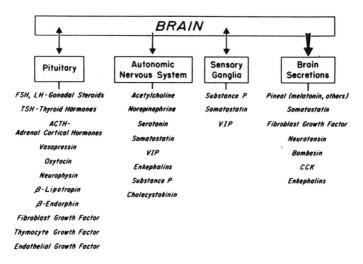

Figure 1. Summary of neuroendocrine mechanisms by which the brain might modulate immune function. Several of the neuropeptides are secreted by more than one anatomic subdivision of the nervous system.

may also be under hypothalamic regulatory control. Because hypothalamic activity is in turn influenced by neural impulses from the visceral brain, by environmental stimuli, and by intrinsic circadian rhythms, any pituitary secretion is potentially capable of being influenced by stress and affective state. Hypothalamic effects on immune function in animals have been demonstrated (see other chapters in this volume; also Janković *et al.*, 1973; Stein *et al.*, 1976) which may be mediated by neuroendocrine mechanisms. Feedback control of the hypothalamus by some component of the immune response has also been postulated (Besedovsky *et al.*, 1977; Srebro and Brodzicki, 1978).

Brain modulation of the immune response may possibly be mediated by direct secretion of brain peptides into the general circulation. The best characterized of the peptides of brain origin that enter the peripheral circulation are vasopressin (antidiuretic hormone, ADH), oxytocin, and neurophysin, all of which are synthesized in the hypothalamus, stored in the neural lobe of the hypophysis, and released into the general circulation under the influence of neural signals. The hypothalamus and other parts of the brain also contain a wide variety of biologically active peptides of established structure, some or all of which can enter the peripheral circulation. Most of these substances are secreted by other structures in the body, especially the gastrointestinal tract; in fact, the brain contribution to peripheral blood is only a minor component of total circulating peptide. (See Table 1 for a detailed summary). In addition to the established neuropeptides, several other biologic activities of potential interest to the immunologist have been identified in brain extracts. These include endothelial growth factor (Maciag *et al.*,

1979) and brain growth factor (Tanaka *et al.*, 1979). Whether these substances are true secretions is not known.

Another neurosecretion derived from neural tissue, and under control of the brain, is melatonin, the indole secretion of the pineal. Melatonin is released into the blood in response to both an endogenous rhythm and to a "lights off" signal by mechanisms mediated through the sympathetic ganglia innervating the pineal. The effects of melatonin on the immune process are unknown; a number of other pineal factors also of unknown relevance to immunity have been identified in pineal extracts.

A fourth potential mechanism of neuroendocrine modulation of the immune response is by the way of the autonomic or peripheral nervous system. In addition to the secretion of classical neurotransmitters, acetylcholine and noradrenalin, the autonomic nervous system is now recognized to secrete a variety of neuroregulatory peptides including somatostatin and vasoactive intestinal peptide (VIP). A subpopulation of primary sensory neurons secrete Substance P and somatostatin from nerve endings. The autonomic nervous system and the sensory afferent system thus constitute nerve networks capable of modifying the peripheral cellular milieu.

Finally, a fifth mechanism by which the brain could modulate the immune response is indirectly through changes in behavior and autonomic regulation that are closely linked to neuroendocrine mechanisms. These include changes in nutritional state brought about by altered feeding behavior, elevated or depressed body temperature, abnormal sleep–wake cycles, altered circadian rhythms, major modifications in distribution of vascular volumes, and modifications of local vascular reactions.

The possible sites of action of any or all of the above mechanisms are potentially as complex as the immune system itself. Any of the subclasses of immune cells may be affected, for example, helper or suppressor lymphocytes, B-lymphocytes, macrophages, and killer cells (e.g., Cantor and Gershon, 1979; Dutton and Scavulli, 1975; Eidinger and Garrett, 1972). Effects on cells can be specific by modifying secretion of immune factors, such as migration inhibition factor or other lymphokines, or by nonspecific metabolic changes in immune cell function. Neuroendocrine influences could be mediated by changing the secretion of thymus factors, by modifying patterns of blood flow through immunogenic tissues, or by influencing the secondary components of the immune response such as complement generation, vascular reactivity, and local release of tissue damaging factors from leukocytes and platelets (e.g., Roubinian *et al.*, 1979). A summary of potential neuroendocrine regulatory mechanisms is outlined schematically in Figure 1.

A review of the known effects of established hormones on the immune response are reviewed in this volume by Alqvist and Pierpaoli; see also Dougherty (1952), Medawar and Sparrow (1956), Talwar *et al.* (1975), Gisler and Schenkel-Hulliger (1971), Maor *et al.* (1974), Ahlqvist (1976), and Nagy and Berczi (1979). In this chapter we will deal with brain control of hormones and neuropeptides rather than with hormonal effects on the immune response. For reviews of neuroendocrine mechanisms see Martin *et al.* (1977), Martini and Besser (1977), and Reichlin *et al.* (1978).

NEUROSECRETION

The Scharrers first (1940) hypothesized that the peptides of the neurohypophysis, oxytocin and vasopressin, were in fact formed by specialized hypothalamic neurons and transported within axons to the neural lobe for ultimate release into the peripheral blood. In the late 1940s Harris and collaborators (1948) proposed and elaborated the hypophysial portal chemotransmitter hypothesis of anterior pituitary control which stated that the factors regulating the anterior lobe are formed by hypothalamic neurons (later termed hypophysiotropic neurons), to be released into the hypophysial portal circulation and carried to the anterior pituitary where they stimulate the synthesis and release of pituitary hormones. Both of these hypotheses have been confirmed and rationalized into a unified theory of neurosecretion in which the nervous system controls endocrine function. Neurosecretion is the phenomenon of synthesis and secretion of specific substances by neurons. Some neurosecretions are exported into the peripheral or hypophysial blood and act as true hormones; others, released in close apposition to other neurons, can act as neurotransmitters or neuromodulators. Translation of neuronal signals into chemical signals was termed by Wurtman and Anton-Tay (1969), "neuroendocrine transduction," and the cells themselves, neuroendocrine transductors.

Two types of neurotransducer cells regulate visceral function: (*a*) neurosecretomotor, in which the neurosecretion acts directly through synapses on gland cells; and (*b*) neuroendocrine, in which the neurosecretion passes into the blood and acts on distant targets (Figure 2). Neurosecretory cells, as far as is known, possess in common with other neurons the usual aspects of neuron function. They transmit action potentials along their axons in an electrophysiological manner identical to normal unmyelinated neurons, and the action potential triggers release of secretory granules from nerve endings by calcium-dependent exocytosis (Renaud *et al.*, 1979). The secretory product is synthesized in cell bodies and transported to axon terminals.

THE HYPOTHALAMIC-PITUITARY AXIS

The Tuberohypophysial System

The pituitary gland of man is divided into two main functional units, the neural lobe (posterior lobe) and the adenohypophysis (anterior lobe, pars

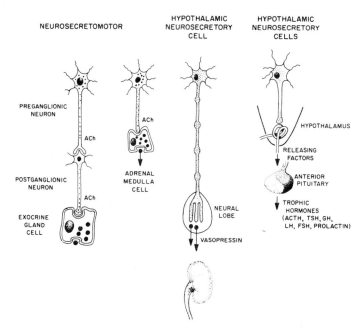

Figure 2. Types of neuroendocrine transducer systems. *Left*, Neurosecretomotor neurons. Postganglionic or preganglionic sympathetic fibers make direct synaptic contact with hormone-secreting cells. *Right*, Hypothalamic neurosecretory neurons. Neurosecretory neurons of the supraoptic system release ADH (vasopressin) into the systemic blood stream. Hypothalamic tuberoinfundibular neurons release hypophysiotropic hormones (releasing factors) into the pituitary portal system to regulate secretion of hormones from the anterior pituitary. *Abbreviations:* ACh, acetylcholine; ACTH, adrenocorticotropin; TSH, thyroid stimulating hormone (thyrotropin); GH, growth hormone (somatotropin); LH, luteinizing hormone: FSH, follicle stimulating hormone. From Martin, *et al.*, (1977), F. A. Davis Company, Philadelphia, with permission.

distalis). In many lower forms, such as the rat, an intermediate lobe (derived embryologically from the same anlage as the anterior lobe) is also present; but, in man, intermediate lobe cells are dispersed throughout the pituitary gland. This point is made here because recent work indicates that in species with defined intermediate lobes the structure contains β-endorphin, CLIP (corticotropin-like intermediate lobe protein), and enzymes that process ACTH in a manner different from the anterior lobe. As a consequence, studies of intermediate lobe in rat, the most commonly used experimental animal, are not directly applicable to man (Liotta *et al.*, 1978).

The neural lobe (Figure 3) is anatomically part of the neurohypophysis which is commonly viewed as consisting of three portions, the neural lobe itself (infundibular process, posterior pituitary), the stalk, and the infundibulum, the latter forming the base of the third ventricle (Reichlin, 1974, 1980; Flerkó, 1980). In fact, there is a fourth intrahypothalamic component

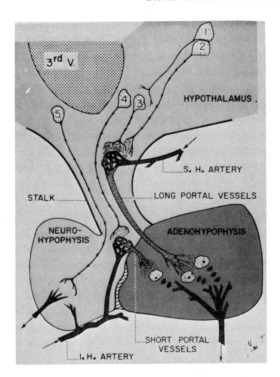

Figure 3. Neural control of pituitary gland. This figure summarizes the types of neural inputs into pituitary regulation. Neuron 5 represents the peptidergic neurons of the supraopticohypophysial and paraventriculohypophysial tracts, with hormone-producing cell bodies in the hypothalamus and nerve terminals in the neural lobe. Neurons 4 and 3 are the peptidergic neurons of the tubero-hypophysial tract, which secrete the hypophysiotropic hormones into the substance of the median eminence. Neuron 4 ends low in the stalk. Neuron 1 represents a monoaminergic neuron ending in relation to the cell body of the peptidergic neuron. Neuron 2 represents a monoaminergic neuron ending on terminals of the peptidergic neuron to give axo-axonic transmission. Neurons 1 and 2 are the functional links between the remainder of the brain and the peptidergic neuron. From Gay (1972). Reproduced with the permission of the publisher. The American Fertility Society.

of the neurohypophysial system that consists of the cells of origin of the two principal nerve tracts that terminate in the neural lobe—supraopticohypophysial and paraventriculohypophysial. Secretions of the neurohypophysial neurons are vasopressin (antidiuretic hormone, ADH), and oxytocin, each of which is synthesized within the cell bodies in association with specific proteins, the neurophysins. Most workers believe that cells of these systems contain one or the other peptide and the respective specific neurophysin (Robinson, 1978). Vasopressin, oxytocin, and at least two forms of neurophysin are secreted into the blood and are known to be under the control of the nervous system, to be responsive to appropriate physiological stimuli, and to be altered by certain stressful conditions.

The anterior lobe receives no direct nerve supply; nevertheless, each of its secretions are under control of the hypothalamus. Control is mediated by chemical factors (hypophysiotropic hormones, releasing factors) secreted by hypothalamic neurons of the tuberohypophysial system, which are released in the interstitial space of the base of the third ventricle (infundibulum, median eminence) and then diffuse into the capillary plexus of the median eminence that is interposed between the peripheral arterial system and the pituitary sinusoidal circulation. By this anatomical arrangement, neurohumoral mediators formed within the hypothalamus are brought into direct contact with the cells of the adenohypophysis.

The hypothalamus itself, a highly primitive portion of the brain with important functions in visceral regulation, homeostasis, behavior, and endocrine control, lies in the lower portion of the diencephalon, bounded anteriorly by the optic chiasm, laterally by the medial sulci of the temporal lobes, and posteriorly by the mammillary bodies (Haymaker et al., 1969). Superiorly, it is bounded by the thalamus. The neurovascular complex that forms the contact area for transfer of the hypophysiotropic factors is the median eminence of the tuber cinereum, the central mound that corresponds externally to the floor of the third ventricle. The median eminence and the subjacent stalk that in the neuroendocrine literature is commonly called the stalk–median eminence (SME) contains most of the termini of the hypophysiotropic neurons and is very rich in hypophysiotropic hormones which are stored in this region.

Two principal groups of peptidergic (peptide secreting) hypothalamic neurons project to the SME and the pituitary gland. In addition, at least one important group of bioaminergic neurons (dopamine secreting) also project to the SME (Joseph and Knigge, 1978). Large neurons of the supraoptic and paraventricular nuclei project to the neural lobe, and also to the median eminence where they may be involved in regulation of the anterior lobe. Small-sized neurons, which are the bulk of regulatory neurons, project from various parts of the hypothalamus, some well-defined nuclei, and others more diffusely distributed as far anteriorly as the preoptic area (Alpert el al., 1976; Krisch, 1978; Fuxe et al., 1979). Their distribution has been plotted most recently by immunohistochemical methods using antisera to identify releasing hormones (Figure 4; Fuxe et al., 1979; Bugnon et al., 1978). By this technique zones of the hypothalamus that have hypophysiotropic function have been defined. Their electrophysiological and biochemical functions have also been characterized. An important fact is that hypophysiotropic neuron cell bodies are distributed most heavily immediately beneath the ependymal lining of the third ventricle, a location of possible importance because of the close contact with the cerebrospinal fluid. From this area, secretions could enter the cerebrospinal fluid, and, contrariwise, substances in the cerebrospinal fluid could enter the hypophysiotropic neurons (Lechan et al., 1980).

Most of the hypophysiotropic neurons are peptide secreting (peptidergic).

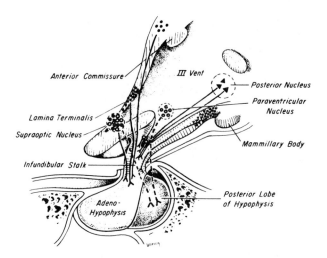

Figure 4. Diagram of basal hypothalamus and pituitary with known pathways of releasing and inhibitory factors. Solid triangles represent the cell bodies of origin of thyrotropin releasing hormone (TRH) tracts which end in the median eminence. Closed circles represent the cell bodies of origin of luteinizing hormone releasing hormone (LHRH) tracts which end in the median eminence and stalk. Open circles represent the cell bodies of origin of the somatostatin tracts which end in the median eminence and posterior pituitary. See text for references. From Molitch and Reichlin (1980).

The important exception is the dopaminergic tuberoinfundibular pathway which arises in cell bodies located principally in the hypothalamic arcuate nuclei and periventricular nuclei and project to the outer zone of the median eminence. Here dopamine acts not as a neurotransmitter but as a hypophysiotropic hormone, entering the portal circulation and inhibiting prolactin and thyrotropin release. Dopaminergic nerve fibers arising from cell bodies outside the hypothalamus terminate on dendrites and soma of some or all hypophysiotropic neurons to form synapses. They may terminate within the substance of the median eminence as well, where after release they may alter the function of other tuberohypophysial neurons. The presence of axoaxonic connections in the median eminence, though postulated on the basis of pharmacologic studies, have not been demonstrated by structural analysis. The several sites in which dopamine can modify pituitary secretion (projections to the hypothalamus, projections from hypothalamus to the pituitary, and the pituitary itself) account for some of the difficulties encountered in interpreting the effects of dopamine agonists and antagonists on pituitary secretion. The hypothalamic dopaminergic nuclei also project to the intermediate lobe in species such as the rat that have a defined structure. In this site they produce tonic suppression of intermediate lobe secretion (Moore and Bloom, 1978).

Connections between the Hypothalamus and Other Brain Centers

Tuberoinfundibular neurons form the final common pathway for neural control of anterior pituitary secretion. These neurons are under control (usually negative feedback) by the hormones whose secretions they regulate. They have a wealth of axonal connections with other parts of the brain that integrate their release with other autonomic, visceral, and emotive functions. Within the hypothalamus, neural centers controlling appetite, temperature, and cardiovascular homeostasis, and diurnal rhythms all project to the medial basal hypothalamus.

The most important ascending pathways to which the tuberohypophysial neurons respond are the dopaminergic, noradrenergic, and serotonergic pathways that arise in the brainstem (Figure 5) (Moore and Bloom, 1979; Palkovits, 1979; Krulich, 1979). These pathways were initially mapped by the formaldehyde-induced fluorescence technique of Falck–Hillarp and more recently by immunohistochemical techniques utilizing antisera directed against the enzymes that synthesize the bioamine neurotransmitters. Dopaminergic cell bodies projecting to the hypothalamus are found in the substantia nigra of the midbrain, and the adjacent ventral tegmental gray area of the midbrain and pons. The principal source of dopamine in the hypothalamus, however, is a distinct tract that arises in the arcuate nucleus itself and terminates in the infundibulum. Noradrenergic neurons projecting to the hypothalamus arise in

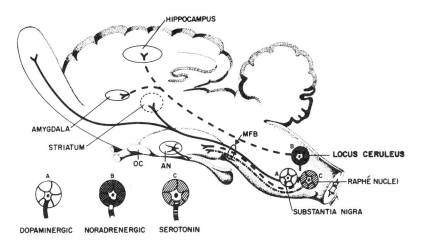

Figure 5. Monoaminergic pathways in mammalian brain—the principal localization of neurons containing norepinephrine, dopamine, and serotonin. *Abbreviations:* MFB, medial forebrain bundle; AN, arcuate nucleus; OC optic chiasm. From Martin, *et al.* (1977), F. A. Davis Company, Philadelphia, with permission.

the locus ceruleus and adjacent regions, but other noradrenergic fibers projecting from hindbrain may indirectly influence the hypothalamus by their impact on visceral brain (septum, amygdala, hippocampus, frontal contex). Unlike the dopaminergic terminals of the median eminence that are in the external zone in contact with the capillary plexus, the noradrenergic fibers are in the inner and middle zones where they more likely are active by modifying the function of adjacent neurons (Hökfelt *et al.*, 1979). Noradrenergic cell bodies of the lateral tegmental area are often bipolar and project heavily to intermediolateral cell bodies of the spinal cord. They are almost certainly direct links in autonomic neuroendocrine reflex arcs connecting sensory components of the autonomic nervous system (e.g., volume receptors) with hypothalamic autonomic and neuroendocrine (e.g., ADH release secondary to volume depletion) responses.

Serotonergic neurons also originate primarily in the raphe nuclei of the hind-brain that are coterminus with the reticular activating system (Ajika and Ochi, 1978). They, too, project downward to the spinal cord and ascend via the medial forebrain bundle to the hypothalamus, limbic system, and cortex. Serotonergic nerve terminal concentrations within the hypothalamus are found in the median eminence (outer zone), arcuate nucleus, suprachiasmatic nucleus, and lining of the third ventricle.

Neuropharmacologic agents that either inhibit or enhance the actions of brain monoamines also thereby alter neuroendocrine function, presumably in part through the pathways described above. Examples of some of their specific effects will be discussed in the following section on the regulation of release of specific pituitary tropic hormones.

Hypothalamic neuroendocrine function is also modulated by higher brain centers controlling more complex social behavior and emotion. Examples of this influence are emotional stress-induced inhibition of ovulation and lactation or increased cortisol secretion. The limbic system, including the septum, amygdala, cingulate gryus, and rhinencephalon, sends several major projections to/or through the hypothalamus that directly affect neuroendocrine function (Martin *et al.*, 1977). These include the striae terminalis and ventral amygdalo-fugal tract from the amygdala, the fornix from the hippocampus, and the medial forebrain bundle (downward projections) from the septum, amygdala, and rhinencephalon. The limbic areas receive hypothalamic inputs via these pathways or indirectly via thalamic nuclei (e.g., Krieger *et al.*, 1979). The medial forebrain bundle also links the brainstem tegmentum with the limbic system, thus completing a circuit between mid- and hind-brain-hypothalamus and limbic system (Haymaker *et al.*, 1969). Evidence regarding direct neocortical–hypothalamic connections is limited, and most neocortical influences (e.g., symbolic thought) are probably mediated via the limbic system.

HYPOTHALAMIC REGULATION OF
INDIVIDUAL PITUITARY TROPIC HORMONES

The established pituitary tropic hormones are large peptides that act on specific target endocrine glands, the thyroid, adrenals, and gonads, that in turn secrete non-peptide hormones, or else act directly on nonendocrine target tissues such as skeleton or liver. All of the pituitary tropic hormones are under both endocrine feedback and neural control and are subject to a wide variety of physical and psychological stresses and other neural factors (for reviews, see Martin *et al.*, 1977; Martini and Besser, 1977; Reichlin, 1980).

Growth Hormone (GH)

Growth hormone secretion is controlled by a dual hypothalamic system, one excitatory, mediated through growth hormone releasing factor (GRF), a substance whose chemical identity has not been characterized, and the other inhibitory, mediated by somatostatin (Brazeau *et al.*, 1973; Chihara *et al.*, 1978b; Arimura *et al.*, 1976). Hormone influences also modify GH secretion (summarized in Figure 6). In man, GH secretion is altered by stress, food intake, physical acitivity, and the sleep cycle (Reichlin, 1975; Cryer and Daughaday, 1977).

The dominant influence of the hypothalamus over GH regulation is that of stimulation. After interruption of the pituitary stalk, or transplantation of the pituitary away from the hypothalamus, GH secretion and pituitary content of GH falls. Secretion is restored by retransplantation of the pituitary to the hypophysiotropic area of the hypothalamus (Halasz, 1969). Destructive lesions of the hypothalamus, or its connections to the pituitary, almost invariably cause decreased GH secretion in man. Increased GH secretion may follow destructive lesions of the somatostatinergic neural system of the rat, but there is no unambiguous evidence for a comparable inhibition of somatostatin release in man. Several examples of paradoxical increase in GH secretion known to occur in patients with anterior hypothalamic lesions, or with several kinds of metabolic encephalopathy, may be due to loss of the normal somatostatin inhibitory component of GH regulation.

In normal individuals, GH is released in both pulsatile and circadian rhythms. Secretory spikes of varying intervals and duration, depending upon the species, occur throughout the day, thus making random GH determinations unreliable indices of total function (Martin 1973). In humans at rest, GH levels are low or undetectable (less than 1 ng/ml) in the morning and rise sharply with exercise. Levels fall after a meal, and then rebound as glucose levels fall. Amino acid ingestion (or infusion) also stimulates GH secretion.

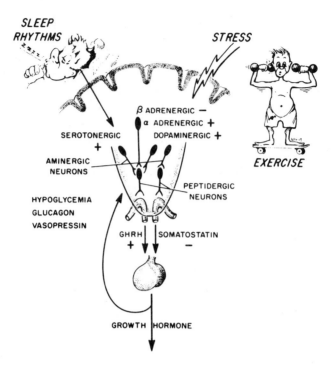

Figure 6. Neuroendocrine factors in growth hormone regulation. Metabolic, physiological, and bioaminergic influences are all mediated through hypothalamic peptidergic neurons. From: Reichlin (1980), W. B. Saunders and Co., Philadelphia, with permission.

The largest secretion of GH occurs during the first 2 hours of the night most usually associated with deep (slow wave Stage III) sleep. Nocturnal GH secretion gradually declines with age, thus accounting for the fact that total GH secretion is less in older individuals.

Stressful stimuli such as hypoglycemia or anesthesia cause increased GH secretion in humans, but, in contrast, inhibit GH secretion in rats (Terry *et al.*, 1976). Several studies comparing GH and ACTH responses to stress in primates have been reported (Brown and Reichlin, 1972). In general, GH responses are not elicited as easily as are ACTH responses, are less sustained, and are more selective. These differences are interpreted to indicate that neural pathways mediating the two stress responses are distinct, or that there are different mechanisms of adaptation intrinsic to the hormone regulatory system itself.

All GH secretory patterns are mediated by the brain, acting mainly through bioamine inputs to the hypophysiotropic neurons. Noradrenergic alpha agonists stimulate and beta adrenergic agonists inhibit GH secretion. Phentolamine, an α-receptor blocker, inhibits hypoglycemia-induced GH rise.

Serotonin antagonists such as methysergide or cyproheptadine inhibit sleep-induced GH release. The role of dopaminergic influences is less clear. L-Dopa, a dopamine precursor, stimulates GH secretion. Although other dopamine agonists also can stimulate GH secretion (at the hypothalamic level) it is more likely that the L-Dopa effect is attributable to dopamine conversion to norepinephrine because the effect is blocked by phentolamine.

In addition to the bioamines, a variety of neuropeptides common to both the brain and the gut (in particular the enkephalins, Substance P, neurotensin, and VIP) influence GH secretion through their actions on hypothalamic neurons. Their relative physiological importance has not been determined.

Growth hormone secretion is also determined by endocrine influences. Growth hormone controls its own secretion by exerting negative feedback control at the level of the hypothalamus, presumably through enhanced secretion of somatostatin (Patel, 1979). Somatomedin (a circulating peptide synthesized under the influence of GH) may also inhibit GH release, a phenomenon used to explain the high levels of GH that are observed in many patients with anorexia nervosa. Estrogens act directly to sensitize the pituitary to GH releasing factor. Release of GH is inhibited by glucocorticoids. Thyroxine is necessary for normal GH secretion—GH secretion is suppressed in hypothyroidism.

Although the mechanisms of regulation of GH secretion have been relatively well worked out, the physiological significance of stress-induced GH release, of its spontaneous variations, and of sleep-related secretion have not been elucidated. The relevance to the immune response of the variations of GH that occur with age, sex, nutritional state, and stress are unknown.

Prolactin

As its name implies, prolactin influences milk production, is essential for normal lactation, and when pathologically elevated may cause inappropriate galactorrhea. Prolactin also has influences on other tissues including brain, adrenal, kidneys, prostate, gonads, and possibly liver. Although estrogens modify prolactin secretion, neural control mechanisms are the principal mode of regulation (Neill, 1980); (Figure 7).

Prolactin is found in high concentration in the blood of neonates, and then falls in infancy and childhood, again rising in adolescence under the influence of sex steroids. Levels fall after the menopause, but secretion persists throughout life. Prolactin is also secreted by normal men. Prolactin is released in response to suckling, and also after a variety of physical and emotional stresses. Prolactin, similar to GH, is secreted in pulses through the day (ultradian rhythm), and like GH rises during sleep, but not in relation to a specific, EEG-defined sleep stage.

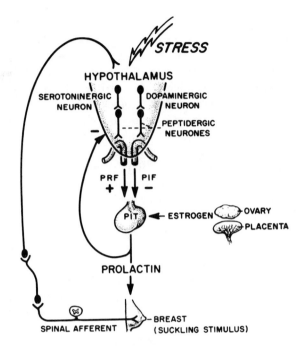

Figure 7. Neuroendocrine regulation of prolactin secretion. Many drugs increase prolactin secretion by inhibiting adrenergic and dopaminergic transmission. See text for details. From Reichlin (1980), W. B. Saunders and Co., Philadelphia, with permission.

In all mammals studied, prolactin rises following stress. Prolactin levels have not been proved to be consistently elevated by chronic emotional stress, and are normal in defined psychiatric illnesses such as schizophrenia and depression.

Prolactin secretion is under tonic inhibition of the tuberohypophysial dopaminergic neurons arising in the arcuate nuclei. Dopamine is released into the hypothalamic portal veins in amounts sufficient to account for almost all of the inhibitory effects of the hypothalamus on prolactin secretion (Gibbs and Neill, 1978).

Although the predominant control of the hypothalamus on prolactin release is inhibitory, there is good evidence that acute release of prolactin (as in stress, anesthesia, and suckling) is mediated by prolactin releasing factors (PRF). Thyrotropic hormone releasing hormone (TRH) is a PRF. That this peptide is not the only PRF is indicated by the fact that TSH responses do not parallel those of prolactin (e.g., in suckling and stress), and that hypothalamic extracts contain PRF activity in amounts greater than can be accounted for by their TRH content.

As in the case of GH regulation, prolactin is under negative feedback control through actions of prolactin on the brain. Most important is the effect of prolactin on the synthesis and secretion of dopamine in the arcuate nucleus complex. There is now good evidence that prolactin stimulates the release of dopamine into the hypophysial portal vessel blood, but it is still uncertain that this response is sufficient to explain all aspects of feedback inhibition.

Prolactin exerts a wide variety of important behavioral effects in lower animals, principally in the area of maternal and nurturing behavior, nest building, and migratory functions. Effects on higher brain functions in man have not been established, but there is good evidence that prolactin can inhibit libido in men, and possibly in women by mechanisms in part, but not exclusively, due to suppression of gonadal function.

Prolactin secretion is regulated by bioamines. As noted, inhibitory control is by dopamine. Excitatory control is by serotonin pathways which are thought to act by releasing PRF(s). Factors regulating secretion of the dopaminergic tuberohypophysial neurons have not been well defined. Noradrenergic influences inhibit prolactin release, presumably by acting on the dopaminergic system, and histamine, acting through H II receptors in the hypothalamus, is thought to inhibit the dopaminergic pathways and thereby stimulate prolactin release (Delitala *et al.*, 1979; Gibbs *et al.*, 1979). Other neurotransmitter substances known to stimulate prolactin release are acetylcholine, and the neuropeptides endorphin, VIP, neurotensin, and Substance P (Chihara *et al.*, 1978a; Kato *et al.*, 1978; Rossier *et al.*, 1979; Samson *et al.*, 1980). Their mode of action and physiological role have not as yet been established.

(ACTH) Adrenocorticotropic Hormone

Studies of the stress-related modulation of the immune response, since the work of Selye, have emphasized cortisol as a potentially critical mechanism of control; however, the role of physiological fluctuations of cortisol secretion on immune function and regulation in man remains to be fully defined.

The secretion of cortisol is stimulated by ACTH, which in turn is under direct neural control (Mangili *et al.*, 1966; Dunn and Critchlow 1973; Rees, 1977; Krieger, 1977; and Figure 8). Like GH and prolactin, ACTH is secreted in an ultradian rhythm with pulses occurring throughout the day, and in a circadian rhythm that is entrained to the sleep–activity cycle. Levels of ACTH fall in late evening to their lowest levels (less than 25 pg/ml) and rise in the early morning hours before waking (Krieger, 1978). (In rats, the activity and ACTH cycle is reversed, with peak activity occurring during the dark.) With time zone or activity change, circadian rhythms of ACTH take several days to alter, unlike PRL and GH which are more directly sleep entrained.

Stress is the most important modulator of ACTH secretion and can interrupt normal diurnal rhythms. Stress can be defined as any new or immediate adaptive challenge to the organism. In humans, there is a consistent ACTH response to physical challenges such as hypoglycemia or anesthesia (Knigge *et*

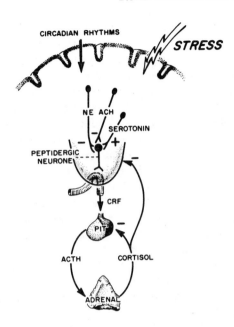

Figure 8. Regulatory elements of ACTH secretion. Secretion of ACTH is stimulated by CRF (corticotrophin releasing factor), and inhibited at the pituitary level and other brain areas by cortisol. See text for details. From Martin *et al.* (1977). F. A. Davis Company, Philadelphia, with permission.

al., 1959). Responses to emotional and intellectual stimuli are more variable; it is the novelty or the inability to adapt to a new environmental challenge that determines the cortisol response. In army officers, secretion rates are actually higher in anticipation of than during military combat (Rose and Sachar, 1980).

Cortisol exerts feedback inhibition on ACTH secretion in a graduated manner that parallels the intensity of the neural stimulus (Kaneko and Hiroshige, 1978). Small doses of exogenous steroids abolish the diurnal rhythm, while large doses affect response to the most severe stresses such as hypotension. Some stresses are so severe that they will "break through" steroid inhibition.

Changes of ACTH secretion are under direct hypothalamic control mediated by release of corticotropin releasing factor (CRF) into the hypophysial portal circulation. Although the identification of this peptide, the first of the releasing factors to be recognized, remains an elusive goal, its existence is certain. Hypothalamic and portal blood CRF activity fluctuates in parallel with ACTH secretion (Vernikos-Danellis, 1964). Corticotropin releasing factor is widely distributed throughout the medial basal hypothalamus. There does not appear to be an important inhibitory influence or inhibitory peptide modulating pituitary ACTH. Rather, inhibitory influences all act at the hypothalamic level to inhibit CRF secretion. Secretion of CRF is under important control by other brain centers. Hypothalamic "islands," produced by stereotatic knife cuts (Halasz, 1969), are associated with tonic increases in ACTH secretion that no longer respond to neural stimuli. Ascending pathways are both stimulatory and inhibitory. From the limbic system, hippocampal and septal afferents modulate stress-induced CRF release and amygdaloid pathways enhance secretion (Mason, 1959; Uhlir et al., 1974).

The classic neurotransmitters all influence CRF and, indirectly, ACTH secretion, although many details remain unresolved. Acethylcholine mediates many of the stress-induced responses (Hedge and Smelik, 1967; Hiroshige and Kaneko, 1978). Serotonin antagonists inhibit sleep and to some extent stress-induced ACTH rise, but serotonin may be acting indirectly on cholinergic neurons (Krieger, 1977). Adrenergic agents exert mixed responses, but overall are inhibitory (Van Loon et al., 1971; Lancranjan et al., 1979). Histamine stimulates ACTH release; whether this effect is entirely indirect via influences on cholinergic and serotonergic pathways is not clear (Morita, 1979). Other neuropeptides such as the enkephalins, VIP, and Substance P also play a role in the complex regulation of CRF.

Thyroid Stimulating Hormone or Thyrotropin (TSH)

Thyrotropin secretion is under triple hypophysiotropic control (Figure 9) that interacts with thyroid hormone feedback at the level of the pituitary and possibly at the level of the hypothalamus as well (Knigge and Joseph 1971; Scanlon et al., 1980).

The predominant effect of the hypothalamus is stimulatory through release of TRH (Greer, 1952; Burgus et al., 1970; Harris et al., 1978; Reichlin et al., 1972). This is shown by experiments in which all hypothalamic inputs are abolished. In such cases, TSH secretion falls to nearly undetectable levels (Reichlin et al., 1972). Somatostatin inhibits TSH secretion, and has recently been shown to exert tonic inhibition under physiological circumstances in the rat and man (Arimura and Schally, 1976; Ferland et al., 1976; Schusdziarra et al., 1978; Weeke et al., 1975). Dopamine also exerts modest inhibitory effects of TSH secretion at the level of the pituitary (Scanlon et al., 1980).

In turn, the secretions of the hypophysiotropic system are influenced by neural functions. In man there is a small amplitude circadian variation, peak levels reached during the night (Chan et al., 1978), and TSH secretion is reduced in severe stress. Cold exposure has little or no effect in the adult, but is stimulatory to the newborn.

The principal neurotransmitter regulators of TSH secretion are noradrenergic, stimulatory to TRH release (Chen and Meites, 1975; Birk-Launidsen et al., 1976; Krulich et al., 1977), and serotonergic inhibitory (Krulich et al., 1979). Because there are three hypothalamic regulatory factors, it has been difficult to sort out the various effects using TSH release as

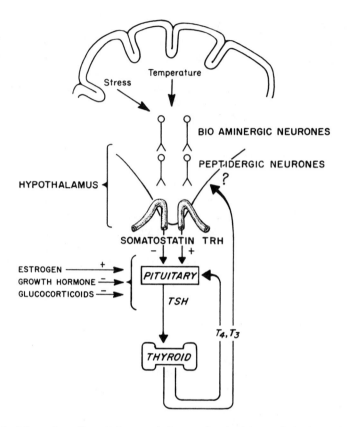

Figure 9. Schematic outline of the neural elements involved in regulation of TSH secretion. Thyroid hormones exert negative feedback at the pituitary, whereas thyrotropin releasing hormone (TRH) stimulates, and somatostatin and dopamine (not shown) inhibit TSH secretion. Reprinted from Martin *et al.* (1977), F. A. Davis Company, Philadelphia, with permission.

the end point of control. Physiological blood levels of thyroid hormone act directly on the pituitary to regulate TSH secretion. It is possible to explain the mode of control of the TSH secretion by postulating a constant level of TRH secretion from the hypothalamus with modulation of pituitary receptors to TRH by thyroid hormone (Perrone and Hinkle, 1978). Glucocorticoids inhibit TSH secretion (Re *et al.*, 1976). Reduced thyroid hormone levels, particularly triiodothyronine (T3), with illness or malnutrition result from both altered TSH secretion and altered peripheral thyroid hormone metabolism.

Direct effects of TSH on tissues other than the thyroid have been demonstrated including stimulation of lipolysis in fat, and inflammation in orbital muscle and connective tissue, but the effects of TSH on the immune response (separate from effects mediated by thyroid hormones) have not been elucidated.

Gonadotropins

Follicle stimulating hormone (FSH) and luteinizing hormone (LH), the hormones that regulate the testes and ovary, are regulated by the hypothalamus as part of a complex interplay of steroid and hypophysiotropic secretion. In relation to the objectives of this chapter, it is sufficient to emphasize that both LH and FSH are under the control of luteinizing hormone releasing hormone (LHRH) and that in its absence gonadotropic function (and dependent gonadal function) virtually ceases (Knobil and Plant, 1978; Franchimont and Roulier, 1977; Yen, 1977). In addition to feedback effects (Fink, 1979) LHRH is under neurotransmitter control in general, α-adrenergic receptors being stimulatory to LHRH release. Dopamine is probably inhibitory to LHRH release. Although chorionic gonadotropin (HCG) may affect local immune responses in the uterus, the gonadotropic hormones themselves have not been shown to act on the immune system independently of gonad secretions (estrogens, progesterone, and testosterone). Estrogens, particularly, may not only modulate immune function directly, but indirectly by effects on other pituitary hormones, particulary prolactin and growth hormone (see preceding sections).

OTHER PITUITARY FACTORS AS POTENTIAL MODULATORS OF THE IMMUNE RESPONSE

In addition to the classic tropic hormones described, the pituitary also secretes or contains a variety of other hormones or factors whose possible effects on the immune response are as yet undefined. Some, such as β-lipotropin and β-endorphin, are under brain–hypothalamic control; the others may prove to be. These, or as yet other undiscovered factors, could modulate any phase of the immune response.

β-Lipotropin and β-Endorphin

β-Lipotropin (β-LPH) (Li, et al., 1965) and its 61–95 subfragment, β-endorphin, are included together with ACTH and the melanocyte stimulating hormone within a larger precursor molecule termed 31-K or pro-opiocortin (Mains et al., 1977; Ling et al., 1976; Lazarus et al., 1976) (Figure 10). Enzymatic cleavage of pro-opiocortin within pituitary corticotrophs or other sites of synthesis results in the release of ACTH. In the pars distalis, only some of the resulting β-LPH is further cleaved to β-endorphin (Fratta et al., 1979). In the rat pars intermedia, β-endorphin and ACTH are the two principal β-peptide fragments formed. In the human, because the pars in-

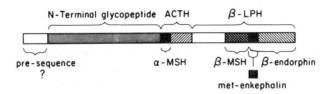

Figure 10. Schematic structure of pro-opiocortin, the common precursor of ACTH, melanocyte stimulating hormone (MSH), and β-endorphin. Reprinted from Herbert *et al.* (1980), Raven Press, NY, with permission.

termedia is rudimentary and dispersed within the pars distalis, it is not known whether differential cleavage of pro-opiocortin occurs (Liotta *et al.*, 1978).

Both β-LPH and β-endorphin are detected in the blood and cerebrospinal fluid of man, and blood levels fluctuate in parallel with ACTH in response to stressor stimuli (Jeffcoate *et al.*, 1978; Wardlaw and Frantz 1979; Wilkes *et al.*, 1980; Nakao *et al.*, 1980). Met-enkephalin, discovered with leu-enkephalin in 1975 (Hughes *et al.*, 1975), is also included within β-LPH (61-65). It is not, however, formed from β-LPH within the pituitary, but is derived from a separate precursor within different cells of origin both within the nervous system and gastrointestinal tract. Circulating leu- and met-enkephalin originate in part from the adrenal medulla (Clement-Jones *et al.*, 1980).

Although β-lipotropin, β-endorphin, and the enkephalins are stress hormones, their physiological roles are uncertain. Except for some lipolytic activity, there is no known physiological role for β-LPH. The potent opioid effects of the endorphins in the brain are evident (Meglio *et al.*, 1977; Guillemin, 1978a), but whether in man peripheral levels of endorphins can produce these effects has not been established (Foley *et al.*, 1979). In rats there is some evidence that secreted endorphin attenuates pain; the locus of this action is unknown. Opiate receptors are present on circulating mononuclear cells, and opiates may alter T-lymphocyte subpopulations (McDonough *et al.*, 1980). ACTH, however, has been shown to have no effect on immune function independent of cortisol (Dougherty, 1952). It is also possible that the endorphins or enkephalins modulate immunity indirectly through their effect on other peripheral neuropeptide secreting cells (see section on the autonomic nervous system).

Fibroblast Growth Factor, Thymocyte Stimulating Factor, and Endothelial Growth Factor

Other pituitary factors of potential interest have also been identified. Thymocyte stimulating factor stimulates thymocytes directly, rather than having an indirect effect on thymic epithelium or bone marrow precursors (Saxena and Talwar, 1977). This substance has not as yet been chemically characterized. Fibroblast growth factor promotes the cellular proliferation *in vitro* of mesodermally and some endodermally derived tissue (Gospoda-rowicz, 1975). Pituitary FGH has not been sequenced, and its specific effect on immune tissue has not been reported.

Hypothalamic and pituitary endothelial growth factor, acting in conjunction with platelet-derived growth factors, stimulates endothelial cells *in vitro* (Maciag *et al.*, 1979). The presence of these factors or putative hormones underscores the possible existence of yet other pituitary peptides with possible immunoregulatory functions. Their identification will most likely come from work with serum-free culture systems (Bottenstein *et al.*, 1979) in which progressively purified pituitary extracts can be evaluated without the high level of background stimulation present in serum-added culture systems and *in vivo*. Possible targets of such factors may not be peripheral lymphocytes which have differentiated maximally under thymic, monocyte, and antigenic influences, but rather thymic epithelium and its secretory products or bone marrow lymphocyte and monocyte precursors.

HYPOTHALAMIC OR BRAIN SECRETIONS AS POTENTIAL IMMUNE MODULATORS

The Blood–Brain Barrier and Periventricular Organs

The possibility must be considered that brain substances could modify the immune process directly. Free passage of brain secretions into the general circulation is prevented by the "blood–brain barrier," formed by tight junctions of brain capillary endothelial cells (Davson, 1967). There are several sites in the brain, however, in which a relatively free brain–blood communication does exist. These are all modified areas of the ependymal lining of the brain to which the general term "periventricular organs" has been applied (Weindl, 1973; Figure 11). All are specialized neurohemal structures. One, the median eminence of the hypothalamus, has been described in a preceding section. Other areas are the subfornical organ (SFO), organum vasculosum of the lamina terminalis (OVLT), pineal gland, subcommissural organ (SCO), and the area postrema of the fourth ventricle. In each site, nerve endings containing secretory vescicles come in contact with a fenestrated capillary plexus. Other pathways by which brain secretions might enter the general circulation are by way of the cerebrospinal fluid via arachnoid villi in the superior sagittal sinus, or by transport from the third ventricle to the blood vessels of the median eminence.

All of these routes are potential exit sites of brain secretions, including peptides. One may ask, however, whether any such secretions do in fact find their way into peripheral blood, where they could alter immune function.

The answer, for some brain peptides, is yes; but the answer must be qualified. Many of the brain peptides are also secreted by the gastrointestinal

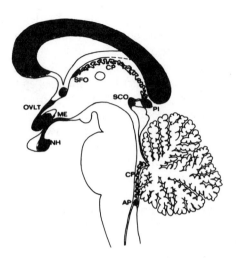

Figure 11. Median sagittal section through the human brain. The circumventricular organs are outlined in black: AP, area postrema; ME, median eminence; NH, neurohypophysis; OVLT, organum vasculosum of the lamina terminalis; PI, pineal body; SFO, subfornical organ; SCO, subcommissural organ; CP, choroid plexus. Reprinted from Weindl (1973).

tract (including pancreas) and by the autonomic nervous system. Peptides common to the brain and gut are listed in Table 1 and include somatostatin, TRH, neurotensin, Substance P, VIP, and the enkephalins. Their presence in blood does not necessarily mean that they arise from brain, although the possibility exists that neural factors do, in some instances, modify gut secretion. Furthermore, most of the brain peptides are degraded very rapidly by enzymes in peripheral blood. Their measurement is fraught with difficulties. Nevertheless, because secretion of brain peptides is a potential route of brain control, current knowledge will be summarized.

Brain Peptides in Peripheral Blood

Somatostatin was first discovered in hypothalamic extracts, but subsequently has been found in other parts of the brain and in many other tissues including gastrointestinal tract and pancreas (Vale *et al.*, 1975). The peptide is found in circulating blood (Pimstone *et al.*, 1978; Schusdziarra *et al.*, 1979); the relative contributions from brain and gut have not been established with certainty (Patel *et al.*, 1979), but available evidence suggests that the bulk of circulating somatostatin is of gut origin and may be regulated by neurotransmitters, the pH of gut lumen contents, or nutrient intake (Schusdziarra *et al.*, 1980). In addition to its action as a paracrine secretion that regulates the function of neighbor cells (Forssmann *et al.*, 1978; Larsson *et al.*, 1979), somatostatin may have modulatory influences on immune function. Infusions of somatostatin have been reported to block endotoxin-induced leukocytosis, an effect independent of the pituitary (Wagner *et al.*, 1979). Somatostatin inhibits release by T lymphoblasts of bone marrow colony stimulating factor (Hintenberger *et al.*, 1977). Recently Bhathena *et al.* (1980) reported that human lymphocytes have somatostatin receptors. The potential importance of somatostatin as a regulator of other lymphocyte functions or of the release of immune-regulating hormones from other tissue such as the thymus is unknown.

Neurotensin, a linear peptide containing 13 amino acids (Carraway and Leeman, 1973) is widely distributed in the brain, autonomic nervous system, and the gut (Leeman *et al.*, 1977; Bissett *et al.*, 1978). Within the brain it is found in highest concentrations in the hypothalamus, and total brain content of neurotensin in the rat is about one sixth that of somatostatin. Ten times this quantity is present in the gut, mostly in the distal small intestine. Significant quantities are also found in the anterior and posterior pituitary. Immunoreactive neurotensin is present in plasma in concentrations between 20 and 80 pmol/l. Because infusions of neurotensin giving rise to blood levels in this range inhibit gastrin secretion in man, it may be assumed that the peptide in blood has physiological effects (Blackburn *et al.,* 1980).

The site of origin of peripheral neurotensin and its possible neuroregulation is unknown. Administered by intravenous or intracerebral routes, neurotensin produces a wide range of actions including vasodilation, hypothermia, hyperglycemia, and a hypothalamically mediated increase in growth hormone secretion (Kaneto *et al.*, 1978; Maeda and Frohman, 1978). Many of the peripheral but not the central actions are blocked by histamine Type I antagonists (Nagai and Frohman, 1978) suggesting that neurotensin may be stimulating the release of histamine. Although neurotensin has been shown to bind to specific receptor sites on mast cells (Lazarus *et al.*, 1977), it does not release histamine from these cells *in vitro*. Neurotensin may also be a chemotactic factor for leukocytes (Leeman *et al.*, 1977), although the *in vivo* significance of this is unknown. Other neuropeptides found in peripheral blood are TRH, Substance P, VIP, and the enkephalins (e.g., Nilsson *et al.*, 1975). Bombesin, a neuropeptide originally isolated from the skin of a particular species of frog (Villarreal and Brown, 1978; Dockray, 1979) has now been shown to be an analog of a peptide distributed widely in mammalian gut and brain, gastrin releasing peptide (McDonald *et al.*, 1979). Each of these substances has a wide spectrum of biologic activities (Rivier *et al.,* 1978; Walsh *et al.*, 1979), but their influence on specific immune functions is unknown. The specific localization in the gut of most of these substances raises the important possibility that they are local regulators (paracrine regulators) of the gut immune system that includes gut lymphocytes and the secretory immunoglobulins (e.g., Jones *et al.*, 1978).

The possible effects of the neural lobe secretions, vasopressin, oxytocin, and neurophysin, on any aspect of immune function are unknown. These hor-

TABLE 1

Peptides Common to Both Nervous System and Gut[a]

Peptide	Distribution		
	Nervous system	Gastrointestinal tract	Other sites
ACTH	Adenohypophysis, hypothalamus, thalamus, brainstem	Duodenum, pancreas	
Angiotensin	Hypothalamus, brainstem, spinal cord	Small intestine	
Bombesin	Hypothalamus, hippocampus, cerebrolcortex	Intestine (bombesin-like peptide)	Amphibian skin
CCK-pancreozymin	Cerebral cortex (C-terminal peptides)	Intestine, especially duodenum	
Enkephalins	Neurohypophysis, hypothalamus, striatum, brainstem, peripheral nerves	Intestine, stomach, pancreas (more met- than leu-enkephalin)	Adrenal medulla
Endorphins	Adenohypophysis and intermediate lobe, hypothalamus; absent in neurohypophysis, striatum, hippocampus	Intestine	Adrenal medulla
Gastrin	Neurohypophysis, adenohypophysis, peripheral nerves, vagus	Stomach, intestine	Placenta

LHRH	Hypothalamus, extrahypothalamic brain	Stomach, intestine, pancreas (?)	
Motilin	Pineal, adenohypophysis, neurohypophysis	Duodenum, stomach, gallbladder	
Neurotensin	Hypothalamus, neurohypophysis, adenohypophysis, thalamus, brainstem, basal ganglia, cerebral cortex	Intestine	
Somatostatin	Hypothalamus, neurohypophysis, cerebrocortex, medulla, pineal, peripheral nerves	Stomach, intestine, pancreas	
Substance P	Hypothalamus, neurohypophysis, adenohypophysis, medulla, striatum, dorsal roots of cord, peripheral nerves	Intestine	
TRH	Hypothalamus	Entire gastrointestinal tract, pancreas	Lung, heart, kidney, spleen
VIP	Cerebral cortex, hypothalamus, amygdala, peripheral nerves, sympathetic ganglia, vagus	Duodenum and entire gastrointestinal tract, pancreas	Adrenal medulla, placenta, lung

[a] From Said (1980) with permission.

mones are of potential interest because vasopressin and its specifically related neurophysin are released during stress, and because oxytocin and its neurophysin are inhibited during stress. Vasopressin has been shown to increase blood concentration of Factor VIII, acting through an as yet unknown intermediate compound (Cash *et al.*, 1978). Vasopressin has potent vasoconstrictor properties and hence might modulate the vascular component to local inflammatory responses.

Secretions of the Pineal Gland

The pineal gland and its functions have been a source of speculation since antiquity. It is now recognized to be a neurohemal organ whose secretions are controlled by its sympathetic nerve innervation, in turn regulated by the suprachiasmatic nucleus, a hypothalamic structure of major importance in determining circadian rhythms. The pineal is also influenced markedly by environmental illumination, and is activated by the signal, "lights off" (Wurtman and Moskowitz, 1977; Wurtman, 1980). The only firmly established secretion of the pineal is melatonin, an indoleamine derived enzymatically from serotonin.

Peptides found in the pineal include somatostatin, TRH, LHRH, and β-endorphin; it is doubtful that the pineal is an important source of circulating peptides. In addition, at least one or more peptides inhibitory to gonadal function (in addition to the established antigonadotropic function of melatonin) have been reported to be present (Fernstrom *et al.*, 1980).

Virtually nothing is known about the effects of pinealectomy, or of the injection of pineal extracts on immune reactions. Pinealectomy was reported to be without effect on humoral antibody formation (Janković *et al.*, 1970; Rella and Lapin, 1976) but was shown to reduce the severity of the immune deficit induced by thymectomy.

THE PERIPHERAL NEUROENDOCRINE SYSTEM

Neurosecretion by Primary Sensory Neurons

Substance P (SP), a peptide with vasodilating properties, was first isolated from gut extracts by von Euler and Gaddum in 1931 and more recently was isolated from hypothalamic extracts, chemically characterized as a linear peptide containing 11 amino acids and shown to be widely distributed (Leeman *et al.*, 1977; Mroz and Leeman, 1977).

In addition to gut and brain (Chan-Palay *et al.*, 1978), it is present in

20-25% of sensory ganglia cell bodies and in the small unmyelinated fibers arising from the ganglia. Substance P is found in the dorsal horn of the spinal cord, in highest concentration in the substantia gelatinosa where it is present in nerve endings projecting centrally from sensory ganglia (Barber *et al.*, 1979; Hökfelt *et al.*, 1975a,b). The recent demonstration of SP in dorsal ganglia, and its known property as a vasodilator, have clarified a number of early observations about the role of peripheral nerves in local vascular responsivity.

Injury to the skin is associated with a prompt local flare corresponding to the second component of the "triple response" of Lewis (1927). Stimulation of peripheral nerves or dorsal root ganglia (Chapman and Goodell, 1964) also produces this dilatation. Based on these and other findings, it has been proposed that local skin injury stimulates retrograde nerve impulse formation, followed by a local axon reflex, with anterograde impulse conduction that depolarizes nerve endings leading to release of a vasodilator substance, now believed to be SP (Hagermark *et al.*, 1978; Olgart *et al.*, 1977). In support of this theory is the finding that capsaicin, a chemical irritant found in Hungarian hot red paprika peppers, when injected into rats abolishes both pain sensation (Hayes and Tyers, 1980) and the neurogenic inflammatory response to chemical irritants (Jancso *et al.*, 1967, 1968) and depletes SP from dorsal ganglia (Yaksh *et al.*, 1979).

These observations give strong evidence that spinal nerves might exert important local effects on components of the inflammatory response, possibly including those induced by antigen–antibody reactions *in situ* (Chapman and Goodell, 1964; Chahl., 1977).

But Substance P is not the only biologically active compound in sensory neurons. Somatostatin is also found there and this peptide, like SP (Brimijoin *et al.*, 1980), is actively transported from cell ganglia to the periphery (Hökfelt *et al.*, 1976; Rasool *et al.*, 1981). The rapid phase of transport of somatostatin is approximately 400 mm/24 hr. The function of somatostatin in ganglia is unknown. In tissue cultures, SP release is inhibited by addition of somatostatin (Mudge *et al.*, 1979), and, in frog spinal cord, somatostatin depresses motoneuron function.

We consider it likely that the distal sensory release of SP, somatostatin, or other neuropeptides might modulate local immune responses. Substance P-mediated vasodilation and increased permeability may have an effect on delayed hypersensitivity and may modify mast cell function (Figure 12).Substance P is a potent releaser of histamine from mast cells *in vitro* (Johnson and Erdos, 1978). *In vivo*, tissue mast cell histamine release is partly dependent on IgE–antigen binding or T cell-macrophage interactions (Graham *et al.*, 1955; Schleimer, 1978). Substance P may well potentiate this process or even serve as an alternative mechanism. Histamine activates a subpopulation of suppressor T lymphocytes (Bourne *et al.*, 1974; Rocklin *et al.*, 1979; Osband *et al.*, 1980; Jouzzo *et al.*, 1980) in man, and Substance P, via histamine, might trigger or sustain this activation. Substance P may have an

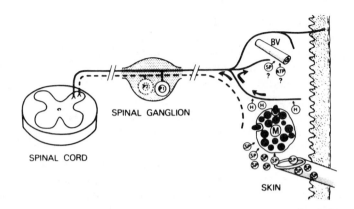

Figure 12. A hypothetical and schematic representation of the actions of Substance P (SP) after distal release from primary sensory neurons, causing vasodilation of blood vessels (BV) and release of histamine (H) from mast cells. Not shown are other hypothetical effects on phagocytes or lymphocytes (see text). Reprinted from O. Hagermark, Hökefelt, T. & Pernew, B. Flare and Itch induced by Substance P in human skin. *Journal of Investigative Dermatology.* 71:233–235. Williams and Wilkins, publishers. Baltimore. Printed with permission.

effect directly on tissue macrophages or lymphocytes in either potentiating or terminating immune responses. An N-terminal fragment of SP has been reported to enhance phagocytosis (Blumberg *et al.*, 1980).

The Nonadrenergic Noncholinergic Autonomic Nervous System

Physiological effects of the autonomic nervous system have traditionally been attributed to the release at nerve terminals of two well-established neurotransmitters, acetylcholine and norepinephrine. However, some of the effects of stimulation of sympathetic and parasympathetic nerves are not blocked by either antiadrenergic or anticholinergic drugs, findings that have led to the recognition that other neurotransmitters must be involved in this system. The first such neurotransmitter to be described was adenosine triphosphate, a purine derivative, and the nonadrenergic, noncholinergic neurons were then termed "purinergic" (Burnstock *et al.*, 1978a). Subsequently, a large number of neuropeptides have been identified within the vagus (Gilbert *et al.*, 1980), sympathetic ganglia, and the intrinsic nervous plexuses of the gut; the term purinergic now appears to be excessively restrictive. Classical sympathetic nerves contain somatostatin, VIP, and enkephalins, and the parasympathetic outflow includes peptidergic neurons containing Sustance P, vasoactive intestinal polypeptide, the enkephalins, somatostatin, cholecystokinin (CCK), and TRH (Gamse *et al.*, 1979; Schultzberg *et al.*, 1978; Hökfelt *et al.*, 1977; Lundberg, 1979; Lundberg *et al.*, 1979).

Best studied of endocrine tissue from the point of view of autonomic regulation is the pancreatic islet cell. Vagal stimulation of the pancreas leads to hyperinsulinism whereas sympathetic stimulation via α-adrenergic receptors inhibits insulin release (Gerich and Lorenzi, 1978). Immunohistochemical studies by Larsson (1979) and collaborators revealed peptidergic nerves containing SP, VIP, enkephalins, and CCK innervating pancreatic ganglia, islets, and blood vessels with specific topographical organization. Only VIP is associated primarily with blood vessels, and CCK is the predominant peptidergic neuron around pancreatic islets themselves. VIP has a physiological role in mediating atropine-resistant pancreatic blood flow, and glucagon release (Said, 1980), whereas the role of the other peptides remains to be determined.

Virtually all parasympathetic fibers have also been shown to contain VIP (Lundberg et al., 1980). The interaction of acetylcholine (ACh) and VIP has been studied in the parotid gland. Acetylcholine stimulates secretion while VIP causes increased blood flow to the gland. Simultaneous release of both neurotransmitters gives rise to a synergistic increase in total secretion. It is likely that similar interactions occur in all peripheral sites of ACh release including other peripheral exocrine glands.

In the sympathetic nervous system, most of the enkephalin-positive fibers are preganglionic, and are believed to depress ganglionic transmission. Somatostatin is located primarily within cell bodies of sympathetic ganglia in cells that in many instances stain positively for dopamine β-hydroxylase (Hökfelt et al., 1977). This suggests that the same neuron may secrete both substances as is the case for ACh–VIP neurons of the parasympathetic system. It also suggests that somatostatin might modulate postganglionic noradrenergic transmission.

With respect to the primary theme of this review, the possibility must be considered that autonomic secretion might modulate immune function. As far as is known, there are no nerve endings directly on the immunocompetent cells, a finding that has been interpreted in the past to indicate that there is no direct neural control of immunocytes. On the other hand, it is now recognized that autonomic fibers contain large secretory varicosities along the length of their terminal branches that are capable of secretion en passant in a range up to 1 to 2 microns from the nerve (Burnstock et al., 1979). It is possible that autonomic fibers that travel with arterioles into thymus, spleen, and bone marrow (e.g., Fillenz, 1970) might influence any neighboring cells that possess physiologically relevant receptors. We may theorize that peptide secretions by autonomic neurons might produce a variety of effects within a given tissue. In the thymus, for example, VIP might regulate cortico-medullary blood flow, somatostatin the secretion of thymic or monocyte peptides. In the skin or gut, mast cell function might be modulated by various peptides (e.g., Theoharides and Douglas, 1978; Cutz, et al., 1978). Hall and Goldstein (this volume) have reviewed the effects of the autonomic nervous system on immune function (see also Bourne et al., 1974; Kashahara et al., 1977).

The peripheral neural effector systems (i.e., sensory and autonomic) can probably be modified by the brain. Hypnotic suggestion can suppress delayed hypersensitivity to tuberculin antigen (Black *et al.*, 1963). Histologic studies show that the vascular rather than the monocyte component is suppressed. The enkephalins, found in high concentration in the dorsal horn, inhibit the transmission of pain sensation at this level. They also inhibit the depolarization of primary sensory neurons (Mudge *et al.*, 1979; Bisbaum and Fields, 1978; Jessell and Iverson, 1977; MacDonald and Nelson, 1978). Enkephalins are also found in pre-ganglionic sympathetic fibers where they may modulate the effects of Substance P on sympathetic ganglia (Konishi *et al.*, 1979; Burnstock *et al.*, 1979) and thus inhibit sensory–autonomic reflex arcs. These brain–sensory relationships raise the possibility of learned or voluntary control of peripheral neuroendocrine systems and thereby potentially of immune responses.

APUD Cells and Paracrine Secretion

In addition to being found in sensory, autonomic, and central nervous neurons, neuropeptides are also located in endocrine cells, mainly in the gut, pancreas, lung, thyroid gland, and carotid body. In lower species such as the frog they are distributed in the skin, and in the toad in the urogenital tract. These endocrine cells were first recognized by Feyrter (1938) who suggested that they might have a paracrine (i.e., side by side) regulatory effect. Subsequently, Pearse pioneered the suggestion that all such cells and related peptidergic neurons are derived in embryological life from primitive neuroectoderm and have migrated to their final sites during embryogenesis (Pearse, 1977; Pictet, 1976; Takor-Takor and Pearse, 1975). Based on common metabolic properties of biogenic amine metabolism, Pearse termed this system of cells the Amine Precursor Uptake and Decarboxylase system (APUD), and postulated that all such cells form part of a diffuse neuroendocrine control system (see also Guillemin, 1978 b).

The common characteristics of peptide and bioamine secreting cells is manifest in their functional unity. In the periphery, neuroendocrine and autonomic nerve cells appear to be part of a single communication network, operating at local, regional, and general levels (Barker *et al.*, 1980; Jessen *et al.*, 1980). Via connections with the central nervous system, the peripheral neuroendocrine system is potentially a specific, though diffuse mechanism by which brain could modulate immune reactions.

Still unresolved is the important question of APUD control of the thymus. Although specific cells with APUD characteristics have not been identified in the human thymus, indirect evidence supports their presence. First is the demonstration of peptides in the thymus, and the histologic evidence of electron dense secretory tissue in thymic epithelium. Second is the common occurrence of ectopic "Apudoma syndromes" (tumors of APUD cells secreting hormones) associated with epithelial thymomas and carcinoids. Most frequent of these are the syndromes of ectopic ACTH and ADH secretion (Azzopardi and Williams, 1968; Liddle *et al.*, 1969; Tischler *et al.*, 1977). Neurotensin and somatostatin have been identified by both immunohistochemistry and immunoassay in the chicken thymus (Sundler *et al.*, 1978) but not to date in the mammalian thymus. We postulate that thymus APUD cells emerge and involute at specific periods in ontogeny as in the case of other organs (see also Czaba and Torok, 1974; LeDouarin and Jotereau, 1975; von Gudecker, 1975). In the rat pancreas, for example, large amounts of TRH are present in the neonate which decline over the first 2 weeks of life whereas pancreatic somatostatin, present in low amounts at birth, rises rapidly over the same time interval (Kowusalo and Leppoluoto, 1979; Ghirlanda *et al.*, 1979). The occurrence of neuropeptides in the thymus would have important implications for neuroendocrine modulation of thymus-dependent immune function.

Nonendocrine Aspects of Hypothalamic Function that May Modulate the Immune Response

The neuroendocrine mechanisms that we have described in this chapter are all either controlled or modified by the hypothalamus and related brain centers. The neuroendocrine response to an internal or environmental stimulus integrates the biochemical, metabolic, or hormonal events that follow from the stimulus. These neuroendocrine pathways in turn are integrated via the nervous system with other complex behavioral and homeostatic responses. The simultaneous initiation of behavioral, neuroendocrine, and autonomic events complicates the task of evaluating the effect of one of those components on the immune response. For example, following bacterial challenge, food intake decreases (Murray and Murray, 1979), body temperature rises, cortisol levels rise, and concentration of the thyroid hormone, triiodothyronine, falls. The extent that these responses play a role in subsequent immune events or are epiphenomena of the immune response are unknown. In this section, we will briefly describe some of the homeostatic functions of the hypothalamus that may play a role in immune modulation, all of which have neuroendocrine correlates and should be considered in experimental studies of hypothalamic lesions.

Temperature

Hyperthermia is one of the most primitive forms of vertebrate defense against pathogen challenge. Poikilothermic animals actively seek a warmer environment after infection, and, if restrained from doing so, suffer increased mortality. In mammals, this process is under hypothalamic control, and fever may play an adaptive role in many immune challenges (Liu and Walford, 1972). *In vitro*, lymphocytes perform better at 40°C than at 37°C (Smith *et al.*, 1978). As an example of the importance of body temperature, cervical dislocation which reduces antibody formation probably does so because the procedure causes hypothermia (Stanton *et al.*, 1942).

Both heat and cold sensors are present in the hypothalamus (Dinarello and Wolff, 1978). They activate autonomic responses that control skin and respiratory heat exchange. Leukocyte and bacterial pyrogens act on the hypothalamus. The overall effect of posterior hypothalamic lesions is to cause hypothermia, and anterior lesions acutely cause hyperthermia (Plum and Van, 1978). Environmental temperature alters thyroid function in animals and cortisol secretion in man (Tuomisto *et al.*, 1976).

Appetite Regulation

The hypothalamus is the dominant center for the control of food intake and related energy metabolism. It contains both a glucostat that controls short-term food consumption and a "lipostat" that monitors long-term maintenance of weight and caloric consumption. The ventral medial nucleus (VMH) plays a dominant role in integrating the hormonal and autonomic concomitants of appetite regulation (Bray, 1974; Panskepp, 1974; Debons *et al.*, 1970; Grossman, 1977). Stimulation of the VMH leads to cessation of food intake, while lesions of this region decrease satiety and produce a distinctive obesity syndrome. The VMH acts in part by suppressing the lateral hypothalamus that controls active feeding behavior and associated vagal anabolic pathways, for example, insulin release (Frohman *et al.*, 1971). Vagotomy abolishes both the hyperinsulinemia and obesity that is associated with VMH lesions. The decreased autonomic activity associated with fasting is also under hypothalamic control. Mice with VMH damage are unable to reduce catecholamine turnover to the same degree as pair fasted controls (Young and Landsberg, 1980). Ascending bioaminergic pathways also modify hypothalamic feeding centers (Baez *et al.*, 1977). Ascending noradrenergic pathways exert both stimulatory (alpha receptors) and inhibitory (beta) effects on food intake (Oltmans *et al.*, 1978; Leibowitz, 1976). Serotonin exerts a braking effect on food intake that relates in part to specific dietary intake (Coscina and Stancer, 1977; Blundell, 1977; Sullivan and Cheng, 1978).

Several excellent reviews have been written about the effect of nutrition on immune function (Gross and Newberne, 1980; McFarlane, 1976; Bistrian, 1977; Scrimshaw *et al.*, 1968). While malnutrition has been most extensively studied, altered dietary content (e.g., increased protein content) may also alter immunoregulatory response (Fernandez *et al.*, 1972). With the exception of the role of cortisol in starvation states, there have been few studies of hormone–nutrition interaction in host defense. Such interactions may be important not only acutely, such as in hospitalization or stress, but also chronically, as in aging-related changes in nutrition, hormone responses, and immune function (Denckla, 1978; Smith et al., 1975; Shank, 1976). Changes in food intake must be well controlled in any study of neurologic lesions.

Sleep–Wake Cycles

Virtually all hypothalamic functions fluctuate diurnally. Some, such as those that regulate GH or prolactin secretion, are directly related to the sleep cycle, while others, such as ACTH regulators, are more loosely entrained to sleep than to the primary diurnal oscillator in the suprachiasmatic nucleus (Moore, 1978). The posterior hypothalamus maintains wakefulness under the tonic influence of the ascending reticular activating system, whereas the anterior hypothalamus and related limbic structures produce synchronous slow wave sleep. Ascending serotonergic and noradrenergic pathways are also necessary for maintenance of slow wave and REM sleep, respectively. And these same pathways affect most neuroendocrine function (see sections on the hypothalamic–pituitary axis).

Vascular Control

We have speculated on the possibility that local microvascular responses mediated by neuropeptides might alter either the early phase of the immune response or delayed hypersensitivity reactions. The hypothalamus exerts control over cardiovascular–respiratory reflexes via the autonomic nervous system. Effector sympathetic and parasympathetic neurons are scattered throughout the hypothalamus in a topographically specific and selective distribution. In general, sympathetic activity increases after stimulation of caudal and medial hypothalamic zones, and parasympathetic activity after anterior and lateral hypothalamic stimulation (Plum and Van, 1978). Selective lesions of the preoptic anterior hypothalamus result in hypertension, hyperthermia, and pulmonary edema (Gamble and Patton, 1953).

Many specific hypothalamic cardiorespiratory reflexes are modulated by both ascending medullary and pontine neural pathways as well as afferents from the visceral brain. As with neuroendocrine responses, the hypothalamus serves as the crucial anatomic and functional integrator of impulses transmitted by these pathways. Control of the microvascular circulation may prove to be a crucial form of brain modulation of immunity (e.g., Luparello et al., 1964). Regional differences in the expression of delayed hypersensitivity are more likely due to regional differences in microvascular responses than to differences in overall immunologic or neuroendocrine reactions (Blecha et al., 1980).

CONCLUDING COMMENTS AND SPECULATIONS

In this chapter, we have discussed the basic mechanisms by which the brain communicates biochemically or hormonally with the non-neuronal components of the organism. Neuroendocrine cells acting through both brain and peripheral neural, endocrine, and paracrine secretion modulate a vast array of peripheral metabolic and hormonal systems. It would be unreasonable to believe that a system as complex as the immune system that determines host defense and maintenance of self would not be modulated by neuroendocrine factors. Such modulation could be relatively crude and nonspecific as during the neuroendocrine and autonomic responses to severe stress, or it might prove to be exquisitely specific such as the day-to-day modulation of both immune stimulating and suppressor functions. Psychic states such as depression, suppressed rage or, conversely, "wellness" might alter immunity (Rogers, *et al.*, 1979; Bartrop *et al.*, 1977; Cohen and Eisdorfer,1977) not only through hypothalamic–pituitary control but by other brain secretions or by spinal–peripheral neuroendocrine mechanisms. Ontogenetic changes in neuropeptide secretion may either specifically alter immunity through thymic hormone secretion, for example, or indirectly via effects on nutrition and energy metabolism (Kishimoto *et al.*, 1979; Antel *et al.*, 1978).

Medical science has progressed largely through a reductionist approach in which the components of homeostatic systems are dissected, analyzed, and eventually synthesized. The study of neuroendocrine modulation of immunity is in its very earliest reductionist phase. Not only are whole body approaches such as hypothalamic lesioning and endocrine ablations required, but also *in vitro* approaches in which specific components of the immune process can be subjected to neuropeptide or hormonal manipulation. Our intention in this review is to emphasize specific elements by which the brain (and hence emotional state) might influence the immune response. Once characterized and made accessible for quantitative measurement, these elements may be fitted into a holistic biobehavioral or psychological approach to the problem of psychological control of the immune response.

REFERENCES

Ahlqvist, J. (1976). Endocrine influences on lymphatic organs, immune responses, inflammation and immunity. *Acta Endocrinol. (Copenhagen), Suppl.* **206.**

Ajika, K., and Ochi, J. (1978). Serotonergic projections to the suprachiastmatic nucleus and the median eminence of the rat: Identification by fluorescence and electron microscope. *J. Anat.* **127,** 563–576.

Alpert, L., Brawer, J., Patel, Y., and Reichlin, S. (1976). Somatostatinergic neurons in anterior hypothalamus: Immunohistochemical localization. *Endocrinology* **98,** 225–258.

Antel, J. P., Weinrick, M., and Arnason, B. (1978). Circulating suppressor cells in man as a function of age. *Clin. Immunol. Immunopathol.* **9,** 134–141.

Arimura, A., and Schally, A. V. (1976). Increase in basal and thyrotropin-releasing hormone

(TRH)-stimulated secretion of thyrotropin (TSH) by passive immunization with antiserum to somatostatin in rats. *Endocrinology* **98**, 1069–1072).

Arimura, A., Smith, W., and Schally, A. (1976). Blockade of the stress induced decrease in blood growth hormone by anti-somatostatin serum in rats. *Endocrinology* **98**, 540–543.

Azzopardi, J. C., and Williams, E. D. (1968). Pathology of 'non-endocrine' tumors associated with Cushing's syndrome. *Cancer* **22**, 274–286.

Baez, L. A., Ahlskog, J. E., and Randall, P. K. (1977). Body weight and regulatory deficits following unilateral nigrostriatal lesions. *Brain Res.* **132**, 467–476.

Barber, R. P., Vaughn, J. E., Slemmon, J. R., Salvaterra, P. M., Roberts, E., and Leeman, S. E. (1979). The origin, distribution and synaptic relationships of Substance P axons in rat spinal cord. *J. Comp. Neurol.* **184**, 331–351.

Barker, J. L., Neal, J. H., Smith, T. G., and MacDonald, R. L. (1978). Opiate peptide modulation of amino acid responses suggests novel form of neuronal communication. *Science* **199**, 1451–1453.

Bartrop, R. W., Lazarus, L., Luckhurst, E., Kiloh, L. G., and Penny, R. (1977). Depressed lymphocyte function after bereavement. *Lancet* **1**, 834–836.

Besedovsky, H., Sorkin, E., Felix, D., and Haas, H. (1977). Hypothalamic change during the immune response. *Eur. J. Immunol.* **7**, 323–325.

Bhathena, S. J., Schecter, G. P., Gazdan, A., Louie, J., and Recant, L. (1980). Glucagon and somatostatin receptors on circulating human mononuclear leukocytes. *62nd Annu. Meet. Endocr. Soc.* Abstract No. 329.

Birk-Launidsen, U., Faber, J., Friis, T., Kirkeegaard, C., and Nerap, J. (1976). Thyrotropin (TSH) release during altered adrenergic alpha and beta receptor influence. *Horm. Metab. Res.* **8**, 406–407.

Bisbaum, A. I., and Fields, H. L. (1978). Endogenous pain control mechanisms: Review and hypothesis. *Ann. Neurol.* **4**, 451–462.

Bissette, G., Mamberg, P., Nemeroff, C. B., and Prange, A. J. (1978). Neurotensin, a biologically active peptide. *Life Sci.* **23**, 2173–2182.

Black, S., Humphrey, J. H., and Nusin, J. S. F. (1963). Inhibition of mantoux reaction by direct suggestion under hypnosis. *Br. J. Med.* **2**, 1649–1652.

Blackburn, A. M., Bloom, S. R., Long, R. G., Fletcher, D. R., Christofides, N. D., Fitzpatrick, M. L., and Baron, J. H. (1980). Effect of neurotensin on gastrin function in man. *Lancet* **1**, 987–989.

Blecha, F., Barry, R. A., and Kelley, K. W. (1980). Stress-induced alterations in cell-mediated immunity of mice *in vivo*. *Fed. Proc.* **39**(3), 479.

Blumberg, S., Teichberg, V. I., Charli, J. L., Hersh, L. B., and McKelvy, J. F. (1980). Cleavage of Substance P to an N-Terminal tetrapeptide and C-terminal heptapeptide by a post proline cleaving enzyme from bovine brain. *Brain Res.* **192**, 477–486.

Blundell, J. E. (1977). Is there a role for serotonin (5-hydrotryptamine) in feeding? *Int. J. Obes.* **1**, 15–42.

Bottenstein, J., Hayashi, H., Hutchings, S., Masul, H., Mather, J., McClure, D. B., Ohasa, S., Rizzino, A., Sato, G., Serrero, G., Wolfe, R., and Wu, R. (1979). The growth of cells in serum-free hormones-supplemented media. *In* "Methods in Enzymology" (W. B. Jakoby and I. H. Pastan, eds.), Vol. 58, pp. 94–109. Academic Press, New York.

Bourne, H. R., Lichtenstein, L. M., and Melmon, K. L. (1974). Modulation of inflammation and immunity by cyclic AMP. *Science* **184**, 19–21.

Bray, G. A. (1974). Endocrine factors in the control of food intake. *Fed. Proc., Fed. Am. Soc. Exp. Biol.* **33**, 1140–1145.

Brazeau, P., Vale, W., Burgus, R., Ling, N., Butcher, M., Rivier, J., and Guillemin, R. (1973). Hypothalamic polypeptide that inhibits the secretion of immunoreactive pituitary growth hormone. *Science* **179**, 77–79.

Brimijoin, S., Lundberg, J. M., Brodin, E., Hökfelt, T., and Nilsson, G. (1980). Axonal transport of Substance P in the vagus and sciatic nerves of the guinea pig. *Brain Res.* **191**, 443–457.

Brown, G. M., and Reichlin, S. (1972) Psychologic and neural regulation of growth hormone secretion. Psychosomatic Med 34, 45–61.

Bugnon, C., Fellman, D., and Block, B. (1978). Immunocytochemical study of the ontogenesis of the hypothalamic somatostatin containing neurons in the human fetus. *Metab. Clin. Exp.* **27**, 1161–1165.

Burgus, R., Dunn, T. F., Desiderio, D., Ward, D. N., Vale, W., and Guillemin, R. (1970). Characterization of the hypothalamic hypophysiotropic TSH-releasing factor (TRF) of ovine origin. *Nature (London)* **226**, 321–325.

Burnstock, G., Iverson, L. I., Hökfelt, T., Kosterlitz, H. W., Gershon, M. D., and Szuszerski, J. H. (1979). Nonadrenergic, noncholinergic autonomic neurotransmission mechanisms. *Neurosci. Res. Program. Bull,* **17**, 379–519.

Bistrian, B. R. (1977). Interaction of nutrition and infection in the hospital setting. *Am. J. Clin. Nutr.* **30**, 1228–1232.

Cantor, H., and Gershon, K. (1979). Immunologic circuits: Cellular composition. *Fed. Proc., Fed. Am. Soc. Exp. Biol.* **38**, 2058–2064.

Carraway, R., and Leeman, S. E. (1973). The isolation of a new hypotensive peptide, neurotensin, from bovine hypothalami. *J. Biol. Chem.* **248**, 6854–6861.

Cash, J. D., Gader, A. M., Mulder, J. L., Cort, J. H. (1978). Structure-activity relations of the fibrinolytic response to vasopressins in man. *Clin. Sci. Mol. Med.* **54**, 403–409.

Chahl, L. A. (1977). Interactions of Substance P with putative mediators of inflammation and ATP. *Eur. J. Pharmacol.* **44**, 45–49.

Chan, V., Jones, A., Liendo-Ch, P., McNeilly, A., Landon, J., and Besser, G. M. (1978). The relationship between circadian variations in circulating thyrotropin, thyroid hormones and prolactin. *Clin. Endocrinol.* **9**, 337–349.

Chan-Palay, V., Jonsson, G., and Palay, S. L. (1978). Serotonin and Substance P co-exist in neurons of the rat's central nervous system. *Proc. Natl. Acad. Sci. U.S.A.* **75**, 1582–1586.

Chapman, L. F., and Goodell, H. (1964). The participation of the nervous system in the inflammatory reaction. *Ann. N.Y. Acad. Sci.* **116**, 990–1017.

Chen, M. J., and Meites, J. (1975). Effects of biogenic amines and TRH on release of prolactin and TSH in the rat. *Endocrinology* **96**, 10–14.

Chihara, K., Arimura, A., Coy, D. H., and Schally, A. V. (1978a). Studies on the interaction of endorphins, Substance P, and endogenous somatostatin in growth hormone and prolactin release in rats. *Endocrinology* **102**, 281–290.

Chihara, K., Arimura, A., Chihara, M., and Schally, A. V. (1978b). Studies on the mechanism of growth hormone and thyrotropin responses to somatostatin antiserum in anesthetized rats. *Endocrinology* **103**, 1916–1923.

Clement-Jones, V., Lowry, P. J., Rees. L. H., and Besser G. M. (1980). Met-enkephalin circulates in human plasma. *Nature,* **283**, 295–297.

Cohen, D., and Eisdorfer, C. (1977). Behavior–immunologic relationships in older men and women. *Exp. Aging Res.* **3**, 225–229.

Coscina, D. V., and Stancer, H. C. (1977). Selective blockade of hypothalamic hyperphagia and obesity in rats by serotonin depleting midbrain lesions. *Science* **195**, 416–418.

Cryer, P. E., and Daughaday, W. H. (1977). Growth hormone. *In* "Clinical Neuroendocrinology" (L. Martini and G. M. Besser, eds.), pp. 243–278. Academic Press, New York.

Csaba, G., and Torok, O. (1974). Examination of the gamori-positive cells of the thymus in tissue culture. *Endocrinol. Exp.* **8**, 3–12.

Cutz, E. Chan, W., Track, N. S., Goth, A., and Said, S. (1978). Release of vasoactive intestinal polypeptide in mast cells by histamine liberators. *Nature (London)* **275**, 661–662.

Davson, H. (1967). "Physiology of the Cerebrospinal Fluid." Little, Brown, Boston, Massachusetts.

Debons, A. F., Krimsky, I., and From, A. (1970). A direct action of insulin on the hypothalamic feeding center. *Am. J. Physiol.* **219**, 938–943.

Delitala, G., Stubbs, W. A., Wass, J. A., Jones, A., Williams, S., and Besser, G. M. (1979). Effect of the H_2 receptor antagonist cimetidine on pituitary hormones in man. *Clin. Endocrinol.* **11**, 161–167.

Denckla, W. D. (1978). Interactions between age and the neuroendocrine and immune systems. *Fed. Proc., Fed. Am. Soc. Exp. Biol.* **37**, 1263–1267.

Dinarello, C. A., and Wolff, S. M. (1978). Pathogenesis of fever in man. *N. Engl. J. Med.* **298**, 607–612.

Dockray, G. J. (1979). Evolutionary relationships of the gut hormones. *Fed. Proc., Fed. Am. Soc. Exp. Biol.* **38**, 2295–2301.

Dougherty, T. F. (1952). Effect of hormones on lymphatic tissue. *Physiol. Rev.* **32**, 379–401.

Dunn, J., and Critchlow, V. (1973). Electrically stimulated ACTH release in pharmacologically blocked rats. *Endocrinolgy* **98**, 835–842.

Dutton, R. W., and Scavulli, J. (1975). Suppressor T cells in the regulation of the immune response. *Res. J. Reticulo endothel. Soc.* **17**, 187–190.

Eidinger, D., and Garrett, T. J. (1972). Studies of the regulatory effects of sex hormones on antibody formation and stem cell differentiation. *J. Exp. Med.* **136**, 1098.

Ferland, L., Labrie, F., Jobin, M., Arimura, A., and Schally, A. V. (1976). Physiological role of somatostatfn in the control of growth hormone and thyrotropin secretion. *Biochem. Biophys. Res. Commun.* **68**, 149–155.

Fernandez, G., Yunis, E. J., Smith, J., and Good, R. A. (1972). Dietary influence on antinuclear antibodies and cell-mediated immunity in NZB mice. *Proc. Soc. Exp. Biol. Med.* **139**, 1189–1196.

Fernstrom, J. D., Fisher, L., Cusack, B. M., and Gillis, M. A. (1980). Radioimmunologic detection and measurement of nonapeptides in the pineal gland. *Endocrinology* **106**, 243–250.

Feyrter, F. (1938). "Uber Diffuse Endokrine Epitheliale Organe." Barth, Leipzig.

Fillenz, M. (1970). The innervation of the cat spleen. *Proc. R. Soc. London* **174**, 459–468.

Fink, G. (1979). Feedback action of target hormones on hypothalamus and pituitary with special references to gonadal steroids. *Annu. Rev. Physiol.* **41**, 571–585.

Flerkó, B. (1980). The hypophysial portal circulation today. *Neuroendocrinology* **30**, 56–63.

Foley, K. M., Kourides, I. A., Intrurissi, C. E., Karko, R. F., Zaroulis, C. G., Poshner, J. B., Houde, R. W., and Haoli, C. (1979). β-Endorphin: Analgesia and hormonal effects in humans. *Proc. Natl. Acad. Sci. U.S.A.* **76**, 5377–5381.

Forssmann, W. G., Helmstaedter, V., Metz, J., Muhlmann, G., Feurle, G. E. (1978). Immuno-histochemistry and ultrastructure of somatostatin cells with special reference to the gastroenteropancreatic (GEP) system. *Metab., Clin. Exp.* **1**, 1179–1190.

Fratta, W., Yang, H. Y. T., Majane, B., and Costa, E. (1979). Distribution of β-endorphin and related peptides in the hypothalamus and pituitary. *Neuroscience* **4**, 1903–1908.

Franchimont, P., and Roulier, R. (1977). Gonadotropin secretion in male subjects. *In* "Clinical Neuroendocrinology" (L. Martini and G. M. Besser, eds.), pp. 197–212. Academic Press, New York.

Frohman, L. A., and Bernardis, L. L. (1971). Effect of hypothalamic stimulation on plasma glucose, insulin, and glucagon levels *Am. J. Physiol.* **221**, 1596–1603.

Fuxe, K., Andersson, K., Hökfelt, T., Mutt, V., Ferland, L., Agnati, L. F., Ganton, D., Said, S., Eneroth, P., Gustafsson, J. A. (1979). Localization and possible function of peptidergic neurons and their interactions with central catecholaminergic neurons, and the central action of gut hormones. *Fed. Proc.* **38**(a), 2333–2340.

Gamble, J. E., and Patton, H. D. (1953). Pulmonary edema and hemorrhage from preoptic lesions in rats. *Am. J. Physiol.* **172**, 623–631.

Gamse, R., Lembeck, F., and Cuello, A. C. (1979). Substance P in the vagus nerve: Immunochemical and immunohistochemical evidence for axoplasmic transport. *Naunyn-Schmiedeberg's Arch. Pharmacol.* **306**, 37–44.

Gay, V. I. (1972). The hypothalamus: Physiology and clinical use of releasing factors. *Fertil. Steril.* **23**, 50.

Gerich, J. E., and Lorenzi, M. (1978). The role of the autonomic nervous system and somatostatin in the control of insulin and glucagon secretion. In "Frontiers in Neuroendocrinology" (W. Ganong and L. Martini, eds.), Vol. 5, pp. 265-288. Raven Press, New York.

Ghirlanda, G. D., Bataille, D., Dubois, M. D., and Rosselin, G. (1979). Variations of the somatostatin content of gut, pancreas, and brain in the developing rat. Metab., Clin. Exp. 27, 1167-1170.

Gibbs, D. M., and Neill, J. D. (1978). Dopamine levels in hypophysial stalk blood in the rat are sufficient to inhibit prolactin secretion in vivo. Endocrinology 102, 1915-1920.

Gibbs, D. M., Plotsky, P. M., De Greef, W. J., and Neill, J. D. (1979). Effect of histamine and acetylcholine on hypophysial stalk plasma dopamine and peripheral plasma prolactin levels. Life Sci. 24, 2063-2070.

Gilbert, R. F. T., Emson, P. C., Tahrenkrug, J., Lee, C. M., Penman, E., and Wass, J. (1980). Axonal transport of neuropeptides in the cervical vagus nerve of the rat. J. Neurochem. 34, 108-113.

Gisler, R. H., and Schenkel-Hulliger, L. (1971). Hormonal regulation of the immune response. II. Influence of pituitary and adrenal activity on immune responsiveness in vitro. Cell. Immunol. 2, 646-657.

Gospodarowicz, D. (1975). Purification of a fibroblast growth factor from bovine pituitary. J. Biol. Chem. 250, 2512-2520.

Graham, H. T., Lowry, O. H., Wahl, N., and Priebat, M. (195). Mast cells as sources of tissue histamine. J. Exp. Med. 102, 307-318.

Greer, M. A. (1952). The role of the hypothalamus in the control of thyroid function. J. Clin. Endocrinol. Metab. 12, 1259-1268.

Gross, R. L., and Newberne, P. M. (1980). Role of nutrition in immunologic function. Physiol. Rev. 1, 188-294.

Grossman, S. P. (1977). The neuroanatomy of eating and drinking behavior. Hosp. Pract. (May), 12, 45-53.

Guillemin, R. (1978a). β-lipotropin and endorphins: Implications of current knowledge. Hosp. Pract. (November), 13, 232-240.

Guillemin, R. (1978b). Peptides in the brain: The new endocrinology of the neuron. Science 202, 390-402.

Hagermark, O., Hökfelt, T., and Pernow, B. (1978). Flare and itch induced by Substance P in human skin. J. Invest. Dermatol. 71, 233-235.

Halasz, B. (1969). The endocrine effects of isolation of the hypothalamus from the rest of the brain. In "Frontiers in Neuroendocrinology" (W. Ganong and L. Martini, eds.), pp. 307-342. Oxford Univ. Press, London, and New York.

Harris, A. R. C., Christianson, D., Smith, M. S., Fang, S.-L., Braverman, L. E., and Vagenakis, A. C. (1978). The physiological role of thyrotropin releasing hormone in the regulation of thyroid stimulating hormone and prolactin secretion in the rat. J. Clin. Invest. 61, 441-448.

Harris, G. W. (1948). Neural control of the pituitary gland. Physiol. Rev. 28, 139-179.

Hayes, A. G., and Tyers. M. B. (1980). Effects of capsaicin on nocioceptive heat, pressure, and chemical thresholds and on Substance P levels in the rat. Brain Res. 189, 561-564.

Haymaker, W., Anderson, E., and Nauta, W. (1969). "The Hypothalamus." Thomas, Springfield, Illinois.

Hedge, G. A., and Smelik, P. G. (1967). Corticotropin release inhibition by intrahypothalamic implantation of atropine. Science 159, 891-892.

Herbert, E., Roberts, J., Phillips, M., Allen, R., Hinman, M., Budarf, M., Policastro, P., and Rosa, P. et al. (1980). Biosynthesis, processing and release of corticotropin, β-endorphin, and melanocyte stimulating hormone in pituitary cell culture systems. In "Frontiers in Neuroendocrinology" (L. Martini and W. F. Ganong, eds.), Vol. 6, 67-101. Raven Press, New York.

Hinterberger, W., Cerny, C., Kinast, H., Pointer, H., and Trag, K. H. (1977). Somatostatin reduces the release of colony-stimulating activity (CSA) from PHA-activated mouse spleen lymphocytes. *Experientia* **34**, 860–862.

Hiroshige, T., and Kaneko, M. (1978). Involvement of brain biogenic amines in the feedback of ACTH secretion under stress in the rat. *Gunma Symp. Endocrinol.* **15**, 69–79.

Hökfelt, T., Kellerth, J. O., Nilsson, G., and Pernow, B. (1975a). Substance P: Localization in the central nervous system and some primary sensory neurons. *Science* **190**, 889–890.

Hökfelt, T., Kellerth, J. O., Nilsson, G., and Pernow, B. (1975b). Experimental immunohistochemical studies on the localization and distribution of Substance P in cat primary sensory neurons. *Brain Res.* **100**, 235–252.

Hökfelt, T., Elde, R. P., Johansson, O., Luft, R., Nilsson, G., and Arimura, A. (1976). Immunohistochemical evidence for separate populations of somatostatin-containing and Substance P-containing primary afferent neurons. *Neuroscience* **1**, 131–136.

Hökfelt, T., Elfvin, L.-G., Elde, R., Schultzberg, M., Goldstein, M., and Luft, R. (1977). Occurrence of somatostatin-like immunoreactivity in some peripheral noradrenergic neurons. *Proc. Natl. Acad. Sci. U.S.A.* **74**, 3587–3591.

Hökfelt, T., Johansson, O., Ljungdahl, A., Lundberg, J., Schultzberg, M., Fuxe, K., Goldstein, M., Steinbusch, H., Verhofstad, A., and Elde, R. (1979). Neurotransmitters and neuropeptides: Distribution patterns and cellular localization as revealed by immunocytochemistry. *In* "Central Regulation of the Endocrine System" (K. Fuxe, T. Hökfelt, and R. Luft, eds.), pp. 31–48. Plenum, New York.

Hughes, J., Smith, T. W., Kosterlitz, H. W., Fothergill, L. A., Morgan, B. A., and Morris, H. R. (1975). Identification of two related pentapeptides from the brain with potent opiate agonist activity. *Nature (London)* **258**, 577–579.

Jancso, N., Jancso-Gabor, A., and Szolescany, J. (1967). Direct evidence for neurogenic inflammation and its prevention by denervation and by pretreatment with Capsaicin. *Br. J. Pharmacol. Chemother.* **31**, 138–151.

Jancsó, N., Jancsó-Gabor, A., and Szolescany, J. (1968). The role of sensory nerve endings in neurogenic inflammation induced in human skin and in the eye and paw of the rat. *Br. J. Pharmacol. Chemother.* **33**, 32–41.

Janković, B. D., and Isaković, K. (1973). Neuroendocrine correlates of immune response. *Int. Arch. Allergy Appl. Immunol.* **45**, 360–372.

Janković, B. D., Isaković, K., and Petrovic, S. (1970). Effect of pinealectomy on immune reactions in the rat. *Immunology* **18**, 1–6.

Jeffcoate, W. J., Rees, L. H., Lowry, P. J., and Besser, G. M. (1978). A specific radioimmunoassay for human β-lipotropin. *J. Clin. Endocrinol. Metab.* **47**, 160–167.

Jessell, T. M., and Iverson, L. L. (1977). Opiate analgesics inhibit Substance P release from rat trigeminal nucleus. *Nature (London)* **268**, 549–551.

Jessen, K. R., Polak, J. M., Van Noorden, S., Bloom, S. R., and Burnstock, G. (1980). Peptide containing neurons connect the two ganglionated plexuses of the enteric nervous system. *Nature (London)* **283**, 391–393.

Johnson, A. R., and Erdos, E. G. (1973). Release of histamine from mast cells by vasoactive peptides. *Proc. Soc. Exp. Biol. Med.* **142**, 1252–1256.

Jones, W. O., Rothwell, T. L. W., and Adams, D. B. (1978). Studies on the role of histamine and 5-hydroxytryptamine in immunity against the nematode *Trichostrongylis colubriformis. Int. Arch. Allergy Appl. Immunol.* **57**, 48–50.

Joseph, S. A., and Knigge, K. M. (1978). The endocrine hypothalamus: Recent anatomic studies. *In* "The Hypothalamus" (S. Reichlin, R. J. Baldessarini, and J. B. Martin, eds.), pp. 15–47. Raven Press, New York.

Jouzzo, J. L., Sams, W. M., Jr., Jegasothy, B. V., and Olansky, J. (1980). Cimetidine as an immunomodulator: Chronic mucocutaneous candidiasis as a model. *Ann. Intern. Med.* **92**, 192–195.

Kaneko, M., and Hiroshige, T. (1978). Fast rate—sensitive corticosteroid negative feedback during stress. *Am J. Physiol.* **234**, 34–35.

Kaneto, A., Kaneko, T., Kajinuma, H., and Kosaka, K. (1978). Effects of Substance P and neurotensin infused intrapancreatically on glucagon and insulin release. *Endocrinology* **102**, 393–401.

Kashahara, K., Tanaka, S., Ito, T., and Hamoshima, Y. (1977). Suppression of the primary immune response by chemical sympathectomy. *Res. Commun. Chem. Pathol. Pharmacol.* **116**, 687–694.

Kato, Y., Iwasaki, Y., Iwasaki, J., Abe, H., Yanaihara, N., and Imura, H. (1978). Prolactin release by vasoactive intestinal polypeptides in rats. *Endocrinology* **103**, 554–558.

Kishimoto, S., Tomino, S., Mitsuya, H., and Fugiwara, H. (1979). Age related changes in suppressor functions of human T cells. *J. Immunol.* **123**, 1586–1593.

Knigge, K. M., and Joseph, S. A. (1971). Neural regulation of TSH secretion: Sites of thyroxine feedback. *Neuroendocrinology* **8**, 273–288.

Knigge, K. M., Penrod, C. H., and Schindler, W. J. (1959). *In vitro* and *in vivo* corticosteroid secretion following stress. *Am. J. Physiol.* **196**, 579–582.

Knobil, E., and Plant, T. M. (1978). Neuroendocrine control of gonadotropin secretion in the female rhesus monkey. *In* "Frontiers of Neuroendocrinology" (W. Ganong and L. Martini, eds.), Vol. 5, pp. 249–265. Raven Press, New York.

Konishi, S., Tsunoo, A., and Otsuka, M. (1979). Enkephalins presynaptically inhibit cholinergic transmission in sympathetic ganglia. *Nature (London)* **282**, 515–516.

Kowusalo, F., and Leppoluoto, J. (1979). High TRH immunoreactivity in the pancreas of fetal and neonatal rats. *Life Sci.* **24**, 1655–1658.

Krieger, D. T. (1977). Serotonin regulation of ACTH secretion. *Ann. N.Y. Acad. Sci.* **297**, 527–535.

Krieger, D. T. (1978). Factors influencing the circadian periodicity of ACTH and corticosteroids. *Med. Clin. North Am.* **62**, 251–259.

Krieger, M. S., Conrad, L. C., and Pfaff, D. W. (1979). An autoradiographic study of the efferent connections of the ventral medial hypothalamus. *J. Comp. Neurol.* **183**, 785–815.

Krisch, B. (1978). Hypothalamic and extrahypothalamic distribution of somatostatin immunoreactive elements in the rat brain. *Cell Tissue Res.* **499**, 499–513.

Krulich, L. (1979). Central neurotransmitters and secretion of prolactin, GH, LH, and TSH. *Annu. Rev. Physiol.* **41**, 603–615.

Krulich, L., Vijayan, E., Coppings, R. J., Giachetti, A., McCann, S. M., and Mayfield, M. A. (1979). On the role of the central serotonergic system in the regulation of the secretion of thyrotropin and prolactin. *Endocrinology* **105**, 276–283.

Krulich, L., Giachetti, A., Marchlewska-koj, A., Hejco, E., and Jameson, H. E. (1977). On the role of central noradrenergic and dopaminergic systems in the regulation of TSH secretion in the rat. *Endocrinology* **100**, 496–505.

Labrie, F., Borgeat, P., Drouin, J., Beaulieu, M., Lagace, L., Ferland, L., and Raymond, V. (1979). Mechanism of action of hypothalamic hormones in the adenohypophysis. *Annu. Rev. Physiol.* **41**, 555–569.

Lancranjan, I., Ohnhaus, E., and Girard, J. (1979). The α-adrenoceptor control of adrenocorticotropin secretion in man. *J. Clin. Endocrinol. Metab.* **49**, 227–230.

Larsson, L.-I. (1979). Innervation of the pancreas by Substance P, enkephalin, vasoactive intestinal polypeptide and gastrin/CCK immunoreactive nerves. *J. Histochem. Cytochem.* **27**, 1293–1294.

Lazarus, L. H., Ling, N., and Guillemin, R. (1976). β-Lipotropin as a prohormone for the morphinomimetic peptides endorphins and enkephalins. *Proc. Natl. Acad. Sci. U.S.A.* **73**, 2156–2159.

Lazarus, L. H., Perrin, M. H., Brown, M. R., and Rivier, J. E. (1977). Mast cell binding of neurotensin. *J. Biol. Chem.* **252**, 7180–7183.

Lechan, R. M., Nestler, J. L., Jacobson, S., and Reichlin, S. (1980). The hypothalamic "tuberoinfundibular" system of the rat as demonstrated by horseradish peroxidase (HRP) microiontophoresis. *Brain Res.* **195**, 13–27.

LeDouarin, N. M., and Jotereau, F. (1975). Tracing of cells of the avian thymus through embryonic life in interspecific chimeras. *J. Exp. Med.* **142**, 17–40.

Leeman, S. E., Mroz, E. A., and Carraway, R. E. (1977). Neurotensin and Substance P. *In* "Peptides in Neurobiology" (H. Gainer, ed.), pp. 99–144. Plenum, New York.

Leibowitz, S. F. (1976). Brain catecholaminergic mechanisms for control of hunger. *In* "Hunger: Basic Mechanisms and Clinical Implications" (D. Novin, W. Wyrwicka, and G. Bray, eds.), pp. 1–18. Raven Press, New York.

Lewis, T. (1927). *The blood vessels of human skin and their responses.* Shaw and Sons, London, England. **11**, 209–265.

Li, C. H., Barnofi, L., and Chrétien, M. (1965). Isolation and amino acid sequence of β-LPH from sheep pituitary glands. *Nature (London)* **208**, 1093–1094.

Liddle, G. W., Nicholson, W. E., Island, D. P., Orth, D. N., Kooru, A., and Lowder, S. C. (1969). Clinical and laboratory studies of ectopic humoral syndromes. *Recent Prog. Horm. Res.* **25**, 283–305.

Ling, N., Burgus, R., and Guillemin, R. (1976). Isolation, primary structure and synthesis of α-endorphin and γ-endorphin, new peptides of hypothalamic-hypophysial origin with morphomimetic activity. *Proc. Natl. Acad. Sci. U.S.A.* **73**, 3942–3946.

Liotta, A. S., Suda, T., and Krieger, D. T. (1978). β-Lipotropin is the major opioidlike peptide of human pituitary and rats pars distalis: Lack of significant β-endorphin. *Proc. Natl. Acad. Sci. U.S.A.* **75**, 2950–2954.

Liu, R. K., and Walford, R. L. (1972). The effect of lowered body temperature on life span and immune and nonimmune processes. *Gerontologia* **18**, 363–388.

Lundberg, J. M. (1979). Enkephalin, Substance P, VIP, somatostatin, gastrin/CCK and neurotensin in peripheral neurons. *Acta Physiol. Scand.* **473**, 19.

Lundberg, J. M., Hokfelt, T., Kewenter, J., Petterson, G., and Ahlmar, H. (1979). Substance P-, VIP-, and enkephalin-like immunoreactivity in the human vagus nerve. *Gastroenterology* **77**, 468–471.

Lundberg, J. M., Anggard, A., Fahrenkrug, J., Hökfelt, T., and Mutt, V. (1980). Vasoactive intestinal polypeptide in cholinergic neurons of exocrine glands: Functional significance of coexisting transmitters for vasodilation and secretion. *Proc. Natl. Acad. Sci. U.S.A.* **77**, 1651–1655.

Luparello, J., Stein, M., and Park, C. D. (1964). Effect of hypothalamic lesions on rat anaphylaxis. *Am. J. Physiol.* **207**, 911–914.

MacDonald, R. L., and Nelson, P. G. (1978). Specific opiate-induced depression of transmitter release from dorsal root ganglion cells in culture. *Science* **199**, 1449–1450.

McDonald, T. J., Jornavall, H., Nilsson, G., Vagne, M., Ghatei, M., Bloom, S. R., and Mutt, V. (1979). Characterization of a gastrin releasing peptide from porcine nonantral gastric tissue. *Biochem. Biophys. Res. Commun.* **90**, 227–233.

McDonough, R. J., Madden, J. J., Falek, A., Shafer, D. A., Pline, M., Gordon, D., Bokos, P., Kuchnle, J. C., and Mendelson, J. (1980). Alteration of T and null lymphocyte frequencies in peripheral blood of Human Opiate Addicts: *In vivo* evidence for opiate receptor sites on T lymphocytes *J. Immunol.* **125**, 2539–2543.

McFarlane, H. (1976). Malnutrition and impaired response to infection. *Proc. Nutr. Soc.* **35**, 263–272.

Maciag, T., Cerundolo, J., Ilsley, S., Kelley, S. P. R., and Forand, R. (1979). Identification and partial characterization of an endothelial growth factor from bovine hypothalamus. *Proc. Natl. Acad. Sci. U.S.A.* **76**, 5674–5678.

Maeda, K., and Frohman, L. A. (1978). Dissociation of systemic and central effects of neurotensin on the secretion of growth hormone, prolactin, and thyrotropin. *Endocrinology* **103**, 1903–1909.

Mains, R. E., Eipper, B. A., and Ling, N. (1977). Common precursor to corticotropins and endorphins. *Proc. Natl. Acad. Sci. U.S.A.* **74**, 3014–3018.

Mangili, G., Motta, M., and Martini, L. (1966). Control of adrenocorticotropic hormone secretion. *In* "Neuroendocrinology" (L. Martini and W. F. Ganong, eds.), pp. 298–360. Academic Press, New York.

Maor, D., Englander, T., Eylan, E., and Alexander, P. (1974). Participation of hormones in the early stages of the immune response. *Acta Endocrinol. (Copenhagen)* **75**, 205–208.

Martin, J. B. (1973). Neural regulation of growth hormone secretion. *N. Engl. J. Med.* **28**, 1384–1393.

Martin, J. B., Reichlin, S., and Brown, G. M. (1977). *Clinical Neuroendocrinology.* F. A. Davis Co., Philadelphia.

Martini, L. and Besser, G. M. (eds.), (1977), *Clinical Neuroendocrinology.* Academic Press, New York.

Mason, J. W. (1959). Plasma 17-hydroxycorticosteroid levels during electrical stimulation of the amygdaloid complex in conscious monkeys. *Am. J. Physiol.* **196**, 44–48.

Medawar, P. B., and Sparrow, E. M. (1956). The effect of adrenocortical hormones, adrenocorticotrophic hormone, and pregnancy in skin transplantation immunity in mice. *J. Endocrinol.* **14**, 240–256.

Meglio, M., Hosobuchi, Y., Loh, H. H., Adams, J. E., and Li, C. H. (1977). β-Endorphin: Behavioral and analgesic activity in cats. *Proc. Natl. Acad. Sci. U.S.A.* **74**, 774–776.

Molitch, M. E., and Reichlin, S. (1980). Absent Septum Pellucidum, Primary empty sella and hypopituitarism: Neuroendocrine aspects. Submitted for publication.

Moore, R. Y. (1978). Central neural control of circadian rhythms. *In* "Frontiers in Neuroendocrinology" (W. F. Ganong and L. Martini, eds.), Vol. 5, pp. 185–207. Raven Press, New York.

Moore, R. Y., and Bloom, F. E. (1978). Central catecholamine neuron systems: Anatomy and physiology of the dopamine systems. *Annu. Rev. Neurosci.* **1**, 129–169.

Moore, R. Y., and Bloom, F. E. (1979). Central catecholamine neuron systems: Anatomy and physiology of the norepinephrine and epinephrine systems. *Annu. Rev. Neurosci.* **2**, 113–168.

Morita, Y. (1979). Histamine induces ACTH secretion and inhibiting effects of antihistaminic drugs. *Jpn. J. Pharmacol.* **29**, 59–65.

Mroz, E. A., and Leeman, S. E. (1977). Substance P. *Vitam. Horm. (N.Y.)* **35**, 209–281.

Mudge, A. W., Leeman, S. E., and Fischbach, G. D. (1979). Enkephalin inhibits release of Substance P from sensory neurons in culture and decreases action potential duration. *Proc. Natl. Acad. Sci. U.S.A.* **76**, 526–530.

Murray, M. J., and Murray, A. B. (1979). Anorexia of infection as a mechanism of host defense. *Am. J. Clin. Nutr.* **32**, 593–596.

Nagai, K., and Frohman, L. A. (1978). Neurotensin hyperglycemia: Evidence for histamine mediation and the assessment of a possible physiologic role. *Diabetes* **27**, 577–582.

Nagy, E., and Berczi, I. (1979). Immunodeficiency in hypophysectomized rats. *Fed. Proc., Fed. Am. Soc. Exp. Biol.* **38**, 1355.

Nakao, K., Nakai, Y., Oki, S., Matsubra, S., Konishi, T., Nishitani, H., and Imura, H. (1980). Immunoreactive β-endorphin in human cerebrospinal fluid. *J. Clin. Endocrinol. Metab.* **50**, 230–233.

Neill, J. (1980). Neuroendocrine regulation of prolactin secretion. *In* "Frontiers in Neuroendocrinology" (L. Martini and W. F. Ganong, eds.), Vol. 6, pp. 129–156. Raven Press, New York.

Nilsson, G., Pernow, B., Fischer, G. H., and Folkers, K. (1975). Presence of Substance P-like immunoreactivity in plasma from man and dog. *Acta Physiol. Scand.* **94**, 542–544.

Olgart, L., Gazelius, B., Brodin, E., and Nilsson, G. (1977). Release of Substance P-like immunoreactivity from dental pulp. *Acta Physiol. Scand.* **101**, 510–512.

Oltmans, G. A., Lorden, J. F., and Margules, D. L. (1978). Food intake and body weight: Effects of specific and nonspecific lesions in the midbrain path of the ascending noradrenergic neurons of the rat. *Brain Res.* **128**, 293–308.

Osband, M., Gallison, D., Miller, B., Agarawel, R. P., and McCaffrey, R. (1980). Concanavalin A activation of suppressor cells mediated by histamine and blocked by cimetidine. *Clin. Res.* **28**, 356A.

Palkovits, M. (1979). Effects of surgical deafferentiation on the transmitter and hormone content of the hypothalamus. *Neuroendocrinology* **29**, 140–148.

Panskepp, J. (1974). Hypothalamic regulation of energy balance and feeding behavior. *Fed. Proc., Fed. Am. Soc. Exp. Biol.* **33**, 1150–1165.

Patel, Y. C. (1979). Growth hormone stimulates hypothalamic somatostatin. *Life Sci.* **24**, 1589–1594.

Patel, Y. C., Hoyte, K., and Martin, J. (1979). Effect of anterior hypothalamic lesions on neurohypophysial and peripheral tissue concentration of somatostatin in the rat. *Endocrinology* **105**, 712–714.

Pearse, A. G. E. (1977). The diffuse neuroendocrine system and the APUD concept: Related "endocrine" peptides in brain, intestine, pituitary, placenta, and annuran cutaneous gland. *Med. Biol.* **55**, 115–125.

Perrone, M. H., and Hinkle, P. M. (1978). Regulation of pituitary receptors for thyrotropin-releasing hormone by thyroid hormones. *J. Biol. Chem.* **253**, 5168–5173.

Pictet, R. L., Rall, L. B., Phelps, P., and Rutter, W. J. (1976). The neural crest and the origin of insulin-producing and other gastrointestinal hormone producing cells. *Science* **191**, 191–192.

Pimstone, B., Berelowitz, M., Kanold, D., Shapiro, B., and Kronheim, S. (1978). Somatostatin-like immunoreactivity (SRIF-Li) in human and rat serum. *Metab., Clin. Exp.* **27**, 1145–1149.

Plum, F., and Van, W. J. (1978). Nonendocrine disease and disorders of the hypothalamus. *In* "The Hypothalamus" (S. Reichlin, R. J. Baldessarini, and J. B. Martin, eds.), pp. 415–473. Raven Press, New York.

Rasool, C. G., Schwartz, A. L., Bollinger, J., and Reichlin, S. (1981). Somatostatin distribution and axoplasmic transport in the rat peripheral nerve. *Endocrinology* **108**, 44–48.

Re, R. N., Kourides, I. A., Ridgway, E. C., Weintraub, B. D., and Maloof, F. (1976). The effect of glucocorticoid administration on human pituitary secretion of thyrotropin and prolactin. *J. Clin. Endocrinol. Metab.* **43**, 338–346.

Rees, L. H. (1977). Human adrenocorticotropin and lipotropin in health and disease. *In* "Clinical Neuroendocrinology" (L. Martini, and G. M. Besser, eds.), pp. 402–442. Academic Press, New York.

Reichlin, S. (1975). Regulation of somatotrophic hormone secretion. *In* "Handbook of Physiology" (R. O. Greep and E. B. Astwood, eds.), Sect. 7, Vol. IV, p. 405. Williams & Williams, Baltimore, Maryland.

Reichlin, S., Martin, J. B., Mitnick, M. A., Boshans, R. L., Grimm, Y., Bollinger, J., Gordon, J., and Malacara, J. (1972). The hypothalamus in pituitary–thyroid regulation. *Recent Prog. Horm. Res.* **28**, 229–286.

Reichlin, S., Baldessarini, R. J., and Martin, J. B., eds. (1978). "The Hypothalamus." Raven Press, New York.

Reichlin, S., (1980). Neuroendocrinology. *In* "Textbook of Endocrinology" (R. H. Williams, ed.), 6th ed., pp. 774–831. Saunders, Philadelphia, Pennsylvania.

Rella, W., and Lapin, V. (1976). Immunocompetence of pinealectomized and simultaneously pinealectomized and thymectomized rats. *Oncology* **33**, 3–6.

Renaud, L. P., Pittman, Q. J., and Blume, H. W. (1979). Neurophysiology of hypothalamic peptidergic neurons. *In* "Central Regulation of the Endocrine System" (K. Fuxe, T. Hökfelt, and R. Luft, eds.), pp. 119–137. Plenum, New York.

Rivier, C., Rivier, J., and Vale, W. (1978). The effect of bombesin and related peptides on prolactin and growth hormone secretion in the rat. *Endocrinology* **102**, 519–522.

Robinson, A. (1978). Neurophysins: An aide to understanding the structure and function of the neurohypophysis. *In* "Frontiers in Neuroendocrinology" (W. F. Ganong and L. Martini, eds.), Vol. 5, pp. 35–60. Raven Press, New York.

Rocklin, R. E., Greineder, D. K., and Melman, K. L. (1979). Histamine-induced suppressor factor (HSF): Further studies on the nature of the stimulus and the cell which produces it. *Cell. Immunol.* **44**, 404–415.

Rogers, M. P., Dubey, D., and Reich, P. (1979). The influence of the psyche and the brain on immunity and disease susceptibility. *Psychosom. Med.* **41**, 147–161.

Rose, R., and Sachar, E. (1980). Psychoneuroendocrinology. *In* "Textbook of Endocrinology" (R. Williams, ed.), 6th ed., Saunders, Philadelphia, Pennsylvania.

Rossier, J., Baltenberg, E., Pittman, Q., Bayon, A., Koda, L., Miller, R., Guillemin, R., and Bloom, F. (1979). Hypothalamic enkephalin neurons may regulate the neurohypophysis. *Nature (London)* **277**, 653–655.

Roubinian, J. R., Talal, N., Greenspan, J. S., Goodman, J. R., and Sliteri, P. K. (1979). Delayed androgen treatment prolongs survival in murine lupus. *J. Clin. Invest.* **63**, 902–911.

Said, S. I. (1980). Peptides common to the nervous system and the gastrointestinal tract. *In* "Frontiers in Neuroendocrinology" (L. Martini and W. F. Ganong, eds.), Vol. 6, pp. 293–331. Raven Press, New York.

Samson, W. K., Snyder, G. D., and McCann, S. M. (1980). Vasoactive intestinal peptide stimulates prolactin release from rat pituitaries *in vitro. Fed. Proc., Fed. Am. Soc. Exp. Biol.* **39**, 374A.

Saxena, R. K., and Talwar, G. P. (1977). An anterior pituitary factor stimulates thymidine incorporation in isolated thymocytes. *Nature (London)* **268**, 57–59.

Scanlon, M. F., Lewis, M., Weightman, D. R., Chan, V., and Hall, R. (1980). The neuroregulation of human thyrotropin secretion. *In* "Frontiers in Neuroendocrinology" (L. Martini and W. F. Ganong, eds.), Vol. 6, pp. 333–380. Raven Press, New York.

Scharrer, E., and Scharrer, B. (1940). Secretory cells within the hypothalamus. *In* "The Hypothalamus," *Res. Publ. Ass. Nerv. Ment. Dis.*, **xx**, Hafner, New York.

Schleimer, R. (1978). Regulatory roles of histamine in the immune system. *Proc. West. Pharmacol. Soc.* **21**, 145–150.

Schultzberg, M., Hökfelt, T., Lundberg, J. M., Terenius, L., Elfvin, L.-G., and Elde, R. (1978). Enkephalin-like immunoreactivity in nerve terminals in sympathetic ganglia and adrenal medulla and in adrenal medullary gland cells. *Acta Physiol. Scand.* **103**, 475–477.

Schusdziarra, V., Rouiller, D., Arimura, A., and Unger, R. A. (1978). Anti-somatostatin serum increases levels of hormones from the pituitary and gut, but not from the pancreas. *Endocrinology* **103**, 1956–1959.

Schusdziarra, V., Rouiller, D., Harris, V., and Unger, R. H. (1979). Plasma somatostatin-like immunoreactivity in depancreatectomized dogs. *Endocrinology* **105**, 595–599.

Schusdziarra, V., Zyzna, E., Rouiller, D., Boden, G., Brown, J. C., Arimura, A., and Unger, R. H. (1980). Splanchic somatostatin: A hormonal regulator of nutrient homeostasis. *Science* **207**, 530–532.

Shank, R. E. (1976). Nutritional characteristics of the elderly—an overview. *In* "Nutrition, longevity, and aging" M. Rockstein and M. L. Sussman (eds.), pp. 9–28. Academic Press, New York.

Smith, J. B., Knowlton, R. P., Agarwall, S. S., (1978). Human lymphocyte responses are enhanced at 40°C. *J. Immunol.* **121**, 691–694.

Smith, S. R., Bledsoe, T., Chhetri, M. K. (1975), Cortisol metabolism and the pituitary-adrenal axis in adults with protein-calorie malnutrition. *J. Clin. Endocrinol. Metab.* **40**, 43–52.

Srebro, Z., and Brodzicki, S. (1978). Changed activity in the hypothalamic neurosecretory centers and the pituitary gland of mice in the course of tetanus toxoid immunization. *Folia Biol. (Krakow)* **26**, 257–262.

Stanton, A. H., Meanning, L., Kopeloff, L., and Kopeloff, N. (1942). Spinal cord section and hemolysin production in the rat. *J. Immunol.* **44**, 237–246.

Stein, M., Schiavi, R. C., and Camerino, M. (1976). Influence of brain and behavior on the immune system. *Science*, **191**, 435–440.

Sullivan, A. C., and Cheng, L. (1978). Appetite regulation and its modulation by drugs. *In* "Nutrition and Drug Interrelations" (J. N. Hathcock, and J. Coon, eds.), pp. 21–81. Academic Press, New York.

Sundler, F., Carraway, R. E., Häkanson, R., Alumets, J., and Dubois, M. P. (1978). Immunoreactive neurotensin and somatostatin in the chicken thymus. *Cell Tissue Res.* **194**, 367–376.

Takor-Takor, T., and Pearse, A. G. E. (1975). Neuroectodermal origin of avian hypothalamo-hypophysial complex: The role of the ventral neural ridge. *J. Embryol. Exp. Morphol.* **34**, 311–325.

Talwar, G. P., Hanjan, S. N. S., Saxena, R. K., Pandian, M. R., Gupta, P. D., and Bhattarai, Q. B. (1975). Regulation of immunologic response by hormones. *In* "Regulation of Growth and Differentiated Function in Eukaryocyte Cells" (G. P. Talwar, ed.), pp. 271–281. Raven Press, New York.

Tanaka, T., Lellett, J., and Rowe, J. (1979). Human brain growth factor (hBGF) analogous to bovine brain fibroblast growth factor (FGF). *61st Annu. Meet. Endocr. Soc.* Abstract No. 588.

Terry, L. C., Willoughby, J. O., Brazeau, P., Martin, J. B., and Patel, Y. C. (1976). Antiserum to somatostatin prevents stress-induced inhibition of growth hormone secretion in the rat. *Science* **192**, 565–567.

Theoharides, T. C., and Douglas, W. W. (1978). Somatostatin induces histamine secretion from rat peritoneal mast cells. *Endocrinology* **102**, 1637–1640.

Tischler, A. S., Dichter, M. A., Biales, B., and Green, L. A. (1977). Neuroendocrine neoplasms and their cells of origin. *N. Engl. J. Med.* **296**, 919–925.

Tuomisto, J., Mannisto, P., Lamberg, A.-A., and Linnoila, M. (1976). Effect of cold exposure on serum thyrotrophin levels in man. *Acta Endocrinol. (Copenhagen)* **83**, 522–527.

Uhlir, I., Seggie, J., and Brown, G. M. (1974). The effect of septal lesions on the threshold of adrenal stress response. *Neuroendocrinology* **14**, 351–355.

Vale, W., Brazeau, P., Rivier, C., Brown, M., Boss, B., Rivier, J., Burgus, R., Ling, N., and Guillemin, R. (1975). Somatostatin. *Recent Prog. Horm. Res.* **34**, 365–397.

Van Loon, G. R., Scapagnini, V., Moberg, G. P., and Ganong, W. F. (1971). Evidence for central adrenergic neural inhibition of ACTH secretion in the rat. *Endocrinology* **89**, 1464–1469.

Vernikos-Danellis, J. (1964). Estimation of corticotropin releasing activity of rat hypothalamus and neurohypophysis before and after stress. *Endocrinology* **75**, 514–520.

Villarreal, J. A. and Brown, M. R. (1978). Bombesin-like peptide in hypothalamus: Chemical and immunologic characterization. *Life Sci.* **23**, 2729–2733.

von Euler, U. S., and Gaddum, J. H. (1931). An unidentified depressor substance in certain tissue extracts. *J. Physiol. (London)* **72**, 74–87.

von Gudecker, R. (1978). Ultrastructure of the age-involuted adult human thymus. *Cell Tissue Res.* **186**, 507–525.

Wagner, H., Hengst, K., Zierden, E., and Gerlach, U. (1979). Investigations of the anti-proliferative effects of somatostatin in man and rats. *Metab., Clin. Exp.* **27**, 1281–1386.

Walsh, J. H., Wong, H. C., and Dockray, G. J. (1979). Bombesin-like peptides in mammals. *Fed. Proc., Fed. Am. Soc. Exp. Biol.* **38**, 2345–2349.

Wardlaw, S. L., and Frantz, A. G. (1979). Measurement of β-endorphin in human plasma. *J. Clin. Endocrinol. Metab.* **48**, 176–180.

Weeke, J., Prange-Hansen, A., and Lundaek, K. (1975). Inhibition by somatostatin of basal levels of serum thyrotropin in normal men. *J. Clin. Endocrinol. Metab.* **41**, 168–171.

Weindl, A. (1973). Neuroendocrine aspects of circumventricular organs. *In* "Frontiers in Neuroendocrinology" (W. F. Ganong and L. Martini, eds.), pp. 3–32. Oxford Univ. Press, New York.

Wilkes, M. M., Stewart, R. D., Bruni, J. F., Quigley, M. E., Yen, S. S. C., Ling, N., and
    Chrétien, M. (1980). A specific homolgous radioimmunoassay for human β-endorphin:
    Direct measurement in biological fluids. *J. Clin. Endocrinol. Metab.* **50**, 309–316.
Wurtman, R. J. (1980). The pineal as a neuroendocrine transducer. *In* "Neuroendocrinology,"
    D. T. Krieger and J. C. Hughes (eds.), pp 102–108. Sinauer Associates, Inc., Sunderland,
    Mass.
Wurtman, R. J., and Anton-Tay, F. (1969). The mammalian pineal as a neuroendocrine
    transducer. *Recent Prog. Horm. Res.* **25**, 493–513.
Wurtman, R. J., and Moskowitz, M. A. (1977). The pineal organ. *N. Engl. J. Med.* **296**,
    1329–1333, 1383–1386.
Yaksh, T. L., Farb, D. H., Leeman, S. E., and Jessell, T. M. (1979). Intrathecal capsaicin
    depletes Substance P in the rat spinal cord and produces prolonged thermal analgesia.
    Science **206**, 481–483.
Yen, S. S. C (1977). Neuroendocrine aspects of cyclic gonadotropin release in women. *In*
    "Clinical Neuroendocrinology" (L. Martini and G. M. Besser, eds.), pp. 175–196. Academic
    Press, New York.
Young, J. B., and Landsberg, L. (1980). Impaired suppression of sympathetic activity during
    fasting in gold thioglucose treated mice. *J. Clin. Invest.* **65**, 1086–1094.

Neurotransmitters and the Immune System

NICHOLAS R. HALL
ALLAN L. GOLDSTEIN

INTRODUCTION

Several neurotransmitter systems have been implicated in modulating the immune system. In some instances, pathways within the brain appear to be involved. In others, peripheral nerves and autonomic projections have been implicated. As is true of much of the research in the area of brain interactions with immunity, some of the data that will be discussed are inconclusive and in some instances implicate a particular neurotransmitter by inference only. Nonetheless, when all of the data are considered together in an attempt to postulate a unified model of immune–CNS interactions, some consistencies are revealed within what at first appears to be a collection of nonsequitous observations.

This chapter will review the evidence implicating serotonergic, catecholaminergic, cholinergic, and endorphinergic systems in the modulation of immunity. A discussion of possible feedback loops involving various products of the activated immune system will also be considered.

SEROTONERGIC SYSTEMS

Although the direct effects of serotonin upon the immune system have not been studied in a systematic manner, the existing indirect evidence suggests

521

that this neurotransmitter exerts a net inhibitory influence over immunogenesis. This conclusion is based upon the demonstration that an inverse
relationship exists between brain serotonin levels and antibody production.

Elevation

Injection of 5-hydroxytryptophan (5-HTP), the immediate precursor of
5-hydroxy-tryptamine or serotonin, has been found to increase the latent
period of antibody formation and to decrease the intensity of both the
primary and secondary immune response (Idova and Devoino, 1972; Devoino
et al., 1970).

Lysergic acid diethylamide (LSD) has similar effects (O'Brian et al., 1962).
Injection of this drug into guinea pigs that had been injected with brain
homogenate decreased the incidence of paralysis, the mortality rate, and the
severity of histopathology when lesions did occur. This effect was attributed
to an antiserotonin effect upon the cerebral vessels. Although this interpretation was consistent with the evidence that LSD interfered with the effects of
serotonin in the periphery, other evidence suggests that LSD may act as a partial serotonergic agonist in the CNS (Cooper et al., 1978). If this mode of action is correct, LSD might exert its effects in a similar way to 5-HTP: by inhibiting the formation of antibodies that would normally have cross-reacted
with the recipient animal's brain cells.

Depression

Reduction of brain serotonin levels has been found to have just the opposite
effect upon immunity. Electrolytic lesioning of serotonin containing neurons
in the midbrain raphe nucleus stimulates antibody production to bovine serum
albumin (BSA) (Eremina and Devoino, 1973). Compared with control
animals, twofold increases in antibody levels were detected in lesioned animals
on the fourth and seventh days following antigen administration. Maximum
titers were detected on Day 7 in the lesioned group, compared with Day 14 in
the controls. The elevated antibody titers and shortened latent phase were
found only during the primary immune response. No differences in the
character or intensity of the secondary response were detected in lesioned versus control subjects.

Reduction of brain serotonin levels by depriving animals of tryptophan may
also result in augmented immunity. Segall and Timiras (1976) reported that
rats with depressed brain serotonin levels due to a tryptophan-deficient diet

not only had increased longevity and a more healthy appearance, but also had delayed onset of tumor growth when compared with ad libitum fed control animals. Direct measures of immunity were not carried out. It is of interest, however, that the rejection of neoplastic growth is thought to depend upon a balanced immunologic state. Therefore, the observation that tryptophan deprivation can delay the onset of tumor growth may be further evidence that the central serotonergic system exerts an inhibitory influence over immunity.

Serotonin is found in very high concentrations within the pineal gland. It is also known that pinealectomy is able to enhance the growth of certain tumors (Rodin, 1963; Lapin, 1974, 1976). Consequently, one might speculate that there exists a relationship between pineal serotonin and the immunocompetence of the host. A partial impairment of T-cell-dependent delayed hypersensitivity and a slight delay in graft rejection following pinealectomy was reported by Janković et al. (1969, 1970), while Rella and Lapin (1976) reported a slight acceleration in the response of spleen cells to T-cell mitogens. Ultrastructural changes in the thymus have also been found in pinealectomized rats (Soriano et al., 1980). It is unlikely, however, that these slight changes in the immune functioning of pinealectomized animals account for the enhanced tumor growth in these animals. Instead, interactions between tumor growth and the pineal are more likely the consequence of nutrient and metabolic changes in tissues supporting the tumor cells (Quay and Gorray, 1980), which in turn are due to an altered endocrine balance. This conclusion is supported by the observation that rats with Dimethylbenzanthracene (DMBA) induced tumors have elevated levels of serotonin in the intermediate lobe of pituitary gland (Aubert et al., 1980).

Altered levels of serotonin in the brain would be expected during the immune response if this neurotransmitter is part of a CNS–immune system axis. Such changes have been reported and they are consistent with the hypothesis that this transmitter is inhibitory. A significant decrease in hypothalamic serotonin concentration has been correlated with the latent phase of antibody production in rabbits after immunization with typhoid vi-antigen (Vekshina and Magaeva, 1974). A "tendency toward a decrease" was also reported in the hippocampus. The existing evidence would suggest that these changes are manifestations of an altered neuroendocrine balance.

Devoino et al. (1970) reported that the inhibitory effects of 5-hydroxytryptophan could not be elicited in rabbits that had been hypophysectomized or in animals with lesions in the pituitary stalk. Furthermore, the inhibitory effects of a variety of pharmacologic manipulations, including administration of 5-HTP, can be reversed with exogenous LH, FSH, and ACTH (Maestroni and Pierpaoli; see chapter in this volume). Since all of these hormones appear to be influenced by serotonergic pathways (Krieger, 1978), the reported changes in immunity are consistent with the hypothesis that brain serotonin can modulate the immune system via a neuroendocrine–immune axis.

CATHECHOLAMINERGIC SYSTEMS

Dopamine

The central dopaminergic system appears to exert a net stimulatory influence upon various parameters of the immune system. This conclusion is based upon reported changes that occur in the immune system in patients with neurologic disorders that involve the dopaminergic pathways, as well as experimental manipulation and measurement of dopamine in animal models.

Neuropathology associated with dopaminergic neurons in the substantia nigra of patients with Parkinson's disease has been correlated with changes involving the lymphocyte population (Hoffman et al., 1978). The total number of T lymphocytes was found to be reduced as was their ability to respond to mitogenic stimulation and in T-dependent skin tests. In contrast to this depression of the T-lymphocyte system, serum concentrations of IgA and IgG, produced by plasma cells of the B-lymphocyte lineage, were significantly elevated in one subgroup of the patients.

Perhaps related to these observations is the reported decrease in dopaminergic activity in the brains of mice with a high propensity for mammary tumors (Cotzias and Tang, 1977). The possibility that this decrease might have been related to an altered state of immunity is supported by another observation reported by the same authors. Injection of the antigen BCG or *Corynebacterium parvum* resulted in a significant increase in dopamine-stimulated adenyl cyclase activity in caudate homogenate. In other studies, it has been found that the incorporation of L-DOPA into the diets of young male mice can lead to a "youthful appearance," as well as a significantly prolonged life span (Cotzias et al., 1974, 1977).

None of these observations alone provides direct support for a role of central dopaminergic systems in modulating the immune system. However, when reviewed together, a consistent correlation does become apparent. An increase in brain dopaminergic activity follows the administration of antigen. When such an increase is impaired due to damage in the substantia nigra, deficiencies in the cellular branch of the immune system have been reported. Correlated with decreased caudate dopaminergic activity is a propensity to develop mammary tumors. Since surveillance against neoplastic disease depends in part upon a viable T-cell system, an influence upon immunity by dopamine can be inferred. Although prolonged longevity might be due to many factors other than altered immunity, the fact that animals do survive longer when L-DOPA is a dietary supplement is not inconsistent with the hypothesis that central dopaminergic systems may exert a stimulatory influence over the immune system.

Norepinephrine and Epinephrine

Norepinephrine and epinephrine have been implicated in modulating immunity but most of the evidence supports a peripheral autonomic link involving these neurotransmitters. Adrenergic fibers showing intense greenish fluorescence have been identified in the interlobular septa of the rat thymus (Fujiwara et al., 1966). Furthermore, during the course of the immune response, spleen levels of norepinephrine have been found to decrease significantly (Besedovsky et al., 1979). Although these findings may be due to changes in the vasculature associated with the release of cells from the thymus, the presence of β-adrenergic receptors on the surfaces of T cells, B cells, and macrophages (Bourne et al., 1974) prompts the consideration of nonvascular mechanisms as well.

Catecholamines produced by both the sympathetic nervous system and by chromaffin cells in the adrenal medulla have been implicated in the modulation of immunity. Chemical sympathectomy, using the drug 6-hydroxydopamine (6-OHDA), has been found to have profound effects upon the immune system. Kasahara et al. (1977) reported that administration of 10–300 mg/kg of 6-OHDA to mice resulted in a significant depression of antibody production to sheep red blood cells (SRBC). Antibodies against this T cell-dependent antigen were measured by a plaque forming cell (PFC) assay and by determining the hemagglutination titer. This inhibition was transitory with treated animals having antibody levels no different from control animals 14 days after the drug treatment. The return to normal of antibody production corresponded to the return to normal of norepinephrine content in the spleen. Our own investigations have found a similar depression of antibody formation in 6-OHDA-treated mice (Hall et al., 1980). Decreased numbers of PFCs and hemagglutination titers to SRBC were found after a single sensitization with SRBC. Mice were treated with either 2 injections of 50 mg/kg 6-OHDA or a single injection of 100 mg/kg. Since the antibody response to SRBC depends upon an interaction of T and B cells, additional parameters of immunity were examined in order to determine if one or both populations of cells had been affected.

Consistent with the decreased amount of antibody produced was the finding that after certain treatments spleen cells were less responsive to the B-cell mitogen, lipopolysaccharide (LPS). In contrast to this observation, the responsiveness of spleen cells to the T-cell mitogen, phytohemagglutinin (PHA) was significantly elevated. The response to concanavalin A (Con-A) was also elevated, but was not statistically different from control values. Following a second exposure to the same antigen, there were no differences between the drug and control groups on any of these measures with the exception of the response to LPS which was still reduced.

The T-cell specific enzyme terminal deoxynucleotidyl transferase (TdT) was measured by enzymatic assay and found to be elevated in thymocytes from mice treated with 6-OHDA. This elevation of TdT levels in thymocytes was observed only after a single exposure to the antigen. Preliminary measures of serum levels of a thymic hormone, thymosin α_1, were elevated in 6-OHDA-treated animals after both primary and secondary exposure to the SRBC.

That these reported effects interfered with the course of immunogenesis is suggested by several lines of evidence. Beta-adrenergic receptors do not appear on B lymphocytes unless the cells are actively producing antibody. This conclusion was reached when it was found that up to two-thirds of sensitized splenic leukocytes could be retained by chromatographic columns of insolubilized isoproterenol (a β-adrenergic agonist) (Melmon et al., 1974). Similar studies using unsensitized cells that were passed over a column and were subsequently used to reconstitute lethally irradiated mice also suggested that the receptors do not appear until after sensitization (Shearer et al., 1972). Recipient animals were able to mount an immunologic response upon injection of SRBC. Had the precursor cells had β-adrenergic receptors on their surface, they would have been retained by the column, diminishing the antibody reaction.

In contrast to the evidence that antibody-producing cells do not develop β-adrenergic receptors until after sensitization has occurred, T lymphocytes appear to possess these receptors at an earlier stage of differentiation (Singh and Owen, 1976). Thymic stem cells were found to be responsive to both cAMP and isoproterenol with respect to the induction of the thy-1 alloantigen. In a subsequent study, Singh et al. (1979) examined the effects of isoproterenol stimulation upon fetal and adult thymocytes. Cyclic-AMP was found to be elevated in both populations after stimulation with this β-adrenergic stimulator. Propranolol, a β-adrenergic antagonist, selectively blocked this rise. However, it was found that although both fetal and adult thymocytes were able to respond to β-adrenergic stimulation, the cAMP rise in fetal thymocytes was of a greater magnitude than in adult cells.

These data would suggest a role for β-adrenergic stimulation during the maturation sequence of lymphocytes. They also implicate cAMP as an intracellular agent responsible for the effects of β-adrenergic stimulation. It would appear that the system is balanced by at least two mechanisms capable of causing a rise in intracellular cGMP. Singh (1979) reported that stimulation of α-adrenergic receptors with phenylephrine and of cholinergic receptors with acetylcholine could result in elevated cGMP.

It is always necessary to consider the possibility that in vitro manipulation of lymphocytes may not necessarily reflect the manner by which these cells are modulated in vivo. However, in view of the changes found in TdT levels in thymocytes from 6-OHDA-treated mice, one has to consider the possibility that the catecholamine-depleting drug might exert its effects by interrupting the normal maturation sequence.

Not all of the published data are consistent with this hypothesis.

Besedovsky *et al.* (1979) reported that 6-OHDA had no effect upon PFC formation. Repeated injections of 6-OHDA were given to newborn rats and then at 2 months of age the animals were challenged with SRBC, followed 5 days later by assessment of splenic PFCs. No differences were observed between the drug and control groups. However, when 6-OHDA treatment was combined with bilateral adrenalectomy, a significant increase in PFCs was observed. Adrenalectomy alone had no effect. These data appear to contradict our own observations and those reported by Kasahara *et al.* (1977). But it is important to realize that different species were used and that, in the rat study, a somewhat different paradigm was used.

Macrophages

Another important component of the immune system is the macrophage population. These cells are responsive to both central and peripheral catecholamine manipulation. The role that macrophages play in the initiation and regulation of the immune response is well established (Unanue, 1972). They also interact in sometimes opposite ways with other elements of the immune system. For an optimal antibody response to T-dependent antigens, interactions between macrophages and T and B cells is necessary (Feldman and Nossal, 1972; Katz and Unanue, 1973). Macrophages are also required for optimal stimulation of T lymphocytes by mitogens (Rosenstreich *et al.*, 1976). Under some conditions, however, macrophages can exert inhibitory influences upon immune measures. Large numbers of macrophages can be inhibitory (Parkhouse and Dutton, 1966; Perkins and Makinodan, 1965). [It is curious that cell density is an important parameter in β-adrenergic stimulation. At high density, macrophages are less responsive to the stimulatory effects of isoproterenol (Welscher and Cruchaud, 1980)]. They can also be inhibitory following stimulation with *C. parvum* (Scott, 1972) or in animals with graft-versus-host disease (Sjöberg, 1972) and certain viral-induced tumors (Kirchner *et al.*, 1974). Since the T-dependent antigen, SRBC, is frequently used in studies of neuro–immune interactions and because mitogen responsiveness has been shown to be altered in various manipulations, it is necessary to include in any review of CNS effects upon immunity a discussion of CNS effects upon macrophages.

Several investigations have revealed that manipulation of the central nervous system can influence cells of the reticuloendothelial system (RES). Some of the earliest investigations have been reviewed by Baciu (1946). In this review, evidence was cited that excitation of the splanchic nerves could increase measures of phagocytosis by 50–100%. On the other hand, vagus nerve excitation decreased phagocytosis by 30–40%. The relevance of this observation to the autonomic nervous system becomes apparent when it is realized that a large number of sympathetic fibers follow the splanchnic nerve and that the dorsal motor nucleus of the vagus nerve contains a large source of preganglionic parasympathetic fibers. Another study cited in the same review purported to have found a decrease in phagocytic activity following the administration of adrenaline and an increase after pilocarpine administration.

Other investigators have reported that lesions in the anterior hypothalamus of cats can inhibit the ability of phagocytic cells to take up carbon particles (Thakur and Manchanda, 1969). Although this finding is consistent with a net inhibitory role of the parasympathetic system over RES cells, the observation (in the same study) that lesions of the middle and posterior hypothalamus produced an even greater decrease is not. It has also been reported that sectioning the spinal cord at either C_3 or L_2 can decrease phagocytic activity after challenging the host with dysentary, typhoid, or proteus antigen (Loverdo, 1958).

Although shedding little light upon the mechanism, other studies implicate the CNS in modulating phagocytic cells. Our own observations have revealed that bilateral lesions in the nucleus locus coeruleus (LC) can significantly reduce the number of granulocyte–macrophage colonies (GM-CFU) that can be cultured from mouse bone marrow (Hall et al., 1978; Hall, 1980). Unilateral lesions produced a decrease in GM-CFUs, but only about half the reduction seen in animals with bilateral lesions. Preliminary data suggested that this decrease due to LC lesions could be partially reversed by the administration of amphetamine. Whether these effects were due to an altered balance of autonomic activity or to disruption of the normal endocrine microenvironment could not be ascertained from these studies.

Other evidence would suggest that at least part of the CNS influence upon phagocytic cells is mediated via autonomic pathways. This conclusion is based upon a complicated series of "isolated head" experiments reported by Baciu (1946, 1978) and Benetato et al. (1949). The technique involved two animals. One, termed the "receptor," had all soft tissue and blood vessels severed at the level of the fourth cervical vertebra. The only connection with the rest of the animal's body was via the vagus nerves and the spinal cord. The head of the receptor was perfused by a "donor" animal. In this procedure, "the cephalic extremity of the receptor's veins and arteries was anastomosed with the cardiac extremity of the corresponding vessels of the donor." Circulation below the level of C4 was carried out by the receptor's own vessels. Input from the medulla was verified by the presence of spontaneous respiratory movements. In the experimental protocol, microbes were injected into the donor animal. Only the head of the recipient animal was exposed to these microbes since only the cephalic end of the jugular and carotid vessels had been anastomosed. It was reasoned by the authors that if changes in the phagocytic activity of the recipient were detected, it would have to be the consequence of neural output channels.

Phagocytosis was measured by determining the number of microbes incorporated in 100 polynuclear cells. In the receptor animal, the phagocytic activity increased by 35% 3 hr after the injection of microbes into the donor. In previously immunized "isolated head" animals, the activity increased by 230% in 1.5 hr. These data supported a previous observation that interrupting autonomic pathways by severing the spinal cord could block phagocytic activity elicited by electrical stimulation of the hypothalamus (Baciu, 1946).

Some of the results described above could have been the consequence of an altered endocrine environment, while other data implicate an autonomic output channel that could exert direct effects at the cell surface. Like the T and B lymphocytes, macrophages have α- and β-adrenergic receptors which, when stimulated, can elevate intracellular cGMP or cAMP (Zurier et al., 1974; Ignarro et al., 1974; Ignarro and George, 1974; Rivkin et al., 1975; Schmidt-Gayk et al., 1975; Higgins and David, 1976; Welscher and Cruchaud, 1976, 1978). With respect to cAMP, elevations of this cyclic nucleotide have been shown to decrease the release of lysosomal hydrolases (Bourne et al., 1974).

Hematopoietic Stem Cells

T lymphocytes, β lymphocytes, and phagocytic cells are derived from a pluripotent stem cell residing in the bone marrow. It is possible that the changes that can be induced by CNS manipulation are not a consequence of modulation of the mature cell population, but rather the indirect consequence of altering the hematopoietic stem cell.

During the course of evaluating the effects of LC lesions upon the development of GM-CFUs, it was observed that there occurred a decrease in total white blood cell count (WBC) in lesioned animals (Hall et al., 1978; Hall, 1980). Since this decrease would have been consistent with an effect at the level of the stem cell, a stem cell assay was carried out in lesioned mice. A sublethal dose of radiation was used to induce colony forming units on the surface of the spleen (CFU-S). Animals received bilateral lesions in either the anterior hypothalamus, posterior hypothalamus, nucleus locus coeruleus, or cerebellum. Only those subjects that had been lesioned in the nucleus locus coeruleus had a significant reduction of CFU-S when compared with controls.

In contrast to the results after destruction of central catecholaminergic neurons, destruction of the peripheral sympathetic nervous system by 6-OHDA was found to increase the number of CFU-S, as well as the spleen weight in mice given sublethal exposure to radiation. These data are consistent with in vitro studies reported by Byron (1975) in which he found that β-adrenergic stimulation and cholinergic receptor stimulation could initiate DNA synthesis in bone marrow stem cells. An extensive network of nerves in the bone marrow could provide the efferent link from the CNS (Kuntz and Richins, 1945; Calvo and Forteza-Vila, 1970; Calvo, 1968). Some of these nerves lie in very close proximity to cellular components, which has led to the speculation that these nerves may play a role in the differentiation of stem cells into myeloid, lymphoid, and erythrocytic end cells (Calvo and Forteza-Vila, 1970). The possibility that these changes might be secondary to an autonomic imbalance at the thymus has to be considered as an alternative hypothesis, especially since T cells and thymic peptides have both been found to influence the course of hematopoiesis (Sharkis et al., 1979).

If the stem cell is being modulated by the CNS, then erythrocytes should also be influenced by manipulations that affect the brain and peripheral nervous system. These cells do not play a direct role in immunologic defense mechanisms. Nonetheless, a discussion of CNS effects upon this population of cells will be included here since they share a common progenitor cell with macrophages and lymphocytes.

Seip et al. (1961) reported that stimulation of the posterior hypothalamus of rabbits led to an increase in the total number of reticulocytes. This increase was blocked by stimulation of the anterior hypothalamus. Electrical stimulation of the posterior hypothalamus of rats has also been found to increase erythropoietic activity (Medado et al., 1967). Autonomic involvement was suggested in this latter study by the observation that atropine, a cholinergic antagonist, was able to block the brain-induced increases.

The catecholamines appear to influence virtually all of the cell types involved in the immune response. Pluripotent stem cells can be stimulated to undergo DNA synthesis following both β-adrenergic and cholinergic stimulation. Pharmacologic manipulation of these receptors on other cell types can influence the activity of T and B lymphocytes and macrophages. Drugs that result in elevated intracellular cAMP tend to be inhibitory, while those that result in elevated cGMP tend to be facilitatory with respect to lymphocytes.

Most of the evidence implicates the catecholaminergic systems in influencing the maturation of lymphocytes. But whether this influence is due to the direct effects of catecholamines from the synaptic vesicles of sympathetic neurons or to the circulating catecholamines produced by chromaffin cells in the adrenal medulla will require further experimentation.

ACETYLCHOLINE

Thymus

Indirect evidence implicating cholinergic systems in the modulation of immunity is to be found in the literature. Several investigators have reported the presence of acetylcholine receptors in thymus tissue (Lindstrom et al., 1976; Engel et al., 1977). In the Engel et al. (1977) study, it was found that peroxidase-labeled α-bungarotoxin bound specifically to viable epithelial cells. Although nicotinic acetylcholine receptors were demonstrated only on epithelial cells, the possibility that they exist on thymocytes as well has been suggested by Singh (1979). Evidence that cholinergic stimulation was able to increase the cell yield from thymus tissue, as well as the ability of these cells to incorporate [^{125}I]UdR (Uridine) was briefly discussed. This observation was described as being preliminary; however, it is consistent with the fact that cholinergic stimulation can stimulate cGMP, which in turn has been shown to activate lymphocytes (Bourne et al., 1974).

Bone Marrow

Studies conducted by Byron (1975, 1976) reveal that bone marrow stem cells bear cholinergic receptors that appear to be involved in the activation of these precursor cells. High specific activity [^{3}H]TdR (Thymidine) was used in cultures of bone marrow cells that had previously been exposed to various drugs. These cells were subsequently injected into irradiated recipient mice for the purpose of measuring CFU-S. Carbamylcholine or acetylcholine in the presence of a cholinesterase inhibitor reduced the number of CFU-S. This reduction was blocked by pretreatment with d-tubocurarine, an effect that could be overcome with high concentrations of carbamylcholine.

Since the lethal effect of high specific activity [^{3}H]TdR is increased in cells actively synthesizing DNA, these data were interpreted as demonstrating that cholinergic stimulation could activate stem cells. This cholinergic activation system appears to be independent of the β-adrenergic system discussed earlier. β-Adrenergic blocking agents were ineffective in inhibiting the effects of cholinergic stimulation. Similarly, cholinergic blockers were ineffective in blocking the effects of β-adrenergic stimulation. That the cholinergic system does play a physiological role in the activation of stem cells is suggested by the observation that cholinesterase is associated with hemopoietic cells.

An earlier study reported the effects of cholinergic and adrenergic stimulation upon the numbers of hemopoietic cells in bone marrow (Terentyeva and Kakhetelidze, 1956). Although many of the cell types examined were altered, most pertinent to this discussion were the effects on lymphocytes and macrophages. Acetylcholine administration was found to decrease both cell types in cat bone marrow, while epinephrine decreased the number of lymphocytes and increased the number of "polyblasts-macrophages." These effects were enhanced following denervation of the bone marrow, suggesting that these cells undergo denervation supersensitivity.

None of these data establish a definite role for the cholinergic system in modulating the immune system. However, the evidence is certainly supportive of such a role and is consistent with the known effects of cGMP. Of great interest is the presence of cholinergic receptors on epithelial cells in the thymus since these cells appear to be a source of thymic hormones (Oosterom et al., 1979; Oosterom and Kater, 1980; Kater et al., 1980). It is possible that, in addition to direct effects upon stem cells and lymphocytes, cholinergic pathways might have additional indirect effects upon the immune system by influencing the production and/or release of thymic hormones.

ENDORPHINS

It has been postulated than an endorphinergic system represents a new division of the autonomic nervous system involved in the conservation of bodily resources and energy (Margules, 1979). The morphinelike substances are thought to exert antisympathetic influences, while an endoloxonergic division opposes this inhibition. While β-endorphin and enkephalin serve as endogenous agents for the former division, the nature of the endogenous "endoloxonergic" substance can only be speculated upon. Whether the immune system is influenced by this proposed system cannot be ascertained based upon the limited evidence. However, it is of interest that some of these substances can influence T lymphocytes.

Wybran et al. (1979) investigated the effects of morphine, dextromoramide, levomoramide, and methionine-enkephalin upon peripheral blood T lymphocytes. Morphine, in a dose-dependent manner decreased the percentage of active and total T-rosette forming cells. Dextromoramide also decreased the active T rosettes, but had no effect on the total. Levomoramide had no effect upon either rosette system.

In contrast to the suppressive effects of morphine and dextromoramide, methionine-enkephalin increased the percentage of active T rosettes. All of these effects were reversed by treatment with the agonist, naloxone. It was suggested by the authors that the existence of two receptors might explain the discrepancy between the inhibitory effects of morphine and dextromoramide and the facilitatory effects of methionine-enkephalin.

It is difficult to relate these findings to the previous discussions, especially with the reported dichotomy. Nonetheless, the data do suggest that receptors for morphine, dextromoramide, and methionine-enkephalin may be present on at least human T lymphocytes. Whether this means that endogenously produced substances serve a physiological role in modulating the immune system is too speculative to predict without additional data.

REFLEX HYPOTHESIS OF ANTIBODY PRODUCTION

Antigen Depot Experiments

It has been proposed that stimulation of antibodies and phagocytic cells can arise following antigen stimulation of neural receptors. A neural impulse is transmitted to the CNS which in turn activates immunity (Gordienko, 1958). Specificity is thought to be encoded by the neural impulse.

This reflex hypothesis of antibody production originated as a consequence of antigen depot experiments. Antigen was deposited on or close to nerves and neural receptors. By removing the antigenic stimulus after a brief exposure, it was argued that absorption of antigen into the circulation could not have occurred, and that subsequent immunologic events were the result of neural stimulation. Using this paradigm, a number of investigators reported stimulation of agglutinating antibody titers (Oshikawa, 1921; Friedberger and Tinti, 1924; Gordienko, 1958). These studies are controversial and subject to the criticism that antigen is absorbed into the circulation and stimulates directly the cells involved in immunity. Nonetheless, they will be discussed briefly since they are of historical interest and may provide anecdotal evidence in support of some of the earlier discussions.

Gordienko *et al.* (1958a) isolated the ears of rabbits from blood circulation, but left the auricularis magnus nerve intact. Intracutaneous application of typhoid vaccine into the ear tip of such animals led to the formation of antibodies within 7 days. Radiolabeled phosphorus was also injected into the ear. The absence of detectable radioactivity in the blood led the authors to conclude that absorption of typhoid vaccine could not have occurred in their rabbit ear preparations.

In a subsequent experiment, the same laboratory reported alterations in electrical activity in antigen-stimulated peripheral nerves (Gordienko *et al.*, 1958b). Measurements were made using isolated auricular and saphenous nerves of the dog before and after intracutaneous administration of various antigens. Changes in amplitude and frequency were detected and were found to vary, depending upon the nature of the antigenic stimulus. Only when the concentration of antigen exceeded a certain level were major changes observed. Typhoid vaccine with 10^4 bacilli per ml caused no change in the potentials. When the concentration was increased to 10^5 bacilli per ml, "a very slight reaction" was observed, but when the concentration exceeded one billion bacilli per ml, major changes were detected. The same was found true using "dysentery vaccine." It was concluded that antigens are capable of causing irritation of skin receptors which in turn can relay a signal via sensory nerves to the brain. Signals from the brain were proposed as initiators of the immune response.

Receptors in the carotid sinus were implicated when electrical changes were detected in the "sinus nerves" after the application of a variety of antigens (Gordienko, 1958). Pharmacologic manipulation was carried out in an attempt to establish a role for the carotid sinus nerve in the process of immunogenesis (Gordienko *et al.*, 1958c). Treatment of carotid sinus receptors with dicaine, sorcaine, and cocaine prevented the formation of antibodies after the application of antigen to the receptor. However, earlier studies by Reitler (1924) had demonstrated that cocaine block of the auricular nerve had no effect on antibody production following the injection of antigen into the innervated ear.

Serious methodological questions have been raised concerning this type of experimentation, especially with respect to absorption of antigen into the surrounding tissue. However, it is possible that some of the electrical changes reported were manifestations of changes in autonomic function. Furthermore, some of the pharmacologic agents might have been exerting their influence at sites other than the proposed antigen receptors, a possibility supported by the more recent evidence discussed earlier in this review.

FEEDBACK SYSTEMS

If the CNS is able to modulate the immune system via autonomic and/or neuro-endocrine links, it is necessary to postulate the manner by which the CNS output channels become activated and subsequently inactivated with respect to the immune system. Several products of the immune response have been implicated in acting in this capacity, including lymphokines, thymic peptides, and components of the complement cascade.

Lymphokines

Fontana *et al.* (1980) studied the effect of lymphocyte supernatant upon glial cells. Brains from fetal rats were used as a source of glial cell cultures, while Con-A-treated spleen cells from adult rats were used as a source of the supernatant. The supernatant was found to stimulate both DNA and RNA synthesis in undifferentiated glioblasts, while only RNA synthesis was stimulated in differentiated glial cells. Immunofluorescence was used to demonstrate the presence of astrocyte-specific glial fibrillary acid protein (GFA). Although the authors designated the stimulatory factor as "glia stimulating factor," or GSF, the possibility that the factor was a previously characterized lymphokine could not be ascertained from the data presented.

Thymic Hormones

Thymic hormones produced by thymus epithelial cells might serve as a means by which information is conveyed from the immune system to the CNS. Thymosin α_1, a potent immunoregulatory peptide (M.W. 3,108, pI 4.2) (Goldstein *et al.*, 1977; Low and Goldstein, 1979; Low *et al.*, 1979), is found in both serum and cerebrospinal fluid (J. E. McClure, Torrey, and Goldstein, unpublished observation). Furthermore, preliminary studies in this laboratory, using ^{125}I-thymosin α_1, have established that the peptide is able to enter the brain. Whether the peptide is binding to specific receptors in discrete brain areas is currently under investigation.

These data certainly do not establish thymosin α_1 as a mediator of immune CNS interaction. However, the possibility that they could influence neuronal functioning has to be considered. This possibility is particularly intriguing in light of recent evidence regarding the induction of the Thy-1 alloantigen. This membrane marker is considered characteristic of T lymphocytes but is also found on certain other tissues, including neurons (Barclay and Hyden, 1978). The markers are similar enough so that antibodies with specificity against Thy-1 on lymphocytes can crossreact with the Thy-1 on brain cells. It is of interest that cAMP has been found to induce the appearance of this marker on the surface of T cells and on cloned lines of neurons (Morris *et al.*, 1980). Thymosin α_1 also can increase the amount of Thy-1 antigen on the surface of T cells. Since cAMP is able to stimulate Thy-1 on both T cells and neurons, thymosin α_1 might be expected to influence both cell populations in a similar way.

Complement

Certain complement components may play a role in providing an afferent link with the brain. Seeman *et al.* (1978) reported that the anaphylatoxin, C3a, could mimic the effects of dopamine in hypothalamic pathways. Implants of norepinephrine and carbamylcholine in the perifornical hypothalamus were found to stimulate feeding and drinking behavior in sated rats. Administration of C3a 20 min before drug stimulation potentiated these effects. It was postulated that the C3a may have released endogenous dopamine or else stimulated dopaminergic receptors since dopamine had the same potentiating effect on the drug-induced behaviors as did the C3a.

Evidence suggesting that these agents are able to alter certain parameters of the CNS does not establish lymphocyte products, thymic peptides, or complement components as being part of a feedback system between the brain and immune system. It is also difficult to discern between feedback and activation. For example, all of these components may constitute a system for the activation of inflammatory or immune responses within the brain. Phagocytic cells of hematopoietic origin are present within the brain (Del Cerro and Monjan, 1979; Fujita and Kitamura, 1976) and so it should not be surprising that they respond to some of the same factors as do phagocytic cells outside the brain.

DISCUSSION

Recognition of nonself antigens and subsequent reaction to these foreign configurations can occur in the absence of both neural and endocrine influences. Cultured lymphocytes can be sensitized to produce antibody, and cultured macrophages can be induced to migrate or engulf foreign particles.

But this implied autonomy of the immune system is limited to only a few specialized functions of these cells. Successful orchestration of the many interactions necessary for host defense to occur requires the influence of the central nervous system and a balanced endocrine environment. The manner by which this influence modulates immunity is not fully understood. Nonetheless, enough data have been reported in the literature to justify the formulation of a hypothetical model by which the neurotransmitters reviewed in this chapter might ultimately influence the endocrine thymus and related parameters of immunity.

Thymic hormones influence the multiple facets of the immune response illustrated in Figure 1 (Goldstein *et al.*, 1976, 1978). Thymosin-activated cells ultimately differentiate into killer cells, memory cells, or types of effector cells to assist in host defense against neoplastic growth, as well as viral, mycobacterial, fungal, and protozoal infections. Other thymosin-stimulated

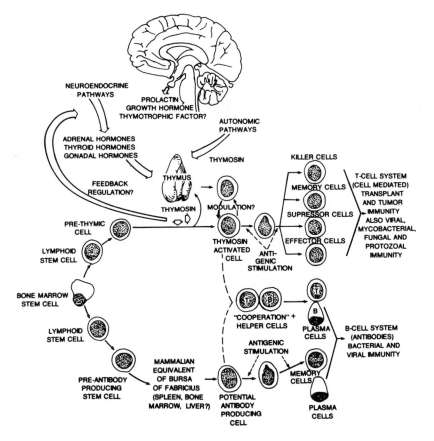

Figure 1. Hypothetical model illustrating interactions between the central nervous system and the endocrine thymus (see text for explanation).

cells exert either "suppressive" or "helper" influence over lymphocytes. In addition, there is evidence that thymic hormones are able to influence the differentiation of bone marrow stem cells.

It may be more than coincidence that the thymic hormones have been implicated in the regulation of many immunologic events that can be altered by manipulating neurotransmitters (See Table 1).

Whether the catecholaminergic and serotonergic-induced changes are due to an imbalanced neuroendocrine system and/or are manifestations of autonomic dysfunction is difficult to ascertain without additional evidence. Both of these CNS output channels have been implicated in the regulation of immunity; therefore, both have been included in Figure 1.

Feedback influences upon the CNS by thymic hormones is a speculative concept but is included in the model for the following reasons: During the immune response, electrical, neurochemical, and morphological changes have been reported in the CNS (see other chapters in this volume, and Hall, 1980). Therefore, it is not unreasonable to postulate that a bidirectional flow of information exists between the immune and nervous systems. That the afferent connection might involve the thymus is suggested by the observation that athymic mice have decreased numbers of oligodendrocytes and increased numbers of astrocytes compared with control mice (Kern and Frank, 1980).

TABLE 1

Effects of Neurotransmitter Substances upon Cellular Components of the Immune Response

Neurotransmitter	B-Cell response	T-Cell response	Macrophages	Pluripotent stem cell
Elevated serotonin	Decrease	No data	No data	No data
Elevated dopamine	Decrease	Increase	Increase	Increase
β-Adrenergic stimulation	Decrease	Decrease	Decrease	Increase
α-Adenergic stimulation	Increase	Increase	No data	Increase
Cholinergic stimulation	Increase	Increase	No data	Increase
Elevated morphine	No data	Decrease	No data	No data
Elevated enkephalin	No data	Increase	No data	No data

Conclusions are based upon surgical or pharmacologic manipulation of the various neurotransmitter (hormonal) systems. In some instances, the summarized effects are based upon incomplete or indirect data and so should be regarded as tentative (see text).

An altered neuroendocrine balance also exists in athymic nude mice (Besedovsky and Sorkin, 1977; Hall, 1980). No direct evidence has yet been obtained to implicate thymic hormones in the feedback regulation of immunity. But preliminary findings from our laboratory reveal that endogenous thymic hormones can be detected in the brain and CSF by radioimmunoassay, and that radiolabeled thymosin α_1 is able to cross the blood–brain barrier and accumulate in discrete subcortical regions. Studies are currently underway to determine if specific receptors are present in the CNS for thymic hormones and the effect that intracerebral thymic hormones have upon thymic-dependent immunity.

If thymic hormones are to be proposed as the hormonal connection in a CNS–immune system axis, autonomic and/or neuroendocrine manipulation might be expected to influence their production. Preliminary evidence indicates that both output channels may do this. Chemical sympathectomy, using 6-OHDA, has been found to cause significant elevation of thymosin α_1 following both the primary and the secondary immune response (Hall et al., 1980). Implicating a neuroendocrine influence is the observation that administration of growth hormone to growth hormone-deficient patients can lead to a several fold elevation in serum thymosin α_1 levels (D. Wara, personal communication).

These observations, coupled with evidence of a direct neural link between the nucleus ambiguus and thymus (Bulloch and Moore, 1980), the presence of GABA, and catecholamines in the thymus (Gerber and Hare, 1979; Fujiwara et al., 1966), the presence of neuronal specific enolases in the thymus (P. J. Marangos, personal communication), and the presence of acetylcholine receptors on the surface of thymosin-producing epithelial cells (Engel et al., 1977) support the existence of a central nervous system–immune system axis as proposed in Figure 1.

ACKNOWLEDGMENTS

The thymosin research discussed in this review was supported in part by grants from the National Cancer Institute, CA-24974 and Hoffman LaRoche, Inc.

REFERENCES

Aubert, C., Janiaud, P., and Lecalvez, J. (1980). Effect of pinealectomy and melatonin on mammary tumor growth in sprague–dawley rats under different conditions of lighting. *J. Neural Transm.* **47**, 121–130.

Baciu, I. (1946). The role of the central nervous system in the inducement of the phagocytic reaction. *Doctoral Dissertation* submitted to the University of Cluji Faculty of Medicine, Institute of Physiology and Medical Physics.

Baciu, I. (1978). Physiologie normale et pathologique: La physiologie du système phagocytaire. *Arch. Union Med. Balk.* **16**, 473–477.

Barclay, A. N., and Hyden, H. (1978). Localization of the Thy-1 antigen by immunofluorescence on neurons isolated from rat brain. *J. Neurochem.* **31**, 1375–1391.

Benetato, G., Oprisiu, C., and Baciu, I. (1949). Sur le rôle du système nerveux central dans le declenchement de la réaction phagocytaire. In "Recueil d'Etudes Médicales," pp. 11–16. Inst. Roumain de Culture Universelle, Bucarest.

Besedovsky, H. O., and Sorkin, E. (1977). Network of immune-neuroendocrine interactions. Clin. Exp. Immunol. 27, 1–12.

Besedovsky, H. D., Del Ray, A., Sorkin, E., Da Prada, M., and Keller, H. H. (1979). Immunoregulation mediated by the sympathetic nervous system. Cell. Immunol. 48, 346–355.

Bourne, H. R., Lichtenstein, L. M., Melmon, K. L., Henney, C. S., Weinstein, Y., and Shearer, G. M. (1974). Modulation of inflammation and immunity by cyclic AMP. Science 184, 19–28.

Bulloch, K., and Moore, R. Y. (1980). Nucleus ambiguus projections to the thymus gland: Possible pathways for regulation of the immune response and the neuroendocrine network. Anat. Rec. 196(3), 25A.

Byron, J. W. (1975). Manipulation of the cell cycle of the hemopoietic stem cell. Exp. Hematol. 3, 44–53.

Byron, J. W. (1976). Cyclic nucleotides and the cell cycle of the hematopoietic stem cell. In "Cyclic Nucleotides and the Regulation of Cell Growth" (M. Abou-Sabe, ed.), pp. 81–93. Dowden, Hutchinson & Ross, Inc., Stroudsburg, Pennsylvania.

Calvo, W. (1968). The innervation of the bone marrow in laboratory animals. Am. J. Anat. 123, 315–328.

Calvo, W., and Forteza-Vila, J. (1970). Schwann cells of the bone marrow. Blood 36, 180–188.

Cooper, J. R., Bloom, F. E., and Roth, R. H. (1978). "The Biochemical Basis of Neuropharmacology," pp. 196–272. Oxford Univ. Press, London and New York.

Cotzias, G. C., and Tang, L. C. (1977). An adenylate cyclase of brain reflects propensity for breast cancer in mice. Science 197, 1094–1096.

Cotzias, G. C., Miller, S. T., Nicholson, A. R., Jr., Mastom, W. H., and Tang, L. C. (1974). Prolongation of the life-span in mice adapted to large amounts of L-Dopa. Proc. Natl. Acad. Sci. U.S.A. 71, 2466–2469.

Cotzias, G. C., Miller, S. T., Tang, L. C., Papavasilious, P. S., and Wang, Y. Y. (1977). Levadopa, fertility and longevity. Science 196, 549–551.

Del Cerro, M., and Monjan, A. A. (1979). Unequivocal demonstration of the hematogenous origin of brain macrophages in a stab wound by a double-label technique. Neuroscience 4, 1399–1404.

Devoino, L. V., Eremina, O. F. N., and Ilyutchenok, R. Yu. (1970). The role of the hypothalamopituitary system in the mechanism of action of reserpine and 5-hydroxytryptophan on antibody production. Neuropharmacology 9, 67–72.

Engel, W. K., Trotter, J. L., McFarlin, D. E., and McIntosh, C. L. (1977). Thymic epithelial cell contains acetylcholine receptor. Lancet 1, 1310.

Eremina, O. F., and Devoino, L. V. (1973). Production of humoral antibodies in rabbits with destruction of the nucleus of the midbrain raphe. Bull. Exp. Biol. Med. (Engl. Transl.) 75, 149–151.

Feldman, M., and Nossal, G. J. V. (1972). Tolerance, enhancement and the regulation of interactions between T cells, B cells and macrophages. Transplant. Rev. 13, 3.

Fontana, A., Grieder, A., Arrenbrecht, S., and Grob, P. (1980). In vitro stimulation of glia cells by a lymphocyte-produced factor. J. Neurol. Sci. 46, 55–62.

Friedberger, E., and Tinti, M. (1924). Über antikörperbildung nach entfernung des antigendepots. II. Die spezifität der agglutinine bei intrakutaner zuführung antigens and entfernung des antigendepots nach kurzer. Zeit. Ztschr. f. Immunitatsforsch. U. exper. Therap. 39, 428–458.

Fujita, S., and Kitamura, J. (1976). Origin of brain macrophages and the nature of the microglia. Prog. Neuropath. 3, 1–50.

Fujiwara, M., Muryobayashi, T., and Shimamoto, K. (1966). Histochemical demonstration of monoamines in the thymus of rats. Jpn. J. Pharmacol. 16, 493–494.

Gerber, J. C., and Hare, T. A. (1979). Gamma-Aminobutyric acid in peripheral tissue, with emphasis on the endocrine pancreas. *Diabetes.* **28,** 1073–1076.

Goldstein, A. L., Cohen, G. H., Thurman, G. B., Hooper, J. A., and Rossio, J. L. (1976). Regulation of immune balance by thymosin: Potential role in the development of suppressor T cells. *In* "Immune Reactivity of Lymphocytes" (M. Feldman and A. Globerson, eds.), pp. 221–228. Plenum, New York.

Goldstein, A. L., Low T.L.K., McAdoo, M., McClure, J., Thurman, G. B., Rossio, J., Lai, C.-Y., Chang, D., Wang, S.-S., Harvey, C., Ramel, A. H., and Meienhofer, J. (1977). Thymosin αl: Isolation and sequence analysis of an immunologically active thymic polypeptide. *Proc. Natl. Acad. Sci. U.S.A.* **74,** 725–729.

Goldstein, A. L., Thurman, G. B., Low, T. L. K., Rossio, J. L., and Trivers, G. E. (1978). Hormonal influences on the reticuloendothelial system: Current status of the role of thymosin in the regulation and modulation of immunity. *Res. J. Reticuloendothel. Soc.* **23,** 253–266.

Gordienko, A. N. (1958). The mechanism of the formation of certain immunological processes. *In* "Control of Immunogenesis by the Nervous System" (A. N. Gordienko ed.), pp. 1–15. Rostov-on-Don. (Translated and Published by The Israel Program for Scientific Translations).

Gordienko, A. N., Kiseleva, V. I., Saakov, B. A., and Tsynkalovskii, R. B. (1958a). The possibility of producing antibodies by direct contact of antigen with cells. *In* "Control of Immunogenesis by the Nervous System" (A. N. Gordienko, ed.), pp. 16–21. Rostov-on-Don. (Translated and Published by The Israel Program for Scientific Translations).

Gordienko, A. N., Kiseleva, V. I., Saakov, B. A., and Leten, A. V. (1958b). Electrophysiological phenomena in the nerve following action of antigens on the skin receptors. *In* "Control of Immunogenesis by the Nervous System" (A. N. Gordienko, ed.), pp. 22–27. Rostov-on-Don. (Translated and Published by The Israel Program for Scientific Translations).

Gordienko, A. N., Kiseleva, V. I., Saakov, B. A., Bondarev, I. M., and Zhigalina, L. I. (1958c). The mechanism of action of antigen on receptors of the carotid sinus in reflex production of antibodies. *In* "Control of Immunogenesis by the Nervous System" (A. N. Gordienko, ed.), pp. 91–95. Rostov-on-Don. (Translated and Published by The Israel Program for Scientific Translations).

Hall, N. R. (1980). Neuroendocrine interactions with immunogenesis. *In* "Molecular and Behavioral Neuroendocrinology" (C. B. Nemeroff and A. J. Dunn, eds.). Spectrum, New York (in press).

Hall, N. R., Lewis, J. K., Schimpff, R. D., Smith, R. T., Trescot, A. M., Gray, H. E., Wenzel, S. E., Abraham, W. C., and Zornetzer, S. F. (1978). Effects of diencephalic and brainstem lesions on haemopoietic stem cells. *Soc. Neurosc. Abstr.* **56,** p. 20

Hall, N. R., McClure, J. E., Hu, S.-K., Tick, N. T., Seales, C. M., and Goldstein, A. L. (1980). Effects of chemical sympathectomy upon thymus dependent immune responses. *Soc. Neurosc. Abstr.* 26.4

Higgins, T. J., and David, J. R. (1976). Effect of isoproterenol and aminophylline on cyclic AMP levels of guinea pig macrophages. *Cell. Immunol.* **27,** 1–10.

Hoffman, P. M., Robbins, D. S., Nolte, M. T., Gibbs, C. S., Jr., and Gajdusek, D. C. (1978). Immunity and immunogenetics in Guamanians with amyotrophic lateral sclerosis (ALS) and Parkinsonism-dementia. *J. Supramol. Struct.* **8,** Suppl. 2 (abstr.).

Idova, G. V., and Devoino, L. V. (1972). Dynamics of formation of γM- and γG-antibodies in mice after administration of serotonin and its precursor 5-hydroxytryptophan. *Bull. Exp. Biol. Med.* (*Engl. Transl.*) **73,** 294–296.

Ignarro, L. J., and George, W. J. (1974). Hormonal control of lysosomal enzyme release from human neutrophils: Elevation of cyclic nucleotide levels by autonomic neurohormones. *Proc. Natl. Acad. Sci. U.S.A.* **71,** 2027–2031.

Ignarro, L. J., Lint, T. F., and George, W. J. (1974). Hormonal control of lysosomal enzyme release from human neutrophils: Effects of autonomic agents on enzyme release, phagocytosis and cyclic nucleotide levels. *J. Exp. Med.* **139,** 1395–1414.

Janković, B. D., Isaković, K., and Petrović, S. (1969). Immune capacity of pinealectomized rats. *Proc. Yugosl. Immunol. Soc.* **1**, 31.

Janković, B. D., Isaković, K., and Petrović, S. (1970). Effect of pinealectomy on immune reactions in rats. *Immunology* **18**, 1–6.

Kasahara, K., Tanaka, S., Ito, T., and Hamashima, Y. (1977). Suppression of the primary immune response by chemical sympathectomy. *Res. Commun. Chem. Pathol. Pharmacol.* **16**, 687–694.

Kater, L., Oosterom, R., McClure, J., and Goldstein, A. L. (1980). Presence of thymosin-like factors in human thymic epithelial conditioned medium. *Int. J. Immunopharmacol.* **1**, 273.

Katz, D. H., and Unanue, E. R. (1973). Critical role of determinant presentation in the induction of specific responses in immunocompetent lymphocytes. *J. Exp. Med.* **137**, 967–990.

Kerns, J. M., and Frank, M. A. (1980). A quantitative study of lymphocytes and neuroglia in the nude mouse spinal cord. *Anat. Rec.* **196**, 96A.

Kirchner, H., Chused, T. M., Herberman, R., Holden, H. T., and Lavrin, D. H. (1974). Evidence of suppressor cell activity in spleens of mice bearing primary tumors induced by Moloney sarcoma virus. *J. Exp. Med.* **139**, 1473–1487.

Krieger, D. T. (1978). Endocrine processes and serotonin. In "Serotonin in Health and Disease" (W. B. Essman, ed.), Vol. 3, pp. 51–67. Spectrum, New York.

Kuntz, A., and Richins, C. A. (1945). Innervation of the bone marrow. *J. Comp. Neurol.* **83**, 213–222.

Lapin, V. (1974). Influence of simultaneous pinealectomy and thymectomy on the growth and formation of metastases of the Yoshida sarcoma in rats. *Exp. Pathol.* **9**, 108–112.

Lapin, V. (1976). Pineal gland and malignancy. *Oesterr. Z. Onkol.* **3**, 51–60.

Lindstrom, J. M., Lennon, V. A., Seybold, M. E., and Whittingham, S. (1976). Experimental autoimmune myasthenia gravis and myasthenia gravis: Biochemical and immunochemical aspects. *Ann. N.Y. Acad. Sci.* **274**, 254–274.

Loverdo, T. V. (1958). Neuroreflex mechanisms in the regulation of phagocytosis. In "Control of Immunogenesis by the Nervous System" (A. N. Gordienko, ed.), pp. 125–135. Rostov-on-Don. (Translated and Published by The Israel Program For Scientific Translation).

Low, T.L.K., and Goldstein, A. L. (1979). The chemistry and biology of thymosin. II. Amino acid sequence analysis of thymosin α_1 and polypeptide β_1. *J. Biol. Chem.* **254**, 987–995.

Low, T.L.K., Thurman, G. B., McAdoo, M., McClure, J., Rossio, J. L., Naylor, P. H., and Goldstein, A. L. (1979). The chemistry and biology of thymosin. I. Isolation, characterization and biological activities of thymosin α_1 and polypeptide β_1 from calf thymus. *J. Biol. Chem.* **254**, 981–986.

Margules, D. L. (1979). Beta-endorphin and endoloxone: Hormones of the autonomic nervous system for the conservation or expenditure of bodily resources and energy in anticipation of famine or feast. *Neurosci. Biobehav. Rev.* **3**, 155–162.

Medado, P., Izak, G., and Feldman, S. (1967). The effect of electrical stimulation of the central nervous system on erythropoiesis in the rat. II. Localization of a specific brain structure capable of enhancing red cell production. *J. Lab. Clin. Med.* **69**, 776–786.

Melmon, K. L., Bourned, H. R., Weinstein, Y., Shearer, G. M., Bauminger, S., and Kram, J. (1974). Hemolytic plaque formation by leukocytes *in vitro*: Control by vasoactive hormones. *J. Clin. Invest.* **53**, 13–21.

Morris, R. J., Gower, S., and Pfeiffer, S. E. (1980). Thy-1 cell surface antigen on cloned cell lines of the rat and mouse: Stimulation by cAMP and by butyrate. *Brain Res.* **183**, 143–159.

O'Brian, D. J., Hughes, F. W., and Newberne, J. (1962). Influence of lysergic acid diethylamide on experimental allergic encephalomyelitis. *Proc. Soc. Exp. Biol. Med.* **111**, 490–493.

Oosterom, R., and Kater, L. (1980). Target cell subpopulations for human thymic epithelial conditioned medium in the mouse thymus. *Clin. Immunol. Immunopathol.* **17**, 183–195.

Oosterom, R., Kater, L., and Oosterom, J. (1979). Effects of human thymic epithelial conditioned medium on mitogen responsiveness of human and mouse lymphocytes. *Clin. Immunol. Immunopathol.* **12**, 460.

Oshikawa, K. (1921). Beziehen zwischen antigen und antikorperbildung. *Immunitactsforsch. Exp. Ther.* **33**, 303-316.

Parkhouse, R.M.E., and Dutton, R.W.J. (1966). Inhibition of spleen cell DNA synthesis by autologous macrophages. *J. Immunol.* **97**, 663-669.

Perkins, E., and Makinodan, T. (1965). The suppressive role of mouse peritoneal phagocytes in agglutinin response. *J. Immunol.* **94**, 765-777

Quay, W. B., and Gorray, K. C. (1980). Pineal effects on metabolism and glucose homeostasis: Evidence for lines of humoral mediation of pineal influences on tumor growth. *J. Neural Transm.* **47**, 107-120.

Reitler, R. (1924). Zur kenntnis der immunkörperbildung im organismus. *Z. Immunitactsforsch. Exp. Ther.* **40**, 453-468.

Rella, W., and Lapin, V. (1976). Immunocompetence of pinealectomized and simultaneously pinealectomized and thymectomized rats. *Oncology* **33**, 3-6.

Rivkin, I., Rosenblatt, J., and Becker, E. L. (1975). The role of cyclic AMP in the chemotactic responsiveness and spontaneous motility of rabbit peritoneal neutrophils: The inhibition of neutrophil movement and the elevation of cyclic AMP levels by catecholamines, prostaglandins, theophylline and cholera toxin. *J. Immunol.* **115**, 1126-1134.

Rodin, A. E. (1963). The growth and spread of Walker 256 carcinoma in pinealectomized rats. *Cancer Res.* **23**, 1545-1550.

Rosenstreich, D. L., Farrar, J. J., and Dougherty, S. (1976). Absolute macrophage dependency of T-lymphocyte activation by mitogens. *J. Immunol.* **116**, 131-139.

Schmidt-Gayk, H. E., Jakobs, K. H. and Hackenthal, E. (1975). Cyclic AMP and phagocytosis in alveolar macrophages: Influence of hormones and dibutyryl cyclic AMP. *Res, J. Reticuloendothel. Soc.* **17**, 251-261.

Scott, M. T. (1972). Biological effects of the adjuvant *Corynebacterium parvum*. II. Evidence for macrophage-lymphocyte interaction. *Cell. Immunol.* **5**, 469-479.

Seeman, B., Schupf, N., and Williams, C. A. (1978). Mimicry of dopamine stimulation of hypothalamic pathways in C3a anaphylatoxin. *Soc. Neurosci. Abstr.* p. 414 1310.

Segall, P. E., and Timiras, P. S. (1976). Patho-physiologic findings after chronic tryptophan deficiency in rats: A model for delayed growth and aging. *Mech. Ageing Dev.* **5**, 109-124.

Seip, M., Halvorsen, S., Anderson, P., and Kaada, B. R. (1961). Effects of hypothalamic stimulation on erythropoiesis in rabbits. *Scand. J. Clin. Lab. Invest.* **13**, 553-563.

Sharkis, S. J., Ahmed, A., Sensenbrenner, L. L., Jedrzejczak, W. W., Goldstein, A. L., and Sell, K. W. (1979). The regulation of hematopoiesis: Effect of thymosin or thymocytes in a diffusion chamber. *In* "Experimental Hematology Today" (S. J. Baum and G. D. Ledney, eds.), Vol. 2, pp. 17-22. Springer-Verlag, Berlin and New York.

Shearer, G. M., Melmon, K. L., Weinstein, Y., and Sela, M. (1972). Regulation of antibody response by cells expressing histamine receptors. *J. Exp. Med.* **136**, 1302-1307.

Singh, U. (1979). Effect of catecholamines on lymphopoiesis in fetal mouse thymic explants. *J. Anat.* **129**, 279-292.

Singh, U., and Owen, J. J. T. (1976). Studies on the maturation of thymus stem cells. The effects of catecholamines, histamine and peptide hormones on the expression of T-cell alloantigens. *Eur. J. Immunol.* **6**, 59-62.

Singh, U., Millson, D. S., Smith, P. A., and Owen, J. J. T. (1979). Identification of β-adrenoreceptors during thymocyte ontogeny in mice. *Eur. J. Immunol.* **9**, 31-35.

Sjöberg, O. (1972). Effect of allogeneic interaction on the primary immune response *in vitro*. *Clin. Exp. Immunol.* **12**, 365-375.

Soriano, F. M., Del Campo, F. J. S., Garcia, J. L., and Agreda, V. S. (1980). Ultrastructural variations in the thymus after pinealectomy. *Morfologia normal y patologica*. **4**:17-26.

Terentyeva, E. I., and Kakhetelidze, M. C. (1956). Influence of acetylcholine and adrenaline on the hematopoietic cells of the bone marrow in a tissue culture. *Bull. Exp. Biol. Med. (Engl. Transl.)* **41**, 1054-1058.

Thakur, P. K., and Manchanda, S. K. (1969). Hypothalamic influence on the activity of reticuloendothelial system of cat. *Indian J. Physiol Pharmacol.* **13**, 10 (abstr.).

Unanue, E. R. (1972). The regulatory role of the macrophage. *Adv. Immunol.* **15**, 95–165.

Vekshina, N. L., and Magaeva, S. V. (1974). Changes in the serotonin concentration in the limbic structure of the brain during immunization. *Bull. Exp. Biol Med. (Engl. Transl.)* **77**, 625–627.

Welscher, H. D., and Cruchaud, A. (1976). The influence of various particles and 3′, 5′-cyclic adenosine monophosphate on release of lysosomal enzymes by mouse macrophages. *Res, J. Reticuloendothel. Soc.* **20**, 405–420.

Welscher, H. D., and Cruchaud, A. (1978). Conditions for maximal synthesis of cyclic-AMP by mouse macrophages in response to β-adrenergic stimulation. *Eur. J. Immunol.* **8**, 180–184.

Wybran, J., Appelboom, T., Famacy, J.-P., and Govaerts, A. (1979). Suggestive evidence for receptors for morphine and methionine-enkephalin on normal human blood T-lymphocytes. *J. Immunol.* **123**, 1068–1070.

Zurier, R. B., Weissman, G., Hoffstein, S., Kammerman, S., and Tai, H. H. (1974). Mechanisms of lysosomal enzyme release from human leukocytes. II. Effects of C-AMP and C-GMP, autonomic agonists, and agents which affect microtubule function. *J. Clin. Invest.* **53**, 297–309.

Immunologic–Neuroendocrine Circuits: Physiological Approaches[1]

H. O. BESEDOVSKY
E. SORKIN

INTRODUCTION

With the progressive unraveling of the cellular and humoral elements of the immune system in recent years, the nature of its regulation has become a matter of major concern. We shall discuss here facts and problems related to the physiological control of the immune system by neuroendocrine mechanisms. Many past attempts to provide facts for dynamic links between the immune system and the neuroendocrine system have been fragmentary, disconnected, and even obscure. Little notice was taken of the progress in immunology of the past 2 decades and there was a tendency to oversimplify the problems inherent in such complex integrative studies of several body systems. It is therefore not altogether surprising that this type of research is not yet popular among immunologists. Nevertheless, recent approaches and experimental findings strongly support the concept of such external immunoregulation. Furthermore, recent developments in physiology and new methodologies for analyzing complex control mechanisms have to be considered when exploring immunoregulation.

Central control of many physiological processes is based most often on regulation of relatively few parameters. Thus, the maintenance of stability

[1] This work was supported by the Swiss National Science Foundation, Grant Nr. 3.213.0.77.

545

and optimal level of blood pressure is achieved by the regulation of cardiac outflow and the diameter of peripheral arterioles. Lung ventilation depends on the rhythmicity and strength of respiratory muscle contraction. Given the enormous heterogeneity and complexity of the immune system and its response, doubtless many more levels of regulatory signals within the system and their interaction and integration with autonomic, hypothalamic, and endocrine controls will have to be considered than in the previously given examples. This paper will concern itself with a critical analysis of concepts and facts on physiological circuits between the immune and the neuroendocrine systems.

THE IMMUNE SYSTEM
AND ITS RESPONSE

The immune system is a complex recognition system with an enormous repertoire of perhaps 10^6–10^7 specificities. It consists in humans of about 10^{12} B lymphocytes and 10^{12} T lymphocytes. Both B and T lymphocytes can recognize macromolecular antigens with a high, but by no means absolute, degree of specificity. Antigenic stimulation leads to clonal expansion of lymphocytes with the participation of lymphocyte- (and macrophage-) derived signals causing proliferation and differentiation.

B lymphocytes have on their surface membranes about 10^4–10^5 of those antibodies which they can produce. The antibody molecules which a given B lymphocyte and its daughter cells produce, all have identical variable domains. It is with these variable domains that antibody molecules can recognize and attach to a fitting area of an antigen molecule or particle. Different classes (12) of antibody molecules exist with different heavy and light chains.

Antibody molecules are themselves good antigens. The antigenic determinants situated on the variable domain of antibody molecules are called idiotypes. These antigenic markers are part of the amino acid sequence that determines the combining site. They constitute an antigenic universe within the immune system itself, that, as it appears now, seems to exert a regulatory function in antibody formation.

T cells constitute about one-half of all lymphocytes. Also, they are diverse with respect to the antigens which they can recognize by still unknown receptors, but they can not be induced to secrete antibody molecules. T-cell precursors arise from multiplying pools of stem cells in the bone marrow of mammals. They pass through the thymus where they acquire a number of maturity and MHC-restriction characteristics. The population of T cells can, apart from their enormous repertoire of specificity, be distinguished by subpopulations with different functions: helper T cells, suppressor T cells, killer T cells, allo-responsive T cells, possibly natural killer (NK) cells, and others. At least some cell types of the subset of T lymphocytes exert immunoregulatory functions. Thus, the attachment of antigen to the combining site of the Ab-like receptor of a B cell usually does not result in triggering this B cell unless a helper or induced T cell recognizes the attached antigen and then secretes several different stimulatory signals. These and other regulatory T-cell mediators are called lymphokines. It is critical that the helper T cell also recognizes on the B-cell surface the Ia antigens, a product of the major histocompatibility (MHC) genes of this animal.

Suppressor T cells are regulatory inhibitors that can prevent B cells from being stimulated by antigen. Like helper T cells, suppressor T cells seem to be antigen specific and nonspecific. Whether they act directly and specifically on B cells or whether they suppress helper cells and/or their precursors is still being investigated.

Cell surface antigens and the pattern of the immune response are encoded in the major histocompatibility complex (MHC) and play an important role in the regulation of the immune system. In man, the MHC is located on the short arm of chromosome six. More than four important loci can be distinguished in the MHC, and dozens of alleles are known to exist in man (and mouse) at each of these loci. Several remarkable facts have recently emerged from MHC studies. (a) The presence or absence of a given L-allele determines whether an animal is capable of producing antibodies to certain antigens. (b) Certain MHC alleles in man determine the susceptibility of a person to a variety of noninfectious diseases (e.g., ankylosing spondylitis, multiple sclerosis). (c) T-killer and T-helper lymphocytes can interact with targets or with other lymphocytes only if these cells, besides presenting foreign antigens, also display the "correct" MHC antigens.

This oversimplified picture of some present-day concepts and facts about the immune system has omitted many other features. No mention was made of the monocyte–macrophage system, which seems of importance in antigen presentation and immunoregulation, nor were other critical effector systems such as lymphokines and complement put in proper perspective. What is evident, however, is the enormous complexity of the immune system which obviously requires for its normal functioning the workings of a great variety of regulatory mechanisms at numerous levels (see also Jerne, 1974, 1976a,b; Melchers and Rajewsky, 1976; Loor and Roelants, 1977).

IMMUNOREGULATION

A major aim of present immunologic research is to gain an understanding of immunoregulation. There are now known to exist several regulatory processes "within the system" (autoregulation) such as T-cell dependent suppression or help, receptor blockade, idiotype anti-idiotype networks, genetic elements, among others. These facts have led to the view that the immune system represents a homeostatic, self-contained and self-monitoring system

(Burnet, 1976). More recently, another possibility has been raised that control of the immune process can also be imposed upon "from without" (external immunoregulation). As we shall discuss, there are now reasons for believing that the immune system, as other body systems, is indeed under *external regulation* by the neuroendocrine system. It is realized, however, that both possibilities of regulation are by no means mutually exclusive and it seems that common pathways exist. Facts and arguments about autoregulation and external regulation are discussed below.

Autoregulation of the Immune System

It has long been evident that the immune system must be subject to internal regulatory mechanisms so as to maintain its homeostatic balance. Such regulation could be visualized as occurring at a number of levels, for example, during differentiation in ontogeny as well as during the various stages of the response to antigen. Accordingly, considerable effort, both theoretical and experimental, has been committed to explore a variety of regulatory mechanisms such as a lymphocyte network (Jerne, 1974), antibody feedback (Uhr and Möller, 1968), the genetic control of immune responsiveness (Benacerraf et al., 1974), and suppressor and helper lymphocytes and their mediators (Gershon, 1979).

The discovery of immune response genes, followed by the mapping of these genes to loci within the major histocompatibility complex, has led to at least a partial understanding of the basic questions concerning mechanisms of intercellular communication and thus autoregulation. The existence of allelic variants of differentiation antigens was used to analyze the T-lymphocyte system and led to the discovery of multiple cell sets, each with functionally distinct genetic programs. Progress has been made in understanding how these interacting cellular networks develop and how the immunocompetent cells communicate with each other via messages passed among the different subsets, thereby determining to an important extent the intensity and type of response.

These regulatory messages include the idiotypic properties of the variable regions of antibodies. There exists a vast number of different idiotypic antigenic determinants close to or within the antibody combining site. They resemble foreign antigens and can react with antibodies (anti-idiotypes) of the same individual. When B cells secrete their antibody molecules, these may interact continuously with lymphocyte receptors carrying fitting idiotypic determinants. Anti-idiotypic antibodies have been demonstrated to inhibit the production of antibodies of the corresponding idiotype. Since every antibody molecule is anti-idiotypic antibody, Jerne (1976a) suggested that the specific immune system be viewed as an enormous functional network of interacting antibody molecules and cell receptors.

The overall effect of these and other interactions, after perturbation of the system by "antigen," may be to restore the homeostatic balance of the system (for a recent discussion of autoregulation, see Gershon, 1979).

Despite the incompleteness of our knowledge of these various regulatory mechanisms, there has developed a kind of consensus that the immune system is a complex self-monitoring, auto-regulated system, which in a purely operational sense, is rather analogous to other well-known self-regulated body systems.

External Regulation of the Immune System

Apart from the briefly discussed autoregulatory mechanisms, the immune system is assumed to be subject to a variety of external hormonal and neural inputs. These may affect several of the mentioned autoregulatory mechanisms. The complexity of the central regulatory signals that have to reach the immune system at the numerous steps of its response implies a need for appropriate communication channels between the responding immune system and the central nervous and endocrine systems. Knowing the complexity of the systems involved, it is not surprising that a considerable degree of scepticism exists as to whether a proper scientific analysis of the neuroendocrine control of the immune system is possible or even necessary at all.

There are in the main probably two groups of workers, the "believers" and those who deny this type of immunoregulation or think it not worthy of serious study. For the believers with clinical experience in psychosomatic medicine the argument runs about as follows: Since the brain controls most body functions, it is obvious that it must also control such essential functions as immune processes. To this declaration of faith we would be entitled to retort that the "obvious" and the "must" of central nervous system control of the immune response needs experimental verification such as identification of the cellular and subcellular immunologic targets for neuroendocrine signals, exploration of the regulatory signals and analysis of the afferent, central and efferent pathways within the network of immune-neuroendocrine interactions.

The opposite attitude ("nonbelievers") is based on the following kind of reasoning: It is possible to obtain a primary induced immune response *in vitro* that closely resembles in quality and magnitude the response in the intact animal. Since regulatory mechanisms also operate in such *in vitro* systems, there is no need to postulate *any* kind of external control over the immune system. Indeed, the nervous system and the immune system seem to avoid each other (Jerne, 1976b). It must be admitted that thanks to their ingenuity, modern immunologists, to a remarkable degree, have been able to mimic under highly artificial *in vitro* culture conditions the immune response as observed in the intact animal. However, there are numerous other physiological examples showing that autoregulation is coordinated with integrative control mechanisms by the central nervous system.

In our view the immune response is subject to external regulatory operations. Internal and neuroendocrine signals are conceived to interact in synergistic or antagonistic fashion or to be integrated in feedback circuits. As a result of the interaction of the various messages, the immune system will be kept in homeostatic balance, possibly at a new level. We shall submit this concept of external regulation to a critical analysis and discuss (a) the evidence needed for acceptance of a central control operating under physiological conditions, and (b) the relevant available experimental data from our and other laboratories.

ESSENTIAL REQUIREMENTS FOR NEUROENDOCRINE CONTROL OF THE IMMUNE SYSTEM

Before neuroendocrine control of the immune system can be accepted as a fact, a number of criteria must be fulfilled:

1. Hormones and neurotransmitters should be able to interfere with processes related to the immune response.
2. Lymphocytes and accessory cells should express receptors for hormones and neurotransmitters.
3. Manipulation of the central nervous system and of endocrine functions should affect the immune response.
4. Dynamic immune–neuroendocrine interactions should exist resulting in: (a) neuroendocrine functional changes capable, in turn, of influencing the immune system, and (b) alterations in immune functions capable of eliciting neuroendocrine changes.
5. Messengers from the activated immune system to central structures should provide information about the ongoing immune response.
6. Lymphocytes and accessory cells should receive regulatory neuroendocrine signals at the time and/or after their activation by antigen.
7. Changes in the activity of integrative nervous centers (e.g., the hypothalamus) should occur, reflecting the reception and processing of signals from the activated immune system.

A discussion of experimental evidence and approaches in terms of the above requirements is given in the following sections.

Hormones and Neurotransmitters Interfere with Processes Related to the Immune Response

Cells involved in the immune response, after their activation by the Ag, proliferate, transform into blasts, and express their genetic potential. This implies metabolic and morphological changes and cell membrane rearrangements. All these processes are known and neurotransmitters can act upon cellular and subcellular mechanisms essential for the immune response such as: lymphoid cell proliferation, lymphoid cell transformation, transport of substances through lymphoid cell membranes, genetic expression, protein synthesis, lymphokine synthesis, antibody formation and cytotoxicity (for references, see Besedovsky and Sorkin, 1977a).

Many hormones and neurotransmitters can modulate intracellular nucleotide levels (cAMP and cGMP) in lymphoid cells. In general, cAMP decreases the immune response, whereas cGMP increases responses. The intracellular levels of these nucleotides can affect antibody formation, cell-mediated immune response, phagocytosis, and allergic reactions (for details, see Braun, 1974; Bourne et al., 1974; Lichtenstein, 1976; Parker, 1979).

Lymphocytes and Accessory Cells Express Receptors For Hormones and Neurotransmitters

An essential requirement for neuroendocrine control of the immune system is the presence of receptors for hormones and neurotransmitters on immunologic cells. In fact, receptors for corticosteroids (Cake and Litwack, 1975; Werb et al., 1978), insulin (Hollenberg and Cuatrecasas, 1974; Helderman and Strom, 1978), growth hormone (Arrenbrecht, 1974), estradiol (Gillette and Gillette, 1979), testosterone (Abraham and Bug, 1976), β-adrenergic agents (Hollenberg and Cuatrecasas, 1974; Singh et al., 1979), and acetylcholine (Strom et al., 1974a; Richman and Arnason, 1979) have been demonstrated in lymphoid and accessory cells.

It seems a reasonable assumption that most of the effects of hormones and neurotransmitters at the cellular and subcellular levels of immunologic cells are exerted via such receptors. β-Adrenergic receptors and insulin receptors were found to appear in lymphocyte membranes only after their activation (Hollenberg and Cuatrecasas, 1974). This event helps to increase the sensitivity of lymphocytes towards these hormones when compared with unstimulated cells and may thereby modulate the magnitude of a given response. It will be important to study in the future the kinetics of appearance or modulation of hormonal receptors in the various subsets of lymphocytes.

MANIPULATION OF NEUROENDOCRINE FUNCTION AFFECTS THE IMMUNE RESPONSE

From the aforegoing it is evident that hormones and neurotransmitters can interfere with essential steps of the immune response. Manipulation of neuroendocrine function should, therefore, affect the immune response in many ways. There is, indeed, a considerable body of evidence to suggest that hormones exert multiple influences on the immune system. It is beyond the scope of this presentation to review the vast literature of this subject. The reader may find the following papers to be especially helpful (Dougherty *et al.*, 1964; Wolstenholme and Knight, 1970; Fabris, 1977; Claman, 1975; Besedovsky and Sorkin, 1977b; see also other chapters in this book.

Investigations on the participation of hormones in the immune response have generally involved either the parenteral administration of hormones or the ablation or blockade of endocrine glands. Numerous reports agree that hormone administration can lead to depressed or stimulated immune responses depending on the kind and dose of the hormones and the timing of administration. In general, glucocorticoids, androgens, estrogens, and progesterone depress the immune response *in vivo,* whereas growth hormone, thyroxine, and insulin increase the response.

Data on the effects of mediators of the autonomic nervous system on the immune system are contradictory, but in the main they indicate that neurotransmitters can influence the immune response, both *in vitro* and *in vivo.* Some of the previously obtained data on catecholamines have been discussed elsewhere (see Besedovsky *et al.*, 1979a). Examples of manipulation of the sympathetic nervous system and its suppressive action on the immune system are described below.

Parasympathetic agents have been reported to increase antibody formation (Marat, 1974) and cytotoxicity (Strom *et al.*, 1972, 1974b).

Numerous studies were performed in the past in order to demonstrate that direct manipulation of the brain can affect the immune response, and by this means to establish the existence of a link between the central nervous system and immunologic function. Thus, electrically-induced lesions or stimulation of different parts of the brain yielded results which were interpreted to be due to direct actions on the immune response or due to alterations of hormonal controls (Janković and Isaković, 1973; Stein *et al.*, 1976; Spector, 1979). Also, stress experiments showed that environmental stimuli acting through the brain can interfere with the immune response. These problems are discussed elsewhere in this book by Monjan and by Palmblad.

We have recently attempted to study a possible link between a major immunologic organ, the spleen, and central structures (Besedovsky *et al.*, 1979a). The effects of surgical denervation of the spleen and chemical sympathectomy by 6-hydroxydopamine on the immune response of such treated animals were examined.

EFFECT OF SPLEEN DENERVATION ON THE IMMUNE RESPONSE

The spleen is known to have a relatively rich noradrenergic sympathetic innervation. Denervation would therefore be expected to result in a diminution of noradrenaline (NA) in spleen which, in turn, could affect the immune response. Denervated and sham-operated rats were injected i.p. with sheep red blood cells (SRBC) and the number of plaque forming cells (PFC) counted 5 days later. Figure 1 shows that an almost 70% increase in number of PFC/spleen was found in denervated animals as compared with sham-operated controls. These findings suggest that interruption of sympathetic nervous innervation removes an important suppressor of the immune response.

Since splenic nerves are not entirely sympathetic, the basis for an increased number of PFC might not be due solely to the interruption of sympathetic fibers. To further clarify this point, sympathectomy was performed by purely chemical means.

EFFECT OF CHEMICAL SYMPATHECTOMY ON THE IMMUNE RESPONSE

Chemical sympathectomy in newborn rats was produced by repeated i.p. administration of 6-hydroxydopamine during the first 5 days of life. At 2 months of age, animals were given an immunizing injection of SRBC i.p. and the number of PFC in the spleen was determined 5 days later. Sympathectomized rats showed a tendency for increased PFC which was not statistically significant. It is known that following 6-hydroxydopamine-(6-OHDA) induced sympathectomy there is a compensatory stimulation of the adrenals so that normal and even high catecholamine (CA) concentrations are present in the

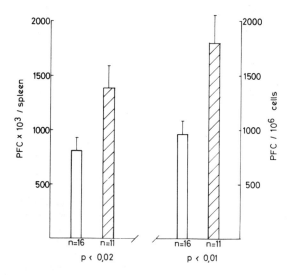

Figure 1. Enhancement of number of PFC by spleen denervation. Denervated or sham-operated rats were injected i.p. with 5×10^9 SRBC and the number of PFC was measured 5 days later. Values are given as mean ± S.E.M. □ = sham-operated rats; ▨ = denervated rats. From "Immunoregulation mediated by the sympathetic nervous system" by Besedovsky, H., *et al., Cellular Immunology*, 1979, **48**, 346–355. Copyright 1979 by Academic Press. Reprinted by permission.

blood and therefore still acting on the spleen. Accordingly, in further experiments rats were first chemically sympathectomized and subsequently adrenalectomized as well. Three other groups served as controls: one injected with solvent and sham-operated; another injected with 6-OHDA and sham-operated, and a third group injected with solvent and adrenalectomized. Figure 2 summarizes the results. Sham-operated rats treated with 6-OHDA (Group 2) again showed a slight increase in number of PFC compared with controls (Group 1). Adrenalectomy alone (Group 3) did not exert any significant effect on numbers of PFC, affirming previous findings (Besedovsky *et al.,* 1979b). In contrast, the combination of chemical sympathectomy via 6-OHDA and adrenalectomy (Group 4) resulted in a 119% increase in the number of splenic PFC.

These experiments support the hypothesis that the sympathetic system exerts a significant influence on the immune response. However, it seemed important to affirm in an *in vitro* model the findings, *in vivo,* that surgical and

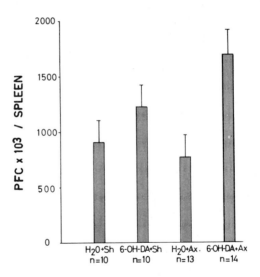

Figure 2. Enhancement of number of PFC in the spleen by chemical sympathectomy combined with adrenalectomy. Group 1: Rats injected i.p. with 2 μl/gm body weight solvent (H_2O) daily during the first 5 days of life and sham-operated at 2 months of age. Group 2: Rats injected i.p. with 150 mg/kg 6-OHDA and sham-operated. Group 3: Rats injected with solvent and adrenalectomized. Group 4: Rats injected with 6-OHDA and adrenalectomized. Group 2 showed a slight increase in the number of PFC when compared with controls (Group 1). Adrenalectomy alone (Group 3) did not significantly change the magnitude of the immune response, whereas combined treatment of 6-OHDA with adrenalectomy (Group 4) resulted in a 119% increase in number of PFC in the spleen ($p < 0.01$). Group 4 also differed significantly from Group 1 ($p < 0.01$). From "Immunoregulation mediated by the sympathetic nervous system," by Besedovsky, H., *et al., Cellular Immunology,* 1979, **48,** 346–355. Copyright 1979 by Academic Press. Reprinted by permission.

chemical sympathectomy both led to diminution of the restraint on the immune response.

NORADRENALINE AND THE SYNTHETIC α-ADRENERGIC AGONIST CLONIDINE SUPPRESS THE IMMUNE RESPONSE IN VITRO

Experiments were designed in anticipation of a direct action by the neurotransmitter NA and its synthetic α-adrenergic agonist, clonidine, on the cells involved in a primary *in vitro* induced immune response. Few and contradictory results had been reported earlier. In the present work, NA was added to mouse spleen cell cultures plus SRBC. A total of 9 experiments were performed in which NA was added in concentrations of 10^{-4}–10^{-8} at zero time. In 6 of these experiments, a suppression of the immune response occurred at all NA concentrations employed, whereas in three other experiments the immune response was either not influenced or an increase was seen. This variation in results is possibly attributable to the instability (oxidized, metabolized) of NA in culture medium.

Since NA stimulates predominantly α-adrenergic receptors, further experimentation *in vitro* was based on the synthetic α-agonist, clonidine, which is a stable compound resistant to monoamine oxidase and catechol-*O*-methyltransferase. As is shown graphically in Figure 3, a strong suppression

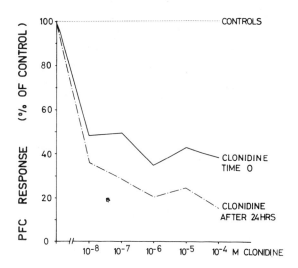

Figure 3. Suppression of the *in vitro* induced primary immune response of mouse spleen cells by the α-adrenergic agonist clonidine. Clonidine was added at the indicated concentration either together with the antigen (SRBC) at the onset of the culture (———) or 24 hr later (·····). Each curve represents the mean of three experiments. The response in the controls varied from 15,000 to 27,000 PFC per culture. From "Immunoregulation mediated by the sympathetic nervous system" by Besedovsky, H. *et al., Cellular Immunology,* 1979, **48,** 346–355. Copyright 1979 by Academic Press. Reprinted by permission.

of the immune response was produced by clonidine at concentrations varying from 10^{-4} to $10^{-8}M$. This immunosuppression was obtained irrespective of whether the agonist was added at the onset of the culture to the spleen cells together with the antigen or 24 hr later. It is noteworthy that the addition of clonidine after 24 hr induced an even more pronounced immunosuppressive effect. Clonidine, in concentrations from 10^{-4} to $10^{-8}M$, did not manifest any discernable toxicity for spleen cells. Indeed, the number of recoverable cells was the same as in the controls after 5 days of culture.

Comments: The aforegoing experiments indicate that manipulation of sympathetic innervation can strongly influence the immune response, but what can be concluded from these and other described manipulations? While our example, a splenic denervation effect on lymphoid organs, represents the disruption of at least an unidirectional link from the central nervous system, it must be admitted that such experiments can not truly prove central regulation. Similarly, the variety of immunologic effects following injection of hormones, ablation of endocrine glands, brain stimulation, or lesions do not really permit one to detect dynamic bidirectional links between the brain and the activated immune system. It is most likely, however, that these manipulations grossly disturb the mutual flow of information and regulatory signals between these systems.

There is indirect evidence for a mutual relationship between the immune system and neuroendocrine mechanisms that can only be explained on the basis of the existence of bidirectional channels of information between the immune system and external, more integrative, structures. In the next section we are going to discuss some of these examples, and in the following section more direct evidence for the operation of physiological neuroendocrine control mechanisms on the immune response will be provided.

PHYSIOLOGICAL DYNAMIC IMMUNE-NEUROENDOCRINE INTERACTIONS DURING DEVELOPMENT AND ADULT LIFE

The first point that bears emphasizing is the remarkable, near-parallel development of the immune and endocrine systems in various mammalian species during early ontogeny. This can hardly be fortuitous. Thus, in species such as mice and rats which at birth have only marginal levels of immunoglobulins and in which immune responses are minimally effective during the first days of extrauterine life (Solomon, 1971), many endocrine mechanisms are also underdeveloped at this time, notably sexual differentiation, functioning of the hypophysis, thyroid, and adrenal glands. There are species, on the other hand, such as guinea pigs, sheep, cow, and man which, to greater or lesser degree, are more mature immunologically at birth; in these species the aforementioned endocrine mechanisms are likewise synchronized in a more advanced stage of development (for references, see Besedovsky and Sorkin, 1977b).

We shall examine, now, the proposition that there also exists a bidirectional influence (i.e., each affects the other) between the endocrine and the immune system. The evidence derives from situations in which a disturbance of this interrelation at one level results in changes at other levels. Such a disturbance is found in conditions where the development of the immune system is impaired or alternatively where the endocrine environment is changed. In either case, the other parameters change in an essentially parallel fashion.

Four kinds of disturbances of the proposed bidirectional interacting systems are given as examples:

1. Changes in hormonal environment produce alterations in immune function. An instructive model is the hypopituitary dwarf mouse with its deficiency in growth hormone and thyrotropin. Cell-mediated immunity, as measured by transplantation criteria, is defective; this deficit can be overcome by injection of STH and thyroxine into such dwarf mice (Fabris et al., 1971a,b). Another animal model, the NZB mouse, is subject to autoimmune disease. The disturbed immune function and expression of the disease was shown to be influenced by sex hormones, for example, when males were castrated their low incidence of the disease was increased to nearly that of females (Talal, 1977).

2. The germ-free state (i.e., lack of antigenic challenge) is manifested in a marked underdevelopment of the total mass of host lymphoid tissue and depressed immunoglobulin levels; it is also expressed in an altered endocrine state (for details and references, see Besedovsky and Sorkin, 1977b). Recent unpublished data from our laboratory show that the noradrenaline content of spleen and thymus of germ-free rats is considerably higher than of specific-pathogen-free (SPF) animals.

3. Congenitally thymusless and neonatally thymectomized mice which have a T-lymphocyte deficiency, display a profoundly disturbed endocrine system. Absence of a thymus in animals kept under conventional, SPF or germ-free conditions, results in degranulation of STH-producing cells in the adenohypophysis (Bianchi et al., 1971), a delay of puberty in females (Besedovsky and Sorkin, 1974; Lintern-Moore and Pantelouris, 1975; Weinstein, 1978), persistence of the reticular zone of the adrenal gland (Pierpaoli and Sorkin, 1972; Shire and Pantelouris, 1974), hypothyroidism (Pierpaoli and Sorkin, 1972; Pierpaoli and Besedovsky, 1975), and alterations in blood levels of gonadal hormones (Pierpaoli and Besedovsky, 1975). A number of these parameters can be normalized only by early thymus implantation (Besedovsky and Sorkin, 1974).

The passive transfer of lymphoid cells makes the recipients immunocompetent, but fails to normalize the aforementioned hormone-dependent parameters (Besedovsky and Sorkin, 1974). Endocrine influences of the thymus on other endocrine glands are being expressed during perinatal life, especially with regard to female sexual function. This finding provides a strong indication that the thymus is involved in the programming of the neuroendocrine system (Besedovsky and Sorkin, 1974; Pierpaoli and Besedovsky, 1975).

4. Surgically bursectomized, 62-hr-old chicken embryos show the following endocrine alterations later in embryonic life or at the time of hatching: underdeveloped oviduct, adrenal hypertrophy, low level production of corticosterone by adrenals, increased testosterone production, and hypertrophy of the testis (Besedovsky et al., 1975a; Pedernera et al., 1979).

The above-mentioned examples of interference at the level of antigenic challenge, development of central and peripheral lymphoid tissue, or at the level of endocrine functions attest to a complex network of interactions between the immune system and the endocrine system.

Other examples for such network interactions include the effects of conditioned reflexes (Ader, this volume; Ader and Cohen, this volume) are discussed elsewhere in this book.

ACTIVATED IMMUNE SYSTEM ELICITS CHANGES IN NEUROENDOCRINE SYSTEM AND RECEIVES REGULATORY SIGNALS

The fact that dynamic interactions do occur between immune and central mechanisms during development supports in our view the argument for a neuroendocrine regulation of the immune system. However, it is an essential requirement for any control mechanism that it can detect changes at those levels which should be regulated by it. Therefore, neuroendocrine changes should occur when the immune system is specifically activated by antigen.

Hormonal Changes during the Immune Response

In order to verify whether such endocrine changes can occur, we performed experiments to elucidate whether the immune response to nontoxic, nonreplicable antigens would *itself* bring about changes in corticosterone and thyroxine blood levels. Therefore, the primary immune response of rats to SRBC or to soluble antigen trinitrophenyl–hemocyanin (TNP–He) and of mice to TNP–horse red blood cells (TNP–HRBC) was studied in relation to a possible endocrine response (Besedovsky et al., 1975b). Rats were immunized by i.p. injection of sheep erythrocytes (SRBC). Nonimmunized rats and animals injected with homologous rat erythrocytes served as controls. Groups of animals were killed rapidly under minimal stress between 9 A.M. and 11 A.M. at various intervals after injection of antigen, and serum hormone levels and PFC were determined. The results in Figure 4A indicate that between days 5 and 7 after immunization with SRBC, the maximum number of PFC in the spleen were observed.

Figure 4B demonstrates a two- to threefold increase in serum corticosterone levels above normal at Days 5, 6, 7, or 8 after immunization with SRBC. The maximum level occurred on Day 5. Rats injected with the same dose of homologous rat red blood cells showed no changes in corticosterone levels at any time. No significant changes in the serum corticosterone level occurred on Day 1 and 3 after immunization. This indicates that the animals were not stressed by the manipulation or the injected cells.

A biphasic change in the serum thyroxine concentration was observed in animals treated with the higher dose of SRBC (Figure 4C). After an initial increase on Day 3, the serum thyroxine decreased to approximately 30% below normal on Days 5–8. No significant change was seen on Day 1.

The observed hormonal changes in blood after injection of SRBC led us to test, as well, a soluble antigen, TNP-hemocyanin, in rats. The results are summarized in Table 1.

Again, the blood corticosterone levels were increased during the immune response, but, in this system, the increase was earlier than in the SRBC-injected rats. Thyroxine blood levels showed a decrease and then an increase that was, in a way, similar to the experiments with SRBC.

Similar hormonal changes were reproduced in another animal species, C3H/He mice, which were immunized with TNP coupled with horse erythrocytes.

These studies have shown that in the course of the immune response to three different antigens in two animal species, major changes occurred in the blood levels of two hormones, corticosterone and thyroxine. Furthermore, corticosterone changes in blood were also noted during skin graft rejection; in this instance, a decrease (Besedovsky et al., 1978). The important implication is that the immune response affects hormonal levels in the blood in such a way that the immune response, itself, can also be influenced. In fact, the corticosterone levels attained at the peak of the immune response to SRBC in rats were of the same magnitude as the concentrations observed in blood of ACTH-treated mice, a treatment which inhibited the capacity of spleen in vitro to respond to SRBC with plaque formation (Gisler and Schenkel-Hulliger, 1971). Our studies imply that the observed hormonal changes could regulate, at least in part by a feedback mechanism, the duration and, possibly, even the magnitude of the immune response.

Antigenic competition was considered by us to be a case in point to prove that such steroid increase is, in fact, of significance in immunologic control. When non-crossreacting red blood cells from two different animal species (horse, sheep) are injected sequentially into a rat, the response to the second antigen is suppressed. This phenomenon which is called antigenic competition is largely unexplained and, strangely, has not been achieved in an in vitro

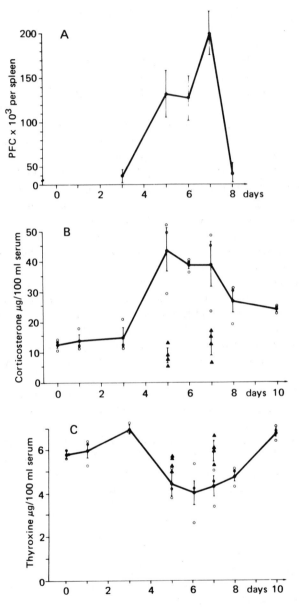

Figure 4. Changes in serum corticosterone and thyroxine levels during the immune response to sheep red cells (SRBC) in rats. (A) Plaque forming cells (PFC) × 10³ per spleen. (B) Corticosterone levels in serum: ○, animals immunized with SRBC: ▲, controls injected with rat red blood cells (RRBC). (C) Thyroxine levels in serum: ○, animals immunized with SRBC; ▲, controls immunized with RRBC. From "Changes in blood hormone levels during the immune response" by Besedovsky, H. *et al., Proceedings of the Society for Experimental Biology and Medicine,* 1975, **150,** 466–470. Copyright 1975 by Academic Press. Reprinted by permission.

TABLE 1.

Serum Corticosterone and Thyroxine Levels, PFC in Spleens of Female Rats Immunized i.p. with 224 μg of TNP-Hemocyanin[a]

Day after immunization	PFC per spleen	Corticosterone (μg/100 ml)[b]	Thyroxine (nmole/liter)[c]
0		13.0 ± 3.9[d]	71.0 ± 2.4
1	5097	24.5 ± 11.3	51.66 ± 4.6
3	576,206	51.0 ± 7.0	60.0 ± 7.4
4	529,611	25.7 ± 9.1	66.5 ± 6.5
6	85,119	36.06 ± 9.3	91.6 ± 7.4

[a] From "Changes in blood hormone levels during the immune response" by Besedovsky, H., et al., *Proceedings of the Society for Experimental Biology and Medicine*, 1975, **150**, 466–470. Copyright 1975 by Academic Press. Reprinted by permission.

[b] Corticosterone (Student's t test): Day 0 versus Day 3, $p < 0.001$; Day 0 versus Days 4 + 6, $p < 0.05$.

[c] Thyroxine (Student's t test): Day 0 versus Day 1, $p < 0.001$; Day 0 versus Days 3 + 4, $p < 0.05$; Day 0 versus Day 6 $p < 0.05$.

[d] All results are expressed as mean ± standard error.

model. The maximum degree of suppression *in vivo* in the above systems is obtained when the second antigen is inoculated 5 days after the first; that is, at a time when the animals have high corticosterone levels because of the immune response to the first antigen (Besedovsky et al., 1979c).

If the increase in corticosterone levels is, in fact, an essential component leading to antigenic competition, it follows that surgical ablation of the adrenals should result in the diminution or elimination of competition. As a detailed analysis of such experiments revealed (Figures 5 and 6), a large proportion of adrenalectomized animals had PFC numbers within the normal range. Thus, adrenalectomy obliterates antigenic competition.

In agreement with our interpretation of antigenic competition as being in part a hormone-dependent phenomenon, we could also show that, in the presence of a physiological concentration of hydrocortisone in an *in vitro* system, a condition occurred which mimicked antigenic competition between horse red blood cells (HRBC) and sheep red blood cells (SRBC) (Besedovsky et al., 1979b).

Our results in a particular model system of sequentially induced antigenic competition indicate that corticosterone is a significant factor in its manifestation. The target cell of this hormonal action remains unknown, although T helper and T suppressor cells are likely to be affected. Recent work by Gillis et al. (1979a,b) would agree with this interpretation, as their results indicate that glucocorticoids inhibit T lymphocyte proliferation via a profound effect on T-cell growth factor (TCGF) production in culture. Furthermore, addition of exogenous TCGF to glucocorticoid-treated human, mouse, or rat T-cell mitogen-stimulated lymphocytes restored normal levels of proliferation.

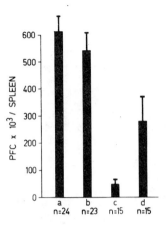

Figure 5. Effect of adrenalectomy on antigenic competition. (a) Sham-operated animals injected i.p. with 5 × 10⁹ SRBC. (b) Adrenalectomized animals injected i.p. with 5 × 10⁹ SRBC. (c) Sham-operated animals injected with 5 × 10⁹ HRBC and with the same dose of SRBC 5 days later. (d) Adrenalectomized animals injected i.p. with 5 × 10⁹ HRBC and with the same dose of SRBC 5 days later. Number of PFC against SRBC were determined in all groups 5 days after injection of SRBC. From "Antigenic competition between horse and sheep red blood cells as a hormone-dependent phenomenon," by Besedovsky, H. *et al., Clinical and Experimental Immunology,* 1979, **37,** 106–113. Copyright 1979 by Blackwell Scientific Publications. Reprinted by permission.

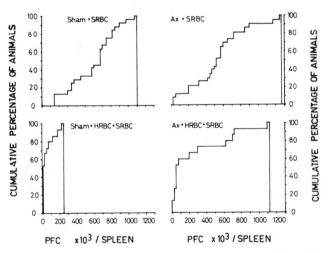

Figure 6. Analysis of the effect of adrenalectomy on antigenic competition. The results are expressed as a cumulative percentage of rats which fall into a given interval of PFC/ spleen. The cumulative percentage in the sham-operated and adrenalectomized animals injected with SRBC only do not differ. The distribution for the sham-operated animals injected with both HRBC and SRBC (antigenic competition) is totally different from all other groups, while the distribution of the adrenalectomized rats injected with both antigens clearly approached that of the corresponding control (Ax + SRBC). From "Antigenic competition beween horse and sheep red blood cells as a hormone-dependent phenomenon" by Besedovsky, H. *et al., Clinical and Experimental Immunology,* 1979, **37,** 106–113. Copyright 1979 by Blackwell Scientific Publications Reprinted by permission.

These observations are compatible with the view that the immunosuppressive effects of glucocorticoid hormones are mediated by controlling the production of the T-cell proliferation-inducing agent TCGF, which, in turn, serves to inhibit the clonal expansion of activated T cells. A link between these and our own results on hormone-dependent antigenic competition seems obvious; the raised glucocorticoid level caused by the response to the first antigen could prevent TCGF production essential for clonal expansion in response to the second antigen.

Local Sympathetic Neurotransmitter Changes in Lymphoid Tissue during the Immune Response

Endocrine signals are mediated by changes in hormonal blood levels and reach the immunologic target cells via microcirculation. Apart from the adrenal medulla, sympathetic signals are mediated by changes of the activity of terminal nerve endings by changes in the local concentration of noradrenaline in close vicinity to target cells.

The rat spleen is known to have sympathetic innervation. When NA distribution in the spleen is estimated with microfluorescence techniques, strong fluorescence is observed in the periarteriolar sheet of the splenic white pulp. This area is highly populated by T lymphocytes and other immune cells. In order to explore whether nerval sympathetic signals reach lymphocytes in the microenvironment in which the immune response takes place, we studied NA content in spleen following immunization with sheep red blood cells. Spleens were each divided into two parts: one portion was used for evaluation of the immune response, the other was decapsulated in order to measure parenchymal NA.

A radiometric–enzymatic assay for measuring femtomole (10^{-15}) quantities of catecholamine (CA) was applied to quantify NA in the spleen. The method consists essentially in conversion of the CA into its O-methylated analogue by catechol-O-methyltransferase in the presence of S-adenosyl-methionine-^{3}H. Serving as a control, the NA content of the heart was determined fluorimetrically.

Groups of rats were immunized i.p. with antigen (SRBC) and the number of PFC and the NA content of the spleen pulp determined at various intervals. Figure 7 shows the results of one of the five experiments performed. The number of PFC followed the usual pattern. The NA content of the spleen slightly decreased on Day 2, but a marked decrease was evident on Days 3 and 4 compared with controls. By Day 8, when relatively few direct PFC were detectable, the NA content had returned to normal. In all five experiments the decrease in NA content of spleen preceded the peak PFC. This reduction ranged from 40 to 70%. When the results were expressed per whole spleen, the NA decrease was also clearly evident. In two experiments, the NA content of a nonlymphoid organ, the heart, was also determined at various intervals

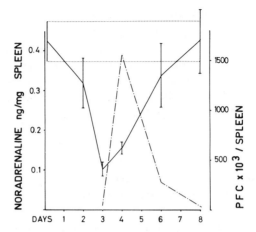

Figure 7. Decreasing NA levels in the splenic pulp during the immune response. Rats were injected with 5×10^9 SRBC or physiological saline and the number of PFC and the NA content determined on Days 3, 4, 6, and 8. Saline-injected controls showed no significant changes in splenic NA content and were used to define the normal control range (Day 0). Each point of the NA curve represents the mean value ± S.E.M. obtained from determinations in spleens of four animals. NA, ———; PFC, ----. From "Immunoregulation mediated by the sympathetic nervous system" by Besedovsky, H., et al., Cellular Immunology, 1979, 48, 346–355. Copyright 1979 by Academic Press. Reprinted by permission.

following immunization. No changes in the NA level in this control organ were discerned during the immune response.

These data constitute the first discrete evidence that a physiologically meaningful change in the splenic content of NA occurs in the environment of antibody-forming cells. This is an event which we would expect to affect the performance of immunocompetent cells. In fact, we have already shown that NA and the synthetic α-agonist, clonidine, can suppress an in vitro induced primary immune response to the same antigen. It is highly significant that this NA decrease occurs in the immediate vicinity of antibody-forming cells. Changes such as these may well be restricted to lymphoid organs, since the content of NA in the heart (for example) remains unmodified during the immune response. The fact that the changes occur several days after administration of antigen seems to exclude any stress effects or, for that matter, any kind of direct effect by the antigen itself. Decreased NA levels might be attributed to its consumption by spleen cells or by other local factors. However, such explanations are viewed as unlikely. The relative constancy of NA content in organs during varying conditions is based on a feedback mechanism operating with a high degree of precision. Free NA influences NA synthesis at the rate limiting step of tyrosine hydroxylase activity. Consequently, unless it is assumed that activated lymphocytes release a specific enzymatic inhibitor, local NA changes will be rapidly compensated for via the aforementioned mechanisms.

Accordingly, it is proposed that changes in NA content during the immune response represent the efferent limb of a reflex mechanism triggered by antigen stimulated cells. It seems to us that the changes in local concentration of NA are most reasonably viewed as regulatory signals capable of modulating the ongoing immune response. Such changes may even be synchronized with appearance of receptors for catecholamine known to occur during activation of lymphoid cells (Hollenberg and Cuatrecasas, 1974).

It is conceivable that, in addition to the direct effect of NA on the immune response, the NA decrease in lymphoid organs during immunization can also affect lymphoid cell traffic (Ernström and Sandberg, 1973).

Afferent Signals from the Activated Immune System Elicit a Response in Neurons of the Hypothalamus

The hypothalamus is known to be involved in many autonomic and endocrine control mechanisms. Therefore, in order to obtain direct evidence for the arrival of signals to the brain during the course of the immune response we looked for physiological changes manifested as electrical activity of individual neurons in the ventromedial nucleus of the hypothalamus of rats after immunization with two different antigens (Besedovsky et al., 1977). Rats were immunized by injection of SRBC or trinitrophenylated-hemocyanin. The kinetics of the immune response and hypothalamic activity were measured at various intervals after antigenic challenge, but each animal was investigated only at one time.

Typical data for animals stimulated with SRBC are summarized in Figure 8. On Day 1, when no plaque forming cells are evident, no changes in firing frequency were demonstrable compared with controls. On Day 5, at the peak of PFC in spleen, there was more than a twofold increase in the firing rate of the ventromedial neurons (control: 3.75 ± 0.28 spikes/sec.; SRBC: 8.82 ± 1.30 spikes/sec.; $p < 0.001$). In several rats which were immunologically nonresponders, no increase in firing rates occurred (not shown in Figure 8). Furthermore, no changes in firing rates were observed in the anterior hypothalamic nucleus (control: 5.77 ± 1.11; SRBC: 5.07 ± 0.96) on Day 5 after SRBC injection.

Hypothalamic responses to TNP-Hae were studied in rats on Days 1 through 5 after injection. The results are depicted in Figure 9. A significant increase in frequency of discharge was noted on Days 1, 2, 4, and 5; the highest activation occurred on Day 2, a time that precedes the peak of the direct PFC (control: 3.23 ± 0.36 spikes/sec.; TNP-Hae; 6.84 ± 0.78 spikes/sec., $p < 0.001$). The reason why there is no change in firing rate on Day 3 cannot be explained.

The results of this study show that two separate, nontoxic, noninfectious antigens elicited, apart from the conventional immune response and the endocrine response (see previous sections on hormonal changes), a distinctive response in the hypothalamus. The only known common feature of these two

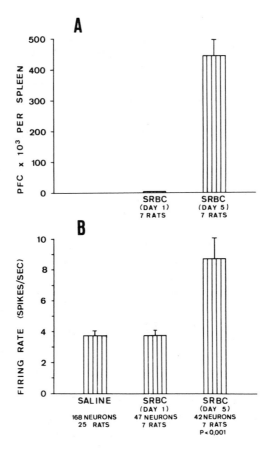

Figure 8. Increase in firing rates of neurons of ventromedial nuclei in the rat hypothalamus after antigenic stimulation. (A) Antibody-producing PFC in rat spleen; (B) firing rates. Rats were injected i.p. with 5×10^9 SRBC. From "Hypothalamic changes during the immune response" by Besedovsky, H., et al., European Journal of Immunology, 1977, **7**, 325–328. Copyright 1977 by Verlag Chemie GMBH. Reprinted by permission.

agents is their immunogenicity, and it is considered most unlikely that these physiological alterations involve the antigen itself. It is more likely that they reflect events linked with the immune response which, in turn, evoke the change in the hypothalamus. In fact, since the highest concentrations of antigen are available after the injection, hypothalamic changes should occur early. However, no such changes have been observed on Day 1 after SRBC injection when no antibody formation is detectable.

The present studies imply that, after antigenic stimulation, signals from lymphoid tissue reach the hypothalamus. The nature of these signals (lymphokines, antibodies, neural), the pathway within the hypothalamus, the type of neurons and whether other brain structures are involved remain to be determined.

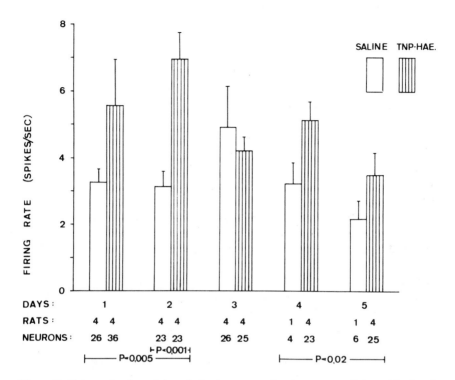

Figure 9. Firing rates by rat hypothalamic neurons in the ventromedial nuclei after intraperitoneal immunization with 250 μg TNP-Hae. From "Hypothalamic changes during the immune response" by Besedovsky, H., *et al.*, *European Journal of Immunology*, 1977, 7, 325–328. Copyright 1977 by Verlag Chemie GMBH. Reprinted by permission.

In summarizing the experimental data and implications of hormonal, autonomic, and hypothalamic changes during the immune response, we believe that more integrated levels also participate in immunoregulation. The fact that the activation of lymphoid cells can bring about neuroendocrine changes, also suggests that in immune processes occurring in ontogeny (such as acquisition of self-tolerance), immune–neuroendocrine interactions play an essential role. We have proposed earlier (Besedovsky and Sorkin, 1977a), and found some experimental evidence (Besedovsky, 1971), that the neuroendocrine environment is a relevant factor in the acquisition of self-tolerance. Self-antigens are expressed during fetal life, and immature lymphocytic cells are likely to interact with them at this time. The result of this interaction can be self-tolerance. (Besedovsky *et al.*, 1979c). Since lymphoid cells can bring about neuroendocrine changes, it is possible, therefore, that a similar process occurs during early ontogeny. The neuroendocrine response which may be elicited by immature lymphocytes after contact with self-antigens is likely to differ from that induced in adult life. It will obviously be based on mechanisms available at this time and may even include still unknown hormones. Such a mechanism may well influence the program of the immune system with regard to its expression of anti-self-reactivity.

Lymphokines as Afferent Signals for Neuroendocrine Changes during the Immune Response

That autonomic, endocrine, and hypothalamic changes follow the induction of an immune response implies the existence of afferent signals derived from the activated immune system which affect the central nervous system and endocrine glands. The nature of these signals is not known, but there is certainly no lack of candidates to be proposed as mediators of such a pathway. The possibility that different lymphokines may be mediating these effects has become more attractive following the observation that some of these mediators are present in blood during the immune response (Adelman *et al.*, 1979; Salvin and Neta, 1980).

Based on this hypothesis, we have carried out experiments in which supernatants, obtained from lymphocytes stimulated *in vitro* with Concanavalin A for 24 hr, were injected i.p. into rats. Such supernatants are known to contain a variety of lymphokine activities. Supernatants from nonstimulated lymphocytes were used to inject control animals. Different groups of animals were killed 30 min, 1, 2, 24, and 48 hr after a single injection of the supernatants, and corticosterone levels in plasma were measured. (Figure 10).

A significant increase in the concentration of this hormone was observed 1 and 2 hr after the injection, the levels of corticosterone returning to normal values after 24 hr.

Since, during the immune response to several different antigens, an increase in corticosterone concentration in blood was observed, we propose that among lymphokines are factors which might be the mediators of this endocrine change. Further work will be needed to clarify which of the numerous "factors" present in the cocktail of lymphocyte supernatants is responsible for this and other neuroendocrine effects, and whether it is exerted via the hypothalamus–adenohypophysial pathway or directly via the adrenal cortex.

GENERAL DISCUSSION AND CONCLUSIONS

After this review of some of the developments in the field of immune–neuroendocrine circuits, we would like to conclude with a critical overall appraisal of this concept, some speculations and look to the future. The experimental facts described, particularly those on the dynamic changes following antigenic stimulation, provide, in our view, a first approximation of a physiological external immunoregulation mediated by the central nervous system. This type of control, with signals derived from outside of the immune

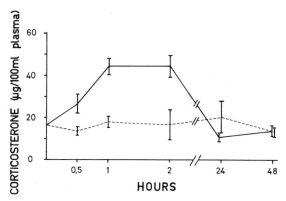

Figure 10. Changes in corticosterone plasma levels after the injection of Con A-stimulated human lymphocytes supernatants.
——, Supernatant from Con A-stimulated lymphocytes; -----, supernatant from nonstimulated lymphocytes.

system, contrasts with "autoregulation" (internal immunologic signals). However, this classification can be misleading if autoregulation versus external regulation are considered to operate in an absolutely independent manner. Rather, it must be assumed that common pathways exist for both control mechanisms. During different stages of the immune response, the performing lymphoid cell clones are likely to receive both internal and external signals which act sometimes synergistically, and sometimes antagonistically. We consider that autoregulation and neuroendocrine immunoregulation operate in a coordinated fashion, analogous, for instance, to the mechanisms which control motor functions. There, segmentary regulation exerted on spinal cord motoneurons ("final common pathway") is well integrated with different hierarchies of suprasegmentary control during postural reactions or voluntary movement.

We propose that, as in this example, the central control of the immune response shares with autoregulation common pathways. Internal and external signals might well be integrated in feedback circuits in which one type of signal influences the other. A few examples of such interactions and common pathways are discussed below.

1. Lymphocyte activation by lymphokines (Pick, 1979), polyclonal or antigenic stimuli, seems to be mediated by changes in the intracellular level of cyclic nucleotides. Since many hormones and neurotransmitters also induce changes in the intracellular concentration of these messengers, it is likely that specific hormone binding to lymphoid cell receptors influences the threshold of lymphoid cell activation by modifying cyclic nucleotide levels.

2. During the immune response, receptors for hormones and neurotransmitters (e.g., insulin, adrenalin) appear in activated lymphoid cells of different subclasses (Hollenberg and Cuatrecasas, 1974). This fact suggests

that hormonal or nerve signals will exert influences which are more effective in activated than in resting cells. When antigen and internal signals activate lymphocytes, the appearance of new or more receptors could make these cells more sensitive to hormonal signals and thereby significantly determine the further development of a response.

3. Hormones and neurotransmitters can affect lymphoid cell metabolism and, by this means, together with the specific internal signals, control essential mechanisms of the immune response, for example, immunoglobulin synthesis and clonal expansion of those lymphoid cells specifically activated by the antigen.

4. The regulatory switch from IgM to IgG production seems to be affected by corticosteroid hormones (Elliott and Sinclair, 1968; Streng and Nathan, 1973).

5. Lymphokines seem to be fundamental factors controlling lymphoid cell activation, transformation, and clonal expansion. There are examples of physiological concentrations of adrenocortical hormones influencing lymphokine production (Wahl et al., 1975; Gillis et al., 1979a,b). These facts, taken together with the increased corticosteroid levels following lymphokine inoculation as observed by us, suggest a hormonally mediated feedback mechanism of regulation of lymphokine production. Further experiments are, however, needed to clarify the physiological significance of these findings.

6. Certain sites within the Fc region of human immunoglobulin molecules have a nonimmunologic affinity to an unknown constituent both on the cell membrane and in the cytoplasm of ACTH producing cells in the human anterior pituitary (Pouplard et al., 1976). The physiological significance of this finding is not yet understood. However, it is conceivable the activity of ACTH producing cells may be affected by the binding of the immunoglobulins. In that case, this could be taken as an example that a product of the immune response is recognized by an endocrine cell and influences its workings.

7. The major histocompatibility complex (MHC) exerts genetic control of the immune response. The complexity of these loci is attested to by evidence of an association of the immune response genes with several diseases. The same MHC controls blood levels of testosterone in mice and other species (Iványi et al., 1973). In our view, this kind of association may not be fortuitous and may reflect immuno-endocrine interactions at the genetic level.

Immunoregulation by the central nervous system implies multiple links between two enormously complex physiological networks. Any proposal of neuroendocrine control of the immune response will certainly be incomplete if it does not take into account that central structures, such as the hypothalamus, which participates in immunoregulation, are involved in many other regulatory mechanisms. In addition, the hypothalamus also integrates brain signals which may affect the basal operation of the neuroendocrine control of the immune response. Furthermore, it should be considered that the hypothalamus receives complex inputs from other superior parts of the central nervous system via its known links with the external world. These latter aspects are discussed by other authors in this book.

Control mechanisms have been acquired in evolution under the selection pressure of the highly variable external world in order to maintain constancy and optimal conditions for body constituents and functions. The intrusion of foreign particles or macromolecules implies an important perturbation of the "milieu interieur." The immune response, being under neuroendocrine control, is probably directed against the antigen, not because it is often associated with harmful microorganisms or other agents, but, rather, because antigens present themselves as foreign to the host. The immune process, like other homeostatic mechanisms, may thus have as a major task the preservation of Self-identity of the body. Indeed, the most relevant question in modern immunology is the dilemma expressed by Burnet and Fenner (1949) of how the immune system can discriminate Self from non-Self. While we are still ignorant of the mechanism of immunologic Self-recognition and acquisition of Self-tolerance, it is nevertheless certain that we are not born as immunologic Selves (nor as Selves in the personal or social context), but that we have to learn to be Selves (Popper, 1977). How this is learned remains one of the major unsolved mysteries in immunology, and it is highly likely that immune-neuroendocrine circuits in ontogeny are a part of this secret.

ACKNOWLEDGMENTS

The authors would like to thank Blackwell Scientific Publications, Oxford, Verlag Chemie, Weinheim and Academic Press, New York for their kind permission to reprint some of the figures. We thank our secretary, Miss Helen Kreuzer for her excellent help during the preparation of the manuscript.

REFERENCES

Abraham, A. D., and Bug, G. (1976). ^{3}H-Testosterone distribution and binding in rat thymus cells *in vivo*. *Mol. Cell. Biochem.* **13**, 157-163.

Adelman, N. E., Hammond, M. E., Cohen, S., and Dvorak, H. F. (1979). Lymphokines as inflammatory mediators. *In* "Biology of the Lymphokines" (S. Cohen, E. Pick, and J. J. Oppenheim, eds.) pp. 13-58. Academic Press, New York.

Arrenbrecht, S. (1974). Specific binding of growth hormone to thymocytes. *Nature (London)* **252**, 255-257.

Benacerraf, B., Katz, D. H., Kapp, J. A., and Pierce, C. W. (1974). Regulatory mechanisms in the immune response. *In* "Cellular Selection and Regulation in the Immune Response" (G. M. Edelman, ed.), pp. 265-281. Raven Press, New York.

Besedovsky, H. O. (1971). Delay in skin allograft rejection in rats grafted with fetal adrenal glands. *Experientia* **27**, 697-698.

Besedovsky, H. O., and Sorkin, E. (1974). Thymus involvement in female sexual maturation. *Nature (London)* **249**, 356-358.

Besedovsky, H. O., and Sorkin E. (1977a). Hormonal control of immune processes. *Endocrinology* **2**, 504–513.

Besedovsky, H. O., and Sorkin, E. (1977b). Network of immune–neuroendocrine interactions. *Clin. Exp. Immunol.* **27**, 1–12.

Besedovsky, H. O. Pedernera, E., and Rossi Alloras, H. (1975a). Influencia de la bursa de Fabricius sobre el desarrollo endocrino del embrion de pollo. *Medicina (Buenos Aires)* **35**, 6–7.

Besedovsky, H. O., Sorkin, E., Keller, M., and Müller, J. (1975b). Changes in blood hormone levels during the immune response. *Proc. Soc. Exp. Biol. Med.* **150**, 466–470.

Besedovsky, H. O., Sorkin, E., Felix, D., and Haas, H. (1977). Hypothalamic changes during the immune response. *Eur. J. Immunol.* **7**, 325–328.

Besedovsky, H. O., Sorkin, E., and Keller, M. (1978). Changes in the concentration of corticosterone in the blood during skin graft rejection in the rat. *J. Endocrinol.* **76**, 175–176.

Besedovsky, H., del Rey, A., Sorkin, E., Da Prada, M., and Keller, H. H. (1979a). Immunoregulation mediated by the sympathetic nervous system. *Cell. Immunol.* **48**, 346–355.

Besedovsky, H., del Rey, A., and Sorkin, E. (1979b). Antigenic competition between horse and sheep red blood cells as a hormone-dependent phenomenon. *Clin. Exp. Immunol.* **37**, 106–113.

Besedovsky, H. O., del Rey, A., and Sorkin, E. (1979c). Role of prethymic cells in acquisition of self-tolerance. *J. Exp. Med.* **150**, 1351–1358.

Bianchi, E., Pierpaoli, W., and Sorkin, E. (1971). Cytological changes in the mouse anterior pituitary after neonatal thymectomy: A light and electron microscopical study. *J. Endocrinol.* **51**, 1–6.

Bourne, H. R., Lichtenstein, L. M., Melmon, K. L., Henney, C. S., Weinstein, Y., and Shearer, G. M. (1974). Modulation of inflammation and immunity by cyclic AMP. Receptors for vasoactive hormones and mediators of inflammation regulate many leukocyte functions. *Science* **184**, 19–28.

Braun, W. (1974). Regulatory factors in the immune response: Analysis and perspectives. *In* "Cyclic AMP, Cell Growth and the Immune Response" (W. Braun, L. M. Lichtenstein, and C. W. Parker, eds.). pp. 4–23. Springer-Verlag, Berlin and New York.

Burnet, F. M. (1976). A homeostatic and self-monitoring immune system. *In* "Immunology" (F. M. Burnet, ed.). pp. 158–161. Sci. Am., New York.

Burnet, F. M., and Fenner, F. (1949). "Production of Antibodies." Macmillan, New York.

Cake, M. H., and Litwack, G. (1975). The glucocorticoid receptors. *In* "Biochemical Actions of Hormones" (G. Litwack, ed.), Vol. 3, pp. 317–390. Academic Press, New York.

Claman, H. N. (1975). How corticosteroids work. *J. Allergy Clin. Immunol.* **55**, 145–151.

Dougherty, T. F., Berliner, M. L., Schneebeli, G. L., and Berliner, D. L. (1964). Hormonal control of lymphatic structure and function. *Ann. N. Y. Acad. Sci.* **113**, 825–843.

Elliott, E. V., and Sinclair, N. R. St. C. (1968). Effect of cortisone acetate on 19S and 7S haemolysin antibody. *Immunology* **15**, 643–652.

Ernström, U., and Sandberg, G. (1973). Effects of adrenergic α- and β-receptor stimulation on the release of lymphocytes and granulocytes from the spleen. *Scand. J. Haematol.* **11**, 275–286.

Fabris, N. (1977). Hormones and aging. *In* "Immunology and Aging" (T. Makinodan and E. Yunis, eds.), pp. 73–89. Plenum, New York.

Fabris, N., Pierpaoli, W., and Sorkin, E. (1971a). Hormones and the immunological capacity. III. The immunodeficiency disease of the hypopituitary Snell-Bagg dwarf mice. *Clin. Exp. Immunol.* **9**, 209–225.

Fabris, N., Pierpaoli, W., and Sorkin, E. (1971b). Hormones and the immunological capacity. IV. Restorative effects of developmental hormones or of lymphocytes on the immunodeficiency syndrome of the dwarf mouse. *Clin. Exp. Immunol.* **9**, 227–240.

Gershon, R. K. (1979). Immune regulation. *Fed. Proc., Fed. Am. Soc. Exp. Biol.* **38**, 2051–2077.

Gillette, S., and Gillette, R. W. (1979). Changes in thymic estrogen receptor expression following orchidectomy. *Cell. Immunol.* **42**, 194–196.

Gillis, S., Crabtree, G. R., and Smith, K. A. (1979a). Glucocorticoid-induced inhibition of T cell growth factor production. I. The effect on mitogen-induced lymphocyte proliferation. *J. Immunol.* **123,** 1624–1631.

Gillis, S., Crabtree, G. R., and Smith, K. A. (1979b). Glucocorticoid-induced inhibition of T cell growth factor production. II. The effect on the *in vitro* generation of cytolytic T cells. *J. Immunol.* **123,** 1632–1638.

Gisler, R. H., and Schenkel-Hulliger, L. (1971). Hormonal regulation of the immune response. II. Influence of pituitary and adrenal activity on immune responsiveness *in vitro. Cell. Immunol.* **2,** 646–657.

Helderman, J. H., and Strom, T. B. (1978). Specific insulin binding site·on T and B lymphocytes as a marker of cell activation. *Nature (London)* **274,** 62–63.

Hollenberg, M. D., and Cuatrecasas, P. (1974). Hormone receptors and membrane glycoproteins during *in vitro* transformation of lymphocytes. *In* "Control of Proliferation of Animal Cells" (B. Clarkson and R. Baserga, eds.). pp. 423–434. Cold Spring Harbor Lab., Cold Spring Harbor, New York.

Iványi, P., Gregorova, S., Mickova, M., Hampl, R., and Starka, L. (1973). Genetic association between a histocompatibility gene (H-2) and androgen metabolism in mice. *Transplant. Proc.* **5,** 189–191.

Janković, B. D., and Isaković, K. (1973). Neuro-endocrine correlates of immune response. I. Effects of brain lesions on antibody production, Arthus reactivity and delayed hypersensitivity in the rat. *Int. Arch. Allergy Appl. Immunol.* **45,** 360–372.

Jerne, N. K. (1974). Towards a network theory of the immune system. *Ann. Immunol. (Paris)* **125,** 373–389.

Jerne, N. K. (1976a). The immune system: A web of V-domains. *Harvey Lect.* **70,** 93–110.

Jerne, N. K. (1976b). The immune system. *In* "Immunology" (F. M. Burnet, ed.), pp. 49–57. Sci. Am., New York.

Lichtenstein, L. M. (1976). Hormone receptor modulation of cAMP in the control of allergic and inflammatory responses. *In* "The Role of Immunologic Factors in Infectious, Allergic, and Autoimmune Processes" (R. F. Beers, Jr. and E. G. Bassett, eds.), pp. 339–354. Raven Press, New York.

Lintern-Moore, S., and Pantelouris, E. M. (1975). Ovarian development in athymic nude mice. I. The size and composition of the follicle population. *Mech. Ageing Dev.* **4,** 385–390.

Loor, F., and Roelants, G. E. (1977). "B- and T-Cells in Immune Recognition." Wiley, New York.

Marat, B. A. (1974). Effect of central cholinolytics on the primary immune response in rabbits. *Bull. Exp. Biol. Med. (Engl. Transl.)* **76,** 971–973.

Melchers, F., and Rajewsky, K. (1976). "The Immune System." Springer–Verlag, Berlin and New York.

Parker, C. W. (1979). The role of intracellular mediators in the immune response. *In* "Biology of the Lymphokines" (S. Cohen, E. Pick, and J. J. Oppenheim, eds.), pp. 541–583. Academic Press, New York.

Pedernera, E., Romano, M., and Aguilar, M. C. (1980). Influence of early surgical bursectomy on the Leydig cells in the chick embryo testis. *J. Steroid Biochem.* **2,** 517–519.

Pick, E. (1979). Mechanism of action of migration inhibitory lymphokines. *In* "Biology of the Lymphokines" (S. Cohen, E. Pick, and J. J. Oppenheim, eds.), pp. 59–119. Academic Press, New York.

Pierpaoli, W., and Besedovsky, H. O. (1975) Role of the thymus in programming of neuroendocrine functions. *Clin. Exp. Immunol.* **20,** 323–338.

Pierpaoli, W., and Sorkin, E. (1972). Alterations of adrenal cortex and thyroid in mice with congenital absence of the thymus. *Nature (London), New Biol.* **238,** 282–285.

Popper, K. R. (1977). *In* "The Self and Its Brain" (K. R. Popper and J. C. Eccles, eds.), p. 109. Springer International, Berlin.

Pouplard, A., Bottazzo, G. F., Doniach, D., and Roitt, I. V. (1976). Binding of human immunoglobulins in pituitary ACTH cells. *Nature (London)* **261,** 142–144.

Richman, D. P., and Arnason, B. G. (1979). Nicotinic acetylcholine receptor: Evidence for a functionally distinct receptor on human lymphocytes. *Proc. Natl. Acad. Sci. U.S.A.* **76**, 4632-4635.

Salvin, S. B., and Neta, R. (1980). "Patterns of *in vivo* Release of Lymphokines: Their Enhancement and Inhibition". In "Biochemical Characterization of lymphokines" (deWeck, A., Kristensen, F. and Landy, M. eds.), pp. 587-590. Academic Press, New York.

Shire, J. G. M., and Pantelouris, E. M. (1974). Comparison of endocrine function in normal and genetically athymic mice. *Comp. Biochem. Physiol.* **47**, 93-100.

Singh, U., Millson, D. S., Smith, P. A., and Owen, J. J. T. (1979). Identification of β adrenoceptors during thymocyte ontogeny in mice. *Eur. J. Immunol.* **9**, 31-35.

Solomon, J. B, (1971) "Foetal and Neonatal Immunology." North-Holland Publ., Amsterdam.

Spector, N. H. The central state of the hypothalamus in health and disease: Old and new concepts. *In* "Handbook of the Hypothalamus" (P. Morgane and J. Panksepp, eds.), Dekker, New York. In press.

Stein, M., Schiavi, P. C., and Camerino, M. (1976). Influence of brain and behavior on the immune system. *Science* **191**, 435-440.

Streng, C. B., and Nathan, P. (1973). The immune response in steroid deficient mice. *Immunology* **24**, 559-565.

Strom, T. B., Deisseroth, A., Morgan-Roth, J., Carpenter, C. B., and Merrill, J. P. (1972). Alteration of the cytotoxic action of sensitized lymphocytes by cholinergic agents and activators of adenylate cyclase. *Proc. Natl. Acad. Sci. U.S.A.* **69**, 2995-2999.

Strom, T. B., Sytkowsky, A. J., Carpenter, C. B. and Merrill, J. P. (1974a). Cholinergic augmentation of lymphocyte-mediated cytotoxicity. A study of the cholinergic receptor of cytotoxic T lymphocytes. *Proc. Natl. Acad. Sci. U.S.A.* **71**, 1330-1333.

Strom, T. B., Sytkowsky, A. J., Carpenter, C. B. and Merrill, J. P. (1974b). The cholinergic receptor of cytotoxic T lymphocytes. *In* "Lymphocyte Recognition and Effector Mechanism" (K. Lindahl-Kiessling and D. Osoba, eds.), pp. 509-513. Academic Press, New York.

Talal, N. (1977). Autoimmunity and lymphoid malignancy: Manifestation of immunoregulatory disequilibrium. *In* "Autoimmunity" (N. Talal, ed.), pp. 194-197. Academic Press, New York.

Uhr, J. W., and Möller, G. (1968). Regulatory effect of antibody on the immune response. *Adv. Immunol.* **8**, 81-127.

Wahl, S. M., Altman, L. C., and Rosenstreich, D. L. (1975). Inhibition of *in vitro* lymphokine synthesis by glucocorticosteroids. *J. Immunol.* **115**, 476-481.

Weinstein, Y. (1978). Impairment of the hypothalamo–pituitary–ovarian axis of the athymic "nude" mouse. *Mech. Ageing Dev.* **8**, 63-68.

Werb, Z., Foley, R., and Munck, A. (1978). Interaction of glucocorticoids with macrophages. Identification of glucocorticoid receptors in monocytes and macrophages. *J. Exp. Med.* **147**, 1684-1694.

Wolstenholme, G. E. W., and Knight, J., eds. (1970). "Hormones and the Immune Response," Ciba Found. Study Group No. 36. Churchill, London.

Integrated Phylogenetic and Ontogenetic Evolution of Neuroendocrine and Identity-Defense, Immune Functions

WALTER PIERPAOLI

INTRODUCTION

This chapter is not meant to be a review of my own published work on the links between neuroendocrine regulation and immunity, or a list of "proofs" or "results" which would only confirm my inadequacy to bind together molecules, tissues, organs, and their functions. I simply wish to profit from the unusual freedom given to me to express some concepts and to supply the isolated pieces of information which give them the right to face criticism or rejection. I will restrict my attention to the links between identity of the individual and its reproduction. Some main "cosmic" primordial factors will appear and will be considered seriously in this connection, namely, the role of the main cycle of day and night in determining the character and the functions of the cellular vehicles of identity and of reproduction. Underestimated ancient organs, the bone marrow and the pineal gland, will be revaluated and forcibly exposed to the daylight from their hiding place in the bones and in the brain. Most important, while writing I tried to avoid boring myself. If I sometimes failed, it was because numbers and tables were in front of me and disturbed my lazy imagination with their misleading evidence. The dialectic and rhetoric which eluded my surveillance may reflect an ancient way of expressing opinions or persuading the interlocutors. Its modern Anglo-Saxon

PSYCHONEUROIMMUNOLOGY

version, called "understatement" or "low key prose," is no less hypocritical and somehow less honest to the audience when seeking condescendence and persuasion through false modesty. Thus, I preferred the more classic, joyful, and frank Mediterranean rhetoric of sunny Greece to the gloomy rhetoric of the Anglo-Saxon "understatement."

THE BARRIER OF THE SPECIES–SPECIFIC CONSTANT

The elusiveness and intricacy of biologic phenomena are popular foci for discussion among scientists. It is conceivable that the constant scientific effort to identify and to describe the essence of body functions meets formidable obstacles whose nature and character is also, per se, a barrier to the comprehension of physiological functions. This seems to me particularly evident when, in addition to species-specific peculiarities, one tries to combine notions deriving from studies in different disciplines of biology and medicine. So, in trying to simplify for understanding, unconsciously we seek an escape to security. These formidable psychological obstacles preclude any insight and real progress and rather prolong the narcotic state of self-contentedness. One of the most serious obstacles is, in my view, what I would call the "species-specific physiology constant."

The "species-specific constant" represents the unique characters of the species in all its parameters. When we extrapolate from one species to another (e.g., mouse to man), we jump over millions of years of evolution of a myriad of adaptive processes which have produced basic differences among the species. In this case, the main difficulty lies in the inconceivable *slowness* by which the species-specific changes have taken place. Therefore, in this case, the slowness of the dynamics for the establishment of these evolutionary changes prevents us from understanding the species-specific diversities.

The other primary obstacle for the understanding of physiological processes at the cellular or molecular levels derives mainly, aside from our ignorance of the mere existence of some basic protagonists of cellular and molecular events, from our inability to realize that the sequential velocity of molecular or even cellular events surpasses by far the threshold of our sensorial sensibility when we are confronted with the speed of enzymatic, chemical, and physicochemical reactions. In other words, while our mind, in spite of lucky intuitions which can fix some end-points, is measuring the time in hours, minutes, and seconds, the cellular and molecular workshop is proceeding at the tremendous speed of 1×10^{-6}, 1×10^{-7}, and 1×10^{-8} seconds, perhaps even faster. In experimental terms, this is even more critical when we consider some of the most commonly used laboratory animals. The mouse, for example, has a short life span and an extremely high metabolic rate when compared to humans, and its growth and differentiative processes are condensed into 2–3 years of life. Therefore, in contrast to the *slowness* of evolutionary events, we are here embarrassed by the *speed* of metabolic events.

These considerations suggest that our inborn physiological mental barriers and our willingness to accept such notions and to refuse what I would call the "existentialism of the biological world" hinder the comprehension of the infinitely more fluid, flexible, and everchanging cell world. Thus, exposition of this proposal for an integrative approach is necessarily incomplete, fragmentary, and also illusory in its simplicity. Millions of years of further brain evolution and new sensorial devices might prepare us to evaluate a "reality" in and around us, whose essential character will forever remain "human." We might rely on a dose of intuition to fill the gap among scattered pieces of information. A few experimental examples will provide only a glimpse into an unknown dimension of physiology.

LINKAGE OF IDENTITY-DEFENSE AND REPRODUCTION: THE TWO COMPONENTS FOR IMMORTALITY

It seems that all living creatures strive for immortality. This noble aim is, in fact, achieved by the evolutionary development of the so-called immune and of the sexual, reproductory systems. It is my aim to clarify the concept and bring experimental evidence to bear on the idea that development and acquisition of identity and capacity to reproduce are synchronous and interdependent, phylogenetic and ontogenetic processes. It is also my intention to produce evidence that development of identity and reproduction of self are based on common organs, cells, and molecules that have shared in evolution the responsibility and have been exposed to the environmental pressure for the common aim: immortality. The emotional component of man's concept of immortality, however, is obviously irrelevant to Nature.

Man is the only species which does not accept the death of an individual as a beneficial event for the maintenance and continuation of life. Therefore, I will insist on the concept that the proliferation of bacteria is as representative of eternal life as is the proliferation of man. However, the evolution of vertebrates and man has perfected the identity-defense or "self" component. In other words, maintenance of "self" and of identity progressed phylogenetically and became a prerequisite for continuation through reproduction. The complex machinery developed by the vertebrates' body needed more sophisticated and complex recognition and defense mechanisms. Moreover, it seems that the same organs, tissues, cells, and molecules that were progressively acquiring these new functions, were also committed to reproductive physiology. Thus, recognition-defense and reproductive structures grew together in phylogeny and still are indissolubly linked in ontogeny. I will try to show how organs such as the thymus, the gonads, the adrenals, the pituitary, and the pineal are directly involved both in immune and reproductive physiology. But, before doing this, we will try to answer two questions: Was this duplicity of functions necessary, and why? In trying to answer these questions, we have to consider the degree of identity and its most ancient links to reproduction of the species.

WHAT IS IDENTITY? IDENTITY AS A FUNCTION OF REPRODUCTION

It is not possible to answer this crucial question unless we escape the "immunologic semantic trap" and direct our attitude toward more Darwinian and unconventional (and seemingly improbable) interpretations. I think that identity is linked to reproduction owing to *economy,* or the species-specific evolutionary pressure to save space and join several functions in a limited space (effector organs, cells, molecular vehicles). In addition, the development of identity has necessarily to do with the need of any species, from protozoa to vertebrates, *to maintain its capacity to reproduce.* This introduces the concept that identity and defense of the species in the broadest sense developed in parallel. Defense of territory or female-male attraction by pheromones, defense of reproductive capacity by mimetization or by production of huge amounts of spermatozoa or ova, defense from parasites, bacteria, viruses, have the common aim of maintaining a sufficient *number* for a species. In this sense, the defense of identity developed together with reproductory capacity in all species. However, at an early stage of evolution, a fundamental influence exerted its *sine qua non* indelible imprint on all life processes, and particularly on defense of identity and reproduction: *the circadian rhythmicity of day and night.* As will be shown by an experimental demonstration in mammals, circadian periodicity was a major evolutionary factor which promoted the development and determined the character of the identity and reproductive systems. That is, circadian periodicity, more than other biorhythms (e.g., circalunar, circannual) superimposed itself and determined the character and the pattern of defense and reproductive mechanisms.

THE NEUROENDOCRINE SUICIDE OF THE SALMON AND THE COLLECTIVE MURDER OF THE BEE

If priority is in reproduction and not in defense-identity, Nature must have provided evidence for it. I was always struck by the story of the spawning salmon and by its death. The atrophy of the alimentary–intestinal tract of the salmon preceding spawning and intensive sexual activity is a tragic prelude to this neuroendocrine death, as if all the vital functions would suddenly become irrelevant in face of the urge for reproduction and maintenance of the species. This is a typical evolutionary example of life priorities and represents, in my view, a sort of accelerated aging, runting, or wasting which, for all its drama,

TABLE 1
Types of Wasting Syndromes[a]

Wasting syndromes with no evident direct participation of endocrine factors	Wasting syndromes with evident direct participation of endocrine factors	Wasting syndromes with possible participation of endocrine factors	Wasting syndromes induced by interruption of endocrine-thymus relationship during ontogenic formation of the immunolymphatic system
Secondary disease after radiation	Hydrocortisone-induced wasting disease	Wasting disease induced by heterologous antilymphocyte serum	Age-dependent wasting disease after injection of heterologous antihypophysis serum in young adult mice
Salmonella typhimurium infection	Testosterone-induced wasting disease	Wasting disease after neonatal thymectomy	Age-dependent wasting disease after injection of antisomatotropic hormone serum into young adult mice
Vaccine-induced wasting syndrome	Wasting disease induced by estrogens	Wasting of thymusless, nude mice	Hypopituitary dwarfism or post-hypophysectomy syndrome
Virus-induced wasting syndrome		Aging	Experimental diabetes (alloxan induced or following pancreatectomy)
Wasting disease induced by heterologous antithymocyte serum		Malnutrition and stress	Age-dependent wasting disease following abolition or inhibition of thyroid function in newborn or young adult mice (treatment with ^{131}I, propylthiouracil or antithyrotropic hormone serum)
Homologous disease or runting disease			

[a] From "Hormones, thymus and lymphocyte functions" by Pierpaoli, W. and Sorkin, E., *Experientia*, 1972, **28**, 1385–1389. Copyright 1972 by Birkhäuser Verlag. Reprinted by permission.

579

TABLE 2
Symptomatology and Pathological Alterations in Wasting Syndromes[a]

Inhibition and progressive decrease of body growth
Thinness of the skin, epidermal changes
Lack of subcutaneous fat (panniculus adiposus)
Length of ears and tail
Microsplancnia and microsomia
Ruffled, juvenile-type hair
Reduction in number and size of hepatic cells
Foci of necrosis in the liver and/or spleen
Hemorrhagic diarrhea
Atrophy of the thymus (in nonthymectomized animals) and of peripheral lymphoid organs; lymphopenia in peripheral blood
Osseal alterations
Hunched posture or kyphosis (deriving from incomplete development or malformation of the vertebrae)
Degranulation of acidophilic cells in the hypophysis
Bone marrow atrophy and focal necrosis
Microcytic anemia
Different sex incidence
Sterility of males or of females, ovarian dysgenesia
Atrophy of thyroid gland
Alterations of adrenal cortex
Lack of appearance of secondary sex characters in males, submaxillary gland and kidney fail to develop, spermatogenesis is incomplete

[a] From "Hormones, thymus and lympocyte functions" by Pierpaoli, W., and Sorkin, E., *Experentia*, 1972, **28**, 1385–1389. Copyright 1972 by Birkhäuser Verlag. Reprinted by permission.

is not present in all kinds of salmon, but only in Pacific species. This is an extreme case illustrating how the use of all resources for reproduction has rendered impossible the maintenance of other functions. This might happen because the systems are interdependent, and the hormones, molecules, and cells share common functions for reproduction and defense.

This evolutionary duplicity of function is most clearly exemplified by the ontogenetic growth of the defense-identity and of the sexual-reproductive systems. In mammals, a harmonious development of the integrated immune-sexual network is needed. This delicate developmental balance during embryologic and postnatal growth can be broken by a very large number of factors. In a long-forgotten and isolated paper I tried to express this concept (Pierpaoli and Sorkin, 1972a). The aim was to find a reasonable interpretation for the wasting, runting, and deteriorating syndromes which appear in the most varied natural or induced situations and which have an almost identical pattern and symptomatology. Ontogenetic development of the integrated neuroendocrine and thymolymphatic systems can be interrupted by so many causes and at so many levels that a listing of them is hopeless. Nowadays, one could add further examples. However, it is still valid to consider that the outcome of this disturbance, whatever the cause, is a block of growth and differentiation, an impairment, not of vital adult functions as in the salmon, but of morphogenesis, of *development* of functions. It is most astonishing to analyze the multitude of possibilities for inducing a runting or wasting syndrome by interventions acting on the still undifferentiated defense-identity and reproductive systems (Pierpaoli and Sorkin, 1972a; Tables 1 and 2). I still believe this is a key for examining how the main mechanisms for defense and reproduction are operating in the adult through humoral (hormones) and cellular (thymus, bone marrow, lymph nodes) effector mechanisms.

Another example of the priority of reproduction over identity is the mass murder of male bees. Although one may dissent on the evolutionary logic of nature, it is clear that male bees are killed because, as sad as it might sound, identity becomes absolutely irrelevant once the continuation of the species has been guaranteed.

DAY AND NIGHT AND THE PRIORITY OF REPLICATION

As mentioned in the preceding section, I think that replication of a species coincides with the need to maintain and prolong its identity and thus achieve immortality through duplication. It seems irrelevant whether immortality is achieved by proliferation or by defense of self. In the economy of Nature, it was more convenient to obtain immortality by replication of a species rather than by maintenance of identity of an individual by defense. However, just to maintain the capacity to reproduce, any species also had to develop the defense of identity. Thus, the infinite systems for protection of the species (reproduction and defense) were integrated although, perhaps, supremacy was achieved by the mechanisms of reproduction over those of defense of individuality. That replication is a much more efficient system than defense is obvious at any level. Demographic pressure has always been, and still is, a major cause for human territorial expansion.

In the course of evolution, marine and terrestrial or amphibious species shaped their reproductive and identity-defense capacities according to a strictly circadian pattern to which circannual (seasonal) and circalunar (lunar) cyclicity added its conditioning effects. The molecules, tissues, organs, which were shaped by evolutionary pressure and by the circadian clock had to acquire the polyvalent ability to provide both for defense and for replication. Thus, the thymus, which acquired progressively new abilities to cope with the increasing complexities of vertebrates and mammalian evolution, was linked to pineal and hypothalamic function and influenced (and was influenced by) sexual-reproductive molecules, tissues, and organs and also developed a regulatory activity with respect to bone marrow. This close link between the ontogeny of thymus, hypothalamus, and pineal gland was recently confirmed by experimental evidence. The following section will be devoted to an illustration of how the genesis of identity-defense and reproduction originated from a common neuroendocrine and cellular network.

TOLERANCE TO SELF OR IMMUNE REACTIVITY
AS END-PRODUCTS OF SEXUAL
DEVELOPMENT IN ONTOGENY

A few years ago I developed a model for studying the links between the neuroendocrine and the immune systems in ontogeny. It had been elaborated for challenging the concept that the endocrine and immune systems are interdependent during embryogenesis. It proposed that, while the hormonal status would be responsible for timing the maturation of the immune system, the same endocrine maturation in embryogenesis would in turn depend on the rate and sequence of appearance of new cells or antigens. Thus, the decreasing rate of cell differentiation (less antigen) and proliferation (less cells) in the later stages of embryonic development might influence (accelerate or retard) sequential neuroendocrine maturation because these same cell dynamics and developmental processes may also be under hormonal control. Conceptual and technical details of this, in my view, most fascinating approach to the genesis of tolerance and immunity are contained in the original paper (Pierpaoli *et al.*, 1977a).

The experiments were based on timed and sequential inoculation of immunologically and endocrinologically immature newborn mice with viable allogeneic cells and on the parallel evaluation of their endocrine status by measurements of hormone levels in peripheral blood. The results are summarized in Figure 1 and Tables 3 and 4. By these means, it was possible to demonstrate that the confrontation of an immature, newborn mouse with alloantigens was inducing (*a*) prolongation of the perinatal time during which specific allotolerance can be induced, and (*b*) alteration and retardation in the maturation of the endocrine system.

It was clear that it was primarily the adrenal and sex steroids that were influenced by the sequential immunologic challenge (Pierpaoli *et al.*, 1977a). Thus, I proposed that: (*a*) the evolutionary and ontogenetic development of the immune and endocrine systems in mammals takes place in a closely interlocked synchronic and interdependent manner, and (*b*) the generation of immunologic tolerance, unresponsiveness, or recognition of "self" components of the body can be regarded as a part of definitive brain programming at the hypothalamic–hypophysis levels.

At that time I ignored the fact that pineal gland function is fundamental for sexual reproductive physiology and that the thymus plays a major role in programming pineal functions. This is discussed in the section on "Ontogenic Thymic Influence."

It is now possible to suggest that massive antigenic challenge in immature mice affects mainly maturation of adrenal–sexual functions, endocrine functions which are closely linked to, and dependent on, thymic and pineal influences during embryologic and perinatal life. Again, the apparently logical conclusion is that there exists a complete evolutionary, somatic, and func-

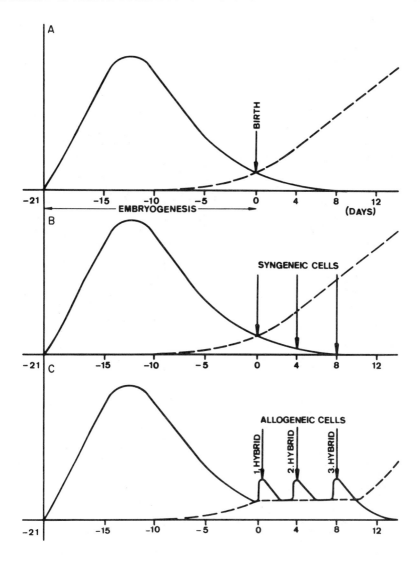

Figure 1. (A) Schematic representation of cell proliferation and differentiation with concomitant maturation of the autonomous endocrine system during embryogenesis and postnatal interval; ————: theoretical rate of cell proliferation and generation of new self antigens; — — — — —: differentiation of the autonomous endocrine system. (B) Inoculation of syngeneic cells does not affect maturation of the developing neuroendocrine system. (C) The sequential and timely critical (4-day interval) inoculation of different allogeneic hybrid cells (2×10^7 spleen cells per inoculation) into mice during the neonatal and perinatal periods results in a prolongation of the perinatal stage, during which tolerance can be induced. Parallel alteration and retardation in the maturation of that section of the endocrine system which normally controls immune differentiation are observed. (From Pierpaoli *et al.* (1977a). "Interdependence between neuroendocrine programming and the generation of immune recognition in ontogeny" by Pierpaoli, W. *et al., Cellular Immunology,* 1977, **29**, 16–27. Copyright 1977 by Academic Press. Reprinted by permission.)

TABLE 3

Experimental Plan for Administration of Allogeneic Cells Postnatally to Prolong Tolerance to Allogeneic Antigens in Mice and to Induce Concomitant Impairment and Retardation of Endocrine Maturation[a]

BALB/c recipients (designation of groups)	Number of transplanted mice	Sequential injections of allogeneic cells (F_1 hybrid donors)			Number of accepted allogeneic skin grafts (BALB/c recipients)
		Birth (C57BL/6J × BALB/c)	Day 4 (DBA/J × BALB/c)	Day 8 (CBA/J × BALB/c)	
A	32	+	−	−	C57BL/6J (30)
B	40	+	+	−	C57BL/6J (35) DBA/J (33)
C	52	+	+	+	C57BL/6J (46) DBA/J (41) CBA/J (40)
D	22	−	+	+	None
E	15	−	−	+	None
F	10	−	−	−	None

[a] Newborn, 4-, and 8-day-old BALB/c mice were injected intravenously (newborns) or intraperitoneally (4 and 8 days old) with 2×10^7 syngeneic (BALB/c) or allogeneic (C57BL/6J × BALB/c, DBA/J × BALB/c, CBA/J × BALB/c) spleen cells. Many of the mice were exsanguinated on Day 12 and levels of hormones were determined in serum (see Table 4). The skin-grafted adult BALB/c mice included an equal number of males and females. The BALB/c mice of all groups (A–F) were first tested for tolerance to C57BL/6J donors. Each single BALB/c mouse of groups A–C that was tolerant to skin from C57BL/6J donors (111/124, or 89%), of the mice showed no sign of rejection after 60 days) was successively transplanted with skin from the other allogeneic donors from the parental hybrid strains (BDA/J and CBA/J) after removal of the first or second accepted graft. The BALB/c mice of groups B and C were considered to be tolerant to DBA/J and CBA/J only when the grafts were accepted permanently. The graftings were repeated when they were technically defective or doubtful. From "Interdependence between neuroendocrine programming and the generation of immune recognition in ontogeny," by Pierpaoli, W. *et al.*, *Cellular Immunology*, 1977, **29**, 16–27. Copyright 1977 by Academic Press. Reprinted by permission.

TABLE 4

Delay and Impairment of Maturation of Adrenal and Sexual Functions Expressed through Changes in Levels of Adrenal and Gonadal Steroids in Postnatal Mice Injected Sequentially with Different Allogeneic Spleen Cells

Newborn BALB/c recipients (identification of groups)	Injection[a]			Thyroxine (µg/100 ml)	Corticosterone (µg/100 ml)
	Birth (BALB/c × C57BL/6J)	Day 4 (BALB/c × DBA/J)	Day 8 (BALB/c × CBA/J)		
(A) Male controls[b]	+	−	−	—	—
	+	−	−	—	5.8 ± 0.2
(A) Female controls	+	−	−	—	3.4 ± 0.4
	+	−	−	—	5.7 ± 0.3
(B) Male controls	+	+	−	—	—
	+	+	−	—	
(B) Female controls	+	+	−	—	—
	+	+	−	—	
(C) Male controls	+	+	+	11.3	6.6 ± 0.2
	+	+	+	10.3	4.5 ± 0.2
(C) Female controls	+	+	+	10.3	21.8 ± 0.7
	+	+	+	12.1	4.5 ± 0.5
(D) Male controls	−	+	+	—	7.1 ± 0.2
	−	+	+	—	10.8 ± 0.2
(D) Female controls	−	+	+	—	10.3 ± 0.3
	−	+	+	—	10.2 ± 0.4
(E) Male controls	−	−	+	—	3.6 ± 0.1
	−	−	+	—	6.8 ± 0.3
(E) Female controls	−	−	+	—	5.6 ± 0.3
	−	−	+	—	6.2 ± 0.2
(F) Male controls	−	−	−	11.5	6.2 ± 0.3
	−	−	−	11.9	4.3 ± 0.4
(G) Males	Bled on day of birth		−	—	8.6 ± 0.2
(G) Females	Bled on day of birth		−	—	10.0 ± 0.3

Hormone levels at 12 days of age[c]

	Testosterone (µg/100 ml)	17β-Estradiol (nM/liter)	Progesterone (ng/100 ml)	GH (ng/ml)	LH (ng/ml)	FSH (ng/ml)	PRL (ng/ml)
A)	398 ± 12	—	—	—	—	104	—
	153 ± 10	—	—	—	—	125	—
A)	—	0.119 ± 0.003	116 ± 4	44	—	—	nd
	—	0.157 ± 0.011	155 ± 6	33	—	—	nd
B)	491 ± 5	—	—	—	—	—	—
	119 ± 17	—	—	—	—	—	—
B)	—	0.183 ± 0.011	232 ± 12	—	—	—	—
	—	0.189 ± 0.010	197 ± 14	—	—	—	—
C)	214 ± 22	—	—	40	33	145	nd
	433 ± 34	—	—	36	34	230	nd
C)	—	0.110 ± 0.004	212 ± 10	34	66	580	nd
	—	0.221 ± 0.012	237 ± 17	46	43	595	0.5
D)	355 ± 18	—	—	16	38	—	—

continued

TABLE 4 (*continued*)

Testosterone (µg/100 ml)	17β-Estradiol (nM/liter)	Progesterone (ng/100 ml)	GH (ng/ml)	LH (ng/ml)	FSH (ng/ml)	PRL (ng/ml)
452 ± 45	—	—	25	58	—	—
(D) —	0.185 ± 0.018	284 ± 16	—	49	—	—
—	0.147 ± 0.16	245 ± 20	—	29	—	—
(E) 118 ± 10	—	—	—	63	—	—
600 ± 24	—	—	—	71	—	—
(E) —	0.192 ± 0.011	287 ± 7	48	52	620	—
—	0.222 ± 0.020	175 ± 10	42	37	560	nd
(F) 222 ± 15	—	—	23	32	292	0.5
—	0.175 ± 0.016	230 ± 12	26	41	550	nd
(G) 119 ± 6	—	—	—	33	—	—
(G) —	0.174 ± 0.011	111 ± 4	—	48	—	—

SOURCE: From "Interdependence between neuroendocrine programming and the generation of immune recognition in ontogeny," by Pierpaoli, W. *et al.*, *Cellular Immunology*, 1977, **29**, 16–27. Copyright 1977 by Academic Press. Reprinted by permission.

[a] Allogeneic or syngeneic (controls) spleec cells (2 × 10⁷).

[b] Control mice of all groups (A–E) were also injected with syngeneic cells at the given schedule.

[c] nd, not detectable; GH, Growth hormone; LH, Luteotropic hormone; FSH, follicle stimulating hormone; PRL, prolactin.

tional identity between those cells and factors which are responsible for identity-defense, immune functions, and those structures responsible for reproduction. New findings on thymic contributions to pineal-directed sexual cyclicity and differentiation of T cells add only more details to the concept that the *priority is for reproduction* because the establishment of cyclicity (pineal and hypothalamic–hypophyseal) *precedes* the cyclicity-dependent maturation of T cells and their differentiation to antigen-reactive cells (see the section on "Ontogenic Thymic Influence"). Such data suggest that the nude mouse, in which no alloreactivity (transplantation immune reaction) or complete sexual maturity develops, represents a living model for challenging my concept.

WHAT IS THE THYMUS FOR?

The idea that the thymus might not be at all what we tend to believe has fascinated me in the last 15 years. In trying to understand more of its significance in phylogeny and ontogeny, I was progressively finding small pieces of evidence in relation to one or another of its possible functions. This progession has been illustrated in a series of reports (see references in the next paragraph). At the present time, the general orientation is toward an unifying concept, but we still lack some experimental evidence for the functions of the multifaceted thymus.

The Thymus as a Programmer

I think that the mammalian thymus is a late product of evolution, functioning in the interest of perfecting, amplifying, and rendering more efficient preexisting defense-identity and morphogenetic functions. In fact, its presence is apparently useful, but not necessary for the maintenance of functions in adult life *under normal conditions*. Early delegation of its functions to the peripheral lymphatic system (lymph nodes, spleen, etc.) is a possible cause for its apparent subsidiary function in adult life. On the contrary, its presence in early ontogeny seems to be required for acquisition of normal adult identity-defense and sexual functions (Pierpaoli and Sorkin, 1967, 1972b; Pierpaoli *et al.*, 1971b, 1976; Pierpaoli and Besedovsky, 1975; Bianchi *et al.,* 1971). Why, then, the very high mitotic activity of thymus cells during late embryologic development and early postnatal life (e.g., in the mouse)? In the light of recent research, this cellular activity of the thymus at a prepubertal time might have to do with the onset of puberty and for the safeguarding of reproduction rather than for "immune" defense mechanisms. The progesterone-inactivating enzymes recently identified in thymocytes (Weinstein *et al.,* 1977; Weinstein, 1977) undoubtedly have an important function for the programming of adult sexual cyclicity in the brain and for the establishment of puberty. Thus, we are now progressively identifying in the thymus, at the subcellular level, the links between edification of identity-defense and reproduction in ontogeny and the mechanisms by which the thymus participates in these maturational processes in mammals. In this sense, the role of the thymus in the programming of hormonal circadian cyclicity of pineal function deserves special attention for all the consequences of cellular (immunologic, morphogenetic) and humoral (sexual cyclicity) character.

It was proposed by Zinkernagel (1979) that the H-2 genotype of the radio-resistant portion of the thymus is responsible for restriction specificity of T cells independently of the T cells' original H-2 genotype and of antigen. Consequently, Zinkernagel suggested that restriction specificity of effector T cells is determined by the H-2 type of the antigen-presenting cells of lymphohemopoietic origin but selection of restriction specificity is operated only by the thymus (Zinkernagel, 1978). These concepts are obviously at variance with the experimental work and the consequent proposition that the thymus is a programmer of neuroendocrine functions in early ontogeny and responsible for cyclicity-dependent maturation of T cells, and with the role of the thymus as an amplifier of precommitted bone marrow-derived germ-line cells (see the following subsection).

The Thymus as an Amplifier

A FUNCTION FOR THE THYMUS IN VERTEBRATES CAN
BE PROPOSED, WHICH COULD SERVE AS A GENERAL
APPROACH FOR UNDERSTANDING ITS ROLE IN
CELL PHYSIOLOGY

The role of the thymus as depicted in Figures 2 and 3 involves expression and maintenance of both immune and nonimmune functions by *amplification* of the inscribed potentialities of the progenitor cells migrating from the bone

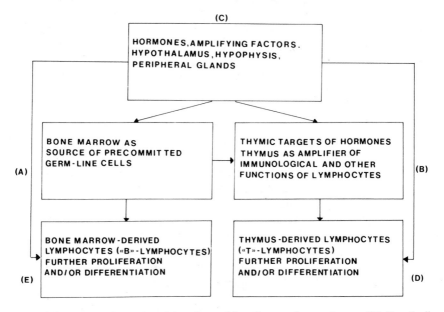

Figure 2. Thymus as amplifer of functions of lymphocytes in vertebrates. (A) Genetically precommitted lymphoid cells migrate to the thymus or to peripheral organs from the bone marrow. These cells (B lymphocytes) are functionally identical with thymus cells and thymus-derived lymphocytes (T lymphocytes) but quantitatively fewer in number. It is suggested that complete, minimally essential immunologic and nonimmunologic information is already present in the lymphoid stem cells of the bone marrow but the number of these cells is low. (B) Amplification of immunologic and other functions occurs in the thymus by proliferation of some of the bone marrow-derived lymphoid cells. Functions of lymphoid cells are expressed and maintained because they reach a measurable dimension by proliferation. In spite of the high mitotic rate, most of the cells in the thymus are in a resting state, do not divide, and then die *in loco*. Some migrate to the peripheral lymphoid tissue. (C) Various hormones, extrinsic or intrisic to the thymus, magnify the innate functions of progenitor cells settling as lymphocytes from the bone marrow in the thymus by inducing their proliferation. However, no final differentiation of these thymic targets of hormones is taking place in the thymus. (D) Thymus-derived lymphocytes originating from the amplifying organ proliferate and differentiate further and provide and maintain immune and other functions. Also, if the thymus is absent, hormones (somatotropic hormone, thyroxine, corticosteroids, and others) determine the final differentiation of lymphocytes (e.g., to plasma cells) in the peripheral lymphatic and nonlymphatic organs (D,E) as spleen, lymph nodes, etc.

marrow, rather than giving rise to new functions or originating, by a further differentiation, new clones of immunologically competent lymphocytes selected by somatic mutation, as suggested by Jerne (1971). Thus this intrinsic innate capacity of progenitor cells from the bone marrow might be expressed by a proliferation in the thymus of cells identical to lymphoid cells in the bone marrow in order that their inscribed functions acquire a measureable and effective dimension. Amplification of functions through proliferation of cells does not necessarily mean ultimate differentiation in the thymus to perform a

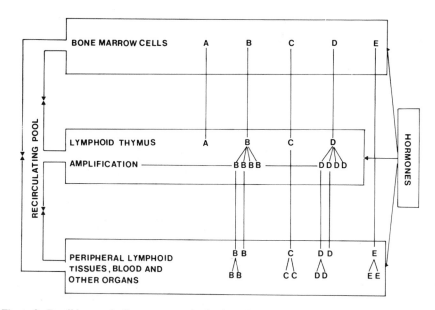

Figure 3. Possible genetically programmed selection of cells and amplification of the function of the selected cells through their hormone-dependent proliferation in the thymus in ontogeny. Lymphoid cells in the bone marrow possess inscribed specificities of functions (A, B, C, D, E). Some of these lymphoid germ-line cells seed in the thymus (A, B, C, D), others in peripheral organs (E). Hormones, extrinsic or intrinsic to the thymus, direct the proliferation of some lymphoid target cells which are sequentially appearing in the thymus during ontogeny and carry receptors for hormones (B, D). After proliferation, some of these cells migrate to the periphery and some remain in the thymus. Proliferation of lymphoid cells determines the amplification of the function only of those cells which are needed in ontogenic sequence for immune and nonimmune performances (B, D). Many lymphocytes in the thymus remain in a quiescent condition and die there when the message to the genetically precommitted lymphocytes to proliferate is not transmitted (A), others migrate to peripheral lymphoid organs where they can eventually proliferate and differentiate further (B, C, D). The restriction of immune or nonimmune function is determined by the presence or absence of the specific immunologic or nonimmunologic stimulus for proliferation of the multifunctional germ-line cells. However, no proliferation of lymphocytes takes place in the thymus or in peripheral lymphoid organs if the message to proliferate is transmitted, but some hormones are absent (e.g., in dwarf mice). Exogenous antigenic *stimuli* induce proliferation in the thymus of antigen-reactive cells only. Tolerance might depend on a lack of proliferation of the potentially responsive cells in the thymus after antigenic stimulation.

specific function. The fact is that very few antibody forming cells are detectable in the thymus.

It had been suggested (and supporting data obtained) that in early ontogeny the thymus acts as an endocrine gland (see this Section, above) and that, consequently, immunologic maturation in mammals is directly dependent on the thymus functioning as an endocrine gland in early ontogeny, thus promoting maturation of other endocrine organs. This proposal, based on findings in genetically athymic mice and other models is not in conflict with the present proposal that the thymus acts as an amplifier through cell proliferation. On the contrary, the concept of a parallel hormonal action of the thymus on differentiating endocrine gland and on amplification of functions through the action of hormones on thymic cells seems logical for an organ where epithelial and lymphoid cells apparently develop in ideal symbiosis during ontogeny. Findings in hormonally-deficient animals indicate that this amplification through proliferation is directed, at least partly, by somatotropic hormone and thyroxine (Pierpaoli and Sorkin, 1968, 1969a,b; Pierpaoli *et al.,* 1969, 1970).

It is entirely conceivable that bone marrow cells which migrate to the thymus contain all possible genetic information and potentialities for immunologic and possible nonimmunologic functions, and that these genetic capacities of bone marrow cells are maintained throughout life. Obviously, such functions would not manifest themselves and would remain undetectable unless and until they are expressed through a process of proliferation by which the potential capacity becomes evident and measureable. This is in accordance with the principles of the germ-line theory of the generation of immunologic diversity (Dreyer, 1971; Hood and Talmage, 1971), and with the elegant experimental work of Silverstein (1970). The studies of Silverstein on immunogenesis and lymphogenesis in ontogeny and the naturally occurring or experimentally induced syndromes which will be discussed later, are all rather convincing arguments in favor of this phylogenetically acquired "adjuvant" or "refining" function of the thymus. As pointed out by Silverstein (1970, see discussion), "progenitor cells from the bone marrow must not pass obligatorily through the thymus for acquiring competence but rather that the thymus has acquired in evolution the capacity to accomplish more efficiently and rapidly an older more primitive function performed earlier in phylogeny by other organs, such as the bone marrow."

Immunodeficiency and other pathological alterations after neonatal thymectomy or in congenital absence of the thymus in many mammalian species indicate that the presence of this organ is crucial at some stage of fetal development, be the function of the thymus that of inducing proliferation of certain lymphocytes, that of secreting humoral factors which promote cell differentiation in other lymphoid or nonlymphoid tissues and organs, or that of acting on differentiation and function of other endocrine glands.

There are many other examples for an "adjuvant" function of the thymus. For example, irradiation of the thymus or large doses of corticosteroids cause death of thymocytes in the thymus cortex, but they can be rapidly replaced by proliferation within the thymus of bone marrow-derived cells which recolonize the depleted organ. After extirpation of the thymus in adult mammals, and subsequent irradiation, the repopulation of the lymphoid organs is slower, but it does take place. As suggested above, it is conceivable that these bone marrow-derived cells are carriers of genetic information which can be expressed and measured *in a more efficient way* in the presence of the thymus. Expression and magnification of the potential capacity of some lymphocytes from the bone marrow develop in a faster and more efficient way in this organ and the functions inscribed in the cell genome are rapidly expressed. This might be the reason for the extremely high mitotic rate and cell proliferation in the thymus cortex which, however, also remains high in the residual thymic cortex in adult age when the thymus atrophies. It is likely that this amplifying activity of the thymus decays with age and that this function is gradually taken over by the peripheral lymphoid tissues. Thymectomy in adult animals has, in fact, no appreciable, short-term consequences. This suggests that the function of the thymus might be functionally identical throughout life but the *quantitative* aspects of its functions varies with age. It is maximal in ontogenic development and declines when the body has built up its species-specific somatic dimension, including immunologic maturity.

The effects of neonatal thymectomy, the different wasting syndromes, hypopituitary dwarfism, and the example of the genetically thymusless "nude" mouse are examples which support these suggestions (see Tables 1 and 2). In nude mice with congenital absence of the thymus, thymus-derived lymphocytes carrying the theta isoantigen marker are found in the peripheral lymphoid tissues, although their number is greatly reduced (Raff and Wortis, 1970). This could mean that the theta-bearing cells are already present in the bone marrow of the athymic mouse but their proliferation is taking place there at a much slower rate than in the thymus. This indicates that the deficiency of theta-bearing cells in the nude mouse is only *quantitative,* and expression of this membrane isoantigen had already taken place in the bone marrow.

It seems logical that the maintenance of proliferative activity for a better expression of immune functions might also be necessary for the control of many cellular processes of a nonimmunologic character (Pierpaoli and Sorkin, 1972a,b).

In view of the foregoing, it is proposed that the genetically inherited immunologic and possibly nonimmunologic capacity present in the progenitor cells derived from the fetal liver or from the bone marrow requires amplification, and that the thymus is the organ where this amplification process would occur most efficiently.

HORMONES, THE AMPLIFYING FACTORS

What is the character of the factors that promote or modulate these proliferative processes in the thymus? All available evidence points to the hormones as fulfilling this role, especially since their mechanism of action has
been partially clarified by the discovery of the function of cyclic AMP (Pastan
and Perlman, 1971). Polypeptide hormones such as adrenocorticotropic hormone (ACTH), thyrotropic hormone (TTH), somatropic hormone (STH), insulin, adrenal and gonadal steroids, and thyroxine, all produce striking modifications in the thymus when their levels decline or rise above physiological
values. Moreover, cyclic AMP levels are influenced by hormones through an
enzyme present on cell membranes. It is entirely possible that hormones, by
regulating the level of cyclic AMP, control most of the processes of proliferation and differentiation of thymocytes. It is, in fact, conceivable that the surface of target cells in the thymus which appear during ontogeny contain
specific receptors for several hormones, as previously suggested (Pierpaoli *et
al.*, 1970). Appearance of new target cells for hormones during ontogeny is a
common event in cell and tissue differentiation and would account for the extraordinary sensitivity of the thymus to any hormone imbalance.

Hormones would be expected to modulate, brake, or accelerate these processes of cell proliferation in the thymus by a feed-back humoral or cellular
system starting at some as yet undefined stage in ontogeny.

It is conceivable that the initially hormone-independent cell proliferation
and morphogenetic processes that occur during embryologic development are
replaced at some stage by the appearance of another system represented by
hormones and target cells in the thymus and in other target tissue. Such a
newly emerging ontogenic system would facilitate the expression, maintenance, or amplification of functions of progenitor cells which derived
from other specialized organs such as the bone marrow and appear during embryologic development. This situation is analogous to that in tissues other
than the thymus and could be likened to metamorphosis in amphibians or to
development of the mammary gland in mammals at puberty and to its
transformation according to menstrual cycle, pregnancy, lactation, and
menopause.

LIMITS OF THE IMMUNE FUNCTION OF THE THYMUS

There are now available varied data consistent with the view that the immunologic function of the thymus represents only one facet of its overall role
in cell physiology. It remains to be determined to what extent the present
general view that the role of the thymus is limited to immune processes is an
oversimplification. This prevailing attitude is understandable in the absence of
hard data on its precise role in other processes, whereas the immunologic
parameters of its function are measured with relative ease. However, the par-

ticipation of the thymus in other functions is rational provided it helps clarify its role in immunity as well as its significance in ontogenic differentiation.

It does not seem unreasonable to consider the thymus as the organ where the phylogenetically acquired specialization enables that fraction of the progenitor cells derived from the bone marrow (responsible for cell-mediated immune reactions and helper function for antibody production) to proliferate and to amplify adequately their immune precommitment. It is, however, evident that this function is minor when compared to the number of cells proliferating in the thymus. For example, massive antigenic stimulation does not affect, positively or negatively, the mitotic activity of the thymus; germ-free mice have a well-developed thymus, in contrast with their poorly developed peripheral lymphoid tissues; the levels of immunoglobulins are practically normal in neonatally thymectomized mice or in thymusless "nude" mice. In my view, the most logical explanation for this lack of immune reactivity of cells in the thymus is that most of them may not have any classical immunologic function (see this Section, below).

It is known that the thymus plays a role in the mechanism of immunologic tolerance, but its function with regard to these processes is not clarified. It has been shown that removal of the thymus in partially "tolerant" or in completely unresponsive animals prolongs tolerance (Claman and Talmage, 1963; Taylor, 1964; Pierpaoli, 1967). As a consequence of what has been proposed above, tolerance might be due to lack of proliferation in the thymus of that fraction of the lymphocytes which are committed to an immune response to a given antigen. Elimination of the thymus (e.g., by neonatal thymectomy or by removal of the thymus in unresponsive animals) would lead to a lack of amplification, possibly by preventing proliferation of the few antigen-reactive cells and, as a consequence, the thymus-dependent immune response would remain undetectable. These considerations are in obvious contrast with the suggestion that the thymus is a "mutant breeding organ" for cells involved in immune reactions in mammals (Jerne, 1971), and with the suggestion that the thymus is an obligatory selector of restriction specificity of effector T cells independently of the T cells original H-2 genotype (Zinkernagel, 1978).

If we try now to consider the process of bone marrow–thymus cooperation (Claman et al., 1966; Mitchel and Miller, 1968; Playfair, 1971) for antibody production in the light of this amplification hypothesis, one has to suggest that the first event in an in vivo transfer experiment of syngeneic bone marrow and/or thymus cells into an irradiated recipient after antigen injection should be a proliferation of antigen-reactive cells in the thymus, the so-called inducers which should later interact with bone marrow cells to render them competent to produce antibody. This seems to be in fact demonstrated by the findings of Shearer and Cudkowicz (1969), which confirm the work of Davies et al. (1966) and Mitchel and Miller (1968). I suppose that these antigen-reactive cells deriving from proliferation in the thymus of progenitor antigen-reactive cells from the bone marrow initiate the response in primary immunization and permit an adequate amplification of it. The same suggestion is valid if the steps following the amplification process are (*a*) direct interaction with other cell types, or (*b*) release of chemical mediators from the antigen-reactive cells, which promote differentiation of other cell types.

The view of the thymus as an amplifier of the inherited genetic capacity of bone marrow-derived cells, where cells proliferate under the regulatory action of hormones, permits one to speculate on a wider function of the bone marrow and *to limit the function of the thymus to a general amplification process*, especially crucial, in some species, in neonatal and early life when this process is quantitatively more relevant. It is known, for example, that in adult animals the bone marrow and not the thymus is the most important source of cells for lymph nodes and spleen (Metcalf, 1967). These views lend support to the different approaches to the development of the immune system, as proposed by the followers of the germ-line theories of antibody formation (Silverstein, 1970; Dreyer *et al.*, 1967; Till *et al.*, 1967; Dreyer, 1971; Hood and Talmage, 1971).

CONCLUSIONS

The present approach to the study of the function of the thymus, although simplified and obviously incomplete, may help explain a number of seemingly obscure findings in immunologic investigations on thymus function as well as recent theories on the generation of immunologic diversity.

While not directly pertinent to the proposed function of the thymus, it might be useful to mention that some crucial unexplained points to be considered are (*a*) how the message for proliferation in the thymus of certain progenitor cells from the bone marrow is transmitted (Figure 3), and (*b*) the fate of most of the thymocytes proliferating in the cortex of the thymus. According to some evidence, a large number of the thymocytes generated in the thymus cortex migrate to the peripheral lymphoid organs (Hess *et al.*, 1967; Michalke *et al.*, 1969). It is unknown if they are directly involved in immune or nonimmune functions or if they provide or produce tissue-specific messengers or mediators for functions, possibly by the amplification mechanism suggested. The same basic (unknown) mechanisms which permit morphogenesis and organogenesis during embryogenesis might be operative. This might well be due to "simple" genetic selection pressure operative during embryogenesis.

It is possible that the short-lived nonstimulated cells in the thymus die after a quiescent, resting stage. Some investigators suggest that a good proportion of lymphocytes are resting cells (Gowans *et al.*, 1961; Porter and Cooper, 1962). Accordingly, it is entirely conceivable that hormones exert a sequential, selective, and conditioning action for the proliferation of specific thymic and peripheral lymphocytes, thus permitting their functions to be expressed, that is, *amplification through proliferation permits expression.*

In order to comprehend the causes and mechanism of cell proliferation in the thymus, whose speed is comparable to that during embryogenesis, it will be necessary to prove that the thymus mimics and prolongs ontogenic development by maintenance of an adequate genetic information through magnification of pre-existing functions by proliferation of suitable cell clones. Should it be established that ontogeny mimics phylogeny, it may also be that "thymogenesis mimics and prolongs ontogeny" (see Figures 2, 3, and 6).

A clear answer to these different interpretations of the role of the thymus is of fundamental clinical and therapeutic relevance. In fact, the possibility to transfer passively alloresistance by transplantation of allogeneic bone marrow is justified only if the recipient will acquire complete donor-type immunologic character of lymphohemopoietic cells (see following sections on bone marrow). Acquisition of a new, complete donor-type competence is excluded if the recipient thymus will prevent acquisition of immunocompetence by the donor lymphohemopoietic cells (Zinkernagel, 1978). On the contrary, our model supports the idea that the transplanted bone marrow acquires complete autonomy in the new recipient and will tolerate its host while maintaining full donor-type character, competence, and immune specificity.

The Thymus-Derived or Processed, Hormone-Dependent Multifunctional Lymphocyte. Its Role in Morphogenesis and Aging

The idea that the thymus-derived lymphocyte and the lymphatic system, in general, regulate in different ways growth and differentiation (morphogenesis) or participate in repairing processes (morphostasis), thus delaying the degenerative phenomena of senescence (of cells, organs, and systems) is not new (Loutit, 1962; Burwell, 1963; Davies *et al.*, 1964; Burch, 1976). The many, although incomplete aspects of this intricate story have been expressed in several articles over the last 2 decades. In particular, a central role for the lymphocyte in connection with growth and aging has been suggested (Pierpaoli and Sorkin, 1972a; Fabris *et al.*, 1972; Pierpaoli *et al.*, 1977b). The essence of these concepts is condensed in a short review which appeared some years ago (Pierpaoli and Sorkin, 1972a) and which, *a posteriori,* seems dramatically supported by the developments concerning the brain-programming function of the thymus (see this section), integration between neuroendocrine and immune functions (Pierpaoli *et al.*, 1977a), and the last proposal on the bone marrow as the center of identity-defense and the consequent medical and therapeutic applications. The reader is asked to consult the original reports if his curiosity is burning (Pierpaoli and Sorkin, 1972a).

ONTOGENETIC THYMIC INFLUENCE ON ESTABLISHMENT
OF PINEAL CYCLICITY AND ON DEVELOPMENT OF
REPRODUCTION AND IDENTITY-DEFENSE MECHANISMS

Earlier observations on the effects of neonatal thymectomy on neuroendo-crine functions and genesis of the wasting syndrome and several other models (Pierpaoli and Sorkin, 1969a, b, 1972a; Tables 1 and 2; Pierpaoli et al., 1969, 1970) have served to demonstrate that developmental hormones condition the onset of immunity. Another model on growth hormone activation of thymo-cytes to immunocompetent cells served to demonstrate that one can accelerate onset of immunity by acting on the still undifferentiated, immunologically "inert" T cells derived from newborn mice (Pierpaoli et al., 1970, 1971a). However, the evidence that thymolymphatic tissues influence neuroendocrine development was still quite indirect (see section on Priority of Replication) and based on much speculation. The natural model of the athymic nude mouse, ideally devoid of allorectivity in its limited life span, served to il-lustrate that, in fact, the thymus was pre-eminent not only for the generation of alloimmunity but also for organization of endocrine functions. Adrenals, thyroid, and gonadal alterations were identified, and it was shown that they did not depend on peripheral defects but on central, hypothalamic deficiencies (Pierpaoli and Besedovsky, 1975; Pierpaoli et al., 1976). These defects could be largely corrected by thymus implantation (Pierpaoli et al., 1976). Thus the basic role of the thymus in hypothalamic–pituitary programming was established (Pierpaoli et al., 1976; and Figure 6).

Almost at the same time, it was shown that passive transfer of thymus cells from newborn normal donors into athymic mice did not restore their inability to reject skin allografts (Pierpaoli, 1975; Table 5). This very useful model served to demonstrate that the environment of the nude mouse does not offer to the unreactive T cells the conditions for differentiating to antigen-reactive, mature T cells. This model was the starting point which led to the findings on the derangements of pineal cyclicity in nude mice. In fact, it was possible to combine progressively the knowledge on the endocrine deficiencies of athymic mice with their inability to activate immature T cells to alloreactive T cells. This was achieved by a progressive understanding of the links between pineal function and reproductive physiology. It was shown that nude mice have a primary alteration of circadian cyclicity. Inoculation of the main pineal neurohormone, melatonin, completely corrected the main immune defects of nude mice that had been transferred with immature T cells. However, this could be accomplished only when injections of melatonin corrected, appar-ently, their anomalous circadian periodicity (Pierpaoli and Maestroni, 1981a). It was thus proposed that the thymus programs pineal cyclicity and the development of that cyclical hormonal "milieu" in which immature T cells can mature to antigen-reactive T cells, as had been suggested earlier (Pier-paoli, 1975). This concept on the role of pineal-sexual cylicity for the genera-

TABLE 5
Skin Graft Rejection by BALB/c Athymic Nude Mice Injected with Thymus Cells from Newborn or Adult Congenic or Allogeneic Donors[a]

Thymus cell donor	Age of donor (days)	Number of thymus cells injected ($\times 10^9$)	Donor of graft	Number of recipients	Age of recipient athymic mice (days)	Rejection time (days)	Life span of mice with or without intact graft (days)	Occurrence of death due to GvH disease after cell injection (days)
BALB/c	30	100–150	C57BL/6	4	30–50	20–40	120–240	—
BALB/c	35–65	350–500	C57BL/6	22	60–200	12–60	120–300	—
BALB/c	1	100–50	C57BL/6 C3H/J	6	45–75	No rejection	120–240	—
BALB/c	1	50	C57BL/6 C3H/J	4	1	No rejection	120–200	—
Charles River	1	100–250	C57BL/6	4	40–70	No rejection	120–200	—
C57BL/6	1	200/250	C57BL/6	3	40	No rejection	120–200	—
C57BL/6	40–300	100–320	C57BL/6 C3H/J	21	20–80	No rejection (GvH disease)	45–100	18–45
C3H/J	40–150	120–200	C57BL/6 C3H/J	8	40	No rejection (GvH disease)	50–110	10–67

[a] Mice were skin-grafted 1–6 weeks after intraperitoneal inoculation of thymus cells. (From "Inability of thymus cells from newborn donors to restore transplantation immunity in athymic mice" by Pierpaoli, W., *Immunology*, 1975, **29**, 465–468. Copyright 1975 by Blackwell Sci. Publ. Reprinted by permission.)

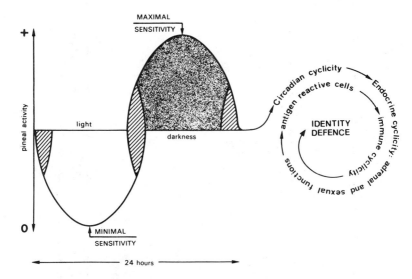

Figure 4. An early programming action of the thymus on the development of the pineal gland imprints the final organization of the pineal-directed hormonal periodicity. This primary cyclicity conditions the establishment of the other cycles (hypothalamic–pituitary, sexual, etc.). Immature T cells do not differentiate to mature, antigen-sensitive cells and consequently to immunocompetent cells unless the hormonal milieu reflects the normal mature endocrine status which is based on the cyclical activities of the different endocrine glands and structures. The athymic nude mouse constitutes a living natural model for this concept (see section on Ontogenetic Thymic Influence.).

tion of transplantation immunity is illustrated schematically in Figures 4 and 6.

THE BONES SHIELD THE INTEGRITY OF THE IDENTITY CELLS: ANCIENT MACROMOLECULES FOR FUTURE PHYSIOLOGY

In trying to follow those complex events accompanying the evolutionary development of the cells and organs committed to identity and reproduction, we might necessarily accept the idea that perhaps the study of physiology considered, first, those structures which most obviously had to do with identity and reproduction, such as sexual organs, glands, and lymph nodes. I feel it was a very unlucky "strategy" which resulted in considering first what was phylogenetically last.

If we dare think that the evolutionary development of some molecules needed for identity and reproductive functions preceded that of the organs, then we might consider the hypothetical existence of some ancient cells, undifferentiated creatures with tremendous acquired potentiality, some kind of brainless multipotent, phylogenetically ancient progenitor creatures. The maintenance of these ancient brainless, but multipotent cells was a consequence of the general principle that more functions and diversification is acquired in evolution by the same *changing* molecules. Thus, there was a time when brainless, monstrous cells had the capacity to provide both identity and replication. We might still carry these "mammalian protozoa" in our body under the name of *bone marrow stem cells*. There is hardly anything more neglected than the *physiology* and function of the bone marrow.

As interferon happened to become the property of virologists, the same unlucky destiny doomed the bone marrow, because its apparent function was only to provide the cells for the hematologists' classifications. It is still a curious phenomenon that only very recently has intense research started on the products of marrow cells at all stages of differentiation. Many molecules are now being identified and their "function" magically revealed by the most varied *in vitro* tests (Metcalf, 1978; Lajtha, 1979; Cline and Golde, 1979). Yet, it seems that phylogenetic hierarchy is also operative in the bone marrow. Keeping this in mind, we were looking for the multivalent "factotum" molecules produced by the "mammalian protozoa" when developing a system for transplantation of foreign, allogeneic bone marrow in lethally irradiated animals. The question was: Are there basic molecules produced by marrow cells which enable engraftment and durable function of foreign marrow in a completely anomalous environment? The answer was yes. Soluble factors were identified which possessed the unsuspected ability to promote rapid engraftment of foreign marrow (allogeneic or interstrain and xenogeneic or interspecies). Apparently, no immunologic or genetic barrier dissuaded the cells to seed the foreign host and *to change its alloidentity*.

In trying to understand how a foreign bone marrow (interspecies or interstrain) can change the identity of its host, we must acknowledge that a radical change of our approach to the concept of identity is needed. In the concept I am trying now to develop, *the bone marrow is the real and only carrier of identity*. In other words, if a host accepts foreign marrow indefinitely and this marrow proliferates undisturbed after replacing the "old" marrow, the "immune" identity resides in the new marrow and not in the host anymore. The host tissues and organs do not certainly assume the new indentity in terms of membrane antigens, antigenic determinants, or major histocompatability antigens, but they are tolerated by the new marrow which will take care of a new defense and identity system which is that of the donor of marrow. *This fact reflects the phylogenetic priority and supremacy of the marrow with respect to its host.* The microcosm of the bone marrow seems, in fact, to contain in itself all the elements for self-regulation or *autonomy,* irrespective of the other mechanisms of neuroendocrine and "immunogenetic" regulation which were superimposed later in phylogeny. The understanding of this apparently simple concept explains why there cannot be a "graft-versus-host reaction" against the host because *it is the marrow's "intelligence" which determines who is foreign.* GVHR would be comparable, in this case, to a suicide. Apparently, the only problem in bone marrow transplantation is not the genetic identity, but the possibility to induce "tabula rasa" in the host marrow. The initiation of a conflict between host and donor marrow is, in my view, the *only* obstacle to bone marrow transplantation (Pierpaoli and Maestroni, 1981b). It is mainly determined by a resistance to the engraftment because even a few residual cells of the host can more easily replicate in that they are the "house master." The experimental proof of this concept for identity is illustrated in the following section, in which a system for transplantation of bone marrow between two immunogenetically different individuals is described.

TRANSPLANTATION OF ALLOGENEIC BONE MARROW

A system for transplanting allogeneic bone marrow is proposed, based on elimination of the endogenous host marrow and on regulation of the donor marrow by substances produced by marrow cells (marrow regulating factors, MRF). Experimental evidence forced us to accept the anomalous and heretical idea that immunology and genetics as presently applied to bone marrow transplantation (BMT) are not relevant to the solution of BMT at the experimental and at the clinical, therapeutic level. On the contrary, we had to recognize the fundamental priority of the *physiology* of bone marrow for achieving a fully functioning, balanced engraftment, in which marrow cells of all categories would proliferate harmoniously in a foreign host. The bone marrow and its well-being in the host became a priority factor irrespective of genetic identity or difference between donor and recipient.

I will list now the main points which were evaluated for achieving consistent and enduring chimerism. One factor was the character and quality of the recipient marrow. A glance at Table 6 will show that different strains of mice

TABLE 6
Number of Bone Marrow Cells Harvested from Tibiae, Femurs, and Humeri of Male and Female, 2- to 4-Month-Old Mice of Different Inbred Strains; Radiosensitivity of Different Strains

Strain	Number of mice	Cells ($\times\ 10^6$) $\pm$ S.D.	Irradiation dose (rad) $LD_{50:30}$ Males	Females
C57BL/6	715	43.2 $\pm$ 7.8	647	670
BALB/c	97	38.5 $\pm$ 7.7	570	585
DBA/2	145	31.0 $\pm$ 5.5		
A/J	145	27.1 $\pm$ 4.4	590	642
C3H/HeJ	60	16.7 $\pm$ 3.7	676	673
AKR/Cu	24	26.7 $\pm$ 5.8		

The mice were killed by cervical dislocation, the long bones were isolated, cut at their ends, and the marrow was flushed off the bones by a needle fitted to a syringe filled with medium TC 199. Cells were suspended by repeated flushing with a needleless syringe, filtered through gauze, adjusted to the desired volume and counted. $LD_{50:30}$ indicates the 50% survival at 30 days after a single dose of irradiation.

display very large variations in *number* of bone marrow cells. This led us to the idea that the much discussed "resistance to engraftment" in certain strains of mice might depend on the *number* and *vitality* (regenerative and proliferative capacity) of their marrow and *not* on some special obstinacy to aggress or reject foreign marrow. As offensive as it might sound, I think that "resistance to engraftment" denotes only the difficulty of eliminating the endogenous marrow in a host which is particularly rich in it and whose marrow has a particularly *high regenerative force*. Thus, the problem became simpler: How to eliminate more efficiently the marrow in a "resistant" host without unduly increasing the dose of irradiation? The system devised was to stimulate the endogenous marrow *before* irradiation with stimulatory factors found in the marrow itself, designated marrow regulating factors (MRF).

The long and complex experiments which resulted in the final simplified model have now been reported extensively (Pierpaoli and Maestroni, 1978, 1979a,b, 1980a,b, 1981b). I will summarize here the basic innovations introduced. They denote that the central issue in BMT is to achieve a rapid and balanced engraftment of the foreign marrow. This can be achieved only if we succeed, first, in abrogating the "resistance to engraftment" which means, in my view, complete elimination of the endogenous host marrow. This was achieved only by the use of factors which apparently participate in the fundamental regulation of bone marrow function (MRF). These substances have not yet been identified in their chemical character, but their activity has been evaluated *in vitro* and *in vivo* (Pierpaoli and Maestroni, 1981b). The timed administration of these substances before lethal, total body irradiation (TBI) changes radically the capacity of the host to accept foreign marrow and to become a permanent chimera (Pierpaoli and Maestroni, 1980a,b, 1981b). This procedure was called "preconditioning." The successive injection of allogeneic bone marrow after TBI was combined with a further inoculation of the MRF and was called "postconditioning." This apparently simple system allowed us to obtain durable chimerism in mice and rabbits, and will be applied to monkey as a prelude to clinical application (Figure 5).

The use of recently isolated substances probably secreted by some cells in the bone marrow allowed us to reconstitute permanently the lethally irradiated host with *histoincompatible* marrow. The interpretation of this achievement is given in our reports. I wish here to stress the fact that these results were obtained thanks to a novel attitude towards bone marrow transplantation (see section "What Is the Thymus for?"). It underlines the proprietary role of the marrow character and activity and the secondary role of its immunogenetic compatibility with the host marrow. As mentioned in the previous section, *the identity of the host is in its marrow.* Therefore, a "new" marrow will recognize the host as its own, provided it will seed and proliferate in a normal fashion. The "immune" identity of the host will be assumed by the "new" marrow, which will carry in itself the "immunologic intelligence" of the host. Thus, BMT is *not,* mainly, an immunologic problem; it concerns the physiology and function of the bone marrow. The endocrine regulation of

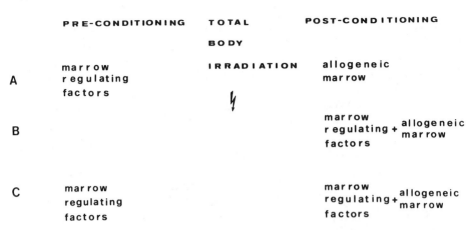

Figure 5. Marrow regulating factors (MRF) are biologically active components of the marrow microenvironment. Administration of MRF only before total body irradiation (TBI) as in (A) allows a more pronounced and efficient eradication of host resistance to the engraftment of foreign, incompatible bone marrow given after TBI. When MRF is administered only after TBI as in (B), it promotes the engraftment only when there is no resistance to engraftment (e.g., parental marrow into F_1 hybrids). A third possibility is offered by administration of MRF before and again after TBI (C). Thus, it is possible to obtain elimination of resistance and/or promotion of engraftment depending on the timing of administration of MRF. Adaptation of the method to different species should allow one to overcome the histocompatibility barrier and thus achieve permanent chimerism.

the marrow through its own secretion was needed for achieving allogeneic chimerism. I am confident that this approach will be of considerable conceptual and practical relevance in medicine and therapy.

BONE MARROW AS A PRIMEVAL
MICROCOSM: MORPHOSTASIS

Is the bone marrow the central physical and functional locus of identity-defense? Did the "mammalian protozoa," the "factotum" cells, maintain their character? Does the bone marrow contain the phylogenetic progenitor cells of identity-defense?

I think that the experimental evidence available now provides an affirmative answer to most of these questions. The data, largely in contradiction with the semantic restriction of "immunology" which confines a vast physiological dimension within dogmatic schemas, document conclusively that the bone marrow constitutes an initial source of precommitted stem cells in embryogenesis and maintains, throughout life, its regulatory function of morphostasis and identity-defense (Figures 2, 3, and 6). If identity-defense means maintenance of the status quo (function and dimension), then we are allowed to consider the defense mechanisms as a part of morphostasis, for the protection of individuality and functions, defense and identity included.

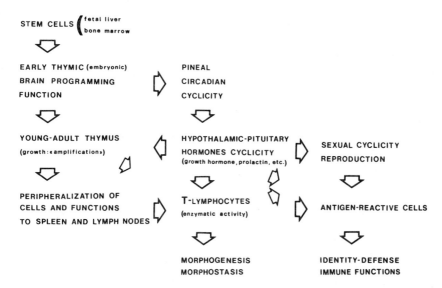

Figure 6. Ontogenetic linkage of thymic–neuroendocrine differentiation and genesis of identity-defense (immunity).

1. The bone marrow contains all the cells and factors which are needed for homeostatic regulation of morphostasis. In fact, replacement of identity-defense is possible *provided the bone marrow is supplied together with its internal regulatory mechanisms to a host which has been deprived of his own marrow* (see section "What Is the Thymus for?" and Fig. 4). The new marrow, thanks to its prominent role and phylogenetic supremacy, will provide for defense-identity and no autoaggression–suicide mechanisms will ensue (Pierpaoli and Maestroni, 1980a,b, 1981b).

2. Runting, wasting, aging could be considered as bone marrow diseases and similar to the "secondary disease" (also called graft-versus-host disease) appearing when no engraftment or a deficient engraftment is manifested after a conditioning regimen (e.g., irradiation) and transplantation of foreign bone marrow. However, the similarity of these syndromes (see Tables 2 and 3) does not mean that they originate from a *primary* involvement of the bone marrow, but that the bone marrow is affected earlier or later. Infusion of syngeneic, compatible bone marrow will cure the secondary disease in lethally irradiated animals. However, that a "marrow therapy" can cure other "runting" or "wasting" syndromes has not been experimentally tested. In fact, this type of research has been quite neglected (Burch, 1976).

3. Regeneration of organs and tissues requires the integrity of marrow function. There is experimental evidence in this direction (Czeizel *et al.,* 1962; Davies *et al.,* 1964).

Thus, the marrow microcosm seems to be central to defense-identity-morphostasis. The *rigidity* of the system seems to be extreme in the sense that the bone marrow monitors carefully that no arbitrary cellular or humoral events modify the spacial and functional status quo (morphostasis), that no intruder survive (defense), and that no foreign element is accepted (identity). On the other side, its *flexibility* is also extreme because, thanks only to such a multitude of functions acquired in evolution, the individual can survive and, consequently, reproduce. The "mammalian protozoa" have survived in us since immemorial time and their humoral multipotential effectors (MRF?) remind us that, not only metaphorically, a crocodile or a monkey can disguise himself in a man and vice versa. I conclude with Figure 6. Time will judge what is illusory or wrong.

REFERENCES

Bianchi, E., Pierpaoli, W., and Sorkin, E. (1971). Cytological changes in the mouse anterior pituitary after neonatal thymectomy: A light and electron microscopical study. *J. Endocrinol.* **51**, 1-6.

Burch, P. R. J. (1976). "The Biology of Cancer, A New Approach." MTP Press, Lancaster, England.

Burwell, R. G. (1963). The role of lymphoid tissue in morphostasis. *Lancet* **2**, 69-74.

Claman, H. N., and Talmage, D. M. (1963). Thymectomy: Prolongation of immunological tolerance in the adult mouse. *Science* **141**, 1193-1194.

Claman, H. N., Chaperon, E. A., and Triplett, R. F. (1966). Thymus–marrow cell combinations. Synergism in antibody production. *Proc. Soc. Exp. Biol. Med.* **122**, 1167-1171.

Cline, M. J., and Golde, D. W. (1979). Cellular interactions in haematopoiesis. *Nature (London)* **277**, 177-181.

Czeizel, S. J., Vaczo, G., and Kertai, P. (1962). Effect of bone marrow on regeneration of liver of X-irradiated rats. *Nature (London)* **196**, 240-41.

Davies, A. J. S., Leuchars, E., Doak, S. M. A., and Cross, A. M. (1964). Regeneration in relation to the lymphoid system. *Nature (London)* **201**, 1097-1101.

Davies, A. J. S., Leuchars, E., Wallis, V., and Kollar, P. C. (1966). The mitotic response of thymus-derived cells to antigenic stimulus. *Transplantation* **4**, 438-451.

Dreyer, W. J. (1971). A proposed new and general chromosomal control mechanism for commitment of specific cell lines during development. *In* "Developmental Aspects of Antibody Formation and Structure" (J. Sterzl and I. Riha, ed.), Vol. 2, pp. 919-932. Academic Press, New York.

Dreyer, W. J., Gray, W. R., and Hood, L. (1967). The genetic, molecular and cellular basis of antibody formation: Some facts and a unifying hypothesis. *Cold Spring Harbor Symp. Quant. Biol.* **32**, 353-367.

Fabris, N., Pierpaoli, W., and Sorkin, E. (1972). Lymphocytes, hormones and ageing. *Nature (London)* **240**, 557-559.

Gowans, J. L., Gesner, B. M., and McGregor, D. D. (1961). The immunological activity of lymphocytes. *Ciba Found. Study Group* **10**, 32-40.

Hess, M. W., Stoner, R. D., and Cottier, H. (1967). Growth characteristics of mouse thymus in the neonatal period. *Nature, (London)* **215**, 426-428.

Hood, L., and Talmage, D. W. (1971). On the mechanism of antibody diversity: Evidence for the germ-line basis of antibody variability. *In* "Developmental Aspects of Antibody Formation and Structure" (J. Sterzl and I. Riha, eds), Vol. 2, pp. 935-962. Academic Press, New York.

Jerne, N. K. (1971). The somatic generation of immune recognition. *Eur. J. Immunol.* **1**, 1-9.

Lajtha, L. G. (1979). Stem cell concepts. *Nouv. Rev. Fr. Hematol.* **21**, 59-65.

Loutit, J. F. (1962). Immunological and trophic functions of lymphocytes. *Lancet* **2**, 1106–1108.

Metcalf, D. (1967). Relation of the thymus to the formation of immunologically reactive cells. *Cold Spring Harbor Symp. Quant. Biol.* **32**, 583–590.

Metcalf, D. (1978). Regulation of hemopoiesis. *Nouv. Rev. Fr. Hematol* **20**, 521–533.

Michalke, W. D., Hess, M. W., Riedwyl, H., Stoner, R. D., and Cottier, H. (1969). Thymic lymphopoiesis and cell loss in newborn mice. *Blood* **33**, 541–554.

Mitchell, G. F., and Miller, J. F. A. P. (1968). Cell-to-cell interaction in the immune response. II. The source of hemolysin-forming cells in irradiated mice given bone marrow and thymus or thoracic duct lymphocytes. *J. Exp. Med.* **128**, 821–837.

Pastan, I., and Perlman, R. L. (1971). Cyclic AMP in metabolism. *Nature (London), New Biol.* **229**, 5–7.

Pierpaoli, W. (1967). Thymectomy and the prolongation of tolerance to bovine serum albumin in adult rats. *Nature (London)* **214**, 802–803.

Pierpaoli, W. (1975). Inability of thymus cells from newborn donors to restore transplantation immunity in athymic mice. *Immunology* **29**, 465–468.

Pierpaoli, W., and Besedovsky, H. O. (1975). Role of the thymus in programming of neuroendocrine functions. *Clin. Exp. Immunol.* **20**, 323–338.

Pierpaoli, W., and Maestroni, G. J. M. (1978). Drug-induced chimerism and prevention of graft-versus-host disease in lethally irradiated mice transplanted with rat bone marrow. *Transplantation* **26**, 456–458.

Pierpaoli, W., and Maestroni, G. J. M. (1979a). A new pre-irradiation conditioning regimen which protects against radiation injury and facilitates engraftment of xenogeneic bone marrow. *Scand. J. Haematol* **22**, 165–172.

Pierpaoli, W., and Maestroni, G. J. M. (1979b). Prevention of graft-versus-host disease and induction of chimerism in lethally irradiated mice reconstituted with rat bone marrow. *J. Clin. Lab. Immunol.* **2**, 125–132.

Pierpaoli, W., and Maestroni, G. J. M. (1980a). The facilitation of enduring engraftment of homologous bone marrow and avoidance of secondary disease in mice. *Cell. Immunol.* **52**, 62–72.

Pierpaoli, W., and Maestroni, G. J. M. (1980b). Induction of enduring allogeneic bone marrow chimerism in rabbits via soluble marrow-derived components. *Immunol. Lett.,* **1**, 255–258.

Pierpaoli, W., and Maestroni, G. J. M. (1981a). Thymus-programmed pineal circadian cyclicity promotes genesis of transplantation immunity. Proc. XXVIII Int. Congress of Physiological Sciences, Budapest, 1980, in press.

Pierpaoli, W., and Maestroni, G. J. M. (1981b). Enduring allogeneic marrow engraftment via non-specific bone-marrow-derived regulating factors (MRF). *Cell. Immunol.,* **57**, 219–228.

Pierpaoli, W., and Sorkin, E. (1967). Relationship between thymus and hypophysis. *Nature (London)* **215**, 834–837.

Pierpaoli, W., and Sorkin, E. (1968). Hormones and immunological capacity. I. Effect of heterologous anti-growth hormone (ASTH) antiserum on thymus and peripheral lymphatic tissue in mice. Induction of a wasting syndrome. *J. Immunol.* **101**, 1036–1043.

Pierpaoli, W., and Sorkin, E. (1969a). Effect of growth hormone and antigrowth hormone on the lymphatic tissue and the immune response. *Antibiot. Chemother.* **15**, 122–134.

Pierpaoli, W., and Sorkin, E. (1969b). Relationship between developmental hormones, the thymus, and immunological capacity. *In* "Lymphatic Tissue and Germinal Centers in Immune Response" (L. Fiore-Donati and M. C. Hanna, Jr., eds.), pp. 397–401. Plenum, New York.

Pierpaoli, W., and Sorkin, E. (1972a). Hormones, thymus and lymphocyte functions. *Experientia* **28**, 1385–1389.

Pierpaoli, W., and Sorkin, E. (1972b). Alterations of adrenal cortex and thyroid in mice with congenital absence of the thymus. *Nature (London), New Biol.* **238**, 282–285.

Pierpaoli, W., Baroni, E., Fabris, N., and Sorkin, E. (1969). Hormones and immunological capacity. II. Reconstitution of antibody production in hormonally deficient mice by somatotropic hormone, thyrotropic hormone and thyroxine. *Immunology* **16**, 217–230.

Pierpaoli, W., Fabris, N., and Sorkin, E. (1970). Developmental hormones and immunological maturation. *Ciba Found. Study Group* **36**, 126–143.

Pierpaoli, W., Fabris, N., and Sorkin, E. (1971a). The effects of hormones on the development of the immune capacity. *In* "Cellular Interaction in the Immune Response" (S. Cohen, G. Cudkowicz, and R. T. McCluskey, eds.), pp. 25–30. Karger, Basel.

Pierpaoli, W., Bianchi, E., and Sorkin, E. (1971b). Hormones and the immunological capacity. V. Modification of growth hormone producing cells in the adenohypophysis of neonatally thymectomized germ-free mice: An electron microscopical study. *Clin. Exp. Immunol.* **9**, 889–901.

Pierpaoli, W., Kopp. H. G., and Bianchi, E. (1976). Interdependence of thymic and neuroendocrine functions in ontogeny. *Clin. Exp. Immunol.* **24**, 501–506.

Pierpaoli, W., Kopp, H. G., Mueller, J., and Keller, M. (1977a). Interdependence between neuroendocrine programming and the generation of immune recognition in ontogeny. *Cell. Immunol.* **29**, 16–27.

Pierpaoli, W., Haemmerli, M., Sorkin, E., and Hurni, H. (1977b). Role of thymus and hypothalamus in ageing. *In* "European Symposium on Basic Research in Gerontology," pp. 141–150. Verlag Dr. med. D. Straube, Erlangen, DRG.

Playfair, J. H. L. (1971). Cell cooperation in the immune response. *Clin. Exp. Immunol.* **8**, 839–856.

Porter, K. A., and Cooper, E. H. (1962). Transformation of adult allogeneic small lymphocytes after transfusion into newborn rats. *J. Exp. Med.* **115**, 997–1007.

Raff, M. C., and Wortis, H. H. (1970). Thymus dependence of theta-bearing cells in the peripheral lymphoid tissues of mice. *Immunology* **18**, 931–942.

Shearer, G. M., and Cudkowicz, G. (1969). Distinct events in the immune response elicited by transferred marrow and thymus cells. I. Antigen requirements and proliferation of thymic antigen-reactive cells. *J. Exp. Med.* **130**, 1243–1261.

Silverstein, A. M. (1970). Lymphogenesis, immunogenesis, and the generation of immunologic diversity. *In* "Developmental Aspects of Antibody Formation and Structure" (J. Sterzl and I. Riha, eds), Vol. 1, pp. 69–77. Academic Press, New York.

Taylor, R. B. (1964). An effect of thymectomy on recovery from immunological paralysis. *Immunology,* **7**, 595–602.

Till, J. E., McCulloch, E. A., Phillips, R. A., and Siminovitch, L. (1967). Analysis of differentiating clones derived from marrow. *Cold Spring Harbor Symp. Quant. Biol.* **32**, 461–464.

Weinstein, Y. (1977). 20a-Hydroxysteroid dehydrogenase: A T lymphocyte associated enzyme. *J. Immunol.* **119**, 1223–1229.

Weinstein, Y., Lindner, H. R., and Eckstein, B. (1977). Thymus metabolises progesterone—Possible marker for T-lymphocytes. *Nature (London)* **266**, 632–633.

Zinkernagel, R. M. (1978). Thymus and lymphohemopoietic cells: their role in T cell maturation, in selection of T cells' H-2-restriction-specificity and in H-2 linked Ir gene control. *Immunol. Rev.* **42**, 224–270.

PART V

Epilogue

Mind, Body,
and Immune Response

ALASTAIR J. CUNNINGHAM

INTRODUCTION

In a science fiction story by Naomi Mitchison (novelist mother of a famous immunologist) there is described a race of intelligent beings that have six arms and radial symmetry. To their minds, polar opposites like "right" and "wrong," "black" and "white" are absurd simplifications: they see issues in shades of gray, and are well equipped to study events which have many contributing causes. We humans, perhaps because of our bilateral symmetry, have an "all or nothing" approach to causality, and experience difficulty understanding the many complex interacting systems that have become important to us, for example, in economic, political, and ecological arenas. Medicine, too, is affected by this limitation of ours. Cures have been found for most conditions where there is a single overwhelmingly obvious cause, notably the infectious diseases, but we are struggling with a formidable list of chronic ailments in which many factors can probably contribute to a disturbance of normal homeostasis, for example, cancer, cardiovascular disease, and autoimmune syndromes. We are simply not accustomed to the conceptual handling of complex entities where many factors, all vital, maintain a balance. The human body is one such entity, and disease (dis-ease) can be viewed as any persistent harmful disturbance of its equilibrium.

609

Within the body are three subsystems all concerned with maintaining this equilibrium, and each highly complex in itself. These are the nervous, endocrine, and immune systems. This book is a bold attempt to promote the study of the interactions between these three, a problem which is intrinsically fascinating and highly relevant to disease. It is also an area where we can test the explanatory power of our conventional reductionist techniques and try to devise new approaches where reductionism has failed.

WHAT IS MEANT BY "UNDERSTANDING" THE INTERACTION BETWEEN MIND OR BRAIN AND IMMUNE SYSTEM?

"Understanding" has to be judged in a pragmatic way. We want to develop predictive theories, to be able to say: "If I do x to the mind, effect y will result in the immune response." Clinical applications follow. Experimental dissection of the mechanisms involved are a means to this end. We need explanations of immune/nervous interactions at many levels, molecular, cellular, tissue, organ, whole animal. It is important to bear in mind that with multilevel organized entities like the body, properties "emerge" (as systems theorists say) at higher levels of organization that could not be predicted solely by analysis of lower level parts (e.g., studying isolated neurones would not allow us to predict consciousness). Mind can be considered an emergent property of brain (at least if one takes an interactionist philosophical position).

Figure 1 attempts to set the study of nervous/immune interactions in a broader context. The whole organism is an open system in dynamic interaction with the environment. We need ultimately an overall theory connecting social, psychological, and somatic events. The individual adapts to his environment, two of the most sophisticated kinds of adaptation being development of mental and immune memory. This raises an important point: the exchanges which take place between environment and organism are transfers of

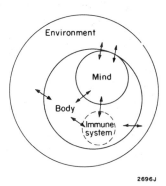

2696J

Figure 1. The interactions between immune system, body, mind, and environment.

energy, but, even more interesting, involve transmission of *information*. Memory is information about specific aspects of the environment. While "stress" is a useful catch-all to describe the stereotyped response to a variety of threatening stimuli, it is too broad to account fully for many of the changes that underly *specific* psychosomatic pathways.

SIMILARITIES BETWEEN IMMUNE AND NERVOUS SYSTEMS

The immune system identifies and reacts against molecular structures which are not part of "self," recognition specificity being provided by antibody molecules. Surveillance of the body for foreign material is carried out by circulating antibodies and lymphocytes, while responses are chiefly made within organized lymphoid tissue. A great deal is known about molecular and cellular effector mechanisms of immunity. By contrast, work on regulation of immune responses is at a much earlier stage, although it is becoming clear that making more detailed predictions about the course of immune responses will depend on better understanding of their regulation. We can already separate three modes of regulation: mechanisms depending on recognition of antigen; genetically determined elements (coded for in the major histocompatibility complex locus) and perhaps related to antigen recognition; idiotypes, the antigenic quality of antibody variable regions which allow immunoglobulin molecules to interact directly, suggesting that the immune system may be connected as a network which self-regulates in the absence of foreign antigen (Jerne, 1974).

The nervous system, like the immune, receives information from outside and inside the body but encodes it in specific patterns of neuronal firing rather than by amplification of specific molecules. Much is known of the anatomy and physiology of nervous tissue, down to cellular levels of transmission of action potentials along nerve-cell processes, and the conversion of electrical to chemical energy at the synapse. Regulation is even more obviously a central issue here. The vast majority of neurones in the brain do not make sensory or motor connections with the body but are used in internal "computation:" the brain largely "talks to itself" as we begin to suspect the immune system also does. The study of the nervous system has traditionally been carried on at several distinct levels, ranging from the "black box" approach of psychology, where environmental inputs are matched with gross behavioral outputs, through neuroanatomy to detailed neurophysiological analysis of events in single cells. Immunologists will recognize parallel approaches in the study of their subject.

There are further interesting similarities in the logic of operation of immune and nervous systems (i.e., while the "hard-ware" or structures are very different, the "soft-ware" shows common features). Both are primarily con-

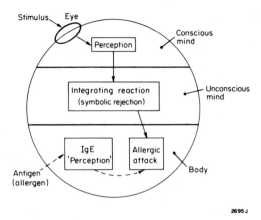

Figure 2. "Information flow" involved in an asthmatic attack produced by a visual stimulus (solid lines) or an antigenic stimulus (dashed lines).

cerned with information processing rather than with energy exchange (by contrast, for example, with muscle tissue). Their complex structures permit this kind of function. Both are concerned with adaptive responses to "unexpected" (i.e., unpredictable) environmental stimuli, as pointed out by Cohn (1968). That is, they must be flexible enough to recognize and deal with entirely new information (perceptions or molecular structures) which neither the individual nor his ancestors has ever encountered before. Recognition of a new stimulus depends however on its association with previously encountered elements. During development both immune and nervous systems unfold in a way that is partly guided by genetics but is also strongly influenced by the cellular environment. Both show memory and tolerance (habituation). Figure 2 is an attempt to dramatize the similarities between immune and psychological reactions to different outside stimuli which may result in the same kind of eventual asthmatic attack.

HOW NERVOUS AND
IMMUNE SYSTEMS INTERACT

Figure 3 shows some of the many levels that information from the mind may pass through in order to produce an effect in the body. Experiments usually involve the correlation of events at two of these levels. Thus psychology generally considers (1) and (10) (see numbered boxes in Figure 3). Much of the work in this book relates levels (4) or (5) or (6) to levels (8) or (9), that is, fluctuations in immune responses are attributed to changes in neuroelectric or hormonal events. Stress research tends to compare (1) and (2) to (8) or (9). The work on psychological conditioning of immune responses described by Ader would be shown in Figure 3 as correlating levels (3) and (8). This seems a

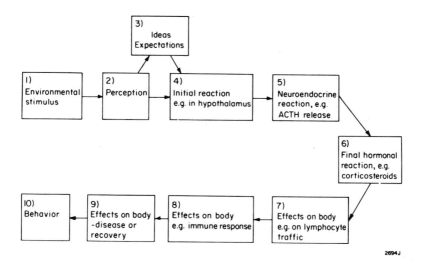

Figure 3. Some of the levels through which an environmental stimulus, perceived by the mind, may affect events in the body and eventually health and behavior.

particularly important kind of study, since most of the stresses affecting western man are not physical but are initiated by his own mental reactions to intrinsically harmless stimuli.

Events at all stages of this pathway are obviously enormously complex. Nevertheless an excellent start has been made in correlating neuroendocrine mechanisms with alterations in immune responses. Some of the clearest patterns reported in this volume are as follows:

1. *Corticosteroids:* tend to depress immune responses, phagocytosis, macrophage activation, and *in vitro* responses of lymphoid cells. Elevating corticosteroid levels changes the ratio of B to T cells in mouse spleen, and changes the recirculation patterns of lymphocytes (e.g., more T cells appear in bone marrow) (see chapters by Monjan and by Besedovsky and Sorkin). Acute stress tends to depress immune responses while chronic stress may elevate them slightly (see chapter by McLean and Reichlin). Manipulating the sympathetic system generally depresses responses, but parasympathetic manipulation may increase them.

2. *Other hormones:* generally androgens, estrogens, and progesterone diminish *in vivo* immune responses, while growth hormone, thyroxine, and insulin may elevate them (Besedovsky and Sorkin). Fluctuations in intrinsic hormone levels take place during immune reactions: during an anti-sheep erythrocyte response, thyroxine is elevated at Day 3 and depressed at Day 5–8, while serum corticosterone levels are raised and spleen noradrenaline levels depressed at the peak of the response (about Day 4), according to Besedovsky and Sorkin.

3. *Hypothalamic effects:* lesions in the hypothalamus can depress imme-

diate and delayed hypersensitivity reactions, while electrical stimulation of this part of the brain can increase some immune responses slightly (see chapter by Stein *et al.*).

4. *Receptors on lymphocytes:* hormone receptors are found much more readily on stimulated than on nonstimulated lymphocytes. Receptors have been described for corticosteroids, growth hormone, estradiol, testosterone, and acetylcholine; β-adrenergic and insulin receptors are only present on stimulated cells (Besedovsky and Sorkin).

5. *Thymus:* a complex relationship between the thymus and other endocrine organs is discussed by Pierpaoli and by Hall and Goldstein. Ahlqvist points out that there is such an involved interaction between growth hormone, the thymus and thymic extracts, corticotropin, adrenal steroids, thyroid hormones, thyroid stimulating hormone, and other factors that a coherent summary is impossible at present.

What strikes the naive reader most forcibly when going through the chapters of this book is the enormous complexity of possible interactions between neurotransmitters, other hormones, and elements of the immune system. This means that when correlations are described, for example, if administration of thyroxine increases an immune response, one can only say that this is a *possible* mechanism in endocrine/immune modifications, not that it necessarily has relevance in most responses. The work of Besedovsky and Sorkin, in which levels of intrinsically produced hormones were assessed during an induced immune response, takes us one step further, but again one cannot infer any causal relationship between the hormone and the effect on immunity. Indeed, as Plaut and Friedman point out, the concept of causality loses much of its meaning in such complex, multivariate, interacting systems; we can only try to uncover a variety of factors which may exert some influence on the immune response and hope that certain simple manipulations will be found to have decisive effects. Explanatory schemes must be simple to be useful. It is unrealistic to expect for psychoneuroimmunologic events (or for immunologic mechanisms alone) a chart similar to those biochemical descriptions of metabolism that hang on the back of many laboratory doors!

THE A PRIORI APPROACH

Faced with the complexity of mechanisms of nervous/immunologic reactions it may be worth approaching this problem "from the other end," setting down (Figure 4) what we know of the way the body controls itself and speculating on influences the nervous system might have on immune events. The specificity of immune responses is initially determined by antigen; any influence of products of the nervous system is likely to be nonspecific, unless the impact of neurosecretory substances on already stimulated lymphocytes is

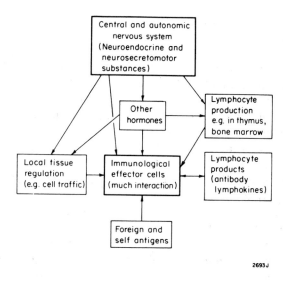

Figure 4. Possible interactions between nervous system and immune system.

significant. Indirect controls seem more likely than direct: the immune system has mechanisms for regulating itself, while the task of the nervous system may be to coordinate immune functions with those of the body as a whole. A promising avenue for nervous control would seem to be through action on the traffic of lymphocytes around the body and through lymphoid tissue. Some direct influence of the nervous system on generation of lymphocytes may be suspected in primary and secondary lymphoid organs.

FURTHER WAYS TO STUDY INTERACTIONS
BETWEEN NERVOUS AND IMMUNE SYSTEMS

It is easier to point to the limitations of existing experiments than to suggest other approaches which might be profitable. Progress in this area is bound to be difficult and slow, but the following points may be worth considering.

First it seems essential to study regulatory events at all levels of organization. At the strictly cellular/biochemical level, further investigation of the effect of hormones on mitogenically-stimulated lymphocytes seems worthwhile. Higher order explanations include the dimensions of space and time: it is valuable to know that a hormone can affect a lymphocyte but also important to find out where and when these reactions occur. The impact of mental and hormonal events on lymphocyte traffic is an obvious but rather neglected area for research at this higher level. In attempting to consider the immune/nervous complex as a whole it may also be useful to draw analogies from other complex systems: for example, mathematical and systems analysis, electrical and other networks, general theory of oscillations and of homeo-stasis.

Multiple correlations should be attempted, that is, between psychosocial stimuli, disease and changes in immune parameters, perhaps also with concur-rent psychological and endocrine measurements. This is obviously difficult and expensive. Most of us are fully extended trying to relate two variables. Yet, as Ahlqvist and others point out in this volume, meaningful patterns will often only emerge from such multiple measures. The problem, to say it again, is to distinguish important actual mechanisms from possible ones. Palmblad suggests following individuals over extended periods, documenting changes in a number of variables. Stress, the common cold, and mucosal Ig levels might be a promising combination.

The use of chronic stress in animals is considered by Riley in this volume. While the temptation with animal experiments is to study "anything that works," perhaps eventually drifting away from relevance to the human condi-tion, it makes sense to attempt such difficult protocols as correlating stress, immune impairment, and the emergence of spontaneous tumors in old mice of normal strains. A stress/immune impairment correlation could then be fol-lowed by attempts to elevate cancer levels through some other manipulation that produces equal immune deficiency. This might at last provide some evidence for or against the common assumption that immune system is impor-tant in protection against naturally-occurring cancer.

Finally, connecting "ideas in the mind" with effects in the immune system is fascinating and potentially important. The animal conditioning experiments described by Ader are a good start. Work with humans might be considered: it has been reported that warts can be removed (Sinclair-Gieben and Chalmers, 1959) and allergic reactions diminished (Black, 1969) by hypnotic suggestion. It seems worth investigating whether white cell migration patterns can be altered by hypnosis or using biofeedback (suggested by D. Bovbjerg). Placebo effects on immune parameters deserve further study, as does the exciting work of Simonton and Simonton (1975) and their colleagues on the use of visual imagery in cancer therapy.

This volume will serve to indicate some of the excitement and also the diffi-culties facing those who wish to study psychoneuroimmunology. Newcomers will be able to draw on a great deal of basic documentation, but will have to develop new research strategies in order to clarify what is obviously a most complex web of events.

REFERENCES

Black, S. (1969). "Mind and Body." William Kimber & Co. Ltd., London.
Cohn, M. (1968). Molecular biology of expectation. *In* "Nucleic Acids in Immunology" (I. J. Plescia and W. Brown, eds.), pp. 671–715. Springer-Verlag, Berlin and New York.

Jerne, N. K. (1974). Towards a network theory of the immune system. *Ann. Immunol. Paris* **125C**, 373–389.

Simonton, O. C., and Simonton, S. S. (1975). Belief systems and management of the emotional aspects of malignancy. *J. Transpersonal Psychol.* **7**, 29–47.

Sinclair-Gieben, A. H. C., and Chalmers, D. (1959). Evaluation of treatment of warts by hypnosis. *Lancet* **2**, 480–482.

Author Index

Simonton, S. S., 616, *617*
Simpson, G. M., 267, *277*
Sims, P., 108, *151*
Sinclair, N. R. St. C., 440, *443,* 570, *572*
Sinclair-Gieben, A. H. C., 616, *617*
Singer, G., 290, 291, 292, 305, 314, *319*
Singh, M. M., 268, *277*
Singh, U., 370, 376, 377, 379, *401,* 410, *428,* 526, 530, *542,* 551, *574*
Singhal, R. L., 361, 372, *401*
Singhal, S. K., 213, *226*
Sinichkin, A. A., 433, *446*
Sjöberg, O., 527, *542*
Sjögren, H. O., 64, 81, 91, *96, 100*
Sklar, L. S., 211, *226*
Skude, G., 238, *256*
Slater, J., 206, 214, *218, 226*
Slemmon, J. R., 501, *509*
Sliteri, P. K., 477, *518*
Smelik, P. G., 491, *512*
Smeraldi, E., 390, *394, 401*
Smeraldi, R. S., 390, *394*
Smiley, R. L., 441, *446*
Smith, A. H., 11, *26, 27*
Smith, E. L., 55, *102*
Smith, G. H., 321, 328, *352*
Smith, J., 506, *511*
Smith, J. B., 506, *518*
Smith, J. W., 442, *446*
Smith, K. A., 561, 570, *573*
Smith, L. M., 191, *226*
Smith, M. S., 491, *512*
Smith, P. A., 526, *542,* 551, *574*
Smith, R. S., 442, *446*
Smith, R. T., 451, 452, *470,* 528, 529, *540*
Smith, S. R., 507, *518*
Smith, T. W., 494, *513*
Smith, W., 485, *509*
Smotherman, W. P., 303, *318*
Snary, D., 356, 357, 380, *394, 396*
Snell, G. D., 193, 194, 197, 215, *223, 226,* 367, *396*
Snell, L., 110, *150*
Snyder, G. D., 489, *518*
Snyder, R. E., 114, *156*
Snyder, S. H., 206, *226*
Soave, O. A., 188, *226*
Sohn, R. J., 434, *445*
Solberg, C. O., 190, *218*
Solomon, J. B., 556, *574*
Solomon, G. F., 8, *29,* 34, 37, 66, 81, 82, *95, 101,* 126, 140, 141, *156,* 160, 161, 165, 170, 171, 172, 174, 178, *180, 181, 182,* 186, 190, 191, 203, 210, *217, 226, 227,*

245, 250, 252, *256, 257,* 260, 263, 264, 267, 268, 270, *272, 274, 277,* 299, 300, 303, 304, 310, *317, 319,* 454, *469, 472*
Solomon, J. C., 198, *218*
Somes, G. W., 22, *28*
Soriano, F. M., 523, *542*
Sorkin, E., 82, *98,* 204, 206, 213, *218, 219,* 224, 348, *349,* 369, 378, 379, *400,* 406, *427,* 436, *443,* 451, 456, 462, *469,* 476, *509,* 525, 527, 538, *539,* 551, 552, 554, 557, 558, 559, 561, 565, 567, *571, 572, 573,* 579, 580, 581, 587, 590, 591, 592, 593, 595, 596, 600, *604, 605, 606*
Southam, A. L., 365, *400*
Sovailescu, L., 451, *469*
Spackman, D. H., 8, *29,* 32, 33, 34, 40, 42, 48, 50, 54, 61, 64, 76, 77, 80, 82, 84, 85, 86, 87, 91, *99, 100, 101,* 110, 131, *155,* 213, *225*
Spahn, G., *102*
Sparrow, E. M., 477, *516*
Sparrow, E. R., 198, *223*
Spear, N. E., 309, *317*
Spector, B. D., 104, 119, 120, *152*
Spector, N. H., 348, *352,* 449, 450, 451, 454, 464, *472, 473,* 552, *574*
Spencer, E. S., *98,* 190, *225,* 299, *318*
Spencer, K. A., 164, *181*
Spilken, A., 9, *28,* 241, *254*
Spitzer, G., 426
Spreafico, F., 127, *148,* 367, 368, *402*
Sprunt, D. H., 72, 87, *101*
Spry, C. J. F., 237, *254*
Srebro, Z., 476, *518*
Sridhara, Rama Roa, B. S., 260, *275*
Stabenau, J. R., 260, *277*
Stancer, H. C., 506, *510*
Stanton, A. H., 506, *518*
Stanton, J. D., 372, *394*
Starka, L., 570, *573*
Starzinski-Powitz, A., 296, *318*
Stastny, P., 383, *401*
Stecher, V. J., 360, *402*
Stefanis, C. N., 271, *277*
Stein, M., 33, *101,* 140, *156,* 186, 203, 205, 227, 351, 431, 432, 433, 434, 435, 436, 437, 438, 439, *444, 445, 446,* 451, 454, 461, *471, 473,* 476, 507, *515, 519,* 552, *574*
Stein, W. H., 54, *101*
Stein, S. P., 9, *29*
Steinberg, A. D., 386, *395*
Steinberg, H. R., 262, *277*
Steinbusch, H., 484, *513*
Steiner, A. L., 442, *446*

Subject Index